A Writer's Resource

A Handbook for Writing and Research

Second Edition

Elaine P. Maimon
University of Alaska Anchorage

Janice H. Peritz
Queens College,
City University of New York

Kathleen Blake Yancey
Florida State University

Boston   Burr Ridge, IL   Dubuque, IA   Madison, WI   New York
San Francisco   St. Louis   Bangkok   Bogotá   Caracas   Kuala Lumpur
Lisbon   London   Madrid   Mexico City   Milan   Montreal   New Delhi
Santiago   Seoul   Singapore   Sydney   Taipei   Toronto

Mc Graw Hill Higher Education

Published by McGraw-Hill, an imprint of The McGraw-Hill Companies, Inc., 1221 Avenue of the Americas, New York, NY 10020. Copyright © 2007. All rights reserved. No part of this publication may be reproduced or distributed in any form or by an means, or stored in a database or retrieval system, without the prior written consent of The McGraw-Hill Companies, Inc., including but not limited to, in any network or other electronic storage or transmission, or broadcast for distance learning.

2 3 4 5 6 7 8 9 0 DOC DOC 0 9 8 7 6

Comb: ISBN-13: 978-0-07-296209-3 Spiral: ISBN-13: 978-0-07-325938-3
      ISBN-10: 0-07-296209-7   ISBN-10: 0-07-325938-1

Editor-in-chief: *Emily Barrosse*
Publisher: *Lisa Moore*
Sponsoring editor:
   Christopher Bennem
Director of development:
   Carla Kay Samodulski
Marketing manager: *Lori DeShazo*
Media producer: *Alex Rohrs*
Managing editor: *David M. Staloch*
Art director: *Jeanne M. Schreiber*
Senior designer: *Cassandra Chu*

Interior and cover designer:
   Maureen McCutcheon
Art manager: *Robin Mouat*
Lead production supervisor:
   Randy Hurst
Photo research coordinator:
   Alexandra Ambrose
Photo researcher: *Christine Pullo*
Composition: *Thompson Type*
Printing: *R.R. Donnelley & Sons*

Cover images: (*from left to right*) © *Philadelphia Museum of Art / CORBIS;* © *NASA / Roger Ressmeyer/CORBIS; Nevros / Folio, Inc.;* © *Jon Hicks / CORBIS*

Credits: *The credits section for this book begins on page C-1 and is considered an extension of the copyright page.*

Library of Congress Cataloging-in-Publication Data
Maimon, Elaine P.
   A writer's resource: a handbook for writing and research / Elaine P. Maimon, Janice H. Peritz, Kathleen Blake Yancey.—2nd ed.
      p. cm.
   Includes index.
   ISBN-13: 978-0-07-296209-3; ISBN-10: 0-07-296209-7 (alk. Paper)
   English language—Rhetoric—Handbooks, manual, etc. 2. English language—Grammar—Handbooks, manuals, etc. 3. Report writing—handbooks, manuals, etc. I. Peritz, Janice. II. Yancey, Kathleen Blake, III. Title.

PE1408/M3366 2005
808'.042—dc22
                             2005054441

The Internet addresses listed in the text were accurate at the time of publication. The inclusion of a Web site does not indicate an endorsement by the authors or McGraw-Hill, and McGraw-Hill does not guarantee the accuracy of the information presented at these sites.

www.mhhe.com

IMPORTANT

HERE IS YOUR REGISTRATION CODE TO ACCESS MCGRAW-HILL PREMIUM CONTENT AND MCGRAW-HILL ONLINE RESOURCES

For key premium online resources you need THIS CODE to gain access. Once the code is entered, you will be able to use the web resources for the length of your course.

Access is provided only if you have purchased a new book.

If the registration code is missing from this book, the registration screen on our website, and within your WebCT or Blackboard course will tell you how to obtain your new code. Your registration code can be used only once to establish access. It is not transferable.

To gain access to these online resources

1. USE your web browser to go to: **www.mhhe.com/awr**

2. CLICK on "First Time User"

3. ENTER the Registration Code printed on the tear-off bookmark on the right

4. After you have entered your registration code, click on "Register"

5. FOLLOW the instructions to setup your personal UserID and Password

6. WRITE your UserID and Password down for future reference. Keep it in a safe place.

If your course is using WebCT or Blackboard, you'll be able to use this code to access the McGraw-Hill content within your instructor's online course.

To gain access to the McGraw-Hill content in your instructor's WebCT or Blackboard course simply log into the course with the user ID and Password provided by your instructor. Enter the registration code exactly as it appears to the right when prompted by the system. You will only need to use this code the first time you click on McGraw-Hill content.

These instructions are specifically for student access. Instructors are not required to register via the above instructions.

The McGraw-Hill Companies

Thank you, and welcome to your McGraw-Hill Online Resources.

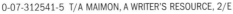
0-07-312541-5 T/A MAIMON, A WRITER'S RESOURCE, 2/E

BRJ6–JT9H–R9K7–3HUC–C9EU

REGISTRATION CODE

REGISTRATION CODE

The McGraw-Hill Companies

Higher Education

Use this registration card to access *Catalyst 2.0: the premier online resource for writing, research, and editing.* Available free with every student and instructor copy of *The New McGraw-Hill Handbook*, online access includes:

- A complete interactive ebook of the text
- The *Factiva* online database with thousands of full text articles and images from periodicals and journals
- Interactive tutorials on document design and visual rhetoric
- Guides for avoiding plagiarism and evaluating sources
- Electronic writing tutors for composing informative, interpretive, and argumentative papers
- *Bibliomaker* software for the MLA, APA, Chicago, and CSE styles of documentation
- More than 4,500 exercises with feedback in grammar, usage, and punctuation

In addition, *Catalyst 2.0* offers writing instructors a new, state-of-the-art course management and peer review system that allows users to do the following:

- Embed comments and links contextually alongside reviewed papers
- Create and select from lists of 'favorite' comments
- Drag and drop editing abbreviations and symbols into papers that link to *Catalyst* grammar coverage online
- Create and comment on multiple drafts among groups of student reviewers
- Use instructor-created review questions to respond to drafts

Preface

As we wrote the first edition of *A Writer's Resource,* our students were in our minds, acting as our chief consultants. We knew that their perspectives on college life were different from those of previous generations of students, and so were their expectations. We understood that they needed a handbook for the twenty-first century, with state-of-the-art resources on writing, researching, and graphic design in cyberspace. They might be using a handbook in an English composition class at 9:00 A.M., but at 10:00 A.M. they might be preparing Power-Points for a speech course, and at 11:00 A.M. they might need the handbook to help with a history assignment. More than any other textbook, their handbook was their guide, not just to writing, but also to learning in college. In revising the first edition, we have endeavored to make it an even stronger and more varied resource for achieving excellence in the ever-changing digital environment that students confront in college.

Changes to the Second Edition

In the second edition of *A Writer's Resource,* we made innumerable small changes—improvements in wording or the presentation of ideas—in addition to the larger modifications mentioned below. In making these changes, we have had the benefit of the considerable expertise of our new co-author, Kathleen Blake Yancey, whose contributions have been particularly welcome in the treatment of visual rhetoric, multimedia writing, and portfolios. Having her join us in this exciting endeavor represents, in itself, the most significant amendment in this edition. The major changes in the second edition include the following:

- **A strong focus on visual rhetoric**
  In keeping with our focus on the needs of today's students, the second edition includes new chapters on "Learning in a

Multimedia World" in Tab 1 and "Finding and Creating Effective Visuals" in Tab 5. Reflecting the many contexts in which students encounter visual rhetoric and design, however, the coverage of these important topics is also integrated throughout the text, particularly in Tab 2, "Writing and Designing Papers," rather than appearing in a separate section, divorced from the rest of the writing process. In addition, the text itself now includes more visuals throughout, with images drawn from various disciplines, time periods, and cultures. Students will see these new visual elements on the tab openers and in numerous examples of the kinds of visuals they will encounter in their reading and use in their writing.

- **A new chapter on multimedia assignments**
  Many students will be asked, or have already been asked, to move beyond traditional college assignments and to write in media other than the printed page. Tab 3, Common Assignments, now includes a chapter with guidelines for such multimedia assignments, including new instruction on creating multimedia presentations, photo and hypertext essays, and blogs, as well as enhanced coverage of how to design an effective Web site.

- **Documentation flowcharts**
  As they conduct research, students today are confronted with more types of sources than ever before. Therefore, Tabs 6 and 7 on the MLA and APA documentation styles now feature foldout, decision-tree-like diagrams that help students identify the kind of source they are dealing with and where to find the proper format for documenting it. These innovative charts offer students an alternate way—in addition to the directories—to locate the model they are looking for.

- **Visual guides for documenting sources**
  To show busy students where to find the information they need to cite their sources properly, the back of each foldout at the beginning of Tabs 6 and 7 provides facsimile pages from books, periodicals, and online subscription services that illustrate where students can find the author's name, the date of publication, and so on.

- **Enhanced coverage of note taking and plagiarism**
  Since students are confronted with more sources than ever before, they need more help with note-taking strategies and clear, straightforward advice on how to join the academic conversation without plagiarizing sources. The second edition provides even more instruction on how to take notes effec-

tively using traditional and online methods, along with more discussion of summary and synthesis and expanded coverage of intellectual property and copyright issues.

- **New boxes that help students recognize and correct errors and use grammar and spelling checkers**
The "Identify and Edit" boxes, which appear in key style, grammar, and punctuation chapters in Tabs 9, 10, and 11, give students—especially visual learners—strategies for identifying and correcting their most serious sentence problems and are especially useful for quick reference. Boxes appearing near the beginning of each chapter in Tabs 9, 10, and 11 warn students of the pitfalls of relying too much on computer grammar and style checkers when editing their work.

- **Expanded coverage for multilingual writers**
Featuring new boxes For Multilingual Students, written by Maria Zlateva, Director of ESL at Boston University, and improved Notes and Tips for Multilingual Writers in Tab 12, *A Writer's Resource* offers extraordinarily rich coverage for non-native speakers and writers of English.

- **Section on further resources, now tabbed for easier reference**
This ground-breaking section, consisting of a Timeline of World History, a glossary of Selected Terms from across the Curriculum, a pull-out map of the world, a Quick Reference for Multilingual Writers, and a Guide to Weights and Measurements, will come in handy for students in a wide variety of courses.

- **New *Catalyst 2.0: A Tool for Writing and Research***
To provide even more online support for today's tech savvy students, or for those students who need to become savvy about technology, *Catalyst* has been revised and expanded. *Catalyst 2.0* features new study tools, including a new interactive tutorial on visual rhetoric and document design; over 4,500 exercises—at several levels of difficulty—in grammar and usage, now with instant feedback; ten new interactive writing guides; and a revised and reorganized tutorial on avoiding plagiarism.

- **Integrated e-book and Interactive Annotated Instructor's Edition**
For ease of use at a home computer or in a lab, a complete e-book is available for students on the text's Web site, with hyperlinks to *Catalyst 2.0* throughout. In addition, the Web

site features the first-ever Interactive Annotated Instructor's Edition, with hundreds of 'pop-up' assignment suggestions and "Teacher to Teacher" advice as well hyperlinks to online sources, links and suggestions for using the resources within *Catalyst 2.0,* and hyperlinks to our Partners in Teaching online resource for teaching composition.

- **Online peer preview and course management utilities** Available for instructors who wish to use them, new class tools for electronic peer review and course management, provided by *Catalyst 2.0,* may be activated for free online. Students can gain access to the course with the *Catalyst* registration code that comes free with every text. Instructors can have their students share drafts of papers and their comments, view their grades online, and link to all the resources in *Catalyst* without ever having to worry about ordering special packages or ISBNs.

Hallmark Features of *A Writer's Resource*

- **A guide for success in college through writing**

  Tab 1: Learning across the Curriculum introduces students to the new territory of college and to college writing. In this unique section, we define concepts such as *discipline* and explain how to use writing as a tool for learning. This edition includes a new chapter (2) on Learning in a Multimedia World, with coverage of online tools for learning.

- **A focus on critical thinking and effective writing** Although instructors in various disciplines may approach subject matter differently, thinking critically and writing logically are underlying expectations across the curriculum. For this reason, Tab 2: Writing Papers begins with a chapter on critical reading, thinking, and writing. Reading and thinking critically lead to writing critically and presenting persuasive arguments.

- **Support for conducting research and managing information** The library's shelves are only the beginning of research for students today. The process continues on the Internet and in the field, the archive, and the lab. To assist students in these varied venues, we provide abundant guidance on posing research questions, understanding the role of ethics in research, conducting keyword searches in the library and on the Web, and thinking critically about sources. We also offer a detailed directory of sources from different disciplines in Chapter 25.

- **Guidelines for college writing assignments**
  Tab 3: Common Assignments across the Curriculum gives students step-by-step advice on writing the three most commonly assigned types of papers: informative, interpretive, and argumentative essays, as well as guidance on other common assignments including personal essays, case studies, lab reports, in-class essay exams, oral presentations with Power-Point, and multimedia assignments. Three full student papers are included as models.

- **Real student writing**
  Because students learn best from practical models that relate to their actual experience, we provide plenty of student writing, including examples from student papers, to show the realities of the processes of drafting, revising, and research. *A Writer's Resource* offers five full student papers, including samples of informative, interpretive, and argumentative writing as well as full MLA and APA papers in Tabs 6 and 7. We have also used student examples in the editing sections, so they illustrate the kinds of problems and concerns that students are most likely to have.

- **Grammar in the context of editing**
  Today's students need to see how grammar fits into the writing process, so they can learn to become effective editors of their own work. For this reason, each tab on the conventions of English usage, grammar, and mechanics starts with the word "Editing." These tabs give students a helpful way to organize their editing and proofreading by using a three-tier approach, beginning with issues of clarity (Tab 9), moving to grammar conventions (Tab 10), and ending with the surface concerns of mechanics, punctuation, and spelling (Tab 11).

- **Strong support for multilingual writers**
  Starting in the very first tab, *A Writer's Resource* offers multilingual writers support for learning in college and for every stage of the writing process. Chapter 3 provides advice to multilingual students on how they can use writing to deal with the unique challenges they often face. In addition, boxes with guidance for multilingual students appear in most of the tabs, and tips for multilingual writers are integrated throughout the basic grammar review in Tab 12. A separate index is provided for multilingual writers following the main index, as well as a complete list of all the For Multilingual Students boxes throughout the book. The handy grammar tips in the pull-out section in Further Resources for Learning provide a

quick reference that is easy to carry as students attend classes
or work in the library.

- **Plenty of advice on using technology**
  Today's student has more opportunities to write than ever before. E-mail, Web sites, chat rooms, and blogs all supplement
  the traditional occasions for writing offered by college course-
  work. Because we recognize that writing in college and in the
  world of work has become less and less a matter of the writer
  alone at a desk and more and more a matter of using technology effectively, we give full attention to technology throughout
  the text, with advice on using online tools for learning in Tab 1;
  specific, practical suggestions for using online resources to collaborate with peer reviewers and to revise; a chapter on designing academic papers and preparing print and online portfolios
  in Tab 2; advice for writing scannable résumés in Tab 4; and
  TextConnex boxes with advice on technology and useful links
  throughout the text.

- **Boxes that offer support for today's diverse student
  population**
  The boxes in *A Writer's Resource* supplement the text discussion with important information and helpful advice.

  > **Learning in College:** Featured throughout the text,
  > these boxed tips offer students information and strategies
  > that will help them become better learners and writers.

  > **Charting the Territory:** These boxes present relevant
  > information on such topics as interpretive assignments
  > in different disciplines and the function of the passive
  > voice in scientific writing, giving students a sense of how
  > requirements and conventions vary across the curriculum.

  > **TextConnex:** Offering advice on using electronic
  > resources and composing on a computer, as well as lists
  > of useful Web sites, the TextConnex boxes help today's
  > hyper-connected students take full advantage of the tech-
  > nology that is available to them.

  > **Writing after College:** Found in Tab 3, these boxes alert
  > students to a variety of related writing situations beyond
  > college.

  > **Boxes for Multilingual Students:** These boxes offer
  > advice on learning in college, writing, research, and se-
  > lected points of grammar.

Supplements for *A Writer's Resource*

Catalyst 2.0: *A Tool for Writing and Research* (**www.mhhe.com/awr**)

Throughout *A Writer's Resource,* Web references in the margin let students know where they can find additional resources on the text's comprehensive Web site. Access to the site—which is powered by *Catalyst 2.0,* the premier online resource for writing, research, and editing—is free with every student and instructor copy of *A Writer's Resource.* The site includes the following resources for students:

- A complete interactive e-book of the text
- Factiva online database, with thousands of full-text articles and images from periodicals and journals
- Interactive tutorials on document design and visual rhetoric
- Guides for avoiding plagiarism and evaluating sources
- Electronic writing tutors for composing informative, interpretive, and argumentative papers
- *Bibliomaker* software for the MLA, APA, Chicago, and CSE styles of documentation
- Over 4,500 exercises in grammar, usage, and punctuation, with feedback for each response

In addition, *Catalyst 2.0* offers writing instructors a new, state-of-the-art course management and peer review system that allows users to do the following:

- Embed comments and links contextually alongside reviewed papers
- Create and select from lists of "favorite" comments
- Drag and drop editing abbreviations and symbols that link to *Catalyst* grammar coverage into papers
- Create and comment on multiple drafts among groups of student reviewers
- Use instructor-created review questions to respond to drafts

Interactive Annotated Instructor's Edition
Deborah Coxwell Teague, Florida State University and
Dan Melzer, California State University, Sacramento

Accessible through *Catalyst,* this online interactive instructor resource will include a complete e-book of the text with the following features:

- Icons in the margins that link to pop-up suggestions for using the text in class
- Links to *Catalyst* and suggestions for using online assets in class

- Links to online resources for writing and research
- Links to the *McGraw-Hill Partners in Teaching* Web site, featuring discussion modules by dozens of the best academics on topics ranging from plagiarism to writing across the curriculum and more
- A printable version of the Instructor's Manual

The McGraw-Hill Exercise Book (ISBN 0-07-232890-8) Santi Buscemi, Middlesex College and Susan Popham, University of Memphis

Featuring numerous sentence-level and paragraph-level editing exercises, as well as exercises in research, documentation, and the writing process, this workbook can be used for any composition course.

The McGraw-Hill Exercise Book for Multilingual Writers (ISBN 0-07-326030-4) Maggie Sokolik, University of California, Berkeley

This workbook features numerous sentence-level and paragraph-level editing exercises tailored specifically for multilingual students.

The McGraw-Hill Writer's Journal (ISBN 0-07-326031-2) Lynée Gaillet, Georgia State University

This elegant, spiral-bound journal for students includes quotations on writing from famous authors as well as advice and tips on writing and the writing process.

The McGraw-Hill Student Planner (ISBN 0-07-322205-4)

This practical, spiral bound date book and planner for students is organized around the academic year, offering them a handy tool to structure and plan their work. It includes a brief almanac at the back with important facts from a variety of disciplines.

Teaching Composition Faculty Listserv at <www.mhhe.com/tcomp>: Moderated by Chris Anson at North Carolina State University and offered by McGraw-Hill as a service to the composition community, this listserv brings together senior members of the college composition community with newer members—junior faculty, adjuncts, and teaching assistants—through an online newsletter and accompanying discussion group to address issues of pedagogy, both in theory and in practice.

Dictionary and Vocabulary Resources

Random House Webster's College Dictionary (ISBN 0-07-240011-0)

This authoritative dictionary includes over 160,000 entries and 175,000 definitions.

The Merriam-Webster Dictionary (ISBN 0-07-310057-9)
Based on the best-selling Merriam-Webster's Collegiate Dictionary, this paperback dictionary contains over 70,000 definitions.

The Merriam-Webster Thesaurus (ISBN 0-07-310067-6)
This handy paperback thesaurus contains over 157,000 synonyms, antonyms, related and contrasting words, and idioms.

**Merriam-Webster's Vocabulary Builder
(ISBN 0-07-310067-6)**
This handy paperback introduces 3,000 words and includes
quizzes to test progress.

**Merriam-Webster's Notebook Dictionary
(ISBN 0-07-299091-0)**
An extremely concise reference to the words that form the core
of English vocabulary, this popular dictionary, conveniently
designed for 3-ring binders, provides words and information
at students' fingertips.

**Merriam-Webster's Notebook Thesaurus
(ISBN 0-07-310068-4)**
Conveniently designed for 3-ring binders, this thesaurus pro-
vides concise, clear guidance for over 157,000 word choices.

**Merriam-Webster's Collegiate Dictionary and Thesaurus,
Electronic Edition (ISBN 0-07-310070-6)**
Available on CD-ROM, this online dictionary contains thousands
of new words and meanings from all areas of human endeavor,
including electronic technology, the sciences, and popular culture.

Acknowledgments

When we wrote *A Writer's Resource,* we started with the premise that it
takes a campus to teach a writer. It is also the case that it takes a community to write a handbook. This text has been a major collaborative
effort for all three of us. And over the years, that ever-widening circle of
collaboration has included reviewers, editors, librarians, faculty colleagues, and family members.

Let us start close to home. Mort Maimon did line editing, checked
sources, and brought to this project his years of insight and experience
as a writer and as a secondary and post-secondary English teacher.
Gillian Maimon, a teacher, a Ph.D. candidate, and a writing workshop
leader, and Alan Maimon, a journalist who is expert in using every
resource available to writers, inspired and encouraged their mother in
this project. Alan also presented a new inspiration to the second edition—first granddaughter, Annabelle Elaine Maimon, who already
shows promise of becoming a writer. Rudy Peritz and Lynne Haney

reviewed drafts of a number of chapters, bringing to our cross-curricular mix the pedagogical and writerly perspectives of, respectively, a law professor and a sociologist. Jess Peritz, a current college student, was consulted on numerous occasions for her expert advice on making examples both up-to-date and understandable.

At Arizona State University West, Beverly Buddee, executive assistant to the provost, worried with us over this project for six years. Our deepest gratitude goes to Lisa Kammerlocher and Dennis Isbell for the guidelines on critically evaluating Web resources in Chapter 21, as well as to Sharon Wilson. Thanks, too, go to C. J. Jeney and Cheryl Warren for providing assistance. ASU West professors Thomas McGovern and Martin Meznar shared assignments and student papers with us. During work on the second edition, Denise Burger, Rosanne Kruckenburg, and Christine Tullius in the Chancellor's Office at the University of Alaska Anchorage showed admirable support and patience.

At Queens College, several colleagues in the English department not only shared their astute reflections on teaching and writing, but also gave us valuable classroom materials to use as we saw fit. Our thanks go to Fred Buell, Nancy Comley, Ann Davison, Joan Dupre, Hugh English, Sue Goldhaber, Marci Goodman, Eric Lehman, Norman Lewis, Charles Molesworth, Beth Stickney, Amy Tucker, and Stan Walker. We are especially grateful to the multitalented Steve Kruger, and to the pedagogically gifted Stuart Cochran, who helped us with writing samples and class tests. The Queens College librarians also gave us various kinds of help with the researching and documentation chapters, and we thank them, especially Sharon Bonk, Alexandra DeLuise, Izabella Taler, and Manny Sanudo.

At Queens, faculty from across the curriculum sent us material to consider for the book and, in some cases, also filled out questionnaires about their own practices as researchers and writers; our thanks go to David Baker, Linda Edwards, Ray Erickson, Peg Franco, Vivian Gruder, Marty Hanlon, Elaine Klein, Michael Krasner, Joel Lidov, Jacqueline Newman, Barbara Sandler, Dean Savage, and John Troynaski. We would also like to thank countless other faculty and administrative colleagues at ASU West, at Queens College, and at the University of Alaska Anchorage, whose commitment to learner-centered education informs this text.

We are also grateful to the following faculty from other institutions who contributed valuable materials and advice: Jane Collins, Jane Hathaway, Jan Tecklin, Christine Timm, Scott Zaluda, Diane Zannoni, and Richard Zeikowitz.

We want to give special thanks to the students whose papers we include in full: Joseph Smulowitz, Rajeev Bector, Nick Buglione, Esther Hoffman, and Audrey Galeano. We also want to acknowledge the following students who allowed us to use substantial excerpts from their work: Diane Chen, Jennifer Koehler, Ilona Bouzoukashvili, Wilma Ferrarella, Jacob Grossman, Umawattie Roopnarian, and Cheryl Pietrocarlo. Our thanks also go to Judy Williamson and Trent Batson for contributing their expertise on writing and computers as well as for sharing what they learned from the Epiphany Project. We also thank Rich Rice of Texas Tech for reviewing the technology coverage and for suggesting the image interpretation assignment in Chapter 14, as well as Dene Grigar of Texas Woman's University, Donna Reiss of Tidewater Community College, Cheryl Ball of Utah State University, and Elizabeth Nist of Anoka-Ramsey Community College for their advice on technology and for suggestions for the chapter on multimedia assignments. We are grateful to Harvey Wiener and the late Richard Marius for their permission to draw on their explanations of grammatical points in the *McGraw-Hill Handbook*. We also appreciate the work of Andras Tapolcai and of Charlotte Smith of Adirondack Community College, who collected many of the examples used in the documentation chapters, and Maria Zlateva, Boston University, our ESL Consultant on the Second Edition, who revised and expanded the coverage for multilingual writers throughout. Thanks also go to librarians Debora Person, University of Wyoming, and Ronelle K. H. Thompson, Augustana College, who provided us with helpful comments on Tab 5: Researching. Our colleague Don McQuade has inspired us, advised us, and encouraged us throughout the years of this project.

Within the McGraw-Hill organization, many wonderful people have been our true teammates. Tim Julet believed in this project initially and signed us on to what has become a major life commitment. From 1999, Lisa Moore, first as executive editor for the composition list, then as publisher for English, has creatively, expertly, and tirelessly led the group of development editors and in-house experts who have helped us find the appropriate form to bring our insights as composition teachers to the widest possible group of students. We have learned a great deal from Lisa. Thanks too to Christopher Bennem, who had the unenviable job of filling Lisa's shoes as sponsoring editor. This book has benefited enormously from two extraordinary development editors: Carla Samodulski, director of development for English, and David Chodoff, senior development editor. Both were true collaborators; as the chapters on editing show, the book has benefited enormously from their care and intelligence. Other editorial kudos go out to Betty Chen for her tireless work on this project over the last two years, Cynthia Ward, Margaret Manos, Laura Olson, James Marquand, and Meg Botteon, as well to Paul Banks, Alex Rohrs, and Manoj Mehta, without whom there would be no *Catalyst 2.0*. David Staloch, managing editor, monitored every detail of production; Cassandra Chu, senior designer, supervised every aspect of the striking text design and cover. Lori DeShazo, marketing manager, and Ray Kelley, Paula Radosevich, Byron Hopkins, Lisa Berry, and Brian Gore, field publishers, have worked tirelessly and enthusiastically to market *A Writer's Resource*. We also appreciate the hands-on attention of McGraw-Hill senior executives Phil Butcher, Emily Barrosse, editor-in-chief of the Humanities, Social Science, and Languages group; and Steve Debow, president of the Humanities, Social Science, and Languages group.

Finally, many, many thanks go to the reviewers who read various versions of this text, generously shared their perceptions, and had confidence in us as we shaped this book to address the needs of their students. In the second edition this included the contributions of the following instructors:

Stephen Adkison, Idaho State University
Angela Albright, Northwest Arkansas Community College
Lauryn Angel-Cann, Colin County Community College
Lisa Ashby, Concordia University
Susan Bailey, Mississippi State
Gwen Ball, Golden Gate University
Greg Barnhisel, Dusquesne University
Evelyn Beck, Piedmont Technical College
John Brinegar, Virginia Commonwealth University
Cheryl Brown, Towson University
Christy Burns, Jacksonville State University
Stephen Calatrello, Calhoun Community College
Elizabeth Canfield, Virginia Commonwealth University
Angier Caudle, Virginia Commonwealth University
Kevin Cavanaugh, Dutchess Community College
Ken Claney, Tulsa Community College
Keith Comer, Idaho State University
Christopher Crane, U.S. Naval Academy
Sara Cushing, Piedmont Technical College
Caron Daugherty, Ozarks Technical Community College
Alexina Fagan, Virginia Commonwealth University
Alexine Fleck, University of Pennsylvania
Kathleen Furlong, Glendale Community College
Karen Gaffney, Raritan Valley Community College
Dane Galloway, Ozarks Technical Community College
Karen Gardiner, University of Alabama
Lynn Grow, Broward Community College
Audrey Hall, Northwest Arkansas Community College
Roberta Henson, Indiana Wesleyan University
Nels Highberg, University of Hartford
Dean Hinnen, University of Texas at Arlington
Stephen Hock, University of Pennsylvania

Glenn Hutchinson, University of North Carolina at Charlotte
Lauren Ingraham, University of Tennessee at Chattanooga
Ron Jenkins, Atlantic Cape Community College
Julie Joki, Rogue Community College
Don Jones, University of Hartford
Betsy Joseph, Dallas County Community College
Pam Kannady, Tulsa Community College
Leah Anne Kleiman, Colin County Community College
Carol Kushner, Tulsa Community College
T. Mera Moore Lafferty, University of Pennsylvania
Don Langford, Ohio State University Newark
Cynthia Lewiecki-Wilson, Miami University of Ohio, Oxford
Barbara Liu, Eastern Connecticut State University
Irma Luna, San Antonio College
Bruce Machart, North Harris Community College
Tom MacLennan, University of North Carolina at Wilmington
Juan Martinez, Florida Central University
Timothy McGinn, Northwest Arkansas Community College
Kathleen McGrory, University of Hartford
Joyce M. Miller, Colin County Community College
Dorothy Minor, Tulsa Community College, Northeast
Tracy Montgomery, Idaho State University
Toni Morris, University of Indianapolis
Carol Nelson-Burns, University of Toledo
Denise Nemec, Northwest Arkansas Community College
Kelly O'Connor-Salomon, Russell Sage College
Danel Olson, North Harris Community College
Catherine Olson, Tomball College
Susan O'Neal, Tulsa Community College
Jean Petrolle, Columbia College Chicago
Claude Pruitt, University of Texas at Dallas
Linda Ranucci, Kent State University
Kirk Richardson, Virginia Commonwealth University
Owen Rogal, St. Ambrose University
Reid Sagara, California State University, Dominguez Hills
Lisa St. Ledger, University of Kansas
David Salomon, Russell Sage College
Christine Shearer-Cremean, Black Hills State University
Jane Stidham, Colin County Community College
Sharon Strand, Black Hills State University
Subashini Subbarao, Oakland Community College
Gayle Thomas, Community College of Southern Nevada
Rebecca Umland, University of Nebraska
Laurie Vickroy, Bradley University
Laura Vorachek, University of Alabama

Ted Walkup, Clayton State University
Cathy Wilson, Colin County Community College
Allison Woods, Franklin University

For their help with the first edition we wish to thank the following reviewers:

Harriet Arnold, University of the Pacific; Jim Baker, Texas A&M University; Jerry Ball, Arkansas State University; Cynthia Bascom, Butler University; Cynthia Bates, University of California, Davis; Anne Beaufort, American University; David Blakesley, Purdue University; Gary Blank, North Carolina State University; Robinson Blann, Trevecca Nazarene University; Philip Blosser, Lenoir-Rhyne College; William Boggs, Slippery Rock University of Pennsylvania; Virginia Bracket, Triton College; William Breedlove, College of Charleston; Karen S. Burge, Wichita State University; Jeff Cain, Sacred Heart University; Patricia Cearley, South Plains College; John Clark, Bowling Green State University; Sandra Clark, Anderson University; Michael Clarke, Loyola University of Chicago; Lauren Sewell Coulter, University of Tennessee, Chattanooga; Michael Delahoyde, Washington State University; Mike DeLong, Oklahoma State University—Oklahoma City; John E. Doyle, Quinnipiac College; William Durfee, University of Minnesota; Deborah Fleming, Ashland University; Shelli Fowler, Washington State University; Lynée Lewis Gaillet, Georgia State University; Ellen Gardiner, University of Mississippi; Sara Garnes, Ohio State University; Susanmarie Harrington, Indiana University—Purdue University Indianapolis; Andrew Harvey, University of North Carolina at Charlotte; Sharon Hatton-Montoya, University of Southern Colorado; Sharon Roger Hepburn, Radford University; Michael Hogan, Southeast Missouri State University; Kathy Houff, University of Georgia; Jodee Hunt, Grand Valley State University; Ronald B. Jenkins, Georgia College and State University; Jim Jeremiah, University of Phoenix; Joan Johnson, Hagerstown Community College; Eunice Johnston, North Dakota State University; Enoch Jordan, Norfolk State University; Bennett M. Judkins, Lenoir-Rhyne College; Rodney D. Keller, Ricks College; Beth Kemper, Campbellsville University; Mary Lynch Kennedy, State University of New York at Cortland; Linda Cooper Knight, Coastal Carolina University; Bill Lamb, Johnson County Community College; David LeNoir, Western Kentucky University; Barbara Liu, Eastern Connecticut State University; Sonia Maasik, University of California at Los Angeles; Mike Mackey, Community College of Denver; Wanda Martin, University of New Mexico; Jonathan Mauk, Owens Community College; Lisa McClure, Southern Illinois University at Carbondale; Angela McGlynn, Mercer County Community College; John David Moore, Eastern Illinois University; Mike Moran, University of Georgia; Ed Nagelhout, University of Nevada, Las Vegas; R. Gerald Nelms, Southern

Illinois University at Carbondale; Phillip F. O'Mara, Bridgewater College; C. R. Orchard, Indiana University of Pennsylvania; Virginia Polanski, Stonehill College; George Pullman, Georgia State University; Claude Reichard, Stanford University; Kelly Ritter, University of Illinois at Chicago; Mike Rose, University of California at Los Angeles; Alison Russell, Xavier University; David R. Russell, Iowa State University; Peter Sattler, Lakeland College; Cathy Sewell, Chesapeake College; Ernest J. Smith, University of Central Florida; Kathleen Sole, University of Phoenix; Madeleine Sorapure, University of California, Santa Barbara; Margot Soven, LaSalle University; Ernest Stromberg, University of Oregon; Lou Suarez, Lorain County Community College; John W. Taylor, South Dakota State University; Christopher Thaiss, George Mason University; Emily Thrush, University of Memphis; Rebecca Umland, University of Nebraska at Kearney; Jeffrey Vail, University of Delaware; Beverly Wall, Trinity College; Amy Walsh, University of South Dakota; Frank Walters, Auburn University; Randal Woodland, University of Michigan—Dearborn; Diane Zannoni, Trinity College; Mary Zdrojkowski, Eastern Michigan University.

Elaine P. Maimon
Janice H. Peritz
Kathleen Blake Yancey

About the Authors

Elaine P. Maimon is Chancellor of the University of Alaska Anchorage, where she is also Professor of English. Previously she was Provost (Chief Campus Officer) at Arizona State University West and Vice President of Arizona State University as a whole. In the 1970s, she initiated and then directed the Beaver College writing-across-the-curriculum program, one of the first WAC programs in the nation. A founding Executive Board member of the National Council of Writing Program Administrators (WPA), she has directed national institutes to improve the teaching of writing and to disseminate the principles of writing across the curriculum. With a PhD in English from the University of Pennsylvania, where she later helped to create the Writing Across the University (WATU) program, she has also taught and served as an academic administrator at Haverford College, Brown University, and Queens College.

Janice Haney Peritz is an Associate Professor of English who has taught college writing for more than thirty years, first at Stanford University, where she received her PhD in 1978, and then at the University of Texas at Austin; Beaver College; and Queens College, City University of New York. From 1989 to 2002, she directed the Composition Program at Queens College where in 1996 she also initiated the College's writing-across-the-curriculum program and the English Department's involvement with the Epiphany Project and cyber-composition. She also worked with a group of CUNY colleagues to develop The Write Site, an online learning center, and more recently directed the CUNY Honors College at Queens College for three years. Currently, she is back in the English Department doing what she loves most: full-time classroom teaching of writing, literature, and culture.

Kathleen Blake Yancey is the Kellogg W. Hunt Professor of English at Florida State University. She has taught at Virginia Tech, Purdue University, the University of North Carolina at Charlotte, and Clemson University, where she held the Pearce Professorship and directed the Pearce Center for Professional Communication. In 2004 she served as Chair for the Conference on College Composition and Communication (CCCC) and has also served as President of the Council of Writing Program Administrators and as Chair of the NCTE College Forum. She is currently the Vice-President Elect of the NCTE. A co-founder and co-leader of the National Coalition on Research into Electronic Portfolios, she consults on curriculum, assessment, and portfolio efforts internationally.

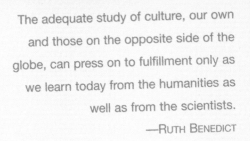

The compass has long been a tool for explorers and mapmakers. This book was designed to be a compass for writing in any discipline.

1

The adequate study of culture, our own and those on the opposite side of the globe, can press on to fulfillment only as we learn today from the humanities as well as from the scientists.

—RUTH BENEDICT

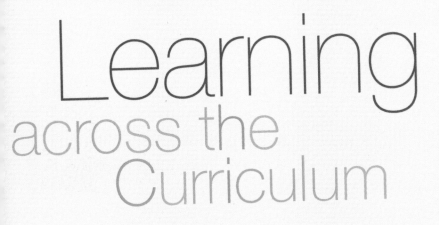

Learning across the Curriculum

1 Learning across the Curriculum

1

Writing to Learn

College is a place for exploration. During your studies, you will travel through many courses, participating in numerous conversations—oral and written—about nature, society, and culture. As you navigate your college experience, use this book as your map and guide:

- **As a map:** this text will help you understand the different approaches to knowledge you may encounter as you move from course to course and see how your studies relate to the larger world of learning.

- **As a guide:** this text will help you write everything from notes to exams to research papers—the record of your participation in the culture of your campus.

`1a` Study the world through a range of academic disciplines.

www.mhhe.com/awr

For discipline-related resources, go to

Learning > Links across the Curriculum

Each department in your college represents a specialized field of academic study, or area of inquiry, called a **discipline.** Each discipline has its own history, terminology, and concerns. Sociology, for example, is concerned with the conditions, patterns, and problems of people in groups and societies. Sociologists collect, analyze, and interpret data about groups and societies; they also debate the data's reliability and the credibility of various ways to interpret the data. These debates occur in journals, books, conferences, and classrooms—sites where knowledge is produced and communicated.

Each discipline is composed of diverse communities or social groups. For example, all economists do not see and say things in the same way. Although they belong to the same discipline—the discipline of economics—economists identify with various groups within their discipline based on their approaches to economic theory.

Your college curriculum is likely to include distribution requirements that will expose you to a range of disciplines. You may be asked to take one or two courses in the humanities (the disciplines of literature, music, and philosophy, for example), the social sciences (sociology, economics, and psychology, for example), and the natural sciences (physics, biology, and chemistry, for example). When you write in each discipline—taking notes, writing papers, answering essay-exam

Getting the Most from a Course

When you take a course, your purpose is not just to amass information about this or that topic. Your purpose is also to understand the kinds of questions people who work in the discipline ask.

- In an art history class, you might ask how a work relates to an artist's life and times.
- In a math class, you might ask what the practical applications of a particular concept are.
- In a sociology class, you might ask how race or gender relate to income.

questions—you will deepen your understanding of how knowledge is constructed. In doing so, you will join the academic conversation. You will also learn to see and think about the world from different vantage points.

www.mhhe.com/ awr
For activities to help strengthen your active reading skills, go to
Learning > Writing to Learn Exercises

1b   Use writing as a tool for learning.

One important goal of this handbook is to help you research and write your papers well. As you go from course to course, however, remember that writing itself is a great aid to learning. Travelers often keep journals and write letters to record what they have seen, heard, and done; to react to their experiences; and to reflect on the meaning of it all. Think of the way a simple shopping list aids your memory once you get to the store, or how taking minutes in a meeting focuses your attention. Writing helps you remember, understand, and create.

- **Writing aids memory.** From taking class notes to jotting down ideas for later development, writing ensures that you will be able to retrieve important information. Many students find it useful to use an informal outline for lecture notes (*see Figure 1.1*) and then go back and fill in details after class. Also write down ideas inspired by your course work—in any form or order—so that you won't forget them. These ideas can be seeds for research projects or some other critical inquiry.

- **Writing sharpens observations.** When you record what you see, hear, taste, smell, and feel, you increase the powers of your senses. Write down each place where a flute is heard in a

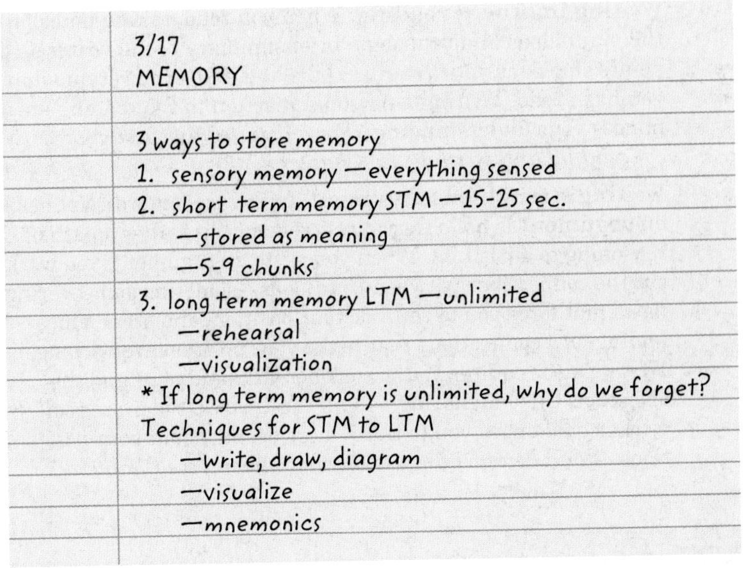

3/17
MEMORY

3 ways to store memory
1. sensory memory —everything sensed
2. short term memory STM —15-25 sec.
   —stored as meaning
   —5-9 chunks
3. long term memory LTM —unlimited
   —rehearsal
   —visualization
* If long term memory is unlimited, why do we forget?
Techniques for STM to LTM
   —write, draw, diagram
   —visualize
   —mnemonics

FIGURE 1.1 An outline for lecture notes. Jotting down the main ideas of a lecture and the questions they raise helps you become a more active listener.

piece of music, and you will hear the instrument more clearly. Note the smells during a chemistry experiment, and you will detect changes caused by reactions more readily.

■ **Writing clarifies thought.** "How do I know what I think until I see what I say?" The writer E. M. Forster's oft-quoted question reminds us that we frequently write our way into a topic. Carefully reading your own early drafts helps you pinpoint what you really want to say. Often, the last paragraph of a first draft becomes the first paragraph of the next one.

■ **Writing uncovers connections.** Maybe a character in a short story reminds you of your next-door neighbor, or an image in a poem makes you feel sad. What is it about your next-door neighbor that is similar to the fictional character? What is it about the image that evokes memories of loss? If you write down answers to these questions, you will learn more about the short story and the poem, and possibly more about yourself.

- **Writing improves reading.** When you read, taking notes on the main ideas and drafting a brief summary of the writer's points sharpens your reading skills and helps you retain what you have read. Writing a personal reaction to the reading enhances your understanding. (*For a detailed discussion of critical reading and writing, see Chapter 4.*)

- **Writing strengthens argument.** In the academic disciplines, an **argument** is not a fiery disagreement but rather a path of reasoning to a position. When you write an argument, you work out the connections between your ideas—sometimes uncovering flaws that force you to rethink your position, and other times finding new connections that make your position even stronger. Writing also requires you to consider your audience and the objections they might raise. In all these cases, the process of writing challenges you to think more deeply about your positions. (*For a detailed discussion of argument, see Chapter 11.*)

www.mhhe.com/ awr

For help with college survival techniques, go to

Learning > Study Skills Tutor

c Take responsibility for reading, writing, and research.

The academic community of college assumes that you are an independent learner, capable of managing your workload without supervision. For most courses, the syllabus will be your primary guide to what is expected of you, serving as a contract between you and your instructor. The syllabus will tell you what reading you need to do before each class, when tests are scheduled, and when papers or stages of papers (topic and research plan, draft, final paper) are due. Use the syllabus to map out your weekly schedule for reading, research, and writing. (*For tips on how to schedule a research paper, see Chapter 18, pp. 207–13.*)

If you are collaborating with a group on a project, it is essential to schedule a series of meetings well in advance to avoid schedule conflicts. It is just as important, however, to schedule time for your solo projects away from all distractions. You will be much more efficient if you work in shorter blocks of concentrated time than if you let your reading and writing drag on for interruption-filled hours.

d Recognize that writing improves with practice.

Composition courses will help you learn to write at the college level, but your development as a writer does not end there. Writing in all your courses will enable you to mature as a writer while preparing you for more writing after college.

2 Learning in a Multimedia World

You are likely to register for courses through your college's Web site, conduct research on the Web, and perhaps even attend lectures in "smart classrooms" equipped to display images from the instructor's computer and DVD/VCR. In this multimedia environment, you will be dealing with images as well as spoken and written texts to a greater degree than has any previous generation. Composing, too, will involve both images and words.

2a Become aware of the persuasive power of images.

As a student, you will not only analyze images but also create them. We live in a world in which images join with words as tools of persuasion as well as instruction. Images, like words, require careful, critical analysis. A misleading chart, such as the one shown in Figure 2.1 on page 8, or an altered photograph can easily distort your perception of a subject. The ability not only to understand visual information but also to evaluate its credibility is an essential tool for learning and writing. (*For details on evaluating visuals, see Chapter 4: Reading, Thinking, Writing, pp. 22–27, and Chapter 11: Arguments, pp. 130–37.*)

2b Make effective use of multimedia elements.

Technology now makes it possible for you to include images and other nonverbal elements in your writing. Not too long ago, students who needed to include a special notation—an equation, say, in a paper for a math or science class, or a musical example in a paper for a music class—probably wrote it out by hand on a separate sheet of paper. Including a photograph was out of the question, except perhaps as a fuzzy black-and-white photocopy on a separate page.

Computers now let you create these elements yourself or import them from other sources and place them where you want them in your writing—like, for example, this passage from Beethoven's Fifth Symphony:

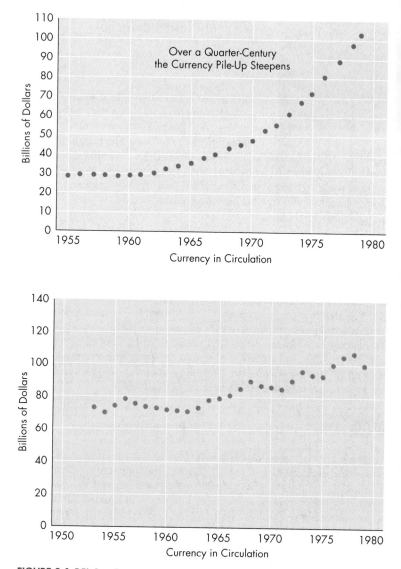

FIGURE 2.1 Misleading (top) and reliable charts. The graph on top, from a 1979 article in the *Wall Street Journal,* shows a dramatic and accelerating increase in currency in circulation in the United States between 1953 and 1979. As a measure of the purchasing power of the people who held the currency, however, the graph is misleading because it fails to take inflation into account. The second graph, corrected for inflation, reveals a steady but far less dramatic rate of increase.

FIGURE 2.2 **Before (top) and after Hurricane Bertha.**

A photograph or diagram or chart can contain information that adds details, makes relationships clearer, and provides dimension to the printed page. In a paper for a geography course, for example, "before" and "after" photographs can illustrate at a glance the effects of a hurricane on a coastline, as the images in Figure 2.2 demonstrate.

A graph can effectively illustrate important trends for a history paper, as Figure 2.3 on page 10 shows. Similarly, a timeline, like the

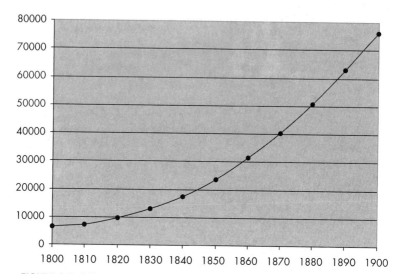

Total U.S. Resident Population 1800–1900, by decade (in thousands)

FIGURE 2.3 **A line graph showing trends over time.**

one in the "Further Resources for Learning" section at the end of this book, can help readers grasp the relationships among important events.

If you can post your paper online or deliver it as an electronic file to be read on a computer, you can include an even greater variety of media. You can supplement a musical passage, for example, with a link to an audio file of the passage. Or you can supplement a paper about political speeches for an American government course with a link to a video clip of a politician giving a speech.

(*For details on creating effective visuals, see Chapter 5: Planning, pp. 53–57; Chapter 6: Drafting, p. 75; Chapter 7: Revising, p. 88; and Chapter 8: Designing the Final Document. For information on creating multimedia presentations, see Chapter 14: Multimedia Writing. For help with finding appropriate visuals, see Chapter 20: Finding and Creating Effective Visuals.*)

www.mhhe.com/ awr
For more about online resources, go to

Additional Links
on Learning

2c Take advantage of online and other electronic tools for learning.

Technology now makes it possible to transcend the constraints of the clock, the calendar, and the car and engage in educational activities 24/7, or twenty-four hours a day, seven days a week.

1. Communicating with e-mail

E-mail, the medium for sending messages and document attachments over the Internet, is the most frequently used form of written communication in the world today. In some classes, you can use e-mail to

---

TEXTCONNEX

Netiquette

The term **netiquette** combines the words *Internet* and *etiquette* to form a new word that stands for good manners in cyberspace. Here are some netiquette guidelines.

- **Remember that you are interacting with real humans,** not machines, and practice kindness, patience, and good humor.
- **Use accurate subject headings to indicate your topic.**
- **Limit each e-mail to a single topic,** particularly if you are sending e-mail to lists, news groups, or conferences.
- **Use words economically, and edit carefully.** Readers' eyes tire and patience evaporates when they encounter all lowercase letters or text that lacks appropriate punctuation.
- **Bear in mind that without cues such as facial expressions, body language, and vocal intonation, your message can easily be misunderstood.** Be extra careful about humor that could be misread as sarcasm. Misunderstandings can escalate quickly into *flaming*—the sending of angry, inflammatory posts.
- **Avoid ALL CAPS.** Typing in all caps is considered shouting.
- **Remember that your e-mail message can be reproduced.** Avoid saying anything you would not want attributed to you or forwarded to others.
- **Include a sufficient portion of the previous text** when responding to an e-mail so that you keep the conversation flowing and provide context.
- **Always seek permission to use other people's ideas.** Electronic text makes sharing ideas easy. If you use another person's online thoughts or words, seek permission first, and always acknowledge the other person properly.
- **Never copy other people's words and present them as your own.** This practice, known as **plagiarism,** is always wrong. (*See Tabs 6–8 for help with citing Internet sources.*)
- **Include your name and contact information at the end of every e-mail you send.**

communicate with your professor, other students, or a consultant in your school's writing center.

Remember, however, that although e-mail is (almost) always available, people are not. Just as your professor may schedule office hours in a campus building, she or he may tell you that you can send e-mail any time but that you should expect an answer only during certain hours.

2. Using instant messaging

Instant messaging allows you to engage in real-time conversations with individuals who are connected to the Internet at the same time as you. It can be used to further your learning in much the same way as e-mail, although you cannot attach papers to an instant message. Use instant messaging sparingly in an academic setting, however. It can distract you from your course work and is rarely appropriate for addressing instructors.

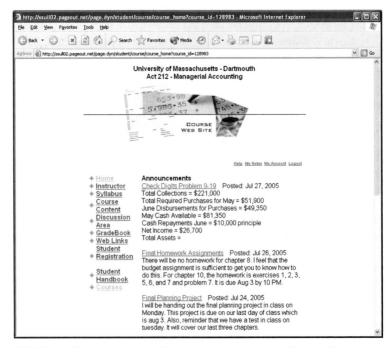

FIGURE 2.4 The home page for a course in accounting at the University of Massachusetts, Dartmouth.

3. Consulting course Web sites

Your instructor may have a Web site for your course, like the one in Figure 2.4 on page 12. If so, check it for late-breaking announcements, the course syllabus, assignments (and their due dates), and course-related links as well as other Web resources.

4. Learning in networked classrooms and virtual classrooms

Some colleges and instructors are experimenting with **networked classrooms**—classrooms in which each student works at one of a network of linked computers. For example, your instructor might post daily assignments and discussion topics, and you might be assigned to work collaboratively on a writing project. Because you are interacting in writing rather than in spoken discussion, you can save ideas and comments for use in the first draft of a paper. Online interactive class sessions also help you become more aware of audience and purpose in your writing because the audience is writing back to you and can ask you for clarifications (*see Chapter 5: Planning and Shaping*). Computers and the Internet also make it possible for students to engage in distance learning—from almost anywhere in the world—in courses conducted entirely online in **virtual classrooms.**

5. Exchanging ideas through blogs

Weblogs (or blogs) provide another forum for online discussion and interaction. A **blog** is a personal online journal. Blog authors might post dated entries with personal commentary on a variety of topics, include links to Web sites they find interesting, and (sometimes) provide a forum for readers' comments. Software and online services now exist that make it possible for almost anyone to create a blog.

6. Using peer review software such as *Catalyst*

www.mhhe.com/
awr
To explore *Catalyst*,
go to

Home

E-mail, instant messaging, networked classrooms, blogs, and many other electronic resources (such as bulletin boards and discussion groups) provide a variety of forums for you and your classmates to discuss assignments and other topics that come up in class. These discussions can help you test ideas and clarify your thoughts as you respond to assignments and work through writing projects.

Peer review is a structured process that goes a step beyond these informal discussions. Often encouraged or required by instructors, peer review gives students an opportunity to respond to one another's work at designated stages in the writing process, to identify and iron out problems and hone arguments. Peer review is possible without computers and the Internet, but specialized software, like the writing environment in the *Catalyst* Web site that accompanies this book, makes peer review an efficient and accessible learning tool. The *Catalyst* software permits you and the other members of your assigned peer group to make comments about one another's writing and to view and respond to those comments; see Figure 2.5 below.

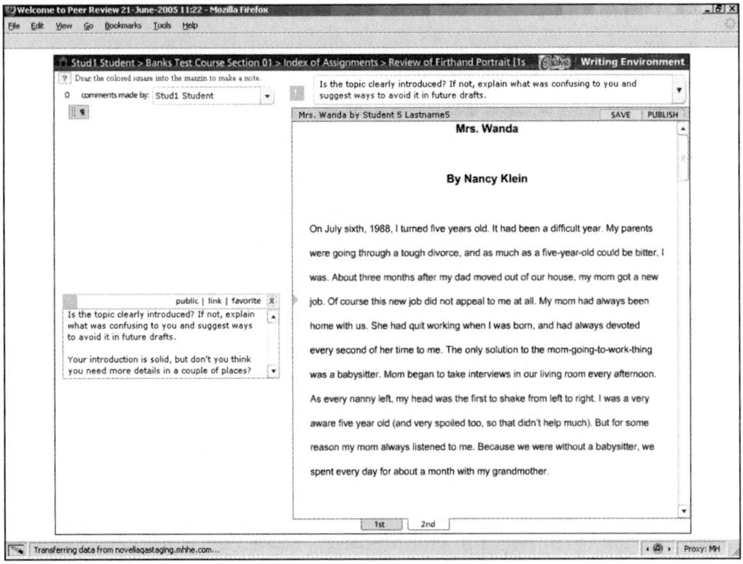

FIGURE 2.5 A peer review screen from *Catalyst*.

3　Learning in English as a Second Language

To some extent, college presents everyone with an unfamiliar culture and its languages. The language of anthropology, for example, probably sounds strange to most students, including those who have been speaking English all their lives. If you spoke another language before learning English, you already have experience trying to feel at home in a new culture and working to acquire a new language.

Asking questions of your professors and others, as well as consulting guidebooks like your course textbooks, can help you orient yourself in college. So, too, can recognizing specialized vocabulary, including common English words that have a special meaning when they are used within a discipline. Like all students, you will have to engage in writing to learn and in critical reading and thinking to succeed in college.

3a　Become aware of cultural differences in communication.

Because you are familiar with at least two languages and cultures, you already know that there is more than one way to interact politely and effectively with other people. In fact, you may wonder about the way people communicate in college classrooms in the United States. Your classmates may pride themselves on being direct; you may think that they sound almost impolite in their enthusiasm to make a point. They may strive to be precise; you may wonder why they are explaining things that attentive people should be able to figure out for themselves.

Colleges in the United States encourage students to openly exchange views, clearly state opinions, and support judgments with examples, observations, and reasons. You may be reluctant to participate because you are concerned about an "accent" or about the fine points of grammar or pronunciation. Don't worry. Communication is your first priority, so gather up your confidence and join the conversation:

- Participate actively in small-group discussions.
- Ask and answer questions during class discussions.
- Approach instructors and fellow students outside class when you need additional help.

3b Use writing to learn more about English.

To develop fluency in English, get into the habit of writing every day.

- **Write a personal journal.** Using English to explore your thoughts and feelings about your studies and college life will help make you feel more comfortable using the language.

- **Keep a writer's notebook.** Every day, write down a quotation from something you have read, and then either comment on it or put the idea into your own words. Write down bits of dialogue you overhear. Make lists of words and phrases that are new to you; many of these will turn out to be English **idioms**—words and phrases with special meanings not necessarily included in a simple dictionary definition. Go over these lists with your writing group, a friend, or a tutor in the writing center.

- **Write letters in English.** Letters are a good way to practice the informal style used in conversation. Write to out-of-town acquaintances who don't speak your first language. Write a letter to the college newspaper about a change you think needs to be made at the college or in response to another letter to the editor. You can also write brief notes, either on paper or through e-mail, to instructors, tutors, librarians, secretaries, and other native speakers of English. Write notes to your roommates, dorm manager, repair person, and others whom you encounter on campus and off.

www.mhhe.com/
awr
For access to online dictionaries, go to

Dictionaries
and Thesauri

3c Use learning tools that are available for multilingual students.

The style of written communication favored in U.S. colleges is often referred to simply as "good writing." This handbook explains this academic style and its variations. This style—which is sometimes described as analytical and argumentative—reflects the Western cultural tradition, one of many traditions in the world.

The following kinds of reference books can help you as you write papers for your college courses. You can purchase them at your college bookstore or find copies in the reference section of your college library.

1. Consulting an ESL dictionary

A good dictionary designed especially for second-language students can be a useful source of information about word meanings. Ordinary dictionaries frequently define difficult words with other difficult words. In the *American Heritage Dictionary,* for example, the word *haze* is defined as "Atmospheric moisture, dust, smoke, and vapor suspended to form a partially opaque condition." An ESL dictionary defines it more simply as "A light mist or smoke."

Do not confuse ESL dictionaries with bilingual or "translation" dictionaries. Translation dictionaries frequently oversimplify word meanings. So, too, do abridged dictionaries because they do not indicate shades of meaning.

Like all standard English dictionaries, an ESL dictionary includes instructions that explain the abbreviations used in the entries. They also list the special notations used for words classified as *slang, vulgar, informal, nonstandard,* or another category worthy of special attention. In the ESL/Learner's Edition of the *Random House Webster's Dictionary of American English* (1997), you will find "pig out" as the sixth entry under the word *pig:*

Pig out (no obj) Slang. to eat too much food: *We pigged out on pizza last night.*

The entry tells you that "pig out" does not take a direct object ("no obj") and that its use is very informal ("Slang"), appropriate in talking with classmates but not in writing papers. You will hear a great deal of slang on your college campus, on the radio, and on television. Make a list of slang phrases, and look them up later. If you do not find them listed in your standard or ESL dictionary, check for them in a dictionary of American slang.

The dictionary will help you with spelling, syllabication, pronunciation, definitions, word origins, and usage. The several meanings of a word are arranged first according to part of speech and then from most common to least common meaning. Examine the entry for the word *academic* in the ESL/Learner's Edition:

ac.a.dem.ic /ˈækəˈdɛmɪk/ *adj.* **1.** (before a noun) Of or relating to a school, esp. one for higher education: *an academic institution.* **2.** Of or relating to school subjects that teach general intellectual skills rather than specific job skills: *academic subjects like English and mathematics.* **3.** Not practical or directly useful: *Whether she wanted to come or not is an academic question because she's here now.*—*n.* (count) **4.** A student or teacher at a college or university—**ac'a.dem'i.cal.ly,** *adv.*

Note that nouns are identified as count or noncount, indicating whether you can place a number in front of the noun and make it plural. You can say, "Four academics joined the group," so when *academic* is used as a noun, it is a count noun. *Honesty* is a noncount noun.

When you look up words or phrases in the dictionary, add them to your personal list. Talk about your list with classmates. They will be happy to explain up-to-date uses of the words and phrases you are learning. To expand your vocabulary, consult a thesaurus for synonyms and use the most precise term.

2. Consulting a dictionary of American idioms

As we explained earlier, an idiom is an expression that is peculiar to a particular language and cannot be understood by looking at the individual words. "To catch a bus" is an idiom.

3. Using a desk encyclopedia

In the reference section of your college library, you will find one-volume encyclopedias on every subject from U.S. history to classical or biblical allusions. You may find it helpful to look up people, places, and events that are new to you for a quick identification, especially if the person, place, or event is referred to often in U.S. culture.

The way the butterfly in this image emerges on a computer screen, as if from a cocoon of written text, suggests the way writers transform words and visuals into finished works through careful planning, drafting, revision, and design.

2

I like to do first drafts at night, when I'm tired, and then do the surgical work in the morning when I'm sharp.

—ALEX HALEY

Writing and Designing Papers

2 Writing and Designing Papers

4 Reading, Thinking, Writing: The Critical Connection

Critical readers, thinkers, and writers get intellectually involved. They recognize that meanings and values are made, not found, so they pose pertinent questions, note significant features, examine relationships, and consider the credibility of what they read, see, and hear. The strategies in this chapter will help you read, think, and write critically.

In this context, the word *critical* means "thoughtful." When you read critically, for example, you recognize the literal meaning of the text, make inferences about implicit or unstated meanings, and then make your own judgments in response.

When they talk about reading texts, most people are thinking of words on a printed page. However, advances in technology have made it easier than ever to receive information in a variety of ways. It is essential to be able to "read" critically not just written texts but visuals, sounds, and spoken texts as well. We use the word *text,* then, to refer to works that readers, viewers, or listeners invest with meaning and that can be critically analyzed.

4a Read critically.

1. Previewing

Critical reading begins with **previewing**—a quick review of the author, publication information, title, headings, visuals, and key sentences or paragraphs.

Previewing written texts   As you preview, be skeptical: just because something is in print does not mean that it is true. Whenever possible, ask questions about the following:

www.mhhe.com/ awr
For help with evaluating sources, go to
Research > CARS Source Evaluation Tutor

- **Author:** Who wrote this piece? What are the writer's credentials? Who is the writer's employer? What is the writer's occupation? Age? What are his or her interests and values?

- **Purpose:** What do the title and first and last paragraphs tell you about the purpose of this piece? Do the headings provide clues to its purpose? What do the visuals suggest about its purpose? What might have motivated the author to write it? Is the main purpose to inform, to interpret, to argue, or to accomplish something else (to entertain or to reflect, for instance)?

- **Audience:** Whom do you suspect the author is trying to inform or persuade? If the piece includes boldfaced terms or a glossary, do the terms give you a sense of what kind of knowledge the author expects his or her audience to have? Is the author addressing you or people like you?

- **Content:** What does the title tell you the piece is about? Does the first paragraph include the main point? What do the headings tell you about the gist of the piece? Does the conclusion say what the author has focused on?

- **Context:** When was the piece published? Is it current? Does the date matter? What kind of publication is it? A book? An article in a periodical or library database? A Web page? Where and by whom was it published? If it has been published electronically, was it posted by the author? By an organization with a special interest?

Tips LEARNING in COLLEGE

Evaluating Context in Different Kinds of Publications

- **For a book:** Are you looking at the original publication, or is this a reprint? What is the publisher's reputation? University presses, for example, are very selective about the books they publish, usually concentrating on scholarly works. A vanity press—one that requires authors to pay to publish their work—is not selective at all.

- **For an article in a periodical:** Look at the list of editors and their affiliations. What do you know about the journal, magazine, or newspaper in which this piece appears? Are the articles reviewed by experts in a particular field before they are published?

- **For a Web page:** Who created the page? A Web page named for a political candidate, for example, may actually have been put on the Web by opponents. (*See the box on p. 244.*)

Previewing visuals You can use most of the previewing questions for written texts to preview visuals. You should also ask some additional questions, however. For example, suppose you were asked to preview the advertisement shown in Figure 4.1.

FIGURE 4.1 ACLU advertisement. The text superimposed on this photograph reads: "I AM NOT AN AMERICAN WHO BELIEVES WE SHOULD ALL HAVE THE SAME OPINIONS. I AM AN AMERICAN who believes that our right to have lively discussion and thorough investigation are the things that make our country great. I AM AN ACLU MEMBER because free speech is the foundation of freedom. Keep America SAFE & FREE. SIGN ON AT: WWW.ACLU.ORG.

Here are some preview questions you might ask and the answers you could give to them:

- **In what context does the visual appear?** This advertisement appeared in the *New York Times Magazine.* The ad does not have an "author," but it is clearly the product of the American Civil Liberties Union (ACLU), as the box in the lower right-hand corner indicates. The box also indicates its purpose—to persuade people to join the ACLU.

- **Does the visual consist of a single image, or is it part of a series of images?** There is one image: a black-and-white photograph that depicts the actor Kristin Davis, best known for playing Charlotte on the television series *Sex and the City.*

- **Is it a representation of a real event, person, or thing, or is it fictional?** The image appears to be nonfiction (even though Davis almost certainly has been posed by the photographer). Davis appears as herself, not as "Charlotte."

- **What does the visual depict?** Davis is standing in what appears to be a gritty urban location.

- **Is the visual accompanied by audio or printed text?**
  Printed text appears over Davis's image, suggesting that the words are hers. Some words are emphasized.

2. Reading and recording initial impressions

A first reading is similar to a first draft—your primary purpose is to get a sense of the whole. Read the selection for its literal meaning. Identify the main topic of the text and the main point the writer makes about the topic. Read the work in one sitting if possible. Note unclear or difficult passages to come back to later as well as ideas that grab your attention. Record your initial impressions:

- If the text or image is an argument, what opinion is being expressed? Were you persuaded by the argument?

- Did you have an emotional response to the text or image? Were you surprised, amused, or angered by anything in it?

- What was your initial sense of the writer or speaker?

- What key ideas did you take away from the work?

3. Using annotation and summary to analyze a text

Once you understand the literal or surface meaning of a text, it is time to dig deeper by analyzing and interpreting it. To **analyze** a text is to consider it in detail by breaking it down into significant parts and examining how those parts relate to each other. We analyze a text in order to **interpret** it and come to a fuller understanding of its meanings.

Using annotation and summary Annotation and summary are techniques that can help as you read to understand, question, analyze, and interpret. **Annotation** combines reading with analysis. To annotate a text, read through it slowly and carefully while asking yourself the *who, what, how,* and *why* questions. As you read, underline or circle words, phrases, and sentences that strike you as significant or puzzling, and write your questions and observations in the margin. If you cannot mark the text, you can make separate notes in a notebook or computer file.

SAMPLE ANNOTATED PASSAGE

Opens with a story about his childhood

Establishes his authority —he's experienced multi-culturalism

Both my parents were immigrants from Russia. In my neighborhood, Yiddish was a first and second language. I grew up in the depths of the Great Depression. There were weeks when my father came home with $5 or less. My mother walked blocks to save a few cents on food.

I went to public school. Some of my friends were sent to the yeshiva—an Orthodox Jewish religious school—but my parents, having experienced the vicious, pervasive anti-Semitism in the Old Country, wanted me to learn what America was all about.

At Boston Latin School and Northeastern University—a working-class college—I took classes that taught a great deal about the fundamental rights and liberties that had to be fought for during this still "unfinished American revolution," as Thurgood Marshall called it. These were required courses, and inspired my lifelong involvement in civil rights and civil liberties.

—NAT HENTOFF, "Misguided Multiculturalism"

Essential?? Supreme Court. Does he assume they would inspire everyone?

You cannot analyze or interpret something if you do not understand it. One way to demonstrate that you understand a text is to summarize it. A **summary** conveys the basic content of a text. When you summarize, your goal is to communicate the text's main points in your own words, not to say what you think of it. A summary is typically about one paragraph in length. Even when you are writing a fuller summary of a longer work, though, you should always use the fewest words possible. Clarity and brevity are important. A summary should never be longer than the original work. Although writing a summary

CHARTING the TERRITORY

Mapping Your Topic

When you are analyzing a text within the framework of a particular discipline, you might begin your analysis by comparing the text you are studying with other texts written on the same topic but from different perspectives—from different places on the disciplinary map.

- **What issues might the topic raise for members of different disciplines?** For historians, the reunification of Germany might raise issues about top-down versus bottom-up modes of change. For economists, the interesting issue might be the unemployment caused by privatizing the former East Germany's industry.

- **How would members of different disciplines investigate the issues that interest them?** What data would historians or economists want? Where and how would they get the data?

- **What kinds of conclusions do members of different disciplines tend to expect and accept?** Historians expect and accept arguments about how people have or have not changed their lives, conditions, or ideas over time. Economists tend to expect and accept conclusions based on some more or less unchanging law or principle, such as the law of supply and demand.

requires simplification, you need to be careful to avoid misrepresenting a writer's points by *oversimplifying* them. (*For specific instructions on how to write a summary, see Chapter 23: Working with Sources and Avoiding Plagiarism, pp. 259–61.*)

Questioning the text Analysis and interpretation require a critical understanding of the *who, what, how,* and *why* of a text:

- **What is the writer's *stance,* or attitude toward the subject?** Does the writer appear to be objective, or does she or he seem to have personal feelings about the subject?

- **What is the writer's *voice?*** Is it like that of a reasonable judge, an enthusiastic preacher, a thoughtful teacher, or a reassuring friend? Does the writer seem to be speaking *at, to,* or *with* the audience?

- **What assumptions does the writer seem to be making about the audience?** Does the writer assume an audience of specialists or a general audience? Does the writer assume that the reader agrees with him or her, or does the writer try to build agreement? Does the writer seem to choose examples and evidence with a certain audience in mind?

- **What is the writer's primary purpose?** Is it to present findings, offer an objective analysis, or argue for a particular action or opinion?

- **How does the writer develop ideas?** What kind of support does the writer rely on to develop the main point? Does she or he define key terms? Tell relevant stories? Provide logical reasons?

- **Does the text appeal to emotions?** Does the writer use words, phrases, clichés, images, or examples that are emotionally charged?

- **Is the text fair?** Does the writer consider opposing ideas, arguments, or evidence? Does he or she deal with them fairly?

- **Is the evidence strong?** Does the writer provide sufficient evidence for his or her position? Where is the argument strongest and weakest?

- **Is the text effective?** What are your beliefs on this subject? Have they been changed by the text?

Visuals, too, can be subjected to critical analysis, as the comments a reader made on the ACLU ad indicate (*see Figure 4.2*).

Davis is projecting a
serious image, and she's
dressed very plainly.
She looks directly at the
camera, directly at the
viewer.

She seems to be in a
dangerous place, a tunnel
entrance with a car
whizzing by, at
night on a slippery road
—but she is unafraid.
Does her statement
require bravery?

Davis's character
"Charlotte" is
associated with
New York City, and
this seems to be a
NYC scene.
Is there a 9/11
connection?

black and white—like
photojournalism—
"real," "serious"

Why are these words
emphasized?

FIGURE 4.2 **Sample annotations on the ACLU ad.**

4. Synthesizing your observations in a critical-response paper

To **synthesize** means to bring together, to make something out of different parts. In the last stage of critical reading, you pull your summary, analysis, and interpretation together into a coherent whole. Whether you realize it or not, you synthesize material every day.

When you hear contrasting accounts of a party from two different people, you assess the reliability and potential bias of each source; you select the information that is most pertinent to you; you evaluate the story that each one tells; and finally, you create a composite, or synthesis, of what you think really went on. When you synthesize information from two or more texts, you follow the same process.

4b   Think critically.

Critical thinking is fundamental not only to college work but also to life in a democratic society. Thinking critically means getting involved, not necessarily finding fault. Critical thinkers never simply gather information and present it without question. They inquire about what they see, hear, and read.

Evaluating a text's argument is not a game of "gotcha," an attempt to catch the bad guys in order to be seen as a good guy. Its purpose is more critical and thoughtful: to figure out a text's promise and limitations, strengths and weaknesses.

1. Recognizing an argument

The word *argument,* when used in the context of critical thinking, does not mean a shouting match. In the college classroom and in reasoned debate outside the classroom, an **argument** means a path of reasoning aimed at persuading people to accept or reject an assertion. The assertion must be arguable: it must be on an issue about which reasonable people can disagree. For example, the assertion that women should be allowed to try out for all college sports teams is arguable.

2. Analyzing and evaluating an argument

There are a number of ways to analyze an argument and evaluate its effectiveness. Two common methods are (1) to concentrate on the type of reasoning the writer is using and (2) to question the logical relation of a writer's claims, grounds, and warrants, using the Toulmin method.

Types of reasoning   Writers may use either inductive or deductive reasoning to make an argument. When writers use **inductive reasoning,** they do not prove that the argument is true; instead, they convince reasonable people that it is probable by presenting evidence (facts and statistics, anecdotes, and expert opinion). When writers use **deductive reasoning,** on the other hand, they are making the claim that a conclusion follows necessarily from a set of assertions, or

premises—in other words, that if the premises are true, the conclusion must be true.

For example, a journalism student writing for the school paper might make the following assertion:

> As Saturday's game shows, the Buckeyes are on their way to winning the Big Ten title.

If the student is reasoning inductively, she will present a number of facts—her evidence—that support her claim but do not prove it conclusively:

FACT 1 With three games remaining, the Buckeyes have a two-game lead over the second-place Badgers.

FACT 2 The Buckeyes' final three opponents have a combined record of 10 wins and 17 losses.

FACT 3 The Badgers lost their two star players to season-ending injuries last week.

FACT 4 The Buckeyes' last three games will be played at home, where they are undefeated this season, giving them the home-field advantage.

A reader would evaluate this student's argument by judging the quality of her evidence, using the criteria listed in the "Tips" box.

Tips LEARNING in COLLEGE

Assessing Evidence in an Inductive Argument

- **Is it accurate?** Make sure that any facts presented as evidence are correct.
- **Is it relevant?** Check to see if the evidence is clearly connected to the point being made.
- **Is it representative?** Make sure that the writer's conclusion is supported by evidence gathered from a sample that accurately reflects the larger population (for example, it has the same proportion of men and women, older and younger people, and so on). If the writer is using an example, make sure that the example is typical and not a unique situation.
- **Is it sufficient?** Evaluate whether there is enough evidence to satisfy questioning readers.

Inductive reasoning is a feature of the **scientific method.** Scientists gather data from experiments, surveys, and careful observations to formulate hypotheses—arguments—that explain the data. Then they test their hypotheses by collecting additional information.

Now suppose the journalism student is using deductive reasoning in an article about great baseball teams; in that case, the truth of her conclusion will depend on the truth of her premises:

PREMISE	Any baseball team that wins the World Series more than twenty-five times in a hundred years is one of the greatest teams in baseball history.
PREMISE	The New York Yankees have won the World Series more than twenty-five times in the past hundred years.
CONCLUSION	The New York Yankees are one of the greatest teams in baseball history.

This is a deductive argument: if its premises are true, its conclusion must be true. To challenge the argument, a reader has to evaluate the premises. Do you think, for example, that the number of World Series wins is a proper measure of a team's greatness? If not, then you could claim that the first premise is false and does not support the conclusion.

In college, deductive reasoning predominates in mathematics and philosophy and some other humanities disciplines. However, you should be alert to both types of reasoning in all your college courses and in your life.

The Toulmin method Philosopher Stephen Toulmin has developed another useful way to understand and implement logical thinking. His analysis of arguments is based on claims (assertions about a topic), grounds (reasons and evidence), and warrants (assumptions or principles that link the grounds to the claims). Consider the following sentence from an argument by a student:

> The death penalty should be abolished because innocent people could be executed.

This example, like all logical arguments, has three facets:

- **The argument makes a claim.** A **claim** is the same thing as a point or a thesis: it is an assertion about a topic. A strong claim responds to an issue of real interest to an audience (for example, the members of a discipline) in clear, precise terms. It also allows for some uncertainty by including qualifying words such as *might* or *possibly*. A weak claim is merely a statement of fact or a statement that few would argue with.

Personal feelings are not debatable and thus are not an appropriate claim for an argument.

WEAK CLAIMS   The death penalty is highly controversial.

The death penalty makes me sick.

■ **The argument presents grounds for the claim.** Here, **grounds** consist of the reasons and evidence (facts and statistics, anecdotes, and expert opinion) that support the claim. A strong argument relies on evidence that is varied, relevant to the claim, and sufficient to support the claim. As grounds for the claim in the example, the student would present anecdotes and statistics related to innocent people being executed. The following box should help you assess the evidence supporting a claim.

TYPES of EVIDENCE for CLAIMS

■ **Facts and statistics:** Facts and statistics can be convincing support for a claim. You should be aware, however, that people on different sides of an issue can interpret the same facts and statistics differently or can cite different facts and statistics to support their point.

■ **Anecdotes:** An anecdote is a brief story used as an illustration to support a claim. Stories appeal to the emotions as well as to the intellect and can be very effective in making an argument. Be especially careful to check anecdotes for logical fallacies (*see pp. 33–34*).

■ **Expert opinion:** The views of authorities in a given field can also be powerful support for a claim. Check that the expert cited has proper credentials to comment on the issue.

■ **The argument depends on assumptions that link the grounds to the claim.** When you analyze an argument, you should be aware of the unstated assumptions, or **warrants,** that underlie both the claim and the grounds that support it. The warrants underlying the example argument against the death penalty include the idea that it is not possible to be completely sure of a person's guilt. Warrants differ from discipline to discipline and even from one school of thought to another within a given discipline. If you were studying the topic of bullfighting and its place in Spanish society in a sociology course, for example, you would probably make different arguments with different warrants than would the writer of a literary analysis of Ernest Hemingway's novel about bullfighting, *Death in the Afternoon.* You might argue that bullfighting serves as a safe outlet for its fans' aggressive feelings. Your warrant would be that sports can have socially useful purposes.

As you read the writings of others and as you write yourself, look for unstated assumptions. What does the reader have to assume—take for granted—to accept the evidence in support of the claim? In particular, hidden assumptions sometimes show **bias**—positive or negative inclinations that can manipulate unwary readers.

3. Recognizing common logical fallacies

Logicians have catalogued some common mistakes that writers commit in their enthusiasm to make a point. These errors are called **fallacies,** or mistakes in logic. Use the box on pages 33–34 to help you identify fallacies when you read and avoid them when you write.

4c Write critically.

Sharpening your ability to think critically and to express your views effectively is one of the main purposes of undergraduate study. When you write critically, you gain a voice in the important discussions and major decisions of our society. Writing can make a difference.

In every classroom, you will gain practice in addressing issues that are important in the larger community. Selecting a topic that you care about will give you the energy to think matters through and to make cogent arguments. Of course, you will have to go beyond your personal feelings about an issue to make the most convincing case. You will also have to empathize with potential readers who may disagree with you about an issue that is close to your heart. (*For more help with writing arguments, see Chapter 11, pp. 130–42.*)

1. Finding a topic worth writing about

Arguments occur in the context of debate and usually concern one or more of the following questions:

- What is true?
- What is good?
- What is to be done?

People seek answers to these questions but often disagree about which ones are best. To enter into the debate, you have to figure out what is at issue, where you stand, and why your position is reasonable.

COMMON LOGICAL FALLACIES

- **Non sequitur:** A conclusion that does not logically follow from the evidence presented or one that is based on irrelevant evidence.

  EXAMPLE   Students who default on their student loans have no sense of responsibility. [*Students who default on loans could be faced with high medical bills or prolonged unemployment.*]

- **False cause:** An argument that falsely assumes that because one thing happens after another, the first event was a cause of the second event. Also known as *post hoc*.

  EXAMPLE   I drank green tea and my headache went away; therefore, green tea makes headaches go away. [*How do we know that the headache didn't go away for another reason?*]

- **Stacking the deck/card-stacking:** An argument that slants the evidence to support a position.

  EXAMPLE   Nine out of ten doctors interviewed prefer X. Therefore X is good for you. [*Which doctors were interviewed? Do they all work for the company that produces X? If so, the writer has stacked the deck.*]

- **False authority:** An argument in which the testimony of an unqualified person is used to support a claim.

  EXAMPLE   "As the actor who plays Dr. Fine on *The Emergency Room*, I recommend this weight-loss drug because . . ." [*Is an actor really qualified to judge the benefits and dangers of a diet drug?*]

- **False analogy:** A comparison in which a surface similarity masks a significant difference.

  EXAMPLE   Governments and businesses both work within a budget to accomplish their goals. Just as business must focus on the bottom line, so should government. [*Is the goal of government to make a profit? Or does government have other, more important goals?*]

- **Red herring:** An argument that diverts attention from the true issue by concentrating on something irrelevant.

  EXAMPLE   Hemingway's book *Death in the Afternoon* is not successful because it glorifies the brutal sport of bullfighting. [*Why can't a book about a brutal sport be successful? The statement is irrelevant.*]

  (continued)

COMMON LOGICAL FALLACIES *(continued)*

- **Begging the question:** A form of circular reasoning that assumes the truth of a questionable opinion.

  EXAMPLE The president's poor relationship with the military has weakened the armed forces. [*Does the president really have a poor relationship with the military?*]

- **Hasty generalization:** A conclusion based on inadequate evidence.

  EXAMPLE Temperatures across the United States last year exceeded the fifty-year average by two degrees, thus proving that global warming is a reality. [*Is this evidence enough to prove this very broad conclusion?*]

- **Bandwagon:** An argument that depends on going along with the crowd, on the false assumption that truth can be determined by a popularity contest.

  EXAMPLE Everybody knows that Hemingway is preoccupied with the theme of death in his novels. [*How do we know that "everybody" agrees with this statement?*]

- **Ad hominem:** A personal attack on someone who disagrees with you rather than on the person's argument.

  EXAMPLE The district attorney is a lazy political hack, so naturally she opposes streamlining the court system. [*Even if the district attorney usually supports her party's position, does that make her wrong about this issue?*]

- **Circular reasoning:** An argument that restates the point rather than supporting it with reasonable evidence.

  EXAMPLE The wealthy should pay more taxes because taxes should be higher for people with higher incomes. [*Why should wealthy people pay more taxes? The rest of the statement doesn't answer this question; it just restates the position.*]

- **Either/or fallacy:** The idea that a complicated issue can be resolved by resorting to one of only two options when in reality there are additional choices.

  EXAMPLE Either the state legislature will raise taxes or our state's economy will falter. [*Are there really only two possibilities?*]

Your purpose in presenting your position to others is not to win but to take part in the ongoing conversation. As you present your argument, keep in mind that reasonable people can see things differently. Acknowledge and respect the views of others. Negotiating differences should become part of your purpose.

2. Making a strong claim

Advancing a strong, debatable thesis on a topic of interest to the discipline or to the public is key to writing a successful argument. Keep in mind, however, that writing itself is a tool for thinking through your position on an issue. As you think, write, and learn about your topic, you will develop, clarify, and sometimes entirely change your views. Think of yourself as a potter working with soft clay. Your thesis is still forming as you work with the topic.

Your personal feelings are not open to debate and so cannot serve as the thesis for an argument. If you write, "I feel that life in the ghetto is dangerous," there is nothing to debate because you are saying something about yourself rather than about the ghetto. But when William Julius Wilson writes, in his article "When Work Disappears," that "joblessness in the ghetto is not a result of welfare dependency," he is making a debatable claim on an issue of real concern. (*For more on theses, see Chapter 5, pp. 48–50.*)

3. Supporting and developing your claim with evidence

The intelligent selection and careful documentation of evidence—facts and statistics, anecdotes, and expert opinion—will determine whether you make a credible case. (*The box on p. 31 describes three types of evidence writers use to support their claims.*)

- **Facts and statistics:** In the article "When Work Disappears," Wilson argues that joblessness prevails in so many inner-city neighborhoods because jobs have disappeared from the ghetto. Wilson supports this claim with the following facts:

    In the neighborhood of Woodlawn, on the South Side of Chicago, there were more than 800 commercial and industrial establishments in 1950. Today, it is estimated that only 100 are left.

- **Anecdotes:** In his article, Wilson uses quotations from long-term residents in several urban ghettos in Chicago. These residents contrast life in their neighborhoods today with local employment opportunities in the 1950s.

- **Expert opinion:** Wilson cites a former secretary of labor to support the claim that educational reform is part of the solution to the problem of joblessness:

Ray Marshall, former secretary of labor, points out that Japan and Germany have developed policies designed to increase the number of workers with "higher-order thinking skills."

In well-written arguments, reasoning often relies on research. As you find and read a variety of sources, you will figure out your claim and amass the evidence you need to support it. You will also want to demonstrate your credibility to readers by properly quoting and documenting the information you have gathered from your sources. (*See the guidelines for documenting sources in Tabs 6–8.*)

4. Appealing to your audience

You want your readers to see you as reasonable, ethical, and empathetic—qualities that promote communication among people who have differences. You display the quality of your thought, character, and feelings—what the ancient Greeks called **logos, ethos,** and **pathos**—by the way you argue for what you believe.

Giving reasons and supplying evidence for your position and arguing responsibly by avoiding fallacies establish your logos. (*For more on fallacies, see pp. 33–34.*) You also need to show that you are sincere (ethos) and that you care about your readers' feelings (pathos). For example, you might refer to a quality or belief you share with others, even those who disagree with you. Establishing common ground in this way will make readers more open to your argument. Do you share an interest in the same issue, topic, or field? Do you have overlapping goals or values? When you read your argument to yourself or to peers, pay attention to how you are coming across. What would readers who have never met you think of you after reading or hearing what you have to say?

5. Considering opposing viewpoints

Don't ignore **counterarguments**—claims that challenge or refute your thesis. Instead, look for ways to refute or accommodate them. For example, you might present at least one counterargument and then refute it by presenting evidence that shows why it is open to question. If you are unable to refute a counterargument, you can often accommodate it by qualifying your thesis with words such as *likely, usually, most,* or *some.* Or you might make a more specific statement of the conditions for or exceptions to your thesis, such as "*If* inflation continues, X" or "*Until* cloning is perfected, Y." These kinds of qualifications often appear in the conclusion of an argument, where it is appropriate to include a more subtle version of the thesis.

6. Checking for errors in your logic

Checking the logic of your own writing is probably the greatest challenge to your ability to read critically. It is essential to step outside yourself and assess your argument objectively for errors in reasoning. (*Use the chart of Common Logical Fallacies on pp. 33–34 to test your reasoning.*) Of course, nothing is more helpful than hearing and responding to your classmates' questions. Peer review is one of the best tools for developing critical thinking and writing skills. (*For advice on peer review, see Chapter 7, pp. 76–79.*)

5 Planning and Shaping

A large part of learning in college involves writing papers that contribute to the ongoing conversation of educated people. The advice in this chapter will help you determine the kind of writing a particular assignment requires and get you started on a first draft.

5a Learn how to approach assignments.

1. Writing about a question

Whether you choose your topic or it is assigned, most topics must be narrowed. To arrive at a manageable topic, it helps to try to write about a question. The particular course you are taking defines a range of questions that are appropriate within a given discipline. Here are examples of the way your course would help define the questions you might ask if, for example, you were writing about Thomas Jefferson:

> **U.S. history:** How did Jefferson's ownership of slaves affect his public stance on slavery?

Political science: To what extent did Jefferson's conflict with the courts redefine the balance of power among the three branches of government?

Education: Given his beliefs about the relationship between democracy and public education, what would Jefferson think about contemporary proposals for a school voucher system?

2. Asking questions about your audience

Who makes up your audience? In college, instructors are usually your primary readers, of course, but they represent a larger group of readers who have an interest or a stake in your topic. An education professor reads and evaluates a paper as a representative of other students in the course, experts in educational policy, school board members, public school principals, and parents of school-age children, among others. Here are some questions to answer about your audience:

- What are the demographics of this audience? What is the education level, social status, occupation, gender, and ethnicity of a typical audience member?

- What common assumptions and differences of opinion do these readers bring to the issue?

- What images do they have, what ideas do they hold, and what actions do they support?

- What is your goal in writing for this audience? Do you want to intensify, clarify, complicate, or change one or more of their assumptions and opinions?

3. Being clear about your purpose

What kind of assignment are you doing? Think beyond the simple statement "I have to write an essay." Are you expected to inform, interpret, or argue?

- **Informing:** writing to transmit knowledge. Terms like *classify, illustrate, report,* and *survey* are often associated with the task of informing.

- **Interpreting:** writing to produce understanding. Terms like *analyze, compare, explain,* and *reflect* are more likely to appear when the purpose is interpreting.

- **Arguing:** writing to assert and negotiate matters of public debate. *Agree, assess, defend,* and *refute* go with the task of arguing.

Some terms, such as *comment, consider,* and *discuss,* do not point to a particular purpose, but many others do. If you are not clear about the kind of work you are expected to do, ask your professor.

4. Selecting the appropriate genre

Genre simply means kind of writing. Poems, stories, and plays are genres of literature, with clear differences in the way they look and sound. Different genres of writing predominate in different disciplines.

Sometimes an assignment will specify the kind of work, or genre, you are being asked to produce. For example, you may be asked to write a report (an informative genre), a comparative analysis (an interpretive genre), or a critique (an argumentative genre).

Some genres, like the case study, are common in a particular field such as sociology but not in other disciplines. Understanding the genre that is called for is very important in successfully fulfilling an assignment. If you are supposed to write a description of a snake for a field guide, you will not be successful if you write a poem—even a very good poem—about a snake. (*See Tab 3: Common Assignments across the Curriculum, pp. 109–80.*)

5. Using appropriate language

Understanding genre helps you make decisions about language. For a description of a snake in a field guide, you would use highly specific terms to differentiate one type of snake from another. A poem would incorporate striking images, vivid words and phrases that evoke the senses, and other forms of literary language.

6. Choosing an appropriate voice

The concept of **voice** is difficult to grasp in a discussion of writing because we think of voice as something we hear. But we also hear voices when we read, and we create voices when we write. The following two passages both deal with the death of a sportswriter named Steve Schoenfeld. Read both passages aloud, and listen to the different voices:

> Tobin originally planned his news conference for Wednesday but postponed it out of respect for Valley sports journalist Steve Schoenfeld, who was killed Tuesday night in a hit-and-run accident in downtown Tempe.
>
> —LEE SHAPPELL, *Arizona Republic*

> Steve Schoenfeld probably would find it amusing that the NFL plans to honor him with a moment of silence in press boxes before

games on Sunday and Monday. He was hardly ever quiet in the press box or anywhere else.

—MARK ARMIJO AND KENT SOMERS, *Arizona Republic*

The first passage is written in an even tone that emphasizes factual reporting. The second passage is written in a poignant style that quietly and movingly celebrates the sportswriter's life.

Different writing situations and assignments allow you to try out different voices. As a college student, you will usually want to inspire trust by sounding informed, reasonable, and fair. Your **stance**—where you stand in relation to your audience and your subject—is seldom that of an expert. Instead, you are writing as an educated person who is sharing what you have learned and what you think about it.

Readers tend to appreciate an even tone of voice, a style that values the middle ground and avoids the extremes of the impersonal or the intimate, the stuffy or the casual.

STUFFY

The epistolary mode of literary expression has assumed numerous distinctive guises since its original manifestation more than four thousand years ago in the cuneiform inscriptions of ancient Sumer.

CASUAL

Letters have been around for a really long time.

APPROPRIATE ACADEMIC VOICE

As Kany points out, letter writing has flourished ever since it first emerged among the ancient Sumerians.

Read your work aloud to yourself or to classmates so that you can literally hear your voice. Does it suit the assignment's topic, purpose, and audience? (*For more about style, see Tab 9: Editing for Clarity.*)

www.mhhe.com/ awr

For more on strategies for exploring your ideas, go to

Writing > Paragraph/Essay Development > Prewriting

5b   Explore your ideas.

You usually explore ideas when you are getting started on a project, but exploration also helps when you are feeling stuck and are searching for something new to say. The following strategies will help you brainstorm and come up with ideas at any stage. You can do much of your exploratory writing in a **journal,** which is simply a place to record your thoughts on a regular basis. (*For more on journals, see p. 45.*) Your class notes constitute a type of academic journal, as do the notes you take on your reading and research.

As you explore, turn off your internal critic and generate as much material as possible, knowing that you will be able to select the best ideas from what you have produced.

1. Reviewing your notes and annotations

If your assignment involves reading one or more texts or researching multiple sources, review your notes and annotations. (*For details on annotating, see Chapter 4. For details on researching and keeping a research journal, see Chapter 23.*) If you are writing about something you have observed, review any notes or sketches you have made. These immediate comments and reactions are one of your best sources for ideas. Look for patterns.

2. Freewriting

When you feel blocked or unsure about what you think, try **freewriting.** Just write whatever occurs to you about a topic. If nothing comes to mind, then write "nothing comes to mind" until something else occurs to you. The trick is to keep pushing forward without stopping. It is especially important not to worry about spelling, punctuation, or grammar rules as you write. Usually, you will discover some implicit point in your seemingly random writing. You might then try doing some **focused freewriting,** where you begin with a point or a specific question. The following is a student's freewriting on the topic of work:

> I want to talk about the difference between a job and work—between a job and a career. If you don't get paid, is it work? If it is, what's the difference between work and play? There are some things I would only do for money—like work as a waiter. But there are other things I would do even if I weren't paid—garden or ride my bike or play with kids. The trick is to find a career that would allow me to get paid for doing those things.

3. Listing

One way to brainstorm is to start with a topic and list the words, phrases, images, and ideas that come to mind. The key to brainstorming is to turn off your internal editor and just jot things down. Later, you can review this list, underline one or more key terms, add or delete items, and look for patterns and connections. You can then zero in on the areas of most interest, add new ideas, and arrange the items into main points and subpoints. Here is a list a student produced on the topic of work:

Work—what is it?
Skilled/unskilled
Most jobs today in service industries
Work and retirement
My dad's retired, but has he stopped working?
If you never want to retire, is your job still considered work?
Jobs I have had: babysitter, camp counselor, salesclerk, office worker—
I'd be happy to retire from those, especially the salesclerk job
Standing all day.
Do this, do that.
Punch the clock.
Do it over again and again
Difference between work and career
I want a career, not a job
Dress for success
High-powered lunches, late dinner.
Travel
Making presentations
Pressure
Making decisions
Big house
Fast car

4. Clustering

Having something down in writing enables you to look for categories and connections. **Clustering,** sometimes called **mapping,** is a brainstorming technique that generates categories and connections from the beginning. To make an idea cluster, do the following:

- Write your topic in the center of a piece of paper, and circle it.
- Surround the topic with subtopics that interest you. Circle each, and draw a line from it to the center circle.
- Brainstorm more ideas, connecting each one to a subtopic already on the sheet or making it into a new subtopic.

Working as a group, the students in a composition course produced the cluster in Figure 5.1 on the topic of "Work in the U.S. today."

5. Questioning

Asking questions is a good way to explore a topic further. The journalist's five *w*'s and an *h* (*who? what? where? when? why?* and *how?*) can help you find specific ideas and details. For example, a student group

FIGURE 5.1 A cluster on the topic of work.

assigned to research and write a paper about some aspect of work came up with the following questions:

- In terms of age, gender, and ethnicity, who is working in the new cyberspace infotainment industry?
- What are the working conditions, benefits, and job security of those employed in the current U.S. service economy?
- Where are all the manufacturing jobs these days?
- When is it best for people to retire from jobs?
- Why are so many U.S. businesses "downsizing"?
- How do people prepare themselves for career changes?

CHARTING the TERRITORY

Different Questions Lead to Different Answers

Always consider what questions make the most sense in the context of the course you are taking. Scholars in different disciplines pose questions related to their fields.

- **Sociology:** A sociologist might ask questions about the ways management and workers interact in the high-tech workplace.
- **History:** A historian might ask how women's roles in the workplace have—or have not—changed since 1960.
- **Economics:** An economist might wonder what effect, if any, the North American Free Trade Agreement (NAFTA) has had on factory layoffs and closings in the United States.

Other questioning techniques include the following:

- Looking at a topic dramatically, as an action (*what*) with actors (*who*), a scene (*where*), means (*how*), and purpose (*why*)
- Looking at a topic as a static thing—a particle—that has its own distinguishing features and parts, as a wave that changes over time, and as a field that operates as a system

STATIC THING

What is work? Do the words *work, job,* and *career* mean the same thing to most people? How do we know when someone is not doing work? What is the opposite of work?

WAVE

How has work changed over time? Over the past thirty years, have there been significant shifts in the number and kinds of jobs available in the United States? Is the computer revolution likely to make a big difference in how business works in the twenty-first century?

FIELD

Where does work fit into our lives? To what extent does a person's self-esteem depend on the job he or she has? What does work mean for a society in which most jobs are in the service and communication areas? How will the new global economy affect the quantity and quality of work in the United States?

For other examples of what and how to question, you should take note of the problems or questions your professor poses in class discussions. If you are using a textbook in your course, check out the study questions.

6. Keeping a journal

You can record your notes and ideas in a journal. However, you may find it helpful to go beyond note taking and start recording ideas and questions inspired by your classes or your exploratory writing as many writers and thinkers have done (*see Figure 5.2*). For example, you might write about connections between your personal life and your academic subjects, connections among your subjects, or ideas touched on in class that you would like to know more about. Jotting down one or two thoughts at the end of class and exploring those ideas at greater length later in the day will help you build a store of essay ideas.

> My economics textbook says that moving jobs to companies overseas ultimately does more good than harm to the economy, but how can that be? When the electronics factory closed, it devastated my town.

FIGURE 5.2 **Pages from Leonardo da Vinci's journal.** The Renaissance artist, scientist, and inventor Leonardo da Vinci filled more than a thousand pages with observations and illustrations. Scholars believe that his original intention was to gather material for a paper on mechanics.

TEXTCONNEX

Electronic Journals

A journal need not be a fancy leatherbound book; in fact, it need not be a book at all. You can use the notes section of a personal digital assistant (PDA) to jot down your thoughts, and a word-processing file works well for longer journal entries. Be sure to label your files so that you can retrieve and review your entries quickly. For a PDA such as Palm, consider creating a new category called Academic Journal in the Note Pad.

7. Browsing in the library or surfing the Net
Your college library is filled with ideas—and it can be a great inspiration when you need to come up with your own. Sometimes it helps to leave your study carrel and browse the bookshelves containing texts that relate to a topic of interest. Exploring a subject on the World Wide Web is the electronic equivalent of browsing in the library. Type keywords related to your topic into a search engine such as *Google,* and visit several sites on the list that results. (*See Tab 5: Researching, pp. 221–25.*)

8. Exchanging ideas
If you read the acknowledgments in the books on your shelves, you will see that writing is a social activity. Most authors thank family members, editors, librarians, and colleagues for help on work in progress. Likewise, you should welcome opportunities to talk about your writing with your classmates, friends, and family.

- Brainstorm within your peer response group if your instructor has set up such groups. Come prepared with ideas and information on your topic to get the discussion started.

- Seek out students who have taken the course previously, and discuss with them their approaches to writing assignments.

- Find out if your college has a writing center that welcomes students for discussions of work in progress.

The online tools that are available to writers offer another way for you to collaborate with others on your papers. Discuss your assignments by exchanging e-mail. If your class has a course Web site, you might also exchange ideas in chat rooms. Other options for exploring your topic and gathering ideas include instant messaging and virtual environments.

Writing e-mail   When you work on papers with classmates, you can use e-mail in the following ways:

- To check out your understanding of the assignment
- To try out various topics
- To ask each other questions about ideas
- To share freewriting, listing, and other exploratory writing
- To respond to each other's ideas, including requests for clarification and additional information

Chatting with each other about ideas   You can also use online chat rooms as well as other virtual spaces to share ideas. Your instructor may include **chat** or **MOO** activities, in which you go into virtual rooms to work on assignments in small groups or visit and interact with classes at other colleges. Some people find that chatting in such virtual rooms, or synchronous spaces, prompts them to become more creative. In the exchange shown in Figure 5.3, for example, two students share ideas about volunteerism.

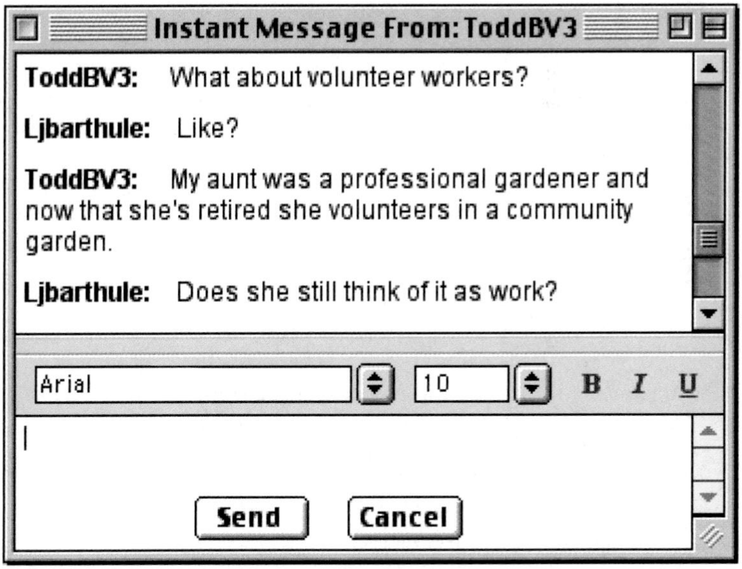

FIGURE 5.3 An exchange in an online chat room. Chatting online with classmates allows you to test ideas, as in this exchange.

www.mhhe.com/
awr
For more help with
developing a thesis,
go to

Writing >
Paragraph/Essay
Development >
Thesis/Central
Idea

5c   Develop a working thesis.

The **thesis** is the central idea of your paper. It needs to communicate a specific point about your topic and suit the purpose of the assignment. As you explore your topic, ideas for your thesis will begin to emerge. You can focus these ideas by drafting a preliminary or working **thesis statement,** which can be one or more sentences long. A preliminary thesis is just that: preliminary. As you draft and revise your paper, you may change your thesis several times to make it stronger.

A good way to develop a thesis is to begin with the answer to a question posed by your assignment. (*For more about questions, see pp. 37–38.*) For example, an assignment in a political science class might ask you to defend or critique "Healthy Inequality," an article by George Will on the increasing gap between rich and poor in the United States. The question your thesis must answer is, "Is George Will's position that inequality is healthy correct?"

To create a strong thesis, you will need to think critically, developing a point of view based on reading course materials and doing research. Not all theses can be stated in one sentence, but all strong theses are suitable, specific, and significant. (*For more on strong theses, see Chapter 4, p. 35.*)

1. Making sure your thesis is suitable

A suitable thesis fits the paper's main purpose. All theses make an assertion, but while a thesis for an argument will take a clear position on an issue or recommend an action, a thesis for an informative or interpretive paper will often preview the paper's content or express the writer's insight into the topic. If you are asked to write a report of your research on the gap between rich and poor in the United States, you should not try to argue a position. An argument will not fulfill the purpose of the assignment, which is to produce an informative paper, a report. All of the following theses are on the same topic, but each is for a paper with a different purpose:

THESIS TO INFORM

In terms of income and wealth, the gap between rich and poor has increased substantially during the past decade.

THESIS TO INTERPRET

The economic ideas George Will expresses in "Healthy Inequality" are politically conservative.

THESIS TO ARGUE

George Will is wrong about economic inequality being good for the United States.

2. Making sure your thesis is specific

Vague theses usually lead to weak, unfocused papers. Watch out in particular for thesis statements that simply announce your topic, state an obvious fact about it, or offer a general observation:

ANNOUNCEMENT

I will discuss the article "Healthy Inequality" by George Will. [*What is the writer's point about the article?*]

STATEMENT OF FACT

The article "Healthy Inequality" by George Will is about the gap between rich and poor. [*This thesis gives us information about the article, but it does not make a specific point about it.*]

GENERAL OBSERVATION

George Will's article "Healthy Inequality" is well written and provocative. [*While this thesis makes a point about the article, the point could apply to many articles. What makes this article worth reading?*]

By contrast, a specific thesis signals a focused, well-developed paper.

SPECIFIC

George Will's argument that economic inequality is healthy for the United States should not be accepted. His interpretation of the recent increase in income inequality is questionable. His reasoning about history is flawed. Above all, his idea of what is healthy is too narrow.

In this example, the thesis expresses the writer's particular point—there are three reasons to reject Will's argument. It also forecasts the structure of the whole paper, providing readers with a sense of direction.

> *Note:* A thesis statement can be longer than one sentence (if necessary) to provide a framework for your main idea. All of the sentences taken together, though, should build to one specific, significant point that fits the purpose of your assignment. (Some instructors may prefer that you limit your thesis statements to one sentence.)

3. Making sure your thesis is significant

A significant thesis asserts something that could potentially make a difference in what readers know, understand, or believe. Chances are that what makes a difference to you will also make a difference to your readers. When you are looking for possible theses, be sure to challenge yourself to develop one that you care about.

5d   Plan a structure that suits your assignment.

Many writers feel that they are more efficient when they know in advance how to develop their thesis and where to fit the information they have gathered. For some, this means organizing their notes into a sequence that makes sense. Others prefer to sketch out a list of ideas in a rough outline, while still others prefer to prepare a formal outline. Whether loose or exact, a guide of some kind can be helpful as you work your way through the first draft of your paper.

Every paper needs the following components:

- A beginning, or **introduction,** that hooks readers and usually states the thesis
- A middle, or **body,** that develops the main idea of the paper in a series of paragraphs—each making a point supported by specific details
- An ending, or **conclusion,** that gives readers a sense of completion, often by offering a final comment on the thesis

It is not essential to have an outline before you start drafting; indeed, some writers prefer to discover how to connect and develop their ideas as they compose. However, even if you prefer to work out your ideas through drafting, outlining still has a place in the writing process. An outline of your first draft will help you spot organizational problems or places where the support for your thesis is weak.

www.mhhe.com/
awr
For more on outlines, go to

Writing >
Paragraph/Essay
Development >
Outlines

1. Preparing an informal plan

A **scratch outline** is a simple list of points, without the levels of subordination found in more complex outlines. Scratch outlines are useful for briefer papers. Here is a scratch outline for a paper on an exhibit of photographs by Sebastião Salgado:

- Photojournalism should be factual and informative, but it can be beautiful and artful too, as Salgado's *Migrations* exhibit illustrates.
- The exhibit overall—powerful pictures of people uprooted, taken in 39 countries over 7 years. Salgado documents a global crisis; over 100 million displaced due to war, resource depletion, overpopulation, natural disasters, extreme poverty.

- Specific picture—"Orphanage"—describe subjects, framing, lighting, emotions it evokes.
- Salgado on the purpose of his photographs. Quote.

A **do/say plan** is a more detailed type of informal outline. To come up with such a plan, review your notes and other relevant material. Then write down your working thesis, and list what you will say for each of the following "do" categories: introduce, support and develop, and conclude. Here is an example:

Thesis: George Will is wrong about economic inequality being good for the United States.

1. **Introduce** the issue and my focus.

   - Use two examples to contrast rich and poor: "approximately 17,000 Americans declared more than $1 million of annual income on their 1985 tax returns" (Mantsios 196). Between 1979 and 1992, there was a 15% decrease in the manufacturing workforce, and in 1993, Sears eliminated 50,000 merchandising jobs (Rifkin 2).
   - Say that the issue is how to evaluate increasing economic inequality, and introduce Will's article "Healthy Inequality." Summarize Will's argument.
   - Give Will credit for raising issue, but then state thesis: he's wrong about more inequality being good for the United States.

2. **Support and develop** thesis that Will's argument is wrong.

   - Point out that Will relies on economic interpretations of Greenwood and Yorukoglu. They see decline ("modest") in labor productivity beginning in 1974. But Rifkin says "manufacturing productivity is soaring"—up 35%.
   - Point out one thing Will and Rifkin agree on: computer revolution is affecting economy/jobs. But Will thinks effects are like "economic turbulence" caused in 1770 by steam engine and in 1840 by electricity.
   - Show that these analogies aren't convincing. Too many differences. Use Aronowitz on "jobless future" and Rifkin for support.
   - Say that Will makes fun of those who "decr[y] . . . injustice," people like Rifkin and Aronowitz. Will thinks inequality motivates people to learn new skills so they can compete. A skilled workforce makes society better/healthy.
   - Will's idea of healthy society is narrow. An economic idea only. And who will pay to train unemployed workers?

3. **Conclude** that Will doesn't ask or answer such key questions because he denies that there is any problem. Earlier he says "suffering is good." Where would he draw the line? Maybe quote from Max Weber?

In outlining his plan, this student has already begun drafting because as he works on the outline, he gets a clearer sense of what he thinks is wrong with Will's argument. He starts writing sentences that he is likely to include in the first complete draft.

www.mhhe.com/
awr
For help with
outlining, go to

Writing >
Outlining Tutor

2. Preparing a formal outline

A **formal outline** classifies and divides the information you have gathered, showing main points, supporting ideas, and specific details by organizing them into levels of subordination. You may be required to include a formal outline for some assignments.

Formal outlines come in two types. A **topic outline** uses single words or phrases; a **sentence outline** states every idea in a sentence. Because the process of division always results in at least two parts, in a formal outline every I must have a II; every A, a B; and so on. Also, items placed at the same level must be of the same kind; for example, if I is London, then II can be New York City but not the Bronx or Wall Street. Items at the same level should also be grammatically parallel; if A is "Choosing screen icons," then B can be "Creating away messages" but not "Away messages."

Here is a formal sentence outline for a paper on Salgado's *Migrations* exhibit:

Thesis: Like a photojournalist, Salgado brings us images of newsworthy events, but he goes beyond objective reporting, imparting his compassion for refugees and migrants to the viewer.

I. The images in *Migrations,* an exhibit of his work, suggest that Salgado does more then simply point and shoot.
II. Salgado's photograph "Orphanage attached to the hospital at Kibumba, Number One Camp, Goma Zaire" illustrates the power of his work.
  A. The photograph depicts three infants who are victims of the war in Rwanda.
    1. The label indicates that there are 4000 orphans in the camp and 100,000 orphans overall.
    2. The numbers are abstractions that the photo makes real.
  B. Salgado's use of black and white gives the photo a documentary feel, but he also uses contrasts of light and dark to create a dramatic image of the babies.
    1. The vertical black-and-white stripes of the blanket direct viewers' eyes to the infants' faces and hands.

         2. The whites of their eyes stand out against the darkness of the blankets.

         3. The camera's lens focuses sharply on the babies' faces, highlighting their expressions.

            a. The baby on the left has a heart-wrenching look.

            b. The baby in the center has a startled look.

            c. The baby on the right has a glazed and sunken look and is near death.

     C. The vantage point of this photograph is one of a parent standing directly over his or her child.

         1. The infants seem to belong to the viewer.

         2. The photo is framed so that the babies take up the entire space, consuming the viewer with their innocence and vulnerability.

III. Salgado uses his artistic skill to get viewers to look closely at painful subjects, illustrating a big, complex topic with a collection of intimate, intensely moving images.

5e   Use visuals effectively.

As you plan your paper, you should consider whether one or more visuals would help you support your thesis. Used judiciously, visuals such as tables, charts, and graphs provide clarity. Effective visuals are used for a specific purpose, not for decoration, and each type of visual illustrates some kinds of material better than others. For example, compare the table on page 54 and the line graph on page 56. Both present similar types of data, but do both have the same effect? Does one strike you as clearer or more powerful than the other?

    Effective visuals are simple and clear. If a chart is overloaded with information, separate it into several charts instead.

> *Caution:* Because the inclusion of visual elements in papers is more accepted in some fields than in others, you may want to ask your instructor for advice before planning to include visuals in your paper.

1. Tables

Tables are used to display information in a way that can be easily scanned by readers. They are made up of rows and columns of cells; each cell presents an element of textual, numeric, or graphic information. Tables organize data for readers. Consider this example taken from the Web site of the Environmental Protection Agency:

TABLE 34.

U.S. Emissions of Criteria Pollutants, 1989–1996
(million metric tons of gas)

SOURCE	1989	1990	1991	1992	1993	1994	1995	1996
Carbon monoxide	93.5	91.3	88.3	85.3	85.4	89.6	83.5	**NA**
Nitrogen oxides	21.1	20.9	20.6	20.7	21.1	21.5	19.7	**NA**
Nonmethane VOCs	21.7	21.4	20.8	20.3	20.5	21.1	20.7	**NA**

NA = not available.

Note: Data in this table are revised from the data contained in the previous EIA report, *Emissions of Green-house Gases in the United States 1995*, DOE/EIA-0573(95) (Washington, DC, October 1996).

SOURCE: U.S. Environmental Protection Agency, Office of Air Quality Planning and Standards, *National Air Pollutant Emission Trends*, 1900–1995, EPA-454/R-96-007 (Research Triangle Park, NC, October 1996), pp. A-5, A-9, and A-16.

It would be more difficult to compare the numbers for different years if this data were presented in paragraph form, and because the measurements include decimals, it would also be difficult to place them precisely on a graph. A table is ideal for displaying this type of precise data.

TEXTCONNEX

Preparing Tables

You can usually create and edit tables using your word-processing software. If you use Microsoft Word, for example, you can size columns proportionally to avoid distorting their contents and make them fit your text. Under the "Table" pulldown menu, select "Insert," then click on "Table." You will see a dialogue box. Choose "Autofit to content" instead of "Fixed column width." As you create the table, the borders will automatically increase. You can also create tables using database, spreadsheet, presentation, and Web site construction software.

2. Bar graphs

Bar graphs show relationships and highlight comparisons between two or more variables, such as the cost of tuition and fees at different public universities. Tables can accomplish the same goal, but bar graphs allow readers to see relative sizes quickly, as in Figure 5.4.

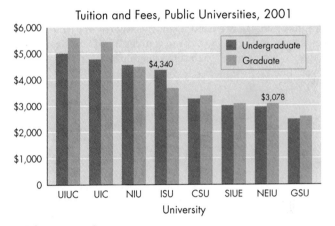

FIGURE 5.4 **Bar graph.**

3. Pie charts

Pie charts are circles divided into segments. They are useful for showing differences between parts in relation to a whole, as long as the differences are significant and there are not too many parts. Pie charts can show only static data, not changes in data over time. The segments of a pie chart should add up to 100% of something, such as the sources of water contamination shown in Figure 5.5.

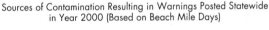

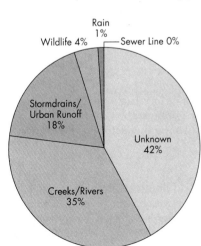

FIGURE 5.5 **Pie chart.**

4. Line graphs

Line graphs or charts are used to show changes over time, such as the changes shown in Figure 5.6, three sources of nitrous oxide emissions over a sixteen-year period, or to show the relationship between two variables over time.

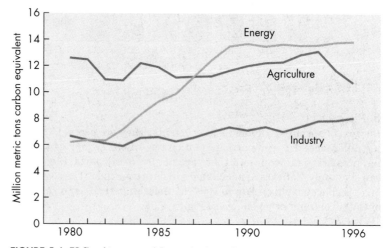

FIGURE 5.6 **U.S. nitrous oxide emissions by source, 1980–1996.**

5. Diagrams

Used to show processes or structures visually, diagrams include such visuals as time lines, organization charts, and decision trees. The diagram in Figure 5.7 shows the factors involved in the decision to commit a burglary.

6. Photographs and illustrations

Photographs and illustrations can reinforce a point you are making in your text in ways that words cannot, showing readers what your subject actually looks like or how it has been affected or changed. For example, the photograph in Nicholas Buglione's paper on the NFL illustrates his point about players' injuries (*see Chapter 11: Arguments, p. 138*). The

FIGURE 5.7 **Event model for a burglary.**

picture in Esther Hoffman's paper on Louis Armstrong and his manager (*see Chapter 30: MLA Documentation Style, p. 328*) provides further evidence of the relationship Hoffman is describing.

When you use photographs or illustrations, always credit your source, and be aware that most photographs and illustrations are protected by copyright. If you plan to use a photograph as part of a Web page, for example, you will usually need to obtain permission from the copyright holder.

6 Drafting

This book offers detailed advice on planning, drafting, revising, and editing in separate chapters, but you will move back and forth as you plan, draft, revise, and edit, and you may circle back and go through the entire process again as you write. Even though the parts of the writing process are interconnected, make sure to give yourself enough time not only to draft but also to revise and edit your work.

Think of drafting as an attempt to discover a beginning, a middle, and an end for what you have to say, but remember that a draft is preliminary. Avoid putting pressure on yourself to make it perfect.

Tips LEARNING in COLLEGE

Avoiding Writer's Block

While it is important to allot time for generating and organizing your ideas, do not put off writing the first draft. If you find it difficult to get started, consider the tips below.

- **Resist the temptation to be a perfectionist.** The poet William Stafford said, "There's no such thing as writer's block for writers whose standards are low enough." Reserve your high standards for the revising and editing stages. For your first draft, do not worry about getting the right word, the stylish phrase, or even the correct spelling.
- **Take it "bird by bird."** Writer Anne Lamott counsels students to break down writing assignments into manageable units and then make a commitment to finishing each unit in one session. She passes along her father's advice to her brother, who had procrastinated on a report about birds and was paralyzed by the enormity of the project: "Bird by bird, buddy. Just take it bird by bird."
- **Start anywhere.** If you are stuck on the beginning, pick a section where you have a clearer sense of what you want to say. You can go back later and work out the transitions.
- **Generate more ideas.** If you hit a section where you are drawing a blank, it may be that you need to do more reading, research, or brainstorming. Be careful, though, not to use reading and research as a stalling tactic.

6a Use online tools for drafting.

www.mhhe.com/
awr
For more on drafting,
go to
Writing >
Paragraph/Essay
Development >
Drafting and
Revising

If you have not already done so, set up a folder for your paper before you start drafting. The following tips will make this process go smoothly.

- **Save your work.** Always protect your creativity and hard-won drafts from power surges and other mishaps. Save often, and make backups.

- **Label revised drafts with different file names.** Use a different file name for each successive version of your paper. For example, you might save drafts of a paper on work as Work1, Work2, Work3, and so on.

- **Print hard copies early and often.** If you save and print the original, you can feel free to experiment.

When you are collaborating with other students on a paper, you can use the "Versions" feature in the "File" menu to save various drafts. Too many versions can get confusing, though, so you should create versions only when your project requires it.

6b Develop ideas and use visuals strategically.

www.mhhe.com/
awr
For more on developing
paragraphs, go to
Writing > Paragraph
Patterns

When you develop ideas, you give your writing texture and depth. The following strategies can help you develop the ideas that support your thesis into a complete draft. Depending on the purpose of your paper, you may use a few of these strategies throughout or a mix of all of them.

Photographs and other kinds of visuals can also serve as rhetorical strategies. As with paragraphs, you can use a mix of visuals in a paper. Keep in mind, though, that any visuals you use should always serve the overall purpose of your work. (*See pp. 53–57, for more on types of visuals and their purposes.*)

1. Narration

When you narrate, you tell a story. (*See Figure 6.1 on p. 60 for an example of a narrative visual.*) The following paragraph comes from a personal essay on the goods that result from "a lifetime of production":

> My dad changed too. He had come to that job feeling—as I do now—that everything was still possible. He'd served his time in the Air Force during the Korean War. Then, while my mother worked as a secretary to support them, he earned a college degree courtesy of the GI Bill. After graduation, my father painted houses for a season until he was offered a position scheduling the production of corrugated board. He took it, though he has

FIGURE 6.1 Visuals that narrate. Using images that narrate can be a powerful way to reinforce a message or portray events you discuss in your paper. Images like this one help tell one of many stories about the conflict in Iraq.

www.mhhe.com/
awr
For help with the
use of narration,
go to

Writing >
Writing Tutors >
Narration

told me that he never planned to stay. It was not something he envisioned as his life's work. I try to imagine what it is like suddenly to look up from a stack of orders and discover that the job you started one December day has watched you age.

—MICHELLE M. DUCHARME, "A Lifetime of Production"

Notice that Ducharme begins with two sentences that state the topic and point of her narration. Then, using the past tense, she recounts in chronological sequence some key events that led to her father's taking a job in the box manufacturing business.

2. Description

To make an object, person, or activity vivid for your readers, describe it in concrete, specific words that appeal to the senses of sight, sound, taste, smell, and touch. (*See Figure 6.2 for an example of a descriptive visual.*) In the following paragraph, Diane Chen describes her impression of a photograph:

> The vertical black-and-white stripes of the blanket direct our eyes to the infants' faces and hands, which are framed by a horizontal white stripe. The whites of their eyes in particular stand out against the darkness created by the shell of the blankets. The camera's lens also seems to be in sharper focus on the faces

FIGURE 6.2 Visuals that describe. Although it may seem obvious that images can serve a descriptive purpose, you should pay careful attention to the effect a particular image will have on your paper. This photograph of Kurt Cobain, for example, could add dimension to a portrayal of the musician as a talented, but conflicted, artist.

than on the blankets, again focusing our attention on the babies' expressions.

—DIANE CHEN, "The Caring Eye of Sebastião Salgado," student paper

www.mhhe.com/
awr
For help with the
use of classification,
go to
Writing >
Writing Tutors >
Classification

3. Classification

Classification is a useful way of grouping individual entities into identifiable categories. (*See Figure 6.3.*) Classifying occurs in all academic disciplines and often appears with its complement—**division,** or breaking a whole entity into its parts.

In the following passage, Robert Reich first classifies future work into two broad categories: complex services and person-to-person services. Then in the next paragraph, he develops the idea of complex services in more detail, in part by dividing that category into more specific—and familiar—categories like engineering and advertising.

[M]ost of America's traditional, routinized manufacturing jobs will disappear. So will routinized service jobs that can be done from remote locations, like keypunching of data transmitted by satellite. Instead, you will be engaged in one of two broad categories of work: either complex services, some of which will be sold to the rest of the world to pay for whatever Americans want to buy from the rest of the world, or person-to-person services, which foreigners can't provide for us because (apart from new immigrants and illegal aliens) they aren't here to provide them.

Complex services involve the manipulation of data and abstract symbols. Included in this category are insurance, engineering, law, finance, computer programming, and advertising. Such activities now account for almost 25 percent of our GNP, up from 13 percent in 1950. They have already surpassed manufacturing (down to about 20 percent of GNP).

—ROBERT REICH, "The Future of Work"

www.mhhe.com/
awr
For help with the
use of definition,
go to
Writing >
Writing Tutors >
Definition

4. Definition

You should define any concepts that readers might need to understand to follow your ideas. (*See Figure 6.4 on p. 64 for an example of a visual that defines.*) Interpretations and arguments often depend on one or two key ideas that cannot be quickly and easily defined. In the following example, John Berger defines "image," a key idea in his televised lectures on the way we see things:

An image is a sight which has been recreated or reproduced. It is an appearance, or a set of appearances, which has been detached from the place and time in which it first made its appearance and preserved—for a few moments or centuries.

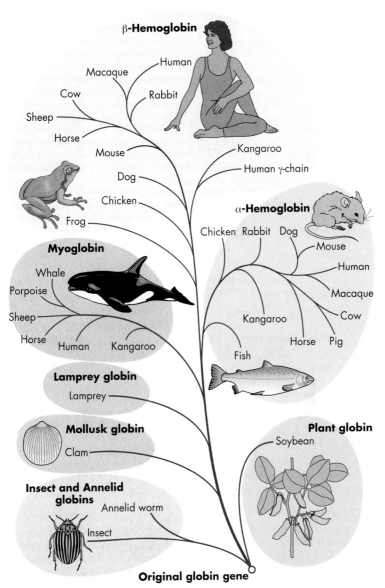

FIGURE 6.3 Visuals that classify or divide. An image can help you make the categories in or parts of complex systems or organizations easier for readers to understand. The image shown here, for example, helps readers comprehend the evolution of a common gene. The image of an Ionic column on p. 64 identifies the parts of that structure.

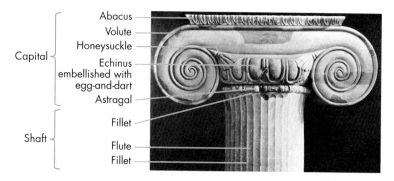

FIGURE 6.4 Visuals that define. Visuals can be extremely effective when used to support a written definition or to identify parts of a whole. This image uses labels and leader lines to identify the characteristics of an Ionic column.

> Every image embodies a way of seeing. Even a photograph. For photographs are not, as is often assumed, a mechanical record. Every time we look at a photograph, we are aware, however slightly, of the photographer selecting that sight from an infinity of other possible sights. This is true even in the most casual family snapshot. The photographer's way of seeing is reflected in his choice of subject.
>
> —JOHN BERGER, *Ways of Seeing*

www.mhhe.com/
awr
For help with the
use of illustration,
go to

Writing >
Writing Tutors >
Exemplification

5. Illustration

No matter what your purpose and point may be, to appeal to readers you will have to show as well as tell. Detailed examples and well-chosen visuals (*see Figure 6.5*) can make abstractions more concrete and generalizations more specific, as the following paragraph shows:

As Rubin explains, "for much of the Accord era, the ideal-typical family . . . was composed of a 'stay-at-home-mom,' a working father, and dependent children. He earned wages; she cooked, cleaned, cared for the home, managed the family's social life, and nurtured the family members" (97). Just such an arrangement characterized my grandmother's married life. My grandmother, who had four children, stayed at home with them, while her husband went off to work as a safety engineer. Sadly, when he died, she was left with nothing. She needed to support herself, yet had no work experience, no credit, and little education. But even though society frowned on her for seeking employ-

FIGURE 6.5 Visuals that illustrate. This map illustrates the political contours of Allied and Axis powers in Europe at the height of World War II.

ment, my grandmother eventually found a clerical position—a low-level job with few perks.

—JENNIFER KOEHLER, "Response to Exercise 6,"
student paper

Caution: Although any image you choose to include in your paper will be illustrative, images should not function merely as decoration. Ask yourself if each image you are considering truly adds information to your paper.

www.mhhe.com/
awr
For help with the
use of comparison and
contrast, go to

Writing >
Writing Tutors >
Comparison/
Contrast

6. Comparison and contrast

When you *compare,* you explore the similarities and differences among various items. When the term *compare* is used along with the term *contrast, compare* has a narrower meaning: "to spell out key similarities." *Contrast* always means "to itemize important differences." (*See Figure 6.6.*)

In the following example, the student writer uses a **subject-by-subject** pattern to contrast the ideas of two social commentators, Jeremy Rifkin and George Will:

> Rifkin and Will have different opinions about unemployment due to downsizing and the widening income gap between rich and poor. Rifkin sees both the decrease in employment and the increase in income disparity as evils that must be immediately dealt with lest society fall apart: "If no measures are taken to provide financial opportunities for millions of Americans in an era of diminishing jobs, then . . . violent crime is going to increase" (3). Will, on the other hand, seems to believe that both unemployment and income differences are necessary to the health of American society. Will writes, "A society that chafes against stratification derived from disparities of talents will be a society that discourages individual talents" (92). Apparently, the society that Rifkin wants is just the kind of society that Will rejects.
>
> —JACOB GROSSMAN, "Dark Comes before Dawn,"
> student paper

Notice that Grossman comments on Rifkin first and then turns to his second subject, Will. To ensure paragraph unity, he begins with a topic sentence that mentions both subjects.

In the following paragraph, the student writer organizes her comparison **point by point** rather than subject by subject. Instead of saying everything about Smith's picture before commenting on the AP photo, the writer moves back and forth between the two images as she makes and supports two points: (1) that the images differ in figure and scene and (2) that they are similar in theme.

> Divided by an ocean, two photographers took pictures that at first glance seem absolutely different. W. Eugene Smith's well-known *Tomoko in the Bath* and the less well-known AP photo *A Paratrooper Works to Save the Life of a Buddy* portray distinctively different settings and people. Smith brings us into a darkened room where a Japanese woman is lovingly bathing her malformed child, while the AP staff photographer captures two soldiers on the battlefield, one intently performing CPR on his wounded friend. But even though the two images seem as different as women and men, peace and war, or life and death, both

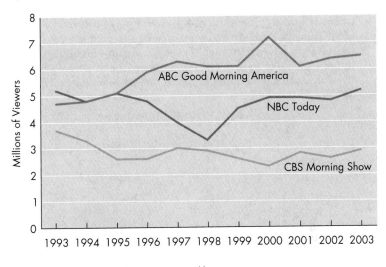

FIGURE 6.6 Visuals that compare and contrast. Graphs and charts are effective for comparing parallel sets of data. This line graph tracks the population of viewers for the three most popular morning shows over ten years.

pictures figure something similar: a time of suffering. It is the early 1970s—a time when the hopes and dreams that modernity promoted are being exposed as deadly to human beings. Perhaps that is why the bodies in both pictures seem humbled. Grief pulls you down onto your knees. Terror impels you to crawl along the ground.

—ILONA BOUZOUKASHVILI, "On Reading Photographs," student paper

7. Analogy

An **analogy** compares topics that at first glance seem quite different (*see Figure 6.7 on p. 68*). A well-chosen analogy can make new or technical information appear more commonplace and understandable:

The human eye provides a good starting point for learning how a camera works. The lens of the eye is like the *lens* of the camera. In both instruments the lens focuses an image of the surroundings on a *light-sensitive surface*—the *retina* of the eye and the *film* in the camera. In both, the light-sensitive material is protected within a light-tight container—the *eyeball* of the eye and the *body* of the camera. Both eye and camera have a mechanism for shutting off light passing through the lens to the interior of the container—the *lid* of the eye and the *shutter* of the camera. In both, the size of the lens opening, or *aperture,* is regulated by an *iris diaphragm.*

—MARVIN ROSEN, *Introduction to Photography*

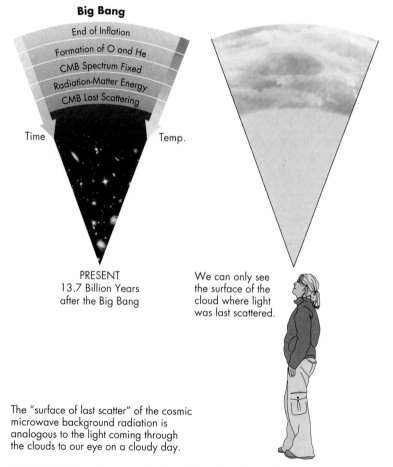

Big Bang

End of Inflation

Formation of O and He

CMB Spectrum Fixed

Radiation-Matter Energy

CMB Last Scattering

Time   Temp.

PRESENT
13.7 Billion Years
after the Big Bang

We can only see
the surface of the
cloud where light
was last scattered.

The "surface of last scatter" of the cosmic
microwave background radiation is
analogous to the light coming through
the clouds to our eye on a cloudy day.

FIGURE 6.7 Visuals as analogies. Visual analogies operate in the same way as written analogies. This graphic presents an analogy to explain the concept of "surface of last scatter," a concept physicists use in describing the Big Bang.

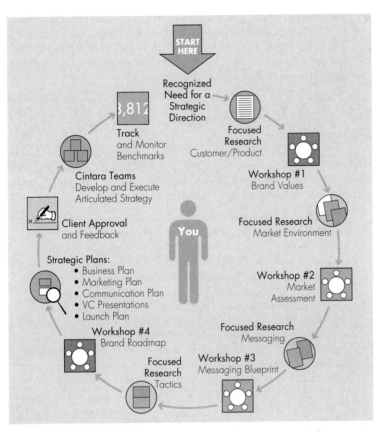

FIGURE 6.8 Visuals that show a process. Flow charts and diagrams such as this one, developed by Cintara, are especially useful when illustrating a process.

8. Process

When you need to explain how to do something or show readers how something is done, you use process analysis (*see Figure 6.8*), explaining each step in the process in chronological order, as in the following example:

> To end our Hawan ritual of thanks, *aarti* is performed. First, my mother lights a piece of camphor in a metal plate called a *taree*. Holding the taree with her right hand, she moves the fire in a circular, clockwise movement in front of the altar. Next, she stands in front of my father and again moves the fiery *taree* in a circular, clockwise direction. After touching his feet and receiving

www.mhhe.com/ awr
For help with describing a process, go to

Writing >
Writing Tutors >
Process Analysis

his blessing, she attends to each of us children in turn, moving the fire in a clockwise direction before kissing us, one by one. When she is done, my father performs his *aarti* in a similar way and then my sister and I do ours. When everyone is done, we say some prayers and sit down.

—U. ROOPNARIAN, student paper

9. Cause and effect

You can use this strategy when you need to trace the causes of some event or situation, to describe its effects, or both (*see Figure 6.9*). In the following example, Rajeev Bector explains the reasons for a character's feelings and actions in a short story:

Given the differences between Mrs. Chestny's and her son's values, as well as the oppressiveness of Mrs. Chestny's racist views, we can understand why Julian struggles to "teach" his mother "a lesson" (185) throughout the entire bus ride. Goffman would point out that "each individual is engaged in providing evidence to establish a definition of himself at the expense of what can remain for the other" (29). But in the end, neither character wins the contest. Julian's mother loses her sense of self when she is pushed down to the ground by a "colored woman" wearing a hat identical to hers (187). Faced with his mother's breakdown, Julian feels his own identity being overwhelmed by "the world of guilt and sorrow."

—RAJEEV BECTOR, "The Character Contest in
Flannery O'Connor's 'Everything That
Rises Must Converge,'" student paper

6c Write focused, clearly organized paragraphs.

Readers expect a piece of writing to be divided into paragraphs—sets of sentences that develop an idea or example in support of the thesis. Paragraphs break the text into blocks for your readers, allowing them to see how your essay builds step by step. Introductory and concluding paragraphs have special functions in a piece of writing, but all paragraphs should have a single, clear focus and a clear organization.

1. Focusing on one main point or example

In a strong paragraph, the sentences form a unit that explores one main point or elaborates on one main example. When you are drafting, start a new paragraph when you introduce a new reason in support of your thesis, a new step in a process, or a new element in an analysis. The

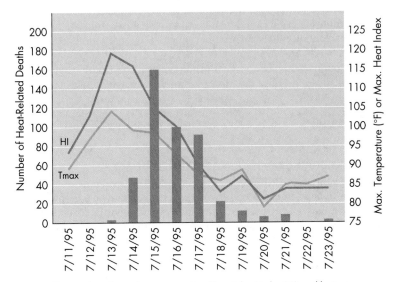

This graph tracks maximum temperature (Tmax), heat index (HI), and heat-related deaths in Chicago each day from July 11 to 23, 1995. The orange line shows maximum daily temperature, the green line shows the heat index, and the bars indicate number of deaths for the day.

FIGURE 6.9 Visuals that show cause and effect. Visuals can provide powerful evidence when you are writing about causes and effects. Although graphs like this one may seem self-explanatory, you will still need to analyze and interpret them for your readers.

paragraphs in your first draft may not all be perfectly unified, and you will likely need to revise for paragraph unity later on. (*See Chapter 7: Revising and Editing, pp. 84–85.*) However, as you draft, if you bear in mind that each paragraph develops a main point or example, then ideas will flow and revising will be easier.

In the following example, the paragraph focuses on a theory that the writer will refer to later in his essay. The main idea is highlighted:

> Current thinking on the topic of loss and mourning rests on foundations constructed by the British psychiatrist, John Bowlby. Using examples from animal and human behavior, Bowlby (1977) posited "attachment theory" as a means of understanding the powerful bonds between humans and the disruption that comes when the bonds are jeopardized or destroyed.

The bonds are formed because of a need for security and safety, are developed early in life, are long enduring, and are directed toward a few special individuals. In normal maturation, the child becomes ever more independent, moving away from the figure of attachment, and returning periodically for safety and security. If the bonds are threatened, the individual will try to restore them through crying, clinging, or other types of coercion; if they are destroyed, withdrawal, apathy, and despair will follow.

—Jonathan Fast, "After Columbine: How People
Mourn Sudden Death"

Details of attachment theory are developed in the rest of the paragraph.

2. Signaling the main idea of your paragraph with a topic sentence

While a topic sentence is not always essential, it can be a helpful starting point as you draft a paragraph. In the following paragraph, the topic sentence (highlighted) provides the writer with a launching point for a series of details:

The excavation also revealed dramatic evidence for the commemorative rituals that took place after the burial. Four cattle had been decapitated and their skulls symbolically placed in a ditch enclosing the burial pit. In the soil above the skulls archaeologists found the butchered bones of at least 250 slaughtered cattle, evidence for a huge ceremonial feast. Clearly this was an expensive way to commemorate a leader. Indeed, the huge quantity of meat suggests that the entire tribe may have gathered at the grave to take part in a ritual feast. Perhaps this was one way the bonds between scattered communities were strengthened.

—Damian Robinson, "Riding into the Afterlife"

The topic sentence announces that the paragraph will focus on a certain kind of evidence.

Sometimes the sentences in a paragraph will lead to a unifying conclusion, as in this example:

Table 1 presents the 15 mechanisms for gaining prestige that were reported for girls and for boys. There were few differences in the avenues to prestige between those in public and private high schools, particularly for girls. Avenues to prestige for girls that focus on their physical attributes, such as attractiveness, popularity with boys, clothes, sexual activity, and participation in sports, were more prominent in public schools than in private schools. In private schools the avenues more indicative of personality attributes, such as general sociability, having a good reputation/virginity, and participating in school clubs/government and cheerleading, were more prominent. Contrary to what parents may expect, avenues considered to be more negative, such as partying and being class clown, appeared more prevalent in private schools than in public schools. However, only clothes remained a significantly more important route to prestige for girls in public schools compared to girls in private schools once controls were introduced for region, size of community, year of graduation, and gender of respondent. Thus, taken together, type of high school had little effect on the ways in which girls accrued prestige in high school.

> —J. JILL SUITOR, REBECCA POWERS, AND RACHEL BROWN,
> "Avenues to Prestige among Adolescents"

If a topic sentence would simply state the obvious, it can be omitted. In the following example, it is not necessary to state that the paragraph is about Igor Stravinsky's preprofessional life:

> Stravinsky was born in Russia, near St. Petersburg, grew up in a musical atmosphere, and studied with Nikolai Rimsky-Korsakov. He had his first important opportunity in 1909, when the great impresario Sergei Diaghilev heard his music.
>
> —ROGER KAMIEN, *Music: An Appreciation*

3. Writing paragraphs that have a clear organization

www.mhhe.com/
awr
For more on paragraphs, go to
Writing > Paragraph Patterns

The sentences in your final draft need to be clearly related to one another. As you are drafting, make connections among your ideas and information as a way of moving your writing forward. The strategies covered in 6b are ways of developing your ideas. Another way to make your ideas work together is to use one of the common organizational schemes for paragraphs. (*For advice on using repetition, pronouns, and transitions to relate sentences to one another, see Chapter 7, pp. 85–86.*)

- **Chronological organization:** The sentences in a paragraph with a chronological organization describe a series of events, steps, or observations as they occur in time: this happened, then that, and so on.

- **Spatial organization:** The sentences in a paragraph with a spatial organization present details as they appear to a viewer: from top to bottom, outside to inside, east to west, and so on.

- **General-to-specific organization:** As we have seen, paragraphs often start with a general topic sentence that states the main idea and then proceed with specifics that elaborate on that idea. The general topic sentence can include a question that the paragraph then answers or a problem that the paragraph goes on to solve.

- **Specific-to-general organization:** The general topic sentence can come at the end of the paragraph, with the specific details leading up to that general conclusion (*see the paragraph from "Avenues to Prestige among Adolescents," pp. 72–73*). This organization is especially effective when you are preparing readers for a revelation.

www.mhhe.com/
awr
For more on
introductions and
conclusions, go to

Writing >
Paragraph/Essay
Development

4. Drafting introductions and conclusions

A paper's opening and closing paragraphs are especially important. You need to hook readers at the beginning and leave them with a strong final impression at the end. As you begin your first draft, you may want to skip over the introduction and focus on the body of your paper. After your paper has taken shape, you can then go back and sketch out the main ideas for your introduction.

The best way to get readers' attention is to show why the topic matters. The opening of your paper should encourage readers to share your view of its importance. Here are some opening strategies:

- Tell a brief story related to the issue your thesis raises.
- Begin with a relevant, attention-getting quotation.
- Begin with a paraphrase of a commonly held view that you immediately question.
- State a working hypothesis.
- Define a key term, but avoid the tired opener that begins, "According to the dictionary . . ."
- Pose an important question.

For informative reports, arguments, and other types of papers, your opening paragraph or paragraphs will include a thesis statement, usually at the beginning or near the end of the introduction. If your purpose is analytic, however, you may instead choose to build up to your thesis. For some types of writing, such as narratives, an explicitly stated thesis may not be needed if the main idea is clear without it.

Just as the opening makes a first impression and motivates readers to continue reading, the closing makes a final impression and motivates readers to think further. The purpose of the conclusion is to bring your paper to an interesting close. While you should not merely repeat the main idea that you introduced at the beginning of the paper, you should also avoid introducing a completely new topic. Your conclusion should remind readers of the paper's significance and satisfy those who might be asking, "So what?" Here are some common strategies for concluding a paper effectively:

- Refer to the story or quotation you used in your introduction.
- Answer the question you posed in your introduction.
- Summarize your main point.
- Call for some action on your readers' part.

- Present a powerful image or forceful example.
- Suggest some implications for the future.

6d Integrate visuals effectively.

If you decide to use a table, chart, diagram, or photograph in your paper, keep this general advice in mind:

- **Number tables and other figures** consecutively throughout your paper, and label them appropriately: Table 1, Table 2, and so on. Do not abbreviate *Table*. *Figure* may be abbreviated as *Fig.*

- **Refer to the visual element in your text** before it appears, placing the visual as close as possible to the text in which you state why you are including it. If your project contains complex tables or many other visuals, however, you may want to group them in an appendix. Always refer to a visual by its label—for example, "See Figure 1."

- **Give each visual a title and caption** that clearly explains what the visual shows. A visual with its caption should be clear without the discussion in the text, and the discussion of the visual in the text should be clear without the visual itself.

- **Include explanatory notes below the visuals.** If you want to explain a specific element within the visual, use a superscript letter (not a number) both after the specific element and before the note. This is essentially a footnote, but the explanation should appear directly beneath the graphic, not at the foot of the page or at the end of your paper.

- **Credit sources for visuals.** If you use a visual element from a source, you need to credit the source. Unless you have specific guidelines to follow, you can use the word *Source,* followed by a colon and complete documentation of the source, including the author, title, publication information, and page number if applicable. Note that book publishers typically provide source information for visuals near the beginning or end of the book.

Note: The Modern Language Association (MLA) and the American Psychological Association (APA) provide guidelines for figure captions and crediting sources of visuals that differ from the preceding guidelines. (*See Chapter 29: MLA Style: Paper Format, pp. 318–19, and Chapter 33: APA Style: Paper Format, pp. 356–57.*)

7 Revising and Editing

Once you have a draft of your paper, you can approach it with a critical eye. In the **revising** stage of the writing process, you review the whole paper, adding, deleting, and moving text as necessary. After you are satisfied with the substance of your paper, **editing** begins. When you edit, you polish sentences so that you say what you want to say as effectively as possible.

This chapter focuses on revising. It also introduces the concepts and principles of editing, which are covered in greater detail in Tabs 9–12.

7a   Get comments from readers.

Asking actual readers to comment on your draft is the best way to get fresh perspectives on your writing. (Be sure that your professor allows this kind of collaboration.) Because you can send drafts to readers by e-mail or post them on a class Web site, computers can make it easier to get comments and use them to revise your work.

1. Using peer review

Whether required or optional, **peer review** involves reading and critiquing your classmates' work while they review yours. When you have a fairly solid draft, you can send it to your peer reviewers by e-mail (also print out a hard copy for yourself), or you can meet in person to exchange and read drafts.

Most readers want to be helpful. When sharing your drafts with your peers, help them help you by asking them specific questions. The best compliment they can pay you is to take your work seriously enough to make constructive suggestions. When you share a draft with readers, give them answers to the following questions:

- **What is your assignment?** Readers need to understand the context for your paper—especially your intended purpose and audience.

- **How close is the project to being finished?** Your answer lets readers know where you are in the writing process and how best to assist you in taking the next step.

- **What steps do you plan to take to complete the project?** If readers know your plans, they can either question the direc-

Tips LEARNING in COLLEGE

Re-Visioning Your Paper

Revising is a process of "re-visioning"—of looking at your work through the eyes of your audience. Here are some tips for getting a fresh perspective on your paper:

- **Get feedback from other readers.** Candid, respectful feedback can help you discover the strong and weak areas of your paper. See 7a for advice on making use of readers' reactions to your drafts.
- **Let your draft cool.** Try to schedule a break between drafting and revising. A good night's sleep, a movie break, or some physical exercise will help you view your paper more objectively.
- **Read your paper aloud.** Some people find that reading aloud helps them "hear" their paper the way their audience will.
- **Use revising and editing checklists.** The checklists on pages 81, 90, and 95 will assist you in evaluating your paper systematically.

tion you are taking or give you more specific advice, such as the titles of additional books or articles you might consult.

- **What kind of feedback do you need?** Let your readers know what you are looking for. Do you want readers to summarize your main points so you can determine if you have communicated them clearly? Do you want to know what readers were thinking and feeling as they read or heard your draft? Do you want a response to the logic of your argument or the development of your thesis?

Reading other writers' drafts will help you view your own work more objectively, and comments from readers will help you see your own writing as others see it. As you gain more objectivity, you will become more adept at revising your work. In addition, the approaches that you see your classmates taking to the assignment will give you ideas for new directions in your own writing.

Peer review is possible without computers and the Internet, of course, but specialized software, like the writing environment in the *Catalyst* Web site that accompanies this book, can make it easier for you to obtain and review comments from your readers. (*For more on this feature of* Catalyst, *see Chapter 2, p. 13.*)

Tips WRITING in COLLEGE

Guidelines for Giving Feedback

- **Focus on strengths as well as weaknesses.** Writers need to know what parts of their paper are strongest so they can retain those sections when they revise and use them as models as they work to improve weaker sections. At the same time, do not withhold constructive criticism, or you will deprive the writer of an opportunity to improve the paper.
- **Be specific.** Give examples to back up your general reactions.
- **Be constructive.** Phrase negative reactions in a way that will help the writer see a solution. Instead of saying that an example is a bad choice, explain that you did not understand how the example was connected to the main point, and suggest a way to make the connection clearer.
- **Ask questions.** Jot down any questions that occur to you while reading. Ask for clarification or note an objection that readers of the final version might make.

Guidelines for Receiving Feedback

- **Resist any tendency to be defensive.** Keep in mind that readers are discussing your paper, not you, and their feedback offers a way for you to see your paper differently. Be respectful of their time and effort.
- **Ask for more feedback if you need it.** Some students may be hesitant to share all of their reactions, and you may need to do some coaxing.
- **Try not to be frustrated by conflicting comments.** When you have two or more readers, you may receive differing—and sometimes contradictory—views on your work. Examine points of conflict and rethink the parts of your paper that caused them. You, not your reviewers, are in charge of decisions about your paper.

2. Responding to readers

Consider and evaluate your readers' suggestions, but remember that you are under no obligation to do what they say. Sometimes you will receive contradictory advice: one reader may like a particular sentence that a second reader may suggest you eliminate. Is there common ground? Yes. Both readers stopped at that sentence. Ask yourself why—and whether you want readers to pause there.

For MULTILINGUAL STUDENTS

Peer Review

Peer editing is a part of many writing classes in the United States and is frequently used to teach editing skills and to cultivate collaboration in a student writing community. As a multilingual writer, you will find peer editing helpful in many ways. It will show you that many errors you make are quite common; it will help you improve your ability to detect mistakes and decide which ones to correct first; it will also challenge you to look at your writing with a critical eye and to present your ideas to a diverse audience.

7b Use online tools for revising.

www.mhhe.com/
awr
For help with revising, go to
Writing >
Paragraph/Essay
Development >
Drafting and
Revising

Word-processing programs can make your text look beautiful, with a pleasing format and an easy-to-read typeface. Even though a first draft may look finished, however, it is still a first draft. Be sure to check for problems in content, structure, and style. Move paragraphs around, add details, and delete irrelevant sentences. The computer makes these changes almost effortless. However, it is always a good idea to print out a copy of your draft because the hard copy, unlike the computer screen, allows you to see your paper as a whole.

To work efficiently, you should become familiar with the revising and editing tools in your word-processing program.

- **Comments:** Many word-processing programs have a "Comments" feature that allows you to add notes that pop up when readers run the cursor over highlighted text, as shown in Figure 7.1. This feature is useful for giving feedback on someone else's draft. Some writers also use it to make notes to themselves.

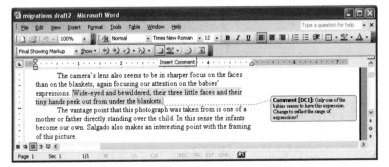

FIGURE 7.1 Using Microsoft Word's Comments feature.

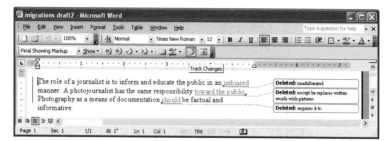

FIGURE 7.2 Showing revisions with Track Changes.

- **Track changes:** The "track changes" feature allows you to edit a piece of writing—either yours or another writer's—while also maintaining the original text. Usually, strike-through marks or marginal notes show what you have deleted or re-placed, as shown in Figure 7.2. Because you can still see the original text, you can judge whether a change has improved the paper and whether any vital information has been lost. If you change your mind, you can restore the deleted text. When collaborating with another writer, you should keep the original text intact while suggesting changes. To do this, track changes onscreen only.

7c Focus on the purpose of your writing.

As you reread your paper and decide how to revise it, base your decisions on the purpose of your paper. Is your primary purpose to inform, to interpret, or to argue? (*For more on purpose, see Tab 2: Learning across the Curriculum, pp. 21–22.*)

Clarity about your purpose is especially important when an assignment calls for interpretation. A description is not the same as an interpretation. With this principle in mind, Diane Chen read over the first draft of her paper on the *Migrations* photography exhibit. Here is part of her description of the photograph she chose to discuss in detail:

FIRST DRAFT

The photograph is black and white, as are the others in the show. The faces of the babies are in sharp focus while the blanket is a bit defocused. Light, which is essential to photography, is disseminated from a single source coming from the upper left-hand corner of the picture. The light source is not too bright as to bathe the babies in light, but just bright enough to illuminate their faces, which have expressions

CHECKLIST

Revising Your Draft for Content and Organization

☐ 1. **Purpose:** Is my purpose for writing clear? If not, how can I revise to make my purpose apparent?

☐ 2. **Thesis:** Is my thesis clear and specific, and do I introduce it early in my draft? (If not, do I have a good reason for withholding it or not stating it at all?)

☐ 3. **Order:** Are my key points arranged effectively? Would another order better support my thesis?

☐ 4. **Paragraphs:** Is each paragraph well developed, unified, and coherent?

☐ 5. **Visuals:** If I am using visuals, do they communicate what I intend them to, without resulting in unnecessary clutter?

of interest and puzzlement. Perhaps they are wondering who Salgado is or what is that strange contraption he is holding.

Keeping her purpose in mind, Chen realized that she needed to discuss the significance of her observations—to interpret and analyze the details. She wanted to show her readers how the formal elements of the photograph functioned. Her revision makes this interpretation clearer.

REVISION

The orphanage photograph is shot in black and white, as are the other images in the show, giving it a documentary feel that emphasizes the truth of the situation. But Salgado's choice of black-and-white photography is also an artistic decision. He uses the contrasts of light and dark to create a dramatic image of the three babies.

The vertical black and white stripes of the blanket direct our eyes to the infants' faces and hands, which are framed by a horizontal white stripe . . .

7d Make sure you have a strong thesis.

Remember that a thesis makes an assertion about a topic. It links the *what* and the *why*. Is your thesis evident on the first page of your draft? Before readers get very far along, they expect an answer to the question "What is the point of all this?" If you do not find the point on the first page, its absence is a signal to revise, unless you are deliberately

www.mhhe.com/ awr
For help with developing a strong thesis, go to

Writing > Paragraph/Essay Development > Thesis/Central Idea

waiting until the end to reveal your thesis. (*For more on strong theses, see Chapter 5, pp. 48–50.*)

Many writers start with a working thesis, which often evolves into a more specific, complex assertion as they develop their ideas. One of the key challenges of revising is to compose a clear statement of this revised thesis. When she drafted a paper on Germany's economic prospects, Jennifer Koehler stated her working thesis as follows:

WORKING THESIS

Germany is experiencing a great deal of change.

During the revision process, Koehler realized that her working thesis was too weak to serve as the thesis of her final draft. A weak thesis is predictable: readers read it, agree, and that's that. A strong thesis, on the other hand, stimulates thoughtful inquiry. Koehler's revised thesis provokes questions:

REVISED THESIS

With proper follow-through, Germany can become one of the world's primary sources of direct investment and maintain its status as one of the world's preeminent exporters.

Sometimes writers find that their ideas change altogether, and the working thesis needs to be completely revised.

Your thesis should evolve throughout the paper. Readers need to see a statement of the main idea on the first page, but they also expect a more complex or general statement near the end. After presenting evidence to support her revised thesis, Koehler concludes her paper by stating her thesis in a more general way:

If the government efforts continue, the economy will strengthen over the next decade and Germany will reinforce its position as an integral nation in the global economy.

7e Review the structure of your paper as a whole.

In a first draft, you are wise to think broadly about the different parts of your paper and how you should order them. Does the paper have a beginning, a middle, and an end, with bridges between those parts? When you revise, however, you can refine and even change this structure so that it supports what you want to say more effectively.

One way to review your structure is by outlining the first draft. (*For help with outlining, see Chapter 5, pp. 50–53.*) Try listing the key points of your draft in sentence form; whenever possible, use sentences that actually appear in the draft. This kind of point-by-point outlining will allow you to see the draft's logic (or lack thereof). Ask yourself if the key points are arranged effectively or if another arrangement would work better. The following structures are typical ways of organizing papers:

- An *informative* structure sets out the key parts of a topic.

- An *exploratory* structure begins with a question or problem and works step-by-step to discover an answer or a solution.

- An *argumentative* structure presents a set of linked reasons plus supporting evidence.

7f Revise for paragraph development, paragraph unity, and coherence.

The structure you choose should be appropriate to the assignment, your purpose, and your thesis, and the paper's parts should develop your ideas in an orderly way. As you revise, examine each paragraph, asking yourself what role it plays—or should play—in the paper as a whole. Keeping this role in mind, check the paragraph for development and unity. You should also check each paragraph for coherence—and consider whether all of the paragraphs together contribute to the paper as a whole.

1. Paragraph development

As you revise your paper, ask yourself: Does each paragraph provide enough detail? Paragraphs in academic papers are usually about a hundred words long. Although sometimes you will deliberately use a one- or two-sentence paragraph for emphasis, short paragraphs generally need to be developed more fully. Would more information make the point clearer? Should a term be defined? Do generalizations need to be supported with examples?

Note how this writer developed one of her paragraphs, adding details and examples to make her argument more effective:

FIRST DRAFT

A 1913 advertisement for Shredded Wheat illustrates Kellner's claim that advertisements sell self-images. The ad suggests that serving Shredded Wheat will give women the same sense of accomplishment as gaining the right to vote.

REVISION

According to Kellner, "advertising is as concerned with selling lifestyles and socially desirable identities . . . as with selling the products themselves" (193). A 1913 ad for Shredded Wheat shows how the selling of self-images works. At first glance, this ad seems to be promoting the women's suffrage movement. In big, bold letters, "Votes for Women" is emblazoned across the top of the ad. But a closer look reveals that the ad is for Shredded Wheat cereal. Holding a piece of the cereal in her hand, a woman stands behind a large bowlful of Shredded Wheat biscuits that is made to look like a voting box. The text claims that "every biscuit is a vote for health, happiness, and domestic freedom." Like the rest of the advertisement, this claim suggests that serving Shredded Wheat will give women the same sense of accomplishment as gaining the right to vote.

—HOLLY MUSETTI, student paper

www.mhhe.com/
awr
For more help with
paragraph unity, go to
Writing >
Paragraph /Essay
Development >
Unity

2. Paragraph unity

A unified paragraph has a single, clear focus. To check for **unity,** identify the paragraph's topic sentence (*see pp. 72–73*). Everything in the paragraph should be clearly connected to the topic sentence.

Compare the first draft of the following paragraph with its revision, and note how the addition of a topic sentence (in bold in the revision) makes the paragraph more clearly focused and therefore easier for the writer to revise further. Note also that the writer deleted ideas that did not directly relate to the paragraph's main point:

FIRST DRAFT

Germany is ranked first on worldwide production levels. Automobiles, aircraft, and electronic equipment are among Germany's most important products for export. As the standard of living of the citizens of what was formerly East Germany increases due to reunification, their purchasing power and productivity will increase. A major problem is that east Germany is not as productive or efficient as west Germany, and so it would be better if less money were invested in the east. Germany is involved in most global treaties that protect business interests, and intellectual property is well protected. A plus for potential ventures and production plans is its highly skilled workforce. Another factor that indicates that Germany will remain strong in the arena of productivity and trade is its physical location in the world. "Its terrain and geographical position have combined to make Germany an important crossroads for traffic between the North Sea, the Baltic, and the Mediterranean. International transportation routes pass through all of Germany," thus utilizing a comprehensive and efficient network of transportation, both on land and over water ("Germany," 1995, p. 185). Businesses can operate plants in Germany and have no difficulties transporting goods and services to other parts of the country. Generally, private enterprise, government, banks, and unions cooperate, making the country more amenable to negotiations for business entry or joint ventures.

REVISION

For many reasons, Germany is attractive both as a market for other nations and as a location for production. As the standard of living of the citizens of what was formerly East Germany increases due to reunification, their purchasing power and productivity increase. Intellectual property is well protected, and Germany is involved in most global treaties that protect business interests. Germany's highly skilled workforce is another plus for potential ventures and production plans. Generally, private enterprise, government, banks, and unions cooperate, making the country amenable to negotiations for business entry or joint ventures. Germany also has an excellent physical location that makes it an "important crossroads for traffic between the North Sea, the Baltic, and the Mediterranean" ("Germany," 1995, p. 185). Equally important, a comprehensive and efficient transportation system allows businesses to operate plants in Germany and easily transport their goods and services to other parts of the country and the world.

—JENNIFER KOEHLER, "Germany's Path to Continuing Prosperity," student paper

3. Coherence

The sentences in a paragraph should "cohere," or stick together as a unit. Likewise, each paragraph should be clearly related to the rest of the essay. A coherent paragraph flows smoothly, with an organization that is easy to follow and each sentence clearly related to the next. (*See Chapter 6, pp. 70–75, for tips on how to develop well-organized paragraphs.*) You can improve coherence both within and among the paragraphs in your draft by using repetition, pronouns, parallel structure, synonyms, and transitions.

www.mhhe.com/awr
For more help with coherence, go to

Writing > Paragraph/Essay Development > Coherence

- Repeat key words to emphasize the main idea:

  A photograph displays a unique *moment*. To capture that *moment* . . .

- Use pronouns and antecedents to form connections between sentences and avoid unnecessary repetition. In the following example, *it* refers back to *Germany* and connects the two sentences:

  Germany imports raw materials, energy sources, and food products. *It* exports a wide range of industrial products, including automobiles, aircraft, and machine tools.

■ Repeat sentence structures to emphasize connections:

Because the former West Germany lived through a generation of prosperity, its people developed high expectations of material comfort. *Because the former East Germany* lived through a generation of deprivation, its people developed disdain for material values.

■ Use **synonyms**—words that are close in meaning to words or phrases that have preceded them:

In the world of photography, critics *argue* for either a scientific or an artistic approach. This *controversy. . .*

■ Use transitional words and phrases. One-word transitions and **transitional expressions** link one idea with another, helping readers understand your logic. (*See the list of common transitional expressions in the box on p. 87.*) Compare the following two paragraphs, the first version without transitions and the second, revised version with transitions (in bold type) that connect one thought to another:

FIRST DRAFT

Glaser was in a position to powerfully affect Armstrong's career and his life. Armstrong acknowledged Glaser's importance, referring to him at one point as "the man who has guided me all through my career" (qtd. in Jones and Chilton 202). There is little evidence that the musician submitted to whatever his business manager wanted or demanded. Armstrong seemed to recognize that he gave Glaser whatever power the manager enjoyed over him. Armstrong could and did resist Glaser's control when he wanted to. That may be one reason why he liked and trusted Glaser as much as he did.

REVISION

Clearly, Glaser was in a position to affect Armstrong's career and his life powerfully. Armstrong acknowledged Glaser's importance, at one point referring to him as "the man who has guided me all through my career" (qtd. in Jones and Chilton 202). **However,** there is little evidence that the musician submitted to whatever his business manager wanted or demanded. **In fact,** Armstrong seemed to recognize that he gave Glaser whatever power the manager enjoyed over him. When he wanted to, Armstrong could and did resist Glaser's control, and that may be one reason why he liked and trusted Glaser as much as he did.

—ESTER HOFFMAN, "Louis Armstrong and Joe Glaser"

TRANSITIONAL EXPRESSIONS

- **To show relationships in space:** above, adjacent to, against, alongside, around, at a distance from, at the . . . , below, beside, beyond, encircling, far off, forward, from the . . . , in front of, in the rear, inside, near the back, near the end, nearby, next to, on, over, surrounding, there, through the, to the left, to the right, up front
- **To show relationships in time:** afterward, at last, before, earlier, first, former, formerly, immediately, in the first place, in the interval, in the meantime, in the next place, in the last place, later on, meanwhile, next, now, often, once, previously, second, simultaneously, sometime later, subsequently, suddenly, then, third, today, tomorrow, until now, when, years ago, yesterday
- **To show something added to what has come before:** again, also, and, and then, besides, further, furthermore, in addition, last, likewise, moreover, next, too
- **To give examples that intensify points:** after all, as an example, certainly, clearly, for example, for instance, indeed, in fact, in truth, it is true, of course, specifically, that is
- **To show similarities:** alike, in the same way, like, likewise, resembling, similarly
- **To show contrasts:** after all, although, but, conversely, differ(s) from, difference, different, dissimilar, even though, granted, however, in contrast, in spite of, nevertheless, notwithstanding, on the contrary, on the other hand, otherwise, still, though, unlike, while this may be true, yet
- **To indicate cause and effect:** accordingly, as a result, because, consequently, hence, since, then, therefore, thus
- **To conclude or summarize:** finally, in brief, in conclusion, in other words, in short, in summary, that is, to summarize

- Use repetition, pronouns, parallelism, transitions, and **transitional sentences,** which refer back to the previous paragraph and move your essay on to the next point, to show how paragraphs in an essay are related to one another:

    The vertical black and white stripes of the blanket direct our eyes to the infants' faces and hands, which are framed by a horizontal white stripe. The whites of their eyes in particular stand out against the darkness created by the shell of the blankets. The camera's lens also seems to be in sharper focus on the faces than on the blankets, again focusing our attention on the babies' expressions.

    Each baby has a different response to the camera. The baby on the left returns our gaze with a heart-wrenching look. . . .

7g   Revise visuals.

If you have used visuals in your paper, you should return to them during the revision stage to eliminate what scholar Edward Tufte calls **chartjunk,** or distracting visual elements. The following are Tufte's suggestions for editing visuals so that your readers will focus on your data rather than your "data containers."

- **Eliminate grid lines or, if the lines are needed for clarity, lighten them.** Tables should not look like nets with every number enclosed. Vertical rules are only needed when space is extremely tight between columns.

- **Eliminate any unnecessary 3D renderings.** Cubes and shadows can distort the information in a visual. For most charts, including pie charts, a flat image makes it easier for readers to compare parts.

- **Label data clearly,** avoiding abbreviations and legends if possible. Make sure that your visual has an informative title.

- **Use bright colors for emphasis,** to focus attention on the key data. For example, if you are including a map, use muted colors over large areas and save strong colors for areas you want to emphasize.

- **Avoid decorating your visual with distracting pictures.** Clip art and other decorative elements seldom make data more interesting or appear more substantial.

- **Look out for and correct distortions of the data.** In the first graph in Figure 7.3, each month gets its own point, except for January, February, March, and April. This creates a misleading impression of hurricane activity by month. The revision corrects this distortion, and also eliminates other elements of chartjunk.

www.mhhe.com/
awr
For additional help
with editing, go to

Editing

7h   Edit sentences.

When you are satisfied with the overall placement and development of your ideas, you can turn your attention to individual sentences, phrases, and words. Tabs 9 and 10 of this handbook address the many specific questions that writers have when they are editing for clarity, word choice, and grammar conventions. The section that follows will give you an overview of editing concerns and techniques.

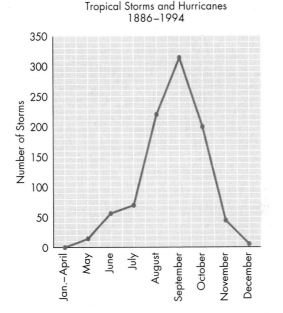

Tropical Storms and Hurricanes
1886–1994

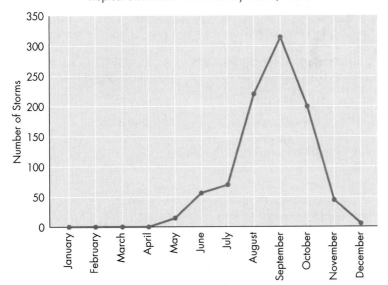

Tropical Storms and Hurricanes by Month, 1886–1994

FIGURE 7.3 Misleading (top) and revised graph. In the graph at the top, the activity in the first part of the year is combined into one point on the axis, misleading readers. The chart at the bottom has been revised to correct this problem.

CHECKLIST

Editing Your Draft for Style and Grammar

To create a personalized editing checklist, fill in the boxes next to your trouble spots, as determined from your instructor's comments on your writing, as well as any diagnostic tests you have taken.

1. **Clarity** (*Tab 9, Chapters 38–46, pp. 401–35*): Does every sentence communicate my meaning in a clear, direct style? Does my paper contain any of the following common causes of unclear sentences?
   - ☐ Wordiness
   - ☐ Missing words
   - ☐ Mixed constructions
   - ☐ Confusing shifts
   - ☐ Faulty parallelism
   - ☐ Misplaced and dangling modifiers
   - ☐ Problem with coordination and subordination
   - ☐ Other: _____

2. **Word choice** (*Tab 9, Chapters 47–50, pp. 435–58*): Is my choice of words as precise as it could be? Have I avoided slang, biased language, clichés, and other inappropriate usages? Have I misused any commonly confused words (for example, *advice* vs. *advise*) or used any nonstandard expressions (for example, *could of*)?

3. **Grammar conventions** (*Tab 10, pp. 459–517*): Does my paper contain any of the common errors that may confuse or distract readers?
   - ☐ Sentence fragments
   - ☐ Comma splices
   - ☐ Run-on sentences
   - ☐ Subject-verb agreement problems
   - ☐ Incorrect verb forms
   - ☐ Inconsistent verb tenses
   - ☐ Pronoun-antecedent agreement problems
   - ☐ Incorrect pronoun forms
   - ☐ Misused adjectives or adverbs
   - ☐ Other: _____

If you are in the process of developing fluency in English, consult Tab 12: Basic Grammar Review for additional editing advice specific to multilingual writers.

1. Editing for clarity

As you edit, you will want to focus on sentence style, aiming for clearly focused and interestingly varied writing. A volley of short, choppy sentences, for example, will probably distract readers from what you have to say, while an unbroken stream of long, complicated sentences is likely to dull their senses. In the example that follows, notice how the revised version connects ideas for readers and, consequently, is easier to read:

DRAFT

My father was a zealous fisherman. He took his fishing rod on every family outing. Often he spent the whole outing staring at the water, waiting for a nibble. He went to the kitchen as soon as he got home. He usually cleaned and cooked the fish the same day he caught them.

REVISED

A zealous fisherman, my father took his fishing rod on every family outing, often spending the whole afternoon by the shore, waiting for a nibble, and then hurrying straight to the kitchen to clean and cook the fish the very same day.

As you edit, you should also condense and focus sentences that are wordy and lack a clear subject and vivid verb:

DRAFT

Although both vertebral and wrist fractures cause deformity and impair movement, hip fractures, which are one of the most devastating consequences of osteoporosis, significantly increase the risk of death, since 12%–30% of patients with a hip fracture die within one year after the fracture, while the mortality rate climbs to 40% for the first two years post fracture.

REVISED

Hip fractures are one of the most devastating consequences of osteoporosis. Although vertebral and wrist fractures cause deformity and impair movement, hip fractures significantly increase the risk of death. Within one year after a hip fracture, 12%–20% of the injured die. The mortality rate climbs to 40% after two years.

More often than not, sentences beginning with *it is* or *there is* or *there are* (*it was* or *there was*)—called **expletive constructions**—are weak and indirect. Using a clear subject and a vivid verb usually makes such sentences more powerful:

DRAFT

There are stereotypes from the days of a divided Germany.

REVISED

Stereotypes formed in the days of a divided Germany *persist.*

2. Editing for word choice

Finding precisely the right word, and then putting that word in the best place, is an important part of revision. In a sense, different disciplines and occupations have their own dialects (terminology) that members of the community are expected to know and use. The word *significant,* for example, has a mathematical meaning for the statistician that it does not have for the literary critic. When taking courses in a discipline, you should use its terminology, not to impress the instructor but to be understood accurately. Whenever you are unsure of a word's denotation (exact meaning), consult a dictionary.

As you review your draft, look for general terms that might need to be made more specific:

DRAFT

Foreign direct investment (FDI) in Germany will probably remain low because of several *factors.* [Factors *is a general word. To get specific, answer the question* "What *factors?*"]

REVISED

Foreign direct investment (FDI) in Germany will probably remain low because of *high labor costs, high taxation, and government regulation.*

Your search for more specific words can lead you to a dictionary and thesaurus, two essential tools for choosing precise words. A dictionary gives the exact definition of a word, its history (etymology), and the parts of speech it belongs to. A thesaurus provides its synonyms—words with the same or nearly the same meaning. (*For more on using a dictionary and a thesaurus, see Chapter 49, pp. 445–8.*) One student used both a thesaurus and a dictionary as aids in revising the following sentence:

DRAFT

Malcolm X had a special kind of power.

Dissatisfied with the lack of precision in the word *power,* this writer checked a thesaurus and found the word *influence* listed as a synonym for *power* and the word *charisma* given as a special kind of influence.

Going back to the dictionary, she found that *charisma* means a "divinely conferred" power and has an etymological connection with *charismatic,* a term used to describe ecstatic (Christian) experiences like speaking in tongues. *Charisma* was exactly the word she needed to convey both the spiritual and the popular sides of Malcolm X:

REVISED

Malcolm X had charisma.

As you edit for word choice, you will also want to make sure that your tone is appropriate for academic writing and that you have avoided biased language. Chapter 47 offers advice on editing to eliminate biased language such as the use of *his* to refer to women as well as men:

BIASED

Every student who wrote *his* name on the class list had to pay a copying fee in advance and pledge to attend every session.

REVISED AS PLURAL

Students who wrote *their* names on the class list had to pay a copying fee in advance and pledge to attend every session.

REVISED TO AVOID PRONOUNS

Every student who signed up for the class had to pay a copying fee in advance and pledge to attend every session.

REVISED WITH *HIS OR HER*

Every student who wrote *his or her* name on the class list had to pay a copying fee in advance and pledge to attend every session.

3. Editing for grammar conventions

Many of us use the rules of English grammar unconsciously to generate sentences that other English speakers can easily understand. Sometimes, however, we will construct a sentence or choose a word form that does not follow the rules of standard written English. In academic writing, these kinds of errors are distracting to readers and can obscure your meaning:

DRAFT

Photographs of illegal immigrants being captured by the U.S. border patrol, of emotional immigrants on the plane to their new country, and of villagers fleeing rebel gangs. [*This is a sentence fragment because it lacks a verb and omits the writer's point about these images.*]

EDITED SENTENCE

Photographs of illegal immigrants being captured by the U.S. border patrol, of emotional immigrants on the plane to their new country, and of villagers fleeing rebel gangs exemplify the range of migration stories.

A list of common abbreviations and symbols used to note errors in a manuscript can be found at the end of this text. Your instructor and other readers may use these, and you may find it helpful to learn them as well. Some writers prefer to circle the sentences that seem wrong to them as they read through their writing, and then go back to figure out each error.

TEXTCONNEX

The Pros and Cons of Grammar and Spell Checkers

Grammar and spell checkers can help you spot some errors, but they miss many others and may even flag a correct sentence. Consider the following example:

Thee neighbors puts there cats' outsider.

A spelling and grammar checker did not catch the five errors in the sentence. (Correct version: *The neighbors put their cats outside.*)

If you are aware of your program's deficiencies, then you can make some use of it as you edit your document. Be sure, however, to review your writing carefully yourself. Throughout the grammar chapters of this book, Grammar Checker boxes warn you of potential pitfalls in using these tools.

7i Proofread carefully.

Once you have revised your paper at the essay, paragraph, and sentence levels, it is time to give your work one last check to make sure that it is free of typos and other mechanical errors.

CHECKLIST

Proofreading

- ☐ Have you included your name, the date, your professor's name, and the paper title? (*See Tabs 6–8 for the formats to use for MLA, APA, Chicago, or CSE style.*)
- ☐ Are all words spelled correctly? Be sure to check the spelling of titles and headings. (*See Chapter 68, pp. 590–94.*)
- ☐ Have you used the words you intended, or have you substituted words that sound like the ones you want but have a different spelling and meaning, such as *too* for *to, their* for *there,* or *it's* for *its*? (*See Chapter 50, pp. 449–58.*)
- ☐ Are all proper names capitalized? Have you capitalized titles of works correctly and either italicized them or put them in quotation marks as required? (*See Chapter 63, pp. 570–77, and Chapter 66, pp. 583–86.*)
- ☐ Have you punctuated your sentences correctly? (*See Tab 12.*)
- ☐ Are sources cited correctly? Is the works-cited or references list in the correct format? (*See Tabs 6–8.*)
- ☐ Have you checked anything you retyped—for example, quotations and tables—against the original?

Proofread a printout of your paper even if you are submitting an electronic version. A ruler placed under each line as you are proofing can make it easier to focus. Another proofreading technique is to start at the end of the paper and proofread your way backwards to the beginning, sentence by sentence.

7j Use campus, Internet, and community resources.

As you revise and edit your paper, you can call on a number of resources outside of the classroom for help.

1. Using the campus writing center

Many campuses maintain writing centers, staffed by tutors, that offer help throughout the writing process. Tutors in the writing center can read and comment on drafts of your work. They can also help you find and correct problems with grammar and punctuation.

www.mhhe.com/
awr
For links to OWLs,
go to
Writing > Writing
Web Links

2. Using online writing labs (OWLs)

Most OWLs offer information about writing that you can access any-time, including lists of useful online resources. Some OWLs are staffed by tutors who support students working on specific writing assign-ments. OWLs with tutors can be useful in the following ways:

- You can submit a draft via e-mail for feedback. OWL tutors will return your work, often within forty-eight hours.

- You can post your paper in a public access space where you will receive feedback from more than just one or two readers.

- You can read papers online and learn how others are handling writing issues.

You can learn more about what OWLs have to offer by checking out the following Web sites:

- Purdue University's Online Writing Lab:
  <http://owl.english.purdue.edu>

- Writing Labs and Writing Centers on the Web (visit almost fifty OWLs): <http://owl.english.purdue.edu/internet/owls/ writing-labs.html>

- Washington State University's Online Writing Lab:
  <http://owl.wsu.edu>

3. Working with experts and instructors

In addition to sharing your work with peers in class, through e-mail, or in online environments, you can use e-mail to consult experts. Sup-pose, for example, that a friend at another college is an expert on your topic. You can use e-mail to interview that friend and then include parts of the interview in your paper, properly crediting your source. (*See Tabs 6–8.*)

You can also consult your instructor or other experts. Many stu-dents don't think to ask their instructor questions by e-mail. If your in-structor is willing, you can quote from his or her response in your paper, as long as you include a proper citation.

Your instructor's comments on an early draft are especially valu-able. He or she will raise questions and make suggestions, but re-member, it is not your instructor's job to "solve" paper problems for you or to tell you how to get an A in the course. It is your responsibility to address the issues your instructor raises and to revise your work accordingly.

7k Learn from one student's revisions.

In the following paragraphs from the second draft of Diane Chen's paper on an exhibit of photographs by Sebastião Salgado, you can see how one writer revised her draft to tighten the focus of her descriptive paragraphs and edited to improve clarity, word choice, and grammar.

The Caring Eye of Sebastião Salgado

Photographer Sebastião Salgado spent seven years ~~of his life~~ travelling to city slums *along migration routes and* refugee camps~~, and migration routes~~ in order to document the lives of people uprooted from their homes *land*. A selection of his photographs can be seen in the exhibit, "Migrations: Humanity in Transition." Like a photojournalist, Salgado brings us images of news-worthy events but he goes beyond objective reporting, imparting his compassion for refugees and migrants to the viewer.

~~So~~ *M*any *of the* photographs in Salgado's show are certain to ~~impress and~~ touch ~~the viewers with their subject matter and sheer beauty~~ *viewers*. Whether capturing the millions of refugee tents in Africa that seem to stretch on for miles or the disheartened faces of ~~small~~ immigrant children, ~~Salgado brings an artistic element to his pictures that~~ *the images in Migrations* suggests *that Salgado* ~~he~~ does so much more with his camera than ~~just~~ point and shoot.

Salgado's photograph of the most vulnerable of these refugees illustrate*s* the power of his work. "Orphanage attached to the hospital at Kibumba, Number One Camp, Goma Zaire," *(Fig. 1)* depicts three ~~apparently newborn or several month old babies,~~ *infants* who are victims of the genocidal war in neighboring Rwanda. The label for the photograph ~~tells us~~ *reveals* that there were 4,000 orphans at this camp and an estimated 100,000 Rwandan orphans overall. Those numbers are mind-numbing, but this *abstractions* picture is not.

8 Designing Academic Papers and Portfolios

As noted in Chapter 7, one of your final writing tasks is to proofread your paper to make sure it is free of distracting errors. Another is to format your text so that readers can "see" your ideas clearly. In this chapter, our main focus is on designing academic papers. (*Advice on designing multimedia presentations and Web sites can be found in Chapter 14, and advice on designing brochures, newsletters, résumés, and other documents in Chapter 15.*)

In your writing course, as well as in other courses and in your professional life, you may be called on to compile a **portfolio**—a collection of your writings. This chapter offers guidelines for designing print and electronic portfolios that showcase your work effectively.

www.mhhe.com/ awr
For links to information on document and Web design, go to

Writing > Writing Web Links > Annotated Links on Design

8a Consider audience and purpose when making design decisions.

As you plan your document, consider your purpose as well as the needs of your audience. If you are writing an informative paper for a psychology class, your instructor—your primary audience—will probably prefer that you follow the guidelines provided by the American Psychological Association (APA). If you are writing a lab report for a biology or chemistry course, you will likely need to follow a well-established format and use the documentation style recommended by the Council of Science Editors (CSE) to cite any sources you use. A history paper might call for the use of the Chicago style. If you are responding to an assignment in a creative nonfiction course, you might have more freedom in making design decisions, though if you cite sources you will need to use the style recommended by the Modern Language Association (MLA). In any paper, however, your goal is to enhance the content of your text, not decorate it. (*For help with these documentation styles, see Tabs 6–8.*)

8b Use the toolbars available in your word-processing program.

The toolbars on your computer give you a range of options for editing, sharing, and, especially, designing your documents. A variety of toolbars are available in most widely used word-processing programs. For example, if you are using Microsoft Word, you can find them by looking at the pulldown menu under "View." In Figure 8.1, three toolbars are open: standard, drawing, and reviewing. The *standard* toolbar allows you to choose different typefaces; bold, italic, or underlined type; numbered or bulleted lists; and so on. The *drawing* toolbar allows you to insert boxes, drawings, and clip art into your text. The *reviewing* toolbar enables you to mark changes, add comments, and even send your document to a reader.

FIGURE 8.1 The Standard, Drawing, and Reviewing Toolbars in Microsoft Word.

If you are using a word-processing program other than Microsoft Word, take some time to learn the different toolbars and formatting options available to you.

8c Think intentionally about design.

For any document that you create, whether for an academic course or for a purpose and an audience outside of college, you need to apply the same basic design principles:

- Organize information for readers.
- Use type style, lists, and other graphic elements to make your text readable and to emphasize key material.
- Format related design elements consistently.
- Include headings to organize long papers.
- Show restraint.

A sample page from a student's report on a local food bank, which includes information that she gathered while serving as a volunteer, illustrates these principles. The content in the sample on page 100 is at a disadvantage because the author has not employed these principles successfully. By contrast, the same material on page 101 is clearer and easier for readers to understand because of its design.

EXAMPLE OF A POORLY DESIGNED REPORT

Emphasis wrong: title of report is not as prominent as heading within report.

Margins are not wide enough, making page look crowded.

Bar chart is not intro-duced in text and does not have caption.

The Caring Express Food Bank

The Caring Express Food Bank serves a varied population of clients, including chronically homeless people, temporarily homeless people, recent immigrants, elderly people on fixed incomes, and people in need of temporary services.

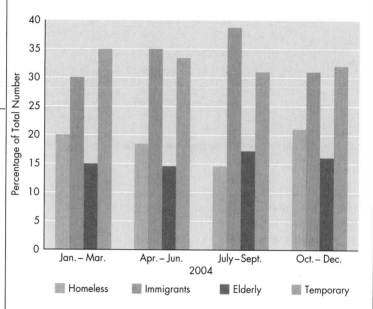

While the number of homeless, both temporary and permanent, that Caring Express assisted in 2004 decreased during the summer months, the number of immigrant workers increased. The percentage of elderly people and people in need of temporary services remained fairly stable throughout the year.

Description of procedure is dense, hard to follow.

Use of bold type and different type-face for no reason.

How Caring Express Helps Clients

When new clients come to Caring Express, a volunteer fills out a **form** with their **address** (if they have one), their **phone number,** their **income,** their **employment situation,** and the help they are receiving, if any, from the local department of human services. Clients who do not live in Maple Valley are referred to a food bank or outreach program in their area. Clients who qualify check off the food they need from a list, and then that food is packed and distributed to them.

EXAMPLE OF A BETTER DESIGN

The Caring Express Food Bank

The Caring Express Food Bank serves a varied population of clients, including chronically homeless people, temporarily homeless people, recent immigrants, elderly people on fixed incomes, and people in need of temporary services. As Figure 1 shows, while the number of homeless, both temporary and permanent, that Caring Express assisted in 2004 decreased during the summer months, the number of immigrant workers increased. The percentage of elderly people and people in need of temporary services remained fairly stable throughout the year.

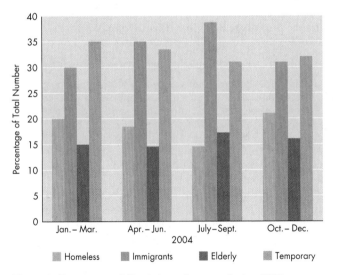

Figure 1. Percentage of clients in each group during 2004

How Caring Express Helps Clients

When new clients come to Caring Express, the volunteers follow this procedure:

1. The volunteer fills out a form with the client's address (if he or she has one), phone number, income, and employment situation.
2. Clients who do not live in Maple Valley are referred to a food bank or outreach program in their area.
3. Clients who qualify check off the food they need from a list.
4. The food is packed and distributed to them.

Title is centered and in larger type than text and heading.

Bar chart is introduced and explained.

Wider margins and white space above and below figure make report easier to read.

Caption explains figure.

Heading is subordinate to title.

Procedure is explained in numbered list. Parallel structure used for list entries.

1. Organizing information for readers

You can organize information visually and topically by grouping related items, using boxes, indents, headings, spacing, and lists. For example, in this book, headings help to group information for readers, and bulleted and numbered lists such as the bulleted list in the Tips box on this page present related points. These variations in text appearance help readers scan, locate information, and dive in when they need to know more about a topic. If a color printer is available to you and your instructor allows you to use color in your paper, then it can serve this purpose as well. For instance, in this text, headings are in blue type.

Tips

LEARNING in COLLEGE

The Basics: Margins, Spacing, Type, Page Numbers, and Printing

Here are a few basic guidelines for formatting academic papers:

- **First page:** In a paper that is no longer than five pages, you can usually place a header with your name, your professor's name, your course and section number, and the date on the first page, above the text. (*See the first page of Esther Hoffman's paper on p. 321.*) If your paper exceeds five pages, page 1 is often a title page. (*See the first page of Audrey Galeano's paper, which is in APA style, on p. 358.*)

- **Type:** Select a common typeface, or font, and choose an 11- or 12-point size.

- **Margins:** Use one-inch margins on all four sides of your text. Adequate margins make your paper easier to read and give your instructor room to write comments and suggestions.

- **Margin justification:** Line up, or justify, the lines of your document along the left margin but not along the right margin. Leaving a "ragged-right"—or uneven—right margin, as in this box, enables you to avoid odd spacing between words.

- **Spacing:** Always double-space your paper unless you are instructed to do otherwise, and indent each paragraph five spaces. Use the ruler at the top of your screen to set this indent automatically. (Many business documents are single-spaced, with an extra line space between paragraphs.)

- **Page numbers:** Number pages in the upper right-hand corner. Some documentation styles require a header next to the page number. (*See Tabs 6–8 for the requirements of the style you are following.*)

- **Printing:** Print final drafts of your academic papers on a laser or an ink-jet printer.

You can also use **white space**—the areas of your document that do not contain type or graphics—to help organize information for your readers. Allowing generous margins and plenty of white space above headings and around other elements makes text easier to read.

You should also introduce any visuals within your text and position them so that they appear near—but never before—this text reference. Strive for a pleasing balance between visuals and other text elements; for example, don't try to cram too many visuals onto one page.

2. Using type style and lists for readability and emphasis

Typefaces are designs that have been established by printers for the letters in the alphabet, numbers, punctuation marks, and special characters. **Fonts** are all of the variations available in a certain typeface and size (for example, 12-point Times New Roman is available in **bold** and *italics*). **Serif** typefaces have tiny lines (serifs) at the ends of letters such as *n* and *y;* **sans serif** typefaces do not have these lines. Standard serif typefaces such as the following are widely used for basic text because they are easy to read.

Times New Roman	Courier
Bookman Old Style	Palatino

For most academic papers, you should choose a standard, easy-to-read typeface and use an 11- or 12-point size. Sans serif typefaces such as the following are sometimes used for headings because they offer a pleasing contrast:

Arial

Verdana

Many typefaces available on your computer are known as **display fonts,** for example:

Curlz

Old English

These should be used rarely, if ever, in academic papers, on the screen, or in presentations. They can be used effectively in other kinds of documents, however, such as brochures, fliers, and posters.

You can emphasize a word or phrase in your text by selecting it and making it **bold,** *italicized,* or underlined. Numbered or bulleted lists help you cluster large amounts of information and make them easier for readers to reference and understand. Because they stand out from your text visually, lists help readers see that ideas are related. You can use a numbered list to display steps in a sequence, present checklists, or suggest recommendations for action.

Format text as a numbered or bulleted list by choosing the option you want from your word-processing program's formatting commands.

Introduce the list with a complete sentence followed by a colon, use parallel structure in your list items, and put a period at the end of each item if the entries are complete sentences. If they are not complete sentences, no punctuation is necessary.

Putting information in a box emphasizes it and also makes it easier for readers to find if they need to refer to it again. Most word-processing programs offer several ways to enclose text within a border or box.

3. Formatting related design elements

In design, simplicity, contrast, and consistency matter. If you emphasize an item by putting it in italic or bold type or in color, or if you use a graphic element such as a box to set it off, consider repeating this effect for similar items so that your document has a unified look. Even a simple horizontal line can be a purposeful element in a long document when used consistently to help organize information.

4. Using headings to organize long papers

In short papers, headings can disrupt the text and are usually not necessary. In longer papers, though, they can help you organize complex information.

Effective headings are brief and descriptive. The headings in academic papers are usually in the form of phrases, although they might be in the form of questions or even imperative sentences. Make sure that your headings are consistent in grammatical structure as well as formatting:

PHRASES BEGINNING WITH _–ING_ WORDS

Fielding Inquiries

Handling Complaints

NOUNS AND NOUN PHRASES

Customer Inquiries

Complaints

QUESTIONS

How Do I Field Inquiries?

How Do I Handle Complaints?

IMPERATIVE SENTENCES

Field Inquiries Efficiently

Handle Complaints Calmly and Politely

Headings at different levels can be in different forms. For example, the first-level headings in a book might be imperative sentences, while the second-level headings might begin with –*ing* words.

Place and highlight headings consistently throughout your paper. If you have not already done so, preparing a formal topic outline will help you decide what your main points and second-level points are and where headings should go. (*For help with topic outlines, see Chapter 5, pp. 50–53.*) You might center all first-level headings, which correspond to the main points in your outline. If you have second-level headings— your supporting points—you might align them at the left margin and underline them. Third-level headings, if you have them, could be aligned at the left margin and set in plain type:

First-Level Heading

<u>Second-Level Heading</u>

Third-Level Heading

A heading should never appear at the very bottom of a page. If a heading falls in this position, move it to the top of the next page.

5. Using restraint

If you use too many graphics, headings, bullets, boxes, or other elements in a document, you risk making it as "noisy" as a loud radio. Standard typefaces and fonts have become standard because they are easy on the eye. Variations from these standard fonts jar the eye. Bold or italic type, underlining, or any other graphic effect should not continue for more than one sentence at a time.

Tips LEARNING in COLLEGE

Standard Headings and Templates

Some types of papers, such as lab reports and case studies, have standard headings, such as "Introduction," "Abstract," and "Methods and Materials" for a lab report. (*See Chapter 12, pp. 147–51.*) These headings give you a head start in organizing your writing.

For some types of documents, **templates,** or preformatted styles, establish the structure and settings for the document and apply them automatically. If you know you will need to produce a certain kind of paper that requires a specific kind of formatting— such as a lab report—on a regular basis, you might consider creating a template for it.

8d Compile an effective portfolio.

When presenting their written work for final submission, students are often asked to collect it in a portfolio. Likewise, when applying for a position that calls for a great deal of writing, job candidates are often asked to provide a portfolio of their writing. Although most portfolios consist of a collection of papers in print form, portfolios can be created in different media. Many students create writing portfolios that are available electronically.

Portfolios, regardless of medium, share at least three common features:

- They are a *collection* of work.
- They offer a *selection*—or subset—of a larger body of work.
- Once assembled, they are introduced, narrated, or commented on by a document that offers the writer's *reflection* on her or his work.

As with any type of writing, portfolios serve a purpose and address an audience—to demonstrate your progress in a course for your instructor, for example, or to present your best work for a prospective employer.

Course requirements vary, so if you are assembling a writing portfolio for a course, you should always follow any guidelines provided by your instructor. Nevertheless, when creating a print writing portfolio, you will usually need to complete the following five activities:

- Gather all your written work.
- Review your work and make appropriate selections.
- Arrange the selections deliberately.
- Include a reflective essay or letter.
- Polish your portfolio.

1. Gathering your writing

Create a list, or inventory, of the writing that you think you might include. You can use this list to make sure that you have every piece of writing you want or need to provide at hand. If you are preparing a portfolio for a writing course, you may need to provide your exploratory writing, notes, and comments from peer reviewers as well as all your drafts for one or more of the papers you include. Be sure that all of your materials have your name on them and that the copy of your final draft does not include errors.

2. Reviewing written work and making selections

Keep the purpose of the portfolio in mind as you review your work, as well as the criteria that will be used to evaluate it. If you are assembling a "showcase" portfolio, you will want to select your very best work. If you are demonstrating your improvement as a writer, you will want to select papers that show your development and achievement.

If no criteria have been provided, consider the audience for the portfolio when deciding which selections will be most appropriate. Who will read it? What qualities will they be looking for as they read?

3. Arranging the selections deliberately

In some situations, you will have specific guidelines for how to arrange your portfolio. For instance, you might be asked to arrange your work in the order that you wrote it. If you have not been told how to organize your portfolio, however, you can think of it as if it were a single text and decide on an arrangement that will best serve your purpose. Does it make sense to organize your work from weakest to strongest? From a less important paper to a more important one? How will you determine importance?

Whatever arrangement you choose, you will need to explain your rationale for it in a letter to the reader, in a brief introduction, or in annotations in your table of contents.

4. Writing a reflective essay or letter

This is one of the most important pieces of writing in the portfolio. It may take the form of an essay or a letter, depending on your purpose or the requirements you have been given. Common topics in the reflective text include the following:

- How you developed various papers
- Which papers you believe are particularly strong and why
- What you learned as you worked on these assignments
- Who you are now as a writer

Once you have written your reflective essay or letter, you should assemble all of the components of your portfolio in a folder.

5. Polishing your portfolio

Although the steps in preparing a portfolio are listed in a sequence, many students find that, as they work through them, they need to backtrack to an earlier step. In the process of writing the reflective letter or

TEXTCONNEX

Preparing an Electronic Portfolio

For some courses or professional purposes, you will need to present your work in an electronic format. Electronic portfolios can be saved on a CD-ROM, or they may be published on a Web site.

Digital portfolios allow you to include different kinds of texts such as audio files and video clips, and they can be connected to other texts using hyperlinks. Their success often depends as much on the use of visual elements as it does on the written word. Here are some additional guidelines for preparing electronic portfolios:

- Use your opening screen to establish your purpose, appeal to your audience, provide links to help readers navigate your portfolio, and suggest who you are as a writer.
- Use links to help readers move within your digital portfolio. You can link to texts from your table of contents, from other texts, and from your reflective letter or essay.
- Consider using links to related files that are external to the work in the portfolio but relevant to it.
- Take advantage of the additional possibilities for presenting your reflective text offered by a digital environment. You might have it cascade across a series of screens, for example, or you might link to an audio or video file where you talk directly to readers.
- Before releasing it, make sure your portfolio works—both conceptually and structurally—by navigating all the way through it yourself.

essay, for example, you might discover a better way to arrange your work, or as you arrange your portfolio, you might find that you would like to re-review all your work. Do not be surprised if you find yourself repeating some of these tasks.

If you want a portfolio that presents you and your work in the best light, it is also wise to share it with classmates or colleagues before submitting it for a class grade, a writing requirement, or a job interview. As with any piece of writing, a portfolio will improve if it is revised on the basis of peer review.

The good news is that most students learn about themselves and their writing as they compile their portfolios and write reflections on their work. The process not only makes them better writers but helps them learn how to demonstrate their strengths as well.

Auguste Rodin's sculpture The Thinker evokes the psychological complexity of human thought and suggests the spirit of critical inquiry common to all disciplines across the curriculum.

Anybody who is involved in working across
the disciplines is much more likely to have a
lively mind and a lively life.

—MARY FIELD BELENKY

Common
Assignments
across the
Curriculum

3 | Common Assignments

Most college courses require writing—from the lab report in chemistry to the policy proposal in economics. This section gives you tips on writing the most common kinds of college assignments and explains the distinctive features of each kind.

9 Informative Reports

Imagine what the world would be like if each person had to learn everything from scratch, by trial and error, with no recipes, no encyclopedias, no textbooks, no newspapers—nothing that records what others have learned. Fortunately, we have many sources of information to draw on, including informative reports.

9a Understand the assignment.

An **informative report** passes on what someone has learned about a topic or issue; it teaches. Because a good way for students to reinforce learning is by teaching it to others, college instructors often assign informative reports. When your instructor assigns an informative report, he or she expects you to find out what is currently known about some specific topic and to present what you discover in a clear, unbiased way.

An informative report gives you a chance to do the following:

- Read more about an issue that interests you.
- Make sense of what you have read, heard, and seen.
- Teach others what you have learned.

9b Approach writing an informative report as a process.

1. Selecting a topic that interests you

An informative report should be clear and reliable but not dull. The major challenge in writing informative reports is engaging readers' interest. Selecting a topic that interests you makes it more likely that your report will interest your readers.

www.mhhe.com/awr
For an interactive tutorial on writing informative reports, go to
Writing > Writing Tutors > Informative Reports

WRITING AFTER COLLEGE

Informative Reports

By writing reports in college, you prepare yourself for future professional and public occasions that will require you to pass on information to others. In many professions, writing informative announcements, manuals, and reports is part of the job:

- In a published article, an anthropologist surveys and summarizes a large body of indigenous material on warfare among the Pueblos before the arrival of the Spanish explorers.
- In a report for their colleagues, three physical therapists define what a critical pathway is, trace its development, and summarize the arguments for and against its use in patient care.
- For an encyclopedia of British women writers, a professor of literature briefly recounts the life and works of Eliza Fenwick, a recently rediscovered eighteenth-century author.
- In a journal for research biologists, two biochemists summarize the findings of more than two hundred recently published articles on defense mechanisms in plants.

Consider connecting what you are learning in one course with a topic you are studying in another course or with your personal experience. For example, one student, Joe Smulowitz, worked part-time for a stockbroker and wanted to make a career in that area. For his topic, he decided to investigate what online stock traders were doing and saying. (*Smulowitz's paper begins on p. 115.*)

2. Considering what your readers know about the topic

Unless the assignment designates a different group, consider your classmates and instructor as your audience. In other words, assume that your readers have some familiarity with the topic but that most of them do not have clear, specific knowledge of it.

3. Developing an objective stance

When writers have an **objective** stance, they do not take sides. Instead, they present differing views fairly, without advocating one view over another. This commitment to objectivity gives an informative report its authority. Ideas and facts are presented methodically, and the emphasis is on the topic, not the writer. By contrast, when writers are **subjective,** they let readers know their views. Although a subjective stance is appropriate for other types of writing, an informative report should come across as objective rather than subjective.

4. Composing a thesis that summarizes your knowledge of the topic

The thesis of an informative report is usually not controversial, even when the report is about a dispute. Because transmitting knowledge is the primary goal, the thesis typically states an accepted generalization or reports the results of the writer's study.

Your thesis should also state the objective of your paper and forecast its content. Before you decide on a thesis, review the information you have collected and divide it into categories, or subtopics. Compose a thesis statement that summarizes—either in general or by category—what the information in your paper shows. (*For more on thesis statements, see Tab 2: Writing and Designing Papers, pp. 48–50.*)

In his paper about online stock trading, Smulowitz's thesis is a generalization that he supports in the body of his paper with information he groups into categories:

> Besides honest investors with various levels of expertise, the Internet grants access to numerous investors who post false information in hopes of making a quick and sometimes large profit. . . . *The one hundred or so postings that I read can be divided into four categories.*

Notice how Smulowitz forecasts the body of his report. We expect to learn something about each of the four categories, and the report is structured to give us that information category by category.

5. Providing context in your introduction

Informative reports usually begin with a relatively simple introduction to the topic and a straightforward statement of the thesis. To orient readers, the introduction may provide some relevant context or background, but writers of informative reports generally get to their topic as quickly as possible and keep it in the foreground. (*For more on introductions, see Tab 2: Writing and Designing Papers, p. 74.*)

6. Organizing your report by classifying and dividing information

Because you are explaining something in an informative report, clarity matters. Informative writers develop their ideas in an organized way, often by classifying and dividing information into categories,

www.mhhe.com/
awr
For more help with developing a thesis, go to
Writing >
Paragraph/Essay
Development >
Thesis/Central
Idea

subtopics, or the stages of a process. (*For more on developing your ideas, see Tab 2: Writing and Designing Papers, pp. 59–70.*)

7. Illustrating key ideas with examples

www.mhhe.com/
awr
For more on
using patterns of
development, go to

Writing >
Paragraph Patterns

Because clarity is so important to the success of an informative report, writers usually use specific examples to help readers understand their most important ideas. In his paper on online stock trading, Smulowitz devotes a lot of space to examples, including messages posted by various investors and an instance of gender-bending. Examples make his report interesting as well as educational. (*For more on using examples, see Tab 2: Writing and Designing Papers, p. 64.*)

8. Defining specialized terms and spelling out unfamiliar abbreviations

Most informative reports include terms that will probably be unfamiliar to most readers, or familiar terms that are being used in a specialized way. Writers usually explain these terms with a synonym or a brief definition. For example, Smulowitz gives a brief definition of the term *online traders* in the first paragraph of his report on online stock trading. (*For more on definition, see Tab 2: Writing and Designing Papers, pp. 62–64.*) Unfamiliar abbreviations like CMC (computer-mediated communication) and GNP (gross national product) are spelled out the first time they are used, with the abbreviation in parentheses.

9. Concluding by answering "so what?"

www.mhhe.com/
awr
For more information
on conclusions, go to

Writing >
Paragraph/Essay
Development >
Conclusions

Because informative writers want readers to remember what they have learned, they often conclude their reports with an image that suggests the information's value or a saying that sums it all up. The conclusion reminds readers of the topic and thesis that were first stated in the introduction. It then answers the "so what?" question.

At the end of his report on online stock trading, Smulowitz answers the "so what?" question with a warning:

> Before buying any stock, investors should investigate it thoroughly. When they read what others say about a company, they should remember that if it sounds too good to be true, it probably isn't true.

(*For more on conclusions, See Tab 2: Writing and Designing Papers, p. 74.*)

9c Student paper: Informative report

www.mhhe.com/
awr
For another sample of
informative writing,
go to

Writing >
Writing Samples >
Informative Paper

In the informative paper that follows, Joe Smulowitz reports what he has learned about the people who are talking online about stocks. As you read his report, notice how Smulowitz provides a context for his topic, cites various sources (using the APA documentation style), categorizes the information, and illustrates his ideas with examples, all hallmarks of a clear, carefully developed paper. The annotations in the margin of this paper point out specific aspects of the informative report.

Note: For details on the proper formatting of a paper in APA style, see Chapter 33 and the sample paper that begins on page 358.

SAMPLE STUDENT INFORMATIVE REPORT

Chatting Online about Stocks

The Internet has produced a new kind of investor: the online stock market investor. Until a few years ago, a person who wanted to invest in the stock market had to hire a professional broker, who might charge $300 per trade as well as a substantial commission. Nowadays, an investor can buy and sell stocks over the Internet at costs ranging from only $7.95 to $25 per trade. As a result, more and more lay people have become online traders—investors who use the Internet to buy and sell stocks. Of the 143 million Americans who are currently using the Internet, 39% use it to trade stocks online (National Telecommunications and Information Administration, 2002, chap. 3). *Silicon Investor,* a popular site for chatting about stocks, receives over 12,000 posts a day from online traders (Lucchetti, 1998).

Who are these online traders, and what are they talking about in investment-related chats? Besides honest investors with various levels of expertise, the Internet grants access to numerous investors who post false information in hopes of making a quick and sometimes large profit. The Internet is rife with "hundreds of fraudulent and abusive

Topic introduced.

Important term defined.

Source information summarized rather than quoted directly.

Thesis stated.

investment schemes, including stock manipulations, pyramid scams, and Ponzi schemes" (Connecticut Department of Banking, 1998, p. 2). State securities agencies and other investment regulators are now looking into cases in which the price of shares in little-known stocks appears to have been manipulated through messages posted on Internet bulletin boards.

Many investors find out about online fraud the hard way. Consider the case of Interlock Consolidated Enterprises, Inc. This Canadian company was reported to have landed a major contract to construct housing in the former USSR. When the company became the topic of online hype in early 1994, its stock jumped from 42 cents a share to $1.30 before falling back to 60 cents (Gardner & Gardner, 1994, "The Fairy Tale" section, para. 4). In this type of scam, known as "pump and dump," investors spread unusually positive news about a stock, then sell it when the price gets unrealistically high. This scam is nothing new to the investment world. In fact, pump-and-dump schemes began in the 1700s (Lucchetti, 1998). But now the schemers can reach hundreds of thousands of people with a single posting, and that kind of reach clearly makes a difference.

An example of what is going on in investment-related chats is the online talk about Chico's, a women's clothing company. *Silicon Investor* includes a chat room called "Miscellaneous," where in 1999 one could read a tip about Chico's: the company was about to release good news, which would raise the price of its stock (Vanier, 1999). A savvy investor would have found out more about Chico's from sources such as *Yahoo! Finance* or *Hoover's Online,* Internet-based business information databases. There investors would have found a history of Chico's; a summary of what Chico's produces; the company's location, phone number, number of employees, names of top management; a list of the company's recent press releases; and most importantly, financial data, including stock price and performance over the past year (Yahoo! Finance, 2004; Hoover's Online, 2004).

Direct quotation: page number included in citation.

Unfamiliar term defined.

Objective stance: "one" used instead of "I."

Having read some facts about Chico's, investors would have been better prepared to understand e-mail messages about the company's stock posted on the *Silicon Investor* bulletin board, messages that fell into four categories. In the first category belonged postings with only positive things to say about Chico's, such as, "CHS [Chico's ticker name] is expected to add 30 stores this year. . . . They are expecting to grow to over 700 stores in the near future" (mfpcpa, 1999). About 75% of the approximately 100 messages belonged to this positive-only category and appeared to be posted by stockholders trying to spread hype about Chico's so that the stock's price would rise. The few replies to these messages expressed agreement.

> Information about Smulowitz's classifications.

In the second category belonged messages that came from investors called "shorts" and "longs." When they think a security's price is going to decrease, shorts borrow the security from a broker or dealer and sell it on the market. The short investor profits if the price goes down, because he or she can replace the borrowed security at a lower cost. Longs, on the other hand, purchase a security because they think its price will increase. The long investor profits if the price goes up, because he or she can sell the security for more than it cost originally. Because the shorts want the price to decrease and the longs want the price to increase, these two kinds of stock traders often feud in online discussions. For example, in the following exchange about Chico's stock, a short's message entitled "Out of Steam" provoked a reaction entitled "Stay LONG" from cag174, a long:

> Categories illustrated with examples and unfamiliar terms defined.

> She can't take it Captain. The stock can't hold its new highs. It keeps closing at the bottom of the range. Shorts will live. We will see 28 again. (Startrader 1975, 1999)
>
> $38 will come before $28. $43 at year end. (cag174, 1999)

> E-mail messages are central to the paper and, thus, are quoted directly, not summarized.

There seemed to be more long investors than short investors on the Chico's bulletin board. Whenever a short posted a negative message aimed at lowering the stock price, several longs retaliated, warning that the short was misleading investors.

In the third category were posts from sneaky investors. For example, the following post appeared to be written by a woman: "Don't know much about stocks, just love the clothes and so do my daughters—31, 35, and 43. Talked hubby into buying in when I read Streisand was buying lots of sweaters . . ." (Katy10121, 1999). Since Chico's is a woman's clothing store, investors are likely to be interested in what women think about the store. But the person who posted this message might not have been female. The poster's online profile listed the poster's sex as "male." This investor could be trying to take advantage of other investors by engaging in gender-bending.

The last category of messages comprised posts from owners of little known and lightly traded stocks called "penny stocks." Here is an example of such messages:

> CHS has given us a great ride, but now would be a good time to get off, while we're on top, and reinvest profits in a little soon-to-be-rediscovered gem, SNKI (Swank). Low volume right now, but check out the P/E and other stats. . . . (gravytrain2030, 1999)

The price of penny stocks such as SNKI ranges from $0.01 to $5 a share. Enthusiasm from seemingly in-the-know observers like gravytrain2030 can sometimes lead to significant increases in the stock price. For that reason, *Yahoo!* does not offer bulletin boards for such stocks. Nevertheless, people still post their messages on other bulletin boards, just as gravytrain2030 did on the Chico's board.

The Internet gives the average person the opportunity to invest in the stock market without going through a broker. All the information essential to investing is available to *anyone* with access to a computer. But hype, manipulation, and fraud are also on the Internet. Before buying any stock, investors should investigate it thoroughly. When they read what others say about a company, they should remember that if it sounds too good to be true, it probably isn't true.

Interpretation provided without bias.

Point and purpose restated in conclusion.

References

cag174. (1999, November 9). Stay LONG. Message posted to Chico's message board, archived at http://finance.yahoo.com/q/mb?s=CHS

Connecticut Department of Banking. (1998). *Investor bulletin: On-line investment schemes.* Hartford, CT: Connecticut Department of Banking.

Lucchetti, A. (1998, May 28). Some Web sites getting tough on stock chat. *The Wall Street Journal,* pp. C1, C12.

Gardner, D., & Gardner, T. (1994). Buy Zeigletics! *The Fool's School.* Retrieved December 8, 2004, from http://www.fool.com/School/Zeigletics/ZFairyTale.htm

gravytrain2030. (1998, July 3). Sell CHCS, reinvest in SNKI. Message posted to Chico's message board, archived at http://finance.yahoo.com/q/mb?s=CHS

Hoover's Online. (2004, December 6). *Chico's FAS Inc.* Retrieved December 6, 2004, from http://premium.hoovers.com/subscribe/co/factsheet.xhtml?ID=16010

Katy10121. (1999, June 24). Just love the clothes. Message posted to Chico's message board, archived at http://finance.yahoo.com/q/mb?s=CHS

mfpcpa. (1999, February 23). Response to Mish's post. Message posted to Chico's message board, archived at http://finance.yahoo.com/q/mb?s=CHS

National Telecommunications and Information Administration. (2002, February). *A nation online: How Americans are expanding their use of the Internet.* (U.S. Department of Commerce Report). Retrieved December 1, 2004, from http://www.ntia.doc.gov/ntiahome/dn/html/anationonline2.htm

Startrader 1975. (1999, November 5). Out of steam. Message posted to Chico's message board, archived at http://finance.yahoo.com/q/mb?s=CHS

References list follows APA style and begins on a new page.

Vanier, G. (1999, May 1). Time to buy Chico's. Message posted to Chico's message board, archived at http://www.siliconinvestor.com/stocktalk/subject.gsp?subjectid=20636

Yahoo! Finance. (2004, December 6.) *Chico's FAS Inc.* Retrieved December 6, 2004, from http://finance.yahoo.com/q/pr?s=chs

---

9d Write reviews of the literature to survey ideas.

In upper-division courses, instructors sometimes assign a special kind of informative report called a **review of the literature.** Here the term *literature* refers to published research reports, not to poems and novels, and the term *review* means that you need to survey others' ideas, not evaluate them or argue for your opinion. A review presents an organized account of the current state of knowledge in a specific area that you and other researchers can use to help determine new projects and new directions for research. The review of the literature may also be a subsection within a research report.

The following paragraph is an excerpt from the review of the literature section in an article by psychologists investigating the motivations for suicide:

> One source of information about suicide motives is suicide notes. International studies of suicide notes suggest that women and men do not differ with regard to love versus achievement motives. For example, in a study of German suicide notes, Linn and Lester (1997) found that women and men did not differ with regard to relationship versus financial or work motives. In a study of Hong Kong suicide notes, Ho, Yip, Chiu, and Halliday (1998) reported no gender or age differences with regard to interpersonal problems or financial/job problems. Similarly, in a UK study, McClelland, Reicher, and Booth (2000) found that men's suicide notes did not differ from women's notes in terms of mentioning career failures. In fact, in the UK study relationship losses were reported more often in men's than in women's suicide notes.

> —SILVIA SARA CANETTO AND DAVID LESTER,
> "Love and Achievement Motives in
> Women's and Men's Suicide Notes"

10 Interpretive Analyses and Writing about Literature

Interpretation is one of the key tasks for educated people. As the phrase "That's open to interpretation" suggests, searching for meaning does not involve looking for a single "right" answer. Instead, it involves figuring out a way of understanding that is meaningful to the writer and convincing to readers.

10a Understand the assignment.

Frequently, college assignments require you to explore the meaning of written documents, literary works, cultural artifacts, social situations, and natural events. When an assignment asks you to compare, explain, analyze, or discuss something, you are expected to study that subject closely, to figure out what it might mean.

Interpretive analyses, including comparative papers, encourage you to move beyond simple description and to examine or compare particular items for a reason: to enhance your readers' understanding of people's conditions, actions, beliefs, or desires.

10b Approach writing an interpretive analysis as a process.

Writing an interpretive analysis typically begins with critical reading. (*See Chapter 4: Reading, Thinking, Writing: The Critical Connection for a discussion of how to read texts and visuals critically.*)

www.mhhe.com/awr
For an interactive tutorial on writing interpretive analyses, go to
Writing > Writing Tutors > Interpretive Analysis

1. Discovering an aspect of the subject that is meaningful to you

Although you will not focus on your personal reflections in the finished version of your interpretive analysis, your interpretation will have more vitality if you take time to discover why the subject is meaningful to you. Think about your own experiences while you read, listen, or observe. Connecting your own thoughts and experiences to what you are studying can help you develop fresh interpretations.

2. Developing a thoughtful stance

Interpretive analyses take your readers with you on an intellectual journey. You are saying, in effect, "Come, think this through with me."

Interpretive Analyses

You can find interpretive analyses in professional journals like *PMLA* (*Publications of the Modern Language Association*) as well as popular publications like the *New Yorker* and the *Atlantic Monthly.* Take a look at some of these publications to see how your work connects with that of professional scholars and critics.

- A cultural critic contrasts the way AIDS and cancer are talked about, imagined, and therefore treated.
- Two geologists analyze photos of an arctic coastal plain taken from an airplane and infer that the effects of seismic exploration vary according to the type of vegetation.
- A musicologist compares the revised endings of two pieces by Beethoven to figure out what makes a work complete and finished.
- A philosopher reflects on personal identity as a complex and shifting concept by investigating how the ideas of the philosophers Descartes and Hume are alike and different.
- A cultural critic explores Freud's anecdotes, showing how they are used both to control and to dramatize the uncanny.

Consequently, your stance should be thoughtful, inquisitive, and open-minded. You are exploring the possible meaning of something. Usually it is wise to admit uncertainty, and sometimes it is good to qualify your interpretations with words like *probably, may,* and *perhaps.* Read your writing aloud, and as you listen to your words, ask yourself whether your stance sounds as exploratory as it should.

3. Using an intellectual framework

To interpret your subject effectively, you need to analyze it using a relevant perspective or intellectual framework. For example, the elements of a work of fiction, such as plot, character, and setting, are often used to analyze stories. Sigmund Freud's theory of conscious and unconscious forces in conflict has been applied to various subjects. In his analysis of Flannery O'Connor's story "Everything That Rises Must Converge," Rajeev Bector uses sociologist Erving Goffman's ideas about "character contests" to interpret the conflict between a son and his mother. (*Bector's analysis begins on p. 128.*)

CHARTING the TERRITORY

Student Analyses across the Disciplines

Students are often called upon to write interpretive analyses such as the following:

- A student in a literature course, Rajeev Bector, asserts that Flannery O'Connor's story "Everything That Rises Must Converge" can be understood as a character contest.
- A student majoring in music spells out the emotional implications of the tempo and harmonic progression in Schubert's *Der Atlas.*
- A student in an economics course demonstrates that, according to an econometric model of nine variables, deregulation has not decreased the level of airline safety.

No matter what framework you use, analysis often entails taking something apart and then putting it back together by figuring out how its parts contribute to a meaningful whole. Because the goal of analysis is to create a meaningful interpretation, you need to treat the whole as more than the sum of its parts and recognize that finding meaning is a complex problem with multiple solutions.

4. Listing, comparing, questioning, and classifying to discover your thesis

To figure out your thesis, it is often useful to explore separate aspects of your subject. If you are analyzing literature, you might consider the plot, the characters, the setting, and the tone before deciding to focus your thesis on one character's personality. If you are comparing two subjects, you can look for and list points of likeness and difference. Note that comparing is not just a way of presenting ideas; it is also a way of discovering them. What features do the items have—and not have—in common? Can you find subtle differences in aspects that at first seem alike? Subtle similarities in aspects that at first seem different? Which do you find more interesting, the similarities or the differences? The answers to such questions can help you figure out your thesis.

As you work on discovering your thesis, try one or more of the following strategies:

- Take notes about what you see or read, and if it helps, write a summary. Look for interesting issues that emerge.

www.mhhe.com/awr
For more help with developing a thesis, go to
Writing > Paragraph/Essay Development > Thesis/Central Idea

- Ask yourself questions about the subject you are analyzing, and write down any interesting answers. Imagine what kinds of questions your professor might ask about the artifact, document, or performance you are considering. In answering these questions, try to figure out the thesis you will present and support.

- Name the class of things to which the item you are analyzing belongs (for example, memoirs), and then identify important parts or features of that class (for example, scene, point of view, helpers, and turning points).

5. Making your thesis focused and purposeful

Because the subject of an interpretative analysis is usually complex, you cannot possibly write about all of its aspects. Instead, focus your paper on one or two issues or questions that are key to understanding the subject. Focusing can help you resist the temptation to describe everything you see. Consider these examples of focused, purposeful theses:

> In O'Connor's short story, plot, setting, and characterization work together to reinforce the impression that racism is a complex and pervasive problem.

> In the first section of Shubert's *Der Atlas,* both the tempo and the harmonic progression express the sorrow of the hero's eternal plight.

Although you want your point to be clear, you also want to make sure that your thesis anticipates the "so what?" question and sets up an interesting context for your interpretation. Unless you relate your specific thesis to some more general issue, idea, or problem, your interpretive analysis may seem pointless to readers. (*For more on developing your thesis, see Tab 2: Writing Papers, pp. 48–50.*)

www.mhhe.com/ awr
For more on crafting introductions, go to

Writing >
Paragraph/Essay
Development >
Introductions

6. Introducing the general issue, a clear thesis or question, and relevant context

In interpretive analyses, it often takes more than one paragraph to do what an introduction needs to do:

- Identify the general issue, concept, or problem at stake. You can also present the intellectual framework that you are applying.

- Provide relevant background information.

- Name the specific item or items you will focus on in your analysis (or the items you will compare).

- State the thesis you will support and develop or the main question(s) your analysis will answer.

You need not do these things in the order listed. Sometimes it is a good idea to introduce the specific focus of your analysis before presenting either the issue or the background information. Just make sure that your introduction does the four things it needs to do, even though you may begin it with a provocative statement or a revealing example designed to capture your readers' attention. (*For more on introductions, see Tab 2: Writing Papers, p. 74.*)

For example, the following is the introductory paragraph from a paper on the development of Margaret Sanger's and Gloria Steinem's feminism that was written for a history class:

> In our male-dominated society, almost every woman has experienced some form of oppression. Being oppressed is like having one end of a rope fastened to a pole and the other end fastened to one's belt: it tends to hold a woman back. But a few tenacious and visionary women have fought oppression and have consequently made the lives of others easier. Two of these visionary women are Margaret Sanger and Gloria Steinem. As their autobiographical texts show, Sanger and Steinem felt compassion for women close to them, and that compassion not only shaped their lives but also empowered them to fight for changes in society.

General issue: feminist struggle against oppression.

Lists items to be compared.

Thesis stated.

In one relatively short paragraph, the student identifies her paper's general issue (women's struggle against oppression), introduces the items to be compared (two autobiographical texts), and in the last sentence states her thesis. Although she has made a good beginning, her readers need additional background information about Sanger and Steinem to give them a context for the two texts that she is comparing. Therefore, the student must expand on the introduction a bit more before moving on to the points she wants to make to support her thesis.

7. Planning your paper so that each point supports your thesis

As with any paper, an interpretive analysis has three main parts: an introduction, a body, and a conclusion. After you pose a key question or state your thesis in the introduction, you need to organize your points to answer the question and support your thesis. Readers must be able to follow the train of thought in your interpretive analysis and see how each point you make is related to your thesis. (*For more on developing your ideas, see Tab 2: Writing Papers, pp. 59–70.*)

For example, if Bector had simply described the events in O'Connor's story or presented a random list of insights, his paper would not shed any light on what the story means. Instead, Bector ends his introduction with a compelling question about one character's motives:

QUESTION   But why would Julian want to hurt his mother, a woman who is already suffering from high blood pressure?

Bector answers this interpretive question in the body of his paper by pointing out and explaining three features of the character contest between mother and son.

For the paper on the roots of Margaret Sanger's and Gloria Steinem's feminism, the student used the following three points to support and develop her interpretive thesis.

> **Thesis:** As their autobiographical texts show, Sanger and Steinem felt compassion for women close to them, and that compassion not only shaped their lives but also empowered them to fight for changes in society.
>
> 1. Steinem and Sanger are both feminists—people intent on exposing and resisting the oppression of women.
> 2. Each of the two women felt compassion for her mother's plight.
> 3. Both Sanger and Steinem saw a connection between their mothers' suffering and the condition of other women.

www.mhhe.com/
awr
For more information
on conclusions, go to

Writing >
Paragraph/Essay
Development >
Conclusions

8. Concluding by answering "so what?"

The conclusion of an interpretive analysis needs to do more than simply repeat the paper's thesis. It needs to answer the "so what?" question by saying why your thesis—as well as the analysis that supports and develops it—is relevant to the larger issue identified in the introduction. What does your interpretation reveal about that issue? (*For information about conclusions, see Tab 2: Writing and Designing Papers, p. 74.*)

For example, the student who wrote about Steinem and Sanger concluded by insisting on the continuing need for a feminist struggle rooted in love for our mothers—including, of course, such mothers of contemporary feminism as Sanger and Steinem.

10c   Student paper: Interpretive analysis

In the following paper, Rajeev Bector uses Erving Goffman's ideas to analyze and interpret the actions of two characters in Flannery O'Connor's short story "Everything That Rises Must Converge." What provoked Bector's interpretation in the first place is this question: How can we understand the mean way Julian and his mother treat

CHARTING the TERRITORY

Ideas and Practices for Writing in the Humanities

Writers in the humanities analyze literature, art, film, theater, music, history, and philosophy. The following ideas and practices are useful in writing interpretive papers in the humanities:

- **Base your analysis on the work itself.** Works of art affect each of us differently, and any interpretation has a subjective element. Also, every film, musical composition, or other work is open to multiple interpretations, as there are numerous critical theories about the significance of art. However, the possibility of different interpretations does not mean that any one interpretation is as valid as any other. Your reading of the work needs to be grounded in details from the work itself.

- **Consider how the concepts you are learning in your course apply to the work you are analyzing.** If your course focuses on the formal elements of art, for example, you might look at how those elements function in the painting you have chosen. If your course focuses on the social context of a work, you might look at how it shares or subverts the belief system and worldview that was common in its time. Use your paper as an opportunity to see the humanities through different critical lenses.

- **Use the present tense when writing about the work and the past tense when writing about its history.** Use the present tense to talk about the events that happen within a work: "In Aristophanes' plays, characters frequently *step* out of the scene and *address* the audience directly." Use the present tense as well to discuss decisions made by the work's creator: "In his version of the Annunciation, Leonardo *places* the Virgin outside, in an Italian garden." Use the past tense, however, to relate historical information about the work or creator: "Kant *wrote* about science, history, criminal justice, and politics as well as philosophical ideas."

each other? As he helps us better understand Julian and his mother, Bector raises the larger issue of racism. To what extent does Bector's interpretive analysis of O'Connor's story also illuminate the workings of racism in our society?

> **Note:** For details on the proper formatting of a paper in MLA style, see Chapter 29 and the sample paper that begins on page 321.

SAMPLE STUDENT ANALYSIS OF A SHORT STORY

The Character Contest in Flannery O'Connor's
"Everything That Rises Must Converge"

Sociologist Erving Goffman believes that every social interaction establishes our identity and preserves our image, honor, and credibility in the hearts and minds of others. Social interactions, he says, are in essence "character contests" that occur not only in games and sports but also in our everyday dealings with strangers, peers, friends, and even family members. Goffman defines character contests as "disputes [that] are sought out and indulged in (often with glee) as a means of establishing where one's boundaries are" (29). Just such a contest occurs in Flannery O'Connor's short story "Everything That Rises Must Converge."

As they travel from home to the Y, Julian and his mother, Mrs. Chestny, engage in a character contest, a dispute we must understand in order to figure out the story's theme. Julian is so frustrated with his mother that he virtually "declare[s] war on her," "allow[s] no glimmer of sympathy to show on his face," and "imagine[s] various unlikely ways by which he could teach her a lesson" (O'Connor 185, 186). But why would Julian want to hurt his mother, a woman who is already suffering from high blood pressure?

Julian's conflict with Mrs. Chestny results from pent-up hostility and tension. As Goffman explains, character contests are a way of living that often leaves a "residue": "Every day in many ways we can try to score points and every day we can be shot down" (29). For many years, Julian has had to live under his racist mother's authority, and every time he protested her racist views he was probably shot down because of his "radical ideas" and "lack of practical experience" (O'Connor 184). As a result, a residue of defeat and shame has accumulated that fuels a fire of rebellion against his mother. But even though Julian rebels against his mother's racist views, it doesn't mean that he isn't a racist himself. Julian doesn't realize that in his own way, he is as prejudiced as his mother. He makes it "a point" to sit next to blacks, in contrast to his mother, who purposely sits next to whites (182). They are two extremes, each biased, for if Julian were truly fair to all, he would not care whom he sat next to.

When we look at the situation from Mrs. Chestny's viewpoint, we realize that she must maintain her values and beliefs for two important reasons: to uphold her character as Julian's mother and to act out her prescribed role in society. Even if she finds Julian's arguments on race relations and integration valid and plausible, Mrs. Chestny must still refute them. If she didn't, she would lose face as Julian's mother—that image of herself as the one with authority. By preserving her self-image, Mrs. Chestny shows that she has what Goffman sees as key to "character": some quality that seems "essential and unchanging" (28).

"We" indicates thoughtful stance, not Bector's personal feelings.

Second point.

Besides upholding her character as Julian's mother, Mrs. Chestny wants to preserve the honor and dignity of her family tradition. Like an actor performing before an audience, she must play the role prescribed for her—the role of a white supremacist. But her situation is hopeless, for the role she must play fails to acknowledge the racial realities that have transformed her world. According to Goffman, when a "situation" is "hopeless," a character "can gamely give everything . . . and then go down bravely, or proudly, or insolently, or gracefully or with an ironic smile on his lips" (32). For Mrs. Chestny, being game means trying to preserve her honor and dignity as she goes down to physical defeat in the face of hopeless odds.

Third point.

Given the differences between Mrs. Chestny's and her son's values, as well as the oppressiveness of Mrs. Chestny's racist views, we can understand why Julian struggles to "teach" his mother "a lesson" (185) throughout the entire bus ride. Goffman would point out that "each individual is engaged in providing evidence to establish a definition of himself at the expense of what can remain for the other" (29). But in the end, neither character wins the contest. Julian's mother loses her sense of self when she is pushed down to the ground by a "colored woman" wearing a hat identical to hers (187). Faced with his mother's

Thesis.

Conclusion—
main point
about Julian
and his mother
related to
larger issue
of racism.

breakdown, Julian feels his own identity being overwhelmed by "the world of guilt and sorrow" (191).

————————————[new page]————————————

Works Cited

"Works Cited"
list follows MLA
style and begins
on a new page.

Goffman, Erving. "Character Contests." Text Book: An Introduction
    to Literary Language. Ed. Robert Scholes, Nancy Comley, and
    Gregory Ulmer. New York: St. Martin's, 1988. 27–33.

O'Connor, Flannery. "Everything That Rises Must Converge."
    Fiction. Ed. R. S. Gwynn. 2nd ed. New York: Addison,
    1998. 179–91.

11 Arguments

In college, reasoned positions matter more than opinions based on personal feelings, and writing arguments is a way to form reasoned positions. Bearing in mind that reasonable people can see things differently, always strive to write well-informed, thoughtful arguments.

11a Understand the assignment.

When you write an **argument paper,** your purpose is not to win but to take part in a debate by stating and supporting your position on an issue. In addition to position papers, written arguments appear in various forms, including critiques, reviews, and proposals.

- **Critiques:** Critiques focus on answering the question "What is true?" A critique fairly summarizes someone's position before either refuting or defending it. Refutations use one of two basic strategies: (1) the presentation of contradictory evidence to show that the position is false or (2) the exposure of inadequate reasoning to show that the position should not be considered true. Defenses make use of three strategies: (1) clarifying a position by explaining in more detail the author's key terms and reasoning, (2) presenting new arguments to support the position, and (3) showing that criticisms of the position are unreasonable or unconvincing.

- **Reviews:** Reviews focus on answering the question "What is good?" The writer evaluates an event, artifact, practice, or institution. Although the evaluation may begin with a gut response—"I like it" or "I don't like it"—such opinions must be transformed into judgments. A trial judge thinks through a

WRITING AFTER COLLEGE

Arguments

Arguments are central to American democracy and its institutions of higher learning because they help create the common ground that is sometimes called public space. In this space, freedom, justice, and equality—the civic ideals set forth in such documents as the Declaration of Independence and the Constitution—are supposed to rule so that reason will prevail over prejudice. All fields of academic study value reason and welcome arguments such as the following:

- A moral philosopher argues that under certain circumstances people have the right to die and, therefore, that democracies should provide them with the means to exercise their right with dignity.

- The board of a national dietetic association publishes a position statement identifying obesity as a growing health problem that dieticians should be involved in preventing and treating.

- A political scientist critiques the idea that the prospects for Russian democracy depend on the country's economy, not on the quality of its political institutions.

- An art critic praises a museum's special exhibition of modern American paintings for its thematic coherence.

- A sociologist proposes four policies that he claims will improve the prospects of people living in inner-city neighborhoods.

decision in light of legal principles. Likewise, judgments in reviews should not be determined by personal taste or the mood of the moment but by commonly accepted criteria.

▪ **Proposals, or policy papers:** Proposals, sometimes called policy papers, focus on answering the question "What should be done?" They are designed to cause change. Readers are encouraged to see a situation in a specific way and take action. Nicholas Buglione's argument about injuries to professional athletes (*see p. 137*) is an example of a proposal.

www.mhhe.com/ awr
For an interactive tutorial on writing arguments, go to
Writing > Writing Tutors > Arguments

11b Approach writing an argument as a process.

In every course you take, you will gain practice in addressing issues that are important in the larger community. Selecting a topic that you care about will give you the impetus to think matters through and make cogent arguments. Of course, you will have to go beyond your personal emotions about an issue to make the most convincing case. You will also have to empathize with potential readers who may disagree with you about a subject that is close to your heart.

1. Figuring out what is at issue

People argue about issues, not topics. Before you can take a position on a topic like air pollution or football injuries, you must figure out what is at issue. Try turning your topic into a problem by asking questions about it. Are there indications that all is not as it should be? Have things always been this way, or have they changed for the worse? From what different perspectives—economic, social, political, cultural, medical, geographic—can problems like a wide receiver's recent knee injury or a quarterback's forced retirement be understood? Do people interested in the topic disagree about what is true, what is good, or what should be done?

Based on your answers to such questions, identify the issues your topic raises and decide which of these issues you think is most important, interesting, and appropriate for you to write about.

2. Developing a reasonable stance that negotiates differences

When writing arguments, you want your readers to respect your intelligence and trust your judgment. Conducting research on your issue can make you well informed; reading and thinking critically about other views can enhance your thoughtfulness. Find out what others have to say about the issue, and make it part of your purpose to negotiate the differences between your position and theirs. Pay attention to the places where you disagree with other people's views, but also note what you have in common—interests, key questions, or underlying values. (*For more on appeals to your audience, see Tab 2: Writing and Designing Papers, p. 36.*)

Always remember that two views on an issue can be similar yet not identical, or different yet not completely opposite. It is important to avoid language that may promote prejudice or fear. Also, misrepresentations of other people's ideas are as out of place in a thoughtful argument as are personal attacks on their character. You should write arguments to open minds, not slam doors shut.

Trying out different perspectives can also help you figure out where you stand on an issue. (*Also see the next section on stating your position.*) Argue with yourself. Make a list of the arguments for and against a specific position; then compare the lists and decide where you stand. Does one set of arguments seem stronger than the other? Do you want to change or qualify your initial position to make it more understandable, reasonable, or believable?

3. Composing a thesis that states your position

Advancing a strong, debatable thesis (a claim) on a topic of interest to the discipline or to the public is key to writing a successful argument. Keep in mind, however, that writing itself is a tool for thinking through your position on a variety of issues. As you think, write, and learn about your topic, you will develop, clarify, and sometimes entirely change your views.

As noted in the section on the Toulmin model of argument, personal feelings and accepted facts are not appropriate claims because they are not debatable (*see 4b, p. 30*).

www.mhhe.com/awr
For more help with developing a thesis, go to
Writing > Paragraph/Essay Development > Thesis/Central Idea

PERSONAL FEELING, NOT A DEBATABLE THESIS

I feel that professional football players are treated poorly.

ACCEPTED FACT, NOT A DEBATABLE THESIS

Many players in the NFL get injured.

DEBATABLE THESIS

Current NFL regulations are not enough to protect players from suffering the hardships caused by game-related injuries.

In proposals and policy papers, the thesis presents a solution in terms of the writer's definition of the problem. The logic behind a thesis for a proposal can be stated like this:

Given these key variables and their underlying cause, one solution to the problem would be . . .

Because this kind of thesis is both complex and qualified, you will often need more than one sentence to state it clearly. You will also need numerous well-supported arguments to make it credible. Readers ultimately want to know that the proposed solution will not cause more problems than it solves; they realize that policy papers and proposals call for actions, and actions have consequences.

4. Supporting and developing your thesis

A strong, debatable thesis needs to be supported and developed with sound reasoning and carefully documented evidence. You can think of an argument as a dialogue between writer and readers. The writer states a debatable thesis, and one reader wonders, "Why do you believe that?" Another reader wants to know, "But what about this factor?" The writer needs to anticipate questions such as these and answer them by presenting claims (reasons) that are substantiated with evidence and by refuting opposing views. (*For more on claims and evidence, see Tab 2: Writing and Designing Papers, pp. 35–36.*)

Usually, a well-developed argument paper includes more than one type of claim and one kind of evidence. Besides generalizations based on empirical data, it often includes authoritative claims based on the opinions of experts and ethical claims based on the application of principle. In his proposal about reducing injuries in professional football, Nicholas Buglione presents facts about the number of injuries in the previous and current seasons to establish the seriousness of the problem. He also includes quotations from an expert in football safety to explain the coach's role in promoting—or failing to promote—team safety (*see p. 139*). As you conduct research, note evidence—facts, examples, and expert testimony—that can be used to support each argument for or against your position.

In developing your argument, you should also pay attention to **counterarguments,** substantiated claims that do not support your position. Think critically about such claims and consider using one of the following strategies to take the most important counterarguments into account:

- Qualify your thesis in light of the counterargument by including a word such as *most, some, usually,* and *likely:* "Although many people—fans and nonfans alike—understand that football is a dangerous sport, few realize just how hard *some* NFL players have it."
- Add to the thesis a statement of the conditions for or exceptions to your position: "The NFL pension plan is unfair to the

players, except for those with more than five years in the league."

- Choose one or two counterarguments and plan to refute their truth or their importance in your paper. Buglione, for example, refutes the counterargument that the NFL has a good pension plan for its players.

5. Creating an outline that includes a linked set of reasons

Arguments are most effective when they present a chain—a linked set—of reasons, so it is a good idea to begin drafting by writing down your thesis and outlining the way you will support and develop it. Your outline should include the following parts:

www.mhhe.com/awr
For more help with creating an outline, go to
Writing > Paragraph/Essay Development > Outlines

- An introduction to the topic and the debatable issue
- A thesis stating your position on the issue
- A point-by-point account of the reasons for your position, including the evidence (facts, examples, authorities) you will use to substantiate each major claim
- A fair presentation and refutation of one or two key counterarguments to your thesis
- A response to the "so what?" question—why your argument matters

6. Emphasizing your commitment to dialogue in the introduction

You want your readers to listen to what you have to say, so make sure that when you present the topic and issue in your introduction, you establish some kind of common ground or shared concern with them. In his essay on the NFL, Buglione begins with a vivid account of a football injury to awaken his readers' concern for injured athletes and make them receptive to his proposal about decreasing the number of injuries in professional football. If possible, you should return to that common ground at the end of your argument.

www.mhhe.com/awr
For more on crafting introductions, go to
Writing > Paragraph/Essay Development > Introductions

7. Concluding by restating your position and emphasizing its importance

After presenting your reasoning in detail, conclude by restating your position. Arguments are always thesis driven, so it is appropriate to remind readers of your thesis. The version of your thesis that you present in your conclusion should be more complex and qualified than the version in your introduction. In the end, readers may not agree with you, but they should know why the issue and your argument matter.

8. Reexamining your reasoning

After you have completed the first draft of your paper, take time to re-examine your reasoning. Checking the logic of your own writing is probably the greatest challenge to your ability to read critically. It is essential to step outside yourself and assess your argument objectively for errors in reasoning. Having peers review your work is especially important. Ask yourself and your peer reviewers the following questions:

■ Have I given a sufficient number of reasons to support my thesis, or should I add one or two more?

■ Have I made any mistakes in logic? (*See the list of common logical fallacies, Tab 2: Writing and Designing Papers, pp. 33–34.*)

■ Have I clearly and adequately developed each claim presented in support of my thesis? Have I defined its key terms, illustrated its meaning, and explained its implications? Is my supporting evidence sufficient? Have I quoted or paraphrased from sources accurately and documented them properly? (*For more on quoting, paraphrasing, and documenting sources, see Tab 5: Researching, pp. 258–61, and Tabs 6–8.*)

For MULTILINGUAL STUDENTS

Learning about Cultural Differences through Peer Review

In some cultures, writing direct and explicit arguments is discouraged, but not so in the United States. When you share your work with peers raised in the United States, you may learn that the way in which you have expressed certain ideas and values—the vocabulary or the style of presentation you have used—makes it difficult for them to understand and accept the point you are making. Ask your peers to suggest different words and approaches, and then decide if their suggestions would really make your ideas more accessible to others.

11c Student paper: Argument

In the following position paper, Nicholas Buglione argues that the National Football League should do more to protect its players from the physical and economic hardships caused by game-related injuries. As you read Buglione's argument, notice how he tries to get readers to sympathize with the players and how he acknowledges what the league has already done to address the injury problem. Buglione asserts that more should be done in two areas: safety and pensions. How suitable, complex, and feasible do you think his solutions are?

***

> *Note:* For details on the proper formatting of a paper in MLA style, see Chapter 29 and the sample paper that begins on page 321.

SAMPLE STUDENT ARGUMENT

www.mhhe.com/
awr
For more samples of argument papers, go to
Writing > Writing Samples > Argument Papers

NFL:

Negligent Football League?

It's fourth down and short on the other team's thirty-five yard line. At this critical point in the game, all eyes are on you, the star running back. The ball is snapped from center into the quarterback's hands. You sprint up into the pocket, receive the hand-off, and race into the hole. At that instant, a rabid 245-pound linebacker drives his massive body into your legs. There is a crunch, followed by excruciating pain: your career in football is over.

Lively opening to hook reader.

Injuries have been a fact of life in the National Football League (NFL) for many years. But in 1995, leg, knee, back, and head injuries piled up, and the NFL decided it was time to take action. Under the auspices of Commissioner Paul Tagliabue, league officials agreed on some basic safety guidelines to solve pro football's woes. These guidelines included the following: (1) making it illegal for players to lead with their heads when they tackle, thereby reducing helmet-to-body contact injuries; (2) allowing the quarterback to ground the ball intentionally in certain situations, thereby lessening the risk of his being injured by a lineman; (3) reducing the size of the helmet's facemask, thereby decreasing its potential as a weapon; and (4) levying a $10,000 to $20,000 fine on any player who hits another player after the play is over.

Topic introduced.

The NFL expected that these regulations would reduce the number of injuries, but the situation got worse, not better. As an example, the

Issue introduced.

1996 season began with an unprecedented seven injuries to starting quarterbacks, all within the first week. As the season went on, more leg, rib, head, and shoulder injuries followed, and one quarterback, Chris Miller, was forced to retire after sustaining his fifth head injury in less than two seasons. The epidemic of injuries carried over into the 1997 season. Steve Young of the San Francisco 49ers suffered his third concussion in ten months, as shown in Fig. 1, and wide receiver Jerry Rice missed much of the season because of a knee injury.

Issue explained
with anecdote.

Injuries have an enormous impact on a player's life after football. Retirees tell horror stories about the aftermath of injuries, which too often turn simple, everyday acts like getting out of bed into backbreaking work. Consider the case of Al Toon. Toon, a wide receiver for the New York Jets, enjoyed a career filled with highlights. Unfortunately, his

Issue
illustrated
with a
photograph.

Fig. 1 Jacksonville Jaguars linebacker Bryce Paup barrels down on San Francisco 49ers quarterback Steve Young (holding the ball) and tackle Jeremy Newberry in a 1999 game. Young suffered his third concussion in ten months during the 1997 season. Mark Wallheiser/Reuters/Corbis.

career was also filled with concussions. After the ninth concussion, he called it quits and tried to put the game behind him. Sadly, those nine head injuries continue to punish Toon. On sunny days, he has to wear dark sunglasses because bright light is too much for his damaged head to handle. Even worse, Toon suffers from memory loss and chronic migraine headaches. Fortunately, he has managed his finances well and can afford to live comfortably with his wife and children. Many other retired players are not so fortunate. Those injured at an early age too often find themselves without a job, without a college degree, and without physical health. Is it any wonder that a few turn to drugs and alcohol, become homeless, or end up in a morgue way before their time?

A significant problem exists in the NFL. Much more must be done to protect players. However, little progress will be made if the league tries to rectify the problem simply by passing rules and amendments to those rules. Such attempts fail to get at the root of the problem: a coaching tradition that emphasizes aggression over safety and a pension plan that fails to support all retired players adequately.

> Thesis stated.

> Causes of problem identified.

Perhaps no one is more responsible for a player's physical welfare than the coach. Although it is true that coaches' need to win games can lead to aggressive methods, and players readily buy into those methods, a coach must balance this need to win with players' safety (SafeUSA, 2002). According to Carl Blyth, an expert on football safety, the head coach's "attitude and leadership" are the "most important" factors in creating this balance (94). Even though coaches should teach players to value safety, they seldom do so; instead, coaches often encourage feelings and behavior that compromise safety. Tommy Chaikin, a former lineman for South Carolina, has pointed out that his coaches encouraged aggressive feelings and behavior during practice. Fighting was not discouraged, and players were trained to fear being ridiculed for exhibiting any compassion (87).

> First point— supported by expert testimony.

> Point also supported with an anecdote.

Because a pugnacious team is more likely to win, it is understandable that coaches want to instill a fighting spirit in their players. What coaches fail to realize, however, is that the aggressive nature of their training programs increases the incidence and severity of injuries. To disregard a player's safety for the purposes of toughening him up is unethical (Lapchick). It is also foolish because ensuring that players stay healthy is in the best interests of the coach and team. According to Rick Reilly, when the Rams' quarterback Kurt Warner was sidelined in 2003 after two years of injuries to his head and shoulders, he was immediately relegated to being the backup for the other quarterback and saw very little play during that season. If he had not been pushed so aggressively during those two years, he probably could have continued to play. Clearly, the coaches of the NFL do not have their players' safety in mind, and this situation must change. Their failure to teach players how to play football safely has made the NFL injury epidemic worse.

Refutes counter-argument that winning is more important than safety.

Injuries often continue to plague players even after they retire. When their football careers are finished, most players still need to work to support themselves and their families. However, as the sportswriter Bob Glauber reports, approximately 70% of today's players have not obtained a college degree (1: B6). Without a college degree, retired football players have little chance of securing white-collar jobs. The alternative, blue-collar work, is closed to many former players who suffer the lingering effects of injury. Glauber's survey of 1,425 former NFL players found that more than 50% are physically limited by previous injuries (2: A64). What compensation is there for these retired players, the ones who have essentially destroyed their bodies playing football for the league?

Second point—supported by statistics.

A pension would seem to be the answer. Though the NFL does have a pension plan, it is not adequate or fair. According to Glauber, the NFL's pension plan pays retired players with five or more years of NFL service $300 a month per year of service (4: A92). The minimum pension is, therefore, $1,500 a month. Although players with permanent injuries certainly deserve more, the bigger problem is that the pension plan applies only to players with five or more years of NFL service. Players injured within the first five years of their career receive no pension at all. What would Kurt Warner have done if he had not recovered from his injuries?

Refutes counter-argument that NFL pensions solve problem.

Why does the NFL treat its players so poorly? One reason may be that professional sports has become big business. In The Political Economy of College Sports (1986), Hart-Nibbrig and Cottingham coined the term "corporate athleticism" to describe the business-minded attitude that has taken over sports (1). Corporate athleticism means that sports organizations like the NFL are primarily concerned with increasing profits. Winning teams make a larger profit, so coaches try to increase the chance of winning by encouraging anger and aggression in their players. Moreover, it is not in the front office's financial interest to support disabled retirees. When players cease to be lucrative for the league's bottom line, the NFL can simply turn to a younger group of men, all of whom are eager to play pro football. The NFL can then exploit this new crop of players.

Third point— supported by expert testimony.

Exploitation can be resisted, especially by the Players Association— the collective bargaining unit of NFL players—even though some observers consider the association part of the problem (Zimmerman). To deal with the injury problem, the Players Association must take three important steps. First, it must make the rest of the sports world aware of the situation. Although many people—fans and nonfans alike— understand that football is a dangerous sport, few realize just how hard some NFL players have it. Second, the Players Association must pressure NFL coaches to monitor the physical well-being of their players closely and stress the value of staying healthy, not the ill-gotten gains of playing through injuries.

Term— *Players Association*— defined.

Proposed solution.

The Players Association must also work to ease the financial burden on injured retirees. It should demand that the NFL amend its pension plan so that coverage is extended to all players, regardless of how many years they played for the league. In the United States, workers injured on the job are eligible for compensation. Why should NFL players be treated differently just because they have been in the league less than five years? In addition, those players who serve five or more years in the NFL deserve more than $1,500 a month, especially if they suffer from debilitating injuries. Finally, young players should receive financial counseling to make them aware of just how short a football career can be. On average, an "NFL career last[s] only 3.6 years," and as Commissioner Paul Tagliabue admits, what follows that career is likely to be both "painful and tragic" for NFL players who have not been "well-advised and well-served" (Glauber 1: B6, B7).

————————————[new page]————————————

Works Cited

Blyth, Carl S. "Tackle Football." Sports Safety. Ed. Charles Peter Yost. Washington: American Association for Health, Physical Education, and Recreation, 1971. 93–96.

Chaikin, Tommy. "The Nightmare of Steroids." Sports Illustrated Oct. 1988: 84–102.

Glauber, Bob. "Life after Football." New York Newsday (four-pt. series) 12 Jan. 1997: B6+ (Pt. 1); 14 Jan. 1997: A64+ (Pt. 2); 15 Jan. 1997: A66+ (Pt. 3); 16 Jan. 1997: A92+ (Pt. 4).

Hart-Nibbrig, N., and Clement Cottingham. The Political Economy of College Sports. Lexington: Heath, 1986.

Lapchick, R. E. "Dying for the Game." Center for the Study of Sport in Society. 2004. 4 April 2004 <http://www.sportinsociety.org/rel-article22.html>.

Reilly, Rick. "Ram Shackled." Sports Illustrated 8 December 2003: 104.

"SafeUSA. Football Safety (American)." SafeUSA 14 July 2002. 9 March 2003 <http://www.safeusa.org/sports/football.htm>.

Zimmerman, Paul. "Union Job: Safety of Its Members Should Be Players' Association Top Priority." Sports Illustrated 1 October 2003. 9 March 2004 <http://www.sportsillustrated.cnn.com/2003/writers/dr_z/10/01/insider/index.html>.

"Works Cited" follows MLA style and begins new page.

12 Other Kinds of Assignments

Personal essays

Personal writing can be found in many places, including diaries and journals, but personal writing is not the same thing as a personal essay. The **personal essay** is one of the most literary kinds of writing. Like a poem, it feels significant—meaningful to readers and relevant to their lives. Like a play, it speaks to readers in a distinctive voice. Like a good story, it is both compelling and memorable.

1. Making connections between your experiences and those of your readers

When you write a personal essay, you are doing much more than fulfilling an assignment; you are exploring your experiences, clarifying your values, and composing a public self. At one level, your purpose is to reveal something about who you are, how you got where you are now, and what you believe. The focus, however, does not need to be on you. You might write a personal essay about a tree in autumn, a trip to Senegal, an encounter with a stranger, or an athletic event. The real topic is how these objects and experiences have become meaningful to you.

WRITING AFTER COLLEGE

Personal Essays

Nowadays it is not uncommon for people from all walks of life to use the personal essay to learn about themselves and explore their experience. Doctors, social workers, nutritionists—as well as novelists—have published memoirs and personal essays.

- Gloria Ladson-Billings, a teacher, reflects on her own experience in the classroom to figure out what makes teachers successful.
- Carol Allen, a philosophy professor, uses Plato's allegory of the cave as a metaphor in *Tea with Demons,* her personal account of going mad and finding her way back.
- Oliver Sacks, a neurologist, writes about his experiences with people whose perceptual patterns are impaired and about what it means to be fully human.

When we read a personal essay, we expect to learn more than the details of the writer's experience; we expect to see the connections between that experience and our own. Depending on your point and what you assume your readers already know or believe, you may decide to intensify, clarify, or complicate the reader's sense of things. You may even try to change readers' minds. But no matter what you intend your essay to accomplish, your point is likely to be more effective if it is not stated directly. The details you emphasize, the words you choose, and the characters you create should all communicate your point implicitly without turning it into "the moral of the story."

2. Turning your essay into a conversation

Personal essayists usually use the first person (*I* and *we*) to create an interpersonal relationship—a sense that the writer and reader are engaged in the open-ended give-and-take of conversation. How you appear in this conversation—shy, belligerent, or friendly, for example—will be determined by the details you include in your essay as well as the connotations of the words you use. Consider how Meghan Daum represents herself in relation to both computer-literate and computer-phobic readers in the following excerpt from her personal essay "Virtual Love," which appeared in a 1997 issue of the *New Yorker:*

> The kindness pouring forth from my computer screen was bizarrely exhilarating, and I logged off and thought about it for a few hours before writing back to express how flattered and "touched"—this was probably the first time I had ever used that word in earnest—I was by his message.
>
> I am not what most people would call a computer person. I have no interest in chat rooms, news groups, or most Web sites. I derive a palpable thrill from sticking a letter in the United States mail.

Besides Daum's conversational stance, notice the emotional effect of her remark on the word *touched* and her choice of words connoting excitement: *pouring forth, exhilarating,* and *palpable thrill.*

3. Structuring your essay like a story

Typically, personal essays are centered around either actions or ideas. There are three common ways to narrate events and reflections:

- **Chronological sequence** uses an order determined by clock time; what happened first is presented first, followed by what happened second, then third, and so on.

- **Emphatic sequence** uses an order determined by the point you want to make; for emphasis, events and reflections are arranged either from least to most or most to least important.

- **Suspenseful sequence** uses an order determined by the emotional effect the writer wants the essay to have on readers. To keep readers hanging, the essay may begin in the middle of things with a puzzling event, then flash back or go forward to clear things up. Some essays may even begin with the end—with the insight achieved—and then flash back to recount how the writer came to that insight.

4. Letting details tell your story

The story of, say, an entire election campaign can be told in one sentence: "He was nominated; he ran; he lost." It is in the details that the story takes shape. No matter what you intend your essay to accomplish, the details you emphasize, the words you choose, and the characters you create all implicitly communicate the point of your essay. Often it is not even necessary to state your thesis.

Consider, for example, the following passage by Gloria Ladson-Billings:

> Mrs. Harris, my third-grade teacher, was quite a sharp dresser. She wore beautiful high-heeled shoes. Sometimes she switched to flats in the afternoon if her feet got tired, but every morning began with the click, click, click of her high heels as she greeted us up and down the rows. I wanted to dress the way Mrs. Harris did. I didn't want to wear old-lady comforters like Mrs. Benn's and I certainly didn't want to wear worn-out loafers like those of my first-grade teacher, Miss Schwartz. I wanted to wear beautiful, shiny, high-heeled shoes like Mrs. Harris's. That was the way a teacher should look, I thought.

> —GLORIA LADSON-BILLINGS, *The Dreamkeepers: Successful Teachers of African-American Children*

Ladson-Billings uses details to make her idea of a good teacher come alive for the reader. At one level—the literal—the "click, click, click" refers to the sound of Mrs. Harris's shoes. At another level, it represents the glamorous teacher. And at the most figurative level, the "click, click, click" evokes the kind of feminine power that the narrator both longs for and admires.

5. Using the present tense strategically

When writers tell stories about themselves, they often use the past tense, as if the experience were over and done with ("once upon a time"). This choice makes sense, but the present tense also has advantages. It creates a sense of immediacy and helps make an essay vivid and memorable. Notice how the student writer of the following passage puts the reader inside the young girl's head by purposefully changing from the past to the present tense:

> As I was learning the switchboard, I caught my Dad watching me out of the corner of his eye. Hmm, I hope he doesn't think that I'm going to give him the satisfaction of not doing a good job. Yes, he's deprived me of my beach days with Joey. But I am on display here. And the switchboard is so vital to this office!

If they have good reason to do so, writers of personal essays may also take liberties with certain conventions of grammar and style. Be sure you understand any rules you may be stretching, however, and if you are writing a personal essay for a class assignment, be sure your instructor will accept the results. Some instructors, for example, might object to the shift from past to present tense in the preceding paragraph. (*See Chapter 41: Confusing Shifts, p. 413*). Some also might object to the last two sentences in the paragraph because they begin with coordinating conjunctions (*but* and *and*).

6. Connecting your experience to a larger issue

To demonstrate the significance of a personal essay to readers, writers usually connect their individual experience to a larger issue. Stories about winning, losing, or arriving in a new place may have self-evident significance for you, but readers will appreciate that significance only if you connect your individual experience with something more social or general. Here, for example, are the closing lines of Daum's essay "Virtual Love":

> The world had proved to be too cluttered and too fast for us, too polluted to allow the thing we'd attempted through technology ever to grow on the earth. PFSlider and I had joined the angry and exhausted living. Even if we met on the street, we wouldn't recognize each other, our particular version of intimacy now obscured by the branches and bodies and falling debris that make up the physical world.

Notice how Daum relates the disappointment of her failed Internet romance with "PFSlider" to a larger social issue: the general contrast between cyberspace and material realities. Her point, however, is surprising; most people do not think of cyberspace as more "intimate"—or touching—than their everyday world of "branches and bodies."

12b Lab reports in the experimental sciences

www.mhhe.com/
awr
For online resources
in various
disciplines, go to

Learning > Links
across the
Curriculum

Without writing, science would not be possible. Scientists form hypotheses and plan new experiments as they observe, read, and write. When they work in the laboratory, they keep well-organized and detailed notebooks. They also write and publish lab reports, using a format that reflects the logic of scientific argument. In this way, they share their discoveries and enable other scientists to use their work.

As a college student, you may be asked to demonstrate your understanding by showing that you know how to perform and report an experiment designed to verify a well-established fact or principle. In advanced courses, you may get to design original experiments as well.

Lab reports usually include seven distinctive sections in the following order: Abstract, Introduction, Methods and Materials, Results, Discussion, Acknowledgments, and References. Begin drafting the report, section by section, while your time in the lab is still fresh in your mind. Start by drafting the methods and materials and results sections, then draft your introduction and discussion sections. Make sure your introduction includes a clearly stated hypothesis. Finally, prepare the literature cited section, the acknowledgments, and the abstract.

Follow the scientific conventions for abbreviations, symbols, and numbers. See if your textbook includes a list of acceptable abbreviations and symbols, or ask your professor where you might find such a

WRITING AFTER COLLEGE

Scientific Research

Research reports by professional scientists are published in journals such as *Science,* the *American Naturalist, Current Directions in Psychological Science,* and the *American Journal of Physics.* Take a look at one of these journals to see how your work relates to the work of professional scientists. Here are some examples of scientific research:

- A biochemist tests the hypothesis that THC (the major active ingredient in marijuana) acts as an estrogen (a female hormone).
- A mechanical engineer tests the hypothesis that 50 pounds of force is sufficient to overcome the thermal contact resistance in the coupling joint of a mechanical switch designed for use on a rocket-borne telescope.
- A social psychologist tests the hypothesis that the more open-ended a question or task is, the more likely it is that an individual will behave in conformity with the will of a group.

list. Use numerals rather than words for dates, time, pages, figures, tables, and standard units of measurement (for example, g/ml and percentages). Spell out numbers between one and nine that are not part of a series of larger numbers.

1. Abstract

An **abstract** is a one-paragraph summary of what your lab report covers in greater detail. Although usually written last, the abstract is the part that is read first. Scientists often read nothing more than the titles and abstracts of articles in journals. Abstracts generally use about 250 words to answer the following questions:

- What methods were used in the experiment?
- What variables were measured?
- What were the findings?
- What do the findings imply?

2. Introduction

www.mhhe.com/
awr
For more on crafting
introductions, go to
Writing >
Paragraph/Essay
Development >
Introductions

The introduction gives readers the information they need to understand the focus and point of your lab report. State your topic, summarize prior research, and present your hypothesis.

As in the example that follows, you should use precise scientific terminology (*α-amylase*), spell out the terms that you will later abbreviate (*gibbelleric acid [GA]*), and whenever possible, prefer the active voice over the passive. (*For a discussion of active and passive voices, see Tab 9: Editing for Clarity, pp. 434–35.*) Use the present tense to state established knowledge ("the rye seed *produces*"); use the past tense to summarize the work of prior researchers ("Haberlandt *reported*"). The writer cites sources using a superscript number system. (*For information on the CSE number style, see pp. 396–400.*)

> According to studies by Yomo,[2] Paleg,[3] and others,[1,4] barley seed embryos produce a gibbelleric acid (GA) which stimulates the release of hydrolytic enzymes, especially α-amylase. It is evident that these enzymes break down the endosperm, thereby making stored energy sources available to the germinating plant. What is not evident, however, is how GA actually works on the molecular level to stimulate the production of hydrolytic enzymes. As several experiments[5–8] have documented, GA has an RNA-enhancing effect. Is this general enhancement of RNA synthesis just a side effect of GA's action, or is it directly involved in the stimulation of α-amylase?

The first sentence names both a general topic, barley seed embryos, and a specific issue, GA's stimulation of hydrolytic enzymes. The last sentence poses a question, one that prepares readers for the hypothesis by focusing their attention on the role enhanced RNA synthesis plays in barley-seed germination.

3. Methods and materials

The purpose of the methods-and-materials section is to answer the *how* and *what* questions so that other scientists can replicate your work. Select the details that they will need to know to replicate the experiment. Using the past tense, recount in chronological order what was done with specific materials, as in the following excerpt from a lab report on α-amylase production in barley seeds:

> After incubating for 48 hours, the seeds were cut in half transversely. Five endosperm halves without embryos were placed in each of 14 small glass test tubes. Next, a solution with a GA_3 concentration ranging from 0 g/ml to 10^5 g/ml was added to each test tube.

Notice that the writer does not mention the time of day or the instrument used to cut the seeds. These details do not influence the results and therefore are not important variables. The student does describe the range of GA concentrations because that is the key variable.

4. Results

In this section, your purpose is to tell readers about the results that are relevant to your hypothesis, especially those that are statistically significant. Results may be relevant to your hypothesis even if they are different from what you expected. An experiment does not need to confirm your hypothesis to be interesting.

To report what you have learned, you might provide a summarizing table or graph. For example, the graph in Figure 12.1 on page 150, which plots the distance covered by a glider over a period of time, was used to summarize the results of an engineering assignment. In this instance, a paper airplane was launched, and the distance it traveled in a specific period of time was measured. Each point on the graph represents the distance the glider traveled in consecutive tenths of a second from 0.1 second to 1.0 second. By reading the positions of the glider on the XY plot (X equals time; Y equals position in centimeters), we can see that the glider traveled a total distance of 98 centimeters in 1.0 second.

Every table and figure you include in a lab report must be referred to in the body of your report. Do not repeat all the information in the table or figure, but do point out and illustrate relevant patterns it reveals. If you run statistical tests on your findings, be careful not to make the tests themselves the focus of your writing. In this section, you should emphasize the results of the tests, not the statistical procedures used to

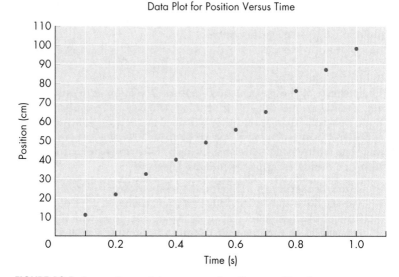

FIGURE 12.1 **A graph used to summarize the results of an engineering assignment.**

analyze the data. Refrain from interpreting why things happened the way they did. Interpretation belongs in the discussion section.

> *Note:* Choose words carefully. Refer to an "increase," for example, as *marked* rather than as *significant.* Like the terms *correlated* and *random,* the term *significant* has a specific statistical meaning for scientists and should therefore be used in a lab report only in relation to the appropriate statistical tests.

5. Discussion

In your discussion section, you need to explain your results. Lab experiments produce results, not facts or laws. To transform results into accepted facts or laws, the scientific community depends on debate and consensus. In discussing your results, interpret your major findings by explaining how and why each finding does or does not confirm the original hypothesis. Connect your research with prior scientific research: how and why do your findings and interpretations agree or disagree with the prior research summarized in your introduction? Also look ahead to future research: where do scientists interested in this area seem to be going?

6. Acknowledgments
You may have reason to include an acknowledgments section. In professional journals, most reports of experimental findings include a brief statement acknowledging those who assisted the author(s) during the research and writing process.

7. References
This final section of your report should include a listing of all manuals, books, and journal articles you consulted during the research and writing process. Do not wait until the last minute to prepare this section, or you may find that you do not have time to track down some missing piece of information. Use one of the citation formats developed by the Council of Science Editors (CSE style), unless another format is favored by those working in the area of your research. (*See Tab 8: Other Documentation Styles.*) If you are uncertain about which format to use, ask your professor for advice.

12c Case studies in the social sciences

www.mhhe.com/awr
For online resources in various disciplines, go to
Learning > Links across the Curriculum

Social scientists are trained observers and recorders of the behavior of individuals and groups, research that depends on writing. Accurate observations are essential starting points for a case study, and writing helps researchers make clear and precise observations.

1. Choosing a topic that raises a question
In doing a case study, your purpose is to connect what you see and hear with issues and concepts in the social sciences. Choose a topic and turn it into a research question. Before engaging in field research, write down your hypothesis—a tentative answer to your research question—as well as some categories of behavior or other things to look for.

2. Collecting data
Make a detailed and accurate record of what you observe and when and how you observe it. Whenever you can, count or measure, and take down word-for-word what is said. Use frequency counts—the number of occurrences of specific, narrowly defined instances of behavior. If you are observing a classroom, for example, you might count the number of teacher-directed questions asked by several children. Your research methodologies course will introduce you to many ways to quantify data.

WRITING AFTER COLLEGE

Case Studies

Using the data they keep in their field notebooks, social scientists write and publish their findings in such journals as the *American Sociological Review, Harvard Business Review,* and *Journal of Marriage and the Family.* Take a look at these journals to see how your work connects with that of professional social scientists:

- A developmental psychologist studies conflict resolution in children by observing a group of four-year-olds in a day care center.
- A sociologist studies how the state enforces gender stereotypes by observing and interviewing women in the juvenile justice system.
- A political scientist studies the legislative process by noting how state senators and representatives negotiate to get a bill passed.
- An anthropologist studies the function of rituals in the formation of inner-city gangs by attending an initiation ceremony.

3. Assuming an unbiased stance

In a case study, you are presenting empirical findings, based on careful observation. Your stance is that of an unbiased observer. Avoid value-laden terms and unsupported generalizations. Do not use words that will evoke emotion or broad statements that you cannot support.

4. Discovering meaning in your data

Your case study is based on the notes you made during your observations. As you review this material, try to uncover connections, identify inconsistencies, and draw inferences. For example, ask yourself why a subject behaved in a specific way, and consider different explanations for the behavior. You will also need to draw upon the techniques for quantitative analysis that you learn in a statistics course.

5. Presenting your findings in an organized way

There are two basic ways to present your findings in the body of a case study: (1) as stages of a process and (2) in analytic categories. Using stages of a process, a student studying gang initiation organized her observations chronologically into appropriate stages. If you organize your study this way, be sure to transform the minute-by-minute history of your observations into a pattern with distinct stages. Using an-

CHARTING the TERRITORY

Case Studies

You will find case studies used in a number of social science disciplines.

- **In sociology:** You may be asked to draw on "insider" knowledge to describe and analyze a small group to which you have belonged or belong now. In this case, your study will address such issues as the group's norms and values, cultural characteristics, stratification and roles, initiation rites, and social control techniques. Your audience will be your professor, who wants to see how your observations reflect current theories on group norms.

- **In nursing:** A case study assignment may be an important part of your practicum in a local hospital. For a nursing class, you will note details of your care for a patient that corroborate or complicate what you have been taught to expect. Your audience will be the supervising nurse, who is interested in your interactions with the patient.

- **In education:** As a student teacher, you may closely observe and write about one student in the context of his or her socioeconomic and family background. Your audience will be the cooperating teacher, who seeks greater insight into the behavior of class members.

alytic categories, a student observing the behavior of a preschool child organized his findings according to three categories from his textbook: motor coordination, cognition, and socialization.

> *Note:* You will find it easier to organize the enormous amount of material you gather for a case study if you develop stages or categories while you are making your observations. In your paper, be sure to illustrate your stages or categories with material drawn from your observations—with descriptions of people, places, and behavior, as well as with well-chosen quotations.

6. Including a review of the literature, a statement of your hypothesis, and a description of your methodology in your introduction

The introduction presents the framework, background, and rationale for your study. Begin with the topic, and review related research, working your way to the specific question that your study addresses. Follow that with a statement of your hypothesis, accompanied by a description of your **methodology**—how, when, and where you made your observations and how you kept records of them.

7. Discussing your findings in the conclusion

The conclusion of your case study should answer these three questions: (1) Did you find what you expected? (2) What do your findings show, or what is the bigger picture? and (3) Where should researchers working on your topic go now?

12d Essay exams

When you take an essay exam, you are pressed for time and uninterested in thinking about how to approach test-taking. If you spend some of your study time thinking about what these tests expect you to do, however, you may feel less stress the next time you take one.

1. Preparing with the course and your instructor in mind

Consider the specific course as your writing context and the course's instructor as your audience. As you study, think about how your instructor approached and presented the course material.

- What questions or problems did your instructor explicitly or implicitly address?
- What frameworks did your instructor use to analyze topics?
- What key terms did your instructor repeatedly use during lectures and discussions?

2. Understanding your assignment

Because essay exams are designed to test your knowledge, not just your memory, working through possible questions is one of the best ways to study. Make up some essay questions that require you to do the following:

- **Explain** what you have learned in a clear, well-organized way. (*See question 1 on the presidency in the box on p. 155.*)
- **Connect** what you know about one topic with what you know about another topic. (*See question 2 on labor supply decisions in the box on p. 155.*)

CHARTING the TERRITORY

Essay Exam Questions across the Curriculum

During finals week, you may be asked to respond to essay questions like the following:

1. Discuss the power of the contemporary presidency as well as the limits of that power. [*from a political science course*]

2. Compare and contrast the treatment of labor supply decisions in the economic models proposed by Greg Lewis and Gary Becker. [*from an economics course*]

3. Describe the observations that would be made in an alpha-particle-scattering experiment if (a) the nucleus of an atom were negatively charged and the protons occupied the empty space outside the nucleus and (b) the electrons were embedded in a positively charged sphere. [*from a chemistry course*]

4. Examine the uses of caesura and enjambment in the following poem, and analyze their effect on the poem's rhythm. [*from a literature course*]

5. In 1800, was Thomas Jefferson a "dangerous radical"? Define your key terms and support your position with evidence from specific events, documents, and so on. [*from an American history course*]

■ **Apply** what you have learned to a new situation. (*See question 3 on a particle-scattering experiment in the box above.*)

■ **Interpret** the causes, effects, meanings, value, or potential of something. (*See question 4 on poetry in the box above.*)

■ **Argue** for or against some controversial statement about what you have learned. (*See question 5 on Jefferson in the box above.*)

3. Planning your time

During the exam period, time management is essential. Quickly look through the whole exam, and determine how much time you will spend on each part or question. Your instructor may give the point credit for each question or suggest the amount of time that should be spent on each part. Move as quickly as possible through the short-answer questions with lower point values so that you can spend the bulk of your time responding to the questions that are worth the greatest number of points.

4. Answering short identification questions by showing the significance of the information

The most common type of short-answer question is the identification question: Who or what is X? In answering questions of this sort, you need to present just enough information to show that you understand X's significance within the context of the course. For example, if you are asked to identify "Judith Loftus" on an American literature exam, don't just write: "character who knows Huckleberry Finn is a boy." Instead, craft one or two sentences that identify Loftus as a character Huckleberry Finn encounters while he is disguised as a girl; by telling Huck how she knows that he is not a girl, Loftus compels readers to think in complex ways about gender.

5. Being tactical in responding to essay questions

When you are faced with an essay question, you may be inclined to start writing down everything you remember about the topic. Don't. Be tactical. Keep in mind that essay questions usually ask you to do something specific. Begin by determining precisely what you are being asked to do. Before you write anything, read the question—all of it—and circle key words.

> Explain two ways in which Picasso's *Guernica* evokes war's terrifying destructiveness.

To answer this question, you need to focus on two of the painting's features, such as coloring and composition, not on Picasso's life.

Sometimes you may be uncertain about what you are being asked to do, either because an essay question says too much or because it says too little. If a question includes more information or direction than necessary, try to isolate the kernel of the question—the main topic and tactic. If a question says too little, try to use the context of the course to give you clues. For example, "Discuss the power of the contemporary presidency as well as the limits of that power" can be made more specific by applying the analytic terms used in class, such as the resources, methods, and conditions of presidential power. You should also consider asking the instructor for clarification.

6. Using the essay question to structure your response

You are unlikely to have time to make a complete outline before you begin writing. Whenever possible, use the question to structure your answer. Usually, you will be able to transform the question itself into the thesis of your answer. For example, if you are asked to agree/disagree with the Federalists' characterization of Thomas Jefferson in the election of 1800, you might begin with the following thesis:

In the election of 1800, the Federalists characterized Jefferson as a dangerous radical. Although Jefferson's ideas were radical for the times, they were not dangerous to the republic.

Take a minute or two to list evidence for each of your main points, and then write the essay.

7. Checking your work

Leave a few minutes to read quickly through your completed answer, looking for words you might have omitted or key sentences that make no sense. Add the missing words, and rewrite the mixed-up sentences. You can usually cross out incorrect words and sentences and make corrections neatly above the original line of text.

12e Coauthored projects

A project is coauthored when more than one person is responsible for producing it. In many fields, working collaboratively is essential. Here are some suggestions to help you make the most of this challenge:

- Working with your partners, decide on some ground rules, including meeting times, deadlines, and ways of reconciling differences. Will the majority rule, or will some other principle prevail? Is there an interested and respected third party who can be consulted if the group's dynamics break down?

- Divide the work fairly so that everyone has a part to contribute to the project. Keep in mind that each group member should do some researching, drafting, revising, and editing.

- In your personal journal, record, analyze, and evaluate the intellectual and interpersonal workings of the group as you

Tips LEARNING in COLLEGE

For Coauthoring Online

Computer networks make it easier for two or more writers to coauthor texts. With e-mail, you can preserve your individual contributions to the final paper and, if need be, share them with your instructor. You will also have a record of how the piece developed and how well you and your coauthor actually worked as a team.

see and experience them. If the group's dynamics begin to break down, seek the assistance of a third party.

- After each group member has completed his or her assigned part or subtopic, gather the whole group to weave the parts together and create a focused piece of writing with a consistent voice. This is the point at which group members usually need to negotiate with one another. Tact is essential. Keep the excellence of the project in the forefront, and all should go well.

13 Oral Presentations

Preparing an oral presentation, like preparing a paper, is a process. As in writing, you will need to consider your audience and purpose as you choose the focus and level of your topic. You will need to gather information, decide on the main idea of your presentation, think through the organization, and choose visuals that support your points. However, unless you are expected to "present a paper" in class or at a conference, it is usually not advisable to write out your presentation like an essay and simply read it aloud. This chapter will help you deliver a presentation that is appropriate, clear, and memorable.

13a Plan and shape your oral presentation.

1. Considering the interests, background knowledge, and attitudes of your audience

Find out as much as you can about your listeners before you prepare the speech. If your audience is composed of your classmates, you will have the advantage of knowing how much background knowledge they have and what their intellectual interests are. What does the audience already think about your topic? What contribution do you most want to make? Do you want to intensify your audience's commitment to what they already think, provide new and clarifying information, provoke more analysis and understanding of the issue, or change what the audience believes about something?

If you are addressing an unfamiliar audience, ask the people who invited you to speak to fill you in on the audience's interests and expectations. It is usually helpful to have a friend listen to your speech in the role of audience member. Ask that friend to stop you every time a term, explanation, or example is unclear. It is also possible to make adjustments to your speech once you get in front of the actual audience, making your language more or less technical, for example, or offering additional examples to illustrate points.

2. Working within the time allotted to your presentation

When you are narrowing your topic (*see Chapter 5, p. 37*), keep in mind how much time you will have for your presentation. Try gauging how many words you speak per minute by reading a passage aloud at a conversational pace (about 120–150 words per minute is ideal). Be sure to time your presentation when you practice it.

13b Draft your presentation with the rhetorical situation in mind.

1. Making your opening interesting

Professional speakers stress the importance of a strong opening both to set the speaker at ease and to gain the audience's confidence and attention. Some suggest that you try out several approaches to your introduction to see which gets the best reactions from friends during rehearsal. Stories, based on your own experience or drawn from your research, often make for an interesting beginning. Brief quotations, striking statistics, and surprising statements are also attention getters. If one of these devices is not appropriate to your subject, craft an introduction that lets your listeners know what they have to gain from your presentation—for example, new information or new perspectives on a subject of common interest.

www.mhhe.com/
awr
For more on crafting
introductions, go to

Writing >
Paragraph/Essay
Development >
Introductions

2. Making the focus and organization of your presentation explicit

Just as signs on the highway tell travelers where to go, signs in your presentation set the direction for your audience. Select two or three ideas that you most want your audience to hear—and remember. Make these ideas the focus of your presentation, and let your audience

know what to expect by previewing the content of your presentation—
"I intend to make three points about fraternities on campus"—and
then listing the three points.

The phrase "to make three points" as in the example signals a top-
ical organization. Of course, there are other common patterns, including
chronological (*at first . . . later . . . in the end*), causal (*because of that . . .
then this follows*), and problem-solution (*given the situation . . . then this
set of proposals*). A question-answer format also works well, either as an
overall strategy or as part of another organizational pattern.

3. Being direct

What your audience hears and remembers has as much to do with how
you communicate your message as it does with what you say. For clarity, use a direct, simple style:

- Choose basic sentence structures.
- Repeat key terms.
- Pay attention to the rhythm of your speech.
- Don't be afraid to use the pronouns *I, you,* and *we.*

Notice how applying these principles transforms the following written sentence into a group of sentences appropriate for oral presentation:

WRITTEN

Although the claim that writing increases student learning has
yet to be substantiated by either an ample body or an exemplary
piece of empirical research, advocates of writing across the curriculum persist in pressing the claim.

ORAL

The more students write, the more they learn. So say advocates
of writing across the curriculum. But what evidence do we have
that writing improves learning? Do we have lots of empirical research or even one really good study? The answer is, "Not yet."

4. Using visual aids

www.mhhe.com/
awr
For an interactive
tutorial on using
PowerPoint, go to
Writing >
PowerPoint
Tutorial

One way to make your focus explicit is with visual aids. A computer
projection of the points from your outline encourages your audience
to make a few notes and discourages you from simply reading from a
script. Consider using slides, posters, objects, video clips, and music.

Presentation software such as PowerPoint can help you stay focused
while you are speaking. The twelve PowerPoint slides in Figure 13.1 on
pages 162–63 offer advice on how to design effective slides for a pre-

sentation. (*For more on using presentation software to incorporate multimedia elements into a presentation, see Chapter 14: Multimedia Writing, pp. 168–71.*)

5. Concluding memorably

Your final comments will be the part of your speech that most members of your audience remember best. Try to make your ending truly memorable: return to that surprising opener, play with the words of your opening quotation, look at the initial image from another angle, or reflect on the story you have told. Make sure your listeners are aware that you are about to end your presentation, using such signal phrases as "in conclusion" or "let me end by saying," if necessary. Keep your conclusion short to hold the audience's attention.

www.mhhe.com/
awr
For more information
on conclusions, go to

Writing >
Paragraph/Essay
Development >
Conclusions

13c Prepare for your presentation.

1. Deciding whether to use notes or a written script

To be an effective speaker, you need to make eye contact with your listeners to monitor their responses and adjust your message accordingly. A written script can be a barrier between you and your audience. You can relate better to your audience if you speak from an outline. Write out only those parts of your presentation where precise wording counts, such as quotations.

For most occasions, it is inappropriate to write out everything you want to say and then read it word for word. In some scholarly or formal settings, however, precise wording may be necessary, especially if your oral presentation is to be published or if your remarks will be quoted by others, including the media. Sometimes the setting for your presentation may be so formal or the audience may be so large that a script feels necessary. In such instances, do the following:

- Triple-space the typescript of your text.
- Avoid carrying sentences over from one page to another.
- Mark your manuscript for pauses, emphasis, and the pronunciation of proper names.

2. Rehearsing, revising, and polishing

Whether you are using an outline or a script, you will need to practice saying your presentation aloud. The rehearsal stage is a time to revise the content of your speech. As you give your speech out loud, you will find transitions that don't quite work, points that need further

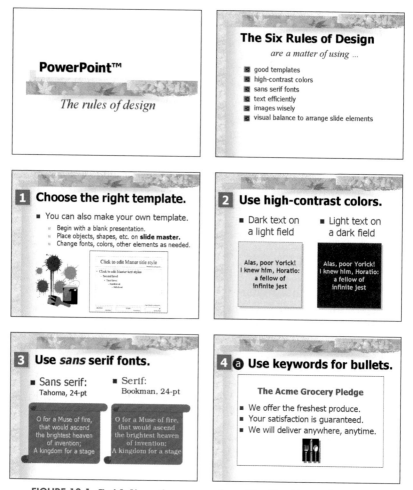

FIGURE 13.1 **Guidelines for preparing effective PowerPoint slides.**

development, and sections that go on too long. After you have settled on the content of your speech and can say it comfortably, focus on polishing the style of your delivery. Ask your friends or use a mirror to check that your body posture is straight but relaxed, that your voice is loud and clear, and that you are making eye contact around the room. Time your final rehearsals, adding and cutting material as necessary. If you will be presenting in an unfamiliar space, try to practice there before your audience arrives. If an on-site rehearsal is not possible, at least be sure to arrive at your site well in advance.

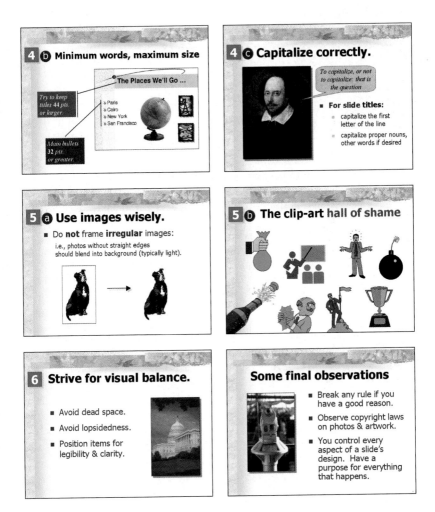

3. Accepting nervousness as normal

Many people dread giving oral presentations and worry that their stage fright will sabotage their delivery. One key to dealing with stage fright is recognizing that the adrenaline surge you feel before a presentation can actually invest your talk with positive energy. Another is knowing that other people usually cannot tell that you are nervous. Practice and revise your presentation until it flows smoothly, and make sure that you have a strong opener to get you through the first, most difficult moments of the speech. If your phobia is extreme, look for a course on overcoming stage fright.

14 Multimedia Writing

Multimedia writing combines words with images, video, or audio into a single composition. The products of multimedia writing can be both dynamic and memorable. To be done well, they require considerable time and effort.

The most common form of multimedia writing is the combination of words and still visuals—such as photographs, maps, charts, or graphs—discussed in many chapters of this handbook. Another form is an oral presentation with any kind of visual support, from a diagram on a blackboard to a PowerPoint slide show (*see Chapter 13, Oral Presentations*). In addition to these forms, digital technology now makes it possible to combine written words with sounds, video, and animation. Of course you cannot include audio or video on a piece of paper the way you can words and still images. Just as you need a computer to create multimedia presentations with audio and video, you also need a computer or other display technology to deliver or read them.

Like any form of writing, multimedia writing allows you to convey a message to a particular audience for a particular purpose—to inform, to interpret, or to persuade with argument. A video or audio segment—like a photograph, map, or chart—must support this purpose in a way that is appropriate to the situations.

TEXTCONNEX

Some Key Concepts in Multimedia Writing

- **File:** A computer file is a collection of information in computer-readable form. Text files store words, image files store pictures, audio files store sounds, and video files store video.
- **Link:** A link is a connection from one file to another, or to another place in the same file. You can link to files stored on your own computer or, through the Internet and World Wide Web, to files stored on other computers.
- **Hypertext:** Hypertext is text with links. (In a sense, the Web is one vast hypertext document with countless links to a nearly endless variety of files.)

14a Learn about tools for creating multimedia texts.

Multimedia writing can take a variety of forms and can be created with a variety of software tools. Here are a few options:

- Most word processors allow you to integrate still visuals with text in a single document, but many also make it possible to write text that permits readers, with the click of the mouse, to connect to various files—including audio, image, and video files (*see section 14b*).

- Most presentation software packages similarly allow you to accompany a presentation with audio and video files as well as still visuals (*see section 14d*).

- A variety of programs and Web-based tools allow you to create your own **Web pages** and **Web sites,** which can include a wide range of multimedia features (*see section 14e*).

- You can create a **weblog** (**blog** for short), on which, in addition to your written entries, you can post your own multimedia files and link to files on other blogs and Web sites (*see section 14f*).

14b Combine text and image using a word-processing program to analyze images.

Texts that combine words and images are, as already noted, the most common form of multimedia writing. Two types of papers you might be called on to write are image interpretations and photographic stories.

1. Composing image interpretations

You may be called on to analyze a single image along the lines described in Chapter 4: Reading, Thinking, Writing: The Critical Connection. Such a paper might combine an image—say, a reproduction of a painting from a museum—with the writer's interpretation of the image. The writer of such an **image interpretation** has two tasks. The first is to describe the picture as fully as possible, using adjectives, comparisons, and words that help readers look at the picture. The second is to analyze the argument the picture seems to be making.

2. Telling photographic stories

In another basic paper that combines words and images—a **photographic story**—a writer tries to imagine the story behind an evocative photograph. Often, as we look at a photograph, we automatically create a story about it that is as much an expression of ourselves as it is a statement about the photograph.

During the Great Depression of the 1930s, for example, the photographer Walker Evans and the writer James Agee traveled to Alabama to take pictures of poor farmers and sharecroppers. These pictures—such as the one in Figure 14.1—invite storytelling. One story this photograph might tell is of a hard-pressed farmer worried about his family and his unpayable debts. Or you might see this one farmer as a symbol of all the hardship brought on by the Depression. Remove him from his Depression-era context, however, and you might see a father suspiciously eyeing the young man coming to take his daughter on her first date. Is there anything in particular that ties this farmer to a specific time and place? What makes you think so?

14c Use a word-processing program to create a hypertext essay.

Most word processors allow writers to create multimedia hypertext essays by inserting links in the document that take readers to other files, including text, image, audio, and video files (*see the TextConnex box on p. 164*). Links can take several forms:

- **Internal links** connect from one place in a document to another place in the same document, or to other files stored on the writer's computer.
- **External links** connect to Web sites on the Internet and any text, image, audio, or video files stored on them.

This ability to link to multimedia files provides writers with a new kind of evidence to use in their work. As with any evidence, however, it must be relevant to the audience and purpose of the essay. It can either complement the essay's verbal claims or, like a good chart or graph, support the claims directly. For example, you might include links to video files of several presidents delivering their inaugural addresses for a political science project. These links might simply complement your thesis, or they might provide direct evidence for an important point about, say, a particular president's delivery. However, unless your assignment includes specific directions to emphasize linked material as evidence, you should probably think of it as supplemental to your written claims.

FIGURE 14.1 **A Walker Evans photograph.**

If you have never created a hypertext essay, start small, with a limited set of links that all clearly serve your audience and purpose. You can create internal links to the full information about works on your works-cited page, to other papers you have written that are related to your current topic, to tangential material that you collected while working on the essay, or to a file in which you raise additional questions about your topic. You can create external links to works on your topic written by your classmates, or you can use external links to take readers to background material on the Web.

> *Caution:* When you revise your hypertext essay, be sure to check all links to make sure they are relevant and functioning correctly. Also, if your essay includes internal links to files on your computer, be sure to include those files with the file for the essay when you submit it to your instructor.

Tips

LEARNING in COLLEGE

Using Hypertext as a Writing Process Tool

Some students insert a variety of links in their essays to help them during the writing process. For example, they might include a link to additional research, or to a source that refutes an argument, or to interesting information that is not directly relevant to the primary subject. These links can help writers refer to supplemental material without undermining the coherence of the text. If a reader of an early draft—an instructor or classmate—thinks the linked material should be in the essay itself, the writer can include it in the next draft.

www.mhhe.com/awr

For an interactive tutorial on using PowerPoint, go to

Writing >
PowerPoint
Tutorial

14d Use presentation software to create multimedia presentations.

Presentation software provides another tool for multimedia composition. Originally intended as an electronic replacement for the traditional kinds of visual aids that had been used to accompany oral presentations, presentation software makes it possible to incorporate audio, video, and animation into a talk. Presentation software can also be used to create a multimedia composition that viewers can go through on their own.

1. Using presentation software for an oral presentation

Presentation slides that accompany a talk should accomplish two tasks: (1) identify major points and (2) display information in a visu-

Tips LEARNING in COLLEGE

Using Presentation Software as a Writing Process Tool

Many students have discovered that presentation software slides provide a useful tool for exploring and organizing their ideas prior to drafting. The slides also give you another way to get feedback from peer reviewers and others, using the following process:

- Well before a paper is due, create a very brief, three- to five-slide presentation—with visuals if appropriate—that previews the key points you intend to make in the paper.
- Present the preview to an audience—friends, classmates, perhaps even your instructor—and ask for reactions and suggestions for improvement.

ally effective way. As you prepare your slides, remember that they support your talk, but they do not replace it; the quickest way to lose your audience is to read to them slides that they can read themselves. In general, keep the amount of information on each slide to a minimum. Finally, plan to show each slide for about one minute. (*For more on preparing and presenting slides for an oral presentation, see Chapter 13: Oral Presentations, pp. 160–61, 162–63.*)

2. Using presentation software to create an independent composition

With presentation software, you can also create compositions that run on their own or at the prompting of viewers. This capability is especially useful in distance-learning settings, in which students attend class and share information electronically. For example, a student might deliver a presentation to the class in the form of an independent composition. The text of the presentation might appear on the slides, or the student might record portions of it, such as the introduction and conclusion, and incorporate them as audio files.

3. Preparing a slide presentation

You should begin thinking about slides while you plan what you are going to say. The two processes work together: as you decide on the words for the talk or independent composition, you will think of visuals that support your points, and as you work out the visuals, you are likely to see additional points you can make and adjust your presentation accordingly. Whether you are preparing slides for an oral presentation or an independent composition, the following guidelines apply:

- **Decide on a slide format.** Before you create your slides, you need to establish their basic appearance. What background color will they have? What typeface or typefaces? What design elements such as borders and rules? You can use the templates provided by the software, although they may force you into a kind of organization that does not fit your talk or that may be overly familiar to your audience. If the templates will not work in your situation, you might modify them or even start from scratch, using the templates as a basis for comparison as you develop your design.

www.mhhe.com/
awr
For more on designing
documents, go to
Writing > Writing
Web Links >
Document and
Web Design

- **Incorporate visuals into your presentation.** Because presentation slides are a visual medium, you will want to include visuals when appropriate. For example, to summarize quantitative information, you might use a chart or graph. Use only visuals that support your purpose. (*For more on choosing visuals, see Chapter 5, pp. 53–57.*)

- **Incorporate other multimedia elements.** Slides can also include audio files. You might record a narrative accompaniment or background information for each slide in an independent composition, or for a presentation on music you might insert audio files to show how a type of music has developed over time. Presentation slides can also include video files and **animation**—visuals that have moving parts or that change over time. An animated diagram of the process of cell division, for example, could help illustrate a presentation on cellular biology. (As you would for any other source, you need to provide documentation if you are using files that belong to others.)

- **Incorporate hypertext links.** Presentation slides, like hypertext essays, can include both internal and external links. You might use an internal link within a slide sequence to jump to another slide that illustrates or explains a particular point or issue, enlivening the presentation and helping the audience remember the information. You can also create external links to files on the Web. The value of this kind of link is that it allows you to showcase resources for your audience. Be careful not to overload your presentation with external

---

Caution: If you plan to make external links part of your presentation, make sure that you have a functioning Web browser on your computer and that a fast connection to the Internet is available where you will be giving the presentation.

links, however, because they can undermine the coherence of a presentation. They can also take a long time to load.

4. Reviewing the presentation

Once you have the text of your presentation in final form and the multimedia elements in place, you should carefully review your slides to make sure they work together coherently:

- Look at the slides in your software's slide sorter window and see how they proceed one to the next. Do you have an introductory slide? Do you need to include transitional effects, such as fades or animation, that reveal the content of a slide item by item? Some of these transitional effects permit audio—do you want that? Do you have a concluding slide? Are the slides consistent with the script of your talk? If the slides are intended as an independent document, do they include enough explanation and an adequate introduction and conclusion?

- Check the arrangement of your slides. You might try printing them as paper handouts and spreading them out over a large surface or printing and cutting apart the handout version of the slides for sorting. You can then rearrange slides physically, if need be, and return to the computer to implement your changes.

- Check the slides to be sure they have a unified look. Make sure, for example, that all the slides have the same background and that each uses the same typeface(s) in the same way.

14e Create a Web site.

Thanks to Web editing software, it is now almost as easy to create a Web site and post it on the Internet as it is to write a paper using word-processing software. Web-based businesses like Yahoo! provide free server space for hosting sites and offer tools for creating Web pages. Many schools also make server space available for student Web sites.

As is true of the other multimedia texts discussed in this chapter, a Web site, to be effective, must be well designed and serve a well-defined purpose for its audience. In creating a Web site, you will need to plan your site, draft content, select visuals, revise, and edit, as you would for any kind of composition. (*See Tab 2: Writing and Designing Papers.*) When you create a Web site, however, each stage involves decisions and requirements that are unique to this medium; the following sections offer guidelines for making some of these decisions.

www.mhhe.com/awr
For more on designing Web sites, go to
Writing > Writing Web Links > Document and Web Design

1. Planning a structure for your site

Like most paper documents, a Web site can have a linear structure, where one page leads to the next, and so on. Because of the hyperlinked nature of this medium, however, a site can also be organized in a hierarchy or with a number of pages that connect to a central page, or hub, like the spokes of a wheel. The diagrams in Figure 14.2 illustrate these two possible structures.

To choose the structure that will work best for your site, consider how you expect visitors to use it. For the site about historic buildings, visitors intrigued by this topic will probably want to explore, following different paths of interest to see where they lead. For the site about resources for caregivers, visitors will probably be looking for specific information. The structure of each site accommodates its users' needs.

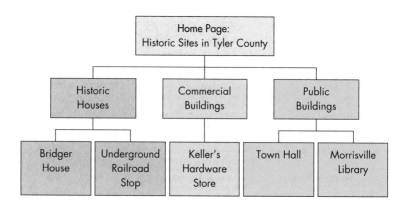

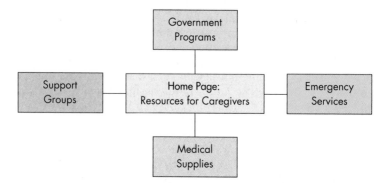

FIGURE 14.2 **Hierarchical (top) and hub structure (bottom).**

2. Gathering content for your site

The content for a Web site will usually consist of written work along with links and graphics. Depending on your topic and purpose, you might also provide audio files, video files, and even animation.

As with any written work, the writing that you do for your site should be clear, well developed, and free of errors. However, there are some special requirements for written content that appears on a Web site:

- Recognize that readers usually do not expect or want lengthy text explanations on your home page. Instead, they want to find the link or button they are looking for quickly.

- In general, create shorter paragraphs, and make sure the text for each page fits on that page. Avoid long passages that require readers to use the scroll bar.

- Use links to connect your interests with those of others and to provide extra sources of information. Avoid using the command "Click here" on your Web site. Instead, make links part of your text. (*Note, for example, the way the text in the Web site in Figure 14.3 on p. 175 incorporates links.*) As with any evidence you use in your writing, your links should lead readers to content that is credible and relevant.

As you prepare your written text, you should also gather any graphics, photographs, and audio and video files that you plan to include. Some sites, such as http://gallery.yahoo.com, allow you to download images, and some images, such as historical photographs available through the Library of Congress, are in the public domain. Whether or not an image is in the public domain, be sure to give proper credit for any material that you have not generated yourself and, if necessary, request permission for its use.

3. Designing Web pages to capture and hold interest

An inviting or interesting photograph or other visual can often grab even a casual Web surfer's attention. On good Web sites, you will also find such easy-to-follow links as "what you'll find here," FAQs (frequently asked questions), or "list of those involved." In planning the structure and content of your site, keep your readers' convenience in mind. For example, in Figure 14.3, notice how easy it is for readers to find what they need.

4. Designing a readable site with a unified look

As you gather your material, you will also need to think about the overall design for your site. Because the Web is a visual medium, readers appreciate a site with a unified look. "Sets" or "themes" are readily

TextConnex

Understanding Web Jargon

- **Browser:** software that allows you to access and view material on the World Wide Web. When you identify a site you want to see on the Web by typing in a URL (see below), your browser (*Netscape Navigator* or *Microsoft Internet Explorer,* for example) tells a distant computer—a **server**—to send that site to you.

- **JPEG and GIF:** formats for photographs and other visuals that are recognized by browsers. Photographs that appear on a Web site should be saved in JPEG format (Joint Photographic Experts Group, pronounced *jay-peg.*) The file extension is .jpg or .jpeg. Clip art should be saved as GIF files (Graphics Interchange Format, pronounced like *gift* without the *t.*)

- **Home page:** the opening page of a Web site. A home page typically includes general information about the site as well as links to various parts of it.

- **HTML/XML:** hypertext markup language/extensible markup language. These languages tag or code text so that your browser can rebuild a document from the compressed files that are sent through the Internet. When your browser retrieves a page, you end up with an "original copy" of the document, usually in a matter of seconds. It is no longer necessary to learn HTML or XML to publish on the Web. Programs such as *FrontPage, PageMill, Dreamweaver,* and *Netscape Composer* now provide a WYSIWYG (What You See Is What You Get) interface for creating Web pages.

- **Protocol:** a set of rules controlling data exchange between computers. **HTTP** (hypertext transfer protocol) is a way of breaking down and then reconstructing a document when it is sent over the Internet.

- **URL:** uniform resource locator or Web address. When you type or paste a URL into your Web browser, you are sending a request through your browser to another computer, asking it to transfer data to your computer.

available at free graphics sites offering banners, navigation buttons, and other design elements. Design your home page to complement your other pages, or your readers may lose track of where they are in the site—and lose their interest in staying.

- Consider including a site map—a Web page that serves as a table of contents for your entire site.

FIGURE 14.3 **The home page of the National Museum of the American Indian.**

- Select elements such as buttons, signs, animations, sounds, and backgrounds with a consistent design.
- Use colors that provide adequate contrast, white space, and sans serif fonts to make text easy to read. Pages that are too busy are not visually compelling. (*For more on design, see Tab 2: Writing and Designing Papers, pp. 98–105.*)
- Avoid using overly wide lines of text; readers find them difficult to process.

The home page and interior page shown in Figure 14.4 illustrate some of these design considerations.

5. Designing a Web site that is easy to access and navigate

Since most Web sites are not linear, writers need to take special care to help their readers find their way to the areas of the site they want

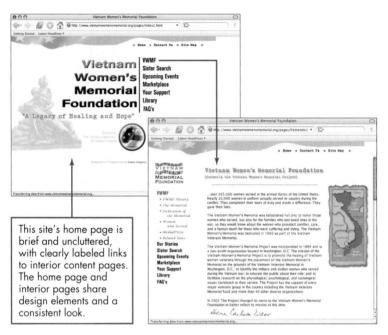

This site's home page is brief and uncluttered, with clearly labeled links to interior content pages. The home page and interior pages share design elements and a consistent look.

FIGURE 14.4 Home page and an interior page from the Web site of the Vietnam Women's Memorial Foundation.

to visit. Writers also need to make it easy for readers to take interesting side trips without wasting their time or losing their way. Here are some guidelines to help you accomplish this:

- **Identify your Web site on each page, and provide a link to the home page.** Remember that readers will not always enter your Web site through the home page. Therefore, you should usually give the title of the site on each page. Provide an easy-to-spot link to your home page as well.

- **Provide a navigation bar on each page.** A **navigation bar** can be a simple line of links that you copy and paste at the top or bottom of each page. Provide a navigation bar on each page to make it easy for visitors to move from the site's home page to other pages and back again. For example, shown on the Web page from the University of Alaska Anchorage (*Figure 14.5 on p. 178*), visitors can choose from five links in the navigation bar under the title.

- **Use graphics that load quickly.** Be considerate of viewers who have older computers that cannot handle huge graphics

TextConnex

Web Resources for Site Design and Construction

- *www.teach.science's Surf and Master the Web: Writing Web Pages:* <http://www2.ncsu.edu/ncsu/pams/science_house/workshops/web/writing.html>
- *Web Guide: Designing a Web Page:* <http://people.depauw.edu/djp/webguide/designwebpage.html>
- *Designing Accessible Web Pages*—information about creating Web pages for people with disabilities <http://nadc.ucla.edu/dawpi.htm>

files. Limit the size of your images to no more than 40 kilobytes so that they will load faster.

- **Use graphics judiciously.** Even though a picture may be worth a thousand words, your Web site should not depend on graphics alone to make its message clear and interesting. Graphics should be used to reinforce your message. The designers of the Library of Congress Web site (*Figure 14.6 on p. 179*) use graphics to help visitors navigate the site.

- **Be aware of the needs of visitors with disabilities.** Visitors to your site may have impaired vision or hearing, so you should provide alternate ways of accessing any visual or auditory information such as descriptions of visual texts and transcriptions of audio files.

For MULTILINGUAL STUDENTS

Designing a Web Site Collaboratively

If you are asked to create a Web site as part of a class assignment, try to make arrangements to work with a partner or a small group. The kind of interaction involved in writing the content and designing the site will provide you with beneficial language support. Periodically, you can invite peers to look over the writing you contribute and make suggestions. At the same time, you will be able to provide the project with the benefit of your unique multicultural viewpoint.

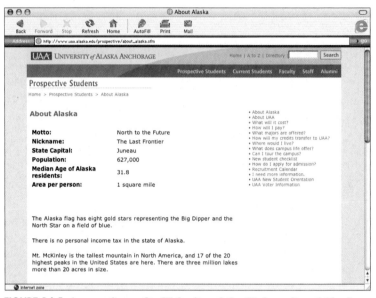

FIGURE 14.5 A page from the Web site of the University of Alaska Anchorage. The navigation bar appears on every page of the site.

6. Using peer feedback to revise your Web site

Before publishing your site, proofread your text carefully, and ask a couple of friends to look at your site and share their responses with you. When you publish on the Web, you offer your work to be read by anyone in the world. Make sure your site reflects favorably on your abilities.

14f Create and interact with weblogs.

Weblogs—called "blogs" for short—provide another site for multimedia writing. Blogs are simply Web sites that can be continuously updated. Some blogs are the exclusive creations of one writer, as in the example in Figure 14.7 on page 180; others provide a group of writers a space for sharing ideas and discussing each other's work. You can include images in a blog and link to other blogs and Web pages.

Unlike standard Web pages, blogs are easily updated and provide a format for compiling material and searching it. Because there are several free servers for creating blogs, and the set-up procedures are outlined clearly, blogs are available to anyone with online access. In

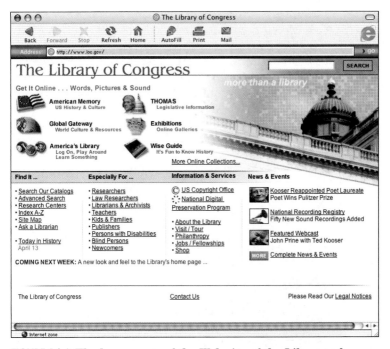

FIGURE 14.6 The home page of the Web site of the Library of Congress.

schools, classes have used blogs to discuss issues, organize work, compile portfolios, and gather and store material and commentary.

In general, blogs are developing more as vehicles for public discussion than as private online journals. Several bloggers, for example, played a prominent role in reporting on the 2004 presidential campaign. Others covered the tsunami disaster later in the same year.

To begin blogging, you will need to set up a blog site with a server such as www.blogger.com. You may at first want to confine yourself to a very specific purpose before launching into wide-ranging commentary.

> *Caution:* Remember that all blogs are more or less public, depending on how much access they allow. Don't post anything you would not want everybody to know about.

FIGURE 14.7 A personal blog. Musician Scott August's blog, hosted on blogger.com, contains posts about his music and travels.

When you begin your blog, consider the following questions:

- What is your purpose?
- To whom will you give access? Will the blog be public, for all to see? Or will it be limited by password protection to specific viewers?
- Do you want to allow others to post on your blog?
- Do you want to set up a schedule of postings or a series of events that will cue you to post?
- Do you want to link to other blogs?

A National
Audubon Society
employee wrote
and designed this
page from one of
the Society's
annual reports to
show donors how
their money helps
this environmental
organization—and
why its cause
matters.

4

The aim of education must be the
training of independently acting and
thinking individuals, who, however, see in
the service of the community their
highest life problem.
—ALBERT EINSTEIN

Writing
beyond
College

4 | Writing beyond College

Although college may be unfamiliar territory to the newcomer, it is part of the larger world. Writing represents an access road—a way of connecting classroom, workplace, and community.

15 Service Learning and Community-Service Writing

Your ability to research and write can be of great value to organizations that serve the community. Courses at every level of the university, as well as extracurricular activities, offer opportunities to work with organizations such as homeless shelters, tutoring centers, and environmental groups.

15a Address the community to effect change.

Your work with community organizations may involve writing newsletters, press releases, or funding proposals. When you are writing for a community group, consider these questions:

- What do community members talk about?
- How do they talk about these issues, and why?
- Who is an outsider (member of the community), and who is an insider (member of the organization)?
- How can you best write from the inside to the outside?

Your answers will help you shape your writing so that it reaches its intended audience and moves that audience to action.

Writing on behalf of a community organization almost always involves negotiation and collaboration. A community organization may revise your draft to fit its needs, and you will have to live with those revisions. In these situations, having a cooperative attitude is as important as having strong writing skills.

Even if you are not writing on behalf of a group, you can still do community-service writing. You can write in your own name to raise an issue of concern to the community in a public forum—for example, a newspaper editorial or a letter to a public official. Any time you address

A WRITER at WORK

When Laura Amabisca entered Glendale Community College, she volunteered to be a tutor in the writing center. Upon transferring to Arizona State University West, she joined the Writing Tutors Club, continuing her service to the campus community. In addition, she became a mentor for other Glendale Community College students who were trying to build the confidence to transfer to the university.

In a course in advanced expository writing, she was able to draw on these experiences for an essay on the special needs of community college transfer students. She also wrote a letter on the same theme to the student newspaper.

The satisfaction and sense of involvement she felt about her on-campus service motivated her to visit the ASU West Volunteer Office for ideas about off-campus service. She then became a volunteer for America Reads, joining students from ASU West and from various community colleges who tutor in this national literacy project.

The Phoenix office of America Reads asked her to help design a public relations campaign to explain the value of America Reads. After writing reflectively in her journal, she volunteered to draft a brochure to convince other college students to join the project. In this way, she moved from involvement on her own campus to service in the wider community.

readers as fellow citizens with the purpose of educating them or advocating change, you are doing community-service writing.

www.mhhe.com/
awr
For interactive help
with design, go to

Writing > Visual
Rhetoric

15b Design brochures, posters, and newsletters with an eye to purpose and audience.

If you are participating in a service learning program or an internship, you may have opportunities to design brochures and newsletters for wide distribution, as well as posters to create awareness and promote events. To create an effective brochure, poster, or newsletter, you will need to integrate your skills in document design with what you have learned about purpose and audience.

Here are a few tips that will help you design effective brochures, posters, and newsletters, whatever your audience and purpose may be:

- Before you begin, consider how readers will gain access to and review the brochure or newsletter. How will it be mailed or distributed? What are the implications for the overall design?

- Sketch the design in pencil before you immerse yourself in the high-tech capacities of the computer. Use the computer to solve design problems, not to create them.

- In making decisions about photographs, illustrations, type fonts, and the design in general, think about the overall image that should be conveyed about the organization sponsoring the brochure, poster, or newsletter.

- If the organization has a logo, include it; if not, suggest designing one. A **logo** is a small visual symbol, like the Nike "swoosh" or the distinctive font used for Coca-Cola.

- Create a template for the brochure, poster, or newsletter so that you can easily produce future editions. In word-processing and document design programs, a **template** is a blank document that includes all of the formatting and codes. When you use a template, you just "plug in" new content and visuals— the format and design are already done.

Notice, for example, how the brochure for the PSFS Building in Philadelphia, Pennsylvania (*Figure 15.1 on p. 186*) purposefully connects the history and importance of an architectural landmark with the prestige of the Loews Philadelphia Hotel, into which "the world's first Modernist skyscraper" has been renovated. The brochure has an informative and also a subtly persuasive purpose. Readers are meant to feel that by staying at this Loews they are participating in a great tradition. The front cover is divided in half, with a striking photo of the building on the left side and an account of its history on the right. The interior page places a photo of the bank above an image of hotel comfort. On both pages, quotations running vertically beside the photographs reinforce the building's architectural significance.

The newsletter from the Harvard Medical School titled "Women's Health Watch" (*Figure 15.2 on p. 187*) has a simple, clear design. The designer keeps in mind the purpose and audience, which are explicitly stated in the title and the headline below the title. The shaded area on the right lists the topics that are covered on the interior pages so that readers can get to the information they need quickly and easily. The Web address is prominently displayed in blue so that readers can find further information. The lead article, "Does Excess Vitamin A Cause Hip Fracture?" is simply designed in two columns, with the headline in bold type, subheadings in blue, a readable typeface, and a graphic strategically placed to break up the text and add visual interest. In all of these ways, the design supports the Harvard Medical School's

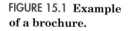

FIGURE 15.1 **Example of a brochure.**

Volume IX Number 7
March 2002

H A R V A R D
Women's Health Watch

INFORMATION FOR ENLIGHTENED CHOICES FROM HARVARD MEDICAL SCHOOL

Does Excess Vitamin A Cause Hip Fracture?

Hip fracture is one of the most dreaded risks of aging. More than 350,000 hip fractures occur annually in the United States, mostly in women over 65. Half of these women never regain the ability to live independently. About 20% die within a year. Many others suffer chronic pain, anxiety, and depression. The consequences are so grim that many older women contacted in surveys on this subject say they'd rather die than suffer a hip fracture that would send them to a nursing home.

Current recommendations on reducing fracture risk advise women to exercise, make sure they get enough calcium and vitamin D, and, if necessary, take medications that help preserve bone strength. Some women also learn strategies for preventing falls or take classes such as tai chi to improve their balance. Now, a new study suggests that we should also pay attention to vitamin A. At high levels, this essential nutrient may actually increase our risk for hip fracture.

NEW STUDY FINDS LINK

Researchers at Harvard Medical School reported in the Jan. 2, 2002, *Journal of the American Medical Association* on the relationship between postmenopausal hip fracture and vitamin A intake. The data came from 72,337 women enrolled in the Nurses' Health Study. The women were divided into five groups according to their average daily consumption, over an 18-year period, of vitamin A from food and supplements.

Researchers then correlated vitamin A intake with hip fracture incidence. They found that women with the highest intake—3,000 micrograms (mcg) or more per day—had a 48% greater risk for hip fractures, compared to women with the lowest intake (1,250 mcg or less per day).

The increased risk was mainly due to *retinol*, a particular form of vitamin A. In fact, women consuming 2,000 mcg of retinol or more daily had a hip fracture risk almost *double* that of women whose daily intake was under 500 mcg. In contrast, consuming high levels of *beta-carotene*, also a source of vitamin A, had a negligible impact on hip fracture risk. Participants taking hormone replacement therapy (HRT) were somewhat protected from the effects of too much retinol.

ABOUT VITAMIN A

Vitamin A is important for vision, the immune system, and the growth of bone, hair, and skin cells. Retinol, also called "preformed vitamin A," is the active form of the vitamin. It occurs naturally in animal products such as eggs, whole milk, cheese, and liver. Other food sources of vitamin A are *carotenoids*, which are found in green leafy vegetables and in dark yellow or orange fruits and vegetables. The body can convert these plant compounds to retinol. Beta-carotene is the most plentiful carotenoid and it converts most efficiently. Even so, you need about 12 times as much beta-carotene as retinol to get the same amount of vitamin A.

Because vitamin A is lost in the process of removing fat, many fat-free dairy products are fortified with retinol. So are some margarines and ready-to-eat cereals. The vitamin A in supplements and multivitamins may come from retinol, beta-carotene, or both. Beta-carotene is preferable because it's also an antioxidant.

Although vitamin A deficiency is a leading cause of blindness in developing countries, it's not a major problem in the United States. The main concern here is excess vitamin A, which can produce birth defects, liver damage, and reduced bone mineral density (BMD). →

15% of women age 50 will suffer a hip fracture before age 80.

www.health.harvard.edu

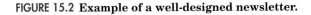

FIGURE 15.2 **Example of a well-designed newsletter.**

(Text continues on p. 188.)

purpose of helping the general public get reliable information about the latest advances in medical research. (*For more information on document design, see pp. 98–105.*)

16 Letters to Raise Awareness and Share Concern

Your ability to write and your willingness to share your opinions and insights can influence local, community, and even national events and decisions. A letter that is clearly argued, concisely phrased, and appropriately directed can accomplish a great deal, whether you are writing to a local politician or to a corporation's board of directors. Your task in writing such a letter is to present yourself as a polite, engaged, and reasonable person who is invested in a particular issue and who can offer a compelling and persuasive case for a particular course of action. Here are some guidelines for writing a letter to raise awareness and share concern:

- Address the letter to the appropriate person(s). If you are writing to a newspaper's or magazine's editorial pages, see how published letters are addressed ("To the editors," for example) and whether any guidelines for letters to the editor are available. If you are writing to a community or nonprofit organization or a private corporation, consult the organization's Web site or call the main number. You will probably be referred to a department called "Consumer Relations" or "Public Relations." It is always best to address your letter to a specific person, or at least a specific department within an organization.

- Use the format for a business letter. (*See the examples of business letters in block format on pp. 195 and 202–3.*)

- Some publications, corporations, and nonprofit organizations include links on their Web sites for forwarding correspondence or submitting letters to the editor. If a Web site includes such a

link, use that instead of writing a print letter. The Web site
will either give you an e-mail address or provide a box for you
to type in your letter. Do not send a document as an attachment to an e-mail. Most corporate and organizational Web
servers are protected by firewalls that screen out e-mail with
attachments. Concisely state your area of concern in the "subject" line of such an e-mail.

- In the first paragraph of your letter, clearly state the area of
  interest or concern you wish to address and why the issue is
  important to you. For example, if you are writing to your local
  school board, you should state in your first paragraph that
  you are a parent of a child at a local school.

- In your second and subsequent paragraphs, provide clear and
  compelling evidence for your concern. If relevant, propose a
  solution.

- Keep it brief. Community organizations and corporations receive hundreds, even thousands, of letters each week. Letters
  to the editor that are selected for publication tend to be no
  more than three or four paragraphs long.

- In your conclusion, thank the reader for taking the time to
  consider your thoughts. If you are writing to request specific
  action—for example, that an item be added to the agenda of
  the next school board meeting—repeat the request. If you
  want a specific response to your concern, politely request a
  letter or telephone call. If you intend to follow up on your letter, note that you will be calling or writing again within a
  week (or however long is appropriate).

TEXTCONNEX

Making Yourself Heard

The Web sites of most major daily newspapers provide access
to their opinion pages and an e-mail address readers can use
to send letters to the editor. The Web site Opinion Pages (<http://
www.opinion-pages.org>) provides links to the editorial and opinion pages of more than six hundred mainstream and alternative
English-language publications worldwide, as well as to more than
two hundred letter-to-the-editor pages.

For MULTILINGUAL STUDENTS

Writing Letters

In formal correspondence, as in most forms of academic writing, American culture favors directness, clarity, and simplicity, regardless of the writer's purpose or audience.

If you come from a culture that instead favors a subtle, indirect approach to a topic, or one that values embellishing a topic with richly digressive paragraphs, you may have to make a conscious effort to adopt the more linear style of English.

When you write to persuade, always start by identifying your goals and your audience's expectations, and tailor the format of your writing to both. Regardless of the purpose of your letter, some general rules apply:

- Maintain a confident, direct style in all professional communication.
- Keep introductory remarks to a minimum, approach the topic without hedging, discuss it point by point, and end on a cordial note.
- Familiarize yourself with the format requirements for the document you are creating. Its layout will make the first impression on the recipient.

17 Writing to Get and Keep a Job

Like many students, you may already have a job on or off campus, or you may be serving an internship or volunteering for a community-based organization. Writing is one way to connect your work, your other activities, and your studies. Strong writing skills will also help you find a good job once you leave college and advance in your chosen career.

17a Explore internship possibilities, and keep a portfolio of career-related writing.

www.mhhe.com/
awr
For more on
professional writing,
go to
Learning > College
to Career

An internship, in which you do actual work in your chosen field, is a vital connection between the classroom and the workplace. You gain academic credit, not for the hours you spend on the job, but for what you learn from the job. Writing and learning go together. Keep a journal to record and analyze your experiences, as well as a file of any writing you do on the job. Your final project for the internship credit may require that you analyze the file of writing you have produced.

Files of writing from internships, clippings of articles and editorials you have written for the school newspaper, writing you have done for a community organization—these and other documents demonstrate your ability to apply intellectual concepts to real-world demands. Organized into a portfolio, this material displays your marketable skills. Use a tabbed loose-leaf notebook or an actual portfolio with compartments for different categories of work. Arrange your writing samples by project or by kind of writing. Within each category, use reverse chronological order so that your most recent work appears first. (*For more on preparing a portfolio, see Tab 2: Writing and Designing Papers, pp. 106–8.*) Your campus career resource center can help you assess your skills and determine what kind of internship would best suit your career goals. It may also assist you in compiling a portfolio, keep it on file, and help you send it to potential employers or graduate schools.

17b Keep your résumé up-to-date and available on a computer disk.

A **résumé** is an informative piece of writing, a brief summary of your education and your work experience that you send to prospective employers. It is never finished. As you continue to learn, work, and write, you should be rethinking and reorganizing your résumé, emphasizing different accomplishments and talents for different potential employers. Some employers—for example, banks and accounting firms—expect a résumé from a college student or recent graduate to be no longer than one page. Other organizations with more informal cultures want to see more detail, especially about a future employee's special skills and interests. Saving your résumé as a computer file allows you to tailor it to the needs and requirements of its readers.

Expect the person reviewing your résumé to give it no more than sixty seconds. Make that first impression count. Design a document that is easy to read, attractively formatted, and flawlessly spelled.

Guidelines for writing a résumé

Always include the following *necessary* categories in a résumé:

- Heading (name, address, phone number, e-mail address)
- Education (in reverse chronological order; do not include high school)
- Work experience (in reverse chronological order)
- References (often included on a separate sheet; for many situations, you can add the line "References available on request" instead)

Include the following *optional* categories in your résumé as appropriate:

- Honors and awards
- Internships
- Activities and service
- Special skills

Laura Amabisca organized the information in her résumé (*see p. 193*) by time and by categories. Within each category, she listed items from the most to least recent. This reverse chronological order gives appropriate emphasis to what she had just done and was doing when she prepared the résumé.

Because Amabisca was applying for jobs in public relations, she highlighted her internship in that field by giving it its own category. People who have been working for a while often divide their work experience into separate categories, emphasizing experience pertinent to their career goal and listing other jobs separately. For example, Amabisca might have used the categories "Public Relations Experience" and "Other Work Experience" instead of "Work Experience" and "Internship."

Sometimes career counselors recommend that you list a career objective right under the heading of your résumé. There is a delicate balance, however, between presenting yourself as someone with clear goals and as someone who can be flexible. Unless you have done enough research to know exactly what a particular company is looking for, it is usually best to leave your career objective out of your résumé. Deal with this issue in your application letter instead.

17c Write an application letter that highlights the information on your résumé and demonstrates that your skills match the job you are seeking.

A clear and concise **application letter** should always accompany a résumé. Before drafting a job application letter, do some research

Laura Amabisca
20650 North 58th Avenue, Apt. 15A
Glendale, AZ 85308
(623) 555-7310
lamabisca@peoplelink.com

EDUCATION
B.A., Arizona State University West, Phoenix (May 2005)
    Major: History
    Minor: Global Management
    Senior Thesis: Picturing the Hopi, 1920–1940: A Historical Analysis
Glendale Community College, Glendale, AZ (2001–2003)

HONORS AND AWARDS
Westmarc Writing Prize (2005)
Arizona Regents' Scholarship (2002–2005)

WORK EXPERIENCE
Sears, Bell Road, Phoenix, AZ
    Assistant Manager, Sporting Goods Department (2003–present)
    Sales Associate, Sporting Goods Department (2001–2003)
    Stock Clerk, Sporting Goods Department (1997–2001)

INTERNSHIP
Public Relations Office, Arizona State University West (Summer 2004)

ACTIVITIES AND SERVICE
Tutor, Public-Relations Consultant, America Reads (2005)
Student Coordinator, Multicultural Festival, ASU West (2004)
Tutor, Writing Center, Glendale Community College (2002–2005)

SPECIAL SKILLS
Bilingual: Spanish/English
Skill and experience with Windows, WordPerfect, Word (IBM and Mac), and HTML authoring

REFERENCES
Ms. Carol Martinez
Director, Public Relations
Arizona State University West
PO Box 371000
Phoenix, AZ 85069-7100

Mr. James Corrothers
Sales Manager
Sporting Goods Department
Sears
302 N. Central Avenue
Phoenix, AZ 85043-6011

A file of confidential references is available upon request to Career Services, Arizona State University West.

Laura's entire résumé is just one page. A brief, well-organized résumé is more attractive to potential employers than a multipage, rambling résumé. Laura uses a simple font and no bold or italic type, ensuring that the résumé will be scannable.

Laura includes key-words (highlighted in blue here) that will be most likely to catch the eye of a potential employer. Laura knows that a position in public relations requires computer skills, communication skills, and experience working with diverse groups of people. Key words such as "sales," "bilingual," "HTML," and "public relations" are critical to her résumé.

As Laura's work experience grows, she can make more space on her résumé by not including the names of references and instead adding the notation "References available upon request."

TEXTCONNEX

Electronic Technology and Your Résumé

Many employers now request résumés by e-mail and will electronically scan print résumés. Both of these innovations require you to take additional care with your résumé. (For more information and step-by-step advice on tailoring résumés for specific fields, see Monster.com <http://resume.monster.com/>.)

Scanning allows a human resources department to compile print résumés in keyword-searchable electronic databases. Contact the human resources department of a potential employer and ask if your résumé should be scannable. If so, be sure to use a clear, common typeface in an easily readable size. Do not include any unusual symbols or characters. Print your résumé on white paper.

Sending your résumé by e-mail also allows a potential employer to enter it into a searchable database. Before you apply by e-mail, be sure that the employer accepts electronically submitted résumés. Also find out whether you should include the résumé in the body of an e-mail message or send it as an attached document. If the employer expects the résumé as an attached document, be sure to save it in a widely readable form such as rich text format (RTF) or ASCII. Use minimal formatting and no colors, unusual fonts, or other decorative flourishes. Be aware, too, that many companies have secure firewalls around their servers that screen out all attachments or attachments that include certain words. You can configure your e-mail program to send you an automatic reply when your e-mail has been successfully transmitted.

Because employers use certain specific keywords to search scanned or electronically submitted résumés, you will want to be sure to include those words in your résumé. The résumé section of Monster.com contains industry-specific advice on appropriate words.

about the organization you are contacting. For example, even though Laura Amabisca was already familiar with the Heard Museum when she applied for a position there, she took time to find out the name of the director of public relations instead of mailing her letter and résumé to an unnamed recipient. (*Amabisca's application letter appears on p. 195.*) If the want ad you are answering does not include a name, call the organization and find out the name of the person responsible for your area of interest. If you try but are unable to identify an appropriate name, or if the want ad does not include the name of the organization, it is better to direct the letter to "Dear Director of Public Relations" than to "Dear Sir or Madam."

20650 North 58th Avenue, Apt. 15A
Glendale, AZ 85308
August 17, 2005

Ms. Jaclyn Abel
Director of Public Relations
Heard Museum
2301 North Central Avenue
Phoenix, AZ 85004

Dear Ms. Abel:

I am writing to apply for the position of Public Relations Assistant that you recently advertised in the *Arizona Republic*. I believe that my experience and qualifications fit well with your needs at the Heard, a museum that I have visited and loved all my life.

As the enclosed résumé indicates, I have experience in the public relations field. While at Arizona State University West, I worked as an intern in the Public Relations Office, where I was responsible for analyzing and reporting on the image projected by the university's external publications. I also had a hand in creating the brochure for the University-College Center and participated in planning ASU West's "Dream Big" campaign. In addition I assisted in organizing an opening convocation attended by 800 people. This work in the not-for-profit sector has prepared me well for employment at the Heard.

My undergraduate major in American history has also helped me understand the rich heritage of Native Americans. In my senior thesis, which received the Westmarc Writing Award, I studied the history of the relationship between the Hopis and the Anglo population as reflected in photographs taken from 1920 to 1940. Although my thesis focuses on a specific tribe, I have been interested for many years in Native-American culture and have often made use of resources in the Heard. I think that I would do a superior job of presenting the Heard as the premier museum of Native American culture.

Confidential reference letters are available from ASU West Career Services. I sincerely hope that we will have an opportunity to talk further about the Heard Museum and its outstanding cultural contributions to the Phoenix metropolitan area. Please contact me at 623-555-7310.

Sincerely,

Laura Amabisca

Laura Amabisca

Enc.

Laura writes to a specific person and uses the correct salutation (*Mr., Ms., Dr.,* etc.). Never use only a first name in an application letter, even if you are writing to an acquaintance.

Laura briefly sums up her work experience. This information is also available on her résumé, but she makes evident in her cover letter why she is applying for the job. Without this explanation, a potential employer might not even look at her résumé.

Laura mentions her familiarity with the museum to which she is applying. This demonstrates her genuine interest in joining the organization.

Here are some additional guidelines for composing a letter of application:

- **Use business style.** Use the block form shown on pages 195 and 202–3. Type your address at the top of the page, with each line starting at the left margin; place the date at the left margin two lines above the recipient's name and address; use a colon (:) after the greeting; double-space between single-spaced paragraphs; use a traditional closing (*Sincerely, Sincerely yours, Yours truly*); and make sure that the inside address and the address on the envelope match exactly.

- **Limit your letter to three or four paragraphs.** Many prospective employers will not bother to turn to page two of an application letter. Focus clearly and concisely on what the employer needs to know. In the first paragraph, identify the position you are applying for, mention how you heard about it, and briefly state that you are qualified. In the following one or two paragraphs, explain your qualifications, elaborating on the most pertinent items in your résumé. Because Amabisca was applying for a public relations job at a museum of Native American culture, she chose to highlight her internship and her thesis. In another application letter, however, this time for a management position at American Express, she made different choices. In that letter, she emphasized her work experience at Sears, including the fact that she had moved up in the organization through positions of increasing responsibility.

- **State your expectation for future contact.** Conclude with a one- or two-sentence paragraph informing the reader that you are anticipating a follow-up to your letter.

- **Use *Enc.* if you are enclosing additional materials.** Decide whether it is appropriate to enclose supporting materials other than your résumé, such as samples of your writing. Amabisca decided to do so because she was applying for her ideal job and had highly relevant materials to send. If you have been instructed to send a cover letter and résumé by e-mail as attachments, include the word "Attachments" after your e-mail "signature."

17d Prepare in advance for the job interview.

An interview with a potential employer is like an oral presentation. You should prepare in advance, rehearse before an audience, and be prepared to answer unexpected questions. Many campus career resource

For MULTILINGUAL STUDENTS

Applying for a Job

Different cultures approach the job application process differently. Whatever your experiences may have been, keep the following guidelines in mind as you search for a job in the United States:

- A form letter accompanied by a generic résumé is not an effective way of getting a job interview. Before writing an application letter or preparing a résumé, you need to have a sense of exactly what the employer is looking for. You can then tailor your documents to those exact requirements.

- The main purpose of the application letter is to motivate the employer to read your résumé and to arrange an interview. It is a brief introduction, not the place to present your qualifications and work experience in detail. Your cover letter should be crisp and to the point. Avoid personal details, and be direct and objective in presenting your qualifications. Your tone toward and approach to the prospective employer should be courteous but dignified.

- Your résumé should contain only education- and work-related information. It is better not to include the kind of personal information (ethnicity, age, marital status) that may be expected in other countries.

- Time is of the essence when you send in application materials and when you arrive at the interview. American culture is notoriously time-conscious; a last-minute application or a late appearance at an interview can count heavily against you.

- Before applying for an internship or a job in the United States, you need to be sure that you have the appropriate visa or work permits. American employers are required by law to confirm such documentation before they can hire anyone. (American citizens must prove their citizenship as well.) For more information, visit your campus international student center and the campus career resource center.

centers offer free seminars on interviewing skills and can also arrange for you to role-play an interview with a career guidance counselor.

Here are some additional guidelines for job interviews:

- Call to confirm your interview the day before it is scheduled. If you are unsure of the location of the interview, make a scouting trip at least a day in advance to determine how much time you will need to get there.

- Dress modestly and formally, even if you are interviewing for an unpaid internship or with a company with a relaxed dress code.

- Bring an additional copy of your résumé and cover letter to refer to during your interview.

- Expect to speak with several people—perhaps someone from human resources as well as the person for whom you would actually be working and other people in his or her department. Usually, questions about salary and benefits should be brought up with human resources, *not* with your immediate supervisor.

- *Always* send a handwritten thank-you note or card (something simple and elegant) to everyone who took the time to meet you. Send a separate card to each person, reiterating a particularly interesting point that the person made and your interest in working with him or her. Thank each person for his or her interest in you. Send these cards within twenty-four hours of your interview.

17e Apply what you learn in college to your on-the-job writing.

Once you get a job, writing is a way to establish and maintain lines of communication with your colleagues and other contacts. You will probably be writing much of the time, to internal and external audiences, both on- and off-line. Much of what you have learned in college about writing for different purposes, occasions, and audiences will come in handy. When you write in the workplace, you should imagine a reader who is pressed for time and wants you to get to the point immediately.

1. Writing e-mail and memos in the workplace
In the workplace you will do much of your writing online, in the form of e-mail. Most e-mail programs set up messages in memo format, with "To," "From," "Date," and "Subject" lines, as in Figure 17.1 on page 199.

Whether you are writing an e-mail message or a conventional memo, you need to consider not only what your workplace document says but also how it looks. Various strategies can make your document easier to read. For example, presenting your information as a numbered or bulleted list surrounded by white space aids readability and allows you to highlight important points and to emphasize crucial ideas. (*For more help with document design, see Tab 2: Writing and Designing Papers, pp. 98–105.*)

```
┌─────────────────────────────────────────────────────────┐
│ □ ▧▧▧▧▧▧▧▧▧▧ e-mail ▧▧▧▧▧▧▧▧▧▧ ⊡ ☰ │
├─────────────────────────────────────────────────────────┤
│                                                       ▲ │
│   **To:** Jaclyn Abel, Director of Public Relations     │
│                                                         │
│   **From:** Laura Amabisca, Public Relations Assistant  │
│                                                         │
│   **Date:** October 10, 2005                            │
│                                                         │
│   **Subject:** Estimate of Visitors for Hopi Exhibit    │
│                                                         │
│                                                         │
│   For the exhibit of Hopi kachinas in 1999, we hosted   │
│   22,410 visitors during a three-month period. It seems │
│   likely that we will attract at least 30,000 for a     │
│   major show on the full range of Hopi culture.         │
│                                                       ▼ │
└─────────────────────────────────────────────────────────┘
```

FIGURE 17.1 Sample workplace e-mail.

2. Writing in other business genres

Conventional forms such as the following also increase readability because readers have built-in expectations for the genre and therefore know what to look for. Besides the memo, there are a number of common business genres:

www.mhhe.com/
awr
For help with
PowerPoint, go to
Writing >
PowerPoint Tutorial

- **Business letters:** Use business letters to communicate formally with people outside an organization. Typically, letters in business format have single-spaced block paragraphs with double spacing between the paragraphs. (*See the examples on pp. 195 and 202–3.*)

- **Business reports and proposals:** Like college research papers, business reports and proposals can be used to inform, analyze, and interpret. An abstract, sometimes called an **executive summary,** is almost always required, as are tables and graphs. (*For more on these visual elements, see Tab 2: Writing and Designing Papers, pp. 53–57.*)

- **Evaluations and recommendations:** You might need to evaluate a person, or you might be called on to evaluate a product or a procedure and recommend whether the company

TextConnex

E-mail in the Workplace

Anything you write using a company's or an organization's computers is considered company property. Many people have found themselves in the embarrassing situation of having their personal e-mail accidentally or intentionally broadcast to an entire corporation—and even beyond. If you want to gossip with a coworker, do so over a cup of coffee. If you want to e-mail your best friend about your personal life, do so from your home computer. And do not use the office's computer, fax machine, or photocopy machine to prepare and send your résumé to another company. The following guidelines will help you use e-mail wisely:

- When you are replying to an e-mail that has been sent to several people (the term *cc* means "carbon copy," a mid-twentieth-century form of duplicating documents), determine whether your response needs to go to all of the original recipients or just to the original sender. Avoid cluttering other people's in boxes.

- When responding to an e-mail, either begin an entirely new e-mail or delete most of the original message. Avoid long e-mails with strings of *Re:Re:Re:* in the "subject" box; these become increasingly cumbersome as they pass from one sender to the next.

- File your e-mail as carefully as you would paper documents. Create separate folders in your e-mail program for each client, project, or coworker. One tremendous advantage of e-mail is that these electronic "paper trails" of correspondence can be easily searched, organized, and accessed.

- Recognize that corporations and organizations have a legal right to trace all Internet activity on any computer they own. While it may be acceptable for you to browse news and shopping sites during your breaks and lunchtime, do not visit any sites while in the workplace that would embarrass you if a colleague or your supervisor suddenly looked over your shoulder.

should buy or use it. Like the reviews and critiques that college writers compose, workplace evaluations are supposed to be reasonable as well as convincing. It is important to be fair, so you should always support your account of both strengths and weaknesses with specific illustrations or examples.

- **Presentations:** In many professions, information is presented in ways both formal and informal to groups of people. You might suddenly be asked to offer an opinion in a group meeting; or you

TEXTCONNEX

Writing Connections

- *Job Central* <http://jobstar.org/tools/resume/samples.cfm>: This site provides samples of resumes for many different situations, as well as sample cover letters.
- *Career Collection: Write a Résumé* <http://college.library.wisc.edu/collections/career/careerresume.html>: This site provides help with preparing cover letters and writing resumes.

might be given a week to prepare a formal presentation, with visuals, on an ongoing project. (*For more information on oral presentations, see Tab 3: Common Assignments, pp. 158–63. To learn more about PowerPoint and other presentation tools, see pp. 168–71.*)

17f Write to express your views as a consumer.

Your ability to write can influence how you are treated as a client or a customer by large and seemingly faceless organizations.

1. Writing a letter of complaint

Suppose that the customer service representatives for an airline have bumped you from a flight without offering you any consideration or compensation, leaving you angry and frustrated. You want action. Compose yourself, and then compose a letter of complaint like the one on pages 202–3. Your task is to present yourself as a polite and reasonable person who has experienced rude and unfair treatment by representatives of the company. If you are writing a letter of complaint on behalf of your company or as a representative of your company (if, for example, you were the travel agent for the person who was treated rudely by the airline), you will also want to compose a letter that states the complaint clearly but calmly and that proposes a resolution.

Here are some guidelines for writing a letter of complaint:

- Address the letter to the person in charge by name. (If you do not know the correct name and title to use, call the corporate headquarters.)
- Use the format for a business letter. (*See the example on pp. 202–3.*)

↑ 1"
↓

Return address
and date.

10653 North 53rd Drive
Glendale, AZ 85308-9100
August 12, 2005

Double space.

Inside address.

Mr. Thomas Stern
Chief Executive Officer
Europe Atlantic Airways
PO Box 43
London, England

Double space.

Salutation.

Dear Mr. Stern:

Double space.

Because Europe Atlantic Airways (EA) strives to provide the best
international service possible, my fiancée and I chose to fly EA on
our recent trip to Berlin. The service for most of the trip was
excellent, but unfortunately, on the final leg of our journey, EA failed
to transfer our luggage, leaving us stranded without our clothing for
several days. When we finally did receive our luggage, it was damaged
and items were missing. I am writing to request compensation for
the expenses we incurred because of this problem.

1"
←→

Service was excellent on our flights from Phoenix to Berlin. On
Wednesday, August 2, we flew EA 642 from Berlin to London and
EA 2146 from London to Phoenix. The crew of flight 2146 from
London to Phoenix, in particular, was exceptional.

Body—
paragraphs
single spaced,
double spaced
between
paragraphs.

After arriving in Phoenix, we were told that our luggage had not
been transferred from Heathrow Airport to flight 2146 at Gatwick
Airport. When we requested that our luggage be sent to Denver
once it arrived in Phoenix, EA representative Jane Franklin
informed us, rather impolitely, that EA would not transfer our
luggage because we were flying on a different carrier from
Phoenix to Denver. Upon arrival in Denver, we had to purchase
items (clothing and toiletries) necessary for the two-day stay.
Enclosed are receipts for the purchases we made, which total
$377.45.

Upon our return to Phoenix from Denver, we retrieved our luggage
and found that (1) one side of the large suitcase was ripped, (2)
our large duffle bag was missing, and (3) clothing and purchases

↑ 1"
↓

Mr. Thomas Stern
Page 2
August 12, 2005

↑ 2 to 5 spaces
↓ depending on
the length of
the second
page.

we had made in Berlin were missing. While the sentimental value
of these items cannot be quantified, I have enclosed receipts
showing the replacement cost for the duffle bag: $125.

I suggest EA reimburse us $502.45 (please see enclosures). Your
doing so would go a long way toward restoring our confidence
in EA. Review of this matter would be greatly appreciated.

I look forward to hearing from you.

Sincerely, ————————————————————————— Close.

Jonathan Corrigan ⎤

———————————— Signature.

Jonathan Corrigan ⎦

Name of
person to
cc: Ms. Jane Franklin ——————————— whom copy
will be sent.

- In the first paragraph, concisely state the problem and the
  action you request.
- In the following paragraphs, narrate clearly and objectively
  what happened, referring to details such as the date and
  time of the incident so that the person you are writing to can
  follow up.
- Recognize those who tried to help you as well as those who
  did not.

- Mention previous positive experiences with the organization, if you can. Your protest will have more credibility if you come across as a person who does not usually complain but is forced to do so in this instance.

- Increase your credibility by proposing reasonable recompense and enclosing receipts, if appropriate. Keep the original receipts and documentation, enclosing photocopies with your letter.

- Conclude by thanking the person you are writing to for his or her time and expressing the hope that you will be able to continue as a customer.

- Send copies to the people whom you mention.

- Keep copies of all correspondence for your records.

Consider, for example, the letter on pages 202–3 by Jonathan Corrigan. Notice how Corrigan's letter adheres to the guidelines just presented.

2. Writing a letter of praise

On the other hand, suppose that an airline employee has been exceptionally helpful to you when you missed a connecting flight, and you are grateful. Express your gratitude by writing a letter of praise. Like letters of complaint, letters of praise are intended to shape future action. In the workplace, you might write a letter of praise to a colleague who worked long hours to complete a project, or to congratulate a team for bringing in new clients. The writing techniques are very similar. Always send copies of such letters to your colleague's supervisor.

Here are some guidelines for writing a letter of praise:

- Address the letter to the person in charge by name. (If you do not know the correct name and title to use, call the corporate headquarters.)

- Use the format for a business letter.

- In the first paragraph, concisely state the situation and the help that was provided.

- In the following paragraphs, narrate what happened, referring to details such as the date and time of the incident so that the person you are writing to can follow up with the person who helped you.

- Conclude by thanking the person you are writing to for his or her time and expressing your intention to continue doing business with the company.

- Send copies to the people whom you mention.

Interplanetary probes help astronomers research the far reaches of the solar system. Voyager 2 sent this image of Saturn's rings to Earth.

For all knowledge and wonder (which is the seed of knowledge) is an impression of pleasure in itself.

—FRANCIS BACON

Researching

5 | Researching

18 Understanding Research

You do research all the time. For example, when you shop for a car, you talk with friends about their cars, read *Consumer's Digest,* interview car dealers, and take a number of test drives. When your doctor says that you have a particular medical condition, you find out as much as possible about the condition and the conventional and latest treatments for it.

Your campus or neighborhood library provides valuable resources for almost any kind of research. These libraries offer not just books, magazines, and journals but also specialized online databases and the expert guidance of research librarians.

Doing research in the twenty-first century, however, is hardly limited to the library. The Internet now provides rapid, direct access to an abundance of information unimaginable to earlier generations of students. The results of Internet searches, however, can sometimes provide an overwhelming flood of sources, many of them of questionable legitimacy.

The goal of the research section of this book (*Chapters 18–25*) is to help you learn to navigate today's research landscape skillfully, manage the information you discover within it, and use that information to write research papers.

18a Understand the purpose of primary and secondary research.

Academic inquiry calls for both primary and secondary research. **Primary research** means working in a laboratory, in the field, or with an archive of raw data, original documents, and authentic artifacts to make firsthand discoveries. **Secondary research** means looking to see what other people have learned and written about a field or topic.

Knowing how to identify facts, interpretations, and evaluations is key to good secondary research:

- **Facts** are objective. Like your body weight, facts can be measured, observed, or independently verified in some way.

- **Interpretations** spell out the implications of facts. Are you as thin as you are because of your genes or because you exercise every day? The answer to this question is an interpretation.

▪ **Evaluations** are debatable judgments about a set of facts or a situation. The assertion that "one can never be too rich or too thin" is an evaluation.

Once you are up-to-date on the facts, interpretations, and evaluations in a particular area, you will be able to design a research project that adds your *perspective* on the sources you found and read:

▪ Given all that you have learned about the topic, what strikes you as important or interesting?

▪ What patterns do you see, or what connections can you make between one person's work and another's?

▪ Where is the research going, and what problems still need to be explored?

18b Recognize the connection between research and college writing.

In many ways research informs all college writing. To write a personal essay, you have to search through your memory, reflect on past events, and select a person, event, or other topic to write about. When you write essay exams, you rely on what you have read in textbooks and learned from lectures.

But some assignments require more rigorous and systematic research than others. **Research project** assignments offer you a chance to find and read both classic and current material on a specific issue.

CHARTING the TERRITORY

Classic and Current Sources

Classic sources are well known and respected older works that made such an important contribution to a discipline or a particular area of research that contemporary researchers use them as touchstones for further research in that area. In many fields, sources published within the past five years are considered current.

A paper based on research is not just a step-by-step account of your "search and find" mission. Nor is it a string of quotations from other writers or a set of summaries based on your sources. A research paper constitutes your contribution to the ongoing academic conversation about a specific issue.

When you are assigned to write a research paper for any of your college courses, the project may seem overwhelming at first. If you break it down into phases, however, and allow enough time for each phase, you should be able to manage your work and write a paper that will become your contribution to the academic conversation.

18c Choose an interesting research question for critical inquiry.

Approach your assignment in a spirit of critical inquiry. "Critical" in this sense does not mean "fault finding," "skeptical," "cynical," or even "urgent." Rather, it refers to a receptive, but reasonable and discerning, frame of mind. Choosing an interesting topic will help you make the results of your inquiry meaningful—to yourself and your readers.

1. Choosing a question with personal significance

Even though you are writing for an academic assignment, you can still get personally involved in your work. Begin with the wording of the assignment, analyzing the project's required scope, purpose, and audience (*see Tab 2: Writing and Designing Papers, pp. 37–40*). Then browse through the course texts and your class notes, looking for a match between your interests and topics, issues, or problems in the subject area.

CHARTING the TERRITORY

Typical Lines of Inquiry in Different Disciplines

Research topics and questions differ from one discipline to another, as the following examples show:

- **History:** How did India's experience of British imperialism affect its response to globalization?
- **Marketing:** How do corporations develop strategies for marketing their products to an international consumer audience?
- **Political science:** Why did many nations of Europe agree to unite, creating a common currency and an essentially "borderless" state of Europe (the European Union, or EU)?
- **Anthropology:** What is the impact of globalization on the world's indigenous cultures?

For example, suppose you are assigned to write a report on a country's global economic prospects. If you have visited Mexico, you might find it interesting to explore that country's prospects.

www.mhhe.com/
awr
For more on
narrowing your
topic, go to

Writing >
Paragraph/Essay
Development >
Thesis/Central
Idea

2. Making your question specific

The more specific your question, the more your research will have direction and focus. To make a question more specific, use the "five w's and an h" strategy by asking about the *who, what, why, when, where,* and *how* of a topic (*see Tab 2: Writing and Designing Papers, pp. 42–43*).

After you have compiled a list of possible research questions, look through the list and choose one that is relatively specific or rewrite a broad one to make it more specific and therefore answerable. For example, as Audrey Galeano worked to develop a topic for a research paper on the impact of globalization for an anthropology course, she rewrote the following broad question to make it answerable:

TOO BROAD	How has globalization affected the Amazon River Basin?
ANSWERABLE	How has large-scale agriculture in the Amazon Basin affected the region's indigenous peoples?

(*Galeano's finished paper appears in Chapter 34, pp. 358–67.*)

3. Finding a challenging question

To be interesting, a research question must be challenging. If it can be answered with a yes or no, a dictionary-like definition, or a textbook presentation of information, you should choose another question or rework it to make it more challenging.

NOT CHALLENGING	Has economic globalization contributed to the destruction of the Amazon rain forest?
CHALLENGING	How can agricultural interests and indigenous peoples in the Amazon region work together to preserve the environment while creating a sustainable economy?

4. Speculating about answers

Sometimes it can be useful to speculate on the answer to your research question so that you have a **hypothesis** to work with during the research process. Don't forget, though, that a hypothesis is a tentative answer that must be tested and revised based on the evidence you turn up in your research. Be aware of the assumptions embedded in your hypothesis or research question. Consider, for example, the following:

HYPOTHESIS   The global demand for agricultural products will destroy the Amazon rain forest.

This hypothesis assumes that destructive farming practices in the Amazon region are the only possible response to global demand. But assumptions are always open to question. Researchers must be willing to adjust their ideas as they learn more about a topic.

18d Make sure you understand the research assignment.

Once you have chosen a topic and framed a tentative research question, spend some time considering your audience and your purpose. Although your audience will most likely include only your instructor and perhaps your classmates, thinking critically about their needs and expectations will help you to plan a research strategy and create a schedule for writing your paper.

Consider the following questions about your audience:

- What do they already know about your topic? How much background information and context will you need to provide? (Your research should include **facts.**)

- Is your topic controversial or challenging? How should you accommodate and acknowledge different perspectives and viewpoints? (Your research should include **interpretations,** and you will need to be careful to balance interpretations that might be opposed to each other.)

- Will you expect the audience to take action based on the results of your research? (Your research should include **evaluations,** carefully supported by facts and interpretations, that demonstrate clearly why readers should adopt a course of action or point of view.)

Your purpose for writing a research paper depends on both the specifics of the assignment as set by your instructor and your own engagement with, and interest in, your topic. Your purpose might be *informative*—to educate your audience about an unfamiliar subject or point of view (*see Chapter 9: Informative Reports, p. 111*). Your purpose might be *interpretive*—to reveal the meaning or significance of a work of art, a historical document, a literary work, or a scientific study (*see Chapter 10: Interpretive Analyses and Writing about Literature, p. 121*). Your purpose might be *persuasive*—to convince your audience, with logic and evidence, to accept your point of view on a controversial issue or to act on the information in your paper (*see Chapter 11: Arguments,*

Tips

LEARNING in COLLEGE

Scheduling Your Research Project

Task	Date
Phase I: Five days	
▪ Complete general plan for research.	_____
▪ Decide on topic and research question.	_____
▪ Consult reference works and reference librarians.	_____
▪ Make a list of relevant keywords for online searching (*see Chapter 19, p. 216*).	_____
▪ Compile **working bibliography** (*see Chapter 23, p. 253*).	_____
▪ Sample some items in bibliography	_____
▪ Make arrangements for primary research (if necessary).	_____
Phase II: Twelve days	
▪ Locate, read, and evaluate selected sources.	_____
▪ Take notes.	_____
▪ Cross-check notes with working bibliography.	_____
▪ Conduct primary research (if necessary).	_____
▪ Confer with instructor or Writing Center (optional).	_____
▪ Outline or plan organization of paper.	_____
Phase III: Ten days	
▪ Write first draft, deciding which primary and secondary source materials to include.	_____
▪ Have peer review (optional).	_____
▪ Revise draft.	_____
▪ Confer with instructor or Writing Center (optional).	_____
▪ Do final revision and editing.	_____
▪ Create Works Cited or References page.	_____
Due date	_____

p. 130). Review your original assignment for keywords that signal its purpose. Note, however, that some terms can signal more than one type of assignment, depending on the context. Here are some examples:

- **Informative:** Explain, describe, define, review
- **Interpretive:** Analyze, compare, explain, interpret
- **Persuasive:** Assess, justify, defend, refute, determine

18e   Create a research plan.

Your research will be more productive if you create a general plan and a detailed schedule immediately after you receive your assignment. A general plan ensures that you understand the full scope of your assignment. A detailed schedule helps you set priorities and meet your deadlines. Use the box on page 212, which outlines the steps in a research project, as a starting point, adjusting the time allotments based on the amount of time you have to complete the assignment.

19 Finding and Managing Print and Online Sources

Your research will take place both in the library and on the Internet. The amount of information available in these places is vast, so a search for useful sources entails three activities:

- Collecting keywords from reference works
- Using library databases
- Finding material in the library and on the Web

www.mhhe.com/
awr
For more information
and links, go to
Research > Using
the Library

19a Use the library in person and online.

Your college librarians are your consultants. They know what is available at your library and how to get material on loan from other libraries. They can also show you how to access the library's computerized book catalog, periodical databases, and electronic resources or how to use the Internet to find information relevant to your project. Most college libraries list their holdings online. Your library's Web site may also have links to important reference works available on the Internet, as shown in Figure 19.1.

In addition, **help sheets** can be found at most college libraries. These documents provide information about the location of both general and discipline-specific periodicals and noncirculating reference books, along with information about special databases, indexes, and sources of information on the Internet. You may be able to access your library's help sheets online from the library's Web site or its online catalog.

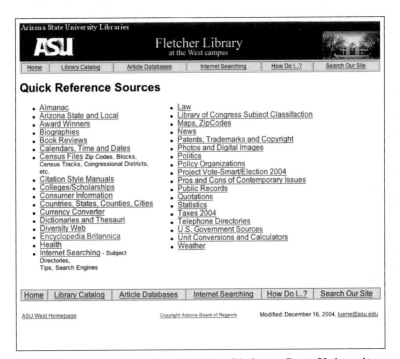

FIGURE 19.1 A page from the Web site of Arizona State University West. The Web page provides links to a variety of Web-based reference sources.

19b Consult various kinds of sources.

The number and kinds of sources you need to consult will vary from one research project to another. You should always review more than one source, however, and usually more than one kind of source. Chances are, you will consult more sources during your research than you will cite in your final project.

Your assignment may specify how many print and electronic sources you are expected to consult and cite. If you are uncertain, talk to your instructor early in the research process to determine the range of sources you should consult. These are some of the kinds of sources available to you:

- **General reference works**

  Encyclopedias, annuals, almanacs

  Computer databases, bibliographies, abstracts

- **Specialized reference works**

  Discipline-specific encyclopedias, almanacs, and dictionaries

- **Books and electronic texts**

- **Periodical articles**

  In newspapers

  In magazines

  In scholarly and technical journals

  On the World Wide Web

- **Web sites**

- **News groups, ListServs, and e-mail**

- **Virtual communities**

  MUDs (multiuser dimensions)

  MOOs (multiuser dimensions, object oriented)

- **Pamphlets, government documents, census data**

- **Primary sources**

  Original documents like literary works, art objects, performances, manuscripts, letters, and personal journals

  Museum collections; maps; photo, film, sound, and music archives

  Field notes, surveys, interviews

  Results of observation and lab experiments

Tips

LEARNING in COLLEGE

Popular or Scholarly?

The audience and purpose of a source, especially a publication, determines whether it should be considered *scholarly* or *popular.* You may begin your inquiry into a research topic with popular sources, but to become fully informed about your topic, you need to delve into scholarly sources. Some newsstand periodicals (such as the *Atlantic* and *Psychology Today*) include writing and reporting that is comparable to that in academic sources. Other popular sources may be appropriate for the early stages of inquiry but cannot by themselves provide the basis of your research.

Popular sources:

- Are widely available on newsstands and in retail stores
- Accept advertising for a wide range of consumer goods
- Are themselves widely advertised (in the case of books)
- Are printed on magazine paper with a color cover
- Are published by a commercial publishing house or media company (such as Time Warner)
- Include a wide range of topics in each issue, from international affairs to popular entertainment

Scholarly sources:

- Are found generally in libraries, not on newsstands
- Include articles with extensive citations and bibliographies
- Are **refereed,** which means that each article has been reviewed, commented on, and accepted for publication by other scholars in the field
- List article titles and authors on the cover
- Include articles mostly by authors who are affiliated with a college, a museum, or some other scholarly institution
- Are published by a scholarly or nonprofit organization, often in association with a university press
- Focus on discipline-specific topics

19c   Understand keywords and keyword searches.

Most online research—whether in your library's catalog, in a specialized database, or on the World Wide Web—requires an understanding of **keyword searches.** In this context, a **keyword** is a term (or terms) you enter into a **search engine** (searching software) to find sources that have information you need.

A successful keyword search returns a manageable number of relevant sources. For your search to be successful, your keyword should be a term that occurs in the sources you need but not in an even greater number of sources that you don't need. If you entered the keyword *Armstrong* in a search engine, for example, you would get information about Louis Armstrong the musician as well as Neil Armstrong the astronaut, Lance Armstrong the cyclist, and many other individuals, companies, or institutions with "Armstrong" as part of their names.

To hone in on your subject, you will often need to refine your initial search term. The "Tips" box below describes a variety of techniques for doing so that work in most search engines. Many search engines also have an advanced search feature that can help with the refining process.

Tips   LEARNING in COLLEGE

Refining Keyword Searches

Although search engines vary, the following guidelines should work for many of the search engines you will use:

- **Group words together.** Put quotation marks or parentheses around the phrase you are looking for. For example, "Dixieland Jazz" tells the search engine to find only sites with those two words in sequence.
- **Use Boolean operators.**

  AND (+)   Use AND or + when you need sites with both of two or more words: Armstrong + Glaser.

  OR   Use OR when you want sites with either of two or more terms: jazz OR "musical improvisation".

  NOT   Use NOT in front of words that you do not want to appear together in your results: Armstrong NOT Neil.

- **Use truncation or a "wildcard."** To find sites that include all the variations on a word with a single root word, combine part of a keyword with an asterisk (*) used as a wildcard: music* (for "music," "musician," "musical," and so forth).
- **Search the fields.** Some search engines permit you to search within fields, such as the title field of Web pages or the author field of a library catalog. Thus TITLE + "Louis Armstrong" will give you all pages that have "Louis Armstrong" in their title.

www.mhhe.com/
awr
For disciplinary
resources to begin
your search, go to

Research >
Discipline
Specific
Resources

19d Use printed and online reference works for general information.

Reference works provide an overview of a subject area. The information contained in general encyclopedias like *Encyclopedia Britannica* and *Encyclopedia Americana* is less authoritative than the specialized knowledge found in discipline-specific encyclopedias, academic journals, and scholarly books. There is nothing wrong with starting your research by consulting a general encyclopedia, but for college research, you need to explore your topic in more scholarly sources. Often, the list of references at the end of an encyclopedia article can lead you to useful sources on your topic.

Reference books do not circulate, so plan to take notes or make photocopies of the pages you may need to consult later. Many college libraries subscribe to services that provide access to online encyclopedias. Check your college library's home page for appropriate links.

Here is a list of some other kinds of reference materials available in print, on the Internet, or both:

ALMANACS   *Almanac of American Politics*
                 Information Please Almanac
                 World Almanac

BIBLIOGRAPHIES *Bibliographic Index*
                 Bibliography of Asian Studies
                 MLA International Bibliography

BIOGRAPHIES   *African American Biographical Database*
                 American Men and Women of Science
                 Dictionary of American Biography
                 Dictionary of Literary Biography:
                    Chicano Writers
                 Dictionary of National Biography
                 Webster's New Biographical Dictionary
                 Who's Who

DICTIONARIES *American Heritage Dictionary of the*
                    English Language
                 Concise Oxford Dictionary of Literary Terms
                 Dictionary of American History
                 Dictionary of Philosophy
                 Dictionary of the Social Sciences
                 Oxford English Dictionary (OED)

For MULTILINGUAL STUDENTS

Researching a Full Range of Sources

Your mastery of a language other than English can sometimes give you access to important sources that would be beyond the reach of your monolingual classmates. You should not limit yourself to sources in your first language, however. Even if you find researching in English challenging, it is important to broaden the scope of your search as soon as you can to include a range of print and Internet resources written in English.

19e Use print indexes and online databases to find articles in journals and other periodicals.

www.mhhe.com/
awr
For access to an online database through *Catalyst,* go to
Research >
Factiva™
PowerSearch

1. Periodicals

Newspapers, magazines, and scholarly journals that are published at regular intervals—be it daily, weekly, monthly, or quarterly—are classified as **periodicals.** The articles in scholarly and technical journals, written by experts and based on up-to-date research, are generally more reliable than articles in popular newspapers and magazines. Although newspapers and magazines can provide useful background information, the journalists who write for them are often not specialists in the field they are writing about, and they sometimes oversimplify complex issues. If you do not know which periodicals are considered important in a discipline, ask your instructor or librarian.

2. Indexes and databases

Articles published in periodicals are cataloged in general and specialized **indexes.** Indexes are available on subscription-only **databases** and as print volumes. If you are searching for articles that are more than twenty years old, you should use print indexes, which can be found in the reference section of your library. Print indexes can be searched by author, subject, or title. Electronic databases can also be searched by date and keyword and will provide you with a list of articles that meet your search criteria. Each entry in the list will include the information you need to find and cite the article. Depending on the database and the agreement it has with the publications it lists, you may also be able to see an abstract of each article, or even its full text.

The "Tips" box on page 221 lists common formats for database information. The "TextConnex" box on pages 222–23 lists some of the major online databases, and the screen shots in Figure 19.2 on page 220 illustrate a search on one of them, ProQuest. Keep in mind that not all libraries subscribe to all databases.

A. Multiple databases will be searched for articles that mention both Armstrong and Glaser.

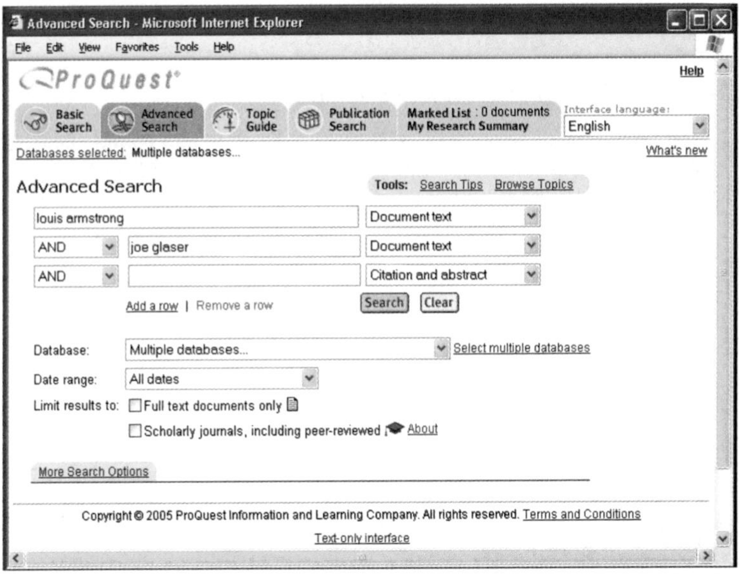

B. Entries include title, author, name of journal, viewing options (e.g., abstract).

FIGURE 19.2 ProQuest's Advance Search page (A) and partial results of search (B).

Tips LEARNING in COLLEGE

Formats for Database Information

When searching a database, you will encounter both abstracts and full articles, and full-text articles may be available in either .pdf or .html format.

- **Abstract:** An abstract is a brief summary of a full-text article. Abstracts appear at the beginning of articles in some scholarly journals and are used in databases to summarize complete articles.

- **Full text:** When an article is listed as "full text," the database provides you with a link to the complete text. Full-text articles accessed through databases do not always include accompanying photographs or other illustrations, however.

- **PDF** and **HTML:** Articles in databases and other online sources may be in either .pdf or .html format (or both). Documents in .html (hypertext markup language) have been formatted to read as Web pages. Documents in .pdf (portable document format) appear as a facsimile of the original pages. To read a .pdf document, you need to have a program like *Adobe Acrobat Reader* installed on your computer.

19f Use search engines and subject directories to find Internet sources.

www.mhhe.com/ awr
For more information and links, go to

Research > Using the Internet

Searches of subscription-only databases available through your library will link you to reliable sources of published information. They usually will not link you to other Web sites, however. To find information that has been published in Web pages, you will need to use an Internet search engine. Because each search engine searches the Web in its own way, you will probably use more than one. (*See the box on p. 226 for a list of popular Internet search engines.*)

Each search engine's home page provides a link to advice on how to use the search engine efficiently and refine a search. Click on the link labeled "search help," "about us," or something similar to learn how that search engine can best serve your needs.

Some Internet search engines provide for specialized searches—for images, for example (*see Chapter 20*). Google offers a service called "Google Scholar" that locates only scholarly sources in response to a

TEXTCONNEX

Some Online Databases

- **ABC-CLIO:** This service offers access to two history-related databases: *America: History and Life,* covering the United States and Canada from prehistory to the present, and *Historical Abstracts,* providing similar resources relating to the history of the world (excluding the United States and Canada) from 1450 to the present.

- **EBSCOhost:** The Academic Search Premier service provides full-text coverage for more than 8,000 scholarly publications and indexes articles in all academic subject areas.

- **ERIC:** This database lists publications in the area of education. It provides information on 1.1 million articles back to 1966 and access to 107,000 full-text documents.

- **Factiva:** This database offers access to the Dow Jones and Reuters news agencies, including newspapers, magazines, journals, newsletters, and Web sites.

- **General Science Index:** This index is general and therefore most appropriate for beginning science students. It lists articles by biologists, chemists, and other scientists.

- **GDCS:** Updated monthly, the Government Documents Catalog Service (GDCS) contains records of all publications printed by the United States Government Printing Office since 1976.

- **GPO Access:** This service of the U.S. Government Printing Office provides free electronic access to government documents.

- **Humanities Index:** This index lists articles from journals in language and literature, history, philosophy, and similar areas.

- **InfoTrac Web:** This Web-based service searches bibliographic and other databases such as the *General Reference Center Gold, General Business File ASAP,* and *Health Reference Center.*

- **JSTOR:** This archive provides full-text access to journals in the humanities, social sciences, and natural sciences.

- **LexisNexis Academic:** Updated daily, this online service provides full-text access to around 6,000 newspapers, professional publications, legal references, and congressional sources.

www.mhhe.com/awr
To conduct a search using the Factiva database, go to
Research > Factiva™ PowerSearch

search term. Many of the links, however, are to online journals that charge a fee for access to full-text articles.

Many Internet search engines also include sponsored links—links that a commercial enterprise has paid to have appear in response to specific search terms. These are usually clearly identified.

Internet keyword searches need to be carefully worded to provide

- *MLA Bibliography:* Covering 1963 to the present, the *MLA Bibliography* indexes more than 4,000 journals, dissertations, and serials published worldwide in the fields of modern languages, literature, literary criticism, linguistics, and folklore. Coverage includes all modern national literatures.
- *New York Times Index:* This index lists major articles published by the *Times* since 1913.
- *Newspaper Abstracts:* This database provides an index to 50 national and regional newspapers.
- *PAIS International:* Produced by the Public Affairs Information Service, this database indexes literature on public policy, social policy, and the social sciences from 1972 to the present.
- *Periodical Abstracts:* This database indexes more than 2,000 general and academic journals covering business, current affairs, economics, literature, religion, psychology, and women's studies from 1987 to the present.
- *ProQuest:* This database provides access to dissertations; newspapers and journals including many full-text articles back to 1996; information on sources in business, general reference, the social sciences, and humanities back to 1986; and historical sources dating back to the nineteenth century.
- *PsycInfo:* Sponsored by the American Psychological Association (APA), this database indexes and abstracts books, scholarly articles, technical reports, and dissertations in psychology and related disciplines.
- *PubMed:* The National Library of Medicine publishes this database, which indexes and abstracts 15 million journal articles in biomedicine and provides links to related databases.
- *Sociological Abstracts:* For researchers in sociology and related disciplines, this database indexes and abstracts articles from more than 2,600 journals, as well as books, conference papers, and dissertations.
- *Social Science Index:* This index lists articles from such fields as economics, psychology, political science, and sociology.
- *WorldCat:* This is a catalog of books and other resources available in libraries worldwide.

relevant results. For example, a search of Google using the keywords *louis armstrong* yields a list of more than 3.8 *million* Web sites, as shown in Figure 19.3 on page 224, a staggering number of links, or **hits.**

Refining the search by putting quotes around *louis armstrong* and linking that term to the term *jazz* with the Boolean operator AND (which will find all sites with the words *louis* and *armstrong*

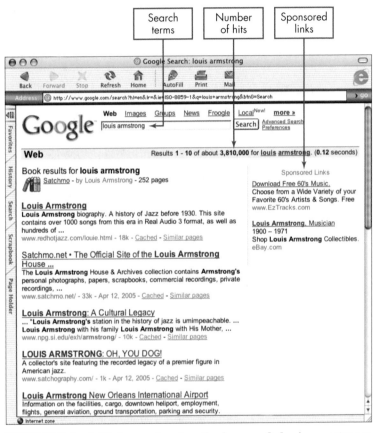

FIGURE 19.3 An initial search using the keywords louis armstrong.
This search yields more than 3.8 million hits.

together and also the word *jazz*) reduces the number of hits to a still unmanageable 942,000. Altering the keywords to make them even more specific narrows the results significantly, as shown in Figure 19.4.

In addition to keyword searches, many Internet search engines offer a **subject directory**—a listing of broad categories. Clicking on a category brings you to a more specific array of choices. Clicking through this hierarchy of choices eventually brings you to a list of sites related to a specific topic.

Just as with online databases and print indexes, some Web sites provide content-specific subject directories designed for research in a particular field. These sites are often reviewed or screened and are excellent starting points for academic research.

www.mhhe.com/
awr
For a variety of
search engines, go to

Research >
Additional Links
on Research

Number
of hits

Further
refined search

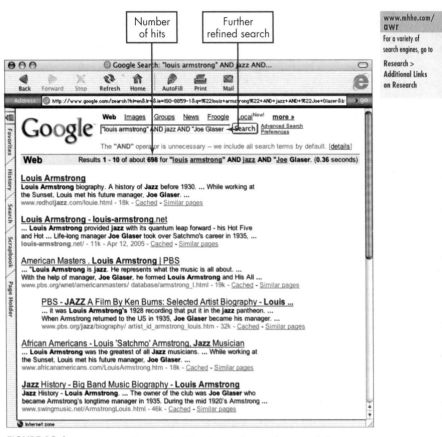

FIGURE 19.4 A narrowed search. Further refining the search by
adding Joe Glaser (Armstrong's long-time manager) reduces the number
of hits to an almost manageable 698. (Note that AND could have been
omitted in this search—with no effect on the results—because Google
treats terms by default as if they were joined by AND.)

19g Use your library's online catalog or card catalog to find books.

Books in most libraries are shelved by **call numbers** based on the Library of Congress classification system. In this system, books on the
same topic have similar call numbers and are shelved together. Some
libraries use the Dewey decimal system of call numbering, which classifies knowledge in divisions of 10 from 000 to 990. Whichever system

TEXTCONNEX

Popular Internet Search Engines

General search engines: These sites allow for both category and keyword searches.

- *AltaVista* <http://www.altavista.com>
- *Google* <http://www.google.com>
- *HotBot* <http://www.hotbot.com>
- *Vivisimo* <http://vivisimo.com>
- *WebCrawler* <http://www.webcrawler.com>
- *Yahoo!* <http://www.yahoo.com>

Meta search engines: These sites search several different search engines at once.

- *Dogpile* <http://www.dogpile.com>
- *Internet Public Library* <http://www.ipl.org>
- *Ixquick* <http://www.ixquick.com>
- *Librarian's Index to the Internet* <http://lii.org>
- *Library of Congress* <http://loc.gov>
- *MetaCrawler* <http://www.metacrawler.com>

Mediated search engines: These sites have been assembled and reviewed by people who sometimes provide annotations and commentary about topic areas and specific sites.

- *About.com* <http://www.about.com>
- *Looksmart* <http://search.looksmart.com>

your library uses, you will need the call number to locate the actual book on the library's shelves. Therefore, when consulting an online library catalog, be sure to jot down (or print out) the call numbers of books you want to consult.

You can conduct a keyword search of most online library catalogs by author, by title, or by subject. For example, a search of the term *Louis Armstrong* by author would produce a list of works by Louis Armstrong; a search by title would produce a list of works with "Louis Armstrong" in the title; and a search by subject would produce a list of works that are all or partly about Louis Armstrong. The *Library of Congress Subject Heading (LCSH)* shows you how your research topic is classified and provides you with a set of key terms that you can use in your search.

TEXTCONNEX

Starting Points for Research in the Disciplines

General academic research

- *The WWW Virtual Library* <http://vlib.org/>

Humanities

- *Artcyclopedia* <http://artcyclopedia.com/>
- *Arts and Letters Daily* <http://www.aldaily.com>
- *Project Gutenberg* <http://www.promo.net/pg/>
- *Voice of the Shuttle* <http://vos.ucsb.edu/>

Social sciences

- *New York Times* "Politics Navigator"
  <http://www.nytimes.com/ref/politics/POLI_NAVI.html>
- *Social Science Information Gateway*
  <http://sosig.esrc.bris.ac.uk/>

Current events

- *NewsLink* <http://newslink.org/menu.html>

Science and health

- *HealthWeb* <http://healthweb.org/>
- *Scirus* <http://www.scirus.com/srsapp/>
- *Virtual Library: Science* <http://vlib.org/Science.html>

The results of a keyword search of a library's online catalog will provide a list composed mostly of books. In the examples in Figures 19.5 and 19.6 of a search of the City University of New York library's online catalog (*pp. 228 and 229*), notice that under the column "Format" other kinds of media that match a keyword subject search are also listed; you can alter the terms of a search to restrict the formats to a specific medium.

As with any keyword search, whether you get what you really need—a manageable number of relevant sources—depends on your choice of keywords. If your search terms are too broad, you will get too many hits; if they are too narrow, you will get few or none.

Figures 19.5 and 19.6 show the results of experimenting with different keywords on the topic of jazz in general and Louis Armstrong in particular. The first, a subject search using only the keyword *jazz,* resulted in too many hits to be practical. The second, a subject search using the key term *louis armstrong,* produced a workable number.

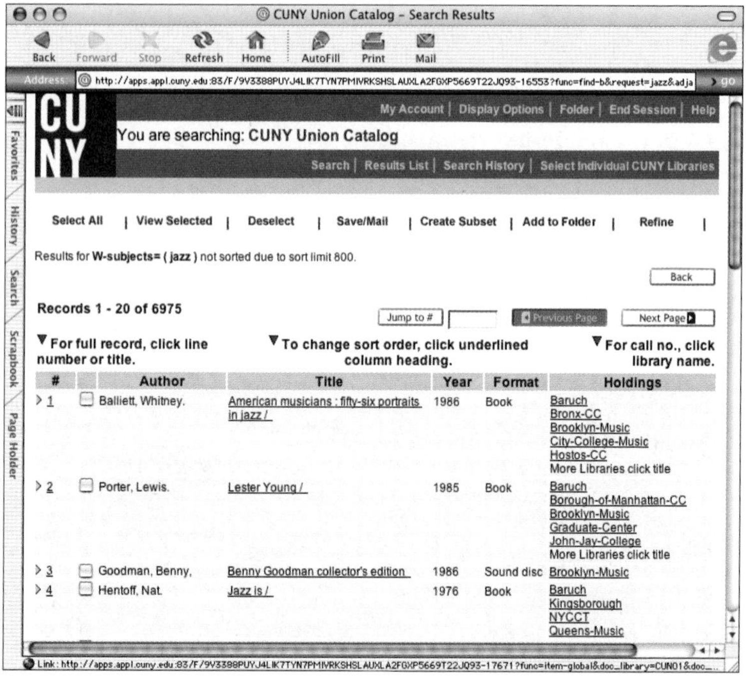

FIGURE 19.5 Initial search using the keyword *jazz*. Using the word *jazz* as a keyword in a subject search produces an unmanageable 6,975 sources. The "Holdings" column indicates which libraries in the CUNY system have the book. Clicking on a library name gives the book's call number at that library.

19h Take advantage of printed and online government documents.

The U.S. government publishes an enormous amount of information and research every year, most of which is available online. At your library's reference desk, ask for the *Monthly Catalog of U.S. Government Publications* and the *U.S. Government Periodicals Index* (both of which are available as online databases). The Government Printing Office's own Web site, *GPO Access* <http://www.gpoaccess.gov/>, is an excellent resource for identifying federal government publications and where to find them. Other online government resources include the following:

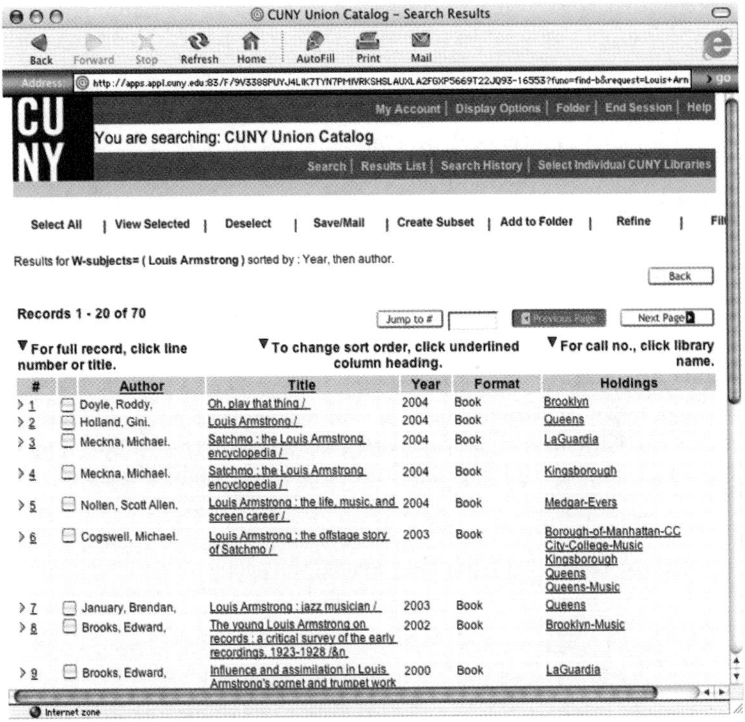

FIGURE 19.6 Second search with a narrower keyword. A keyword search using the term *Louis Armstrong* produces 70 results, a manageable number.

- *FedWorld Information Network* (maintained by the National Technical Information Service) <http://www.fedworld.gov/>
- *FirstGov* (the U.S. government's "Official Web Portal") <http://firstgov.gov/>
- *The National Institutes of Health* <http://www.nih.gov>
- *U.S. Census Bureau* <http://www.census.gov>

19i   Explore online communication.

In addition to providing information, the Internet provides access to communities with common interests and varying levels of expertise on different subjects. Among the online forums for these communities are discussion lists (electronic mailing lists), Usenet news groups, and

Weblogs (blogs), as well as various forms of synchronous communication in which people interact in real time. Online forums can help you with research in the following ways:

- You can get an idea for a paper by finding out what topics interest and concern people.

- You can learn what people think about almost any topic, from food to pop culture to sports to science.

- You can zero in on a very specific topic, such as a comic book character, a vintage TV show, a singer, or a scientific theory.

- You can query an expert in the field about your topic.

Discussion lists (electronic mailing lists) are networked e-mail conversations on particular topics that may be relevant to your research topic. Lists can be open (anyone can join) or closed (only certain people can join). If the list is open, you can subscribe by sending a message to a computer that has list-processing software installed on it.

> *Caution:* The level of expertise among the people who participate in online forums, and the scholarly seriousness of the forums themselves, varies widely.

Usenet news groups may exist on topics relevant to your research. Unlike lists, however, news groups are posted to a **news server**—a computer that hosts the news group and distributes postings to participating servers. You must subscribe to read postings, and they are not automatically distributed by e-mail.

Interactively structured Web sites provide another medium for online communication. **Blogs,** for example (*see Chapter 14*), can be designed to allow readers to post their own comments and queries. **Wikis,** sites designed for online collaboration, go further, allowing people both to comment on and modify one another's contributions.

Chat rooms are one form of **synchronous communication,** which involves various types of real-time electronic exchanges between individuals. In these sites on the Internet, people can carry on real-time discussions. Chat rooms are usually organized by topic, so the people who use a room are likely to share an interest in its topic. **Instant messaging (IM)** is another medium for real-time communication, but it involves only people who have agreed to form a group. Other, less common formats for synchronous communication include multiuser dimensions and object-oriented multiuser dimensions (MUDs and MOOs), both of which are used for role-playing simulations and can be adapted for scholarly interaction.

20 Finding and Creating Effective Visuals

Visuals are often included as support for a writer's thesis, sometimes to enhance an argument and other times to make the writer's own argument. A relief organization, for example, might post a series of compelling visuals on its Web site to persuade potential donors to contribute money following a catastrophic event. In some writing situations, you will be able to prepare or provide your own visuals. You may, for example, create bar graphs from data that you collected. In other situations, however, you may decide to create a visual from data that you found in a source or to search in your library or on the Internet for a visual to use.

www.mhhe.com/ awr
For resources to begin your search, go to

Research >
Discipline Specific
Resources

20a Find quantitative data and display it visually.

Research writing in many disciplines, especially the sciences, social sciences, business, and other technical fields often requires reference to quantitative information, and quantitative information often has more impact when it is displayed visually in a chart, graph, or map. Pie charts, for instance, are used to show percentages of a whole; bar graphs are used to show comparisons of one group to another over time. Line graphs can also show trends over time, such as rates of immigration, to make a point about the effect of events such as wars or economic downturns on population movements. In other words, in addition to documenting patterns and events, these ways of showing information are tools of analysis. (*For examples of graphs and charts, and a discussion of what situations to use them in, see Tab 2: Writing and Designing Papers, pp. 53–57.*)

Caution: Whether you are using data from a source to create an image or incorporating an image created by someone else into your paper, you must give credit to the source of the data or image, just as you do when you paraphrase or quote the work of others. Furthermore, if you plan to publish a visual you selected from another source on a Web site or in another medium, you must obtain permission to use it from the copyright holder. If the copyright holder refuses permission, you must remove the image.

231

www.mhhe.com/
awr
For an interactive
tutorial, go to

Writing >
Visual Rhetoric

1. Finding existing graphs, charts, and maps

As you search for print and online sources for your research project (*see Chapter 19*), take notes on useful graphs, charts, or maps that you can incorporate (with proper acknowledgment) into your paper. Some you may find in online sources. A Google search, for example, turned up a site affiliated with Columbia University that had the map shown in Figure 20.1, which might be useful for a paper on population trends in Africa.

If your source is available in print only, you may be able to use a scanner to capture and digitize it. No matter how you incorporate an existing visual showing data, however, be sure that you do so according to fair-use guidelines (*see Chapter 23*).

2. Creating visuals from quantitative data

Sometimes you may find data presented in writing or in tables that would be more effective as a chart or graph. Using spreadsheet or other software, you can create a visual on your own.

For example, suppose you are writing about population trends in the United States in the nineteenth century and want to illustrate the country's population growth in that period with a line graph, using data from the U.S. Census Bureau, which is in the public domain. Most census data, however, appears in tables like the one shown in Figure 20.2. If you transfer the data you need from a table like this to a spreadsheet program like *Microsoft Excel,* you can use it to create graphs that you can insert into a paper, as in Figure 20.2.

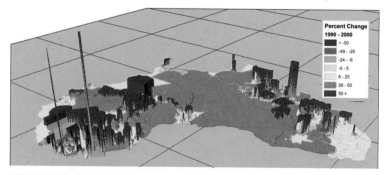

FIGURE 20.1 Africa Population Change, 1990–1995. Both negative and positive change are extruded vertically proportional to percent change.

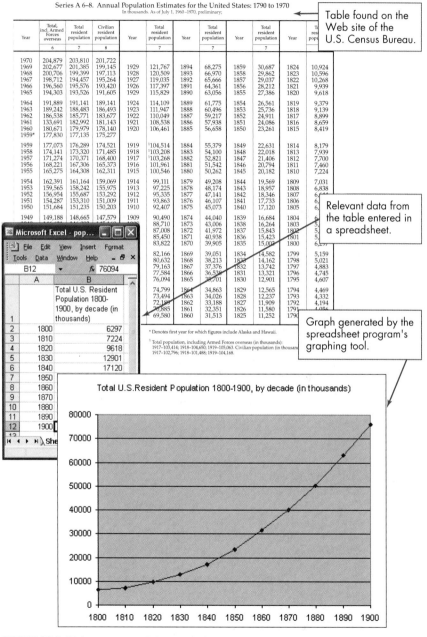

Series A 6–8. Annual Population Estimates for the United States: 1790 to 1970
In thousands. As of July 1, 1960–1970, preliminary;

Table found on the Web site of the U.S. Census Bureau.

Relevant data from the table entered in a spreadsheet.

Graph generated by the spreadsheet program's graphing tool.

FIGURE 20.2 **Using a spreadsheet program to create a graph from data in a table.**

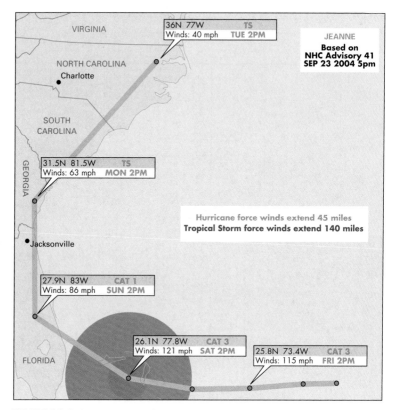

FIGURE 20.3 An accurate display of hurricane data.

3. Displaying the right data

Make sure that you display data in a way that is consistent with your purpose and that what you display does not deceptively leave out information that could undermine your claims. Consider, for example, two maps of the paths of hurricanes in 2004 (Figures 20.3 and 20.4). The first (Figure 20.3) shows the position of Hurricane Jeanne on September 23, 2004, and its predicted path for the next five days and incorporates quantitative data such as the storm's predicted wind speed. The purpose of the map is to help the people in its path understand the risk they face from the storm.

The map in Figure 20.4 is comparative, showing the paths of two hurricanes that were active at the same time. This map does not provide information about the intensity of either storm, making them

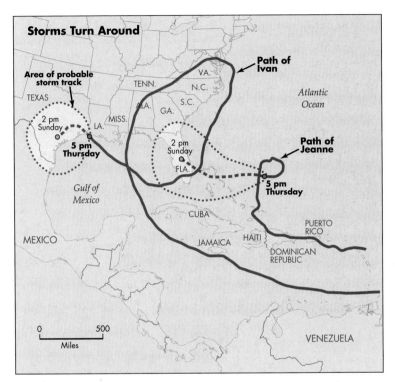

FIGURE 20.4 A display of hurricane data that could be used deceptively.

appear equal. Were the intent to deceive—to support the erroneous claim, say, that coastal Texas suffered as badly from Hurricane Ivan as did coastal Alabama—this seeming equivalence would be a problem. Always consider what a visual leaves out as well as what it displays.

20b Search for appropriate images in online collections, with an Internet search engine, or in books and journals and other print sources.

Photographs, pictures of artwork, drawings, diagrams, and maps can provide visual support for many kinds of papers, particularly in subjects like history, English and other languages, philosophy, music, theater, and other performing arts. As with the display of quantitative

Tips LEARNING in COLLEGE

Deciding When to Use an Image in Your Paper

Regardless of the kind or number of images you use, there are several questions you will want to consider as you look for them:

- How many images do you need?
- Where will each image appear in the text?
- What contribution will each image make to the text?
- What contribution do the images taken as a whole make to the text?
- Does the audience have enough background information to interpret each image in the way you intend?
- If not, is there additional information that should be included in the text or in a caption?
- If no additional information is needed, does the image nonetheless need a caption?
- Have you reviewed your own text (and perhaps asked a friend to review it as well) to see how well the image is "working"—in terms of appropriateness, location, and context?

data, you might *choose* an image from another source, or you might *create* one. If you were doing a report comparing the way different corporations are organized, for example, you might use organizational charts that appear in corporate reports. Alternatively, you might use your word processor's drawing feature to create your own organizational charts based on information you find in the corporate reports.

Similarly, when appropriate, you could use photographs you have taken yourself in your work. For a geology paper, for example, you might use a picture you took of a geological formation.

The following are three sources of images that you can draw on:

www.mhhe.com/
awr

For a wide range of visual and text sources, go to

Research >
Factiva™
PowerSearch

- **Online image collections:** Several libraries and other archives maintain collections of images online. The Library of Congress, for example, is a rich source of images (most in the public domain) relating to American history and culture. The Schomburg Center for Research in Black Culture, part of the New York Public Library, is an excellent source for images and other resources relating to African-American studies. See the "TextConnex" box on page 238 for the URLs of these and other collections.

Tips LEARNING in COLLEGE

Deciding What Kind of Chart or Graph to Use

In deciding the kind of chart or graph you want to use, you will want to consider the following questions:

- What information do you want to show, and why?
- What options do you have for displaying this information?
- How much context do you want to include, and why?
- How many graphs do you think you might need?
- How detailed should your graph be, and why?
- Will your visual be used as a tool of analysis for the future, or will it be used to report on what was?
- What information will be left out or minimized, and how important is that omission?
- What other information—an introduction, an explanation, a summary, an interpretation—will readers need to make sense of the graphed information?

- **Images on the Internet:** Many search engines have the ability to search the Web for images alone. You can conduct an image search on Google, for example, by clicking on the "images" option, entering the key term, and then clicking on "search."

www.mhhe.com/awr
For a selection of search engines, go to
Research > Additional Links on Research

- **Images scanned from a book or journal:** You can use a scanner to scan some images from books and journals into a paper, but as always, only if you are sure your use is within fair-use guidelines. Also, be sure to credit the source of the image as well as the publication in which you found it.

Caution: The results of Internet image searches, like those of any Internet search, need to be carefully evaluated for relevance and reliability. (*See Chapter 21: Evaluating Sources, pp. 241–42.*) Make sure you have proper source information for any images you use that you find in this way.

TEXTCONNEX

Some Online Image Collections

- *Art Institute of Chicago* (selected works from the museum's collection) <http://www.artic.edu/aic/index.html>
- *The Library of Congress* <http://www.loc.gov/>
- *National Archives Digital Classroom* (documents and photographs from American history) <http://www.archives.gov/digital_classroom/index.html>
- *National Aeronautics and Space Administration* (images and multimedia features on space exploration) <http://www.nasa.gov/vision/universe/features/index.html>
- *National Park Service Digital Image Archive* (thousands of public domain photographs of U.S. national parks) <http://photo.itc.nps.gov/storage/images/index.html>
- *New York Public Library* <www.nypl.org/digital/>
- *Schomburg Center for Research in Black Culture* <www.nypl.org/research/sc/sc.html>
- *VRoma: A Virtual Community for Teaching and Learning Classics* (images and other resources related to ancient Rome) <http://www.vroma.org/>

21 Evaluating Sources

New technologies may grant fast access to a tremendous variety of sources, but they cannot by themselves help you decide which of those sources to use for your research. It is up to you to evaluate each potential source to determine whether it is both *relevant* and *reliable*. A source is relevant if it pertains to your research topic. A source is reliable if it provides trustworthy information.

Evaluating sources requires you to think critically and make judgments about which sources will be useful for answering your research question. This process helps you manage your research and focus your time on those sources that deserve close scrutiny.

21a Question print sources.

Just because something is in print does not make it true or relevant. How can you determine if a print source is likely to be both reliable and useful? Here are some questions to ask about any source you are considering:

Reliability

- **What information can you find about the writer's credentials?** Obtain biographical information about the writer by checking the source itself, consulting a biographical dictionary, or conducting an Internet search of the writer's name. Is the writer affiliated with a research institution that contributes knowledge about an issue? Is the writer an expert on the topic? Is the writer cited frequently in other sources about the topic?

- **Who is the publisher?** University presses and academic publishers are considered more scholarly than the popular press because they usually publish only work that is based on research and subjected to rigorous peer review.

- **Does the work include a bibliography of works consulted or cited?** Reliable research is always part of a conversation among specialists. To show familiarity with what other researchers have said about a topic, trustworthy writers cite a variety of sources and document their citations properly. Does this source do so? Does the source include a variety of citations?

TEXTCONNEX

Evaluating Sources

- *Primary or secondary? Popular or scholarly?*
  <http://www.sport.ussa.edu/library/primary.htm>: Discusses the difference between primary and secondary research sources, as well as the difference between popular and scholarly sources.
- *Evaluating sources of information*
  <http://owl.english.purdue.edu/handouts/research/:r_evalsource .html>: From the Purdue Online Writing Lab; provides guidelines for evaluating print and online sources.

- **Is the work balanced in tone, or does the writer appear biased?** What kind of tone does the author use? Is the work objective or subjective? Are the writer's arguments clear and logical? What is the author's point of view? Does he or she present opposing views fairly? (*For more on evaluating arguments, see Tab 2: Writing and Designing Papers, pp. 28–34.*)

Relevance

- **Do the source's title and subtitle indicate that it addresses your specific research question?**

- **What is the publication date?** Is the material up-to-date (published within the past five years)? If you have a reason for working with older sources, is the publication date appropriate for your research?

- **If the source is a book, does the table of contents indicate that it covers useful information?**

- **If the source is a book, does it have an index?** Scan the index for keywords related to your topic to see how useful the book might be.

- **If the source is an article, does it have an abstract at the beginning or a summary at the end?** An abstract or a summary presents the main points made in the article and can help you decide if the source is likely to be useful.

- **Does the work contain headings?** Skim the headings to see if they indicate that the source covers useful information.

In college research, relevance can be a tricky matter. For example, your sociology instructor will expect you to give special preference to sociological sources in a project on the organization of the workplace. Your business management instructor will expect you to use material from that field in a project on the same topic. Be prepared to find that some promising sources turn out to be less relevant than you first thought.

21b Question Internet sources.

With print sources, you can have at least some confidence that the material has been filtered through editors and publishers. But anyone can design an attractive Web page that looks authoritative but contains utter nonsense. The Internet is a free-for-all. You may find up-to-the-minute material there, but you must question every source.

When you use sources from the Internet, you must analyze their reliability carefully and critically. Here are some points to keep in mind and guidelines to follow.

- **Authority and credibility:** Are the author and producer of the Web site identifiable? Does the author include biographical information? Is there any indication that the author has relevant expertise on the subject? Look for information about the individual or organization sponsoring the site; such information can indicate its reliability. The following extensions in the Web address, or uniform resource locator (URL), can help you determine the type of site (which often tells you something about its purpose):

.com commercial (business)	**.edu** educational	**.mil** military
.org nonprofit organization	**.gov** U.S. government	**.net** network

  A tilde (~) followed by a name in a URL usually means the site is a personal home page not affiliated with any organization.

- **Audience and purpose:** To evaluate a Web site's intended audience, you should apply the same criteria as for a print source, but you should also consider additional factors: Does the site assume special technical knowledge, capabilities, and access? Does the appearance of the site and the tone of any written material suggest an audience? A site's purpose also influences the way it presents information and the reliability of that information. Is the site's main purpose to promote a cause, raise money, advertise a product or service, provide factual information, present research results, provide news, share personal information, or offer entertainment? If you access a Web page through a search engine, always try to view the site's home page so that you can best evaluate its audience and purpose.

■ **Objectivity and bias:** Don't take the information that the site presents at face value. Look carefully at the purpose and tone of the text. Is there evidence of obvious bias? Clues that indicate a lack of reasonableness or bias include an intemperate tone, broad claims, exaggerated statements of significance, conflicts of interest, no recognition of opposing views, and strident attacks on opposing views. (*For more on evaluating arguments, see Tab 2: Writing and Designing Papers, pp. 28–34.*)

■ **Relevance and timeliness:** Keep your thesis or topic in mind as you browse online. In what ways does the information from an online source specifically support (or refute) your thesis or topic? Do the site's intended audience and purpose include an academic audience? Does the site name its authors and sponsors, give additional links and resources, and make its purposes clear? Does the site indicate how recently it has been updated, and are most of the included links still working? (If many of the links lead to "dead" sites, the page probably hasn't been updated for some time.)

Notice how in Figure 21.1 on page 243 the home page establishes the Web site's authority and credibility, identifies its audience and purpose, and suggests its objectivity and relevance. (*See also the TextConnex box on pp. 244–45.*)

www.mhhe.com/
awr
For an interactive
tutorial using the CARS
checklist, go to
Research > CARS
Source Evaluation
Tutor

21c Evaluate a source's arguments.

As you read the sources you have selected, you should continue to assess their reliability. Does the writer of a piece appeal to your emotions, to your reason, or to both in a balanced way? Regardless of where a source comes from, always ask yourself whether a particular writer is objective and fair-minded. Look for arguments that are qualified, supported with evidence, and well documented. Avoid relying on biased sources that appeal to emotions instead of rational thought or that promote one-sided political or religious agendas instead of inquiry and discussion.

The debate surrounding the use of stem cells for research on neurological diseases is an excellent example of the need to evaluate arguments for possible bias. Web sites and print publications that support the use of cells taken from frozen embryos stored in fertility clin-

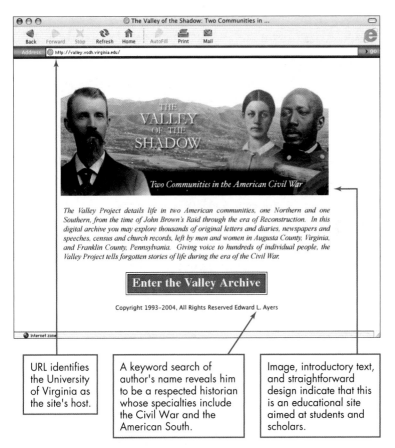

FIGURE 21.1 **The home page for the Valley Project.** This Web site provides a collection of primary-source documents related to two communities in the years before, during, and after the American Civil War.

ics and slated to be discarded are likely to cite facts and arguments favorable to their position. Web sites and print publications opposed to this research, however, are more likely to challenge the credibility of claims about its potential benefits and to cite arguments about the sanctity of all life.

A fair-minded researcher needs to read and evaluate sources on both sides of this and other issues.

TextConnex

Using the CARS Checklist to Evaluate Web Sites

A Web site that is **C**redible, **A**ccurate, **R**easonable, and **S**upported (CARS) should meet the following criteria:

Credibility

- The source is trustworthy; you would consider a print version to be authoritative (for example, an online edition of a major newspaper or news magazine).
- The argument and use of evidence are clear and logical.
- The author's or sponsor's credentials are available.
- Quality control is evident (for example, spelling and grammar are correct, and links are functional).
- The source is a known or respected authority; it has organizational support (such as a university, a research institution, or a major news publication).
- The source appears at or near the top of a Google search (Google.com ranks sites according to their popularity; sites near the top of a list of "hits" are the most frequently accessed by people looking for the same information you seek).

Accuracy

- The site is updated frequently, if not daily (and includes "last updated" information).
- The site provides evidence for its assertions.
- The site is detailed; text appears in full paragraphs.
- The site is comprehensive, including archives, links, and additional resources. A search feature and table of contents or tabs allow you to quickly find the information you need.
- The site's purpose includes completeness and accuracy.

Reasonableness

- The site is fair, balanced, and objective.
- The site makes its purpose clear (Is it selling something? Prompting site visitors to sign a petition? Promoting a new film?).
- The site contains no conflict of interest.
- The site does not include fallacies or a slanted tone. (*For more on fallacies, see Chapter 4, pp. 33–34*).

TEXTCONNEX

Support

- The site lists sources for its information, providing links where available.
- The site clarifies which content it is responsible for and which links are created by unrelated authors or sponsors.
- The site provides contact information for its authors and/or sponsors.
- If the site is an academic resource, it follows the conventions of a specific citation style (MLA, APA, or another accepted style).

22 Doing Research in the Archive, Field, and Lab

Research involves using both primary and secondary sources of information. When you consult books, journal articles, and other print and online resources, you are doing **secondary research**—gathering information from sources that have already been created by another writer or researcher. When you conduct **primary research**—looking up old maps, consulting census records, polling community members about a current issue—you participate in the discovery of knowledge.

The Internet has transformed primary research. For example, meteorological databases housed in Colorado are now available on the Internet in a format that students as well as specialists can use. Laboratory research is being transformed by the development of dry labs—computer-based experimental arenas in which research is conducted through simulations. Also, researchers can now use e-mail to carry out surveys and interviews.

The three kinds of primary research discussed in this chapter are archival research, field research, and laboratory research.

- **Archival research:** An **archive** is a cataloged collection of documents, manuscripts, and other materials, possibly including receipts, wills, photographs, sound recordings, and other kinds of media. Archives are found in campus libraries, museums, performing arts centers, and municipal buildings, among other places. Usually, an archive is organized around one key person, movement, circumstance, or phenomenon.

- **Field research:** Field research takes you out into the world to gather and record information. For example, you might conduct field research in a school, among a group of workers, or at a sporting event.

- **Laboratory research:** Every science course you take will most likely involve a laboratory component. In the laboratory, you work individually or as a team to carefully record each step of an experiment.

22a Adhere to ethical principles when doing primary research.

In the archive, field, or lab, you are working directly with something precious and immediate: an original record, a group of people, or special materials. An ethical researcher shows respect for materials, experimental subjects, fellow researchers, and readers.

CHARTING the TERRITORY

Primary Research in the Disciplines

Different disciplines engage in characteristically different forms of primary research. Here are some examples:

- **Archival research:** languages and literature; education; music and the performing arts; visual arts; media and popular culture; social sciences
- **Field research:** social sciences; marketing and advertising; media and communication
- **Laboratory research:** life sciences; physical sciences; computer science; engineering

Ethics also require you to describe accurately and completely what your primary research reveals—even if it means revising your thesis or reconsidering your entire argument. An ethical researcher does not overlook or conceal data that don't support a hypothesis and, of course, an ethical researcher never fabricates supporting data.

Here are some guidelines for ethical research:

- Handle original documents and materials with great care, always leaving sources and data available for other researchers.
- Accurately report your sources and results.
- Follow the procedures mandated by your college and your field when working with human participants.

Research with human participants that you do as an undergraduate should also adhere to the following basic principles:

- **Confidentiality:** People who fill out surveys, participate in focus groups, or respond to interviews should be assured that their names will not be used without their permission.
- **Informed consent:** Before participating in an experiment, all participants must sign a statement affirming that they understand the general purpose of the research. Researchers agree that observations of crowds in a shopping mall or children in a classroom do not require informed consent, unless your observations intrude on the lives of the people you are observing.
- **Minimal risk:** Researchers must design experiments so that participants do not incur any risks greater than they do in everyday life.
- **Protection of vulnerable groups:** Researchers must be held strictly accountable for research done with participants in the following categories: the physically disabled, prisoners, the mentally impaired or incompetent, minors, the elderly, and pregnant women.

22b Prepare yourself before undertaking archival research.

Archives are found in libraries, museums, other institutions and private collections, and on video- and audiotape. Your own attic may contain family archives—letters, diaries, and photograph collections that could have value to a researcher. Some archival collections are accessible through audio- and videotape as well as the Internet; others you must visit in person (*see the box on p. 248*).

The more you know about your area of study, the more likely you will be to see the significance of an item in an archival collection. Reading about your topic in books, journals, and Internet documents will provide a framework for discovery and lead you to questions that can be answered only by consulting original materials in an archive.

Archives generally require that you call or e-mail to arrange a time for your visit, and some are restricted. If you find an archive on the Internet that you would like to visit, phone or e-mail well in ad-

TEXTCONNEX

Online Information about Archives

Here are some Internet sites that will help you find and understand a wide range of archival sources:

- *American Memory* <http://memory.loc.gov>: This site offers access to more than seven million digital items from over a hundred collections of material on U.S. history and culture.
- *ArchivesUSA* <http://archives.chadwyck.com>: This subscription service is available via ProQuest. It provides information about 80,000 manuscript collections, more than 50,000 document collections, and more than 5,000 other archival repositories.
- *U.S. National Archives and Record Administration* (*NARA*) <http://www.nara.gov>: Learn how to use the National Archives in this site's research room, and then search the site for the documents you want.
- *Radio Program Archive* <http://www.people.memphis.edu/ ~mbensman>: This site lists radio archives available from the University of Memphis and explains how to obtain cassettes of programs.
- *Repositories of Primary Sources* <http://www.uidaho.edu/ special-collections/OtherRepositories.html>: This site lists more than 4,800 Web sites describing holdings of manuscripts, rare books, historical photographs, and other archival materials.
- *Television News Archive* <http://tvnews.vanderbilt.edu>: This site provides summaries of television news broadcasts and information on how to order videocassettes.
- *Virtual Library Museums Page* <http://icom.org/vlmp>: This site lists online museums throughout the world.
- *Women Writers Project* <http://www.wwp.brown.edu/texts/ wwoentry.html>: This site lists archived texts by pre-Victorian women writers that are available through the project.

vance to find out if you will need references, a letter of introduction, or other qualifying papers. Archives also generally require you to present a photo ID and to leave personal items in a locker or at a coat check, have strict policies about photocopying or otherwise reproducing materials, and rarely if ever allow anything to leave the premises. The more you know about the archive's policies and procedures before you visit, the more productive your visit will be.

22c Plan your field research carefully.

Field research involves observing and recording observations as well as eliciting information with interviews and surveys. Effective field research requires a strong research design and a plan for keeping accurate records.

To conduct field research at a particular site, such as a place of business or a school, you will need to call first and obtain permission from the department or person with the authority to grant access. Explain the nature of your project, the date and time you would like to visit, how much time you think you will need, and exactly what it is that you will be doing: Will you merely be observing? Interviewing people? Taking photographs? Also ask for a confirming letter or e-mail. Always write a thank-you note after you have concluded your research. Do *not* attempt to conduct your research without first obtaining permission. To do so is unethical.

1. Observing and writing field notes

When you use direct observation, you need to keep careful records. Figure 22.1 on page 250 shows a scientist taking field notes. Here are some guidelines to follow:

- Be systematic and purposeful in your observations, but be alert to unexpected behavior.
- Record what you see and hear as objectively as possible.
- Take more notes than you think you will ever need.
- When appropriate, categorize the types of behavior you are looking for, and devise a system for counting instances of each type.
- When you have recorded data over a significant period of time, group your observations into categories for more careful study and discussion.

(*For advice on conducting direct observations for a case study, see Tab 3: Common Assignments across the Curriculum, pp. 151–54.*)

FIGURE 22.1 **Archaeologist Anna Roosevelt taking notes during the excavation of a site in the Amazon region of South America.** Systematic, purposeful observation and careful note taking are crucial to the success of all fieldwork.

2. Conducting interviews

Asking relevant questions of experts or people who are members of a specific population is a powerful research tool. Group interviews, called "focus groups," are used in marketing, education, psychology, and other fields. Interviews should be conducted in a relaxed atmosphere, but they are not simply conversations. To be useful, interviews require systematic preparation and implementation:

- Identify appropriate people for your interviews.
- Do background research, and plan your questions.

- Take careful notes, and if possible, tape-record the interview (but be sure to obtain your subject's permission if you use audiotape).
- Follow up on vague responses with questions that get at specific information.
- Politely probe inconsistencies and contradictions.
- Write thank-you notes to interviewees, and later send them copies of your report.

3. Taking surveys

Surveys collect the responses of a group of subjects to a series of structured questions, or **questionnaire.** The researcher might read from the questionnaire like a script and then record the subjects' responses, or the subjects might read and respond to the questionnaire on their own. Survey research is much more complex than it looks. In fact, students in advanced social science courses spend a great deal of time studying the design and analysis of surveys, and surveys or polls used by political campaigns and the news media are designed with the help of statisticians and tabulated according to complex mathematical equations. The following suggestions will help you prepare informal surveys.

- Define your purpose. Are you trying to gauge attitudes, learn about typical behaviors, or both?
- Write clear directions and questions. For example, if you are asking multiple-choice questions, make sure that you cover all possible options and that none of your options overlap.
- Make sure that your questions are neutral, that they do not suggest a preference for one answer over another.
- Make the survey brief and easy to complete. Informal surveys should be no longer than one page (front and back).

22d Keep a notebook when doing lab research.

All experimenters, from undergraduates to professional scientists, are required to keep careful records of their laboratory work in a notebook. This notebook provides a complete and accurate account of the testing of a hypothesis in the controlled environment of the laboratory. Whether or not you are using a lab manual for your notes, the following guidelines will help you take accurate notes on your research:

- Record immediate, on-the-spot, accurate notes on what happens in the lab. Write down as much detail as possible. Measure precisely; do not estimate. Identify major pieces of apparatus, unusual chemicals, and laboratory animals in enough detail so that, for example, a reader can determine the size or type of equipment you used (instead of "physiograph," write "physiograph, Grass model 7B"). Use drawings, when appropriate, to illustrate complicated equipment setups. Include tables, when useful, to present results.

- Follow a basic format. If you are working without a lab manual or if no standard format is provided, you will be expected to present your results in a format that allows you to communicate all the major features of an experiment. The five basic sections that must be included are title, purpose, materials and methods, results, and conclusions. (*For more advice on preparing a lab report, see Tab 3: Common Assignments across the Curriculum, pp. 147–51.*)

- Write in complete sentences, even if you are filling in answers to questions in a lab manual. Resist using shorthand to record your notes. Writing in complete sentences will ensure that you understand the concepts in the experiment. Later, when you study your lab notebook, the complete sentences will provide a clear record of your procedures and results. For example, in responding to the question "Why is water readily polluted?" in your lab manual, the short answer "universal solvent" does not give the same information as this more detailed response: "Water is a universal solvent. Consequently, many compounds, including pollutants, dissolve in water." Also, highlight connections in your sentences by using the following transitions: *then, next, consequently, because,* and *therefore.* Cause-effect relationships are important to working scientists and should have similar importance in your lab notebook.

- When necessary, revise and correct your laboratory notebook in visible ways. If you make a mistake in recording laboratory results, correct it as clearly as possible, either by erasing or by crossing out and rewriting on the original sheet. If you make an uncorrectable mistake in your lab notebook, do not tear the sheet out. Simply fold the sheet lengthwise and mark *omit* on the face side. No matter how much preparation you do, unanticipated results often occur in the lab, and you may find yourself jotting down notes on a convenient piece of scrap paper or even a paper towel. Attach these notes to your laboratory notebook.

23 Working with Sources and Avoiding Plagiarism

Once you have a research question to answer, an idea about what the library and Internet have to offer, and some sense of the kinds of materials you need, you are ready to begin selecting and using sources. Paying attention to detail and keeping careful records at this stage will help you avoid plagiarism later.

23a Maintain a working bibliography.

www.mhhe.com/
awr
For help with creating
a bibliography, go to

**Research >
Bibliomaker**

As you research, compile a **working bibliography**—a list of those books, articles, pamphlets, Web sites, and other sources that seem most likely to help you answer your research question. It is essential to maintain an accurate and complete record of all sources you consult.

For each source, record the following bibliographic information:

- Call number of the book, reference work, or other print source; the URL of each Web site
- All authors, editors, and translators
- Title of the chapter, article, or Web page
- Title of the book, periodical, or Web site in which the chapter, article, or page appears
- For books, the date of publication, place, and publisher as well as the edition or volume number, if applicable
- For periodical articles, the date and edition or volume number, issue, and page numbers if applicable
- For a Web source, the date you consulted it

(*See the foldouts following Tabs 6 and 7 for examples of these elements.*)

You can record bibliographic information on note cards or in a word-processing file; you can print out bibliographic information obtained from online searches in databases and library catalogs; or you can record bibliographic information directly on photocopies of source material. You can also save most Web pages and other online sources to your own computer. Many professional researchers use bibliographic software such as *Endnote, ProCite,* and *Reference Manager* to help them keep track of sources and format bibliographic information. The *Catalyst* Web site that accompanies this handbook includes *Bibliomaker,* a program that can automatically format citations in the most common documentation styles: MLA, APA, CSE, and Chicago (*see Tabs 6–8*).

1. Using note cards or a word processor

Before computers became widely available, most researchers used 3-by-5-inch or 4-by-6-inch note cards to compile the working bibliography, with each potential source getting a separate card. This method is still useful. Besides including all the information you need to document the source, you can also use the cards to record brief quotations from or comments on those sources you decide to read and use (Figure 23.1).

Instead of handwriting on cards, you can also record bibliographic information in a word-processing file. Or you can combine the two methods, recording bibliographic information in a word-processing file, then printing it, cutting it out, and taping it on a note card.

2. Printing the results of online searches in databases and library catalogs

The results of searches in online indexes and databases usually include complete bibliographic information about the sources they list. (*See the example of a database search in Chapter 19, p. 220.*) You can print these

BMCC Library ML419.A75 B47 1997

Bergreen, Laurence. <u>Louis Armstrong:</u>
<u>An Extravagant Life.</u> New York:
Broadway, 1997.

Ostwald, David. "All That Jazz." Rev. of
<u>Louis Armstrong: An Extravagant Life,</u>
by Laurence Bergreen.
<u>Commentary</u> Nov. 1997: 68–72.

"Satchmo!" <u>New Orleans Online.</u> 1998.
New Orleans Tourism Marketing
Corporation. 26 Feb. 2004
< http://www.neworleansonline.com/
neworleans/music/satchmobio.html >

FIGURE 23.1 Three sample bibliography note cards. The cards are for a book (top), for a journal article (middle), and for a Web site (bottom).

results directly from your browser or, in some cases, save them to disk and transfer them to a word-processing file. Be sure also to record the name and URL of the database and the date of your search.

> *Caution:* If you download the full text of an article from a database and refer to it in your paper, your citation must include information about the database as well as bibliographic information about the article itself.

You can similarly print out or save bibliographic information from the results of searches in online library catalogs. Some college libraries make it possible for you to send your list of sources to yourself by e-mail. (*See Figure 23.2 on p. 256.*)

3. Using photocopies and printouts from Web sites
If you photocopy articles, essays, or pages of reference works from a print or a microfilm source, take time to note the bibliographic information on the photocopy. Similarly, if you print out a source you found on a Web site or copy it to your computer, be sure to note the site's complete URL and the date you visited it.

23b Take notes on your sources.

www.mhhe.com/ awr
For more information and interactive exercises, go to

Research > Research Techniques

Taking notes helps you think through the answer to your research question. You can take notes on the information you glean from your sources by annotating photocopies or printouts or by noting useful quotations and ideas on paper, on note cards, or in a computer file.

1. Annotating
One way to take notes is to annotate photocopied articles and printouts from online information services or Web sites. (*See Figure 23.3 on p. 257 for an annotated Web site printout.*) As you read, write the following notes directly on the page:

- On the first page, write down complete bibliographic information for the source.
- As you read, record questions, reactions, and ideas in the margins.
- Comment in the margins on ideas that agree with or differ from those you have already learned about.

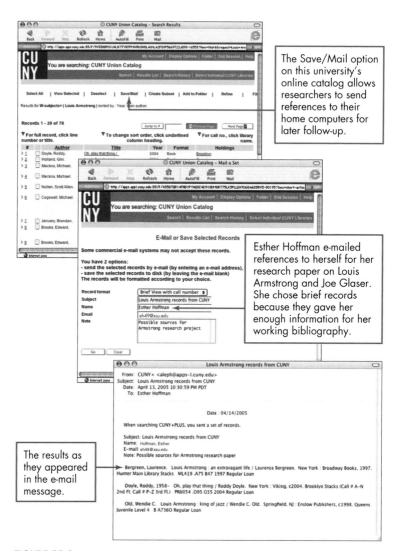

The Save/Mail option on this university's online catalog allows researchers to send references to their home computers for later follow-up.

Esther Hoffman e-mailed references to herself for her research paper on Louis Armstrong and Joe Glaser. She chose brief records because they gave her enough information for her working bibliography.

The results as they appeared in the e-mail message.

FIGURE 23.2 Three sample screens showing the results of an online search of a library database.

- Put important and difficult passages into your own words by paraphrasing or summarizing them in the margins. (*For help with paraphrasing and summarizing, see pp. 258–61.*)

- Use a highlighter to mark statements that you may want to quote because they are key to your readers' understanding of the issue or are especially well expressed.

FIGURE 23.3 **An annotated Web page printout.**

2. Taking notes in a research journal or log

A **research journal** or **research log** is a tool for keeping track of your research. It can be a spiral or loose-leaf notebook, a box of note cards, or a word-processing document on a laptop computer—whatever you are most comfortable with. Use the journal to write down leads for sources to consult and to record ideas and observations about your topic as they occur to you.

When you have finished annotating a photocopy or printout of an article, use your research journal to explore some of the comments, connections, and questions you recorded in the margins. If you do not have photocopies or printouts to annotate, take notes directly in your journal. Writing down each idea on a separate card, notebook page, or word-processing page will make it easier to organize the material later. Whatever method you use, be sure to record the source's bibliographic information as well as the specific page number for each idea.

Enclose in quotation marks any exact words from a source. If you think you may forget that the phrasing, as well as the idea, came from someone else, label the passage a "quote," as Esther Hoffman did in the following excerpt from her research notebook:

> Notes on Dan Morgenstern. "Louis Armstrong and the Development and Diffusion of Jazz." *Louis Armstrong: A Cultural Legacy.* Ed. Marc H. Miller. Seattle: U of Washington P and Queens Museum of Art, 1994. 95–145.
>
> ■ Armstrong having trouble with managers. Fires Johnny Collins in London, 1933. Collins blocks Armstrong from playing with Chick Webb's band (pp. 124–5).
>
> ■ Armstrong turned to Glaser, an old Chicago acquaintance. Quote: "Joe Glaser . . . proved to be the right man at the right time" (p. 128).

Unless you think you might use a particular quotation in your paper, it is usually better to express the author's ideas in your own words by using a paraphrase or a summary.

3. Paraphrasing

www.mhhe.com/
awr
For more information
and interactive
exercises, go to

Research > Avoiding
Plagiarism >
Summarize/
Paraphrase

When you **paraphrase,** you put someone else's statements into other words. Keep in mind that a paraphrase is not a word-for-word translation. Instead, you need to express the source's ideas *in your own way,* a way that will usually be shorter and less detailed than the original. Even though the sentences are yours, you must still give credit for the ideas to the original writer by citing his or her work properly. If your paraphrase includes any exact phrasing from the source, put quotation marks around those phrases.

In the first, unacceptable paraphrase that follows, the writer has done a word-for-word translation, using synonyms for some terms but retaining phrases from the original and failing to enclose them in quotation marks ("nonsense syllables," "free invention of rhythm, melody, and syllables"). The borrowed phrases are highlighted. Notice also how close the sentence structures in the faulty paraphrase are to the original. The acceptable paraphrase, by contrast, is more concise than the original, and although it quotes a few words from the source, the writer has expressed the definition in a new and different way.

SOURCE

Scat singing. A technique of jazz singing in which onomato-poeic or nonsense syllables are sung to improvised melodies. Some writers have traced scat singing back to the practice, common in West African musics, of translating percussion patterns into vocal lines by assigning syllables to characteristic rhythms. However, since this allows little scope for melodic improvisation and the earliest recorded examples of jazz scat singing involved the free invention of rhythm, melody, and syllables, it is more likely that the technique began in the USA as singers imitated the sounds of jazz instrumentalists.

—J. BRADFORD ROBINSON,
The New Grove Dictionary of Jazz

UNACCEPTABLE PARAPHRASE: PLAGIARISM

Scat is a way of singing that uses nonsense syllables and extemporaneous melodies. Some people think that scat goes back to the custom in West African music of turning drum rhythms into vocal lines. But that doesn't explain the free invention of rhythm, melody, and syllables of the first recorded instances of scat singing. It is more likely that scat was started in the U.S. by singers imitating the way instrumental jazz sounded (Robinson 515).

ACCEPTABLE PARAPHRASE

Scat, a highly inventive type of jazz singing, combines "nonsense syllables [with] improvised melodies." Although syllabic singing of drum rhythms occurs in West Africa, scat probably owes more to the early attempts of American singers to mimic both the sound and the inventive musical style of instrumental jazz (Robinson 515).

4. Summarizing

www.mhhe.com/
awr
For more information
and interactive
exercises, go to

Research >
Avoiding
Plagiarism >
Summarize/
Paraphrase

When you **summarize,** you state the main point of a piece, condensing a few paragraphs into one sentence or a few pages into one paragraph. Here are some suggestions for approaching the task:

- **Write down the text's main point.** Compose a sentence that identifies the text, the writer, the approach (reports, explores, analyzes, argues), and the key point the writer makes about the topic.
- **Divide the text into sections.** To develop the main point, writers move from one subtopic to another or from the

Tips LEARNING in COLLEGE

Using Sources to Establish Your Credibility

As noted in Chapter 4, effective writers appeal to their audience by demonstrating that they are *reasonable, ethical,* and *empathetic (see p. 36).* When you present relevant evidence from reliable sources, you demonstrate that you are reasonable. When you take care to put other writers' ideas into your own words and indicate the sources of all ideas and quotations that are not your own and that are not common knowledge *(see p. 265),* you demonstrate that you are ethical, and therefore trustworthy. When you carefully follow the citation formats required by the discipline that you are writing in, you demonstrate your consideration, or empathy, for your readers by making it easier for them to consult your sources if they wish to.

statement of an idea to the reasons, evidence, and examples that support it. If you own the text, annotate it to indicate where sections begin and end.

- **In one or two sentences, sum up what each of the text's sections says.** When you summarize, you in effect compose your own topic sentence for each major section of the text. If you own the text, highlight key sentences in each section to help focus your summary.

- **Combine your sentence stating the writer's main point with the sentences summarizing each of the text's major sections.** Now you have a summary of your source.

Here is a passage by John Ephland followed by two summaries. The unacceptable first summary is simply a restatement of Ephland's thesis, using much of his phrasing (highlighted). The second, acceptable summary states Ephland's main point in the writer's own words.

SOURCE

The origins of jazz, an urban music, stemmed from the countryside of the South as well as the streets of America's cities. It resulted from two distinct musical traditions, those of West Africa and Europe. West Africa gave jazz its incessant rhythmic drive, the need to move and the emotional urgency that has served the music so well. The European ingredients had more to do with classical qualities pertaining to harmony and melody.

The blending of these two traditions resulted in a music that played around with meter and reinterpreted the use of notes in new combinations, creating blue notes that expressed feelings both sad and joyous. The field hollers of Southern share-cropping slaves combined with the more urban, stylized sounds of musicians from New Orleans, creating a new music. Gospel music from the church melded with what became known in the 20th century as the blues offered a vocal ingredient that translated well to instruments.

—JOHN EPHLAND, "Down Beat's Jazz 101: The Very Beginning"

UNACCEPTABLE SUMMARY: PLAGIARISM

The origins of jazz are two distinct musical traditions, those of West Africa and Europe. New meters and new note combinations capable of expressing both sad and joyous feelings resulted from the blending of these two traditions.

ACCEPTABLE SUMMARY

Jazz has its roots in the musical traditions of both West Africa and Europe. It combines rhythmic, harmonic, and melodic features of both traditions in new and emotionally expressive ways.

5. Quoting directly

Sometimes the writer of a source will say something so eloquently and perceptively that you will want to include that writer's words as a **direct quotation.** In general, you will want to quote directly from writers who are themselves primary sources. For example, in a research paper about Louis Armstrong, a direct quotation from Armstrong himself (or a direct quotation from someone who worked with him) would add nuance and texture to the paper. To avoid inadvertent plagiarism, be careful to indicate that the content is a direct quotation when you copy it into your note cards or your research notebook, and place quotation marks around it.

www.mhhe.com/awr

For more information and interactive exercises, go to

Research > Avoiding Plagiarism > Using Quotations

Note: Beware of writing a paper that consists of a string of quotations, one after another. If you notice that you have used more than one quotation every two or three paragraphs, convert most of the quotations into paraphrases (*see pp. 258–59*).

ptSTART

23c Take stock of and synthesize
what you have learned.

When you take stock, you assess the research you have done. You also synthesize what you have learned from the sources you have consulted.

In college writing, the credibility of your work depends on the relevance and reliability of your sources as well as the scope and depth of your reading and observation. A paper on Louis Armstrong is unlikely to be credible if it relies on only one source of information. For lab reports, detailed observations are likely to be most important because they are the main kind of source that experimenters use when writing up their work.

As the context and kind of writing change, so too do the requirements for types and numbers of sources. As a general rule, however, you should consult more than two sources and use only sources that are both reliable and respected by people working in the field. Ask yourself the following questions about the sources you have consulted:

- Are your sources trustworthy? (*See Chapter 21, pp. 239–45, for more on evaluating sources.*)

- If you have started to develop a tentative answer to your research question, have your sources provided you with a sufficient number of facts, examples, and ideas to support that answer?

- Have you used sources that examine the issues from several different perspectives?

It is also important to think about how the sources you have read relate to one another. Ask yourself when, how, and why your sources agree or disagree, and consider where you stand on the issues they raise. Did anything you read surprise or disturb you? Writing down your responses to such questions can help you clarify what you have learned from working with sources.

www.mhhe.com/ awr
For more information and interactive exercises, go to
Research > Avoiding Plagiarism > Using Sources Accurately

23d Integrate quotations, paraphrases, and summaries properly and effectively.

Ultimately, you will use some of the paraphrases, summaries, and quotations you have collected during the course of your research to support and develop the ideas you present in your paper. Here are some guidelines for integrating them properly and effectively.

1. Integrating quotations

Quotations should be short, enclosed in quotation marks, and well integrated into your sentence structure, as in the following example from Esther Hoffman's paper on Louis Armstrong and Joe Glaser:

> In his dedication to the unpublished manuscript "Louis Armstrong and the Jewish Family in New Orleans," Armstrong calls Glaser "the best friend that I ever had," while in a letter to Max Jones, he writes, "I did not get really happy until I got with my man—my dearest friend—Joe Glaser" (qtd. in Jones and Chilton 16).

When you are integrating someone else's words into your writing, use a **signal phrase** that indicates whom you are quoting. The signal phrases "Armstrong calls Glaser" and "he writes" identify Armstrong as the source of the two quotations in the preceding passage. The box on page 264 lists common signal phrases.

Brackets within quotations   Sentences that include quotations must make sense grammatically. Sometimes you may have to adjust a quotation to make it fit your sentence. Use brackets to indicate any such minor adjustments. For example, *my* has been changed to *his* to make the quotation fit in the following sentence:

> Armstrong confided to a friend that Glaser's death "broke [his] heart" (Bergreen 490).

Ellipses within quotations   Use **ellipses** (. . .) to indicate that words have been omitted from the body of a quotation, but be sure that what you omit does not significantly alter the source's meaning.

> As Morgenstern put it, "Joe Glaser . . . proved to be the right man at the right time" (128).

(For more on using ellipses, see Tab 12: Editing for Correctness, pp. 568–69.)

Quotations in block format   Quotations longer than four lines should be used rarely because they tend to break up your text and make readers impatient. If you include a longer quotation, put it in block format (*see Tab 12: Editing for Correctness, pp. 554–56*), and be especially careful to integrate it into your paper. Tell your readers why you want them to read the block quotation, and afterwards, comment on it.

2. Integrating paraphrases and summaries

The principles for integrating paraphrases and summaries into your text are similar to those for including direct quotations. Provide a

Tips

LEARNING in COLLEGE

Varying Signal Phrases

When a writer relies on the same signal phrase throughout a paper, readers quickly become bored. Vary your signal phrases. Instead of using the verbs *says* and *writes* again and again, consider including some of the following:

acknowledges	denies	points out
adds	describes	proposes
admits	emphasizes	proves
argues	explains	refutes
asks	expresses	rejects
asserts	finds	remarks
charges	holds	reports
claims	implies	responds
comments	insists	shows
complains	interprets	speculates
concedes	maintains	states
concludes	notes	suggests
considers	observes	warns
contends		

smooth transition between a source's point and your own voice, and give credit to the source. Use signal phrases to introduce ideas you have borrowed from your sources. Besides crediting others for their work, signal phrases make ideas more interesting by giving them a human face. Here are some examples:

> As Bergreen points out, Armstrong easily reached difficult high notes, the F's and G's that stymied other trumpeters (248).

In this passage, Esther Hoffman uses the signal phrase "As Bergreen points out" to identify Bergreen as the source of the paraphrased information about Louis Armstrong's extraordinary technical abilities.

> A 1960 letter from Glaser to Lucille Armstrong corroborates Gold's account; it shows that Glaser assumed responsibility for buying the musician and his wife a new car as well as for filing the paperwork needed to retain the old license plate number.

Tips   LEARNING in COLLEGE

Determining What Is "Common Knowledge"

Information that an audience could be expected to know about from a wide range of sources is considered common knowledge. For example, the structure of DNA and the process of photosynthesis are considered common knowledge among biologists. However, a recent scientific discovery about genetics would not be common knowledge, and so you would need to cite the source of this information.

Maps, charts, graphs, and other visual displays of information are not considered common knowledge. Even though everyone knows that Paris is the capital of France, a reproduction of a map of France in your paper should be credited to the map's creator. (*For more information on properly citing visual and numerical resources in MLA style, see pp. 289, 304–5, and 314.*)

In this passage, Hoffman uses "corroborates" to signal her paraphrase of an original letter she found in the Louis Armstrong archives. She names the source (the author of the letter), so she does not need additional parenthetical documentation.

23e   Avoid plagiarism and copyright infringement.

www.mhhe.com/ awr
For information on material that does not need citing, go to
Research > Avoiding Plagiarism > Common Knowledge

Integrity and honesty require us to acknowledge others, especially when we use their words or ideas. Researchers who fail to acknowledge their sources—either intentionally or unintentionally—commit **plagiarism.** Buying a term paper from an online paper mill or "borrowing" a friend's completed assignment are obvious forms of plagiarism. But plagiarism also includes paraphrasing or summarizing material without properly citing its source. (*See pp. 258–61 for more on paraphrasing and summarizing.*)

Students who plagiarize may receive a failing grade for an assignment or course and face other disciplinary action—including expulsion. Your campus probably has a written policy regarding plagiarism and its consequences.

TEXTCONNEX

Learning More about Plagiarism, Copyright and Fair Use, and Intellectual Property

- **Plagiarism:** For the Council of Writing Program Administrator's "Defining and Avoiding Plagiarism: The WPA Statement on Best Practices," see <www.wpacouncil.org/positions/index.html>. Educators at Indiana University offer tips on avoiding plagiarism at <www.Indiana.edu/~wts/wts/plagiarism.html>. Georgetown University's Honor Council offers an example of a campus honor code pertaining to plagiarism and academic ethics at <www.georgetown.edu/honor/plagiarism.html>.

- **Copyright and fair use:** For information and discussion of fair use, see Copyright and Fair Use at <fairuse.stanford.edu>, and the U.S. Copyright Office at <www.loc.gov/copyright>.

- **Intellectual property:** For information about what constitutes intellectual property and related issues, see the World Intellectual Property Organization Web site at <www.wipo.int/>. For a legal perspective, the American Intellectual Property Law Association offers information and overviews of recent cases at <www.aipla.org/>.

1. Learning how plagiarism relates to copyright and intellectual property

Understood broadly, plagiarism is theft of property—in this case intellectual property—that belongs to someone else, the copyright holder. **Copyright** is the legal right to control the reproduction of any original work—a piece of writing, a musical composition, a play, a movie, a computer program, a photograph, a work of art. A copyrighted work is the **intellectual property** of the copyright holder, whether that entity is a publisher, a record company, an entertainment conglomerate, or the individual creator of the work. Here is some additional information on these important legal concepts:

- **Copyright:** A copyrighted text cannot be reprinted without the written permission of the copyright holder. The copyright protects the right of authors and publishers to make money from their productions.

- **Fair use:** The concept of **fair use** protects most academic use of copyrighted sources. Under this provision of copyright law, you can legally quote a brief passage from a copyrighted text without infringing on copyright. Of course, to avoid plagiarism you must identify the passage as a quotation and cite it properly.

- **Intellectual property:** In addition to works protected by copyright, intellectual property includes patented inventions, trademarks, industrial designs, and similar intellectual creations that are protected by other laws.

2. Avoiding inadvertent and deliberate plagiarism

Students under the pressure of a deadline can sometimes make poor choices. Inadvertent plagiarism occurs when busy students take notes carelessly, forgetting to jot down the source of a paraphrase. Deliberate plagiarism occurs when students wait until the last minute and then "borrow" a paper from a friend or cut and paste large portions of an online article into their own work. No matter how tired or pressured you may be, there is no justification for plagiarism.

Aside from managing your time and planning your research and writing carefully, here are some suggestions for avoiding plagiarism:

- Do not rely too much on one source, or you may easily slip into using that person's thoughts as your own.

- Keep accurate records while doing research and taking notes, or you may lose track of where an idea came from. If you do not know where you got an idea or a piece of information, do not use it in your paper until you find out.

- When you take notes, be sure to put quotation marks around words, phrases, or sentences taken verbatim from a source.

For MULTILINGUAL STUDENTS

Cultural Assumptions and Misunderstandings about Plagiarism

Respect for ownership of ideas is a core value of Western society. Your culture may consider the knowledge in classic texts a national heritage and, therefore, common property. As a result, you may have been encouraged to incorporate words and information from those texts into your writing without citing their source. American academic culture, however, requires you to identify any use you make of someone else's original work and to cite the work properly in an appropriate documentation style (*see Tabs 6–8*). You must similarly credit the source of ideas that are not considered common knowledge. You should accept these rules as non-negotiable and apply them conscientiously to avoid plagiarism and its serious consequences. When in doubt about citation rules, ask your instructor.

Tips **LEARNING in COLLEGE**

Avoiding Inadvertent Plagiarism:
Some Questions to Ask Yourself

- Is my thesis my own idea, or did I find it in one of my sources?
- Have I relied extensively on only one or two sources, instead of a variety of sources?
- Have I used uncommon terms, distinctive phrases, or quotations from a source but failed to enclose them in quotation marks?
- Have I included any words, phrases, or ideas that I don't really understand or explain?
- Have I indicated my source for all quotations, paraphrases, and summaries, either within the text or in a parenthetical citation?
- Have I included page numbers as required for all quotations, paraphrases, and summaries?
- Does every in-text citation have a corresponding entry in the list of works cited or references?

If you use any of those words, phrases, or sentences when summarizing or paraphrasing the source, put them in quotation marks. Keep in mind that changing a word here and there while keeping a source's sentence structure or phrasing constitutes plagiarism even if you credit the source for the ideas. (*See p. 259 for an example.*)

- Cite the source of all ideas, opinions, facts, and statistics that are not common knowledge.

- Choose an appropriate documentation style, and use it consistently and properly. (*See Tabs 6–8 for information about the most common documentation styles for academic writing.*)

- Print out any online source you consult, note the date on which you viewed it, and be sure to keep the complete URL of the site for correct citation.

- If you cut and paste a passage from a Web site into a word-processing file, use a different font to identify that material, and also copy the URL for the passage and note the date on which you visited the site.

www.mhhe.com/
awr
For more information
and interactive
exercises, go to

Research > Avoiding
Plagiarism > Using
Copyrighted
Materials

3. Using copyrighted materials fairly
All written materials, including student papers, letters, and e-mail, are covered by copyright even if they do not bear an official copyright sym-

bol. A copyright grants its owner exclusive rights to the use of a protected work, including reproducing, distributing, and displaying the work. The popularity of the World Wide Web has led to increased concerns about the fair use of copyrighted material. Before you post your paper on the Web or produce a multimedia presentation that includes audio, video, and graphic elements copied from a Web site, make sure that you have used copyrighted material fairly.

The following four criteria are used to determine if copyrighted material has been used fairly:

- **What is the purpose of the use?** Educational, nonprofit, and personal use are more likely to be considered fair than is commercial use.

- **What is the nature of the work being used?** In most cases, imaginative and unpublished materials can be used only if you have the permission of the copyright holder.

- **How much of the copyrighted work is being used?** If a writer uses a small portion of a text for academic purposes, this use is more likely to be considered fair than if he or she uses a whole work for commercial purposes.

- **What effect would this use have on the market for the original?** The use of a work is usually considered unfair if it would hurt sales of the original.

24 Writing the Paper

You have chosen a challenging research question and have located, read, and evaluated a variety of relevant sources. Now you need to come up with a thesis that will allow you to share what you have learned as well as your perspective on the issue.

24a Plan and draft your paper.

Begin by recalling the context and the purpose of your paper. If you have an assignment, review it to see if the paper is supposed to be primarily informative, interpretive, or argumentative. Keep your purpose and context in mind as you decide on your thesis.

1. Gathering and evaluating your information

Your note-taking strategies will determine how you collect and organize your information. If you have taken notes on index cards, group them according to topic and subtopic. For example, Esther Hoffman could have used the following categories to organize her notes:

Biography – Armstrong
Biography – Glaser
Glaser as manager
Conflict – A & G
Armstrong – media image
Jazz – general info

Sorting index cards into stacks that match up topics and subtopics allows you to see what you have gathered. A small stack of cards for a particular subtopic might mean that the subtopic is not as important as you originally thought—or that you need to do additional research focused on that specific subtopic.

If your notes are primarily on your computer, you can create a new folder or page for each topic and subtopic, and then cut and paste to move information to the appropriate category.

2. Deciding on a thesis

www.mhhe.com/
awr
For help with
developing a thesis,
go to

Writing >
Paragraph/Essay
Development >
Thesis/Central
Idea

Consider the question that guided your research as well as others provoked by what you have learned during your research. Revise the wording of your question to make it intriguing as well as suitable (*see Chapter 18, pp. 209–11*). After you write down this question, compose an answer that you can use as your working thesis, as Esther Hoffman did in the following example:

HOFFMAN'S FOCAL QUESTION

What kind of relationship did Louis Armstrong and Joe Glaser actually have?

HOFFMAN'S WORKING THESIS

Armstrong and Glaser enjoyed not only a successful business partnership but also a complex friendship based on mutual respect and caring.

(For more on devising a thesis, see Tab 2: Writing and Designing Papers, pp. 48–50.)

3. Outlining a plan for supporting and developing your thesis

www.mhhe.com/
awr
For interactive help
with outlines, go to
Writing >
Outlining Tutor

Guided by your tentative thesis, outline a plan that uses your sources in a purposeful way. Decide on the kind of structure you will use—explanatory, exploratory, or argumentative—and choose facts, examples, and ideas drawn from a variety of sources to support your thesis. (*See Chapters 9–11 in Tab 3 for more on these structures.*)

For her interpretive paper on Armstrong and Glaser, Hoffman decided on an exploratory structure, an approach organized around raising and answering a central question:

- Introduce Armstrong as a great musician who was once a poor waif.
- Introduce Glaser, Armstrong's manager for thirty-four years.
- State the question: What kind of relationship did these two actually have? Did Glaser dominate Armstrong?
- Discuss Glaser as Armstrong's business manager—support for idea that it was Glaser who made Armstrong a star.
- Discuss Armstrong's resistance to being controlled by Glaser.
- Conclude: Armstrong and Glaser worked well together as friends who respected and cared for each other.

To develop this outline, Hoffman needed to list supporting facts, examples, or ideas for each point. (*For more on developing an outline, see Tab 2: Writing and Designing Papers, pp. 50–53.*)

4. Writing a draft that you can revise, share, and edit

www.mhhe.com/
awr
For more information
and interactive
exercises, go to
Writing >
Paragraph/Essay
Development >
Drafting and
Revising

When you have a tentative thesis and a plan, you are ready to write a draft. As her outline shows, Hoffman planned to use a few pages to set up the context for her issue, but many writers find that they can present their thesis or focal question at the end of an introductory paragraph or two.

As you write beyond the introduction, be prepared to reexamine and refine your thesis as you discover interesting connections as well as new ways to express your ideas. Such discoveries often occur when writers use what they have read in various sources to support and develop their ideas. As you draw on ideas from your sources, be sure to quote and paraphrase properly. (*For advice on quoting and paraphrasing, see Chapter 23, pp. 258–61.*)

Make your conclusion as memorable as possible. In the final version of Hoffman's paper, on pages 328–29, note how she uses a visual and a play on words—"more than meets the eye"—to end her paper. In doing so, she enhances her concluding point—that the two men were different, yet complementary, and that their relationship was complex.

Hoffman came up with the last line of her paper as she revised her first draft. Often writers will come up with fresh ideas at this stage, one reason it is important to spend time revising and editing your paper. (*For more on revising, see Tab 2, pp. 76–88. For help with editing, see Tabs 9–12.*)

5. Integrating visuals

Well-chosen visuals can sometimes help illustrate your argument. Hoffman found two images in her archival research about Louis Armstrong. She described both of them in her paper and was able to include a reproduction of one of them. Two additional things to consider when integrating a visual into your paper are figure numbers and captions.

- **Figure numbers:** Both MLA and APA style require writers to number each image in a research paper. In MLA style, the word "figure" is abbreviated to "Fig." In APA style, the full word "Figure" is written out.

- **Captions:** Each visual that you include in your paper must be followed by a caption that includes the title of the visual (if given; otherwise, a brief description will do) and its source. In MLA style, each caption begins with the figure number and a period after the number (Fig. 1.); in APA style, use italics for the figure number (*Figure 1.*).

24b Revise your draft.

After you have completed a draft of your research paper, you may be asked to share it with other members of your class for peer review and feedback. Similarly, academic researchers often present their papers at conferences to get feedback from others working in their field, and sales professionals work as teams on quarterly reports.

You may prefer to revise a hard copy of your draft by hand, or you might find it easier to use the "track changes" feature in your word-processing program. Either way, be sure to keep previous versions of your drafts. It is useful to have a record of how your paper evolved—especially if you need to track down a particular source or want to reincorporate something that you used earlier in the process.

Tips LEARNING in COLLEGE

Guidelines for Revising Your Research Paper

Consider these questions as you read your draft and gather feedback from your instructor and peers:

- Is your thesis clear and engaging? Where in your draft do you most clearly state your thesis?
- Does each paragraph include a topic sentence? Are the transitions between paragraphs clear and logical?
- Have you provided an adequate in-text citation for each source?
- Do you have enough evidence to support each point you make? Where should you include additional research?
- Does your introduction give a specific and interesting overview of your topic and thesis? Does your conclusion provide a compelling synthesis of your research and clearly sum up the support for your thesis?
- Have you integrated quotations, summaries, and paraphrases smoothly and used a variety of signal phrases?
- Do all of your illustrations have complete and accurate captions?
- Do all of your in-text citations match your Works Cited or References page? Is there anything on your Works Cited or References page that is not in the text of your paper?

24c Document your sources.

www.mhhe.com/
awr
For help with
documenting sources,
go to

Research >
Avoiding
Plagiarism >
Citing Sources

Whenever you use information, ideas, or words from someone else's work, you must acknowledge that person. As noted in the box on page 265, the only exception to this principle is when you use information that is common knowledge, such as the chemical composition of water or the names of the thirteen original states. When you tell readers what sources you have consulted, they can more readily understand your paper as well as the conversation you are participating in by writing it.

How sources are documented varies by field and discipline. Choose a documentation style that is appropriate for the particular course you are taking, and use it properly and consistently.

If you are not sure which of the four styles covered in this handbook to use, ask your instructor. If you are required to use an alternative, discipline-specific documentation style, consult the list of manuals on page 275.

For her paper on Louis Armstrong and Joe Glaser, Esther Hoffman used the MLA documentation style. (*The final draft of the paper appears in Tab 6: MLA Documentation, on pp. 321–32.*)

CHARTING the TERRITORY

Documentation Styles Covered in This Text

TYPE OF COURSE	DOCUMENTATION STYLE MOST COMMONLY USED	WHERE TO FIND THIS STYLE IN THE HANDBOOK
Humanities (English, religion, music, art, philosophy)	MLA (Modern Language Association) or Chicago (*Chicago Manual of Style*)	MLA: *pp. 281–332* Chicago: *pp. 371–90*
Social sciences (anthropology, psychology, sociology, education, business)	APA (American Psychological Association)	*pp. 333–67*
Sciences (mathematics, natural sciences, engineering, computer science)	CSE (Council of Science Editors)	*pp. 391–400*

TEXTCONNEX

Presenting and Publishing Your Work

There are many ways to share the results of your research. New technologies allow for the creation of sophisticated audio and video presentations and Web sites. In both your academic and your professional career, you will likely be called upon to present your ideas and research using media such as PowerPoint or through visual tools such as iDVD. You might use desktop publishing software to prepare a manuscript for publication. Make the presentation of your research suit your audience and your purpose.

(*For more information on oral presentations, see pp. 158–63. To learn more about using PowerPoint and other visual presentation tools, see pp. 168–71. For a discussion of document design, see pp. 98–105.*)

CHARTING the TERRITORY

Style Manuals for Specific Disciplines

SPECIFIC DISCIPLINE	POSSIBLE STYLE MANUAL
Chemistry	Dodd, Janet S., ed. *The ACS Style Guide: A Manual for Authors and Editors.* 2nd ed. Washington: American Chemical Society, 1997.
Geology	Bates, Robert L., Rex Buchanan, and Marla Adkins-Heljeson, eds. *Geowriting: A Guide to Writing, Editing, and Printing in Earth Science.* 5th ed. Alexandria: American Geological Institute, 1995.
Government and law	Garner, Diane L., and Diane H. Smith, eds. *The Complete Guide to Citing Government Information Resources: A Manual for Writers and Librarians.* Rev. ed. Bethesda: Congressional Information Service, 1993.
	Harvard Law Review et al. *The Bluebook: A Uniform System of Citation.* 17th ed. Cambridge: Harvard Law Review Assn., 2000.
Journalism	Goldstein, Norm, ed. *Associated Press Stylebook and Briefing on Media Law.* Revised and updated ed. New York: Associated Press, 2000.
Linguistics	Linguistic Society of America. "LSA Style Sheet." *LSA Bulletin.* Published annually in the December issue.
Mathematics	American Mathematical Society. *AMS Author Handbook: General Instructions for Preparing Manuscripts.* Providence: AMS, 1997.
Medicine	Iverson, Cheryl, ed. *American Medical Association Manual of Style: A Guide for Authors and Editors.* 9th ed. Baltimore: Williams & Wilkins, 1998.
Physics	American Institute of Physics. *Style Manual for Guidance in the Preparation of Papers.* 5th ed. New York: AIP, 1995.
Political science	American Political Science Association. *Style Manual for Political Science Papers.* Rev. ed. Washington: APSA, 2001.

25

Discipline-Specific Resources in the Library and on the Internet

The list that follows will help you get started doing research in specific disciplines. Both print and electronic resources are listed because you should use both types in your research. (Print entries precede electronic entries.) Most major academic disciplines have computerized bibliographies, databases, and indexes that you can access through your college's library. (*For a list of online databases, see pp. 222–23.*)

www.mhhe.com/ awr

For an updated listing of resources, go to

Research > Discipline Specific Resources

Note: Remember that Web addresses change frequently, so if you get the 4040 (File not found) message, try doing a search for the page using a search engine.

Anthropology

Abstracts in Anthropology
Annual Review of Anthropology
Dictionary of Anthroplogy
Encyclopedia of World Cultures
American Anthropology Association
  <http://www.aaanet.org>
National Anthropology Archives
  <http://www.nmnh.si.edu/naa/>
WWW Virtual Library: Anthropology
  <http://vlib.anthrotech.com>

Art and Architecture

Art Abstracts
Art Index
BHA: Bibliography of the History of Art
Encyclopedia of World Art
McGraw-Hill Dictionary of Art
Artcyclopedia
  <http://www.artcyclopedia.com>
The Louvre
  <http://www.louvre.fr/ louvrea.htm>
The Metropolitan Museum of Art (New York)
  <http://www.metmuseum.org>
The National Gallery (Washington, D.C.)
  <http://www.nga.gov>

Voice of the Shuttle Art History and Architecture
  <http://vos.ucsb.edu/index.asp>

Biology

Biological Abstracts
Biological and Agricultural Index
Encyclopedia of the Biological Sciences
Henderson's Dictionary of Biological Terms
Zoological Record
Biology Online
  <http://www.biology-online.org/>
Harvard University Biology Links
  <http://mcb.harvard.edu/ BioLinks.html>
National Science Foundation: Biology
  <http://www.nsf.gov/news/ overviews/biology/index.jsp>

Business

Accounting and Tax Index
Encyclopedia of Business Information Sources
ABI/Inform
Business Periodicals
Business and Industry

Newslink Business Newspapers
    <http://newslink.org/biznews.html>

Chemistry

Chemical Abstracts (CASEARCH)
*McGraw-Hill Dictionary of
    Chemistry*
*Van Nostrand Reinhold
    Encyclopedia of Chemistry*
American Chemical Society
    <http://www.acs.chemistry.org>
Sheffield ChemDex
    <http://www.chemdex.org>
WWW Virtual Library: Chemistry
    <http://www.liv.ac.uk/chemistry/
    links/links.html>

Classics

Oxford Classical Dictionary
*Princeton Encyclopedia of Classical
    Sites*
Perseus Digital Library
    <http://www.perseus.tufts.edu>

Communications and Journalism

Mass Media Bibliography
Communication Abstracts
*International Encyclopedia of
    Communications*
Journalism Abstracts
*American Communication
    Association*
    <http://www.americancomm.org>
*Journalism and Mass
    Communications Abstracts*
    <http://www.aejmc.org/abstracts/>
The Poynter Institute
    <http://www.poynter.org>

Computer Science and Technology

Computer Abstracts
Dictionary of Computing
Encyclopedia of Computer Science
*McGraw-Hill Encyclopedia of
    Science and Technology*
*FOLDOC (Free Online Dictionary of
    Computing)*
    <http://wombat.doc.ic.ac.uk/
    foldoc/>

*MIT Laboratory for
    Computer Science and Artificial
    Intelligence Laboratory*
    <http://www.csail.mit.edu/
    index.php>

Cultural Studies, American and Ethnic Studies

Encyclopedia of World Cultures
*Dictionary of American Negro
    Biography*
*Gale Encyclopedia of Multicultural
    America*
Mexican American Biographies
American Studies Web
    <http://lumen.georgetown.
    edu/projects/asw/>
*National Museum of the
    American Indian*
    <http://www.nmai.si.edu>
*Schomburg Center for Research in
    Black Culture*
    <http://www.nypl.org/research/
    sc/sc.html>
*Smithsonian Center for Folklife and
    Cultural Heritage*
    <http://www.folklife.si.edu/
    index.html>

Economics

EconLit
*PAIS: Public Affairs Information
    Service*
American Economic Association
    <http://www.aeaweb.org>
Internet Resources for Economists
    <http://www.oswego.edu/
    ~economic/econweb.htm>
*Resources for Economists on the
    Internet*
    <http://www.rfe.wustl.edu>

Education

Dictionary of Education
Education Index
*Encyclopedia of Educational
    Research*
*International Encyclopedia of
    Education*

Resources in Education
The Educator's Reference Desk
    <http://www.eduref.org>
EdWeb
    <http://edwebproject.org>
U.S. Department of Education
    <http://www.ed.gov>

Engineering

Applied Science and Technology
    Index
Engineering Index
McGraw-Hill Encyclopedia of
    Engineering
IEEE Spectrum
    <http://www.spectrum.ieee.org>
WWW Virtual Library: Engineering
    <http://www.eevl.ac.uk/
    wwwvl.html>

Environmental Sciences

Dictionary of the Environment
Encyclopedia of Energy, Technology,
    and the Environment
Encyclopedia of the Environment
Environment Abstracts
Environment Index
Envirolink
    <http://envirolink.org>
U.S. Environmental Protection
    Agency
    <http://www.epa.gov>

Film

Dictionary of Film Terms
The Film Encyclopedia
Film Index International
Film Literature Index
Internet Movie Database
    <http://us.imdb.com>

Geography

Geographical Abstracts
Longman Dictionary of Geography
Modern Geography: An Encyclopedic
    Survey
CIA World Factbook
    <http://www.cia.gov/cia/
    publications/factbook/index.html>

Resources for Geographers
    <http://www.colorado.edu/
    geography/virtdept/resources/
    contents.htm>

Geology

Bibliography and Index of Geology
Challinor's Dictionary of Geology
The Encyclopedia of Field and
    General Geology
American Geological Institute
    <http://www.agiweb.org>
U.S. Geological Survey
    <http://www.usgs.gov>

Health and Medicine

American Medical Association
    Encyclopedia of Medicine
Cumulated Index Medicus
Medical and Health Information
    Directory
Nutrition Abstracts and Reviews
U.S. National Library of Medicine
    <http://www.nlm.nih.gov>
World Health Organization
    <http://www.who.int>

History

America: History and Life
Dictionary of Historical Terms
Encyclopedia of American History
An Encyclopedia of World History
Historical Abstracts
Electronic Documents in History
    <http://www.tntech.edu/history/
    edocs.html>
History Cooperative
    <http://historycooperative
    .press.uiuc.edu>
History World
    <http://www.historyworld.net/>
NARA Archival Research Catalog
    <www.archives.gov/research_
    room/arc/index.html>

Languages and Linguistics

Cambridge Encyclopedia of
    Language

An Encyclopedic Dictionary of
    Language and Languages
International Encyclopedia of
    Linguistics
LLBA: Linguistics and Language
    Behavior Abstracts
MLA International Bibliography
Center for Applied Linguistics
    <http://www.cal.org>
SIL International Linguistics
    <http://www.sil.org/linguistics>

Literature

Concise Oxford Dictionary of
    Literary Terms
MLA International Bibliography
The New Princeton Encyclopedia of
    Poetry and Poetics
Electronic Text Center at the
    University of Virginia Library
    <http://etext.lib.virginia.edu>
Project Gutenberg
    <http://www.gutenberg.org>
Voice of the Shuttle
    <http://vos.ucsb.edu/index.asp>

Mathematics

American Statistics Index
Facts on File Dictionary of
    Mathematics
International Dictionary of Applied
    Mathematics
Mathematical Reviews (MathSciNet)
American Mathematical Society
    <http://www.ams.org>
Math Forum
    <http://mathforum.com>

Music

Music Index
New Grove Dictionary of Music and
    Musicians
New Oxford Companion to Music
New Oxford Dictionary of Music
RILM Abstracts of Musical
    Literature
All Music
    <http://allmusic.com>

Philosophy

Dictionary of Philosophy
Philosopher's Index
Routledge Encyclopedia of Philosophy
American Philosophical Association
    <http://www.apa.udel.edu/apa/
    index.html>
EpistemeLinks.com
    <http://www.epistemelinks.com>

Physics

Dictionary of Physics
McGraw-Hill Encyclopedia of Physics
Physics Abstracts
American Institute of Physics
    <http://aip.org>
American Physical Society
    <http://www.aps.org>
Institute of Physics
    <http://iopublishing.com>
PhysicsWeb
    <http://physicsweb.org/>

Political Science

Almanac of American Politics
Congressional Quarterly Almanac
Encyclopedia of Government and
    Politics
International Political Science
    Abstracts
Political Resources on the Web
    <http://www.politicalresources
    .net>
Public Affairs Information Service
    (PAIS)
Non-Western Sources on
    Contemporary Political Issues
    <http://library.lib.binghamton
    .edu/subjects/polsci/home.html>
Thomas: Legislative Information
    on the Internet
    <http://thomas.loc.gov>
United Nations
    <http://www.un.org>

Psychology

International Dictionary of
    Psychology

*International Encyclopedia
of Psychiatry, Psychology,
Psychoanalysis, and Neurology*
Psychological Abstracts
American Psychological Association
  <http://www.apa.org>
American Psychological Society
  <http://www.psychologicalscience.
  org>
Encyclopedia of Psychology
  <http://www.psychology.org/>
PsychWeb
  <http://www.psywww.com>

Religion

ATLA Religion
Dictionary of Bible and Religion
Encyclopedia of Religion
Religion Index
Religions and Scriptures
  <http://www.wam.umd.edu/
  ~stwright/rel>

Sociology

Annual Review of Sociology
Encyclopedia of Social Work
Encyclopedia of Sociology
Sociological Abstracts
*Academic Info Sociology:
  Databases and Centers*
  <http://www.academicinfo.net/
  socdata.html>

American Sociological Association
  <http://asanet.org>
The SocioWeb
  <http://www.socioweb.com/
  ~markbl/socioweb/indexes>

Theater and Dance

*International Encyclopedia
  of the Dance*
*McGraw-Hill Encyclopedia
  of World Drama*
American Theater Web
  <http://www.american
  theaterweb.com/>
*The WWW Virtual Library:
  Theater and Drama*
  <http://ul-theatre.com>

Women's Studies

Women Studies Abstracts
*Women's Studies: A Guide to
  Information Sources*
Women's Studies Encyclopedia
*Feminist Majority Foundation
  Online*
  <http://www.feminist.org>
National Women's History Project
  <http://www.nwhp.org>

6

Next to the originator of a good sentence is the first quoter of it.

—RALPH WALDO EMERSON

MLA
Documentation
Style

6

MLA Documentation Style

MLA style requires writers to provide bibliographic information about their sources in a works-cited list at the end of a paper. In order to format works-cited entries correctly, it is important to know first of all what kind of source you are citing. The directory on pages 293–94 will help you find the appropriate sample to use as your model. As an alternative, you can use the charts on the foldout pages that follow to help you locate the right example. Answering the questions provided in the charts will usually lead you to the sample entry you need. If you cannot find what you are looking for after consulting the appropriate directory or chart, ask your instructor for help.

Entries in a Works-Cited List: BOOKS OR OTHER PRINT SOURCES

❓ Is your source a complete book?

No Yes

	Go to this entry
Is it a complete book with one named author?	
Is it the only book by this author that you are citing?	1
Are you citing more than one book by this author?	2
Does it also have an editor or translator?	6, 15
Is it a published doctoral dissertation?	36
Is it a complete book with more than one named author?	3
Is it a complete book without a named author?	
Is the author an organization?	4
Is the author anonymous or unknown?	22
Is it a complete book with an editor or a translator?	
Is there an editor instead of an author?	5
Does it have both an editor and an author?	6
Is it an anthology?	12
Is it a translation?	15
Is it the published proceedings of an academic conference?	35
Is it a complete book with a volume or an edition number?	
Is it part of a multivolume work (e.g., Volume 3)?	18
Is it one in a series?	19
Does it have an edition number (e.g., Second Edition)?	16
Is it a complete book but not the only version?	
Is your book a republished work (e.g., a classic novel)?	20
Is your book a religious text (e.g., the Bible)?	17
Is the book from a publisher's imprint?	13
Does the book's title include the title of another book?	21

❓ Is your source part of a book?

No Yes

	Go to this entry
Is it from an edited book?	
Is it a work in an anthology?	7
Is it a chapter in an edited book?	7
Are you citing two or more items from the same anthology?	8
Is it an article from a collection of reprinted articles?	11
Is it a published letter (e.g., part of a published collection)?	43
Is it from a reference work (e.g., an encyclopedia)?	
Is it an article with an author?	9
Is it an article without a named author?	10
Is it a preface, an introduction, a foreword, or an afterword?	14

Check the next panel or the directory on pages 293–94 or consult your instructor.

Entries in a Works-Cited List: PRINT PERIODICALS OR OTHER PRINT SOURCES

❓ Is your source from a journal, a magazine, or a newspaper?

No Yes

	Go to this entry
Is it from an academic journal?	
Are the page numbers continued from one issue to the next?	23
Do the page numbers in each issue start with 1?	24
Is your source an abstract (a brief summary) of an article?	31
Is it from a magazine?	
Is the magazine published monthly?	25
Is the magazine published weekly?	26
Is your source a letter to the editor?	32
Is it a review (e.g., a review of a book or film)?	29
Is it an interview?	39
Is it stored on microfiche, microform, or microfilm?	47
Is it from a newspaper?	
Is it an article?	27
Is it an interview?	39
Is it an editorial?	30
Is it a letter to the editor?	32
Is it a review (e.g., a review of a book or film)?	29
Is it stored on microfiche, microform, or microfilm?	47
Is the author unknown?	28

❓ Is it a print source but not a book, a part of a book, or an article in an academic journal, a magazine, or a newspaper?

No Yes

	Go to this entry
Is it published by the government or a nongovernment organization?	
Is it a pamphlet or other type of document?	33, 34
Is it a court case or other legal document?	46
Is it from the *Congressional Record*?	62
Is it an academic work?	
Is it an unpublished dissertation or essay?	37
Is it an abstract of a dissertation?	38
Is it a personal letter or a letter from an archive?	44, 45
Is it a visual text or an advertisement?	
Is it a map or chart?	40
Is it a cartoon?	41
Is it an advertisement?	42
Is it stored in an archive?	45
Is it published in more than one medium (e.g., a book and a CD-ROM)?	48

Check the directory on pages 293–94 or consult your instructor.

Entries in a Works-Cited List: ELECTRONIC OR OTHER NONPRINT SOURCES

❓ Did you find your nonprint source online?

No Yes

	Go to this entry
Is it a Web site?	
Is it a professional or personal Web site?	50
Is it a home page for a course?	51
Is it authored by a person using a pseudonym?	52
Is it an entry from a Weblog (blog)?	64
Is it an article from an online scholarly journal?	
Is it an article from a journal that is available only online?	54
Is it an article from a journal that is also available in print?	55
Is it an article you found through a subscription database service (e.g., EBSCO or ProQuest)?	68
Is it from an online magazine or newspaper?	
Is it an article from an online version of a print periodical?	56
Is it an article from a periodical that is only available online?	57
Is it an article from an online newspaper?	58
Is it an editorial?	59
Is it a letter to the editor?	60
Is it a review?	63
Is it an online book or scholarly project?	
Is it an online book?	53
Is it an online scholarly project?	49
Is it sponsored by or related to the government?	61, 62
Is it an online communication?	
Is it a posting to a news group or other type of online forum?	69, 70
Is it an e-mail communication?	71
Is it an e-mail interview?	83
Is your source an online graphic, audio, or video file?	72–75

❓ Is your source a nonprint source that is not published online?

No Yes

	Go to this entry
Is your source stored on a CD-ROM or DVD?	
Is it a CD-ROM or DVD with or without a print version?	65–67
Is it computer software on a CD-ROM or DVD?	76
Is it a film, DVD, or videotape?	77
Is it a television or radio program?	78
Is it a broadcast interview?	79
Is it a personal or telephone interview?	83
Is it a sound recording, musical composition, or work of art?	80–82
Is it a lecture, speech, or performance?	84, 85

Check the directory on pages 293–94 or consult your instructor.

The Elements of an MLA Works-Cited Entry: Books

Author → Bergreen, Laurence.

Book title → Louis Armstrong: An Extravagant Life.

New York: Broadway, 1997.

Place of publication ↗ ↑ Publisher ↑ Date of publication ↖

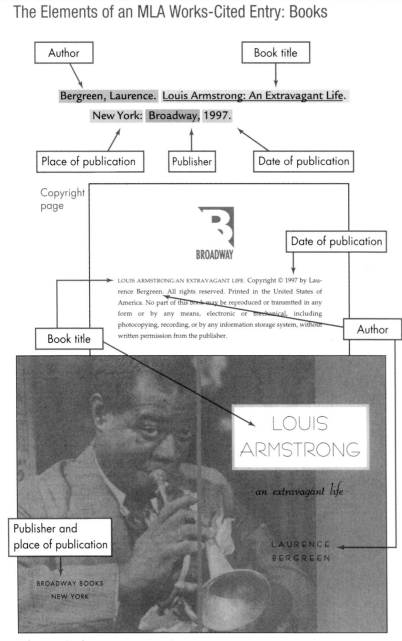

Copyright page

Book title

Publisher and place of publication

Date of publication

Author

Title page (in this case, two pages)

Information for a book citation can be found on the book's title and copyright pages.

The Elements of an MLA Works-Cited Entry: Journal Articles

Author → Edwards, Brent Hayes. "Louis Armstrong and the Syntax of Scat." ← Article title

Critical Inquiry 28 (2002): 618-49.

Journal title ↗ Volume number ↑ Year of publication ↑ Page numbers ↖

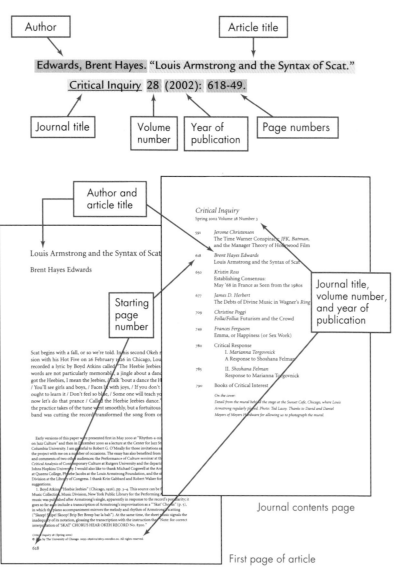

Author and article title

Starting page number

Journal title, volume number, and year of publication

Journal contents page

First page of article

Some academic journals, like this one, provide most of the information needed for a citation on the first page of an article as well as, like others, on the cover or contents page. You will need to look at the article's last page for the last page number. This journal is paged continuously throughout each yearly volume, so only the volume number is needed in the works-cited entry.

The Elements of an MLA Works-Cited Entry: Journal Articles from an Online Subscription Service

Author, title, and other information about the print version of the article

Edwards, Brent Hayes. "Louis Armstrong and the Syntax of Scat." Critical Inquiry 28 (2002): 618-49. ProQuest.

Columbia U. Libraries. 5 May 2005 <http://proquest.com/proquest/>.

Subscribing library system ↑ Date of access ↑ Subscription service home page ↑ Name of subscription service ↗

Link to home page for subscription service (for home page URL)

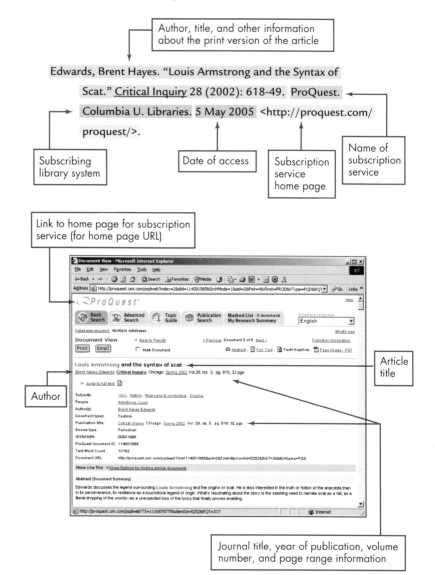

Author

Article title

Journal title, year of publication, volume number, and page range information

A citation for an article obtained from an online subscription database service like ProQuest includes information about the service, the subscribing library, and the date of access in addition to information about the print version of the article. Information about the library and the date of access comes from the researcher's notes.

College papers include information, ideas, and quotations from sources that must be accurately documented. Documentation allows others to see the path you have taken in researching and writing your paper—be it informative, interpretive, or argumentative. (*For more on what to document, see Tab 5: Researching, pp. 273–74.*)

The documentation style developed by the Modern Language Association (MLA) is used by many researchers in the arts and humanities, especially language and literature. The guidelines presented here are based on the sixth edition of Joseph Gibaldi's *MLA Handbook for Writers of Research Papers* (New York: MLA, 2003).

MLA documentation style has three parts:

- In-text citations
- List of works cited
- Explanatory notes

In-text citations and a list of works cited are mandatory; explanatory notes are optional.

www.mhhe.com/
awr
For links to Web sites for documentation styles used in various disciplines, go to

Research > Links to Documentation Sites

26 MLA Style: In-Text Citations

In-text citations let readers know that they can find full information about the source of a quotation or an idea you have paraphrased or summarized in the works-cited list at the end of your paper.

MLA IN-TEXT CITATIONS: DIRECTORY to SAMPLE TYPES

(See pp. 293–317 for works-cited examples.)

(continued)

1. Author named in sentence: You can use the last name only, unless two or more of your sources have the same last name.

signal phrase
As Hennessey explains, record deals were usually negotiated by "white middlemen" (127).

Note that the parenthetical page citation comes after the closing quotation mark but before the period.

2. Author named in parentheses: If you do not name the source's author in your sentence, then you must provide the name in the parentheses.

Armstrong easily reached difficult high notes, the F's and G's that
no punctuation within parentheses
stymied other trumpeters (Bergreen 248).

Note that there is no comma between the author's name and the page number. If you cite two or more distinct pages, however, separate the numbers with a comma: (Bergreen 450, 457).

GENERAL GUIDELINES
for MLA IN-TEXT CITATIONS

- Name the author, either in a signal phrase such as "Bergreen maintains" or in a parenthetical citation.

- Include a page reference in parentheses. No "p." precedes the page number, and if the author is named in the parentheses, there is no punctuation between the author's name and the page number.

- Place the citation as close to the material being cited as possible and before any punctuation marks that divide or end the sentence, such as commas, semicolons, or periods—except in a block quotation, where the citation comes one space after the period or other closing punctuation mark.

- Underline titles of books and magazines, and place quotation marks around the titles of articles, poems, and plays. Do not use italics.

- For Internet sources, follow the same general guidelines as for print sources. Keep the parenthetical citations as simple as possible, providing enough information for readers to find the full citation in your works-cited list. (Do not, for example, provide a long URL within a parenthetical citation; instead, cite either the author's name or the title of the site or article.)

3. Two or more works by the same author: You must identify which work you are citing, either in your sentence or in an abbreviated form in parentheses.

title underlined
In Louis Armstrong, an American Genius, Collier reports that Glaser paid Armstrong's mortgage, taxes, and basic living expenses (330).

During those years, Glaser paid Armstrong's mortgage, taxes, and basic living expenses (Collier, Louis Armstrong 330).

4. Two or three authors of the same work: If a source has up to three authors, you should name them all either in your text, as shown below, or in parentheses: (Jones and Chilton 160, 220).

According to Jones and Chilton, Glaser's responsibilities included booking appearances, making travel arrangements, and paying the band members' salaries (160, 220).

Tips

LEARNING in COLLEGE

What Is the Modern Language Association?

The Modern Language Association (MLA) is a professional organization of language teachers that was founded in the United States in 1883. Its purpose is to support the study and teaching of languages. The MLA published its first handbook in 1977, and since then the book has become a widely accepted guide to rules for writing research papers. The *MLA Handbook* focuses on the mechanics of academic writing, including punctuation, quotation, and documentation of sources. In addition, the MLA guidelines are used by academic journals, newsletters, magazines, and university presses in both the United States and Canada. Recently, translated versions have also appeared in Japan and China. Following the MLA guidelines will help you document your research and write a clear and credible research paper.

5. More than three authors: If the source has more than three authors, either list all the authors or give the first author's last name followed by *et al.,* the abbreviation for the Latin phrase meaning "and others."

> Changes in social regulations are bound to produce new forms of
>
> subjectivity (Henriques et al. 275).

6. Authors with the same last name: If two or more of your sources have the same last name, include the first initial of the author you are citing; if the first initial is also shared, use the full first name, as shown below.

> In the late nineteenth century, the sale of sheet music spread rapidly
>
> in a Manhattan area along Broadway known as Tin Pan Alley
>
> (Richard Campbell 63).

7. Organization as author: To cite works by organized groups, government agencies, associations, or corporations, treat the organization as the author. If the name is long, either put it in a signal phrase or use an abbreviated version in the parentheses.

> The Centre for Contemporary Cultural Studies claims that
>
> "there is nothing inherently concrete about historiography" (10).

> Historiography deals with abstract issues (Centre 10).

8. Unknown author: When no author is given, cite a work by its title, using either the full title in a signal phrase or an abbreviated version in the parentheses. Be sure to abbreviate in a way that points clearly to the corresponding entry in your list of works cited.

> title of article
> "Squaresville, U.S.A. vs. Beatsville" makes the Midwestern small-town
>
> home seem boring compared with the West Coast artist's "pad" (31).

> The Midwestern small-town home seems boring compared with the
>
> West Coast artist's "pad" ("Squaresville" 31).

9. Entire work: When you want to acknowledge an entire work, such as a film or a book, you should do so in your text, not in a parenthetical citation. Be sure to include the work in your list of works cited.

> Sidney J. Furie's film Lady Sings the Blues presents Billie Holiday as a
>
> beautiful woman in pain rather than as the great jazz artist she was.

10. Paraphrased or summarized source: If you include the author's name in your paraphrase or summary, include only the page number or numbers in your parenthetical citation. Signal phrases clarify that you are paraphrasing or summarizing.

> signal phrase
> Bergreen recounts how in southern states, where blacks were
>
> prohibited from entering many stores, Glaser sometimes had to
>
> shop for the band's food and other supplies (378, 381).

11. Source of a long quotation: For a quotation of four or more typed lines, do not use quotation marks. Instead, indent the material to be quoted by one inch (most word-processing programs will automatically set the correct indention if you use the "increase indent" command or button). Allow one space before the parenthetical information after the final punctuation mark of the quotation.

> Glaser managed the Sunset Café, a club where Armstrong often
>
> performed:
>
> > There was a pronounced gangster element at the Sunset,
> >
> > but Louis, accustomed to being employed and protected by

> mobsters, didn't think twice about that. Mr. Capone's men
> ensured the flow of alcohol, and their presence reassured
> many whites. (Bergreen 279)

12. Source of a short quotation: Close the quotation before the parenthetical citation. If the quotation concludes with an exclamation point or a question mark, include that punctuation mark before the closing quotation mark and insert a period after the parenthetical citation.

> His innovative singing style also featured "scat," a technique that
>
> brackets enclose word that substitutes for omitted text
> combines "nonsense syllables [with] improvised melodies"
>
> (Robinson 515).

13. One-page source: You need not include a page number in the parenthetical citation for a one-page printed source, but doing so is never wrong.

PAGE NUMBER

> Knittle notes that a benefit of deep breathing and relaxation is the
> "circulation of lymph throughout the body, a process that removes
> toxins from the tissues and organs" (34).

NO PAGE NUMBER

> Knittle notes that a benefit of deep breathing and relaxation is the
> "circulation of lymph throughout the body, a process that removes
> toxins from tissues and organs."

14. Government publication: To avoid an overly long parenthetical citation, give the name of the government agency that published the source within your text.

> According to a report issued by the Bureau of National Affairs, many
> employers in 1964 needed guidance to apply new workplace rules that
> ensured fairness and complied with the Civil Rights Act of 1964 (32).

> The President's Council on Bioethics documents the disturbing trend
> towards using genetic engineering to "enhance" lifestyles rather than
> cure disease (Beyond Therapy).

15. Photograph, map, graph, chart, or other visual:

Visual included within the text of your paper:

> An aerial photograph of Manhattan (Fig. 3), taken by the United States Geographical Survey, demonstrates how creative city planning can introduce parks and green spaces within even the most densely populated urban areas.

The caption you write for the image should include citation information.

Visual not included within the text of your paper:

> An aerial photograph of Manhattan taken by the United States Geographical Survey demonstrates how creative city planning can introduce parks and green spaces within even the most densely populated urban areas (TerraServer-USA).

Because you are not including the image, you need to provide a parenthetical citation that directs your reader to your works-cited list and further information about the image, such as the full URL of the site where it can be viewed, if you found it on a Web site (*see no. 16*).

16. Web site or other online electronic source:

For online sources such as Web sites, the MLA recommends using the guidelines already established for print sources. If you cannot find the author of an online source, then identify the source by title, either in your text or in a parenthetical citation. Because most online sources do not have set page, section, or paragraph numbers, they must usually be cited as entire works.

> In the 1920s, many young black musicians from New Orleans migrated north to Chicago, hoping for a chance to perform with the best ("Chicago").

17. Work with numbered paragraphs or screens instead of pages:

Give the paragraph or screen number(s) after the author's name and a comma. To distinguish them from page numbers, use the abbreviation *par(s).* or the word *screen(s).*

> Goodman understood how to balance the public's demand for pop with his own desire to push his players (Edgers, screen 1).

18. Work with no page or paragraph numbers: When citing an online or print source without page, paragraph, or other reference numbers, try to work the author's name into your text instead of putting it in a parenthetical citation.

author's name

> Crouch argues that Armstrong remains a driving force in present-day
>
> music, from country and western music to the chanted doggerel of rap.

19. Multivolume work: When citing more than one volume, include the volume number, followed by a colon, a space, and the page number.

> Schuller argues that even though jazz's traditional framework appears
>
> European, its musical essence is African (1: 62).

If you consult only one volume of a multivolume work, it is unnecessary to cite the volume number in the parenthetical reference. You should include it as part of the works-cited entry (*see p. 299*).

20. Literary work:

Novels and literary nonfiction books: Include the relevant page number, followed by a semicolon, a space, and the chapter number.

> Louis Armstrong figures throughout Ellison's <u>Invisible Man</u>, including
>
> in the narrator's penultimate decision to become a "yes" man who
>
> "undermine[s] them with grins" (384; ch. 23).

If the author is not named in your sentence, add the name in front of the page number: (Ellison 384; ch. 23).

Poems: Use line numbers, not page numbers.

> In "Trumpet Player," Hughes says that the music "Is honey / Mixed with
>
> liquid fire" (lines 19-20). This image returns at the end, when Hughes
>
> concludes that "Trouble / Mellows to a golden note" (43-44).

Note that the word *lines* (not *l.* or *ll.*) is used in the first citation to establish what the numbers in parentheses refer to; subsequent citations need not use the word *lines*. (*See pp. 554–56 and 569–70 for more information about quoting poetry.*)

Plays and long, multisection poems: Use division (act, scene, canto, book, part) and lines, not page numbers. In the following example, notice that arabic numerals are used for act and scene divisions as well as for line numbers: (*Hamlet* 2.3.22-27). The same is true for canto, verse, and lines in the following citation of Byron's *Don Juan:* (*DJ* 1.37.4-8).

21. Religious text: Cite material in the Bible, Upanishads, or Koran (Qu'ran) by book, chapter, and verse, using an appropriate abbreviation when the name of the book is in parentheses rather than in your sentence. Name the edition from which you are citing.

> As the Bible says, "There is nothing new under the Sun" (Revised
>
> Standard Version, Eccles. 1.9).

Note that titles of biblical books are not underlined.

22. Historical document: Cite familiar documents such as the Constitution and the Declaration of Independence in your text, providing the name and the numbers of the parts you are citing.

> Judges are allowed to remain in office "during good Behaviour," a vague
>
> standard that has had various interpretations (US Const., art. 3, sec. 1).

It is not necessary, however, to include a familiar document in your list of works cited.

23. Indirect source: When you quote or paraphrase a quotation you found in someone else's work, put *qtd. in* (meaning "quoted in") before the name of your source.

> Armstrong confided to a friend that Glaser's death "broke [his] heart"
>
> (qtd. in Bergreen 490).

In your list of works cited, list only the work you consulted, in this case the indirect source by Bergreen.

24. Two or more sources in one citation: When you credit two or more sources, use a semicolon to separate the citations.

Giving up his other business ventures, Glaser now became Armstrong's
exclusive agent (Bergreen 376-78; Collier 273-76; Morgenstern 124-28).

25. Two or more sources in one sentence: Include a parenthetical reference after each idea or quotation you have borrowed.

Americans lavish more money each year on their pets than they spend
on children's toys (Merkin 21), but the feral cat population--consisting
of abandoned pets and their offspring--is at an estimated 70 million
and growing (Mott).

26. Work in an anthology: Give the name of the specific work's
author, not the name of the editor of the whole collection.

When Dexter Gordon threatened to quit, Armstrong offered him
a raise--without consulting with Glaser (Morgenstern 132).

Here, Morgenstern is cited as the source even though his work appears in a collection edited by Marc Miller. Note that the list of works
cited must include an entry for Morgenstern (*see p. 332*).

27. E-mail, letter, or personal interview: Cite by name the person
you communicated with, using either a signal phrase or parentheses.

Much to Glaser's surprise, both "Hello, Dolly" and "What a Wonderful
World" became big hits after the rights had been sold (Jacobs).

In the works-cited list, you will need to identify the kind of communication and its date (*see pp. 305, 313, and 316*).

27 MLA Style: List of Works Cited

Besides in-text citations, MLA documentation style requires a works-cited page, where readers can find full bibliographic information about the sources you used. The list of works cited should appear at the end of your paper, beginning on a new page titled "Works Cited." Include only those sources you cite in your paper, unless your instructor tells you to prepare a works-consulted list.

www.mhhe.com/
awr
To download
Bibliomaker software
for MLA, go to
Research >
Bibliomaker

MLA WORKS-CITED ENTRIES: DIRECTORY to SAMPLE TYPES

(See pp. 283–92 for examples of in-text citations.)

(continued)

MLA WORKS-CITED ENTRIES: DIRECTORY to SAMPLE TYPES *(continued)*

Books

1. Book with one author: Underline the book's title. Only the city, not the state, is included in the publication data. Notice that in the example the publisher's name, *Wayne State University Press,* is abbreviated to *Wayne State UP.*

Hennessey, Thomas J. From Jazz to Swing: African-Americans and Their

Music 1890-1935. Detroit: Wayne State UP, 1984.

2. Two or more works by the same author(s):

When you list more than one work by the same author, give the author's name in the first entry only. For subsequent works authored by that person, replace the name with three hyphens and a period. Multiple works by one author are alphabetized by title.

Collier, James Lincoln. Jazz: The American Theme Song. New York:

Oxford UP, 1993.

---. Louis Armstrong, an American Genius. New York: Oxford UP, 1983.

3. Book with two or more authors:

Name the two or three authors in the order in which they appear on the title page, putting the last name first for the first author only. When a work has more than three authors, you may use the abbreviation *et al.* (meaning "and others") to replace the names of all authors except the first.

Davis, Miles, and Quincy Troupe. Miles: The Autobiography. New York:

Simon, 1989.

Henriques, Julian, et al. Changing the Subject: Psychology, Social

Regulation, and Subjectivity. New York: Methuen, 1984.

4. Organization as author:

Consider as an organization any group, commission, association, or corporation whose members are not identified on the title page.

Centre for Contemporary Cultural Studies. Making Histories: Studies

in History Writing and Politics. London: Hutchinson, 1982.

5. Book by an editor or editors:

If the title page lists an editor instead of an author, treat the editor as an author but put the abbreviation *ed.* after the name. Use *eds.* when more than one editor is listed. Only the first editor's name should appear in reverse order.

Miller, Paul Eduard, ed. Esquire's Jazz Book. New York: Smith, 1944.

GENERAL GUIDELINES
for the MLA WORKS-CITED LIST

- Begin on a new page.
- Begin with the centered title "Works Cited."
- Include an entry for every in-text citation.
- Include author, title, and publication data for each entry, if available. Use a period to set off each of these elements from the others. Leave one space after the periods.
- Do not number the entries.
- Put entries in alphabetical order by author's or editor's last name. (If the author is unknown, use the first word of the title, excluding the articles *a, an,* or *the*). If the work has more than one author, see no. 3. Do not add academic titles such as *Ph.D.* to the author's name.
- Underline titles of books and periodicals. Put quotation marks around titles of articles and poems. Do not use Italics. Give all titles, including titles of works in a foreign language, exactly as they appear on the title page.
- Capitalize the first and last and all important words in all titles and subtitles. Do not capitalize articles, prepositions, coordinating conjunctions, and the *to* in infinitives.
- In the publication data, abbreviate publishers' names and months; (*Oxford UP* instead of *Oxford University Press; Dec.* rather than *December*), and include the name of the city in which the publisher is located but not the state: *Danbury: Grolier.* If a source does not give the date of publication, give the approximate date, enclosed in brackets: [c. 1975]. If you cannot approximate the date, write *n.d.* for "no date."
- Do not use *p., pp.,* or *page(s).* Numbers alone will do. When page spans over 100 have the same first digit, use only the last two digits of the second number: 243-47.
- Abbreviate all months (for newspaper, magazine, and some online sources) except *May, June,* and *July.*
- For articles and other print sources that skip pages, provide the page number for the beginning of the article followed by a plus (+) sign.
- Use a hanging indent: Start the first line of each entry at the left margin, and indent all subsequent lines of the entry five spaces (or one-half inch on the computer).
- Double-space within entries and between them.

6. Book with an author and an editor: Put the author and title first, followed by *Ed.* (meaning "edited by") and the name of the editor. However, if you cited something written by the editor rather than the author, see no. 14.

editor's name not in reverse order

Armstrong, Louis. <u>Louis Armstrong--A Self-Portrait</u>. Ed. Richard

Meryman. New York: Eakins, 1971.

7. Work in an anthology or chapter in an edited book: List the author and title of the selection, followed by the title of the anthology, the abbreviation *Ed.* for "edited by," the editor's name, publication data, and page numbers.

Smith, Hale. "Here I Stand." <u>Readings in Black American Music</u>.

Ed. Eileen Southern. New York: Norton, 1971. 286-89.

8. Two or more items from one anthology: Include a complete entry for the anthology. Each selection from the anthology that you are citing should have its own entry in the alphabetical list that includes only the author, title of the selection, editor, and page numbers.

entry for a selection from the anthology

Johnson, Hall. "Notes on the Negro Spiritual." Southern 268-75.

entry for the anthology

Southern, Eileen, ed. <u>Readings in Black American Music</u>. New York:

Norton, 1971.

entry for a selection from the anthology

Still, William Grant. "The Structure of Music." Southern 276-79.

9. Signed article in a reference work: Cite the author's name, title of the entry (in quotation marks), title of the reference work (underlined), and publication information.

Robinson, J. Bradford. "Scat Singing." <u>The New Grove Dictionary</u>

<u>of Jazz</u>. Ed. Barry Kernfeld. Vol. 3. London: Macmillan, 2002.

515-16.

10. Unsigned entry in a reference work: Start the entry with the title. For well-known reference works such as general-interest encyclopedias and dictionaries, the city and publisher can be omitted.

"Scat." Merriam-Webster's Collegiate Dictionary. 11th ed. 2003.

11. Article from a collection of reprinted articles:

Prager, Joshua Harris. "The Longest Replay." Wall Street Journal July

    abbreviation for "reprinted"

    1998. Rpt. in Floating off the Page: The Best Stories from the Wall

    Street Journal's Middle Column." Ed. Ken Wells. New York: Wall

    Street Journal-Simon, 2002. 149-53.

12. Anthology:

Eggers, Dave, ed. The Best American Nonrequired Reading 2003.

    Boston: Houghton, 2003.

13. Publisher's imprint: For books published by a division within a publishing company, known as an "imprint," put a hyphen between the imprint and publisher.

Wells, Ken, ed. Floating off the Page: the Best Stories from the Wall

    Street Journal's "Middle Column." New York: Wall Street Journal-

    Simon, 2002.

14. Preface, foreword, introduction, or afterword: When the writer of the part is different from the author of the book, use the word *By* after the book's title and cite the author's full name. If the book's author wrote the part, use only the author's last name after *By*.

    name of part of book

Crawford, Richard. Foreword. The Jazz Tradition. By Martin Williams.

    New York: Oxford UP, 1993. v-xiii.

Fowles, John. Preface. Islands. By Fowles. Boston: Little, 1978. 1-2.

15. Translation: Cite the work under the author's name, not the translator's. The translator's name goes after the title, with the abbreviation *Trans.* (meaning "translated by").

> Goffin, Robert. Horn of Plenty: The Story of Louis Armstrong. Trans.
>
> James F. Bezov. New York: Da Capo, 1977.

16. Edition other than the first: Include the number of the edition: *2nd ed., 3rd ed.,* and so on. Place the number after the title, or if there is an editor, after that person's name.

> Panassie, Hugues. Louis Armstrong. 2nd ed. New York: Da Capo, 1980.

17. Religious texts: Give the version, underlined; the editor's or translator's name (if any); and the publication information.

> New American Standard Bible. La Habra: Lockman Foundation, 1995.

> The Upanishads. Trans. Eknath Easwaran. Tomales: Nilgiri, 1987.

18. Multivolume work: Your citation should indicate whether you used more than one volume of a multivolume work. The first example indicates that the researcher used more than one volume; the second shows that only the second volume of the work was used.

> Lissauer, Robert. Lissauer's Encyclopedia of Popular Music in America.
>
> 3 vols. New York: Facts on File, 1996.

> Lissauer, Robert. Lissauer's Encyclopedia of Popular Music in America.
>
> Vol. 2. New York: Facts on File, 1996.

19. Book in a series: After the title of the book, put the name of the series and, if available on the title page, the number of the work.

> Floyd, Samuel A., Jr., ed. Black Music in the Harlem Renaissance.
> Name of series not underlined
> Contributions in Afro-American and African Studies 128.
>
> New York: Greenwood, 1990.

20. Republished book: Put the original date of publication, followed by a period, before the current publication data. In the following example, the writer cites a 1974 republication of a book that originally appeared in 1936.

> Cuney-Hare, Maud. <u>Negro Musicians and Their Music</u>. 1936. New York:
>
> Da Capo, 1974.

21. Title in a title: When a book's title contains the title of another book, do not underline the second title. In the following example, the novel *Invisible Man* is not underlined.

> O'Meally, Robert, ed. <u>New Essays on</u> Invisible Man. Cambridge:
>
> Cambridge UP, 1988.

22. Unknown author: The citation begins with the title. In the list of works cited, alphabetize the citation by the first important word, not by articles like *A, An,* or *The.*

> <u>Webster's College Dictionary</u>. New York: Random; New York:
>
> McGraw, 1991.

Note that this entry includes both of the publishers listed on the dictionary's title page; they are separated by a semicolon.

Periodicals

Periodicals are published at set intervals, usually four times a year for scholarly journals, monthly or weekly for magazines, and daily or weekly for newspapers. Between the author and the publication data are two titles: the title of the article, in quotation marks, and the title of the periodical, underlined. (*For online versions of print periodicals and periodicals published only online, see pp. 310–11.*)

23. Article in a journal paginated by volume: Many scholarly journals are published a handful of times each year and are then bound together by libraries into yearly volumes. For journals paginated by yearly volume, not individual issue, put the volume number after the title. Give the year of publication in parentheses, followed by a colon, a space, and the page numbers of the article.

Tirro, Frank. "Constructive Elements in Jazz Improvisation." Journal of
the American Musicological Society 27 (1974): 285-305.

24. Article in a journal paginated by issue: For scholarly journals
paginated by issue, not volume, you must also give the issue number.
Place a period after the volume number, and follow it with the issue
number. In the example, the volume is 25 and the issue is 4.

Aguiar, Sarah Appleton. "'Everywhere and Nowhere': Beloved's 'Wild'
Legacy in Toni Morrison's Jazz." Notes on Contemporary
Literature 25.4 (1995): 11-12.

25. Article in a monthly magazine: Provide the month and year,
abbreviating the names of all months except *May, June,* and *July.*

Walker, Malcolm. "Discography: Bill Evans." Jazz Monthly
June 1965: 20-22.

26. Article in a weekly magazine: Include the complete date of
publication: day, month, and year.

Taylor, J. R. "Jazz History: The Incompleted Past." Village Voice
3 July 1978: 65-67.

27. Article in a newspaper: Provide the day, month, and year.
If an edition is named on the masthead (the top of the first page, which
includes the name of the newspaper), specify the edition (*natl. ed.* or
late ed., for example) after the date and use a comma between the date
and the edition. Whenever possible, give a section designation (*E* in the
example) along with the page number. If the article appears on non-
consecutive pages, put a plus sign (+) after the first page number.

Blumenthal, Ralph. "Satchmo with His Tape Recorder Running."
New York Times 3 Aug. 1999: E1+.

28. Unsigned article: The citation begins with the title and is alphabetized by the first word other than an article like *A, An,* or *The.*

"Squaresville, U.S.A. vs. Beatsville." Life 21 Sept. 1959: 31.

29. Review: Begin with the name of the reviewer and, if there is one, the title of the review. Add *Rev. of* (meaning "review of") and the title plus the author or performer of the work being reviewed. Notice that the word *by* precedes the author's name.

> Ostwald, David. "All That Jazz." Rev. of Louis Armstrong:
>
> An Extravagant Life, by Laurence Bergreen. Commentary
>
> Nov. 1997: 68-72.

30. Editorial: Treat editorials as articles, but add the word *Editorial* after the title. If the editorial is unsigned, begin with the title.

> Shaw, Theodore M. "The Debate over Race Needs Minority Students'
>
> Voices." Editorial. Chronicle of Higher Education 25 Feb. 2000:
>
> A72.

31. Abstract of a journal article: Collections of abstracts from journals in specific disciplines can be found in the reference section of your library. Include the publication information for the original article, followed by the title of the publication that provides the abstract, the volume, the year in parentheses, and the item or the page number.

> Theiler, Anne M. and Louise G. Lippman. "Effects of Mental Practice
>
> and Modeling on Guitar and Vocal Performance." Journal of
>
> General Psychology 122.4 (1995): 329-43. Psychological Abstracts
>
> 83 (1996): item 30039.

32. Letter to the editor:

> Tyler, Steve. Letter. National Geographic Adventure Apr. 2004: 11.

Other Print Sources

33. Government document: Either the name of the government and agency or the document's author's name comes first. If the government and agency names come first, follow the title of the document with the word *By* for a writer, *Ed.* for an editor, or *Comp.* for a compiler. Publication information, abbreviated, comes last.

United States. Bureau of National Affairs. The Civil Rights Act of 1964:

Text, Analysis, Legislative History; What It Means to Employers,

Businessmen, Unions, Employees, Minority Groups. Washington:

BNA, 1964.

For the format to use when citing the *Congressional Record,* whether in print or online, see no. 62.

34. Pamphlet: Treat as you would a book. If the pamphlet has an author, list his or her name first; otherwise, begin with the title.

All Music Guide to Jazz. 2nd ed. San Francisco: Miller Freeman, 1996.

35. Conference proceedings: Cite as you would a book, but include information about the conference if it is not in the title.

Mendel, Arthur, Gustave Reese, and Gilbert Chase, eds. Papers Read

at the International Congress of Musicology held at New York

September 11th to 16th, 1939. New York: Music Educators' National

Conference for the American Musicological Society, 1944.

36. Published dissertation: Cite as you would a book. After the title, add *Diss.* for "dissertation," the name of the institution, and the year the dissertation was written.

Fraser, Wilmot Alfred. Jazzology: A Study of the Tradition in Which Jazz

Musicians Learn to Improvise. Diss. U of Pennsylvania, 1983.

Ann Arbor: UMI, 1987.

37. Unpublished dissertation or essay: For a dissertation, begin with the author's name, followed by the title in quotation marks, the abbreviation *Diss.,* the name of the institution, and the year the dissertation was written.

Reyes-Schramm, Adelaida. "The Role of Music in the Interaction of

Black Americans and Hispanos in New York City's East Harlem."

Diss. Columbia U, 1975.

For an unpublished essay, include the phrase *Unpublished essay* after the title.

> Pollack, Bracha. "A Man ahead of His Time." Unpublished essay, 1997.

38. Abstract of a dissertation: Use the format for an unpublished dissertation. After the dissertation date, give the abbreviation *DA* or *DAI* (for *Dissertation Abstracts* or *Dissertation Abstracts International*), then the volume number, date of publication, and page number.

> Quinn, Richard Allen. "Playing Together: Improvisation in Postwar
>
> American Literature and Culture." Diss. U of Iowa, 2000.
>
> DAI 61 (2001): 2305A.

39. Published interview: Name the person interviewed and give the title of the interview or the descriptive term *Interview,* the name of the interviewer (if known and relevant), and the publication information.

> Armstrong, Louis. "Authentic American Genius." Interview with
>
> Richard Meryman. Life 15 Apr. 1966: 92-102.

40. Map or chart: Cite as you would a book with an unknown author. Underline the title of the map or chart, and add the word *Map* or *Chart* following the title.

> Let's Go Map Guide to New Orleans. Map. New York:
>
> St. Martin's, 1997.

41. Cartoon: Include the cartoonist's name, the title of the cartoon (if any) in quotation marks, the word *Cartoon,* and the publication information.

> Myller, Jorgen. "Louis Armstrong's First Lesson." Cartoon.
>
> Melody Maker Mar. 1931: 12.

42. Advertisement: Name the item or organization being advertised, include the word *Advertisement,* and indicate where the ad appeared.

> Hartwick College Summer Music Festival and Institute. Advertisement.
>> New York Times Magazine 3 Jan. 1999: 54.

43. Published letter: Treat like a work in an anthology, but include the date. Include the number, if one was assigned by the editor. If you use more than one letter from a published collection, follow the instructions for cross-referencing two or more items from an anthology in no. 8.

> Hughes, Langston. "To Arna Bontemps." 17 Jan. 1938.
>> Arna Bontemps--Langston Hughes Letters 1925-1967.
>>> Ed. Charles H. Nichols. New York: Dodd, 1980. 27-28.

44. Personal letter: To cite a letter you received, start with the writer's name, followed by the descriptive phrase *Letter to the author* and then the date.

> Cogswell, Michael. Letter to the author. 15 Mar. 1998.

To cite someone else's unpublished personal letter, see the guidelines in no. 45.

45. Manuscripts, typescripts, and material in archives: Give the author, a title or description of the material (*Letter, Notebook*), the form (*ms.* if manuscript, *ts.* if typescript), any identifying number, and the name and location of the library or other institution housing the material.

> Glaser, Joe. Letter to Lucille Armstrong. 28 Sept. 1960. Box 3.
>> Armstrong Archives. Queens College CUNY, Flushing, NY.

46. Legal source: Cite familiar government documents such as the Constitution within the body of your text only (*see no. 22 on* *p. 291).* To cite a specific act, give its name, Public Law number, the date it was enacted, and its Statutes at Large number.

> Microenterprise Results and Accountability Act of 2004. Pub. L.
>
> 108-484. 23 Dec. 2004. Stat. 3922.

To cite a law case, provide the names of the plaintiff and defendant, the case number, the court that decided the case, and the date of the decision.

> Hamdi v. Rumsfeld. No. 03-6696. Supreme Ct. of the US. 28 June 2004.

For more information about citing legal documents or case law, MLA recommends consulting *The Blue Book: A Uniform System of Citation,* published by the Harvard Law Review Association and available in the reference section of your library.

47. Microfiche/microform/microfilm: Sources that have been photographed, greatly reduced, and stored on microfilm, which you view with the help of a projector, are cited exactly as you would the print version.

48. Publication in more than one medium: If you are citing a publication that consists of several different media (for example, a book accompanied by a CD-ROM and a Web site), list all of the media included.

> Kamien, Roger. Music: An Appreciation. 8th ed. Book, CD-ROM,
>
> interactive online site. New York: McGraw, 2000.

Electronic Sources

The examples that follow are based on the guidelines for the citation of electronic sources in the sixth edition of the *MLA Handbook for Writers of Research Papers* (2003).

Note: The Internet address for an electronic source is its uniform resource locator, or URL. If you need to divide a URL between lines, divide it after a slash. Do not insert a hyphen. If the URL is too long and complex to enter, give the URL of the site's search page.

GENERAL GUIDELINES for CITING ONLINE PERIODICALS

- Begin with the writer's name.
- Put the title of the article in quotation marks.
- If there is no title, use a descriptive term such as "editorial" or "comment."
- Underline the name of the publication. Note that the online versions of some print magazines and newspapers have slightly different titles than the print versions; be sure to cite the online version (*see nos. 55, 56, and 58*).
- Cite the volume, issue, or other identifying number, if relevant, just as you would for the print version.
- Cite the publication date of the original print version of an article, or the "posted" date for an article that appeared only on the online version of the publication.
- If the article is divided into separate pages or numbered paragraphs or sections, indicate the total number of those pages or sections (*see no. 54*).
- If the article is not divided into sections or pages, don't impose an artificial division (for example, "on the second screen"). Just leave that portion of the citation out.
- Include your original date of access to the specific article (not the general site), even if you return to the site several times in the course of your research.
- Conclude the citation with a reasonable URL. If the URL for a specific article is too long (if it takes up much more than one full line of your citation), just give the search page or, if the site does not have a search page, the home page for the site. If your readers can access the document through a series of links from the home page, include them after the word *Path* and a colon. Separate the links with semicolons.
- If you need to break a URL, do so after a slash (/) mark. Do not include extra spaces or hyphens.
- Do not create a "hyperlink" for the URL. See page 308 for instructions on how to turn off automatic hyperlinking in most word-processing programs.

49. Online scholarly project:

Entire Web site: Begin with the title (underlined) of the source, followed by the name of the editor (if any) and the electronic publication

TextConnex

URL Addresses

Some popular word-processing programs automatically turn all URLs into hyperlinks. The MLA recommends disabling this automatic hyperlinking before you print your document. To turn off automatic hyperlinking, go to "AutoFormat as You Type" in the "AutoCorrect" part of the "Tools" menu and remove the check mark next to "Internet and network paths with hyperlinks."

data, which includes, if relevant, the version number, the date of publication or update, and the name of the sponsoring institution (if any). End with the date you used the project and, in angle brackets (< >), the source's complete URL.

> William Ransom Hogan Archive of New Orleans Jazz. Ed. Bruce Boyd
> Raeburn. 30 Oct. 2004. Tulane U. 3 May 2005 <http://
> www.tulane.edu/~lmiller/jazzHome.html>.

URL divided after slash

Part of a scholarly Web site: When citing one part, document, or page of a project, add the author (if known) and the title of the part in quotation marks. If the author is unknown, start with the title of the part in quotation marks.

> Raeburn, Bruce Boyd. "An Introduction to New Orleans Jazz." William
> Ransom Hogan Archive of New Orleans Jazz. Ed. Bruce Boyd
> Raeburn. 30 Oct. 2004. Tulane U. 3 May 2005 <http://
> www.tulane.edu/~lmiller/BeginnersIntro.html>.

> "Armstrong Biography." Satchmo.Net: The Official Site for the Louis
> Armstrong House and Archives. 2003. Queens College CUNY.
> 3 May 2005 <http://www.satchmo.net/bio/>.

50. Professional or personal Web site: Name the person responsible for the site, the title of the site (underlined), the name of the associated institution or organization (if any), the date of access, and the URL. If no title is available, use a descriptive term such as *Home page* (without underlining or quotation marks).

Henson, Keith. The Keith Henson Jazzpage. 3 May 2005 <http://

home.earthlink.net/~keithhenson>.

Wildman, Joan. The World of Jazz Improvisation. U of Wisconsin,

Madison. 3 May 2005 <http://hum.lss.wisc.edu/jazz>.

51. Home page for a course: After the instructor's name, list the course title; if there is no course title on the home page, use the title from the school's catalog, if available, or the course number. Include the dates of the course, then the department and school names.

Marshall, S. A. Insects in Relation to Wildlife. Course home page.

Jan. 2005-May 2005. Dept. of Environmental Biology, U of

Guelph. 18 Apr. 2005 <http://www.uoguelph.ca/OAC/env/

co_3090.shtml>.

52. Site authored by a person using a pseudonym: Provide the name given on the Web site, even if it is obviously not the author's real name. You may provide the real name in brackets. (*See also no. 64.*)

Instapundit [Glenn Reynolds]. Weblog posting. Instapundit.com.

3 Sept. 2005. 20 Sept. 2005 <http://instapundit.com/archives/

week_2005_08_28.php>.

53. Online book:

Entire book: Cite as for print books, including author; title (underlined); editor, translator, or compiler (if any); and publication data for the print version. Add, if available, the name of the database or project, date of electronic publication, sponsoring organization, date of access, and URL.

database underlined

Sandburg, Carl. Chicago Poems. New York: Holt, 1916. Bartleby.com.

Aug. 1999. 3 May 2005 <http://www.bartleby.com/165>.

Work in an online book: Add the title of the work after the author and put it in quotation marks, unless the part cited is an introduction, foreword, preface, or afterword.

Sandburg, Carl. "Chicago." Chicago Poems. New York: Holt,

1916. Bartleby.com. Aug. 1999. 3 May 2005 <http://

www.bartleby.com/165>.

54. Article in an online scholarly journal, published only on-line: Any legitimate journal, whether published in print or online, will have a volume and possibly an issue number, as is true for print journals (see nos. 23 and 24). Include these after the journal's name, with the year of publication in parentheses. Follow this information with access information, as you would do with any online source. On-line scholarly periodicals do tend to number the paragraphs or sections of their articles. When this is the case, indicate the number of sections or paragraphs in your citation.

Schmalfeldt, Janet. "On Keeping the Score." Music Theory

Online 4.2 (1998). 20 pars. 3 May 2005 <http://

www.societymusictheory.org>.

55. Article in an online scholarly journal that is also published in print: List information about the print source, including the volume number, issue number, publication year, and page numbers, before listing information about the online source.

Tsal, Yehoshua, Lilach Shalev, and Carmel Mevorach. "The Diversity

of Attention Deficits in ADHD: The Prevalence of Four Cognitive

Factors in ADHD Versus Controls." Journal of Learning

Disabilities 38.2 (2005): 142-57. IngentaConnect. 5 Aug. 2005

<http://www.ingentaconnect.com/content/proedcw/

jld/2005/>.

56. Article in an online version of a print magazine or period-ical: Provide the publication date—day, month, and year, or month and year—rather than the volume and issue numbers.

Web site for the *Atlantic* magazine

Davis, Francis. "Jazz--Religious and Circus." Atlantic Online. Feb. 2000.

3 Apr. 2004 <http://www.theatlantic.com/issues/2000/

002davis.html>.

57. Article in a periodical that appears only online:

> Ross, Michael E. "The New Sultans of Swing." <u>Salon</u>. 18 Apr. 1996.
>
> > 3 May 2005 <http://www.salon.com/weekly/music1.html>.

58. Article in an online newspaper: Follow the format used for an article in an online magazine.

> "Bulletin Board: Louis Armstrong Centenary." <u>New York Times on the</u>
>
> > <u>Web</u>. 7 Nov. 2001. 3 May 2005 <http://www.nytimes.com>.
> >
> > > overly long URL abbreviated

59. Editorial in an online newspaper: Include the word *Editorial* after the published title of the editorial.

> "A New Pope's Old Message." Editorial. <u>San Francisco Chronicle</u>
>
> > 20 Apr. 2005. 20 Apr. 2005 <http://www.sfgate.com>.

60. Letter to the editor in an online newspaper: Include the name of the letter writer, as well as the word *Letter*.

> Hughan, Wade C. Letter. <u>San Francisco Chronicle</u> 20 Apr. 2005.
>
> > 20 Apr. 2005 <http://www.sfgate.com>.

61. Online government publication except the *Congressional Record*: Begin with the name of the country, followed by the name of the sponsoring department, the title of the document, and the names (if listed) of the authors.

> United States. National Commission on Terrorist Attacks upon the
>
> > United States. <u>The 9/11 Commission Report</u>. By Thomas H. Kean
> >
> > et al. 5 Aug. 2004. 30 Mar. 2005 <http://www.gpoaccess.gov/
> >
> > 911/index.html>.

62. *Congressional Record* (online or in print): Abbreviate the title and include the date and page numbers.

> <u>Cong. Rec.</u> 28 Apr. 2005: D419-D428.

63. Online review:

> Kot, Greg. "The Mekons Find Renewal in Their Loud, Punky Past." Rev
>
> of Punk Rock CD, the Mekons. Chicago Tribune Online Edition.
>
> 26 Mar. 2004. 2 Apr. 2004 <http://www.chicagotribune.com>.

64. Weblog ("blog") posting: A Weblog, or "blog," is an online diary. (*For more on blogs, see Tab 3: Common Assignments, p. 178.*) Citing a blog entry is similar to the citation of other online postings.

> Sullivan, Andrew. "The Grim Task in Iraq." Weblog posting.
>
> Andrewsullivan.com: The Daily Dish. 25 Nov. 2003. 24 Feb. 2004
>
> <http://www.andrewsullivan.com/index.php?dish_inc=archives>.

65. CD-ROM or DVD: Works on CD-ROM are usually cited like books or parts of books, but the term *CD-ROM* and the name of the vendor, if different from the publisher, are added before the publication data.

> "Armstrong, (Daniel) Louis 'Satchmo.'" Microsoft Encarta Multimedia
>
> Encyclopedia CD-ROM. Redmond: Microsoft, 1994.

66. CD-ROM or DVD—Material with no print version:

> "Aristotle." Encarta 2000. CD-ROM. Redmond: Microsoft, 1999.

67. CD-ROM or DVD—Entire book:

> Jones, Owen. The Grammar of Ornament. CD-ROM. Palo Alto:
>
> Octavo, 1998.

68. Work from a library or personal subscription service: For material that you accessed through a library subscription service such as *EBSCO, InfoTrac, ProQuest,* and *LexisNexis,* add the following to your citation: the name of the online service used; the library's name; the date of access; and, if known, the URL of the site's home page.

Hardack, Richard. "'A Music Seeking Its Words': Double-Timing

and Double Consciousness in Toni Morrison's Jazz."

Callaloo 18 (1995): 451-72. Expanded Academic ASAP.

InfoTrac. Rosenthal Lib., Queens College CUNY. 3 May 2005

<http://web7.infotrac.galegroup.com>.

If you used a personal subscription service such as America Online, and you retrieved information by using a keyword or a topic path, identify the online service, the date accessed, and either the keyword used or the path taken. Use a colon after the capitalized words *Keyword* or *Path,* and use semicolons to separate topics.

"Jazz." World Book Online Reference Center. 2005. America Online.

3 May 2005. Path: Research and Learn; References; Encyclopedia;

Site Contents; Jazz.

69. Posting to a news group: Begin with the author and (in quotation marks) the title or subject line; the words *Online posting,* without quotation marks or underlining, follow. End with the posting date, the list or group name, the date of access, and the URL of the list or the e-mail address of the moderator if no URL is available.

Mopsick, Don. "Favorite Jazz Quotes." Online posting. 17 Mar. 2000.

Big Band-Music Fans. 17 June 2000 <http://www.remarq.com/

list/4755?nav+FIRST&rf+1&si+grou>.

70. Synchronous communication: Include a description and the date of the event, the title of the forum, the date of access, and the URL. If relevant, the speaker's name can begin the citation.

Curran, Stuart, and Harry Rusche. Discussion: Plenary Log 6. Third

Annual Graduate Student Conference in Romanticism. 20 Apr.

1996. Prometheus Unplugged: Emory MOO. 4 Jan. 1999

<http://prometheus.cc.emory.edu/plen/plenary6.txt>.

71. E-mail: Include the author; the subject line (if any) in quotation marks; the descriptive term *E-mail* plus the name of the recipient; and the date of the message.

Hoffman, Esther. "Re: My Louis Armstrong Paper." E-mail to J. Peritz.

5 Aug. 2005.

72. Online graphic: Base the form of your citation on the most closely related print or nonprint model. When possible, include the creator's name, the title or description of the source, the title of the larger work in which the source appears (underlined), the publication data, the date of access, and the URL.

Hirschfeld, Al. Louis "Satchmo" Armstrong. Margo Feiden Galleries.

5 May 2005 <http://www.alhirschfeld.com/cgi-bin/

cat_alpha?CAT=A2#L>.

73. Online audio or video file: Follow the guidelines in no. 72.

Adderley, Nat. Interview with Jimmy Owens. Video clip. Louis

Armstrong Jazz Oral History Project. 2 Apr. 1993. Schomburg

Center for Research in Black Culture. 3 May 2005 <http://

www.nypl.org/research/sc/scl/MULTIMED/JAZZHIST/

jazzhist.html>.

74. Online cartoon:

Toles, Tom. "The Rubik's Food Pyramid." Cartoon.

Washingtonpost.com. 21 Apr. 2005. 29 Apr. 2005

<http://www.washingtonpost.com/wp-srv/

opinion/toles_archive.html>.

75. Online map:

"New Orleans." Map. Lonely Planet. 2 May 2005 <http://

www.lonelyplanet.com/mapshells/north_america/

new_orleans/new_orleans.htm>.

76. Computer software: Provide the author's or editor's name, if available; the title (underlined); the medium; the version number; and the publication information, including place of publication, publisher, and date. If you downloaded the software from the Internet, replace the publication information with the date of access and the URL.

> AllWrite! 2.1 with Online Handbook. CD-ROM. Vers. 2.1. New York:
>
> McGraw, 2003.

Audiovisual and Other Nonprint Sources

77. Film, videotape, or DVD: Begin with the title (underlined). For a film, cite the director and the lead actors or narrator (*Perf.* or *Narr.*), followed by the distributor and year. For a videotape or DVD, add the medium (*Videocassette* or *DVD*) before the name of the distributor.

> Artists and Models. Dir. Raoul Walsh. Perf. Louis Armstrong, Martha
>
> Raye, and Connee Boswell. Paramount Pictures, 1937.

78. TV or radio program: Give the episode title (in quotation marks), the program title (underlined), the name of the series (if any), the name of the network, the city, and the broadcast date.

> "The Music of Charlie Parker." Jazz Set. WBGO-FM, New York.
>
> 2 Dec. 1998.

79. Broadcast interview: Give the name of the person interviewed, followed by the word *Interview* and the name of the interviewer if you know it. End with information about the broadcast.

> Knox, Shelby. Interview with David Brancaccio. NOW. PBS. WNET,
>
> New York. 17 June 2005.

80. Sound recording: The entry starts with the composer, conductor, or performer, depending on your focus. Include the work's title (underlined); the medium (*LP* below), unless it is a compact disc; the artist(s), if not already mentioned; the manufacturer; and the date of release.

> Armstrong, Louis. Town Hall Concert Plus. LP. RCA Victor, 1957.

81. Musical composition: Include only the composer and title, unless you are referring to a published score. Published scores are treated like books except that the date of composition appears after the title. Note that the titles of instrumental pieces are underlined only when they are known by name, not just by form and number, or when the reference is to a published score.

> Ellington, Duke. Satin Doll.

> Haydn, Franz Josef. Symphony no. 94 in G Major.
> reference to published score
> Haydn, Franz Josef. Symphony No. 94 in G Major. 1791.
> Ed. H. C. Robbins Landon. Salzburg: Haydn-Mozart, 1965.

82. Artwork: Provide the artist's name, the title of the artwork (underlined), and the institution or private collection and city in which the artwork can be found.

> Leonard, Herman. Louis Armstrong: Birdland. Barbara Gillman Gallery,
>
> Miami.

If you used a photograph of a work of art from a book, treat it like a work in an anthology (*see no. 7*), but underline the titles of both the work and the book, and include the institution or collection and city where the work can be found.

83. Personal, telephone, or e-mail interview: Begin with the person interviewed, followed by *Personal interview, Telephone interview,* or *E-mail interview* and the date of the interview. (*See no. 39 for a published interview and no. 79 for a broadcast interview.*)

> Jacobs, Phoebe. Personal interview. 5 May 2005.

84. Lecture or speech: To cite an oral presentation, give the speaker's name, the title (in quotation marks) or a descriptive label such as *Address* or *Lecture,* the name of the forum or sponsor, the location, and the date.

> Taylor, Billy. "What Is Jazz?" John F. Kennedy Center for the Performing
>
> Arts, Washington. 14 Feb. 1995.

85. Performance: To cite a play, opera, ballet, or concert, begin with the title; followed by the authors (*By*); pertinent information about the live performance, such as the director (*Dir.*) and major performers; the site; the city; and the performance date.

Ragtime. By Terrence McNally, Lynn Athrens, and Stephen Flaherty.
Dir. Frank Galati. Ford Performing Arts Center, New York.
11 Nov. 1998.

28 MLA Style: Explanatory Notes and Acknowledgments

Explanatory notes are used to cite multiple sources for borrowed material or to give readers supplemental information. Their purpose is to avoid distracting readers with an overly long parenthetical citation or an interesting but not directly relevant idea. You can also use explanatory notes to acknowledge people who helped you with research and writing. Acknowledgments are a courteous gesture in academic as well as workplace writing, even if you do not intend your paper for publication. If you acknowledge someone's assistance in your explanatory notes, be sure to send that person a copy of your paper. Because they contributed in some way to your work, they are likely to be very interested in your final product.

TEXT

One answer to these questions is suggested by a large (24-by-36-inch) painting discovered in Armstrong's house.[1]

NOTE

[1]I want to thank George Arevalo of the Louis Armstrong Archives for his help on this project. When I was low on inspiration and in search of some direction, George showed me the two pictures I describe in this

paper. Seeing those pictures helped me figure out what I wanted to say—and why I wanted to say it. For introducing me to archival research and to the art of Louis Armstrong, I also want to thank the head of the Louis Armstrong Archives, Michael Cogswell, and my English teacher, Professor Amy Tucker.

29 MLA Style: Paper Format

The following guidelines will help you prepare your research paper in the format recommended by the sixth edition of the *MLA Handbook for Writers of Research Papers*. For an example of a research paper that has been prepared using MLA style, see pages 321–32.

Materials
Before printing your paper, make sure that you have stored your final draft on a backup disk. Use a high-quality printer and high-quality, white 8 1/2-by-11-inch paper. Put the printed pages together with a paper clip, not a staple, and do not use a binder unless you have been told to do so by your instructor.

Heading and title
Unless your instructor requires one, no separate title page is needed. In the upper left-hand corner of the first page, one inch from the top and side, type on separate, double-spaced lines your name, your instructor's name, the course number, and the date. Double-space between the date and the paper's title and the title and the first line of text, as well as throughout your paper. The title should be centered and properly capitalized (*see p. 321*). Do not underline the title or put it in quotation marks or bold type.

Margins and spacing

Use one-inch margins all around, except for the top right-hand corner, where the page number goes. Your right margin should be ragged (not "justified," or even).

Double-space lines throughout the paper, including in quotations, notes, and the works-cited list. Indent the first word of each paragraph one-half inch (or five spaces) from the left margin. For block quotations, indent one inch (or ten spaces) from the left.

Page numbers

Put your last name and the page number in the upper right-hand corner of the page, one-half inch from the top and flush with the right margin.

TEXTCONNEX

Electronic Submission of Papers

Some instructors may request that you submit your paper electronically. (You may also need to submit documents electronically in other situations, such as job or internship applications or as business correspondence.) Keep the following tips in mind:

- Confirm your instructor's e-mail address in advance of submitting the paper.
- Find out in advance how your instructor would like you to submit documents. Some instructors prefer that shorter documents be cut and pasted into the body of an e-mail message. Others might prefer that you submit documents attached to e-mail messages. However, people with dial-up modems can be inconvenienced by very long documents or documents that contain visuals. *Always ask permission before sending an attached document to anyone.*
- If you are asked to send a document as an attachment, confirm that the format of your document is compatible with the receiver's computer. Documents with a great deal of formatting tend to get garbled, or appear full of strange characters, when "translated" from one program to another. Save your document as a "rich text format" (RTF) file or in ASCII format, which simplifies the formatting of your document and makes it easier to share.
- As a courtesy, run a virus scan on the file you intend to submit electronically before sending it. You should also scan for viruses if you are submitting the document on a disk or CD-ROM.
- Send the submission to your own e-mail address as well so that you can make sure the paper has been transmitted successfully.

Visuals

Place visuals (tables, charts, graphs, and images) close to the place in your text where you refer to them. Label and number tables consecutively (*Table 1, Table 2*) and give each one an explanatory caption; put this information above the table. The term *Figure* (abbreviated *Fig.*) is used to label all other kinds of visuals, except for musical illustrations, which are labeled *Example* (abbreviated *Ex.*). Place figure or example captions below the visual. Below all visuals, cite the source of the material and provide explanatory notes as needed. *(For more on using visuals effectively, see Tab 2: Writing and Designing Papers, pp. 53–57.)*

30 Student Paper in MLA Style

As a first-year college student, Esther Hoffman wrote the following paper for her composition course. She knew little about Louis Armstrong and jazz before her instructor took the class to visit the Louis Armstrong Archives. She did archival research based on what she had learned from consulting online and print sources.

www.mhhe.com/
awr
For another sample
of a paper in
MLA style, go to

Research > Sample
Research Papers >
MLA Style

Note: If your instructor requires a title page, prepare it according to his or her instructions. If you do not have instructions to follow, you can center the title approximately one-third from the top of the page, with the word *by* and your name centered approximately one inch below the title and your instructor's name, the course name, and the date centered on separate lines approximately one inch below your name. Double-space all elements. If your instructor requires a final outline, place it between the title page and the first page of the paper.

Esther Hoffman

Professor Tucker

English 120

10 May 2005

Louis Armstrong and Joe Glaser:

More Than Meets the Eye

In the 1920s, jazz music was at its height in creativity and popularity. Chicago had become one of the jazz capitals of America, and its clubs showcased the premier talents of the time, performers like Jelly Roll Morton and Joe Oliver. It has always been difficult to break into the music business, and the jazz scene of the twenties was no exception. Eager for fame and fortune, though, many young black musicians who had honed their craft in New Orleans migrated north to Chicago, hoping for a chance to perform with the best ("Chicago").

Among these émigrés was Louis Armstrong, a gifted musician who developed into the "first true virtuoso soloist of jazz" ("Armstrong"). Armstrong played the trumpet and sang with unusual improvisational ability as well as technical mastery. As Bergreen points out, Armstrong easily reached difficult high notes, the F's and G's that stymied other trumpeters (248). His innovative singing style also featured "scat," a technique that combines "nonsense syllables [with] improvised melodies" (Robinson 425). According to one popular anecdote, Armstrong invented scat during a recording session; mid-song, he dropped his lyrics sheet and--not wanting to disrupt a great take--began to improvise (Edwards 619). Eventually Armstrong's innovations became the standard, as more and more jazz musicians took their cue from his style.

Armstrong's beginnings give no hint of the greatness that he would achieve. In New Orleans, he was born into poverty and

---

On every page: writer's last name and page number.

Title centered, no underline.

Double-spaced throughout.

Background scene sketched.

Web source cited by title.

Paragraph indent 5 spaces or ½"

Topic introduced.

MLA in-text citation: author named in signal phrase.

MLA in-text citation: author named in parentheses.

received little formal education. As a youngster, Armstrong had
to take odd jobs like delivering coal and selling newspapers so
that he could earn money to help his family. At the age of twelve,
Armstrong was placed in the Colored Waifs' Home to serve an
eighteen-month sentence for firing a gun in a public place. There
"Captain" Peter Davis gave him "basic musical training on the
cornet" ("Satchmo!"). Older, more established musicians soon
noticed Armstrong's talent and offered him opportunities to play
with them. In 1922, Joe Oliver invited Armstrong to join his band
in Chicago, and the twenty-one-year-old trumpeter headed north.

It was in Chicago that Armstrong met Joe Glaser, the man
who eventually became his longtime manager. According to
Bergreen, Glaser had a reputation for being a tough but
trustworthy guy who could handle any situation. He was raised in
a middle-class home by parents who were Jewish immigrants from
Russia. As a young man, Glaser got caught up in the Chicago
underworld and soon had a rap sheet that included indictments
for running a brothel as well as for statutory rape.[1] Glaser's mob
connections also led to his involvement in Chicago's club scene, a
business almost completely controlled by gangsters like Al Capone.
During the era of Prohibition, Glaser managed the Sunset Cafe,
a club where Armstrong often performed:

> There was a pronounced gangster element at the Sunset,
> but Louis, accustomed to being employed and protected
> by mobsters, didn't think twice about that. Mr.
> Capone's men ensured the flow of alcohol, and their
> presence reassured many whites. (Bergreen 279)

By the early thirties, Armstrong had become one of the most
popular musicians in the world. He attracted thousands of fans

Development by narration (*see pp. 59–60*).

Focus introduced.

Superscript number indicating explanatory note.

Block quotation indented 10 spaces or 1″.

Hoffman 3

during his 1930 European tour, and his "Hot Five" and "Hot
Seven" recordings were considered some of the best jazz ever
played. Financially, Armstrong should have been doing very well,
but instead he was having business difficulties. He owed money to
Johnny Collins, his former manager, and Lil' Hardin, his ex-wife,
was suing him for a share of the royalties on the song "Struttin'
with Some Barbecue." At this point, Armstrong asked Glaser to be
his business manager. Glaser quickly paid off Collins and settled
with Lil' Hardin. Giving up his other business ventures, Glaser now
became Armstrong's exclusive agent (Morgenstern 124-28; Collier
273-76; Bergreen 376-78). For the next thirty-four years, his
responsibilities included booking appearances, organizing the
bands, making travel arrangements, and paying the band
members' salaries (Jones and Chilton 160, 220).

    Under Glaser's management, Armstrong reached the pinnacle
of his fame, an achievement for which he was profoundly grateful.
Once, while discussing the creation of the All-Star bands,
Armstrong even credited his musical accomplishments to Glaser,
saying, "Anything that I have done musically since I signed up with
Joe Glaser at the Sunset, it was his suggestions" (qtd. in Jones and
Chilton 175). Was Glaser really as central to Armstrong's work and
life as this comment makes him seem? To what extent did Glaser
create and control the star known nowadays as a "King of Jazz"?
What kind of relationship did Joe Glaser and Louis Armstrong
actually have?

    One answer to these questions is suggested by a large (24-by-
36-inch) oil painting discovered in Armstrong's house.[2] Joe Glaser
is pictured in the middle of the canvas. Four black-and-white
quadrants surround the central image of Glaser. One quadrant

Summary of
material from
a number of
sources.

Citation of
multiple
sources.

Use of
information
from two
separate
pages in
one source.

Indirect
source.

Poses key
questions that
thesis will
answer.

Hoffman 4

Development by description (*see pp.* 60–62).

depicts a city scene, the scene in which Glaser thrived. The bottom two quadrants picture dogs, a reminder that Glaser raised show dogs. The remaining quadrant presents an image of Louis Armstrong. By placing Glaser in the center and Armstrong off in a corner, the unknown artist seems to suggest that even though Armstrong was the star, it was Glaser who made him one.

Presents claim plus supporting evidence.

In fact, Glaser did advance Armstrong's career in numerous important ways. In 1935, he negotiated the lucrative record contract with Decca that led to the production of hits like "I'm in the Mood for Love" and "You Are My Lucky Star" (Bergreen 380). Glaser also decided when to sell the rights to Armstrong's songs. Determined to make as much money as possible, he sometimes sold the rights to a song as soon as it was released, especially when he thought the song might not turn out to be a big hit. However, in at least two instances, this money-making strategy backfired: much to Glaser's surprise, both "Hello, Dolly" and "What a Wonderful World" became big hits after the rights had been sold (Jacobs).

Development by illustration (*see pp.* 64–65).

To expand Armstrong's popularity, Glaser increased his exposure to white audiences in the United States. In 1935, articles on Armstrong appeared in Vanity Fair and Esquire, two magazines with a predominantly white readership (Bergreen 385). Glaser also promoted Armstrong's movie career. At a time when only a handful of black performers were accepted in Hollywood, Armstrong had roles in a number of films, including Pennies from

Note use of transitional expressions (*see pp.* 86–87).

Heaven (1936) with Bing Crosby. Moreover, "Jeepers Creepers," a song Armstrong sang in Going Places (1938), received an Academy Award nomination (Bogle 149, 157). Of course, more exposure sometimes meant more discomfort, if not danger, especially when

Hoffman 5

Armstrong and his band members were touring in the South. Bergreen recounts how in southern states, where blacks were prohibited from entering many stores, Glaser sometimes had to shop for the band's food and other supplies (378, 381).

As Armstrong's manager, Glaser also exerted some control over the musician's personal finances and habits. According to Dave Gold, an accountant who worked for Associated Booking, it was Glaser who paid Armstrong's mortgage, taxes, and basic living expenses (Collier 330). A 1960 letter from Glaser to Lucille Armstrong corroborates Gold's account; it shows that Glaser assumed responsibility for buying the musician and his wife a new car as well as for filing the paperwork needed to retain the old license plate number. More personal were Glaser's attempts to control Armstrong's habitual use of marijuana. In 1931, Armstrong received a suspended sentence after his arrest for marijuana possession. He continued to use the drug, however, especially during performances, and told Glaser that he wanted to write a book about marijuana's positive effects. Glaser flatly rejected the book idea and, fearful of a scandal, also forbade Armstrong's smoking any marijuana while on tour in Europe (Pollack).

Clearly, Glaser was in a position to affect powerfully Armstrong's career and his life. Armstrong acknowledged Glaser's importance, at one point referring to him as "the man who has guided me all through my career" (qtd. in Jones and Chilton 175). However, there is little evidence that the musician submitted to whatever his business manager wanted or demanded. In fact, Armstrong seemed to recognize that he gave Glaser whatever power over him the manager enjoyed. When he wanted to, Armstrong could and did resist Glaser's control, and

Support by expert opinion (*see p. 31*).

Support by key fact (*see p. 31*).

Support by anecdote (*see p. 31*).

Thesis paragraph.

that may be one reason why he liked and trusted Glaser as much as he did.

After Glaser became his manager, Armstrong no longer had to worry about the behind-the-scenes details of his career. He was free to concentrate on creating music and making the most of the opportunities his manager worked out for him. Glaser booked Armstrong into engagements with legendary performers like Benny Goodman, Ella Fitzgerald, and Duke Ellington. He also worked with the record companies to ensure that Armstrong would make the best and most profitable recordings possible (Bergreen 457). During the thirty-four years they worked together, both Armstrong and Glaser made lots of money. More important, their relationship freed Armstrong to make extraordinary music.

If Armstrong acquiesced to most of Glaser's business decisions, it may have been because he had no reason to resist them. However, when he deemed it necessary, Armstrong acted on his own. For example, in 1944 a talented band member named Dexter Gordon threatened to quit, so Armstrong offered him a raise--without consulting first with Glaser (Morgenstern 132). In 1957, when Armstrong wanted to put a stop to backstage crowding, he not only directed Glaser to make a sign prohibiting guests from going backstage but also told him exactly what to say on the sign (Armstrong, Backstage Instructions). As these incidents suggest, when Armstrong was displeased with the way his career was being handled, he acted to amend the situation.

Armstrong also knew how to resist Glaser's attempts to control the more personal aspects of his life. In a recent interview, Phoebe Jacobs, formerly one of Glaser's employees, shed new light on the relationship between the manager and the musician.

Source cited: archival material.

Source cited: personal interview.

Hoffman 7

Armstrong's legendary generosity was tough on his pocketbook. It was well known that if someone needed money, Armstrong would readily hand over some bills. At one point, Glaser asked Jacobs to give Armstrong smaller denominations so that he would not give away so much money. The trumpeter soon figured out what was going on and admonished Jacobs for following Glaser's orders about money that belonged to him, not Glaser. On another occasion, Armstrong declined an invitation to join Glaser for dinner at a Chinese restaurant, saying, "I want to eat what I want to eat" (qtd. by Jacobs).

   Even though he sometimes pushed Glaser away, Armstrong obviously loved and trusted his manager. In all the years of their association, the two men signed only one contract and, in the musician's words, "after that we didn't bother" (qtd. in Jones and Chilton 240). A picture of Joe Glaser in one of Armstrong's scrapbooks bears the following label in the star's handwriting: "the greatest." In his dedication to the unpublished manuscript "Louis Armstrong and the Jewish Family in New Orleans," Armstrong calls Glaser "the best friend that I ever had," while in a letter to Max Jones, he writes, "I did not get really happy until I got with my man--my dearest friend--Joe Glaser" (qtd. in Jones and Chilton 16). In 1969, Joe Glaser died. Referring to him again as "the greatest," Armstrong confided to a friend that Glaser's death "broke [his] heart" (qtd. in Bergreen 490).

   Although there are hints of a struggle for the upper hand, the relationship between Louis Armstrong and Joe Glaser seems to have been genuinely friendly and trusting. Armstrong gave Glaser a good deal of authority over his career, and Glaser used that authority to make Armstrong a musical and monetary success.

Authoritative quotation (*see p. 31*).

Memorable quotation (*see p. 261*).

Wording of quote adjusted (*see pp. 567–68*).

Concludes with qualified version of thesis.

Hoffman 8

Effective visual
(*p. 75*).

Fig. 1 An anonymous watercolor caricature of Armstrong with his manager, Joe Glaser, c. 1950. Louis Armstrong Archives, Queens College, City University of New York, Flushing.

Armstrong was happy to take the opportunities that Glaser provided for him, but he was not submissive. This equitable and friendly relationship is depicted by another picture found in Armstrong's house. The 25-by-21-inch picture, shown in Fig. 1,

Memorable
illustration.

Hoffman 9

is a caricature of Armstrong and Glaser. The pair stand side by
side, and Glaser has his hand on Armstrong's shoulder. Armstrong,
who is dressed for a performance, looks and smiles at us as if he
were facing an audience. But Glaser looks only at Armstrong, the
musician who was his main concern from 1935 to the day he died.
In appearance alone, the men are clearly different. But seen in their
longstanding partnership, the two make up a whole--one picture
that offers us more than meets the eye.

Hoffman 10

Notes

[1]Bergreen 372-76. Even though Ostwald points out a few mistakes in Bergreen's <u>Louis Armstrong: An Extravagant Life</u>, I think the book's new information about Glaser is useful and trustworthy.

[2]I want to thank George Arevalo of the Louis Armstrong Archives for his help on this project. When I was low on inspiration and in search of some direction, George showed me the two pictures I describe in this paper. Seeing those pictures helped me figure out what I wanted to say--and why I wanted to say it. For introducing me to archival research and to the art of Louis Armstrong, I also want to thank the head of the Louis Armstrong Archives, Michael Cogswell, and my English teacher, Professor Amy Tucker.

Gives supplemental information about key source.

Indent first line 5 spaces or ½".

Acknowledges others who helped.

Hoffman 11

Works Cited

"Armstrong, (Daniel) Louis 'Satchmo.'" Microsoft Encarta
    Multimedia Encyclopedia. CD-ROM. Redmond: Microsoft,
    1994.

Armstrong, Louis. Backstage instructions to Glaser. April 1957.
    Accessions 1997-26. Louis Armstrong Archives. Queens
    College CUNY, Flushing, NY.

---. "Louis Armstrong and the Jewish Family in New Orleans."
    Unpublished ms. 31 March 1969. Louis Armstrong Archives.
    Queens College CUNY, Flushing, NY.

Bergreen, Laurence. Louis Armstrong: An Extravagant Life. New
    York: Broadway, 1997.

Bogle, Donald. "Louis Armstrong: The Films." Louis Armstrong: A
    Cultural Legacy. Ed. Marc H. Miller. Seattle: U of Washington
    P and Queens Museum of Art, 1994. 147-79.

"Chicago: Early 1920s." Wolverine Antique Music Society. Ed.
    R. D. Frederick. 1998. 3 May 2005 <http://www.shellac.org/
    wams/wchicag1.html>.

Collier, James Lincoln. Louis Armstrong, an American Genius.
    New York: Oxford UP, 1983.

Edwards, Brent Hayes. "Louis Armstrong and the Syntax of Scat."
    Critical Inquiry 28 (2002): 618-49.

Glaser, Joe. Letter to Lucille Armstrong. 28 Sept. 1960. Box 3.
    Armstrong Archives. Queens College CUNY, Flushing, NY.

Jacobs, Phoebe. Personal interview. 5 May 2005.

Jones, Max, and John Chilton. Louis: The Louis Armstrong Story,
    1900-1971. Boston: Little, 1971.

nging
dent
spaces
½".

New page,
title centered.

Entries in
alphabetical
order.

Source:
archival
material.

3 hyphens used
instead of
repeating
author's name.

Source:
whole book.

Source:
Web site
document.

Source:
journal
paginated
by volume.

Source:
personal
interview.

Source:
selection in
edited book.

Morgenstern, Dan. "Louis Armstrong and the Development and
Diffusion of Jazz." <u>Louis Armstrong: A Cultural Legacy</u>.
Ed. Marc H. Miller. Seattle: U of Washington P and Queens
Museum of Art, 1994. 95-145.

Source: review
in a monthly
magazine.

Ostwald, David. "All That Jazz." Rev. of <u>Louis Armstrong</u>:
<u>An Extravagant Life</u>, by Laurence Bergreen. <u>Commentary</u>
Nov. 1997: 68-72.

Source:
classmate's
paper.

Pollack, Bracha. "A Man ahead of His Time." Unpublished essay,
1997.

Robinson, J. Bradford. "Scat Singing." <u>The New Grove Dictionary</u>
<u>of Jazz</u>. Ed. Barry Kernfeld. Vol. 3. London: Macmillan, 2002.
515-16.

"Satchmo!" <u>New Orleans Online</u>. 2005. New Orleans Tourism
Marketing Corporation. 3 May 2005 <http://
www.neworleansonline.com/neworleans/music/
satchmobio.html>.

7

Take the whole range of imaginative literature, and we are all wholesale borrowers. In every matter that relates to invention, to use, or beauty or form, we are borrowers.

—WENDELL PHILLIPS

APA
Documentation Style

7 APA Documentation Style

APA style requires writers to provide bibliographic information about their sources in a list of references at the end of a paper. In order to format entries for the list of references correctly, it is important to know what kind of source you are citing. The directory on pages 341–42 will help you find the appropriate sample to use as a model. Alternatively, you can use the charts on the foldout pages that follow to help you locate the right example. Answering the questions in the charts will usually lead you to the sample entry you need. If you cannot find what you are looking for after consulting the appropriate directory or chart, ask your instructor for help.

The Elements of an APA References Entry: Books

Author → | Date of publication → | Book title →

Brookfield, H. (2001). *Exploring agrodiversity*. New York:
Columbia University Press.

↑ Publisher | ↑ Place of publication

Date of publication →

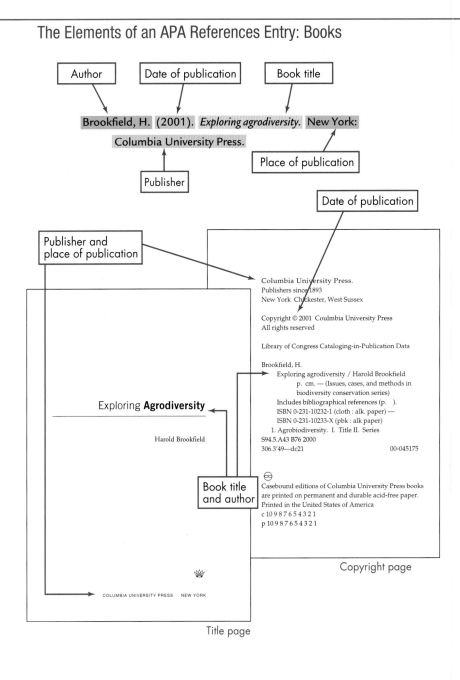

Publisher and place of publication

Columbia University Press.
Publishers since 1893
New York Chichester, West Sussex

Copyright © 2001 Coulmbia University Press
All rights reserved

Library of Congress Cataloging-in-Publication Data

Brookfield, H.
    Exploring agrodiversity / Harold Brookfield
        p. cm. — (Issues, cases, and methods in
            biodiversity conservation series)
    Includes bibliographical references (p.   ).
    ISBN 0-231-10232-1 (cloth : alk. paper) —
    ISBN 0-231-10233-X (pbk : alk. paper)
    1. Agrobiodiversity. I. Title II. Series
S94.5.A43 B76 2000
306.3'49—dc21   00-045175

Casebound editions of Columbia University Press books
are printed on permanent and durable acid-free paper.
Printed in the United States of America
c 10 9 8 7 6 5 4 3 2 1
p 10 9 8 7 6 5 4 3 2 1

Copyright page

Exploring **Agrodiversity**

Harold Brookfield

Book title and author →

COLUMBIA UNIVERSITY PRESS   NEW YORK

Title page

Information for a book citation can be found on the book's title and copyright pages.

The Elements of an APA References Entry: Journal Articles

Author → | Year of publication → | Article title → | Journal title →

Epstein, J. (2002). A voice in the wilderness. *Latin Trade,*
10(12), 26.

↑ Volume | ↑ Issue number | ↑ Page number

Journal title →

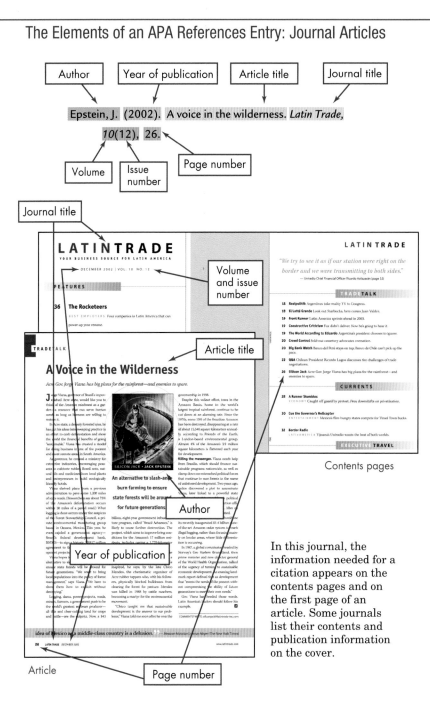

Contents pages

Article

Volume and issue number

Article title

Year of publication

Author

Page number

In this journal, the information needed for a citation appears on the contents pages and on the first page of an article. Some journals list their contents and publication information on the cover.

The Elements of an APA References Entry: Journal Articles from an Online Subscription Service

Author, title, and other information about the print version of the article →

Epstein, J. (2002). A voice in the wilderness. *Latin Trade,*
10(12), 26. Retrieved March 15, 2004, from EbscoHost
Research Databases.

↑ Date of access | ↑ Subscription database service

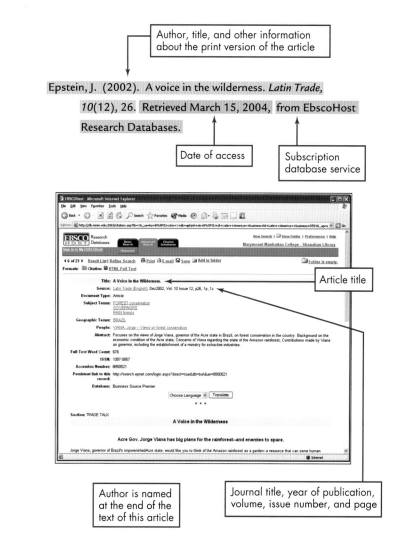

Article title

Author is named at the end of the text of this article

Journal title, year of publication, volume, issue number, and page

A citation for an article obtained from an online subscription database service like EBSCO includes the name of the service and the date of access in addition to information about the print version of the article. In this database listing, the author's name appears at the end of the full text of the article; usually you can also find the author's name in the listing.

❓ Is your source a complete book?

No   Yes

	Go to this entry
Is it a complete book with one named author?	
Is it the only book by this author that you are citing?	1
Are you citing more than one book by this author?	4
Does it also have an editor or translator?	5, 7
Is it a complete book with more than one named author?	2
Is it a complete book without a named author or editor?	
Is the author an organization?	3
Is the author anonymous or unknown?	10
Is it a complete book with an editor or translator?	
Is there an editor instead of an author?	5
Is it a translation?	7
Is it an entire reference work?	9
Is it a complete book with a volume or an edition number?	
Is it part of a multivolume work (e.g., Volume 3)?	12
Does it have an edition number (e.g., Second Edition)?	11
Is it a republished work (e.g., a classic study)?	13

❓ Is your source part of a book?

No   Yes

	Go to this entry
Is it a work from an anthology or a chapter in an edited book?	6
Is it an article in a reference work (e.g., an encyclopedia)?	8
Is it a published presentation from a conference?	27

Check the next panel or the directory on pages 341–42 or consult your instructor.

❓ Is your source from an academic journal, a magazine, or a newspaper?

No   Yes

	Go to this entry
Is it from an academic journal?	
Are the page numbers continued from one issue of the journal to the next?	14
Do the page numbers in each issue of the journal start with 1?	15
Is the article from a journal supplement?	16
Is it an abstract (a brief summary) of a journal article?	17
Is it a review (e.g., a review of a book)?	24
Is it a published presentation from a conference?	27
Is it from a monthly or weekly magazine?	
Is it an article?	19
Is it a letter to the editor?	21
Is it a review (e.g., a review of a book)?	24
Is it from a newspaper?	
Is it an article?	20
Is it an editorial or a letter to the editor?	21
Is it a review (e.g., a review of a book)?	24
Is it from a newsletter?	23
Is the author unknown?	22
Are you citing two or more articles published in the same year by the same author?	18

❓ Is it a print source but not a book, a part of a book, or an article in an academic journal, a magazine, or a newspaper?

No   Yes

	Go to this entry
Is it published by the government or a nongovernment organization?	
Is it a government document?	25
Is it a report or a working paper?	26
Is it a brochure, pamphlet, or fact sheet?	29
Is it from the *Congressional Record*?	42
Is it an unpublished work?	
Is it an unpublished conference presentation?	27
Is it an unpublished dissertation or a dissertation abstract?	28

Check the directory on pages 341–42 or consult your instructor.

❓ Did you find your nonprint source online?

No   Yes

	Go to this entry
Is it an article you found through a subscription database service (e.g., EBSCO or ProQuest)?	32
Is it from an online scholarly journal?	
Is it an article from a journal that is available only online?	33
Is it an article from a journal that is also available in print?	34
Is it from an online publication?	
Is it an article from an online newspaper?	35
Is it an article from an online newsletter?	40
Is it from a personal or organizational Web site?	
Is it a document or visual from a Web site?	36
Is it produced by one organization but posted on another organization's Web site?	37
Is it part of a long online document?	38
Is it a document on a university's Web site?	39
Is it an entry from a Weblog (blog)?	45
Is it a government publication?	
Is it a government document available online?	41
Is it from the *Congressional Record*?	42
Is it an online document without a date or an author?	43
Is it a posting to a news group or other online forum?	44

❓ Is your source a nonprint source that is not published online?

No   Yes

	Go to this entry
Is it a film, a DVD, a videotape, a CD-ROM, or an audio recording?	30
Is it a television program?	31
Is it computer software?	46

Check the directory on pages 341–42 or consult your instructor.

Instructors of social science and professional courses in psychology, sociology, political science, communications, education, and business usually prefer a documentation style that emphasizes the author and the year of publication, in part because the style makes it easy to tell if the sources cited are current.

www.mhhe.com/ awr
For links to Web sites for documentation styles used in various disciplines, go to

Research > Links to Documentation Sites

The American Psychological Association (APA) has developed a widely used version of the author-year style; the information in Chapters 31–34 is based on the fifth edition of its *Publication Manual* (Washington: APA, 2001). For updates to the APA documentation system, check the APA-sponsored Web site at <http://www.apastyle.org>.

APA documentation style has two mandatory parts:

- In-text citations
- List of references

31 APA Style: In-Text Citations

In-text citations let readers know that they can find full information about the source of an idea you have paraphrased or summarized, or the source of a quotation, in the list of references at the end of your paper.

APA IN-TEXT CITATIONS: DIRECTORY to SAMPLE TYPES

Tips

LEARNING in COLLEGE

What Is the American Psychological Association?

The American Psychological Association (APA) is the largest psychological organization in the world, with more than 155,000 members. It supports advances in psychological research and in the practice of psychology. Now in its fifth edition, the *Publication Manual of the American Psychological Association* has become an accepted guide for writers in many areas of science, not just psychology. Like the *MLA Handbook (see p. 286)*, the APA *Publication Manual* is concerned with the mechanics of academic writing. The manual is especially useful in helping students prepare and present scientific facts and figures, and it contains special sections on how to construct tables, present statistics, and cite scientific references.

1. Author named in your sentence: Follow the author's name with the year of publication (in parentheses).

signal phrase
According to Brookfield (2001), nearly 12% of the Amazonian rain

forest in Brazil has been shaped or influenced by thousands of years

of indigenous human culture.

2. Author named in parentheses: If you do not name the source's author in your sentence, you must include the name in parentheses, followed by the date and, if you are giving a quotation or a specific piece of information, the page number. The name, date, and page number are separated by commas.

The Organization of Indigenous Peoples of the Colombian Amazon

attempted in 2001 to take legal action to ban such fumigation over

indigenous lands. Their efforts were not supported by the Colombian
ampersand used within parentheses
government (Lloyd & Soltani, 2001, p. 5).

3. Two to five authors: If a source has five or fewer authors, name all of them the first time you cite the source.

GENERAL GUIDELINES for APA IN-TEXT CITATIONS

- Identify the author(s) of the source, either in the sentence or in a parenthetical citation. Use only the last name of the author(s). (*For additional information on in-text naming procedures, see pp. 336–38.*)
- Indicate the year of publication of the source following the author's name, either in parentheses if the author's name is part of the sentence or, if the author is not named in the sentence, after the author's name and a comma in a parenthetical citation.
- Include a page reference for a quotation or a specific piece of information. Put a *p.* before the page number. If the author is named in the text, the page number appears in the parenthetical citation following the borrowed material. Page numbers are not necessary when you are summarizing the source as a whole or paraphrasing an idea found throughout a work. (*For more on summary, paraphrase, and quotation, see Tab 5: Researching, pp. 258–65.*)
- If the source does not have page numbers (as with many online sources), do your best to direct readers toward the specific part of the text you are citing (for example, citing the section title of the online source). If the source has no page or paragraph numbering or easily identifiable headings, just use the source name and date.

As Kaimowitz, Mertens, Wunder, and Pacheco (2004) report in "Hamburger Connection Fuels Amazon Destruction," there are three key factors behind the burgeoning demand for Brazilian beef and the resulting burning of the Amazon rain forest for pasture land.

If you put the names of the authors in parentheses, use an ampersand (&) instead of *and*.

There are three key factors behind the burgeoning demand for Brazilian beef and the resulting burning of the Amazon rain forest for pasture land (Kaimowitz, Mertens, Wunder, & Pacheco, 2004, p. 3).

After the first time you cite a work by three or more authors, use the first author's name plus *et al.* Always use both names when citing a work by two authors.

Another key factor is concern over livestock diseases in other countries (Kaimowitz et al., 2004, p. 4).

4. Six or more authors: For in-text citations of a work by six or more authors, always give the first author's name plus *et al.* In the reference list, however, list the first six authors' names, followed by *et al.*

As Barbre et al. (1989) have argued, using personal narratives enables researchers to connect the individual and the social.

5. Organization as author: Treat the organization as the author and spell out its name the first time the source is cited. If the organization is well known, you may use an abbreviation thereafter.

According to a report issued by the Inter-American Association for Environmental Defense (2004), a significant population of Colombia's indigenous peoples live within these protected parklands.

Public service announcements were used to inform parents of these findings (National Institute of Mental Health [NIMH], 1991).

In subsequent citations, only the abbreviation and the date need to be given: (*NIMH, 1991*).

6. Unknown author: When no author or editor is given, use the first one or two important words of the title. Use quotation marks for titles of articles or chapters and italics for titles of books or reports.

The transformation of women's lives has been hailed as "the single most important change of the past 1,000 years" ("Reflections," 1999, p. 77).

7. Two or more authors with the same last name: If the authors of two or more sources have the same last name, always include their first initial, even if the year of publication differs.

M. Smith (1988) showed how globalization has restructured both cities and states.

8. Two or more sources cited at one time: When you are in-debted to two or more sources, cite the authors in the order in which they appear in the list of references, separated by a semicolon.

> Other years see greater destruction from large-scale economic
> and industrial initiatives, such as logging (Geographical, 2000;
> Kaimowitz et al., 2004, p. 2).

9. E-mail, letters, conversations: To cite information received from unpublished forms of personal communication, such as conver-sations, letters, notes, and e-mail messages, give the source's initials and last name, and provide as precise a date as possible.

> According to ethnobotanist G. Freid (personal communication, May 4,
> 2004), the work of research scientists in the Brazilian Amazon has been
> greatly impeded in the last 10 years because of the destruction of
> potentially unrecorded plant species.

> *Note:* Because readers do not have access to them, you should not include personal communications—e-mail, notes, and letters—in your reference list.

10. Indirect source: When referring to a source that you know only from reading another source, use the phrase *as cited in,* followed by the author of the source you actually read and its year of publication.

> According to the Center for International Forestry Research,
> an Indonesia-based NGO (as cited in Prugh, 2004), an area of
> land the size of Uruguay was deforested in the years 2002 and
> 2003 alone.

> *Note:* The work by the Center for International Forestry Research would not be included in the reference list, but the work by Prugh would be included.

11. Electronic source: Cite an electronic source the same way you would a print source, with the author's last name and the publication date. If the document is a PDF (portable document format) file with stable page numbers, cite the page number as you would a print source. If the source has paragraph numbers instead of page numbers, use *para.* or ¶ instead of *p.* when citing a specific part of the source (*see no. 12*).

> Applications of herbicides have caused widespread damage to
> biodiversity, livestock, and crops, and have caused "thousands"
> of peasants and indigenous peoples to flee these lands (Amazon
> Alliance, 2004).

> *Note:* If the specific part lacks any kind of page or paragraph numbering, cite the heading and the number of the paragraph under that heading where the information can be found. If you cannot find the name of the author, or if the author is an organization, follow the appropriate guidelines for print sources (*see nos. 5 and 6*). If you cannot determine the date, use the abbreviation "n.d." in its place: (*Wilson, n.d.*).

12. Two or more sources in one sentence: Include a parenthetical reference after each fact, idea, or quotation you have borrowed.

> By one estimate, nearly 12% of the Amazonian rain forest in Brazil
> has been shaped or influenced by thousands of years of indigenous
> human culture (Brookfield, 2001); the evidence is as basic as the *terra*
> *preta do Indio,* or "Indian black soil," for which the Brazilian region of
> Santarem is known (Rough Guides, para. 2).

13. Sacred or classical text: Cite these within your text only, and include the version you consulted as well as any book, part, or section numbers that are standard for all versions.

> The famous song sets forth a series of opposites, culminating in
> "a time to love, and a time to hate; a time of war, and a time of peace"
> (Eccles. 3:8, King James Bible).

32 APA Style: References

APA documentation style requires a list of references where readers can find complete bibliographical information about the sources referred to in your paper. The list of references should appear at the end of your paper, beginning on a new page titled "References."

www.mhhe.com/
awr
To download
Bibliomaker software
for APA, go to

Research >
Bibliomaker

APA REFERENCE ENTRIES: DIRECTORY to SAMPLE TYPES

(See pp. 335–40 for examples of in-text citations.)

(continued)

Books

1. Book with one author:

> Brookfield, H. (2001). *Exploring agrodiversity.* New York: Columbia
> University Press.

2. Book with two or more authors:

> Goulding, M., Mahar, D., & Smith, N. (1996). *Floods of fortune:*
> *Ecology and economy along the Amazon.* New York: Columbia
> University Press.

3. Organization as author: To credit a subdivision like "Economics Department," put its name after the name of the parent organization. When the publisher is the same as the author, use *Author* instead of repeating the organization's name as the publisher.

> Deutsche Bank, Economics Department. (1991). *Rebuilding eastern*
> *Europe.* Frankfurt, Germany: Author.

4. Two or more works by the same author: List the works in publication order, with the earliest one first.

GENERAL GUIDELINES for APA LIST OF REFERENCES

- Begin on a new page.
- Begin with the centered title "References."
- Include a reference for every in-text citation except personal communications (*see no. 9 on p. 339*).
- Put references in alphabetical order by author's last name.
- Give the last name and first or first and second initials for each author. If the work has more than one author, see no. 2. Do not add academic titles such as *Ph.D.* to the author's name.
- Put the publication year in parentheses following the author's or authors' names.
- Capitalize only the first word and proper nouns in titles. Also capitalize the first word following the colon in a subtitle.
- Use italics for titles of books but not articles. Do not enclose titles of articles in quotation marks.
- Include the city and publisher for books. If the city is not well known, include the state, using its two-letter postal abbreviation.
- Include the periodical name and volume number (both in italics) as well as the page numbers for an article.
- Separate the author's or authors' names, date (in parentheses), title, and publication information with periods.
- Use a hanging indent: Begin the first line of each entry at the left margin, and indent all subsequent lines of an entry one-half inch (five spaces).
- Double-space within and between entries.

Wilson, S. (Ed.). (1997). *The indigenous people of the Caribbean.*
   Gainesville, FL: University Press of Florida.

Wilson, S. (1999). *The emperor's giraffe and other stories of cultures
   in contact.* Boulder, CO: Westview Press.

If the works were published in the same year, put them in alphabetical order by title and add a letter (*a, b, c*) to the year to distinguish each entry in your in-text citations (*see no. 18*).

5. Book with editor(s):   Add (*Ed.*) or (*Eds.*) after the name. If a book lists an author and an editor, treat the editor like a translator (*see no. 7*).

Lifton, K. (Ed.). (1998). *The greening of sovereignty in world politics.*

Cambridge, MA: M.I.T. Press.

6. Selection in an edited book or anthology: The selection's author, year of publication, and title come first, followed by the word *In* and information about the edited book. Note that the page numbers of the selection go in parentheses after the book's title.

Wilmer, F. (1998). Taking indigenous critiques seriously: The enemy 'r'

us. In K. Lifton (Ed.), *The greening of sovereignty in world politics* (pp.

55–60). Cambridge, MA: M.I.T. Press.

7. Translation: After the title of the translation, put the name(s) of the translator(s) in parentheses, followed by the abbreviation *Trans.*

Jarausch, K. H., & Gransow, V. (1994). *Uniting Germany: Documents*

and debates, 1944-1993 (A. Brown & B. Cooper, Trans.).

Providence, RI: Berg.

8. Article in a reference work: Some encyclopedias and similar reference works name the authors of individual selections. Begin with the author's name, if given. If no author is given, begin with the title.

title of the selection
Arawak. (2000). In *The Columbia encyclopedia* (p. 2533). New York:

Columbia University Press.

9. Entire dictionary or reference work: Unless an author is indicated on the title page, list dictionaries by title, with the edition number in parentheses, followed by the date and publication information. (The in-text citation should include the title or a portion of the title.) (*See no. 8 for information on listing an article in a reference book and no. 10 on alphabetizing a work listed by title.*)

The American Heritage dictionary of the English language (4th ed.). (2000).

Boston: Houghton Mifflin.

Hinson, M. (2004). *The pianist's dictionary.* Bloomington: Indiana

University Press.

10. Unknown author or editor: Start with the title. When alphabetizing, use the first important word of the title (excluding articles such as *The, A,* or *An*).

> *Give me liberty.* (1960). New York: World.

11. Edition other than the first: After the title, put the edition number in parentheses, followed by a period.

> Smyser, W. R. (1993). *The German economy: Colossus at crossroads*
>
> (2nd ed.). New York: St. Martin's Press.

12. One volume of a multivolume work: If the volume has its own title, put it before the title of the whole work. No period separates the title and parenthetical volume number.

> Handl, G. (1990). *The Mesoamerican biodiversity legal project.* In
>
> *Yearbook of international environmental law* (Vol. 4). London: Graham
>
> & Trotman.

13. Republished book:

> Le Bon, G. (1960). *The crowd: A study of the popular mind.* New York:
>
> Viking. (Original work published 1895)

> *Note:* In-text citations should give both years: "As Le Bon
> (1895/1960) pointed out . . ."

Periodicals

14. Article in a journal paginated by volume: Do not put the article title in quotation marks, and do not use *pp.* before the page numbers. Italicize the title of the periodical and the volume number.

> da Cunha, M. C., & de Almeida, M. (2000). Indigenous people, traditional
>
> people and conservation in the Amazon. *Daedalus, 129,* 315.

15. Article in a journal paginated by issue: Include the issue number (in parentheses). Notice that the issue number is not italicized as part of the journal's title.

> Epstein, J. (2002). A voice in the wilderness. *Latin Trade, 10*(12), 26.

16. Journal supplement: Begin with the names of the author(s) or editor(s) followed by the date and supplement title, the journal name and volume number, and—if needed—the issue number in parentheses and the word *Suppl.* with supplement number, if there is one, in parentheses.

> Barnsteener, J. H., Burke, K. G., & Rich, V. (Eds.). (2005, March).
>
> State of the science on safe medication administration.
>
> *American Journal of Nursing 2005, 105*(3)(Suppl.), 1-56.

17. Abstract: For an abstract that appears in the original source, add the word *Abstract* in brackets after the title. If the abstract appears in a printed source that is different from the original publication, include the publication information for the complete article and original publication, followed by the publication information for the source of the abstract.

> Burnby, J. G. L. (1985, June). Pharmaceutical connections: The Maw's
>
> family [Abstract]. *Pharmaceutical historian, 15*(2), 9-11.

> Murphy, M. (2003). Getting carbon out of thin air. *Chemistry & Industry,*
>
> *6,* 14-16. Abstract obtained from *Fuel and Energy Abstracts,* 2004,
>
> *45*(6), 389.

> *Note:* If the dates of the publications differ, cite them both, with a slash between them, in the in-text citation: *Murphy (2003/2004).*

18. Two or more works in one year by the same author: Alphabetize by title, and attach a letter to each entry's year of publication, beginning with *a*. In-text citations must use the letter as well as the year so that readers know exactly which work is being cited.

Agarwal, J. P. (1996a). *Does foreign direct investment contribute to unemployment in home countries?—An empirical survey* (Discussion Paper No. 765). Kiel, Germany: Institute of World Economics.

Agarwal, J. P. (1996b). Impact of Europe agreements on FDI in developing countries. *International Journal of Social Economics, 23*(10/11), 150–163.

> *Note:* Also see no. 26, which explains the format for a report or working paper.

19. Article in a magazine: After the year, add the month for magazines published monthly or the month and day for magazines published weekly. Note that the volume number is also included.

Gross, P. (2001, February). Exorcising sociobiology.
New Criterion, 19, 24.

20. Article in a newspaper: Use *p.* or *pp.* with the section and page number. List all page numbers, separated by commas, if the article appears on discontinuous pages: *pp. C1, C4, C6.* If there is no identified author, begin with the title of the article.

Smith, T. (2003, October 8). Grass is green for Amazon farmers.
The New York Times, p. W1.

21. Editorial or letter to the editor:

Krugman, P. (2000, July 16). Who's acquiring whom? [Editorial].
The New York Times, Sec. 4, p. 15.

Deren, C. (2005, May 5). The last days of LI potatoes? [Letter to the editor]. *Newsday,* p. A49.

22. Unsigned article: Begin the entry with the title, and alphabetize it by the first important word (excluding articles such as *The, A,* or *An*).

Reflection on a thousand years: Introduction. (1999, April 18).

  The New York Times Magazine, p. 77.

23. Newsletter article: Add the season or month of the newsletter after the year in parentheses. If the article has no author, begin the listing with the title. If the pages are discontinuous, separate the page numbers with a comma.

Gardiner, P. (2005, April). Can you say cold turkey? California's prisons

  set to go smoke-free. *Burning Issues, 7*(2), 1-4, 9-10.

Largest ever study of osteoarthritis of the knee is seeking volunteers.

  (2004, Winter). *Johns Hopkins Arthritis Center Newsletter, 2*(2), 3.

24. Review:

Kaimowitz, D. (2002). Amazon deforestation revisited [Review of the

  book *Brazil, forests in the balance: Challenges of conservation with*

  development]. *Latin American Research Review, 37,* 221-236.

Scott, A. O. (2002, May 10). Kicking up cosmic dust [Review of the

  motion picture *Star wars*]. *The New York Times,* p. B1.

> **Note:** If the review is untitled, use the bracketed description in place of a title.

Other Print and Audiovisual Sources

25. Government document: When no author is listed, use the government agency as the author.

U.S. Bureau of the Census. (1976) *Historical statistics of the United States:*

  Colonial times to 1970. Washington, DC: U.S. Government Printing

  Office.

For the format to use when citing an enacted resolution or piece of legislation, see no. 42.

26. Report or working paper: If the issuing agency numbered the report, include that number in parentheses after the title.

> Agarwal, J. P. (1996a). *Does foreign direct investment contribute to*
> *unemployment in home countries?—An empirical survey* (Discussion
> Paper No. 765). Kiel, Germany: Institute of World Economics.

> *Note:* For reports from a deposit service like the Educational Resources Information Center (ERIC), put the document number in parentheses at the end of the entry.

27. Conference presentation: Treat published conference presentations as a selection in a book (*no. 6*), as a periodical article (*no. 14 or 15*), or as a report (*no. 26*), whichever applies. For unpublished conference presentations, including poster sessions, provide the author, the year and month of the conference, the title of the presentation, and information on the presentation's form, forum, and place.

> Markusen, J. (1998, June). *The role of multinationals in global economic*
> *analysis.* Paper presented at the First Annual Conference in
> Global Economic Analysis, West Lafayette, IN.

> Desantis, R. (1998, June). *Optimal export taxes, welfare, industry*
> *concentration and firm size: A general equilibrium analysis.* Poster
> session presented at the First Annual Conference in Global
> Economic Analysis, West Lafayette, IN.

28. Unpublished dissertation or dissertation abstract:

> Weinbaum, A. E. (1998). Genealogies of "race" and reproduction in
> transatlantic modern thought (Doctoral dissertation, Columbia
> University, 1998). *Dissertation Abstracts International, 58,* 229.

If you used the abstract but not the actual dissertation, treat the entry like a periodical article, with *Dissertation Abstracts International* as the periodical.

Weinbaum, A. E. (1998). Genealogies of "race" and reproduction in

transatlantic modern thought. *Dissertation Abstracts International,*

58, 229.

29. Brochure, pamphlet, fact sheet: Identify the type of publication in brackets. If there is no date of publication, put *n.d.* in place of the date. If the publisher is an organization, list it first, and name the publisher as *Author.*

United States Postal Service. (1995, January). *A consumer's guide to postal*

services and products [Brochure]. Washington, DC: Author.

Union College. (n.d.) *The Nott Memorial: A national historic landmark at*

Union College [Pamphlet]. Schenectady, NY: Author.

Department of Health and Human Services, Centers for Disease

Control and Prevention. (2003, July 31). *Anthrax: What you*

need to know [Fact sheet]. Washington, DC: Author.

30. Film, DVD, videotape, CD-ROM, recording: Begin with the cited person's name and, if appropriate, a parenthetical notation of his or her role. After the title, identify the medium in brackets, followed by the country and name of the distributor.

Towner, R. (1989). *City of eyes* [Record]. Munich: ECM.

Wenders, W. (Director). (1989). *Wings of desire* [Videotape]. Germany:

Orion Home Video.

For films and videotapes that might be hard to find, add the name and address of the distributor in parentheses after the bracketed medium information. For audio recordings for which an identification number is needed, add the number immediately following the medium description and use parentheses instead of brackets; add the name and address of the distributor.

National Geographic Society (Producer). (1993). *Killer whales: Wolves*

of the sea [Videotape]. (Available from the National Geographic

Society, 3400 Riverside Drive, Burbank, CA 91505-4627).

Bollas, R. N. (Speaker/Author). (2000). *What color is your parachute?*
2000: A practical manual for job-hunters and career changers [Cassette
recording]. San Bruno, CA: Audio Literature.

31. Television program: When citing a single episode, treat the
writer as the author and the producer as the editor of the series.

Weissman, G. (Writer). (2000). Mississippi: River out of control
[Television series episode]. In J. Towers (Producer), *Wrath of God.*
New York: The History Channel.

When citing a whole series or a specific news broadcast, name the
producer as author.

Towers, J. (Producer). (2000). *Wrath of God.* New York: The History
Channel.

Crystal, L. (Executive Producer). (2000, July 18). *The NewsHour
with Jim Lehrer* [Television broadcast]. Washington, DC:
Public Broadcasting Service.

Electronic Sources

32. Online article or abstract from a database: When you use
material from databases such as *PsycInfo, Sociological Abstracts, General BusinessFile ASAP,* and *LexisNexis,* include a retrieval date and
the name of the database in addition to the standard information
about author, year, title, and publisher.

Epstein, J. (2002). A voice in the wilderness. *Latin Trade, 10*(12), 26.
Retrieved March 15, 2004, from EbscoHost Research Databases.

Haas, R. (1994). Eastern Europe: A subsidy strategy for ecological
recovery. *Global Energy Issues 6*(3), 133-138. Abstract retrieved
April 22, 2001, from Lexis-Nexis database.

Note: When citing an abstract instead of the article, add the
word *abstract* to the retrieval statement.

33. Online article from a journal published only online: Include a retrieval date and the URL.

> Amazon Alliance. (2004). Columbia: US acknowledges funding for
>
> fumigations in national parks and protected areas. *Amazon*
>
> *Update, 98.* Retrieved April 7, 2004, from http://
>
> www.amazonalliance.org/upd_jan04_en.html

34. Online article from a journal previously published in print: To cite an electronic version of an article from a print journal, use the standard format for a periodical article (*see no. 14*) and add [*Electronic version*] after the article title. If the article appears not to have been altered from the print version, you need not include the URL. If the article has been altered from the print version, include the retrieval date and URL, as you would for online-only articles (*see no. 33*).

> Cook, B. G., & Cook, L. (2004). Bringing science into the classroom by
>
> basing craft on research [Electronic version]. *Journal of Learning*
>
> *Disabilities, 37,* 240-247.

35. Article in an online newspaper:

> Feller, B. (2005, May 6). GM, Ford get "junk" rating. *The Detroit News*
>
> *Online.* Retrieved May 6, 2005, from http://www.detnews.com/
>
> 2005/autosinsider/0505/06/A01-173553.htm

36. Document on a Web site: If the document is an entire article or report, include the basic information for an online document. If you have used a graph, chart, map, or image, give the source information following the figure caption (*for an example, see p. 360*).

> Lloyd, J., & Soltani, A. (2001, December). *Report on: Plan Columbia*
>
> *and indigenous peoples.* Retrieved April 2, 2004, from http://
>
> www.amazonwatch.orgamazon/CO/uwa/reports/
>
> plancol_march02.pdf

37. Article or report from a secondary source's Web site: Include information about the host organization's Web site after the retrieval date.

World Health Organization. (1992). *ICD-10 criteria for borderline personality disorder.* Retrieved March 28, 2005, from the BPD Sanctuary Web site: http://www.mhsanctuary.com/borderline/icd10.htm

38. Chapter or section of an online document: Include the chapter title, if there is one, before the title of the work.

Fielding, H. (1749). Book XV: In which the history advances about two days. In *The history of Tom Jones, a foundling* (chap. 15). Retrieved September 18, 2005, from http://www. bartleby.com/302/1501.html

39. Document on a university's Web site: Include relevant information about the university and department after the retrieval date.

Tugal, C. (2002, February). *Islamism in Turkey: Beyond instrument and meaning.* Retrieved August 16, 2005, from University of California-Berkeley, Department of Sociology Web site: http://sociology.berkeley.edu/public%5Fsociology/

40. Article in an online newsletter:

Shenandoah Chapter, Virginia Native Plant Society. (2005, April). Conservation. *Shenandoah Chapter Newsletter.* Retrieved May 6, 2005, from http://www.vnps.org/shenan.htm

Lekwa, S. (2003, October-November). Cougars in Iowa pose little threat to people and animals. *Acreage Living: A Bi-monthly Newsletter for Rural Residents Highlighting Timely Topics on Country Living.* Retrieved May 6, 2005, from http://www.extension.iastate.edu/acreage/AL2003/aloctnovt03.html

41. Online government document except the *Congressional Record:*

> National Commission on Terrorist Attacks upon the United States.
> (2004, August 5). *The 9/11 Commission report.* Retrieved March 30,
> 2005, from http://www.gpoaccess.gov/911/index.html

> Centers for Disease Control and Prevention. (2003, July 31). *Anthrax:*
> *What you need to know.* Retrieved March 30, 2005, from
> http://www.bt.cdc.gov/agent/anthrax/needtoknow.asp

42. *Congressional Record* (online or in print):

To cite enacted resolutions or legislation, give the number of the congress after the number of the resolution or legislation, the volume number for the *Congressional Record,* the page number(s), and the year, followed by *(enacted).*

> H. Res. 2408, 108th Cong., 150 Cong. Rec. 1331-1332
> (2004)(enacted).

Give the full name of the resolution or legislation when citing it within your sentence, but abbreviate it when it appears in a parenthetical in-text citation: *(H. Res. 2408, 2004).*

43. Online document without a date or author:

Use the abbreviation *n.d.* (no date) for any undated document. Begin the entry with the document's title if no author is given.

> Center for Science in the Public Interest. (n.d.). *Food additives to avoid.*
> Retrieved July 10, 2005, from http://www.mindfully.org/Food/
> Food-Additives-Avoid.htm

> *Raw food vegans thin, but healthy.* (2005, March 28). Retrieved April 23,
> 2005, from CNN.com: http://www.cnn.com/2005/HEALTH/
> diet.fitness/03/28/raw.vegans.reut/index.html

44. Online posting to an archived news group, discussion forum, or mailing list:

Provide the message's author, its date, and the subject line as the title. After the phrase *Message posted to,* give

Tips

APA EXPLANATORY NOTES

APA discourages the use of explanatory content notes to supplement the ideas in your paper, but they *are* an option. If you decide it is necessary to include a few content notes, put superscript numbers at appropriate points in your text. Type the notes, double spaced, on a separate page with the centered title "Footnotes." Indent the first line of each note five spaces, and type the appropriate superscript number followed by the note, with all lines after the first flush with the left margin.

the name of the discussion forum or news group, followed by the address of the message.

> Red Wave. (2000, April 8). Pareto/allocative efficiency of gift economy.
>
> Message posted to alt.society. economic-dev message board,
>
> archived at http://www.remarq.com/read/9755/
>
> qAyjNymZ61SoC-vwH#LR

45. Weblog ("blog") posting:

> Sullivan, A. (2003, November 23). The grim task in Iraq.
>
> *Andrewsullivan.com: The Daily Dish.* Retrieved February 24, 2004, from
>
> http://www.andrewsullivan.com/index.php?dish_inc=archives

46. Computer software:

> AllWrite! 2.1 with Online Handbook. (2003). [Computer software].
>
> New York: McGraw-Hill.

33 APA Style: Paper Format

The following guidelines will help you prepare your research paper in the format recommended by the *Publication Manual of the American Psychological Association,* fifth edition. For an example of a research paper that has been prepared using APA style, see pages 358–67.

Materials. Before printing your paper, make sure that you have stored your final draft on a backup disk. Use a high-quality printer and high-quality, white 8 1/2-by-11-inch paper. Do not justify your text or hyphenate words at the right margin; it should be ragged right.

Title page. The first page of your paper should be a title page. Center the title between the left and right margins in the upper half of the page, and put your name a few lines below the title. Most instructors will also want you to include the course number and title, the instructor's name, and the date. (*See p. 358 for an example.*)

Margins and spacing. Use one-inch margins all around, except for the right-hand top corner, where the page number goes.

Double-space lines throughout the paper, including in the abstract, within any notes, and in the list of references. Indent the first word of each paragraph one-half inch (or five spaces).

For quotations of more than forty words, use block format and indent five spaces from the left margin. Double-space the quoted lines.

Page numbers and abbreviated titles. All pages, including the title page, should have a number preceded by a short (one- or two-word) version of your title. Put this information in the upper right-hand corner of each page, about one-half inch from the top.

Abstract. Instructors sometimes require an abstract—a 75- to 120-word summary of your paper's thesis, major points or lines of development, and conclusions. The abstract appears on its own numbered page, entitled "Abstract," and is placed right after the title page.

Headings. Although headings are not required, most instructors welcome them. The primary headings should be centered, and all keywords in the heading should be capitalized.

You can also use secondary headings if you need them; they should be italicized and should appear flush against the left-hand margin. Do not use a heading for your introduction, however. (*For more on headings, see Tab 2: Writing and Designing Papers, pp. 104–5.*)

Visuals. Place visuals (tables, charts, graphs, and images) close to the place in your text where you refer to them. Label each visual as a table or a figure, and number each kind consecutively (Table 1, Table 2). You will also need to provide an informative caption for each visual. Cite the source of the material, preceded by the word *Note* and a period, and provide explanatory notes as needed. (*For more on using visuals effectively, see Tab 2: Writing and Designing Papers, pp. 53–57.*)

34 Student Paper in APA Style

Audrey Galeano researched and wrote the following report on the indigenous peoples of the Amazon for her anthropology course Indigenous Peoples and Globalization. Her sources included books, a journal, articles, and Web sites.

www.mhhe.com/awr
For another sample of a paper in APA style, go to
Research > Sample Research Papers > APA Style

All pages:
short title and
page number.

Saving the Amazon:

Globalization and Deforestation

Full title,
centered.

Audrey Galeano

Anthropology 314: Indigenous Peoples and Globalization

Title appears
on separate
page,
centered,
with course
information,
and date.

Professor Mura

May 3, 2005

Abstract
appears on
new page
after title
page. First
line is not
indented.

Abstract

The impact of globalization on fragile ecosystems is a complex problem. In the Amazon river basin, this impact has led to massive deforestation as multinational corporations exploit the rain forest's natural resources. In particular, large-scale industrial agriculture has caused significant damage to the local environment. In an effort to resist the loss of this ecosystem, indigenous peoples in the Amazon basin are reaching out to each other, to nongovernmental organizations (NGOs), and to other interest groups to combat industrial agriculture and promote sustainable regional agriculture. Although these efforts have had mixed success, it is hoped that the native peoples of this region can continue to live on their homelands without feeling intense pressure to acquiesce to industrialization or to relocate.

Objective stance
used, with no
reference to
essay. Essay
concisely sum-
marized—key
points included,
but not details
or statistics.

Paragraph
should be no
longer than
120 words.

Saving the Amazon   3

Saving the Amazon:
Globalization and Deforestation

For thousands of years, the indigenous peoples of the Amazon river basin have practiced forms of sustainable agriculture. These peoples developed ways of farming and hunting that enabled them to provide food and trade goods for their communities with minimal impact on the environment. These methods have endured despite colonization and industrialization. Today, the greatest threat to indigenous peoples in the Amazon river basin is posed by the massive deforestation caused by industrial-scale farming and ranching, as revealed in satellite images taken by Brazil's National Institute of Space Research since 1988. (See Figure 1.)

Because of the injury to ecosystems and native ways of life, indigenous peoples and antiglobalization activists have joined forces to promote sustainable agriculture and the rights of native peoples throughout the Amazon river basin.

Sustainable Lifeways, Endangered Lives

Recent work in historical ecology has altered our understanding of how humans have shaped what is romantically called "virgin forest." As anthropologist Anna Roosevelt (as cited in Society for California Archaeology, 2000) observes, "People adapt to environments but they also change them. There are no virgin environments on earth in areas where people lived." By one estimate, nearly 12% of the Amazonian rain forest in Brazil has been shaped or influenced by thousands of years of indigenous human culture (Brookfield, 2001); the evidence is as basic as the *terra preta do Indio*, or "Indian black soil," for which the Brazilian region of Santarem is known (Rough Guides, para. 2).

(Margin annotations:)

Full title repeated on first page only.

Figure introduced and commented on.

Thesis statement.

Primary heading, centered, subtly reveals writer's stance.

Parenthetical citation of source with organization as author.

Information from two different sources combined in one sentence.

Saving the Amazon   4

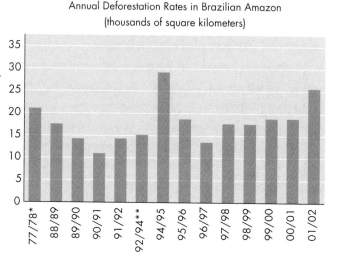

Graph presents statistics in visual form for readers.

Figure 1. Annual deforestation rates in the Brazilian Amazon, 1988-2002 (square kilometers). *Note.* From National Institute of Space Research. (2002). In D. Kaimowitz, B. Mertens, S. Wunder, & P. Pacheco, *Hamburger connection fuels Amazon destruction: Cattle ranching and deforestation in Brazil's Amazon.* Retrieved July 16, 2004 from http://www.cifor.cgiar.org/ publications/pdf_files/media/Amazon.pdf

Informative caption and source note appear below figure.

     The previous thousands of years of human influence on the Amazon is slight, however, compared to the modern-day destruction of rain forests around the globe, and in the Amazon river basin in particular. The sources of this destruction vary from country to country and year to year, with certain years affected more by climate change and other years seeing greater destruction from human initiatives, such as logging (Walker, Moran, & Anselin, 2000).

Support by key facts (*see p. 31*).

Saving the Amazon   5

According to the Center for International Forestry Research, an
Indonesia-based NGO, an area of land the size of Uruguay was
deforested in 2002-2003 alone. Nearly all of this land was cleared
for industrial agriculture and cattle ranching (Prugh, 2004).

Globalization and Agricultural Destruction

Large-scale industrial agriculture seeks out the least expensive
ways to produce the largest amounts of crops. Perhaps the largest
cash crop of the late twentieth and early twenty-first centuries is
soy, which has numerous uses and is among the least expensive
crops to produce. According to Roberto Smeraldi, director of the
environmental action group Friends of the Earth, "Soybeans are
the single biggest driver for deforestation" in the Brazilian Amazon;
in the 12 months ending in August 2003, 9,169 square miles of rain
forest had been cleared by soy farmers, ranchers, and loggers in
Brazil (as cited in Stewart, 2004, paras. 4-5). Although Brazilian
officials have attempted to regulate the depredations of the rain
forest by multinational soy producers, Stewart notes that, in 2003,
soybean production brought nearly $8 billion to the Brazilian
economy, forcing indigenous and small-scale farmers off their
lands and damaging local climate.

An Associated Press (AP) report reprinted on the Organic
Consumer's Association Web site describes the impact of soy
production on Brazil's Xingu National Park, a protected rain forest
reserve that is home to 14 indigenous tribes. "The soy is arriving
very fast. Every time I leave the reservation I don't recognize
anything anymore because the forest keeps disappearing," a
director of the Xingu Indian Land Association is quoted as
observing (AP, 2003, para. 11). Although the industrial soy farms
have not crossed the borders of the Xingu National Park, they

---

Paragraph
expands on
introductory
paragraph.

Discussion of
details begun
and linked to
broader issue
of globalization.

Abbreviation
given at first
mention of
organization.

Abbreviation
for organiza-
tion used in
parenthetical
citation.

surround the protected lands and have raised fears that chemical pesticides and deforestation will dry up rivers and kill fish. "Our Xingu is not just what's here. It's a very long thread, and when it rains the soy brings venom down the same river that passes by our door," says Capivara chief Jywapan Kayabi (para. 24).

Cattle ranching has also led to the deforestation of the Amazon. The cattle population of the Amazon nations increased from 26 million in 1990 to 57 million in 2002 (Prugh, 2004). Attention to the destruction caused by industrial cattle-ranching began in the late 1980s. Barrett (2001) points out that ranchers were following onto lands already depleted of fertility and biodiversity by logging, road building, and colonization of the Brazilian Amazon in the 1960s and 1970s. Ranching, Barrett observes, "doesn't require nutrient-rich soil" and therefore "took the place vacated by other activities, along with the blame for soil erosion and loss of biodiversity" (p. 1).

Indigenous Peoples and Regional Activism

Depopulation of these lands as a result of colonization meant that traditional agricultural practices were no longer sustained. In recent years, antiglobalization NGOs, the international movement for indigenous peoples' rights, and increased understanding of the consequences of deforestation are helping native peoples reclaim lands and reestablish traditional agricultural practices. However, some kinds of alliances and interventions are not as productive as others.

Anthropologists da Cunha and de Almeida ask a provocative question: "Can traditional peoples be described as 'cultural conservationists'?" (2000, p. 315). Although as many as 50 indigenous groups in Amazonia still have no contact with the

---

First main cause of deforestation discussed.

Second main cause of deforestation discussed.

Page number given for quotation.

Contributing factor in problem of deforestation shows complexity of situation.

Saving the Amazon   7

outside world, other indigenous peoples have secured their land
rights through international efforts over the past 20 years. Some of
these efforts, da Cunha and de Almeida argue, are influenced by
romantic ideas about "noble savages" and fail to acknowledge the
ways in which indigenous peoples in contemporary Brazil make a
living from rain forest resources.

Barham and Coomes (1997) also note that a better
understanding of how indigenous peoples live is necessary for the
efforts of international groups such as Amazon Alliance to
succeed. Indigenous peoples need to see some material benefit
from conservationist practices. After all, as da Cunha and de
Almeida write, "traditional peoples are neither outside the central
economy nor any longer simply in the periphery of the world
system" (2000).

Franke Wilmer (1998) suggests that "human action and its
impact in the world are directed by a view that is dangerously out
of touch with natural laws which, according to indigenous peoples,
govern all life on this planet" (p. 57). For instance, although the
Kayapo people of south central Amazonia have been devastated by
colonization, they still "used their knowledge to manipulate
ecosystems in remarkable ways . . . to maximize biological
diversity" (Brookfield, 2001, p. 141). Among the Kayapo's
sustainable practices are crop rotation, the use of ash to fertilize
fields, and the transition of older fields back to secondary forest
(Brookfield, 2001).

Some socially conscious global corporations have attempted
to assist indigenous Amazonian farmers in developing sustainable,
profitable crops. Two of the best-known efforts, described in a
2003 *New York Times* article by Tony Smith, provide a cautionary

Local culture,
history, and
economics
shown to be
linked to
global
systems.

Ellipses
indicate
omission in
quotation.

Saving the Amazon   8

tale. In the 1990s, the British multinational "green" cosmetics company The Body Shop and American ice cream manufacturer Ben and Jerry's both developed "eco-friendly" products from the Amazon. Ben and Jerry's Rainforest Crunch ice cream used Brazil nuts that were harvested in a sustainable fashion by an Amazonian cooperative, and The Body Shop also used the oils from Brazil nuts in some of its cosmetics. But Rainforest Crunch proved so popular that the cooperative couldn't meet the demand, and Ben and Jerry's had to turn to other suppliers, "some notorious for their antilabor practices" (Smith, 2003, p. W1). The Body Shop wound up being sued by a chief of the Kayapo tribe, whose image was used in Body Shop advertising without permission (Smith).

The best solution might be for Brazilian business, developers, government officials, and indigenous peoples to work together. One new initiative described in the *Times* article is the cultivation of the sweet-scented native Amazon grass called priprioca, on which the Sao Paulo cosmetics company Natura is basing a new fragrance. Farmer Jose Mateus, who has grown watermelons and manioc on his small farm near the Amazon city of Belem, has agreed to grow priprioca instead--and he expects to get twice the price for the grass than he would for his usual crop (Smith, 2003). Eduardo Luppi, director of innovation for Natura, comments, "We do have the advantage that we are Brazilian and we are in Brazil. If you are in England or America and want to manage something like this in the Amazon by remote control, you can forget it" (as cited in Smith, 2003, p. W1).

Although indigenous peoples face extraordinary obstacles in their quest for environmental justice, some political officials support their struggles. In the Acre state of Brazil, Governor Jorge

Problems caused by one solution discussed.

Solutions described, backed up with quotations from experts, which come from secondary source.

Saving the Amazon   9

Viana was inspired by the example of martyred environmental activist Chico Mendes to secure financing from Brazil's federal development bank for sustainable development in his impoverished Amazonian state (Epstein, 2002). Viana, who holds a degree in forest engineering, told the journal *Latin Trade* that "we want to bring local populations into the policy of forest management. . . . We have to show them how to exploit without destroying" (as cited in Epstein, p. 26).

Conclusion

The social, economic, climate-related, and political pressures on the Amazonian ecosystem may prove insurmountable; report after report describes the enormous annual loss of rain forest habitat. The best hope for saving the rain forest is public pressure on multinational agricultural corporations to practice accountable, safe, and sustainable methods. In addition, it is important to encourage indigenous peoples to practice their age-old sustainable agriculture and land-management strategies while guaranteeing their rights and safety. Much in the Amazon has been ruined, but cooperative efforts like those discussed in this paper can nurture and sustain what remains for future generations.

Essay concludes on optimistic note, balancing writer's and sources' concerns.

References

Associated Press. (2003, December 18). *Soybeans: The new threat to Brazilian rainforest.* Retrieved April 8, 2004, from http://www.organicconsumers.org/corp/soy121903.cfm

Barham, B. L., & Coomes, O. T. (1997). Rain forest extraction and conservation in Amazonia. *The Geographical Journal, 163*(2), 180.

Barrett, J. R. (2001). Livestock farming: Eating up the environment? *Environmental Health Perspectives, 109*(7), 1.

Brookfield, H. (2001). *Exploring agrodiversity.* New York: Columbia University Press.

da Cunha, M. C., & de Almeida, M. (2000). Indigenous people, traditional people and conservation in the Amazon. *Daedalus, 129,* 315.

Epstein, J. (2002). A voice in the wilderness. *Latin Trade, 10*(12), 26. Retrieved March 15, 2004, from EbscoHost Research Databases.

Prugh, T. (2004). Ranching accelerates Amazon deforestation. *World Watch, 17*(4), 8.

Rough Guides. (2003). *Santarem.* Retrieved July 25, 2004, from http://www.travelingo.org/south-america/brazil/amazon/eastern-amazonia/santarem/

Smith, T. (2003, October 8). Grass is green for Amazon farmers. *The New York Times,* p. W1.

Society for California Archaelogy. (2000). *Interview with Dr. Anna Roosevelt.* Retrieved July 20, 2004, from http://www.scahome.org/educational_resources/2000_Roosevelt. html

New page, heading centered.

Entries in alphabetical order and double-spaced.

Hanging indent 5 spaces or ½".

Saving the Amazon   11

Stewart, A. (2004, July 14). Brazil's soy success brings
environmental challenges. *Dow Jones.* Retrieved July 15, 2004
from http://www.amazonia.org.br/English/noticias/
noticia.cfm?id=116059

Walker, R., Moran, E., & Anselin, L. (2000). Deforestation and
cattle ranching in the Brazilian Amazon: External capital and
household processes. *World Development 28*(4), 683-699.

Wilmer, F. (1998). Taking indigenous critiques seriously: The
enemy 'r' us. In K. Lifton (Ed.), *The greening of sovereignty in
world politics* (pp. 55-60). Cambridge, MA: M.I.T. Press.

The DNA molecule is like a blueprint that documents the process for constructing living organisms.

8

Nothing gives an author so much pleasure as to find his works respectfully quoted by other learned authors.

—BENJAMIN FRANKLIN

Other
Documentation
Styles
Chicago and
CSE

8

Other Documentation Styles

There are many documentation styles besides those developed by the Modern Language Association (*see Tab 6*) and the American Psychological Association (*see Tab 7*). In this section, we cover three additional documentation styles: the *Chicago Manual* style and the two styles developed by the Council of Science Editors. To find out where you can learn about other style types, consult the list of style manuals on page 275. If you are not sure which style to use, ask your instructor.

www.mhhe.com/
awr
For links to Web sites for documentation styles used in various disciplines, go to

Research > Links to Documentation Sites

For MULTILINGUAL STUDENTS

Deciding Which Documentation Style to Use

Always check with your instructor if you are not sure which documentation style you should use for a particular paper. Each of the styles presented in this book is academically sound, and it is possible that any one of several styles could provide the guidance you need to format and document your paper. The choice of which style to use is often guided by the personal preference of the professor.

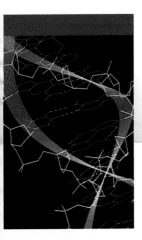

35 Chicago Documentation Style

The note and bibliography style presented in the fifteenth edition of *The Chicago Manual of Style* (Chicago: University of Chicago Press, 2003) is used in many disciplines, including history, art, philosophy, business, and communications. This style has three parts:

- Numbered in-text citations
- Numbered footnotes or endnotes
- A bibliography of works consulted

The first two parts are necessary; the third is optional, unless your instructor requires it. (The *Chicago Manual* also has an alternative author-date system that is similar to APA style.) For more information on this style, consult the *Chicago Manual* or *A Manual for Writers of Term Papers, Theses, and Dissertations,* sixth edition, by Kate L. Turabian (Chicago: University of Chicago Press, 1996). For updates and answers to frequently asked questions about this style, go to the *Chicago Manual*'s Web site at <http://www.Press.uchicago.edu> and click on "Chicago Manual of Style Web site."

35a Use numbered in-text citations and notes.

Whenever you use information or ideas from a source, you need to indicate what you have borrowed by putting a superscript number in the text ([1]) at the end of the borrowed material. These superscript numbers are placed after all punctuation marks except for the dash.

> As Bergreen points out, Armstrong easily reached difficult high notes, the F's and G's that stymied other trumpeters.[3] And his innovative singing style featured "scat," a technique that combines "nonsense syllables [with] improvised melodies."[4]

If a quotation is fairly long, you can set it off as a block quotation. Indent it five spaces or one-half inch from the left margin, and double-space the quotation, leaving an extra space above and below it. Place the superscript number after the period that ends the quotation. (*See p. 388 for an example.*)

Each in-text superscript number must have a corresponding note either at the foot of the page or at the end of the text. Indent the first

TEXTCONNEX

Superscript Numbers

To find the superscript option in your computer's word-processing program, click on "Format" on your tool bar and then choose "Font." Superscript is one of many font options.

line of each footnote like a paragraph. Footnotes begin with the number and are single-spaced, with a double space between notes.

If you are using endnotes instead of footnotes, they should begin after the last page of your text on a new numbered page titled "Notes." Single-space within and double-space between endnotes.

The first time you cite a source in either a footnote or an endnote, you should include a full citation. Subsequent citations require less information.

FIRST REFERENCE TO SOURCE

3. Laurence Bergreen, *Louis Armstrong: An Extravagant Life* (New York: Broadway Books, 1997), 248.

ENTRY FOR SOURCE ALREADY CITED

6. Bergreen, 370.

If several pages pass between references to the same title, include a brief version of the title to clarify the reference.

ENTRY FOR SOURCE ALREADY CITED IN LONGER PAPER

7. Bergreen, *Louis Armstrong*, 370.

If you quote from the same work immediately after providing a full footnote, use the abbreviation *Ibid.* (Latin for "in the same place"), followed by the page number.

8. Ibid., 370.

35b Prepare a separate bibliography if your instructor requires one.

Some instructors require a separate list of works cited or of works consulted. If you are asked to provide a works-cited list, do so on a separate, numbered page titled "Works Cited." If the list should include all works you consulted, title it "Bibliography."

Bergreen, Laurence. *Louis Armstrong: An Extravant Life*. New York: Broadway Books, 1997.

www.mhhe.com/
awr
To download
Bibliomaker software
for Chicago style,
go to

**Research >
Bibliomaker**

35c Use the correct Chicago style for notes and bibliography entries.

CHICAGO STYLE: DIRECTORY to SAMPLE TYPES

Books

1. Book with one author:

NOTE

> 1. James Lincoln Collier, *Louis Armstrong: An American Genius* (New York: Oxford University Press, 1983), 82.

BIBLIOGRAPHY ENTRY

> Collier, James Lincoln. *Louis Armstrong: An American Genius*. New York: Oxford University Press, 1983.

> ## GENERAL GUIDELINES for a BIBLIOGRAPHY or a WORKS-CITED LIST in CHICAGO STYLE
>
> - Begin on a new page.
> - Begin with the centered title "Works Cited" if you are including only works referred to in your paper. Use the title "Bibliography" if you are including every work you consulted.
> - List sources alphabetically by author's (or editor's) last name.
> - Capitalize the first and last words in titles as well as all important words and words that follow colons.
> - Indent all lines except the first of each entry five spaces, using your word processor's hanging indent feature.
> - Use periods between author and title as well as between title and publication data.
> - Single-space each entry; double-space between entries.

2. Multiple works by the same author: After providing complete information in the first footnote, include only a shortened version of the title with the author's last name and the page number in any subsequent footnotes. In the bibliography, list entries either in alphabetical order by title or in chronological order from earliest to most recent. After the first listing, replace the author's name with a "3-em" dash (type three dashes in a row).

NOTES

7. Collier, *Jazz,* 154.

12. Collier, *Louis Armstrong,* 32.

BIBLIOGRAPHY ENTRIES

Collier, James Lincoln. *Jazz: The American Theme Song.* New York: Oxford University Press, 1993.

——. *Louis Armstrong, An American Genius.* New York: Oxford University Press, 1983.

3. Book with two or more authors: In notes, you can name up to three authors. When there are three authors, put a comma after the first name and a comma plus *and* after the second.

NOTE

2. Miles Davis and Quincy Troupe, *Miles: The Autobiography* (New York: Simon & Schuster, 1989), 15.

BIBLIOGRAPHY ENTRY

Davis, Miles, and Quincy Troupe. *Miles: The Autobiography.* New York: Simon & Schuster, 1989.

When more than three authors are listed on the title page, use *and others* or *et al.* after the first author's name in the note.

NOTE

3. Julian Henriques and others, *Changing the Subject: Psychology, Social Regulation and Subjectivity* (New York: Methuen, 1984), 275.

BIBLIOGRAPHY ENTRY

Henriques, Julian, Wendy Holloway, Cathy Urwin, Couze Venn, and Valerie Walkerdine. *Changing the Subject: Psychology, Social Regulation and Subjectivity.* New York: Methuen, 1984.

Notice that *and others* or *et al.* is not used in bibliography entries, even when a book has more than three authors.

4. Book with an author and an editor or a translator: Put the author's name first and add the editor's (*ed.*) or translator's (*trans.*) name after the title. Spell out *Edited* or *Translated* in the bibliography entry.

NOTE

4. Louis Armstrong, *Louis Armstrong--A Self-Portrait,* ed. Richard Meryman (New York: Eakins Press, 1971), 54.

BIBLIOGRAPHY ENTRIES

Armstrong, Louis. *Louis Armstrong--A Self-Portrait.* Edited by Richard Meryman. New York: Eakins Press, 1971.

Goffin, Robert. *Horn of Plenty: The Story of Louis Armstrong.* Translated by James F. Bezov. New York: Da Capo Press, 1977.

5. Book with editor(s):

NOTE

5. Paul Eduard Miller, ed., *Esquire's Jazz Book* (New York: Smith & Durrell, 1944), 31.

BIBLIOGRAPHY ENTRY

Miller, Paul Eduard, ed. *Esquire's Jazz Book.* New York: Smith & Durrell, 1944.

6. Organization as author:

NOTE

6. Centre for Contemporary Cultural Studies, *Making Histories: Studies in History Writing and Politics* (London: Hutchinson, 1982), 10.

BIBLIOGRAPHY ENTRY

Centre for Contemporary Cultural Studies. *Making Histories: Studies in History Writing and Politics.* London: Hutchinson, 1982.

7. Work in an anthology or part of an edited book: Begin with the author and title of the specific work or part.

NOTES

7. Hale Smith, "Here I Stand," in *Readings in Black American Music,* ed. Eileen Southern (New York: Norton, 1971), 287.

8. Richard Crawford, foreword to *The Jazz Tradition,* by Martin Williams (New York: Oxford University Press, 1993).

BIBLIOGRAPHY ENTRIES

Smith, Hale. "Here I Stand." In *Readings in Black American Music,* edited by Eileen Southern, 286-89. New York: Norton, 1971.

Crawford, Richard. Foreword to *The Jazz Tradition,* by Martin Williams. New York: Oxford University Press, 1993.

In notes, descriptive terms such as *foreword* are not capitalized. In bibliography entries, these descriptive terms are capitalized.

8. Article in an encyclopedia or a dictionary: For well-known reference works, publication data can be omitted from a note, but the edition or copyright date should be included. There is no need to include page numbers for entries in reference works that are arranged alphabetically; the abbreviation *s.v.* (meaning "under the word") plus the entry's title can be used instead.

NOTES

9. J. Bradford Robinson, "Scat Singing," in *The New Grove Dictionary of Jazz* (2002).

10. *Encyclopedia Britannica,* 15th ed., s.v. "Jazz."

Reference works are not listed in the bibliography unless they are unusual or crucial to your paper.

BIBLIOGRAPHY ENTRY

Robinson, J. Bradford. "Scat Singing." In *The New Grove Dictionary of Jazz*. Edited by Barry Kernfeld. Vol. 3. London: Macmillan, 2002.

9. The Bible: Abbreviate the name of the book, and use arabic numbers for chapter and verse, separated by a colon. Name the version of the Bible cited only if it matters, and do not include the Bible in your bibliography.

NOTE

11. Eccles. 8:5 (Jerusalem Bible).

10. Edition other than the first: Include the number of the edition after the title or, if there is an editor, after that person's name.

NOTE

12. Hugues Panassie, *Louis Armstrong,* 2d ed. (New York: Da Capo Press, 1980), 12.

BIBLIOGRAPHY ENTRY

Panassie, Hugues. *Louis Armstrong.* 2d ed. New York: Da Capo Press, 1980.

11. Multivolume work: Put the volume number in arabic numerals (even if the volume number is spelled out or in roman numerals in the original), followed by a colon, before the page number.

NOTE

13. Robert Lissauer, *Lissauer's Encyclopedia of Popular Music in America* (New York: Facts on File, 1996), 2:33-34.

BIBLIOGRAPHY ENTRY

Lissauer, Robert. *Lissauer's Encyclopedia of Popular Music in America.* Vol. 2. New York: Facts on File, 1996.

12. Work in a series: Include the name of the series as well as the book's series number. The series name should not be italicized or underlined.

NOTE

> 14. Samuel A. Floyd, ed., *Black Music in the Harlem Renaissance,* Contributions in Afro-American and African Studies, no. 128 (New York: Greenwood Press, 1990), 2.

BIBLIOGRAPHY ENTRY

> Floyd, Samuel A., ed. *Black Music in the Harlem Renaissance.* Contributions in Afro-American and African Studies, no. 128. New York: Greenwood Press, 1990.

13. Unknown author: Cite anonymous works by title, and alphabetize them by the first word, ignoring *A, An,* or *The.*

NOTE

> 15. *The British Album* (London: John Bell, 1790), 2:43-47.

BIBLIOGRAPHY ENTRY

> *The British Album.* Vol. 2. London: John Bell, 1790.

Periodicals

14. Article in a journal paginated by volume: When journals are paginated by yearly volume, your citation should include the following: author, title of article in quotation marks, title of journal, volume number and year, and page number(s).

NOTE

> 16. Frank Tirro, "Constructive Elements in Jazz Improvisation," *Journal of the American Musicological Society* 27 (1974): 300.

BIBLIOGRAPHY ENTRY

> Tirro, Frank. "Constructive Elements in Jazz Improvisation." *Journal of the American Musicological Society* 27 (1974): 285-305.

15. Article in a journal paginated by issue: If the periodical is paginated by issue rather than by volume, add the issue number, preceded by the abbreviation *no.*

NOTE

> 17. Sarah Appleton Aguiar, "'Everywhere and Nowhere': *Beloved*'s 'Wild' Legacy in Toni Morrison's *Jazz,*" *Notes on Contemporary Literature* 25, no. 4 (1995): 11.

BIBLIOGRAPHY ENTRY

Aguiar, Sarah Appleton. "'Everywhere and Nowhere': *Beloved*'s 'Wild' Legacy in Toni Morrison's *Jazz.*" *Notes on Contemporary Literature* 25, no. 4 (1995): 11-12.

16. Article in a magazine: Identify magazines by week (if available) and month of publication. In the note, give only the specific page cited; in the bibliography, give the full range of pages.

NOTE

18. Malcolm Walker, "Discography: Bill Evans," *Jazz Monthly,* June 1965, 22.

BIBLIOGRAPHY ENTRY

Walker, Malcolm. "Discography: Bill Evans." *Jazz Monthly,* June 1965, 20-22.

If the article cited does not appear on consecutive pages, do not put any page numbers in the bibliography entry. You can, however, give specific pages in the note. In Chicago style, the month precedes the date, and months are not abbreviated.

NOTE

19. J. R. Taylor, "Jazz History: The Incompleted Past," *Village Voice,* July 3, 1978, 65.

BIBLIOGRAPHY ENTRY

Taylor, J. R. "Jazz History: The Incompleted Past." *Village Voice,* July 3, 1978.

17. Article in a newspaper: Citations for newspaper articles in Chicago format provide four basic pieces of information: the author's name (if known), the title of the article, the name of the newspaper, and the date of publication. Because newspapers publish in multiple editions, do not give a page number. Instead, give the section number or title if it is indicated. If applicable, indicate the edition (for example, *national edition*) before the section number.

NOTE

20. Ralph Blumenthal, "Satchmo with His Tape Recorder Running," *New York Times,* August 3, 1999, sec. E.

Newspaper articles that you have cited in the text of your paper do not need to be included in a bibliography or reference list. However, if you are asked to include newspaper articles in the bibliography or reference list, or if you did not provide full citation information in the essay or the note, format the entry as follows.

BIBLIOGRAPHY ENTRY

Blumenthal, Ralph. "Satchmo with His Tape Recorder Running," *New York Times,* August 3, 1999, sec. E.

18. Unsigned article or editorial in a newspaper: Begin the note and the bibliography or reference list entry with the name of the newspaper.

NOTE

21. *New York Times,* "A Promising Cloning Proposal," October 15, 2004.

BIBLIOGRAPHY ENTRY

New York Times, "A Promising Cloning Proposal," October 15, 2004.

Other Sources

19. Review: If the review is untitled, start with *review of* for a note or *Review of* for a bibliography entry.

NOTE

22. David Ostwald, "All That Jazz," review of *Louis Armstrong: An Extravagant Life,* by Laurence Bergreen, *Commentary,* November 1997, 72.

BIBLIOGRAPHY ENTRY

Ostwald, David. "All That Jazz." Review of *Louis Armstrong: An Extravagant Life,* by Laurence Bergreen. *Commentary,* November 1997, 68-72.

20. Interview: Start with the name of the person interviewed, and note the nonprint medium (tape recording, video). Only interviews accessible to your readers are listed in the bibliography.

NOTES

23. Louis Armstrong, "Authentic American Genius," interview by Richard Meryman, *Life,* April 15, 1966, 92.

24. Michael Cogswell, interview by author, tape recording, Louis Armstrong Archives, Queens College CUNY, Flushing, NY, May 3, 2005.

BIBLIOGRAPHY ENTRY

Armstrong, Louis. "Authentic American Genius." Interview by Richard Meryman. *Life,* April 15, 1966, 92-102.

21. Government document: If it is not already obvious in your text, name the country first.

NOTE

25. Bureau of National Affairs, *The Civil Rights Act of 1964: Text, Analysis, Legislative History; What It Means to Employers, Businessmen, Unions, Employees, Minority Groups* (Washington, DC: BNA, 1964), 22-23.

BIBLIOGRAPHY ENTRY

U.S. Bureau of National Affairs. *The Civil Rights Act of 1964: Text, Analysis, Legislative History; What It Means to Employers, Businessmen, Unions, Employees, Minority Groups.* Washington, DC: BNA, 1964.

22. Unpublished dissertation or document: Include a description of the document as well as information about where it is available. If more than one item from an archive is cited, include only one entry for the archive in your bibliography (*see p. 390*).

NOTES

26. Adelaida Reyes-Schramm, "The Role of Music in the Interaction of Black Americans and Hispanos in New York City's East Harlem" (Ph.D. diss., Columbia University, 1975), 34-37.

27. Joe Glaser to Lucille Armstrong, 28 September 1960, Louis Armstrong Archives, Rosenthal Library, Queens College CUNY, Flushing, NY.

BIBLIOGRAPHY ENTRIES

Reyes-Schramm, Adelaida. "The Role of Music in the Interaction of Black Americans and Hispanos in New York City's East Harlem." Ph.D. diss., Columbia University, 1975.

Glaser, Joe. Letter to Lucille Armstrong. Louis Armstrong Archives. Rosenthal Library, Queens College CUNY, Flushing, NY.

23. Musical score or composition: Treat a published score as a book, and include it in the bibliography.

NOTE

> 28. Franz Josef Haydn, *Symphony No. 94 in G Major,* ed. H. C. Robbins Landon (Salzburg: Haydn-Mozart Press, 1965), 22.

BIBLIOGRAPHY ENTRY

> Haydn, Franz Josef. *Symphony No. 94 in G Major.* Edited by H. C. Robbins Landon. Salzburg: Haydn-Mozart Press, 1965.

For a musical composition, give the composer's name, followed by the title of the work. Put the title in italics unless it names an instrumental work known only by its form, number, and key.

NOTES

> 29. Duke Ellington, *Satin Doll.*

> 30. Franz Josef Haydn, Symphony no. 94 in G Major.

24. DVD or Videocassette: Include the original release date before the publication information if it differs from the release date for the DVD or videocassette.

NOTE

> 31. *Wit,* DVD, directed by Mike Nichols (New York: HBO Home Video, 2001).

BIBLIOGRAPHY

> *Wit.* DVD. Directed by Mike Nichols. New York: HBO Home Video, 2001.

25. Sound recording: Begin with the composer or other person responsible for the content.

NOTE

> 32. Louis Armstrong, *Town Hall Concert Plus,* RCA INTS 5070.

BIBLIOGRAPHY ENTRY

> Armstrong, Louis. *Town Hall Concert Plus.* RCA INTS 5070.

26. Artwork: Begin with the artist's name, and include both the name and the location of the institution holding the work. Works of art are usually not included in the bibliography.

NOTE

> 33. Herman Leonard, *Louis Armstrong: Birdland,* black-and-white photograph, 1956, Barbara Gillman Gallery, Miami.

27. Performance: Begin with the author, director, or performer—whoever is most relevant to your study.

NOTE

> 34. Terrence McNally, Lynn Athrens, and Stephen Flaherty, *Ragtime,* dir. Frank Galati, Ford Performing Arts Center, New York, November 11, 1998.

BIBLIOGRAPHY ENTRY

> McNally, Terrence, Lynn Athrens, and Stephen Flaherty. *Ragtime.* Directed by Frank Galati. Ford Performing Arts Center, New York, November 11, 1998.

28. CD-ROM or other electronic non-Internet source: Indicate the format after the publication information.

NOTE

> 35. *Microsoft Encarta Multimedia Encyclopedia,* s.v. "Armstrong, (Daniel) Louis 'Satchmo'" (Redmond, WA: Microsoft, 1994), CD-ROM.

BIBLIOGRAPHY ENTRY

> *Microsoft Encarta Multimedia Encyclopedia.* "Armstrong, (Daniel) Louis 'Satchmo.'" Redmond, WA: Microsoft, 1994. CD-ROM.

Online Sources

The fifteenth edition of *The Chicago Manual of Style* specifically addresses the documentation of electronic and online sources. In general, citations for electronic sources include all of the information required for print sources, in addition to a URL and, in some cases, the date of access. There are three key differences between Chicago- and MLA-style online citations:

- Chicago does not require URLs to be enclosed in angle brackets.

- Names of months are not abbreviated, and the date is usually given in the following order: month, day, year (September 13, 2004).

- Dates of access are necessary only for sites that are frequently updated (such as news media sites or blogs) and for books.

29. Online book: Include the date of access in parentheses.

NOTE

36. Carl Sandburg, *Chicago Poems* (New York: Henry Holt, 1916), http://www.bartleby.com/165/index.html (accessed May 3, 2005).

BIBLIOGRAPHY ENTRY

Sandburg, Carl. *Chicago Poems*. New York: Henry Holt, 1916. http://www.bartleby.com/165/index.html (accessed May 3, 2005).

30. Online journal:

NOTE

37. Janet Schmalfeldt, "On Keeping the Score," *Music Theory Online* 4, no. 2 (1998), http://smt.ucsb.edu/mto/issues/mto.98.4.2.schmalfeldt.html.

BIBLIOGRAPHY ENTRY

Schmalfeldt, Janet. "On Keeping the Score." *Music Theory Online* 4, no. 2 (1998). http://smt.ucsb.edu/mto/issues/mto.98.4.2.schmalfeldt.html.

31. Online database, Web site, or discussion group: Identify as many of the following items as you can: author, title, kind of source (in brackets), publication data, and URL. It is not necessary to include bibliography entries for postings to a discussion group.

NOTES

38. Bruce Boyd Raeburn, "An Introduction to New Orleans Jazz," in *William Ransom Hogan Archive of New Orleans Jazz* (Tulane University, October 30, 2004), http://www.tulane.edu/~1miller/BeginnersIntro.html.

39. Don Mopsick, "Favorite Jazz Quotes," in Big Band Music Fans, October 30, 2004, http://www.remarq.com/list/4755?nav+FIRST&rf+1&si+grou.

BIBLIOGRAPHY ENTRY

Raeburn, Bruce Boyd. "An Introduction to New Orleans Jazz."
In *William Ransom Hogan Archive of New Orleans Jazz.* Tulane
University, October 30, 2004. http://www.tulane.edu/~.1miller/
BeginnersIntro.html.

32. Article from an online magazine or newspaper: Include
the date of access if required or if the material is time sensitive.

NOTES

40. Michael E. Ross, "The New Sultans of Swing," *Salon,* April 18,
1996, http://www.salon.com/weekly/music1.html.

41. Don Heckman, "Jazz, Pop in Spirited Harmony," *Los Angeles
Times,* August 10, 2005, http://www.calendarlive.com/music/jazz/
cl-et-hancock10aug10,0,7414710.story?coll=cl-home-more-channels
(accessed August 12, 2005).

BIBLIOGRAPHY ENTRIES

Ross, Michael E. "The New Sultans of Swing." *Salon,* April 18, 1996.
http://www.salon.com/weekly/music1.html.

Heckman, Don. "Jazz, Pop in Spirited Harmony." *Los Angeles Times,*
August 10, 2005. http://www.calendarlive.com/music/jazz/
cl-et-hancock10aug10,0,7414710.story
?coll=cl-home-more-channels (accessed August 12, 2005).

www.mhhe.com/
awr
For another sample of
a paper in Chicago
style, go to
Research > Sample
Research Papers >
CMS Style

35d Sample from a student paper in Chicago style

The following excerpt from Esther Hoffman's paper on Louis Armstrong has been put into Chicago style so that you can see how citation
numbers, endnotes, and bibliography work together. (Hoffman's entire
paper, in MLA style, can be found on pages 321–32.)

Chicago style allows you the option of including a title page. If you
do provide a title page, count it as page 1, but do not include the number on the page. Put page numbers in the upper right-hand corner of
the remaining pages, except for the pages with the titles "Notes" and
"Bibliography" or "Works Cited"; on these pages, the number should be
centered at the bottom of the page.

2

In the 1920s, jazz music was at its height in creativity and popularity. Chicago had become one of the jazz capitals of America, and its clubs showcased the premier talents of the time, performers like Jelly Roll Morton and Joe Oliver. It has always been difficult to break into the music business, and the jazz scene of the twenties was no exception. Eager for fame and fortune, though, many young black musicians who had honed their craft in New Orleans migrated north to Chicago, hoping for a chance to perform with the best.[1]

Among these emigres was Louis Armstrong, a gifted musician who developed into the "first true virtuoso soloist of jazz."[2] Armstrong played the trumpet and sang with unusual improvisational ability as well as technical mastery. As Bergreen points out, he easily reached difficult high notes, the F's and G's that stymied other trumpeters.[3] And his innovative singing style featured "scat," a technique that combines "nonsense syllables [with] improvised melodies."[4] Eventually, Armstrong's innovations became the standard, as more and more jazz musicians took their cue from his style.

Armstrong's beginnings give no hint of the greatness that he would achieve. In New Orleans, he was born into poverty and received little formal education. As a youngster, Armstrong had to take odd jobs like delivering coal and selling newspapers so that he could earn money to help his family. At the age of twelve, Armstrong was placed in the Colored Waifs' Home to serve an eighteen-month sentence for firing a gun in a public place. There "Captain" Peter Davis gave him "basic musical training on the cornet."[5] Older, more established musicians soon noticed Armstrong's talent and offered him opportunities to play with

3

them. In 1922, Joe Oliver invited Armstrong to join his band in Chicago, and the twenty-one-year-old trumpeter headed north.

It was in Chicago that Armstrong met Joe Glaser, the man who eventually became his longtime manager. According to Bergreen, Glaser had a reputation for being a tough but trustworthy guy who could handle any situation. He was raised in a middle-class home by parents who were Jewish immigrants from Russia. As a young man, Glaser got caught up in the Chicago underworld and soon had a rap sheet that included indictments for running a brothel as well as for statutory rape.[6] Glaser's mob connections also led to his involvement in Chicago's club scene, a business almost completely controlled by gangsters like Al Capone. During the era of Prohibition, Glaser managed the Sunset Café, a club where Armstrong often performed:

> There was a pronounced gangster element at the Sunset, but Louis, accustomed to being employed and protected by mobsters, didn't think twice about that. Mr. Capone's men ensured the flow of alcohol, and their presence reassured many whites.[7]

Notes

1. R. D. Frederick, ed., "Chicago; Early 1920s," Wolverine Antique Music Society, http://www.shellac.org/wams/wchicag1.html.

2. *Microsoft Encarta Multimedia Encyclopedia,* s.v. "Armstrong, (Daniel) Louis 'Satchmo' " (Redmond, WA: Microsoft, 1994), CD-ROM.

3. Laurence Bergreen, *Louis Armstrong: An Extravagant Life* (New York: Broadway Books, 1997), 248.

4. J. Bradford Robinson, "Scat Singing," in *The New Grove Dictionary of Jazz* (2002).

5. "Satchmo!" *New Orleans Online* (New Orleans Tourism Marketing Corporation, 2005), http://www.neworleansonline .com/neworleans/music/satchmobio.html.

6. Bergreen, 372-76.

7. Ibid., 279.

Bibliography

Armstrong, Louis. "Authentic American Genius." Interview by
   Richard Meryman. *Life,* April 15, 1966, 92-102.

———. Louis Armstrong Archives. Rosenthal Library, Queens College
   CUNY, Flushing, NY.

———. *Town Hall Concert Plus.* RCA INTS 5070.

Bergreen, Laurence. *Louis Armstrong: An Extravagant Life.* New York:
   Broadway Books, 1997.

Bogle, Donald. "Louis Armstrong: The Films." In *Louis Armstrong:
   A Cultural Legacy,* ed. Marc H. Miller, 147-79. Seattle: University
   of Washington Press and Queens Museum of Art, 1994.

Collier, James Lincoln. *Jazz: The American Theme Song.* New York:
   Oxford University Press, 1993.

———. *Louis Armstrong: An American Genius.* New York: Oxford University
   Press, 1983.

Crawford, Richard. Foreword to *The Jazz Tradition,* by Martin
   Williams. New York: Oxford University Press, 1993.

Davis, Miles, and Quincy Troupe. *Miles: The Autobiography.*
   New York: Simon & Schuster, 1989.

Frederick, R. D., ed. "Chicago; Early 1920s." Wolverine Antique
   Music Society. http://www.shellac.org/wams/wchicag1.html.

Jones, Max, and John Chilton. *Louis: The Louis Armstrong Story,
   1900-1971.* Boston: Little, Brown, 1971.

Morgenstern, Dan. "Louis Armstrong and the Development and
   Diffusion of Jazz." In *Louis Armstrong: A Cultural Legacy,* edited
   by Marc H. Miller, 95-145. Seattle: University of Washington
   Press and Queens Museum of Art, 1994.

Writer in-
cludes *all*
sources she
consulted, not
just those she
cited in body
of paper.

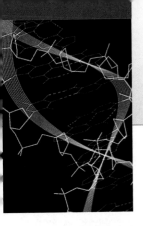

36 CSE Documentation: Name-Year Style

The Council of Science Editors (CSE), formerly known as the Council of Biology Editors (CBE), endorses two documentation styles in the sixth edition of *Scientific Style and Format: The CBE Manual for Authors, Editors, and Publishers* (New York: Cambridge University Press, 1994):

www.mhhe.com/ awr
For links to Web sites for documentation styles used in various disciplines, go to

Research > Links to Documentation Sites

- **A name-year style,** described in this chapter, that includes the last name of the author and year of publication in the text. (This system resembles APA style; *for APA style, see pp. 333–67.*)

- **A number style,** described in Chapter 37, that includes a superscript number (^{1}) in the text and a list of references in citation sequence. (This system is distinctive to the natural and applied sciences.)

These two styles cannot be mixed within a paper. Consult your instructor for the preferred style, and use it consistently. A major new edition of *The CSE Manual* is being prepared. This new edition will specifically address online and electronic citations. For more information, go to the Council of Science Editors' Web site at <http://www.councilscienceeditors.org/publications/ssf_7th.cfm>.

36a In-text citations

Include the source's author, the publication date, and, if you are citing a particular passage, the page number(s).

> According to Gleason (1993), a woman loses 35% of cortical bone and 50% of trabecular bone during her lifetime.

> Osteoporosis has been defined as "a disease characterized by low bone mass, micro-architectural deterioration of bone tissue, leading to enhanced bone fragility and a consequent increase in fracture risk" (Johnston 1996, p 30S).

Note: When a page number is cited, no period follows the *p.*

36b   List of references

Every source cited in your paper must correspond to an entry in your list of references, which should be prepared according to the guidelines in the box on page 393.

CSE NAME-YEAR STYLE: DIRECTORY to SAMPLE TYPES

Books

Include the author(s), last name first; publication year; title; place and publisher; and number of pages.

1. One author:

> Bailey C. 1991. The new fit or fat. Boston: Houghton Mifflin. 167 p.

2. Two or more authors:

> Begon M, Harper JL, Townsend CR. 1990. Ecology: Individuals, populations, and communities. 2nd ed. Boston: Blackwell. 945 p.

3. Selection in an edited book:

> Bohus B, Koolhaas JM. 1993. Psychoimmunology of social factors in rodents and other subprimate vertebrates. In: Ader R, Felten DL,

GUIDELINES for the CSE LIST of REFERENCES: NAME-YEAR STYLE

- Begin the list on a new page after your text but before any appendixes, tables, and figures.
- Use the centered title "References."
- Include only references that are cited in your paper.
- Indent all lines except the first in each entry.
- Arrange the entries alphabetically by author's last name.
- Single-space within each entry, and double-space between entries.
- Do not underline or italicize titles.
- Capitalize only the first word and proper nouns in titles.

> Cohen N, editors. Psychoneuroimmunology. San Diego (CA): Academic Pr. p 807-30.

4. Technical report or government document:

> Gleeson P. 1993. Osteoporosis. Rockville (MD): Public Health Service of the US Dept. of Health and Human Services; Agency for Health Care Policy Research [AHCPR] Publication nr 92-0038. 27 p.

5. Organization as author:

> [NIH] National Institutes of Health. 1993. Clinical trials supported by the National Eye Institute: celebrating vision research. Bethesda (MD): US Dept. of Health and Human Services. 112 p.

6. Book with editor(s):

> Wilder E, editor. 1988. Obstetric and gynecologic physical therapy. New York: Churchill Livingstone. 225 p.

Periodicals

When listing periodical articles, include the following information: author(s); year; title of article; title of journal; number of the volume and, if needed, of the issue; and page numbers.

> *Note:* Up to ten authors can be listed by name; periodical titles are abbreviated; an issue number is needed only when a journal is not paginated by volume; year, month, and day are listed for magazines.

7. Article in a journal paginated by volume:

Devine A, Prince RL, Bell R. 1996. Nutritional effect of calcium supplementation by skim milk powder or calcium tablets on total nutrient intake in postmenopausal women. Am J Clin Nutr 64:731-7.

8. Article in a journal paginated by issue:

Hummel-Berry K. 1990. Obstetric low back pain, a comprehensive review, part 2: evaluation and treatment. J Ob Gyn PT 14(2):9-11.

9. Article in a supplement to a journal:

Seeman E, Tsalamandris C, Bass S, Pearce G. 1995. Present and future of osteoporosis therapy. Bone 17(2 Suppl):23S-29S.

10. Article in a magazine:

Sternfeld P. 1997 Jan 1. Physical activity and pregnancy outcome review and recommendations. Sports Med:33-47.

Online Sources

11. Online journal article:

Krieger D, Onodipe S, Charles PJ, Sclabassi RJ. 1998. Real time signal processing in the clinical setting. Ann Biomed Engn [Internet] [cited 2000 Jul 6];26(3);462-72. Available from: http://www.kluweronline.com/issn/0090-6964

12. Online book (monograph):

Kohn LT, Corrigan JM, Donaldson MS. 2000. To err is human: building a safer health system [online book]. Washington, DC: National

Academy Press: 2000 [cited 2000 Jul 6]. 312 p. Available from: http://www.nap.edu/books/0309068371/html

13. Online database or Web site:

National Osteoporosis Foundation. 2000. Osteoporosis and related bone disease—national resource center [Internet]. Bethesda (MD): National Institutes of Health [NIH] [cited 2000 Jul 6]. Available from: http://www.osteo.org/osteo.html

36c   Sample references list: CSE name-year system

www.mhhe.com/
awr
For a complete sample
paper in CSE style,
go to

Research > Sample
Research Papers >
CSE Style

References

American Association of Clinical Endocrinologists. 1991. Clinical practice guidelines for the prevention and treatment of postmenopausal osteoporosis. J Fla Med Assoc 83:552-66.

Caldwell JR. 1996. Epidemiologic and economic considerations of osteoporosis. J Fla Med Assoc 83:548-51.

Gleeson P. 1993. Osteoporosis. Rockville (MD): Public Health Service of the US Dept. of Health and Human Services. AHCPR Publication nr 92-0038. 27 p.

Johnson CC. 1996. Development of clinical practice guidelines for prevention and treatment of osteoporosis. Calci Tiss Int 59(1 Suppl):30S-33S.

Roberts MM. 1997. Osteoporosis: update on prevention and treatment [lecture handout]. Pennsylvania Physical Therapy Assn [PPTA] Conference. Harrisburg.

Seeman E, Tsalamandris C, Bass S, Pearce G. 1995. Present and future of osteoporosis therapy. Bone 17(2 Suppl):23S-29S.

37 CSE Documentation: Number Style

www.mhhe.com/
awr
For links to Web sites
for documentation
styles used in various
discplines, go to

Research > Links
to Documentation
Sites

37a In-text citations

To cite a source, insert a superscript number immediately after the relevant name, word, or phrase.

> As a group, American women over 45 years of age sustain approximately 1 million fractures each year, 70% of which are due to osteoporosis.[1]

That number now belongs to that source, and it should be used if you refer to that source again later in your paper.

> A BMD value more than 1 SD but less than 2.5 SD below the young adult mean is considered as osteopenia,[4] while osteoporosis is defined as a BMD 2.5 SD below the young adult mean.[1]

Credit more than one source at a time by referring to each source's number. Separate the numbers with a comma.

> According to studies by Yomo,[2] Paleg,[3] and others,[1,4] barley seed embryos produce a substance which stimulates the release of hydrolytic enzymes.

If the numbers are in sequence, however, separate them with a hyphen.

> As several others[1-4] have documented, GA has an RNA-enhancing effect.

www.mhhe.com/
awr
To download
Bibliomaker software
for CSE style, go to

Research >
Bibliomaker

37b List of references

Every source cited in your paper must correspond to an entry in your list of references, which should be prepared according to the guidelines in the box on page 398.

CSE NUMBER STYLE: DIRECTORY to SAMPLE TYPES

Books and Reports

1. One author   *397*
2. Two or more authors   *397*
3. Organization as author   *397*
4. Chapter in a book   *397*
5. Book with editor(s)   *398*
6. Selection in an edited book   *398*
7. Technical report or government document   *398*

Periodicals

8. Article in a journal paginated by volume   *399*

9. Article in a journal or supplement paginated by issue   *399*
10. Article in a magazine or newspaper   *399*

Online Sources

11. Online journal article   *399*
12. Online book (monograph)   *400*
13. Online database or Web site   *400*

Books and Reports

1. One author:

1. Bailey C. The new fit or fat. Boston: Houghton Mifflin; 1991. 167 p.

2. Two or more authors:
List up to ten authors; if there are more than ten, use the first author's name with the phrase *and others*.

2. Begon M, Harper JL, Townsend CR. Ecology: Individuals, populations, and communities. 2nd ed. Boston: Blackwell; 1990. 945 p.

3. Organization as author:

3. National Institutes of Health. Clinical trials supported by the National Eye Institute: celebrating vision research. Bethesda (MD): US Dept. of Health and Human Services; 1993. 112 p.

4. Chapter in a book:
Note that the author of the chapter and the book are the same. Consult no. 6 on page 398 when the authors are not the same person.

GUIDELINES for the CSE LIST of REFERENCES: NUMBER STYLE

- Assign numbers to the sources cited in your paper, in the order in which you cite them.
- In the list of references (titled "References"), list sources in the numerical order of their citation, not in alphabetical order.
- Align the second and subsequent lines of the entry with the first word of the first line, not with the number.
- Single-space within each entry, and double-space between entries.
- Do not underline or italicize titles.
- Capitalize only the first word and proper nouns in titles.
- Give the names of up to ten authors with the last name first, followed by the first initial or initials.
- Do not place a period at the end of a URL.

4. Castro J. The American way of health: how medicine is changing and what it means to you. Boston: Little, Brown; 1994. Chapter 9, Why doctors, hospitals, and drugs cost so much; p 131-53.

5. Book with editor(s):

5. Ader R, Felten DL, Cohen N, editors. Psychoneuroimmunology. San Diego (CA): Academic Pr; 1993. 1218 p.

6. Selection in an edited book:

6. Bohus B, Koolhaas JM. Psychoimmunology of social factors in rodents and other subprimate vertebrates. In: Ader R, Felten DL, Cohen N, editors. Psychoneuroimmunology. San Diego (CA): Academic Pr; 1993. p 807-30.

7. Technical report or government document: Include the name of the sponsoring organization or agency as well as any report or contract number.

7. Gleeson P. Osteoporosis. Rockville (MD): Public Health Service of US Dept. of Health and Human Services; 1993 Mar. Agency for Health Care Policy Research [AHCPR] Publication nr 92-0038. 27 p.

Periodicals

8. Article in a journal paginated by volume: There is no need to designate issue number and month for journals paginated by yearly volume rather than issue. Note that titles of journals are abbreviated.

> 8. Devine A, Prince RL, Bell R. Nutritional effect of calcium supplementation by skim milk powder or calcium tablets on total nutrient intake in postmenopausal women. Am J Clin Nutr 1996; 64:731-7.

9. Article in a journal or supplement paginated by issue: Include the year, the month, the volume number, and the issue number (in parentheses). Be sure to indicate when the article is in a supplement rather than in the issue itself. Note that semicolons are used to separate the month from the volume number.

> 9. Hummel-Berry K. Obstetric low back pain, a comprehensive review, part 2: evaluation and treatment. J Ob Gyn PT 1990 Jun;14(2):9-11.
>
> 10. Seeman E, Tsalamandris C, Bass S, Pearce G. Present and future of osteoporosis therapy. Bone 1995 Aug; 17(2 Suppl):23S-29S.

10. Article in a magazine or newspaper: Indicate the year, month, and day of publication. For newspapers, identify the section before the page number: *NY Times 2000 Jul 9;Sect C:2.*

> 11. Sternfeld P. Physical activity and pregnancy outcome review and recommendations. Sports Med 1997 Jan 1:33-47.

Online Sources

In addition to the information that is normally required, CSE requires the following data: type of document, availability information, and date of access.

11. Online journal article:

> 12. Krieger D, Onodipe S, Charles PJ, Sclabassi RJ. Real time signal processing in the clinical setting. Ann Biomed Engn [Internet] 1998 [cited 2000 Jul 6];26(3):462-72. Available from: http://www.kluweronline.com/issn/0090-6964

12. Online book (monograph)

13. Kohn LT, Corrigan JM, Donaldson MS. To err is human: building a safer health system [online monograph]. Washington, DC: National Academy Press; 2000. Available from: National Academy Press at http://www.nap.edu/books/0309068371/html

13. Online database or Web site:

14. National Osteoporosis Foundation. Osteoporosis and related bone diseases--national resource center [Internet]. [cited 2000 Jul 6]. Available from: http://www.osteo.org/osteo.html

www.mhhe.com/ awr
For a complete sample paper in CSE style, go to
Research > Sample Research Papers > CSE Style

37c Sample reference list: CSE number system

References

1. American Association of Clinical Endocrinologists. Clinical practice guidelines for the prevention and treatment of postmenopausal osteoporosis. J Fla Med Assoc 1991; 83:552-66.

2. Johnston CC. Development of clinical practice guidelines for prevention and treatment of osteoporosis. Calci Tiss Int 1996;59(1 Suppl):30S-33S.

3. Caldwell JR. Epidemiologic and economic considerations of osteoporosis. J Fla Med Assoc 1996;83:548-51.

4. Seeman E, Tsalamandris C, Bass S, Pearce G. Present and future of osteoporosis therapy. Bone 1995 Aug; 17(2 Suppl):23S-29S.

5. Roberts MM. Osteoporosis: update on prevention and treatment [lecture handout]. Pennsylvania Physical Therapy Assn [PPTA] Conference. 1997 Oct. Harrisburg.

6. Gleeson P. Osteoporosis. Rockville (MD): Public Health Service of US Dept. of Health and Human Services; 1993 Mar. AHCPR Publication nr 92-0038. 27 p.

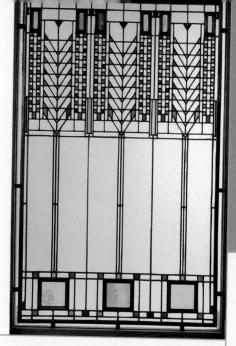

Frank Lloyd Wright's Robie House features 174 stained-glass windows. Sunlight brings out the clarity of each window's design; in turn, the designs—a variety of geometric, colorful patterns—transform the light.

9

I . . . believe that words can help us move or keep us paralyzed, and that our choices of language and verbal tone have something—a great deal—to do with how we live our lives and whom we end up speaking with and hearing.

—ADRIENNE RICH

Editing
for Clarity

9 Editing for Clarity

Like drafting and revising, editing can be creative. Sometimes, being creative means focusing on your sentences and asking whether the parts fit together well. Other times, it means assessing your word choices.

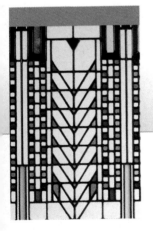

38 Wordy Sentences

A sentence does not have to be short and simple to be concise. Instead, every word in it must count.

Wordiness and Grammar Checkers

Most computer grammar checkers recognize many wordy structures, but inconsistently so. One style checker flagged most passive verbs and some *it is* and *there are* (expletive) constructions, but not others. It also flagged the redundant expression *true fact*, but missed *round circle* and the empty phrase *it is a fact that*.

www.mhhe.com/
awr
For more information
on and practice
eliminating
redundancies,
go to

Editing >
Wordiness

38a   Eliminate redundancies.

Redundancies are meaningless repetitions that result in wordiness. Be on the lookout for such commonplace redundancies as *first and foremost, full and complete, final result, past histories, round in shape,* and *refer back.*

➤ Students living ~~in close proximity~~ in the dorms need to

cooperate ~~together if they want~~ to live in harmony.

Sometimes, modifiers such as *very, rather,* and *really* and intensifiers such as *absolutely, definitely,* and *incredibly* do not add meaning to a sentence but are simply redundant.

➤ That film was ~~really~~ hard to watch, but ~~absolutely~~ worth

seeing.

➤ The ending ~~definitely~~ shocked us ~~very much~~.

38b   Do not repeat words unnecessarily.

Although repetition is sometimes used for emphasis, unnecessary repetitions weaken sentences and should be removed.

➤ The children enjoyed watching television more than ~~they~~

~~enjoyed~~ reading books.

➤ They watched cartoons in the morning and ~~cartoons~~ in the

late afternoon.

38c   Replace wordy phrases.

Make your sentences more concise by replacing wordy phrases with appropriate one-word alternatives.

➤ ~~It is necessary at this point in time that tests~~ *Tests must now* be run ~~for the~~

~~purposes of measuring~~ *to measure* the switch's strength.

ALTERNATIVES for COMMON WORDY PHRASES

Wordy Phrases	Concise Alternatives
at this point in time	now
at the present time	now
in the not-too-distant future	soon
in close proximity to	near
is necessary that	must
is able to	can
has the ability to	can
due to the fact that	because
for the reason that	because
in spite of the fact that	although
in the event that	if
in the final analysis	finally
in order to	to
for the purpose(s) of	to

38d Reduce clauses and phrases.

For conciseness and clarity, simplify your sentence structure by turning modifying clauses into phrases.

➤ **The film *Dirty Pretty Things*, ~~which was~~ directed by Stephen Frears, portrays the struggles of illegal immigrants in London.**

Also look for opportunities to reduce phrases to single words.

➤ **Stephen Frear's film *Dirty Pretty Things* portrays the struggles of illegal immigrants in London.**

38e Combine sentences.

Sometimes, you can combine several short, repetitive sentences into a single, more concise sentence.

IDENTIFY AND EDIT
Wordy Sentences

W

To make your writing concise, ask yourself these questions as you edit your writing:

? *1. Do any sentences contain wordy or empty phrases such as at this point in time? Do any of them contain redundancies or other unnecessary repetitions?*

- ~~The fact is that at this point in time~~ _{More} ~~more~~ women than men _{now} attend college.

- Total college enrollments have increased steadily ~~upward~~ since the 1940s, but since the 1970s women have enrolled in greater numbers than men ~~have~~.

? *2. Can any clauses be reduced to phrases, or phrases to single words? Can any sentences be combined to reduce repetitive information?*

- ~~Reports that come from~~ _{College} ~~college~~ officials ~~indicate~~ _{report} that applications from women exceed those from men/ ~~This~~ , *indicating* ~~pattern indicates~~ that women will continue to outnumber men in college for some time to come.

? *3. Do any sentences include there is, or there are, or it is expressions; weak verbs; or nouns derived from verbs?*

- In 1970, _{men outnumbered women in college by} ~~there were~~ more than 1.5 million. ~~more men in college than women.~~

- This trend ~~is a reflectiopn of~~ _{reflects} broad changes in gender roles throughout American society.

 Hurricane Floyd ~~had a devastating effect on~~ _{'s torrential rains devastated} our town/, ~~The destruction resulted from torrential rains. Flooding~~ submerged _{ing} Main Street under eight feet of water. ~~The rain~~ _{and} ~~also~~ triggered _{ing} mudslides that destroyed two nearby towns.

38f Make your sentences straightforward.

Concise sentences get to the point quickly instead of in a roundabout way. Eliminate expletive constructions like *there is, there are,* and *it is,* and replace the static verbs *to be* and *to have* with active verbs. (*For more on active verbs, see pp. 433–35.*)

ROUNDABOUT

There are stylistic similarities between "This Lime-Tree Bower" and "Tintern Abbey," which are indications of the influence that Coleridge had on Wordsworth.

STRAIGHTFORWARD

The stylistic similarities between "This Lime-Tree Bower" and "Tintern Abbey" indicate that Coleridge influenced Wordsworth.

Eliminating the expletive *There are* makes the main subject of the sentence—*similarities*—clearer. To find the action in the sentence, ask what *similarities* do here; they *indicate*. Do the same for the sentence's other subject, *Coleridge,* by asking what he did: *Coleridge . . . influenced.*

39 Missing Words

When editing, make sure you have not omitted any words readers need to understand the meaning of your sentence.

39a Add words needed to make compound structures complete and clear.

For conciseness, words can sometimes be omitted from compound structures: *His anger is extreme and his behavior* [is] *violent.*

www.mhhe.com/awr
For information and exercises on missing words, go to

Editing > Word Choice

Do not leave out part of a compound structure unless both parts of the compound are the same, however.

> *with*
> ➤ **The gang members neither cooperated ˄ nor listened to the**
>
> **authorities.**

39b Include *that* when it is needed for clarity.

The subordinator *that* should be omitted only when the clause it introduces is short and the sentence's meaning is clear: *Faith Hill sings the kind of songs many women love.* Usually, *that* should be included.

> *that*
> ➤ **The attorney argued ˄ men and women should receive equal**
>
> **pay for equal work.**

39c Make comparisons clear.

To be clear, comparisons must be complete. If you have just said "Peanut butter sandwiches are boring," you can say immediately afterward "Curried chicken sandwiches are more interesting." Saying "Curried chicken sandwiches are more interesting" in isolation does not give your audience enough information, however. You need to name who or what completes the comparison.

Sometimes, what is being compared can be unclear. To clarify, add the missing words.

> *did*
> ➤ **I loved my grandmother more than my sister. ˄**
> *I loved*
> ➤ **I loved my grandmother more than ˄ my sister.**

When you use *as* to compare people or things, be sure to use it twice.

> *as*
> ➤ **Napoleon's temper was ˄ volatile as a volcano.**

Include *other* or *else* to indicate that people or things belong to the group with which the subject is being compared.

> ➤ **High schools and colleges stage *The Laramie Project* more**
> **than any *other* play.**

➤ Professor Koonig wrote more books than anyone *else* in the department.

Use a possessive form when comparing attributes or possessions.

➤ Plato's philosophy is easier to read than ~~that of Aristotle.~~ *Aristotle's.*

39d Add articles (*a, an, the*) where necessary.

In English, omitting an article usually makes an expression sound odd, unless the omission occurs in a series of nouns.

➤ A dog that bites should be kept on *a* leash.

➤ He gave me *the* books he liked best.

➤ The classroom contained a fish tank, birdcage, and rabbit hutch.

Note: If the articles in a series are not the same, each one must be included.

➤ The classroom contained an aquarium, *a* birdcage, and

a rabbit hutch.

(For more information about the use of articles, multilingual writers should consult Tab 12: Basic Grammar Review, pp. 606–8.)

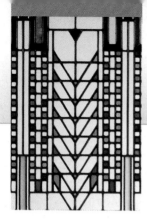

40 Mixed Constructions

Sentence parts that do not fit together either grammatically or logically confuse readers and must be revised to make meaning clear.

www.mhhe.com/awr
For information and exercises on mixed constructions, go to
Editing > Mixed Constructions

40a Untangle mixed-up sentence structures.

Mixed constructions occur when writers start a sentence one way and then, midway through, change grammatical direction. The following sentence begins with a prepositional phrase (a phrase introduced by a preposition such as *at, by, for, in,* or *of*) but then tries to make that phrase into the subject. A prepositional phrase cannot be the subject of a sentence, however. Eliminating the preposition *for* makes it clear that *family members* is the subject of the verb *decide*.

> *Family*
> ~~For family~~ members who enjoy one another's company
>
> often decide on a vacation spot together.

In the following example, the dependent clause *when a Curandero is consulted* cannot serve as the subject of the sentence. Transforming the dependent clause into an independent clause with a subject and predicate (a complete verb) solves the problem.

> *can be*   *for*
> In Mexican culture, ~~when~~ a Curandero ~~is~~ consulted ~~can~~
>
> ~~address~~ spiritual or physical illness.

Sometimes you may have to separate your ideas into more than one sentence to clarify your point. This sentence is trying to do two things at one time: to contrast England and France in 1805 and to define the difference between an oligarchy and a dictatorship. Using two sentences instead of one makes both ideas clear.

MIXED UP

In an oligarchy like England was in 1805, a few people had the power rather than a dictatorship like France, which was ruled by Napoleon.

410

REVISED

In 1805, England was an oligarchy, a state ruled by the few. In contrast, France was a dictatorship, a state ruled by one man: Napoleon.

Mixed Constructions and Grammar Checkers

Computer grammar checkers are unreliable at detecting mixed constructions. For example, a grammar checker failed to highlight the three examples of mixed-up sentences in section 40a.

40b Make sure predicates fit their subjects.

A **predicate** (the verb plus its object or complement) must connect logically to a sentence's subject. When it does not, the result is faulty predication.

> ~~The best kind of education for me would be a~~ university
>   A
>   ^ would be best for me.
> with both a school of music and a school of government./
>   ^

A university is an institution, not a type of education, so the sentence needs revision.

40c Edit sentences with *is when, is where,* and *the reason . . . is because* to make the subject clear.

The phrases *is where* and *is when* may sound logical, but they usually result in faulty predication.

>   the production of carbohydrates from the interaction of
> Photosynthesis is ~~where~~ carbon dioxide, water, and
>   ^
>
> chlorophyll ~~interact~~ in the presence of sunlight. ~~to form~~
>   ^
>
> ~~carbohydrates.~~

Photosynthesis is not a place, so *is where* is illogical.

Although *the reason . . . is because* may seem logical, it creates an awkward sentence. To fix this kind of faulty predication, change *because* to *that,* or change the subject of the sentence.

>   *that*
> **The reason the joint did not hold is ~~because~~ the coupling**
>
> **bolt broke.**

or

>   *The*
> **~~The reason the~~ joint did not hold ~~is~~ because the coupling**
>
> **bolt broke.**

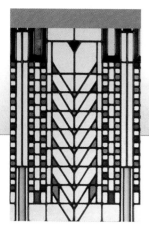

41 Confusing Shifts

When you are editing, look for jarring shifts and revise to make your sentences consistent.

Confusing Shifts and Grammar Checkers

Because confusing shifts can occur in sentences that are otherwise grammatically correct, computer grammar checkers rarely flag them. Consider this blatant example:

> **The teacher entered the room and then roll is called.**

Although it shifts confusingly from past to present tense and from active to passive voice, at least one grammar checker failed to highlight it.

41a Make your point of view consistent.

Once you choose a point of view, you should use it consistently. Writers have three points of view to choose from:

- First person (*I* or *we*) emphasizes the writer and is used in personal writing.
- Second person (*you*) focuses attention on readers and is used to give orders, directions, or advice.
- Third person (*he, she, it, one,* or *they*) is topic oriented and so is prevalent in academic writing.

Writers sometimes make jarring shifts in point of view when they compose generalizations. For example, the writer of the following sentence initially shifted from the third person (*students*) to the second person (*you*), a common kind of confusing shift.

> **Students will have no trouble getting access to a computer**
>
> *they*
> **if ~~you~~ arrive at the lab before noon.**

Do not switch from singular to plural or plural to singular for no reason. When editing such shifts, choose the plural to avoid using *his or her* or introducing gender bias. (*See Tab 10: Editing for Grammar Conventions, pp. 501–2.*)

> *People are*
> **~~A person is~~ often assumed to be dumb if they are attractive**
>
> **and smart if they are unattractive.**

41b Keep your verb tenses consistent.

www.mhhe.com/
awr
For information and exercises on shifts in verb tense and voice, go to

Editing > Verb and Voice Shifts

Verb tenses show the time of an action in relation to other actions. Choose a time frame—present, past, or future—and use it consistently, changing tense only when the meaning requires it.

Confusing shifts in time from past to present may occur when you are narrating events that are still vivid in your mind.

> **The wind was blowing a hundred miles an hour when**
>
> *was* *fell*
> **suddenly there is a big crash, and a tree ~~falls~~ into the**
>
> **living room.**

CHARTING the TERRITORY

Present Tense and Literary Works

By convention, the present tense is used to write about the content of literary works. When you write about literary works, be careful not to shift out of the present tense.

➤ David Copperfield observes other people with a fine

and sympathetic eye. He describes villains such as

Mr. Murdstone and heroes such as Mr. Micawber in

unforgettable detail. But Copperfield ~~was~~ *is* not himself

an especially interesting person.

You may also introduce inconsistencies when you are using the present perfect tense, perhaps because the past participle causes you to slip from present tense to past tense.

➤ She has admired many strange buildings at the university

but ~~thought~~ *thinks* that the new Science Center ~~looked~~ *looks* out of place.

41c Avoid unnecessary shifts in mood and voice.

Besides tense, verbs in a sentence also have a mood and a voice. There are three basic moods: (1) the **indicative,** used to state or question facts, acts, and opinions; (2) the **imperative,** used to give commands or advice; and (3) the **subjunctive,** used to express wishes, conjectures, and hypothetical conditions. Unnecessary shifts in mood can confuse and distract your readers. Be on the lookout for shifts between the indicative and the subjunctive and between the indicative and the imperative.

➤ If he ~~goes~~ *could go* to night school, he would take a course in

accounting.

➤ The sign says that in case of emergency passengers should

should not
follow the instructions of the train crew and ~~don't~~ leave
                                            ^

the train unless instructed to do so.

Most verbs have two voices. In the **active voice,** the subject does the acting; in the **passive voice,** the subject is acted upon. Do not shift abruptly from one voice to the other.

They favored violet,
➤ The Impressionist painters hated black. ~~Violet,~~ green, blue,
                                            ^

pink, and red. ~~were favored by them.~~
              ^

41d Avoid awkward shifts between direct and indirect quotations and questions.

Indirect quotations report what others wrote or said without repeating their words exactly. **Direct quotations** report the words of others exactly and should be enclosed in quotation marks. (*For more on punctuating quotations, see Tab 11: Editing for Correctness, pp. 557–59.*) Do not shift from one form of quotation to the other within a sentence.

➤ In his inaugural speech, President Kennedy called on

Americans not to ask what their country could do for them

to   they could   their
but instead "ask what ~~you~~ can do for ~~your~~ country."
             ^   ^   ^

The writer could have included the quotation in its entirety: *In his inaugural speech, President Kennedy said, "My fellow Americans, ask not what your country can do for you; ask what you can do for your country."*

Similarly, do not shift from an indirect to a direct question.

whether
➤ The performance was so bad the audience wondered ~~had~~
                                                   ^
had
the performers ever rehearsed.
              ^

As an alternative, the writer could ask the question directly: *Had the performers ever rehearsed? The performance was so bad the audience wasn't sure.*

IDENTIFY AND EDIT
Confusing Shifts

shift

To avoid confusing shifts, ask yourself these questions as you edit your writing:

 1. Does the sentence shift from one point of view to another? For example, does it shift from third person to second?

> ◆ Over the centuries, millions of laborers helped build and
> maintain the Great Wall of China, and ~~if you were one, you~~
> *most of them*
> ~~probably~~ suffered great hardship as a result.

 2. Are the verbs in your sentence consistent in the following ways?

> *In tense (past, present, or future):*
> ◆ Historians call the period before the unification of China the
> Warring States period. It ~~ends~~ when the ruler of the Ch'in
> *ended*
> state conquered the last of his independent neighbors.
>
> *In mood (statements vs. commands or hypothetical conditions):*
> ◆ If a similar wall ~~is~~ built today, it would cost untold amounts
> *were*
> of time and money.
>
> *In voice (active vs. passive):*
> ◆ The purpose of the wall was to protect against invasion, but
> commerce ~~was promoted by it also.~~
> *it also promoted.*

 3. Are quotations and questions clearly phrased in either direct or indirect form?

> ◆ The visitor asked the guide ~~when~~ did construction of the
> *, "When*
> Great Wall begin?*"*
>
> ◆ The visitor asked the guide when ~~did~~ construction of the
> Great Wall ~~begin?~~
> *began.*

42 Faulty Parallelism

Parallel constructions enhance clarity by presenting equally important ideas in the same grammatical form.

➤ **At Gettysburg in 1863, Lincoln said that the Civil War was being fought to make sure that government *of the people, by the people,* and *for the people* might not perish from the earth.**

When you notice that items in a series or paired ideas do not have the same grammatical form, correct them by making them parallel.

Note: If you are writing a paper that includes a formal outline or headings, make sure the items at each level of your outline or heading structure are parallel.

42a Edit items in a series to make them parallel.

www.mhhe.com/ awr
For information and exercises on parallelism, go to
Editing > Parallelism

A list or series of equally important items should be parallel in grammatical structure.

➤ **The Census Bureau classifies people as employed if they receive payment for any kind of labor, are temporarily absent from their jobs, or ~~working~~ *work* at least fifteen hours as unpaid laborers in a family business.**

In the next example, the writer changed a noun to an adjective. Notice that the writer also decided to repeat the word *too* to make the sentence more forceful and memorable.

➤ **My sister obviously thought that I was too young, *too* ignorant, and *too troublesome.* ~~a troublemaker.~~**

417

42b Edit paired ideas to make them parallel.

Paired ideas connected with a coordinating conjunction (*and, but, or, nor, for, so, yet*), a correlative conjunction (*not only . . . but also, both . . . and, either . . . or, neither . . . nor*), or a comparative expression (*as much as, more than, less than*) must have parallel grammatical form.

➤ Successful teachers must ^both^ inspire ~~students~~ and ~~challenging~~ ^challenge their students.^

~~them is also important.~~

➤ I dreamed not only of getting the girl but also of the ^winning^ gold

medal.

➤ Many people find that having meaningful work is more

important than ^earning^ high pay.

42c Repeat function words as needed to keep parallel structures clear.

Function words give information about a word or indicate the relationships among words in a sentence.

FUNCTION WORDS

- Articles (*the, a, an*)
- Prepositions (for example, *to, for,* and *by*)
- Subordinating conjunctions (for example, *although* and *that*)
- The word *to* in infinitives

You can omit repeated function words whenever the parallel structure is clear without them, as in the first example, below. Otherwise, you should include them, as in the second example, on page 420.

➤ Her goals for retirement were to travel, ~~to~~ study art

history, and ~~to~~ write a book about Michelangelo.

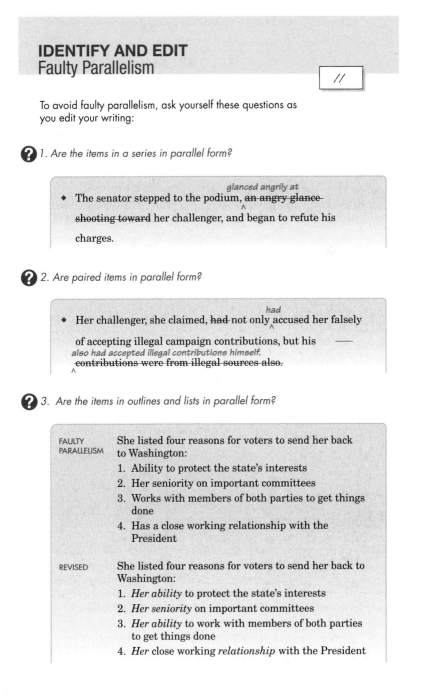

IDENTIFY AND EDIT
Faulty Parallelism

//

To avoid faulty parallelism, ask yourself these questions as
you edit your writing:

? 1. Are the items in a series in parallel form?

> *glanced angrily at*
> ◆ The senator stepped to the podium, ~~an angry glance~~
> ^
> ~~shooting toward~~ her challenger, and began to refute his
> charges.

? 2. Are paired items in parallel form?

> *had*
> ◆ Her challenger, she claimed, ~~had~~ not only ‸accused her falsely
>
> of accepting illegal campaign contributions, but his ——
> *also had accepted illegal contributions himself.*
> ~~contributions were from illegal sources also.~~
> ‸

? 3. Are the items in outlines and lists in parallel form?

FAULTY
PARALLELISM

She listed four reasons for voters to send her back
to Washington:
1. Ability to protect the state's interests
2. Her seniority on important committees
3. Works with members of both parties to get things
   done
4. Has a close working relationship with the
   President

REVISED

She listed four reasons for voters to send her back to
Washington:
1. *Her ability* to protect the state's interests
2. *Her seniority* on important committees
3. *Her ability* to work with members of both parties
   to get things done
4. *Her* close working *relationship* with the President

➤ **The project has three goals: to survey the valley for**

to
Inca-period sites, ₍ₐ₎excavate a test trench at each site,

to
and ₍ₐ₎excavate one of those sites completely.

The writer added *to* to make it clear where one goal ends and the next begins.

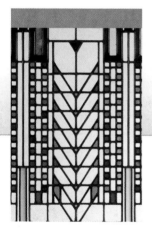

43 Misplaced and Dangling Modifiers

For a sentence to make sense, its parts must be arranged appropriately. When a modifying word, phrase, or clause is misplaced or dangling, readers get confused.

www.mhhe.com/
awr
For information and
exercises on misplaced
modifiers, go to

Editing > Misplaced
Modifiers

43a Put modifiers close to the words they modify.

For clarity, modifiers should come immediately before or after the words they modify. In the following sentence, the clause *after the police arrested them* modifies *protesters,* not *property.* Putting the clause before the word it modifies makes it clear that if any property destruction occurred, it occurred before—not after—the arrest.

After the police arrested them, the
➤ ~~The~~ protesters were charged with destroying college

property. ~~after the police had arrested them.~~

Misplaced Modifiers and Grammar Checkers

Some grammar checkers will reliably highlight split infinitives (*see 43d*) but only occasionally highlight other types of misplaced modifier. One grammar checker, for example, missed the misplaced modifier *with a loud crash* in this sentence.

➤ The valuable vase *with a loud crash* fell to the floor and broke into hundreds of pieces.

The following sentence was revised to make it clear that the hikers were watching the storm from the porch:

➤ ~~The~~ From the cabin's porch, the hikers watched the storm gathering force. ~~from the~~

~~cabin's porch.~~

43b Clarify ambiguous modifiers.

Adverbs can modify what precedes or follows them. Make sure the adverbs you use are not ambiguously placed. The following revision clarifies that it is the objection that is vehement, not the argument.

➤ Historians who object vehemently to this account ~~vehemently~~ argue

that the presidency was never endangered.

Problems occur with limiting modifiers such as *only, even, almost, nearly,* and *just.* Check every sentence that includes one of these modifiers. In the following sentence, does the writer mean that vegetarian dishes are the only dishes served at dinner or that dinner is the only time when vegetarian dishes are available? Editing clears up the ambiguity.

AMBIGUOUS

The restaurant *only offers* vegetarian dishes for dinner.

REVISED

The restaurant *offers only* vegetarian dishes for dinner.

or

The restaurant *offers* vegetarian dishes *only* at dinner.

Misplacing *not,* another limiting modifier, can result in an inaccurate sentence.

       Not all
➤ ~~All~~ of the vegetarian dishes are ~~not~~ low in fat and calories.

43c Move disruptive modifiers.

When you separate grammatical elements that belong together with a lengthy modifying phrase or clause, the resulting sentence can be difficult to read. In the following sentence, the phrase beginning with *despite* initially came between the subject and verb, disrupting the flow of the sentence. With the modifying phrase at the beginning of the sentence, the edited version restores the connection between subject and verb.

    Despite their similar conceptions of the self,
➤ **Descartes and Hume, ~~despite their similar conceptions~~**

    ~~of the self,~~ deal with the issue of personal identity in

    different ways.

43d Check split infinitives for ambiguity.

An **infinitive** couples the word *to* with the present tense of a verb. In a **split infinitive,** one or more words intervene between *to* and the verb form. Avoid separating the parts of an infinitive with a modifier unless keeping them together results in an awkward or ambiguous construction.

    In the following example, the modifier *successfully* should be moved. The modifier *carefully* should probably stay where it is, however, even though it splits the infinitive *to assess. Carefully* needs to be close to the verb it modifies, and putting it after *assess* would cause ambiguity because readers might think it modifies *projected economic benefits.*

                           successfully,
➤ **To ~~successfully~~ complete this assignment students have**

    to carefully assess projected economic benefits in relation

    to potential social problems.

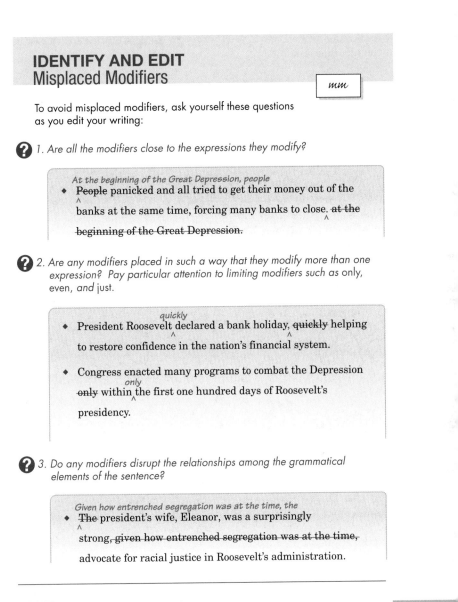

IDENTIFY AND EDIT
Misplaced Modifiers

mm

To avoid misplaced modifiers, ask yourself these questions
as you edit your writing:

❓ *1. Are all the modifiers close to the expressions they modify?*

♦ ~~People~~ *At the beginning of the Great Depression, people* panicked and all tried to get their money out of the
banks at the same time, forcing many banks to close. ~~at the~~
~~beginning of the Great Depression.~~

❓ *2. Are any modifiers placed in such a way that they modify more than one
expression? Pay particular attention to limiting modifiers such as* only*,*
even*, and* just*.*

♦ President Roosevelt declared a bank holiday, *quickly* ~~quickly~~ helping
to restore confidence in the nation's financial system.

♦ Congress enacted many programs to combat the Depression
~~only~~ *only* within the first one hundred days of Roosevelt's
presidency.

❓ *3. Do any modifiers disrupt the relationships among the grammatical
elements of the sentence?*

♦ ~~The~~ *Given how entrenched segregation was at the time, the* president's wife, Eleanor, was a surprisingly
strong, ~~given how entrenched segregation was at the time,~~
advocate for racial justice in Roosevelt's administration.

43e Fix dangling modifiers.

A **dangling modifier** is a descriptive phrase that implies an actor
different from the sentence's subject. When readers try to connect the
modifying phrase with the actual subject, the results may be humor-
ous as well as confusing. To fix a dangling modifier, you must name

www.mhhe.com/
awr
For information and
exercises on dangling
modifiers, go to

Editing > Dangling
Modifiers

its implied actor explicitly, either as the subject of the sentence or in the modifier itself.

DANGLING MODIFIER	*Swimming toward the boat on the horizon,* the crowded beach felt as if it were miles away.
REVISED	Swimming toward the boat on the horizon, *I* felt as if the crowded beach were miles away.
	or
	As *I swam* toward the boat on the horizon, the crowded beach seemed miles away.

Note that simply moving a dangling modifier will not fix the problem. To make the meaning clear, you must make the implied actor in the modifying phrase explicit.

DANGLING MODIFIER	*After struggling for weeks in the wilderness,* the town pleased them mightily.
REVISED	After struggling for weeks in the wilderness, *they* were pleased to come upon the town.
	or
	After *they had struggled* for weeks in the wilderness, the town was a pleasing sight.

Dangling Modifiers and Grammar Checkers

Computer grammar checkers cannot distinguish a descriptive phrase that properly modifies the subject of the sentence from one that implies a different actor. As a result, they do not flag dangling modifiers, and writers must rely on their own judgment to identify and correct them.

IDENTIFY AND EDIT
Dangling Modifiers

dm

To avoid dangling modifiers, ask yourself these questions when you see a descriptive phrase at the beginning of a sentence:

? 1. What is the subject of the sentence?

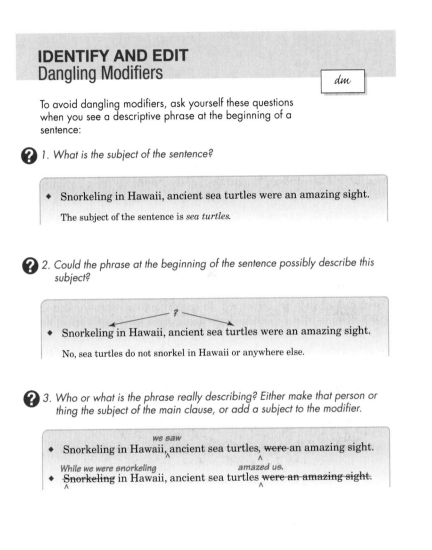

♦ Snorkeling in Hawaii, ancient sea turtles were an amazing sight.

The subject of the sentence is *sea turtles*.

? 2. Could the phrase at the beginning of the sentence possibly describe this subject?

♦ Snorkeling in Hawaii, ancient sea turtles were an amazing sight.

No, sea turtles do not snorkel in Hawaii or anywhere else.

? 3. Who or what is the phrase really describing? Either make that person or thing the subject of the main clause, or add a subject to the modifier.

♦ Snorkeling in Hawaii, we saw ancient sea turtles, were an amazing sight.

While we were snorkeling
♦ Snorkeling in Hawaii, ancient sea turtles amazed us. were an amazing sight.

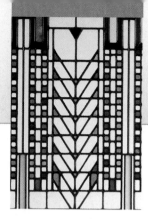

44 Coordination and Subordination

Coordination and subordination allow you to combine and develop ideas in ways that readers can follow and understand. Coordination should be used only when two or more ideas deserve equal emphasis. Subordination should be used to indicate that information is of secondary importance and to show its logical relation to the main idea.

www.mhhe.com/awr

For information and exercises on coordination and subordination, go to

Editing > Coordination and Subordination

44a Use coordination to express equal ideas.

Coordination gives two or more ideas equal weight. To coordinate parts within a sentence, join them with a coordinating conjunction (*and, but, or, for, nor, yet,* or *so*). To coordinate two or more sentences, use a comma plus a coordinating conjunction, or insert a semicolon. A semicolon is often followed by a conjunctive adverb such as *moreover, nevertheless, however, therefore,* or *subsequently.* (*For more on conjunctive adverbs, see Tab 12: Basic Grammar Review, pp. 621–22.*)

➤ **The auditorium was huge, *and* the acoustics were terrible.**

➤ **The tenor bellowed loudly, *but* no one in the back could hear him.**

➤ **Jones did not agree with her position on health care; *nevertheless,* he supported her campaign for office.**

44b Use subordination to express unequal ideas.

Subordination makes one idea depend on another and is therefore used to combine ideas that are not of equal importance. The main idea is expressed in an independent clause, and the secondary ideas are expressed in subordinate clauses or phrases. Subordinate clauses start with a relative pronoun (*who, whom, that, which, whoever, whomever, whose*) or a subordinating conjunction such as *after, although, because, if, since, when,* or *where.*

➤ **The blue liquid, *which will be added to the beaker later,* must be kept at room temperature.**

➤ **Christopher Columbus discovered the New World in 1492,** *although he never understood just what he had found.*

➤ *After writing the opening four sections,* **Wordsworth put the work aside for two years.**

Note: Commas often set off subordinate ideas, especially when the subordinate clause or phrase opens the sentence. (*For more on using commas, see Tab 11: Editing for Correctness, pp. 522–39.*)

44c Do not subordinate major ideas.

Major ideas belong in main clauses, not in subordinate clauses or phrases. The writer revised the following sentence because the subject of the paper was definitions of literacy, not people who value literacy.

INEFFECTIVE SUBORDINATION

Literacy, which has been defined as the ability to talk intelligently about many topics, is highly valued by businesspeople as well as academics.

REVISION

Highly valued by businesspeople as well as academics, literacy has been defined as the ability to talk intelligently about many topics.

44d Combine short, choppy sentences.

Short sentences are easy to read, but several of them in a row can become so monotonous that meaning gets lost.

CHOPPY

My cousin Jim is not an accountant. But he does my taxes every year. He suggests various deductions. These deductions reduce my tax bill considerably.

You can use subordination to combine a series of short, choppy sentences into a longer, more meaningful sentence. Put the idea you want to emphasize in the main clause, and use subordinate clauses and phrases for the other ideas. In the following revision, the main clause is italicized.

REVISED

Even though he is not an accountant, *my cousin Jim does my taxes every year,* suggesting various deductions that reduce my tax bill considerably.

If a series of short sentences includes two major ideas of equal importance, use coordination for the two major ideas and subordinate the secondary information.

CHOPPY

Bilingual education is designed for children. The native language of these children is not English. Smith supports expanding bilingual education. Johnson does not support expanding bilingual education.

REVISED

Smith supports bilingual education for children whose native language is not English; Johnson, however, does not support bilingual education.

44e Avoid overloading sentences with excessive subordination.

When a sentence seems overloaded, try separating it into two or more sentences.

OVERLOADED

Big-city mayors, who are supported by public funds, should be cautious about spending taxpayers' money for personal needs, such as home furnishings, especially when municipal budget shortfalls have caused extensive job layoffs, angering city workers and the general public.

REVISED

Big-city mayors should be cautious about spending taxpayers' money for personal needs, especially when municipal budget shortfalls have caused extensive job layoffs. They risk angering city workers and the general public by using public funds for home furnishings.

45 Sentence Variety

Enliven your prose by using a variety of sentence patterns. Varying your sentence structure helps you keep your readers interested.

Sentence Variety and Grammar Checkers

Monotony is not a grammatical error; sentence variety is an issue of style, not syntax. A computer grammar checker might flag a very long sentence, but it cannot decide whether the sentence is too long.

45a Vary your sentence openings.

www.mhhe.com/awr
For information and exercises on sentence variety, go to
Editing > Sentence Variety

When all the sentences in a passage begin with the subject, you risk losing your readers' attention. Vary your sentences by moving a modifier to the beginning. The modifier may be a single word, a phrase, or a clause.

➤ *Eventually,* Armstrong's innovations ~~eventually~~ became the standard.

➤ *In at least two instances, this* ~~This~~ money-making strategy backfired. ~~in at least two instances.~~

➤ *After Glaser became his manager,* Armstrong no longer had to worry about business. ~~after Glaser became his manager.~~

A **participial phrase** begins with an *-ing* verb (*driving*) or a past participle (*moved, driven*) and is used as a modifier. You can often move it to the beginning of a sentence for variety, but if you move it, make sure that the phrase describes the explicit subject of the sentence or you will end up with a dangling modifier (*see pp. 423–25*).

➤ *Pushing the other children aside,* Joseph, ~~pushing the other children aside,~~ demanded that the teacher give him a cookie first.

429

For MULTILINGUAL STUDENTS

Adverbial Modifiers and Subject-Verb Order

In standard English word order, the subject of a sentence precedes the verb. When certain adverbs come at the beginning of a sentence, however, they force changes in this order, usually requiring the subject to fall between a helping verb and the main verb. Adverbs that have this effect include *never, not since, seldom, rarely, in no case,* and *not until.*

helping main
subject verb verb

FAULTY Rarely Simon has tried harder at work than he did today.

helping main
verb subject verb

REVISED Rarely has Simon tried harder at work than he did today.

➤ *Stunned by the stock market crash, many*
~~Many~~ brokers, ~~stunned by the stock market crash,~~

committed suicide.

45b Vary the length and structure of your sentences.

Short, simple sentences will keep your readers alert, but only if these sentences occur in a context that also includes longer, complex sentences.

As you edit your work, check to see if you have overused one kind of sentence structure. Are most of your sentences short and simple? If so, use subordination to combine some of them (*see p. 427*). But if most of your sentences are long and complex, put at least one of your ideas into a short, simple sentence. Your goal is to achieve a good mix.

DRAFT

I dived quickly into the sea. I peered through my mask at the watery world. It turned darker. A school of fish went by. The distant light glittered on their bodies, and I stopped swimming. I waited to see if the fish might be chased by a shark. I was satisfied that there was no shark and continued down.

REVISED

I dived quickly into the sea, peering through my mask at a watery world that turned darker as I descended. A school of fish went by, the distant light glittering on their bodies. I stopped swimming and waited. Perhaps the fish were being chased by a shark? Satisfied that there was no shark, I continued down.

(*For more information on sentence types, see Tab 12: Basic Grammar Review, pp. 633–35. For more on sentence variety, see Tab 2: Writing and Designing Papers, p. 91.*)

45c Include a few cumulative and periodic sentences and rhetorical questions.

Cumulative sentences add a series of descriptive participial or absolute phrases to the basic subject-plus-verb pattern, making your writing more forceful and detailed. (*See Tab 12: Basic Grammar Review, pp. 630–31 for more on these phrases.*) They can also be used to add details, as the following example shows.

➤ **The motorcycle spun out of control,** *plunging down the ravine, crashing through the fence,* **and** *coming to rest on its side.*

Another way to increase the force of your writing is to use a few **periodic sentences,** in which the key word, phrase, or idea appears at the end, where readers are most likely to remember it.

    In 1946 and 1947, young people
➤ ~~Young people fell in love with the jukebox in 1946 and 1947~~
                                   and fell in love—with the jukebox.
~~and~~ **turned away from the horrors of World War II.**

To get your readers to participate more actively in your work, you can ask a question. Because you do not expect an answer, this kind of question is called a **rhetorical question.**

➤ **Players injured at an early age too often find themselves without a job, a college degree, and their health. Is it any wonder that a few turn to drugs and alcohol?**

Rhetorical questions work best in the middle or at the end of a long, complicated passage. They can also help you make a transition from one topic to another. Avoid using them more than a few times in a paper, however, and never begin an essay with a broad rhetorical question such as "How did the Peace Corps begin?"

45d Try an occasional inversion.

You might occasionally try using an inverted sentence pattern or another sentence type, such as a rhetorical question or an exclamation, to vary the normal sentence pattern of subject plus verb plus object. (*For more on sentence types, see Tab 12: Basic Grammar Review, pp. 633–35.*)

You can create an **inversion** by putting the verb before the subject. Because many inversions sound odd, they should be used infrequently and carefully. In a passage on the qualities of various contemporary artists, the following inversion makes sense and adds interest.

➤ **Characteristic of Smith's work are bold design and original thinking.**

CHARTING the TERRITORY

Exclamation Points in Academic Writing

In academic writing, exclamations are rare, perhaps because they seem adolescent. If you decide to use one for special effect, be sure that you want to express strong emotion about the idea and can do so without losing credibility.

➤ **Wordsworth completed the thirteen-book *Prelude* in 1805, after seven years of hard work. Instead of publishing his masterpiece, however, he devoted himself to revising it—for thirty-five years! The poem, in a fourteen-book version, was finally published in 1850, after he had died.**

46 Active Verbs

Active verbs such as *run, shout, write,* and *think* are more direct and forceful than forms of the *be* verb (*am, are, is, was, were, been, being*) or passive-voice constructions. The more active verbs you use, the stronger and clearer your writing will be.

www.mhhe.com/awr

For information and exercises on active verbs, go to

Editing > Verbs and Verbals

Active Verbs and Grammar Checkers

Computer grammar checkers generally do not flag weak uses of the *be* verb because they cannot tell when a usage is appropriate and when it clutters a sentence. A grammar checker did not flag the sentence *The paper was an argument for a stronger police presence* because it is grammatically correct. The writer would need to notice the weak *be* verb and change the sentence to *The paper argued . . . .*

Some grammar checkers do flag most passive-voice sentences (*see 46b*), but their suggestions for revising them can sometimes make the sentence worse. Again, it requires a writer's judgment to determine how best—if at all—to revise a passive-voice sentence.

46a Consider alternatives to some *be* verbs.

Although it is not a strong verb, *be* does a lot of work in English.

As a linking verb:

➤ Germany *is* relatively poor in natural resources.

➤ Decent health care *is* a necessity, not a luxury.

As a helping verb:

➤ Macbeth *was* returning from battle when he met the three witches.

Be verbs are so useful that they can easily get overworked. Watch for weak, roundabout sentences with *be* verbs, and consider replacing those verbs with active verbs. (*See also Chapter 38: Wordy Sentences, p. 407.*)

➤ **The mayor's refusal to meet with our group ~~is a~~**
    demonstrates
   ~~demonstration of~~ his lack of respect for us, as well
          ^

as for the environment.

46b   Prefer the active voice.

Verbs can be in the active or passive voice. In the **active voice,** the subject of the sentence acts; in the **passive voice,** the subject is acted upon.

    ACTIVE   The Senate finally passed the bill.

    PASSIVE   The bill was finally passed by the Senate.

The passive voice downplays the actors as well as the action, so much so that the actors are often left out of the sentence.

    PASSIVE   The bill was finally passed.

CHARTING the TERRITORY

Passive Voice in Scientific Writing

The passive voice is often used in scientific reports to keep the focus on the experiment and its results rather than on the experimenters.

➤ **The bacteria were treated carefully with nicotine and were observed to stop reproducing.**

Unless you have a good reason to use the passive voice, prefer the active voice. It is more forceful, and readers usually want to know who or what does the acting.

    PASSIVE   Polluting chemicals were dumped into the river.

    ACTIVE   Industrial Products Corporation dumped polluting chemicals into the river.

When the recipient of the action is more important than the doer of the action, however, the passive voice is the more appropriate choice.

➤ **After her heart attack, my mother was taken to the hospital.**

Mother and the fact that she was taken to the hospital are more important than who took her to the hospital.

47 Appropriate Language

Language is appropriate when it fits your topic, purpose, and audience. Whether you are preparing to write about literature or natural science or history, take some time to read how writers in the field have handled your topic.

www.mhhe.com/
awr
For information
and exercises on
appropriate language,
go to

Editing >
Word Choice

47a In college writing, avoid slang, regional expressions, and nonstandard English.

Slang, regional sayings, and nonstandard English appear often in conversation but are too informal for college writing—unless that writing is reporting conversation.

Slang words change frequently. (Remember *phat?*). In college writing, slang terms and the hip tone that goes with them should be avoided.

SLANG   In *Heart of Darkness,* we hear a lot about a *dude* named Kurtz, but we don't see the *guy* much.

REVISED   In *Heart of Darkness,* Marlow, the narrator, talks almost continually about Kurtz, but we meet Kurtz himself only at the end.

Like slang, regional and nonstandard expressions such as *y'all,* *hisself,* and *don't be doing that* work fine in conversation but not in formal college writing. In American colleges, professions, and businesses, the dominant dialect is standard written English. Most of your instructors will expect you to write in this dialect, unless you have a good reason not to.

47b Use an appropriate level of formality.

College writing assignments usually call for a style that avoids the extremes of the stuffy and the casual, the pretentious and the chatty. Revise passages that veer toward one extreme or the other.

> **PRETENTIOUS** Romantic lovers are characterized by a preoccupation with a deliberately restricted set of qualities in the love object that are viewed as means to some ideal end.

> **REVISED** People in love see what they want to see, usually by idealizing the beloved.

47c Avoid jargon.

When specialists communicate with each other, they often use technical language that can sound incomprehensible to nonspecialists. Such language is appropriate in many contexts and has a place in college writing. **Jargon** is the inappropriate use of specialized or technical language. If you want to be understood, you should not use discourse that is appropriate for specialists when you are writing for a general audience.

As you edit, look for jargon and revise any you find.

> **JARGON** An *opposition education theory* holds that children learn Spanish best *under strict discipline conditions.*

> **REVISED** An *alternative theory of education* holds that children learn Spanish best *when strict discipline is enforced.*

If you need to use technical terms when writing for nonspecialists, be sure to define them.

Discourse Communities

People who share certain interests and knowledge and customary ways of communicating constitute a **discourse community.** Members of the discourse community of baseball fans, for example, talk and write about *switch-hitters, batting averages, and earned run averages*—terms that are probably unfamiliar to people outside the community. Each of us belongs to several discourse communities. The more familiar you are with a discourse community, the more you will know about the language that is appropriate in that community.

➤ **Armstrong's innovative singing style featured "scat," a technique that combines "nonsense syllables [with] improvised melodies" (Robinson 515).**

47d Avoid most euphemisms and all doublespeak.

Euphemisms and doublespeak have one goal: to cover up the truth. **Euphemisms** substitute words like *correctional facility* and *passing away* for such harsh realities as *prison* and *death*. On some occasions, a euphemism like *passing away* may serve a useful purpose; for example, you may wish to avoid upsetting a grieving person. Usually, however, words should not be used to evade or deceive.

Doublespeak is another word for deceit. Its purpose is to confuse or mislead readers. As the following example shows, bureaucrats sometimes use doublespeak to obscure facts and evade responsibility.

➤ **Pursuant to the environmental protection regulations enforcement policy of the Bureau of Natural Resources, special management area land use permit issuance procedures have been instituted.**

47e Do not use biased or sexist language.

1. Recognizing biased language

Words can wound. Be on the lookout for stereotypes that demean, ignore, or patronize people on the basis of gender, race, religion, national origin, ethnicity, physical ability, sexual orientation, occupation, or any other human condition. Revise for inclusiveness.

For example, do not assume that Irish Catholics have large families.

> ~~Although the~~ *The* Browns are ~~Irish~~ *an* Irish ~~Catholics, there are only~~ *Catholic family with*

> two children. ~~in the family.~~

In addition, remember that a positive stereotype is still a stereotype.

> ~~Because Asian students are whizzes at math, we~~ *We* all wanted

> ~~them~~ *math whizzes* in our study group.

CHARTING the TERRITORY

Biased Language

When writing on topics in history and the social sciences, take special care not to use terms like *underprivileged* or *culturally deprived.* The American Psychological Association recommends this test: Substitute your own group for the group you are discussing. If you are offended by the resulting statement, revise your phrasing to eliminate bias.

---

2. Recognizing sexist language

Sexist language demeans or stereotypes women and men, but women are usually the explicit targets. Many labels and clichés imply that women are not as able or as mature as men. Consider the meaning of words and phrases like *the weaker sex, [acting like a] girl, poetess,* and *coed.*

3. Avoiding stereotypes

Avoiding bias means avoiding subtle stereotypes. For example, not all heads of state are or have to be men.

BIASED	Wives of heads of state typically choose to promote a charity that benefits a cause they care about.
REVISED	Spouses of heads of state typically choose to promote a charity that benefits a cause they care about.

4. Avoiding the generic *he*

Traditionally, the pronoun *he* has been used to represent either gender. Today, however, the use of *he* to represent everyone in a group is considered offensive.

BIASED   Everybody had his way.

REVISED   We all had our way.

5. Revising sexist language

Review your writing to see if it is unintentionally biased. As you revise, follow these simple principles.

■ Replace terms that indicate gender with their genderless equivalents:

No	Yes
chairman	chair, chairperson
congressman	representative, member of Congress
forefathers	ancestors
man, mankind	people, humans
man-made	artificial
policeman	police officer
spokesman	spokesperson

■ Do not make unnecessary references to or overemphasize a woman's marital status, relationship to children, or appearance. Refer to men and women in parallel ways: *ladies and gentlemen* [not *ladies and men*], *men and women, husband and wife.*

BIASED   D. H. Lawrence and Mrs. Woolf met each other, but Lawrence did not like the Bloomsbury circle that revolved around Virginia.

REVISED   D. H. Lawrence and Virginia Woolf met each other, but Lawrence did not like the Bloomsbury circle that revolved around Woolf.

■ Replace the masculine pronouns *he, him, his,* and *himself* when they are being used generically to refer to both women and men. One satisfactory way to replace masculine pronouns is to use the plural.

BIASED   It's every man for himself.

REVISED   All of us have to save ourselves.

Some writers alternate *he* and *she,* and *him* and *her.* This strategy may be effective in some writing situations, but switching back and forth can also be distracting. The constructions *his or her* and *he or she* are acceptable as long as they are not used excessively or more than once in a sentence.

AWKWARD   Each student in the psychology class was to choose a different book according to *his or her* interests, to read the book overnight, to do without *his or her* normal sleep, to write a short summary of what *he or she* had read, and then to see if *he or she* dreamed about the book the following night.

REVISED   Every student was to choose a book, read it overnight, do without sleep, write a short summary of the book the next morning, and then see if *he or she* dreamed about the book the following night.

The constructions *his/her* and *s/he* are not acceptable in academic writing.

Note: Using the neuter impersonal pronoun *one* can sometimes help you avoid masculine pronouns, but *one* can make your writing sound stuffy.

STUFFY   The American creed holds that if *one* works hard, *one* will succeed in life.

REVISED   The American creed holds that those who work hard will succeed in life.

(*For more on editing to avoid the generic use of* he, him, his, *or* himself, *see Tab 10: Editing for Grammar Conventions, pp. 501–2.*)

48 Exact Language

To convey your meaning clearly, you need to choose the right words. As you revise, be on the lookout for problems with diction: Is your choice of words as precise as it should be?

48a Choose words with suitable connotations.

www.mhhe.com/awr
For information and exercises on exact language, go to
Editing >
Word Choice

Words have denotations and connotations. **Denotations** are the primary meanings of the word. **Connotations** are the feelings and images associated with a word.

Consider, for example, the following three statements:

Murdock *ignored* the no-smoking rule.
Murdock *disobeyed* the no-smoking rule.
Murdock *flouted* the no-smoking rule.

Even though the three sentences depict the same event, each sentence describes Murdock's action somewhat differently. If Murdock *ignored* the rule, it may simply have been because he did not know or care about it. If he *disobeyed* the rule, he must have known about it and consciously decided not to follow it, but what if he *flouted* the rule? Well, there was probably a look of disdain on his face as he made sure that others would see him puffing away at a cigarette.

As you revise, consider replacing any word whose connotations do not exactly fit what you want to say.

> The players' union should ~~request~~ *demand* that the NFL amend its

   pension plan.

If you cannot think of a more suitable word, consult a thesaurus (*see p. 448*) for **synonyms**—words with similar meanings. Keep in mind, however, that most words have connotations that allow them to work in some contexts but not in others. To find out more about a synonym's connotations, look the word up in a dictionary.

48b Include specific and concrete words.

In addition to general and abstract terms, clear writers use specific and concrete words.

441

For MULTILINGUAL STUDENTS

Usage Problems

Most students whose first language is not English consider vocabulary use a major challenge in analyzing and responding to academic texts. Even though you learn the meaning of a word, you may have trouble using it correctly in your speaking and writing. Certain types of word combinations are determined by conventional use rather than by their literal meaning (for example, *you do homework* but *you make a plan*).

Conscious or unconscious translation from your native language will always be part of your learning, but you should try to study English words and phrases in context, with sensitivity to their connotations. It helps to keep a dictionary close by (*see Chapter 49, pp. 445–48*).

General words name broad categories of things, such as *trees, books, politicians,* and *students.* **Specific words** name particular kinds of things or items, such as *pines* and *college sophomores.*

Abstract words name qualities and ideas that do not have physical properties, such as *charity, beauty, hope,* and *radical.* **Concrete words** name things we can sense by touch, taste, smell, hearing, and sight, such as *velvet, vinegar, smoke, screech,* and *sweater.*

By creating images that appeal to the senses, specific and concrete words make writing more precise.

VAGUE	The trees were affected by the bad weather.
PRECISE	The tall pines shook in the gale.

As you edit, make sure that you have developed your ideas with specific and concrete details. Also check for overused, vague terms—such as *factor, thing, good, nice,* and *interesting*—and replace them with more specific and concrete alternatives.

➤ The protesters were charged with ~~things~~ they never ~~did.~~
 crimes   *committed.*

48c Use standard idioms.

Idioms are habitual ways of expressing ideas. They are not always logical and can be hard to translate. Often they involve selecting the right preposition: We do not go *with* the car but *in* the car or simply *by* car; we do not abide *with* a rule but *by* a rule. If you are not sure which preposition to use, look up the main word in a dictionary. (*For more on idioms and multilingual writers, see Tab 12: Basic Grammar Review, pp. 616–17, 618–19.*)

Some verbs, called **phrasal verbs,** include a preposition to make their idiomatic meaning complete:

Henry *made up* with Gloria.
Henry *made off* with Gloria.
Henry *made out* with Gloria.

(*For more on phrasal verbs, see p. 619.*)

48d Avoid clichés.

A **cliché** is an overworked expression. If someone says, "She was as mad as a ———," we expect the next word to be *hornet*. We have heard this expression so often that it no longer creates a vivid picture in our imagination. It is usually best to rephrase clichés in plain language.

CLICHÉ   When John turned his papers in three weeks late, he had to *face the music.*

BETTER   When John turned his papers in three weeks late, he had to *accept the consequences.*

The list that follows gives some common clichés to avoid.

COMMON CLICHÉS

acid test
agony of suspense
beat a hasty retreat
beyond a shadow
  of a doubt
blind as a bat
brave as a lion
brutal murder
calm, cool, and
  collected
cold, hard facts
cool as a cucumber
crazy as a loon
dead as a doornail
deep, dark secret
depths of despair
face the music

few and far between
flat as a pancake
gild the lily
give 110 percent
green with envy
heave a sigh of
  relief
hit the nail on the
  head
last but not least
the other side of
  the coin
pale as a ghost
pass the buck
pretty as a picture
quick as a flash
rise to the occasion

sadder but wiser
shoulder to the
  wheel
sink or swim
smart as a whip
sneaking suspicion
straight and narrow
tempest in a teapot
tired but happy
tried and true
ugly as sin
untimely death
wax eloquent
white as a sheet
worth its weight in
  gold

48e Create suitable figures of speech.

Figures of speech make writing vivid, most often by using a comparison to supplement the literal meaning of words. A **simile** is a comparison that contains the word *like* or *as*.

➤ **His smile was like sunshine after a rainstorm.**

A **metaphor** is an implied comparison. It treats one thing or action, such as a critic's review, as if it were something else.

➤ **The critic's slash-and-burn review devastated the cast.**

Because it is compressed, a metaphor is often more forceful than a simile.

Comparisons can make your prose more vivid, but only if they suit your subject and purpose. Be careful not to mix metaphors; if you use two or more comparisons together, make sure they are compatible.

MIXED His presentation of the plan was so *crystal clear* that in a *burst of speed* we decided *to come aboard.*

REVISED His clear presentation immediately convinced us to support the plan.

48f Avoid misusing words.

Avoid mistakes in your use of new terms and unfamiliar words by consulting a dictionary whenever you include an unfamiliar word in your writing.

➤ **The aristocracy** ~~exuded~~ *exhibited* **numerous vices, including greed**

and ~~license.~~ *licentiousness.*

49 The Dictionary and the Thesaurus

A dictionary and a thesaurus are essential tools for all writers. You should also find out about specialized dictionaries for the subject area of your major.

49a Make using the dictionary a habit.

A standard desk dictionary—such as the *Random House Webster's College Dictionary,* the *Webster's New World Dictionary,* or the *American Heritage College Dictionary*—contains 140,000 to 180,000 entries. These dictionaries also provide information such as the correct spellings of important place names, the official names of countries with their areas and populations, the names of capital cities, biographical entries, lists of abbreviations and symbols, names and locations of colleges and universities, titles and correct forms of address, and conversion tables for weights and measures.

CHARTING the TERRITORY

Dictionaries

In the library's reference section, you can find specialized dictionaries such as biographical and geographical dictionaries; foreign language dictionaries; dictionaries of first lines of poems and of famous quotations; dictionaries of legal and medical terms; and dictionaries of philosophy, sociology, engineering, and other disciplines. Ask the reference librarian to help you locate a useful specialized dictionary for your topic or field.

All dictionaries include guides to their use. The guides explain the terms and abbreviations that appear in the entries as well as special notations such as *slang, nonstandard,* and *vulgar.*

An entry from the *Random House Webster's College Dictionary* follows. The labels point to the kinds of information discussed in the following sections.

Phonetic symbols showing pronunciation.

Word endings and grammatical abbreviations.

Dictionary entry.

com•pare (kəmpâr´), *v.*, **-pared, -par • ing,** *n.* —*v.t.* **1.** to examine (two or more objects, ideas, people, etc.) in order to note similarities and differences. **2.** to consider or describe as similar; liken: *"Shall I compare thee to a summer's day?"* **3.** to form or display the degrees of comparison of (an adjective or adverb). —*v.i.* **4.** to be worthy of comparison: *Whose plays can compare with Shakespeare's?* **5.** to be in similar standing; be alike: *This recital compares with the one he gave last year.* **6.** to appear in quality, progress, etc., as specified: *Their development compares poorly with that of neighbor nations.* **7.** to make comparisons. —*n.* **8.** comparison: *a beauty beyond compare.* —*Idiom.* **9. compare notes,** to exchange views, ideas, or impressions. [1375–1425; late ME < OF *comperer* < L *comparāre* to place together, match, v. der. of *compar* alike, matching (see COM-, PAR)] —**com•par´er,** *n.* —**Usage.** A traditional rule states that COMPARE should be followed by *to* when it points out likenesses between unlike persons or things: *she compared his handwriting to knotted string.* It should be followed by *with,* the rule says, when it examines two entities of the same general class for similarities or differences: *She compared his handwriting with mine.* This rule, though sensible, is not always followed, even in formal speech and writing. Common practice is to use *to* for likeness between members of different classes: *to compare a language to a living organism.* Between members of the same category, both *to* and *with* are used: *Compare the Chicago of today with* (or *to*) *the Chicago of the 1890s.* After the past participle COMPARED, either *to* or *with* is used regardless of the type of comparison.

Definitions as transitive verb (v.t.).

Definitions as intransitive verb (v.i.).

Definition as noun (n.).

Etymology.

Special meaning

Usage note.

1. Spelling, word division, and pronunciation

Entries in a dictionary are listed in alphabetical order according to their standard spelling. In the *Random House Webster's College Dictionary,* the verb *compare* is entered as **com•pare.** The dot separates the word into its two syllables. If you had to divide the word *compare* at the end of a line, you would place a hyphen where the dot appears.

Phonetic symbols in parentheses following the entry show its correct pronunciation. The second syllable of *compare* receives the greater stress when you pronounce the word correctly: you say "com-PARE." In this dictionary, an accent mark (´) appears after the syllable that receives the primary stress.

Plurals of nouns are usually not given if they are formed by adding an *s,* unless the word is foreign (*gondolas, dashikis*). Irregular plurals—such as *children* for *child*—are noted.

Note: Some dictionaries list alternate spellings, always giving the preferred spelling first or placing the full entry under the preferred spelling only.

Tips LEARNING in COLLEGE

Using a Dictionary

- **Use the guide words.** At the top of each dictionary page are guide words (usually in bold type) that tell you the first and last words on the page. Because all the entries are in alphabetical order, you can locate the word you are seeking by looking for guide words that would appear before and after your word.
- **Try alternate spellings.** If you cannot find a word on the first try, think of another way to spell it.
- **Use the pronunciation key.** The letters and symbols that indicate each word's pronunciation are explained in a separate section at the front or back of a dictionary. In some dictionaries, they are also summarized at the bottom of each right-hand page of entries. Pronouncing new words aloud will help you learn them.
- **Pay attention to the parts of speech in a definition.** The same word can have different meanings depending on how it is used in a sentence—that is, its part of speech.
- **Always test the meaning you find.** To check whether you have selected the correct word, substitute the meaning for the word in your sentence and see if the sentence makes sense.

2. Word endings and grammatical labels

The abbreviation *v.* immediately after the pronunciation tells you that *compare* is most frequently used as a verb. The next abbreviation, *n.,* indicates that *compare* can sometimes function as a noun, as in the phrase *beyond compare.*

Here is a list of common abbreviations for grammatical terms:

adj.	adjective	*prep.*	preposition
adv.	adverb	*pron.*	pronoun
conj.	conjunction	*sing.*	singular
interj.	interjection	*v.*	verb
n.	noun	*v.i.*	intransitive verb
pl.	plural	*v.t.*	transitive verb
poss.	possessive		

The *-pared* shows the simple past and past participle form of the verb; the present participle form, *-paring,* follows, indicating that *compare* drops the final *e* when *-ing* is added.

3. Definitions and word origins

In the sample entry, the definitions begin after the abbreviation *v.t.,* which indicates that the first three meanings relate to *compare* as a transitive verb. A little further down in the entry, *v.i.* introduces definitions of *compare* as an intransitive verb. Next, after *n.,* comes the definition of *compare* as a noun. Finally, the word *Idiom* signals a special meaning not included in the previous definitions.

Included in most dictionary entries is an **etymology**—a brief history of the word's origins—set off in brackets. There we see the date of the first known use of the word in English together with the earlier words from which it is derived. *Compare* came into English between 1375 and 1425 and was derived from the Old French word *comperer,* which came from Latin.

4. Usage

Some main entries in the dictionary conclude with examples of and comments about the common usage of the word.

49b　Consult a thesaurus for words that have similar meanings.

A **thesaurus** is a dictionary of synonyms. Several kinds of thesauruses are available, many called *Roget's* after Peter Mark Roget (pronounced ro-ZHAY), who published the first one in 1852. Today, thesauruses are included in most word-processing software packages.

Most writers find a thesaurus a pleasure to use, but you need to be cautious when using one. Consider the connotations as well as the denotations of the words you find in the thesaurus. Do not choose a word just because it sounds smart or fancy.

Tips　LEARNING in COLLEGE

Using a Thesaurus

- Use a thesaurus to find a more precise word, not a fancier one.
- Become familiar with how the words in your thesaurus are arranged. In *Roget's International Thesaurus,* the words are listed in numbered categories. In other thesauruses, the words are arranged in alphabetical order. Usually, an online thesaurus will provide synonyms for words that you highlight in your text.
- Never use an unfamiliar word from a thesaurus without first looking it up in the dictionary.
- Make sure that your replacement word has appropriate connotations as well as the correct denotation.

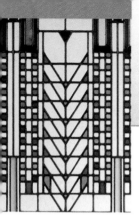

50 Glossary of Usage

The following words and expressions are often confused (such as *advice* and *advise*), misused (such as *etc.*), or considered nonstandard (such as *could of*). Consulting this list will help you use these words precisely.

www.mhhe.com/
awr
For an online glossary of usage and exercises, go to

Editing >
Word Choice

a, an   Use *a* with a word that begins with a consonant sound: *a cat, a dog, a one-sided argument, a house.* Use *an* with a word that begins with a vowel sound: *an apple, an X ray, an honor.*

accept, except   *Accept* is a verb meaning "to receive willingly": *Please accept my apologies. Except* is a preposition meaning "but": *Everyone except Julie saw the film.*

adapt, adopt   *Adapt* means "to adjust or become accustomed to": *They adapted to the customs of their new country. Adopt* means "to take as one's own": *We adopted a puppy.*

advice, advise   *Advice* is a noun; *advise* is a verb: *I took his advice and deeply regretted it. I advise you to disregard it, too.*

affect, effect   As a verb, *affect* means "to influence": *Inflation affects our sense of security.* As a noun, *affect* means "a feeling or an emotion": *To study affect, psychologists probe the unconscious.* As a noun, *effect* means "result": *Inflation is one of the many effects of war.* As a verb, *effect* means "to make or accomplish": *Inflation has effected many changes in the way we spend money.*

agree to, agree with   *Agree to* means "consent to"; *agree with* means "be in accord with": *They will agree to a peace treaty, even though they do not agree with each other on all points.*

ain't   A slang contraction for *is not, am not,* or *are not, ain't* should not be used in formal writing or speech.

all/all of, more/more of, some/some of   Except before some pronouns, the "of" in these constructions can usually be eliminated: *All France rejoiced. Some students cut class.* But: *All of us wish you well.*

all ready, already   *All ready* means "fully prepared." *Already* means "previously." *We were all ready to go out when we discovered that Jack had already ordered a pizza.*

all right, alright   The spelling *alright* is an alternate, but many educated readers still think it is incorrect in standard written English. *He told me it was all right to miss class tomorrow.*

all together, altogether   *All together* expresses unity or common location; *altogether* means "completely," often in a tone of ironic understatement. *At the casino, it was altogether startling to see so many kinds of gambling all together in one place.*

allude, elude, refer to   *Allude* means "to refer indirectly": *He alluded to his miserable adolescence. Elude means "to avoid" or "to escape from": She eluded the police for nearly two days.* Do not use *allude* to mean "to refer directly": *The teacher referred* [not *alluded*] *to page 468 in the text.*

almost, most   *Almost* means "nearly." *Most* means "the greater part of." Do not use *most* when you mean *almost. He wrote to me about almost* [not *most*] *everything he did. He told his mother about most things he did.*

a lot   *A lot* is always two words. Do not use *alot.*

A.M., AM, a.m.   These abbreviations mean "before noon" when used with numbers: 6 A.M., 6 a.m. Be consistent, and do not use the abbreviations as a synonym for *morning: In the morning* [not *a.m.*]*, the train is full.*

among, between   Generally, use *among* with three or more nouns, and *between* with two: *The distance between Boston and Knoxville is a thousand miles. The desire to quit smoking is common among those who have smoked for a long time.*

amoral, immoral   *Amoral* means "neither moral nor immoral" and "not caring about moral judgments." *Immoral* means "morally wrong." *Unlike such amoral natural disasters as earthquakes and hurricanes, war is intentionally violent and therefore immoral.*

amount, number   Use *amount* for quantities you cannot count; use *number* for quantities you can count. *The amount of oil left underground in the United States is a matter of dispute, but the number of oil companies losing money is tiny.*

an   *See* a, an.

anxious, eager   *Anxious* means "fearful": *I am anxious before a test. Eager* signals strong interest or desire: *I am eager to be done with that exam.*

anymore, any more   *Anymore* means "no longer." *Any more* means "no more." Both are used in negative contexts: *I do not enjoy dancing anymore. I do not want any more peanut butter.*

anyone/any one, anybody/any body, everyone/every one, everybody/every body   *Anyone, anybody, everyone,* and *everybody* are indefinite pronouns: *Anybody can make a mistake.* When the pronoun *one* or the noun *body* is modified by the adjective *any* or *every,* the words should be separated by a space: *A good mystery writer accounts for every body that turns up in the story.*

as   Do not use *as* as a synonym for *since, when,* or *because: I told him he should visit Alcatraz since* [not *as*] *he was going to San Francisco. When* [not *as*] *I complained about the meal, the cook said he did not like to eat there himself. Because* [not *as*] *we asked her nicely, our teacher decided to cancel the exam.*

as, like   In formal writing, avoid the use of *like* as a conjunction: *He sneezed as if* [not *like*] *he had a cold. Like* is perfectly acceptable as a preposition that introduces a comparison: *She handled the reins like an expert.*

at   Avoid the use of *at* to complete the notion of *where:* not *Where is Michael at?* but *Where is Michael?*

awful, awfully   Use *awful* and *awfully* to convey the emotion of terror or wonder (awe-full): *The vampire flew out the window with an awful shriek.* In writing, do not use *awful* to mean "bad" or *awfully* to mean "very" or "extremely."

awhile, a while   *Awhile* is an adverb: *Stay awhile with me. A while* is an article and a noun. Always use *a while* after a preposition: *Many authors are unable to write anything else for a while after they publish their first novel.*

being as, being that   Do not use *being as* or *being that* as synonyms for *since* or *because: Because* [not *being as*] *the mountain was there, we had to climb it.*

belief, believe   *Belief* is a noun meaning "conviction"; *believe* is a verb meaning "to have confidence in the truth of": *Her belief that lying was often justified made it hard for us to believe her story.*

beside, besides   *Beside* is a preposition meaning "next to" or "apart from": *The ski slope was beside the lodge. She was beside herself with joy. Besides* is both a preposition and an adverb meaning "in addition to" or "except for": *Besides a bicycle, he will need a tent and a pack.*

between   *See* among, between.

better   Avoid using *better* in expressions of quantity: *Crossing the continent by train took more than* [not *better than*] *four days.*

bring, take   Use *bring* when an object is being moved toward you, and *take* when it is being moved away: *Please bring me a new disk and take the old one home with you.*

but that, but what   In expressions of doubt, avoid writing *but that* or *but what* when you mean *that: I have no doubt that* [not *but that*] *you can learn to write well.*

can, may   *Can* refers to ability; *may* refers to possibility or permission: *I see that you can rollerblade without crashing into people, but nevertheless you may not rollerblade on the promenade.*

can't hardly   This double negative is ungrammatical and self-contradictory: *I can* [not *can't*] *hardly understand algebra. I can't understand algebra.*

capital, capitol   *Capital* refers to a city; *capitol* refers to a building where lawmakers meet: *Protesters traveled to the state capital to converge on the capitol steps. Capital* also refers to wealth or resources.

censor, censure   *Censor* means "to remove or suppress material." *Censure* means "to reprimand formally." *The Chinese government has been censured by the U.S. Congress for censoring newspapers.*

cite, sight, site   The verb *cite* means "to quote or mention": *Be sure to cite all your sources in your bibliography.* As a noun, the word *sight* means "view": *It was love at first sight. Site* is a noun meaning "a particular place": locations on the Internet are referred to as *sites.*

compare to, compare with   Use *compare to* to point out similarities between two unlike things: *She compared his singing to the croaking of a wounded frog.* Use *compare with* for differences or likenesses between two similar things: *Compare Shakespeare's* Antony and Cleopatra *with Dryden's* All for Love.

complement, compliment   *Complement* means "to go well with": *I consider sauerkraut the perfect complement to sausages. Compliment* means "praise": *She received many compliments on her thesis.*

conscience, conscious   The noun *conscience* means "a sense of right and wrong": *His conscience bothered him.* The adjective *conscious* means "awake" or "aware": *I was conscious of a presence in the room.*

continual, continuous   *Continual* means "repeated regularly and frequently": *She continually checked her computer for new e-mail. Continuous* means "extended or prolonged without interruption": *The car alarm made a continuous wail in the night.*

could of, should of, would of   Avoid these ungrammatical forms of *could have, should have,* and *would have.*

criteria, criterion   *Criteria* is the plural form of the Latin word *criterion,* meaning "standard of judgment": *The criteria are not very strict. The most important criterion is whether you can do the work.*

data   *Data* is the plural form of the Latin word *datum,* meaning "fact." Although *data* is often used informally as a singular noun, in writing, treat *data* as a plural noun: *The data indicate that recycling has gained popularity.*

differ from, differ with   *Differ from* expresses a lack of similarity; *differ with* expresses disagreement: *The ancient Greeks differed less from the Persians than we often think. Aristotle differed with Plato on some important issues.*

different from, different than   The correct idiom is *different from.* Avoid *different than: The east coast of Florida is very different from the west coast.*

discreet, discrete   *Discreet* means "tactful" or "prudent." *Discrete* means "separate" or "distinct." *What's a discreet way of telling them that these are two discrete issues?*

disinterested, uninterested   *Disinterested* means "impartial": *We expect members of a jury to be disinterested. Uninterested* means "indifferent" or "unconcerned": *Most people today are uninterested in alchemy.*

don't, doesn't   *Don't* is the contraction for *do not* and is used with *I, you, we, they,* and plural nouns; *doesn't* is the contraction for *does not* and is used with *he, she, it,* and singular nouns: *You don't know what you're talking about. He doesn't know what you're talking about either.*

due to   *Due to* is an overworked and often confusing expression when it is used for *because of.* Use *due to* only in expressions of time in infinitive constructions or in other contexts where the meaning is "scheduled": *The plane is due to arrive in one hour. He is due to receive a promotion this year.*

each and every   Use one of these words or the other but not both: *Every cow came in at feeding time. Each one had to be watered.*

each other, one another   Use *each other* in sentences involving two subjects and *one another* in sentences involving more than two: *Husbands and wives should help each other. Classmates should share ideas with one another.*

eager   See anxious, eager.

effect   See affect, effect.

e.g., i.e.   The abbreviation *e.g.* stands for the Latin words meaning "for example." The abbreviation *i.e.* stands for the Latin for "that is." *Come as soon as you can, i.e., today or tomorrow. Bring fruit with you, e.g., apples and peaches.* In formal writing, replace the abbreviations with the English words: *Keats wrote many different kinds of lyrics, for example, odes, sonnets, and songs.*

either, neither   Both *either* and *neither* are singular: *Neither of the two boys has played the game. Either of the two girls is willing to show you the way home. Either* has an intensive use that *neither* does not, and when it is used as an intensive, *either* is always negative: *She told him she would not go either.* (*For* either . . . or *and* neither . . . nor *constructions, see p. 480.*)

elicit, illicit   The verb *elicit* means "to draw out." The adjective *illicit* means "unlawful." *The detective was unable to elicit any information about other illicit activity.*

elude   *See* allude, elude, refer to.

emigrate, immigrate   *Emigrate* means "to move away from one's country": *My grandfather emigrated from Greece in 1905. Immigrate* means "to move to another country and settle there": *Grandpa immigrated to the United States.*

eminent, imminent, immanent   *Eminent* means "celebrated" or "well known": *Many eminent Victorians were melancholy and disturbed. Imminent* means "about to happen" or "about to come": *In August 1939, many Europeans sensed that war was imminent. Immanent* refers to something invisible but dwelling throughout the world: *Medieval Christians believed that God's power was immanent through the universe.*

etc.   The abbreviation *etc.* stands for the Latin *et cetera,* meaning "and others" or "and other things." Because *and* is included in the abbreviation, do not write *and etc.* In a series, a comma comes before *etc.,* just as it would before the coordinating conjunction that closes a series: *He brought string, wax, paper, etc.* In most college writing, it is better to end a series of examples with a final example or the words *and so on.*

everybody/every body, everyone/every one   *See* anyone/any one. . .

except, accept   *See* accept, except.

expect   *Expect* means "to hope" or "to anticipate": *I expect a good grade on my final paper. Suppose* means "to presume": *I suppose you did not win the lottery on Saturday.*

explicit, implicit   *Explicit* means "stated outright." *Implicit* means "implied, unstated." *Her explicit instructions were to go to the party without her, but the implicit message she conveyed was disapproval.*

farther, further   *Farther* describes geographical distances: *Ten miles farther on is a hotel. Further* means "in addition" when geography is not involved: *He said further that he didn't like my attitude.*

fewer, less   *Fewer* refers to items that can be counted individually; *less* refers to general amounts. *Fewer people signed up for indoor soccer this year than last. Your argument has less substance than you think.*

firstly   *Firstly* is common in British English but not in the United States. *First, second, third,* and so on are the accepted forms.

flaunt, flout *Flaunt* means "to wave" or "to show publicly" with a delight tinged with pride and even arrogance: *He flaunted his wealth by wearing overalls lined with mink. Flout* means "to scorn" or "to defy," especially in a public way, seemingly without concern for the consequences: *She flouted the traffic laws by running through red lights.*

former, latter *Former* refers to the first and *latter* to the second of two things mentioned previously: *Mario and Alice are both good cooks; the former is fonder of Chinese cooking, the latter of Mexican.*

further *See* farther, further.

get In formal writing, avoid colloquial uses of *get,* as in *get with it, get it all together, get-up-and-go, get it,* and *that gets me.*

good, well *Good* is an adjective and should not be used in place of the adverb *well: He felt good about doing well on the exam.*

half, a half, half a Write *half, a half,* or *half a* but not *half of, a half a,* or *a half of: Half the clerical staff went out on strike. I want a half-dozen eggs to throw at the actors. Half a loaf is better than none, unless you are on a diet.*

hanged, hung People are *hanged* by the neck until dead. Pictures and all other things that can be suspended are *hung.*

hopefully *Hopefully* means "with hope." It is often misused to mean "it is hoped": *We waited hopefully for our ship to come in* [not *Hopefully, our ship will come in*].

i.e. *See* e.g., i.e.

if . . . then Avoid using these words in tandem. Redundant: *If I get my license, then I can drive a cab.* Better: *If I get my license, I can drive a cab. Once I get my license, I can drive a cab.*

illicit *See* elicit, illicit.

imminent *See* eminent, imminent, immanent.

immigrate *See* emigrate, immigrate.

immoral *See* amoral, immoral.

implicit *See* explicit, implicit.

imply, infer *Imply* means "to suggest something without stating it directly": *By putting his fingers in his ears, he implied that she should stop singing. Infer* means "to draw a conclusion from evidence": *When she dozed off in the middle of his declaration of eternal love, he inferred that she did not feel the same way about him.*

in, in to, into *In* refers to a location inside something: *Charles kept a snake in his room. In to* refers to motion with a purpose: *The resident manager came in to capture it. Into* refers to movement from outside to inside or from separation to contact: *The snake escaped by crawling into a drain. The manager ran into the wall, and Charles got into big trouble.*

incredible, incredulous The *incredible* cannot be believed; the *incredulous* do not believe. Stories and events may be *incredible;* people are *incredulous: Nancy told an incredible story of being abducted by a UFO over the weekend. We were all incredulous.*

infer   *See* imply, infer.

inside of, outside of   The "of" is unnecessary in these phrases: *He was outside the house.*

ironically   *Ironically* means "contrary to what was or might have been expected." It should not be confused with *surprisingly,* which means "unexpected," or with *coincidentally,* which means "occurring at the same time or place." *Ironically, his fastball lost speed after his arm healed.*

irregardless   This construction is a double negative because both the prefix *ir-* and the suffix *-less* are negatives. Use *regardless* instead.

it's, its   *It's* is a contraction, usually for *it is* but sometimes for *it has: It's often been said that English is a difficult language to learn. Its* is a possessive pronoun: *The dog sat down and scratched its fleas.*

kind(s)   *Kind* is singular: *This kind of house is easy to build. Kinds* is plural and should be used only to indicate more than one kind: *These three kinds of toys are better than those two kinds.*

lay, lie   *Lay* means "to place." Its main forms are *lay, laid,* and *laid.* It generally has a direct object, specifying what has been placed: *She laid her book on the steps and left it there. Lie* means "to recline" and does not take a direct object. Its main forms are *lie, lay,* and *lain: She often lay awake at night.*

less   *See* fewer, less.

like   *See* as, like.

literally   *Literally* means "actually" or "exactly as written": *Literally thousands gathered along the parade route.* Do not use *literally* as an intensive adverb when it can be misleading or even ridiculous, as here: *His blood literally boiled.*

loose, lose   *Loose* is an adjective that means "not securely attached." *Lose* is a verb that means "to misplace." *Better tighten that loose screw before you lose the whole structure.*

may   *See* can, may.

maybe, may be   *Maybe* is an adverb meaning "perhaps": *Maybe he can get a summer job as a lifeguard. May be* is a verb phrase meaning "is possible": *It may be that I can get a job as a lifeguard, too.*

moral, morale   *Moral* means "lesson," especially a lesson about standards of behavior or the nature of life: *The moral of the story is do not drink and drive. Morale* means "attitude" or "mental condition": *Office morale dropped sharply after the dean was arrested.*

more/more of   *See* all/all of. . . .

more important, more importantly   The correct idiom is *more important,* not *more importantly.*

most   *See* almost, most.

myself (himself, herself, etc.)   Pronouns ending with *-self* refer to or intensify other words: *Jack hurt himself. Standing in the doorway was the man himself.* When you are unsure whether to use *I* or *me, she* or *her, he* or *him* in a compound subject or object, you may be tempted to substitute one of the *-self* pronouns. Don't do it: *The quarrel was between her and me* [not *myself*]. (*Also see Problems with Pronouns beginning on p. 499 in Tab 10.*)

neither   *See* either, neither

nohow, nowheres   These words are nonstandard for *anyway, in no way, in any way, in any place,* and *in no place.* Do not use them in formal writing.

number   *See* amount, number.

off of   Omit the *of: She took the painting off the wall.*

one another   *See* each other, one another.

outside of   *See* inside of, outside of.

plus   Avoid using *plus* as a substitute for *and: He had to walk the dog, do the dishes, empty the garbage, and* [not *plus*] *write a term paper.*

practicable, practical   *Practicable* is an adjective applied to things that can be done: *A space program that would land human beings on Mars is now practicable. Practical* means "sensible": *Many people do not think such a journey is practical.*

precede, proceed   *Precede* means "come before;" *proceed* means "go forward": *Despite the heavy snows that preceded us, we managed to proceed up the hiking trail.*

previous to, prior to   Avoid these wordy and somewhat pompous substitutions for *before.*

principal, principle   *Principal* is an adjective meaning "most important" or a noun meaning "the head of an organization" or "a sum of money": *Our principal objections to the school's principal are that he is a liar and a cheat. Principle* is a noun meaning "a basic standard or law": *We believe in the principles of honesty and fair play.*

proceed   *See* precede, proceed.

raise, rise   *Raise* means "to lift or cause to move upward." It takes a direct object—someone raises something: *I raised the windows in the classroom. Rise* means "to go upward." It does not take a direct object—something rises by itself: *We watched the balloon rise to the ceiling.*

real, really   Do not use the word *real* when you mean *very: The cake was very* [not *real*] *good.*

reason . . . is because   This is a redundant expression. Use either *the reason is that* or *because: The reason he fell on the ice is that he cannot skate. He fell on the ice because he cannot skate.*

refer to   *See* allude, elude, refer to.

relation, relationship   *Relation* describes a connection between things: *There is a relation between smoking and lung cancer. Relationship* describes a connection between people: *The brothers have always had a close relationship.*

respectfully, respectively   *Respectfully* means "with respect": *Treat your partners respectfully. Respectively* means "in the given order": *The three Williams she referred to were Shakespeare, Wordsworth, and Yeats, respectively.*

rise   *See* raise, rise.

set, sit   *Set* is usually a transitive verb meaning "to establish" or "to place." It takes a direct object, and its principal parts are *set, set,* and *set: DiMaggio set the standard of excellence in fielding. She set the box down in the corner. Sit* is usually intransitive, meaning "to place oneself in a sitting position." Its principal parts are *sit, sat,* and *sat: The dog sat on command.*

shall, will   *Shall* was once the standard first-person future form of the verb *to be* when a simple statement of fact was intended: *I shall be twenty-one on my next birthday.* Today, most writers use *will* in the ordinary future tense for the first person: *I will celebrate my birthday by throwing a big party. Shall* is still used in questions. *Shall we dance?*

should of   *See* could of, should of, would of.

site   *See* cite, sight, site.

some   Avoid using the adjective *some* in place of the adverb *somewhat: He felt somewhat* [not *some*] *better after a good night's sleep.*

some of   *See* all/all of. . . .

somewheres   Use *somewhere* or *someplace* instead.

stationary, stationery   *Stationary* means "standing still": *I worked out on my stationary bicycle. Stationery* is writing paper: *That stationery smells like a rose garden.*

suppose   *See* expect, suppose.

sure   Avoid confusing the adjective *sure* with the adverb *surely: The dress she wore to the party was surely bizarre.*

sure and   *Sure and* is often used colloquially. In formal writing, *sure to* is preferred: *Be sure to* [not *be sure and*] *get to the wedding on time.*

take   *See* bring, take.

that, which   Many writers use *that* for restrictive (i.e., essential) clauses and *which* for nonrestrictive (i.e., nonessential) clauses: *The bull that escaped from the ring ran through my china shop, which was located in the square.* (*Also see Commas, pp. 526–30, in Tab 11.*)

their, there, they're   *Their* is a possessive pronoun: *They gave their lives. There* is an adverb of place: *She was standing there. They're* is a contraction of *they are: They're reading more poetry this semester.*

this here, these here, that there, them there   When writing, avoid these nonstandard forms.

to, too, two   *To* is a preposition; *too* is an adverb; *two* is a number: *The two of us got lost too many times on our way to his house.*

try and   *Try to* is the standard form: *Try to* [not *try and*] *understand.*

uninterested   *See* disinterested, uninterested.

utilize   *Utilize* seldom says more than *use,* and the simpler term is almost always better: *We must learn how to use the computer's zip drive.*

verbally, orally   To say something *orally* is to say it aloud: *We agreed orally to share credit for the work, but when I asked her to confirm it in writing, she refused.* To say something *verbally* is to use words: *His eyes flashed anger, but he did not express his feelings verbally.*

wait for, wait on   People *wait for* those who are late; they *wait on* tables.

weather, whether   The noun *weather* refers to the atmosphere: *She worried that the weather would not clear up in time for the victory celebration.* *Whether* is a conjunction referring to a choice between alternatives: *I can't decide whether to go now or next week.*

well   *See* good, well.

which, who, whose   *Which* is used for things, and *who* and *whose* for people: *My fountain pen, which I had lost last week, was found by a child who had never seen one before, whose whole life had been spent with ballpoints.*

whether   *See* weather, whether.

will   *See* shall, will.

would of   *See* could of, should of, would of.

your, you're   *Your* is a possessive pronoun: *Is that your new car? You're* is a contraction of *you are: You're a lucky guy.*

10

There is a core simplicity to the English language and its American variant, but it's a slippery core.

—STEPHEN KING

Editing
for Grammar
Conventions

When you edit, your purpose is to make the sentences in your text both clear and strong. The previous section of the handbook focused on editing for clarity. This section focuses on editing for common grammatical problems.

51 Sentence Fragments

A **sentence fragment** is an incomplete sentence treated as if it were complete. It may begin with a capital letter and end with a period, a question mark, or an exclamation point, but it lacks one or more of the following:

www.mhhe.com/
awr
For information and
exercises on sentence
fragments, go to

Editing > Sentence
Fragments

- A complete verb
- A subject
- An independent clause

Although writers sometimes use them intentionally (*see "Charting the Territory: Intentional Fragments" on p. 465*), fragments are rarely appropriate for college assignments.

51a Learn how to identify sentence fragments.

You can identify fragments in your work by asking three questions as you edit.

THREE QUESTIONS for IDENTIFYING FRAGMENTS

- Do you see a complete verb?
- Do you see a subject?
- Do you see *only* a dependent clause?

1. Do you see a complete verb?

A **complete verb** consists of a main verb and any helping verbs needed to indicate tense, person, and number. (*See Chapter 54: Problems with Verbs, p. 491.*) A group of related words without a complete verb is a phrase fragment, not a sentence.

> **FRAGMENT**   The ancient Mayas were among the first to develop many mathematical concepts. *For example, the concept of zero.* [no verb]

> **SENTENCE**   The ancient Mayas were among the first to develop many mathematical concepts. *For example, they developed the concept of zero.*

2. Do you see a subject?

The **subject** is the *who* or *what* that a sentence is about. (*See Tab 12: Basic Grammar Review, p. 624.*) A group of related words without a subject or complete verb is a phrase fragment, not a sentence.

> **FRAGMENT**   The ancient Mayas were accomplished mathematicians. *Developed the concept of zero, for example.* [no subject]

> **SENTENCE**   The ancient Mayas were accomplished mathematicians. *They developed the concept of zero, for example.*

3. Do you see *only* a dependent clause?

An **independent clause** has a subject and complete verb and can stand on its own as a sentence. A **dependent** or **subordinate clause** also has a subject and complete verb, but it begins with a subordinating word such as *although, because, since, that, unless, which,* or *while.* Dependent clauses function within sentences as modifiers or nouns, but they cannot stand as sentences on their own. (*See Tab 12: Basic Grammar Review, p. 631.*)

FRAGMENT The ancient Mayas deserve a place in the history of mathematics. *Because they were among the earliest people to develop the concept of zero.*

SENTENCE The ancient Mayas deserve a place in the history of mathematics *because they were among the earliest people to develop the concept of zero.*

Fragments and Grammar Checkers

Grammar checkers identify some fragments, but they will not tell you what the fragment is missing or how to edit it. Grammar checkers can also miss fragments without subjects that could be interpreted as commands. Consider the following fragment: *Develop the concept of zero, for example.* Because this fragment has the form of a command, a grammar checker might fail to tag it.

51b Learn how to edit sentence fragments.

You can repair sentence fragments by editing them in one of two ways:

■ Transform them into sentences.

They
➤ **Many people feel threatened by globalization. ~~Because~~**
  ^

  ~~they~~ think it will undermine their cultural traditions.

■ Attach them to a nearby independent clause.

➤ **Many people feel threatened by globalization,/**

  because
  ~~Because~~ they think it will undermine their cultural
  ^

  traditions.

IDENTIFY AND EDIT
Fragments

frag

❓ 1. Do you see a complete verb?

Yes | **No → FRAGMENT**

FRAGMENT   For example, the concept of zero.

                                      subj verb

SENTENCE   For example, they were among the first to develop the concept of zero.

❓ 2. Do you see a subject?

Yes | **No → FRAGMENT**

FRAGMENT   Developed the concept of zero, for example.

                                    subj   verb

SENTENCE   They developed the concept of zero, for example.

❓ 3. Do you see only a dependent clause?

No | **Yes → FRAGMENT**

FRAGMENT   Because they were among the earliest people to develop the concept of zero.

SENTENCE   The Mayas deserve a place in the history of mathematics because they were among the earliest people to develop the concept of zero.

SENTENCE

The approach to take in any particular case is a stylistic decision. Sometimes one approach may be clearly preferable to the other, and sometimes both approaches may seem equally effective.

Intentional Fragments

Advertisers often use attention-getting fragments: "Hot deal! Big savings! Best wireless!" "Nothing but Net." "Because you're worth it." In everyday life, we often speak in fragments: "How are you?" "Fine." As a result, people who write fiction and drama use fragments to create realistic dialogue. Writers also sometimes use fragments deliberately in other contexts for stylistic effect. You, too, may occasionally want to use a sentence fragment for stylistic reasons. Keep in mind, however, that advertising, literary writing, and college writing have different contexts and purposes. In formal writing, use intentional sentence fragments sparingly, if at all.

You may, for example, choose to rewrite a fragment as a sentence for emphasis.

➤ **The ambulance crew gave us tips on handling**

They stressed
emergencies. ~~Stressing~~ the importance of staying calm.

Rewriting long fragments as separate sentences can help keep your writing direct and concise.

➤ **Students with good time management habits start**

Others,
studying right away in the evening. ~~Whereas others,~~ of the

procrastinating variety, may go running first, or make

phone calls, or clean their rooms, or surf the Internet, or

watch television—anything to avoid getting to work.

Attaching a fragment to a related sentence, on the other hand, can highlight the relationship between ideas.

➤ **The Mayas built great cities. ~~Even~~** *even* **though they lacked**

metal tools.

For MULTILINGUAL STUDENTS

Avoiding Fragments

Fragments are almost never acceptable in formal writing in standard written English. Many languages other than English, however, permit constructions that, transferred literally into English, would result in fragments. For example, some languages—Russian and Chinese, to name two—permit the omission of the auxiliary or linking verb *be.* Transferred directly into English, this pattern can result in fragments like *He very happy with the news,* instead of the correct *He is very happy with the news.* Multilingual students need to be aware of these potential pitfalls.

51c Connect a phrase fragment to another sentence, or add the missing elements.

Often unintentional fragments are **phrases**—word groups that lack a subject or a complete verb or both and usually function as modifiers or nouns.

1. Watching for verbals

Phrase fragments frequently begin with **verbals**—words derived from verbs, such as *putting* or *to put.* (*For more on verbals, see p. 629.*)

> **FRAGMENT** That summer, we had the time of our lives. *Fishing in the early morning hours, splashing in the lake after lunch, exploring the woods before dinner, and playing Scrabble until it was time for bed.*

One way to fix this fragment is to transform it into an independent clause with its own subject and verb.

> ➤ That summer, we had the time of our lives. ~~Fishing~~ *We fished* in the
>
> early morning hours, ~~splashing~~ *splashed* in the lake after lunch,
>
> ~~exploring~~ *explored* the woods before dinner, and ~~playing~~ *played* Scrabble
>
> until it was time for bed.

Notice that all of the *-ing* verbals in the fragment need to be changed to keep the phrases in the new sentence parallel. (*For more on parallelism, see Tab 9: Editing for Clarity, pp. 417–20.*)

Another way to fix the problem is to attach the fragment to the part of the previous sentence that it modifies (in this case, *the time of our lives*).

➤ That summer, we had the time of our lives⁄, ~~Fishing~~ *fishing* in the early morning hours, splashing in the lake after lunch, exploring the woods before dinner, and playing Scrabble until it was time for bed.

2. Watching for preposition fragments

Phrase fragments can also begin with one-word prepositions such as *as, at, by, for, from, in, of, on,* or *to.* To correct these types of fragments, you will often find it easiest to attach them to a nearby sentence.

➤ Impressionist painters often depicted their subjects in everyday situations⁄, ~~At~~ *at* a restaurant, perhaps, or by the seashore.

3. Watching for transitional phrases

Some fragments start with two- or three-word prepositions that function as transitions, such as *as well as, as compared with, except for, in addition to, in contrast with, in spite of,* or *instead of.*

➤ For the past sixty-five years, the growth in consumer spending has been both steep and steady⁄, ~~As~~ *as* compared with the growth in gross domestic product (GDP), which fluctuated significantly between 1929 and 1950.

4. Watching for words and phrases that introduce examples

Check word groups beginning with expressions that introduce examples—such as *for example, like, specifically,* or *such as*—to make sure they are complete sentences. If they are fragments, edit to make them into sentences or attach them to an independent clause.

➤ **Elizabeth I of England faced many dangers as a princess.**

  she fell
  For example, ~~falling~~ out of favor with her sister, Queen

  was
  Mary, and ~~being~~ imprisoned in the Tower of London.

5. Watching for appositives

An **appositive** is a noun or noun phrase that renames a noun or pronoun.

➤ **In 1965, Lyndon Johnson increased the number of troops**

  a
  in Vietnam/, ̸A former French colony in southeast Asia.

6. Watching for fragments that consist of lists

Usually, you can connect a list to the preceding sentence using a colon. If you want to emphasize the list, consider using a dash instead.

➤ **In the 1930s, three great band leaders helped popularize**

  jazz/: Louis Armstrong, Benny Goodman, and Duke

  Ellington.

7. Watching for fragments that are parts of compound predicates

A **compound predicate** is made up of at least two verbs as well as their objects and modifiers, connected by a coordinating conjunction such as *and, but,* or *or.* The parts of a compound predicate have the same subject and should be together in one sentence.

➤ **The group gathered at dawn at the base of the mountain/**

  and
  ~~And~~ assembled their gear in preparation for the morning's

  climb.

51d   Connect fragments that begin with a subordinating word (*although, because, since*) to another sentence, or eliminate the subordinating word.

Fragments often begin with a subordinating word such as *although, because, even though, since, so that, whenever,* or *whereas.* Usually, a fragment that begins with a subordinating word can be attached to a nearby independent clause.

➤ **On the questionnaire, none of the thirty-three subjects**

indicated any concern about the amount or kind of fruit

even
the institution served./, ~~Even~~ though all of them identified

diet as an important issue for those with diabetes.

Punctuation tip: A comma usually follows a dependent clause that begins a sentence. If the clause appears at the end of a sentence, it is usually not preceded by a comma unless it is a contrasting thought, as in the example above. (*See Tab 11: Editing for Correctness, p. 538.*)

It is sometimes better to transform such a fragment into a complete sentence by deleting the subordinating word.

➤ **The solidarity of our group was undermined in two ways.**

Participants
~~When participants~~ either disagreed about priorities or

advocated significantly different political strategies.

For MULTILINGUAL STUDENTS

Adding a Subject Pronoun to a Dependent Clause

In English, a dependent clause needs a subject, even if it repeats the subject of the main clause. *The tire lost air because was punctured* should be changed to *The tire lost air because it was punctured*. In a dependent clause that begins with a relative pronoun, however, the pronoun *is* the subject. For example, *that* is the subject of the dependent clause in this sentence: *We replaced the tire that was punctured.*

52 Comma Splices and Run-on Sentences

Comma splices and run-on sentences are sentences with improperly joined independent clauses. Recall that an independent clause has a subject and a complete verb and can stand on its own as a sentence.

www.mhhe.com/awr
For information and exercises on comma splices, go to

Editing >
Comma Splices

52a Learn how to identify comma splices and run-on sentences.

A **comma splice** is a sentence with two independent clauses joined by only a comma.

> **COMMA SPLICE** Dogs that compete in the annual Westminster Dog Show are already champions, they have each won at least one dog show before arriving at Madison Square Garden.

A **run-on sentence,** sometimes called a **fused sentence,** does not even have a comma between the independent clauses.

> **RUN-ON** From time to time, new breeds enter the ring the Border Collie is a recent addition to the show.

Writers may mistakenly join two independent clauses with only a comma or create a run-on sentence in three situations:

- When a transitional expression like *as a result* or *for example* or a conjunctive adverb like *however* links the second clause to the first.

> **COMMA SPLICE** Rare books can be extremely valuable, *for example,* an original edition of Audubon's *Birds of America* is worth over a million dollars.

> **RUN-ON** Most students complied with the new policy *however* a few refused to do so.

- When the second clause specifies or explains the first.

> **RUN-ON** The economy changed in 1991 corporate bankruptcies increased by 40 percent.

- When the second clause begins with a pronoun.

> **COMMA SPLICE** President Garfield was assassinated, he served only six months in office.

470

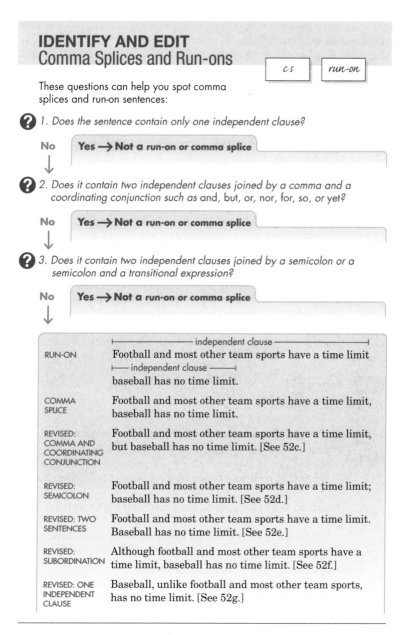

IDENTIFY AND EDIT
Comma Splices and Run-ons

| c s | run-on |

These questions can help you spot comma splices and run-on sentences:

? 1. *Does the sentence contain only one independent clause?*

No   **Yes →Not a run-on or comma splice**
↓

? 2. *Does it contain two independent clauses joined by a comma and a coordinating conjunction such as and, but, or, nor, for, so, or yet?*

No   **Yes →Not a run-on or comma splice**
↓

? 3. *Does it contain two independent clauses joined by a semicolon or a semicolon and a transitional expression?*

No   **Yes →Not a run-on or comma splice**
↓

RUN-ON	├─── independent clause ───┤ Football and most other team sports have a time limit ├── independent clause ──┤ baseball has no time limit.
COMMA SPLICE	Football and most other team sports have a time limit, baseball has no time limit.
REVISED: COMMA AND COORDINATING CONJUNCTION	Football and most other team sports have a time limit, but baseball has no time limit. [See 52c.]
REVISED: SEMICOLON	Football and most other team sports have a time limit; baseball has no time limit. [See 52d.]
REVISED: TWO SENTENCES	Football and most other team sports have a time limit. Baseball has no time limit. [See 52e.]
REVISED: SUBORDINATION	Although football and most other team sports have a time limit, baseball has no time limit. [See 52f.]
REVISED: ONE INDEPENDENT CLAUSE	Baseball, unlike football and most other team sports, has no time limit. [See 52g.]

1. Checking for transitional expressions and conjunctive adverbs

Check those sentences that include transitional expressions or conjunctive adverbs. If a comma precedes one of these words or phrases, you may have found a comma splice. If no punctuation precedes one of them, you may have found a run-on sentence. Can the word groups that precede and follow the conjunctive adverb or transitional expression both stand alone as sentences? If so, you have found a comma splice or a run-on sentence.

2. Reviewing sentences with commas

Check sentences that contain commas. Can the word groups that appear on both sides of the comma stand alone as sentences? If so, you have found a comma splice.

Comma Splices, Run-on Sentences, and Grammar Checkers

Computer grammar checkers are unreliable at distinguishing properly from improperly joined independent clauses. One grammar checker, for example, correctly flagged this sentence for incorrect comma usage: *Many history textbooks are clear, some are hard to follow.* It failed, however, to flag this longer alternative: *Many history textbooks are clear and easy to read, some are dense and hard to follow.*

---

www.mhhe.com/
awr
For information and
exercises on run-on
sentences, go to

Editing > Fused
Sentences

52b Learn five ways to edit comma splices and run-on sentences.

- Join the two clauses with a comma and a coordinating conjunction (*and, but, or, nor, for, so, yet*) (*52c, p. 473*).

  ➤ **Dogs that compete in the annual Westminster Dog Show**

  for
  are already champions, they have each won at least one
  ^

  dog show before arriving at Madison Square Garden.

- Join the two clauses with a semicolon (*52d, p. 473*).

  ➤ **From time to time, new breeds enter the ring; the**
  ^

  Border Collie is a recent addition to the show.

  You can also add an appropriate conjunctive adverb or transitional expression, followed by a comma.

➤ From time to time, new breeds enter the ring the *; for instance,*

Border Collie is a recent addition to the show.

■ Separate the clauses into two sentences (*52e, p. 475*).

➤ Salt air corrodes metal easily ~~therefore~~ automobiles in *. Therefore,*

coastal regions require frequent washing.

■ Turn one of the independent clauses into a dependent clause (*52f, p. 475*).

➤ Treasure hunters shopping in thrift stores and at

garage sales should be realistic; valuable finds are *because*

extremely rare.

■ Transform the two clauses into a single independent clause (*52g, p. 475*).

➤ The best history books are clear; ~~they also~~ tell a *and*

compelling story.

52c Join the two clauses with a comma and a coordinating conjunction such as *and, but, or, nor, for, so,* or *yet.*

If you decide to correct a comma splice or run-on by joining the two clauses, be sure to choose the coordinating conjunction that most clearly expresses the logical relationship between the clauses.

➤ John is a very stubborn person, I had a hard time *so*

convincing him to let me take the wheel.

52d Join the two clauses with a semicolon.

A semicolon tells readers that two clauses are logically connected. However, a semicolon does not spell out the logic of the connection.

➤ Most students complied with the new policy,; a few refused

to do so.

To show the logic of the connection, you can add a conjunctive adverb or transitional expression.

➤ **Most students complied with the new policy**/ **a few refused**

    ; however,

    to do so.

CONJUNCTIVE ADVERBS and TRANSITIONAL EXPRESSIONS

also	incidentally	now
as a result	indeed	nonetheless
besides	in fact	of course
certainly	in other words	on the contrary
consequently	instead	otherwise
finally	in the meantime	similarly
for example	likewise	still
for instance	meanwhile	then
furthermore	moreover	therefore
however	nevertheless	thus
in addition	next	undoubtedly

Note: The conjunctive adverb or transitional expression is usually followed by a comma when it appears at the beginning of the second clause. It can also appear in the middle of a clause, set off by two commas, or at the end, preceded by a comma.

➤ **Most students complied with the new policy**/;

    , however,
    a few refused to do so.

➤ **Most students complied with the new policy**/; **a few**

    , however
    refused to do so.

When the first independent clause introduces the second one, use a colon instead of a semicolon. A colon is also appropriate if the second clause expands on the first one in some way. (*See Tab 11: Editing for Correctness, p. 545.*)

➤ **Professor Johnson then revealed his most important point:**

    the paper would count for half my grade.

52e Separate the clauses into two sentences.

The simplest way to correct comma splices and run-on sentences is to turn the clauses into separate sentences. The simplest solution is not always the best solution, however, especially if the result is one short, simple sentence followed by another. The simplest solution works well in this example because the second sentence is a compound sentence.

➤ I realized that it was time to choose*. Either* ~~either~~ I had to learn

how to drive, or I had to move back to the city.

When the two independent clauses are part of a quotation, with a phrase such as *he said* or *she noted* between them, each clause should be a separate sentence.

➤ "This was the longest day of my life," she said*.*

"Unfortunately,
~~"unfortunately,~~ it's not over yet."

52f Turn one of the independent clauses into a dependent clause.

In editing the following sentence, the writer chose to make the clause about *a few* her main point and the clause about *most* a subordinate idea. Readers will expect subsequent sentences to tell them more about the subject of the main clause.

Although most
➤ ~~Most~~ students complied with the new policy, ~~however~~ a

few refused to do so.

52g Transform the two clauses into one independent clause.

It is seldom easy, but transforming two clauses into one clear and correct independent clause is often worth the work.

➤ I realized that it was time ~~to choose,~~ either ~~I had~~ to learn

how to drive or ~~I had~~ to move back to the city.

Sometimes you can change one of the clauses to a phrase and place it next to the word it modifies.

➤ Baseball cards *, first printed in the nineteenth century,* are an obsession among some collectors/.

~~the cards were first printed in the nineteenth century.~~

53 Subject-Verb Agreement

All verbs must agree with their subjects in person (first, second, or third—*I, we; you; he, she, it, they*) and number (singular or plural).

www.mhhe.com/
awr
For information
and exercises on
subject-verb
agreement, go to

Editing >
Subject-Verb
Agreement

53a Learn the standard subject-verb combinations.

For regular verbs, the present tense *-s* or *-es* ending is added to the verb if its subject is third-person singular; otherwise, the verb has no ending.

Present Tense Forms of a Regular Verb: *Read*

	SINGULAR	PLURAL
First person	I *read.*	We *read.*
Second person	You *read.*	You *read.*
Third person	He, she, it *reads.*	They *read.*

Note, however, that the verb *be* has irregular forms in both the present and the past tense.

Present Tense and Past Tense Forms of the Irregular Verb *Be*

	SINGULAR	PLURAL
First person	I *am/was* here.	We *are/were* here.
Second person	You *are/were* here.	You *are/were* here.
Third person	He, she, it *is/was* here.	They *are/were* here.

The verbs *have* and *do* have the following forms in the present tense.

Present Tense Forms of the Verb *Have*

	SINGULAR	PLURAL
First person	I *have.*	We *have.*
Second person	You *have.*	You *have.*
Third person	He, she, it *has.*	They *have.*

Present Tense Forms of the Verb *Do* and Its Negative *Don't*

	SINGULAR	PLURAL
First person	I *do/don't.*	We *do/don't.*
Second person	You *do/don't.*	You *do/don't.*
Third person	He, she, it *does/doesn't.*	They *do/don't.*

Problems with subject-verb agreement tend to occur when writers do the following:

- Lose sight of the subject (*53b, p. 478*)
- Use compound, collective, or indefinite subjects (*53c–e, pp. 480–83*)
- Have a subject that follows the verb (*53f, p. 483*)
- Confuse a subject complement with the subject (*53g, p. 483*)
- Use a relative pronoun as the subject of a dependent clause (*53h, p. 484*)

- Use a phrase beginning with an *-ing* verb as the subject (*53i, p. 484*)
- Use titles, company names, or words considered by themselves (*53j, pp. 484–85*)

53b Do not lose sight of the subject when a word group separates it from the verb.

To locate the subject of a sentence, find the verb, and then ask the *who* or *what* question about it ("Who is?" "What is?"). Does that subject match the verb in number?

> *oppose*
> ➤ **The leaders of the trade union ~~opposes~~ the new law.**
> ^

The answer to the question "Who opposes?" is *leaders,* a plural noun, so the verb should be in the plural form: *oppose.*

Note: If a word group beginning with *as well as, along with,* or *in addition to* follows a singular subject, the subject does not become plural.

> *opposes*
> ➤ **My teacher, as well as other faculty members, ~~oppose~~ the**
> ^
> **new school policy.**

Subject-Verb Agreement and Grammar Checkers

Computer grammar checkers are unreliable guides to subject-verb agreement. For example, a grammar checker failed to flag this sentence for correction: *The candidate's position on foreign policy issues trouble some voters.* The subject is the singular noun *position,* so the verb should be *troubles.* Apparently, however, the grammar checker interpreted the word *issues* as the subject and so let the sentence pass with an incorrect verb form.

IDENTIFY AND EDIT
Problems with Subject-Verb Agreement

agr

★ *1. Find the verb.*

> verb
> PROBLEM Hamlet and Claudius *brings* down the Danish
> SENTENCE royal family.
>
> Verbs are words that specify action, condition, or state of being.

★ *2. Ask the who or what question to identify the subject.*

> |————— subject —————| |—verb—|
> PROBLEM Hamlet and Claudius *brings* down the Danish
> SENTENCE royal family.
>
> The answer to the question "What brings" is *Hamlet and Claudius.*

★ *3. Determine the person (first, second, or third) and number (singular or plural) of the subject.*

> |————— subject —————|
> PROBLEM Hamlet and Claudius brings down the Danish
> SENTENCE royal family.
>
> The subject of the sentence—*Hamlet and Claudius*—is a compound joined by *and,* and is third-person plural.

★ *4. If necessary, change the verb to agree with the subject.*

> bring
> EDITED Hamlet and Claudius ~~brings~~ down the Danish
> PROBLEM ^
> SENTENCE royal family.
>
> *Bring* is the third-person plural form of the verb.

53c Treat most compound subjects—subjects connected by *and, or, nor, both . . . and, either . . . or*, or *neither . . . nor*—as plural.

Compound subjects are made up of two or more parts joined by either a coordinating conjunction (*and, or, nor*) or a correlative conjunction (*both . . . and, either . . . or, neither . . . nor*).

1. Treating most compound subjects as plural
Most subjects that are joined by *and* should be treated as plural.

➤ *The king and his advisers were* shocked by this turn of events.

➤ This poem's *first line and last word have* a powerful effect on the reader.

2. Treating some compound subjects as singular
There are exceptions to the rule that subjects joined by *and* are plural.

- The two subjects refer to the same entity.

  ➤ *My best girlfriend and most dependable advisor is* my mother.

- The two subjects are considered as a single unit.

  ➤ *Forty acres and a mule continues* to be what is needed.

- The two subjects are preceded by the word *each* or *every*.

  ➤ *Each* man, woman, and child *deserves* respect.

3. Treating some compound subjects as either plural or singular
Compound subjects connected by *or, nor, either . . . or*, or *neither . . . nor* can take either a singular or a plural verb, depending on the subject that is closest to the verb.

SINGULAR	Either the children or *their mother is* to blame.
PLURAL	Neither the experimenter nor *her subjects were* aware of the takeover.

53d Treat most collective subjects—subjects like *audience, family,* and *committee*—as singular.

A **collective noun** names a unit made up of many persons or things, treating it as an entity. Other examples are *group* and *team*.

1. Treating most collective nouns as singular *News, athletics, physics, statistics,* and other words like these are usually singular as well, despite their *-s* endings, because they function as collective subjects. Units of measurement used collectively, such as *six inches* or *20%,* are also treated as singular.

➤ The *audience is* restless.

➤ That *news leaves* me speechless.

➤ *One-fourth* of the liquid *was* poured into test tube 1.

2. Treating some collective subjects as plural
When the members of a group are acting as individuals, the collective subject can be considered plural.

➤ The *group were* passing around a bottle of beer.

You may want to add a modifying phrase that contains a plural noun to make the sentence clearer and avoid awkwardness.

➤ The *group of troublemakers were* passing around a bottle of beer.

> The modifying phrase *of troublemakers* makes the sentence less awkward.

When units of measurement refer to people or things, they are plural.

➤ *One-fourth* of the students in the class *are* failing the course.

53e Treat most indefinite subjects—subjects like *everybody, no one, each, all,* and *none*—as singular.

Indefinite pronouns such as *everybody* and *no one* do not refer to a specific person or item.

1. Recognizing that most indefinite pronouns are singular

The following indefinite pronouns are always singular: *all, anybody, anyone, anything, each, either, everybody, everyone, everything, neither, nobody, no one, none, nothing, one, somebody, someone,* and *something.*

➤ *Everyone* in my hiking club *is* an experienced climber.

None and *neither* are singular when they appear by themselves.

➤ In the movie, five men set out on an expedition, but *none returns.*

➤ *Neither sees* a way out of this predicament.

If a prepositional phrase that includes a plural noun or pronoun follows *none* or *neither,* the indefinite pronoun seems to have a plural meaning. Although some writers treat *none* or *neither* as plural in such situations, others maintain that these two pronouns are always singular. It is a safe bet to consider them singular.

➤ In the movie, five men set out on an expedition, but *none* of them *returns.*

➤ *Neither* of the hikers *sees* a way out of this cave.

2. Recognizing that some indefinite pronouns are always plural

A handful of indefinite pronouns (*both, few, many, several*) are always plural because they mean more than one by definition. *Both,* for example, always indicates two.

➤ *Both* of us *want* to go to the rally for the environment.

➤ *Several* of my friends *were* very happy about the outcome of the election.

3. Recognizing that some indefinite pronouns can be either plural or singular

Some indefinite pronouns (*some, any, all, most*) may be either plural or singular, depending on whether they refer to a plural or singular noun in the context of the sentence.

➤ *Some* of the *book is* missing, but *all* of the *papers are* here.

53f Make sure the subject and verb agree when the subject comes after the verb.

In most English sentences, the verb comes after the subject. Sometimes, however, a writer will switch this order. In the following sentence, you can locate the subject by asking, "Who or what stand?" The answer is the sentence's subject: *an oak and a weeping willow.* Because the subject is a compound subject (two subjects joined by *and*), the verb must be plural.

➤ Out back behind the lean-to *stand an old oak tree and a*

weeping willow.

In sentences that begin with *there is* or *there are,* the subject always follows the verb.

➤ There *is* a worn wooden *bench* in the shade of the two trees.

53g Make sure the verb agrees with its subject, not the subject complement.

A **subject complement** renames and specifies the sentence's subject. It follows a **linking verb**—a verb, often a form of *be,* that joins the subject to its description or definition: *children <u>are</u> innocent.* In the following sentence, the singular noun *gift* is the subject. *Books* is the subject complement. Therefore, *are* has been changed to *is* to agree in number with *gift.*

➤ One gift that gives her pleasure ~~are~~ books.
   is

53h *Who, which,* and *that* (relative pronouns) take verbs that agree with the subject they replace.

When a relative pronoun such as *who, which,* or *that* is the subject of a dependent clause, it is taking the place of a noun that appears earlier in the sentence—its **antecedent.** The verb that goes with *who, which,* or *that* needs to agree with this antecedent. In the following sentence, the relative pronoun *that* is the subject of the dependent clause *that has dangerous side effects. Disease,* a singular noun, is the antecedent of *that;* therefore, the verb in the dependent clause is singular.

> ➤ **Measles is a childhood *disease that has* dangerous side effects.**

The phrase *one of the* implies more than one and so is plural. *Only one of the* implies just one, however, and is singular. Generally, use the plural form of the verb when the phrase *one of the* comes before the antecedent. Use the singular form of the verb when *only one of the* comes before the antecedent.

PLURAL **Tuberculosis is *one of the* diseases *that have* long, tragic histories in many parts of the world.**

SINGULAR **Barbara is the *only one of the* scientists *who has* a degree in physics.**

53i Phrases beginning with *-ing* verbs take the singular form of the verb when they are subjects.

A **gerund phrase** is an *-ing* verb form followed by objects, complements, or modifiers. When a gerund phrase is the subject in a sentence, it is singular.

> ➤ ***Experimenting with drugs is* a dangerous rave practice.**

53j Titles, company names, and words considered as words are singular

> ➤ ***The Two Gentlemen of Verona*** ~~are~~ *is* **considered the weakest of Shakespeare's comedies.**

includes
➤ The McGraw-Hill Companies ~~include~~ many different
^

divisions.

has
➤ In today's highly partisan politics, *moderates* ~~have~~ come to
^

mean "wishy-washy people."

54 Problems with Verbs

Verbs provide a great deal of information. They report action (*run, write*) and show time (*going, gone*). They change form to indicate person (first, second, or third—*I, we; you; he, she, it, they*) and number (singular or plural). They also change to indicate voice and mood.

www.mhhe.com/
awr
For information and
exercises on verbs,
go to
Editing > Verbs
and Verbals

54a Learn the principal forms of regular and irregular verbs.

All English verbs have five main forms, except for the *be* verb, which has eight.

- The **base form** is the form you find if you look up the verb in a dictionary. (*For irregular verbs, other forms are given as well. See pp. 487–88 for a list.*)
- The **present tense** form is used to indicate an action occurring at the moment or habitually, as well as to introduce quotations, literary events, and scientific facts (*54f, pp. 492–94, and 54h, p. 496*).
- The **past tense** is used to indicate an action completed at a specific time in the past (*54f, pp. 492–94*).

- The **past participle** is used with *have, has,* or *had* to form the perfect tenses (*54f, pp. 492–94*); with a form of the *be* verb to form the passive voice, and as an adjective (the *polished* silver).

- The **present participle** is used with a form of the *be* verb to form the progressive tenses (*54f, pp. 492–94*). It can also be used as a noun (the *writing* is finished) and as an adjective (the *smiling* man).

Tips

LEARNING in COLLEGE

Finding a Verb's Principal Forms

If you are unsure of a verb's principal forms, check a dictionary. If the verb is regular, the dictionary will list only the present form, and you will know that you should form the verb's past tense and past participle by adding *-ed* or *-d*. If the verb is irregular, the dictionary will give its principal forms.

Dictionary entry for an irregular verb:

preferred past tense form given first

sing (sing) *v.,* sang or, often, sung; sung; singing

part of speech (v, verb)   past participle   present participle

1. Learning about common irregular verbs

Regular verbs always add *-d* or *-ed* to the base verb to form the past tense and past participle. **Irregular verbs,** by contrast, do not form the past tense or past participle in a consistent way. The box on pages 487–88 lists the principal forms of common irregular verbs, which you can find in the dictionary.

2. Using the correct forms of irregular verbs that end in *-en*

The forms of irregular verbs with past tenses that end in *-e* and past participles that end in *-n* or *-en*, such as *ate/eaten* and *rode/ridden*, are sometimes confused.

>   *eaten*
> ➤ He had ~~ate~~ the apple.
>   ^

>   *ridden*
> ➤ They had ~~rode~~ the whole way on the bus.
>   ^

FORMS of COMMON IRREGULAR VERBS

Base	Past tense	Past participle
awake	awoke	awoke/awakened
arise	arose	arisen
be	was/were	been
beat	beat	beaten
become	became	become
begin	began	begun
blow	blew	blown
break	broke	broken
bring	brought	brought
buy	bought	bought
catch	caught	caught
choose	chose	chosen
cling	clung	clung
come	came	come
do	did	done
draw	drew	drawn
drink	drank	drunk
drive	drove	driven
eat	ate	eaten
fall	fell	fallen
fight	fought	fought
fly	flew	flown
forget	forgot	forgotten/forgot
forgive	forgave	forgiven
freeze	froze	frozen
get	got	gotten/got
give	gave	given
go	went	gone
grow	grew	grown
hang	hung	hung (for things)
hang	hanged	hanged (for people)
have	had	had
hear	heard	heard
know	knew	known
lose	lost	lost

(*continued*)

FORMS of COMMON IRREGULAR VERBS (continued)

Base	Past tense	Past participle
pay	paid	paid
raise	raised	raised
ride	rode	ridden
ring	rang	rung
rise	rose	risen
say	said	said
see	saw	seen
set	set	set
shake	shook	shaken
sit	sat	sat
spin	spun	spun
steal	stole	stolen
spend	spent	spent
strive	strove/strived	striven/strived
swear	swore	sworn
swim	swam	swum
swing	swung	swung
take	took	taken
tear	tore	torn
tread	trod	trod/trodden
wear	wore	worn
weave	wove	woven
wring	wrung	wrung
write	wrote	written

3. Using the correct forms of *went* and *gone*, and *saw* and *seen*

Went and *saw* are the past tense forms of the irregular verbs *go* and *see*. *Gone* and *seen* are the past participle forms.

>   *gone*
> ➤ I had ~~went~~ there yesterday.
>   ^

>   *saw*
> ➤ We ~~seen~~ the rabid dog and called for help.
>   ^

For MULTILINGUAL STUDENTS

Nonstandard Irregular Verb Forms

In many dialects of English, the forms of some irregular verbs vary from those of standard English. In academic writing, however, always use the standard forms. When in doubt, consult the list of irregular verbs on pages 487–88, and if necessary, edit your work accordingly.

> ➤ The neighborhood gardeners ~~growed~~ *grew* their own
>
> vegetables in the empty lot.

> ➤ The Sistene Chapel frescos ~~be~~ *were* cleaned in the 1980s.

> ➤ Achilles ~~drug~~ *dragged* Hector's body three times around the
>
> walls of Troy.

54b Distinguish between *lay* and *lie, rise* and *raise,* and *sit* and *set.*

Even experienced writers confuse the verbs *lay* and *lie, rise* and *raise,* and *sit* and *set.* The correct forms are given below.

Often-Confused Verb Pairs and Their Principal Forms

BASE	PAST	PAST PARTICIPLE	PRESENT PARTICIPLE
lay (to place)	laid	laid	laying
lie (to recline)	lay	lain	lying
rise (to go/get up)	rose	risen	rising
raise (to lift up)	raised	raised	raising
sit (to be seated)	sat	sat	sitting
set (to put on a surface)	sat	set	setting

One verb in each of these pairs (*lay, raise, set*) is **transitive:** an object receives the action of the verb. The other verb (*lie, rise, sit*) is **intransitive** and cannot take an object. You should use a form of *lay, raise,* or *set,* if you can replace the verb with *place* or *put.* (*See Tab 12: Basic Grammar Review, pp. 627–28 for more on transitive and intransitive verbs.*)

> ➤ The dog *lays* a bone at your feet, then *lies* down and closes his eyes.

direct object

> ➤ As the flames *rise,* the heat *raises the temperature* of the room.

direct object

> ➤ The technician *sits* down and *sets the samples* in front of her.

direct object

Tips LEARNING in COLLEGE

Using Lay *and* Lie *Correctly*

Lay (to place) and *lie* (to recline) are also confusing because the past tense of the irregular verb *lie* is *lay* (*lie, lay, lain*). Always double-check the verb *lay* when it appears in your writing.

> ➤ He washed the dishes carefully, then ~~lay~~ *laid* them on a
>
> clean towel.

54c Do not forget to add an -s or -es ending to the verb when it is necessary.

In the present tense, almost all verbs add an -*s* or -*es* ending if the subject is third-person singular. (*See pp. 476–77 for more on standard subject-verb combinations.*) Third-person singular subjects can be nouns (*woman, Benjamin, desk*), pronouns (*he, she, it*), or indefinite pronouns (*everyone*).

> ➤ The stock market ~~rise~~ *rises* when economic news is good.

If the subject is in the first person (*I*), the second person (*you*), or the third-person plural (*people, they*), the verb does *not* add an -*s* or -*es* ending.

➤ **You invests your money wisely.**

➤ **People needs to learn about companies before buying**

their stock.

54d Do not forget to add a -*d* or an -*ed* ending to the verb when it is necessary.

When they are speaking, people sometimes leave the -*d* or -*ed* ending off certain verbs such as *asked, fixed, mixed, supposed to,* and *used to.* However, in writing, the endings should be included on all regular verbs in the past tense and all past participles of regular verbs.

➤ **The driving instructor ask the student driver to pull**
$\qquad\qquad\qquad\qquad$*asked*

over to the curb.

➤ **After we had mix the formula, we let it cool.**
$\qquad\qquad\quad$*mixed*

Also check for missing -*d* or -*ed* endings on past participles used as adjectives.

➤ **The concern parents met with the school board.**
$\quad\;$*concerned*

Verb Forms and Grammar and Spelling Checkers

Grammar checkers will sometimes highlight an incorrect verb form, but they will miss more than they catch. For example, a grammar checker flagged the incorrect form in this sentence: *She had chose to go to the state college.* It also suggested the correct form: *chosen.* However, the checker missed the misuse of *set* in this sentence: *I am going to set down for a while.*

Similarly, spelling checkers will point out misspelled verbs, but they will not highlight a verb form that is used incorrectly in a sentence.

54e Make sure your verbs are complete.

With only a few exceptions, all English sentences must contain complete verbs. A **complete verb** consists of the main verb along with any helping verbs that are needed to express the tense (*see pp. 492–94*) or voice (*see p. 602*). **Helping verbs** include forms of *be, have,* and *do* and the modal verbs *can, could, may, might, shall, should,* and *will.* Helping verbs can be part of contractions (*He's running, we'd better go*), but they cannot be left out of the sentence entirely.

> ➤ They *be going on a field trip next week.*
>   _{*will*}

correction: will inserted before "be"

A **linking verb,** often a form of *be,* connects the subject to a description or definition of it: *Cats <u>are</u> mammals.* Linking verbs can be part of contractions (*She's a student*), but they should not be left out entirely.

> ➤ Montreal a major Canadian city.
>   _{*is*}

correction: is inserted before "a"

54f Use verb tenses accurately.

Tenses show the time of a verb's action. English has three basic time frames—present, past, and future—and each tense has simple, perfect, and progressive verb forms to indicate the time span of the actions that are taking place. (*For a review of the present tense forms of a typical verb and of the verbs* be, have, *and* do, *see 53a, pp. 476–77; for a review of the principal forms of regular and irregular verbs, which are used to form tenses, see 54a, pp. 485–89.*)

1. The simple present and past tenses   These two tenses use only the verb itself, without a helping verb or verbs. The **simple present tense** is used for actions occurring at the moment or habitually. The **simple past tense** is used for actions completed at a specific time in the past.

SIMPLE PRESENT

Every May, she *plans* next year's marketing strategy.

Tips   ## LEARNING in COLLEGE

Checking Verb Tenses

Is the time frame of your paper predominantly present, past, or future? Keep this time frame in mind as you edit, and you will be better able to see and solve problems with the accuracy and consistency of your verb tenses.

SIMPLE PAST

In the early morning hours before the office opened, she *planned* her marketing strategy.

2. The simple future tense

The **simple future tense** takes *will* plus the verb. It is used for actions that have not yet begun.

SIMPLE FUTURE

In May, I *will plan* next year's marketing strategy.

3. Perfect tenses

The **perfect tenses** take a form of *have (has, had)* plus the past participle. They are used to indicate actions that were or will be completed by the time of another action or a specific time. (*For more on the past participle, see p. 486.*)

PRESENT PERFECT

She *has* already *planned* next year's marketing strategy.

PAST PERFECT

By the time she resigned, Mary *had* already *planned* next year's marketing strategy.

FUTURE PERFECT

By May 31, she *will have planned* next year's marketing strategy.

When the verb in the past perfect is irregular, be sure to use the proper form of the past participle.

➤ **By the time the week was over, both plants had ~~grew~~** *grown*

five inches.

4. Progressive tenses

The **progressive tenses** take a form of *be (am, are, were)* plus the present participle. The progressive forms of the simple and perfect tenses are used to indicate ongoing action.

PRESENT PROGRESSIVE

She *is planning* next year's marketing strategy now.

PAST PROGRESSIVE

She *was planning* next year's marketing strategy when she started to look for another job.

FUTURE PROGRESSIVE

During the month of May, she *will be planning* next year's marketing strategy.

For MULTILINGUAL STUDENTS

When Not to Use the Progressive Tenses

Some verbs are not usually used in the progressive tenses, even when they relate to a continuous state or action. Typically, these verbs are about thoughts, preferences, and ownership.

>   *understood*
> I ~~was understanding~~ the lecture until the last
>
> ten minutes.

>   *wants*
> The manager ~~is wanting~~ the report by the end of the day.

>   *own*
> They ~~are owning~~ the house they are renovating.

5. Perfect progressive tenses   The **perfect progressive tenses** take *have* plus *be* plus the verb. These tenses indicate an action that takes place over a specific period of time. The present perfect progressive tense is used for actions that start in the past and continue to the present; the past and future perfect progressive tenses are used for actions that ended or will end at a specified time or before another action.

PRESENT PERFECT PROGRESSIVE

She *has been planning* next year's marketing strategy since the beginning of May.

PAST PERFECT PROGRESSIVE

She *had been planning* next year's marketing strategy when she was offered another job.

FUTURE PERFECT PROGRESSIVE

By May 18, she *will have been planning* next year's marketing strategy for more than two weeks.

54g Use the past perfect tense to indicate an action completed at a specific time or before another event.

When a past event was ongoing but ended before a particular time or another past event, use the past perfect rather than the simple past.

➤ **Before the Johnstown Flood occurred in 1889, people**

           had

  in the area expressed their concern about the safety of
              ^

  the dam on the Conemaugh River.

    People expressed their concern before the flood occurred.

If two past events happened simultaneously, however, use the simple past, not the past perfect.

➤ **When the Conemaugh flooded, many people in the area**

  ~~had~~ **lost their lives.**

CHARTING the TERRITORY

Reporting Research Findings

Although a written work may be seen as always present, research findings are thought of as having been collected at one time in the past. Use the past or present perfect tense to report the results of research:

                           responded

➤ **Three of the compounds (nos. 2, 3, and 6) ~~respond~~**
                                       ^

  positively by turning purple.

           has reviewed

➤ **Clegg (1990) ~~reviews~~ studies of workplace organization**
                 ^

  focused on struggles for control of the labor process.

54h Use the present tense for literary events, scientific facts, and introductions to quotations.

If the conventions of a discipline require you to state what your paper does, do so in the present, not the future, tense.

> ➤ In this paper, I *describe* the effects of increasing NaCl concentrations on the germination of radish seeds.

Here are some other special uses of the present tense:

- By convention, events in a novel, short story, poem, or other literary work are described in the present tense.

  > ➤ Even though Huck's journey down the river ~~was~~ *is* an
  >
  > escape from society, his relationship with Jim ~~was~~ *is* a
  >
  > form of community.

- Like events in a literary work, scientific facts are considered to be perpetually present, even though they were discovered in the past.

  > ➤ Mendel discovered that genes ~~had~~ *have* different forms,
  >
  > or alleles.

- The present tense is also used to introduce a quotation, paraphrase, or summary of someone else's writing.

  > ➤ William Julius Wilson ~~wrote~~ *writes* that "the disappearance
  >
  > of work has become a characteristic feature of the
  >
  > inner-city ghetto" (31).

54i Make sure infinitives and participles fit with the tense of the main verb.

Infinitives and participles are **verbals**—words formed from verbs that have various functions within a sentence. Verbals can form phrases by taking objects, modifiers, or complements. Because they express time, verbals need to fit with the main verb in a sentence.

1. Using the correct tense for infinitives

An **infinitive** has the word *to* plus the base verb (*to breathe, to sing, to dance*). The perfect form of the infinitive is *to have* plus the past participle (*to have breathed, to have sung, to have danced*). If the action of the infinitive happens at the same time as or after the action of the main verb, use the present tense.

➤ I hope *to sing and dance* on Broadway next summer.

If the action of the infinitive happened before the action of the main verb, use the perfect form.

➤ My talented mother would like *to have sung and danced* on Broadway as a young woman, but she never had the chance.

2. Using the correct tense for participles that are part of phrases

Participial phrases can begin with the present participle (*breathing, dancing, singing*), the present perfect participle (*having breathed, having danced, having sung*), or the past participle (*breathed, danced, sung*). If the action of the participle happens simultaneously with the action of the sentence's verb, use the present participle.

➤ *Singing one hour a day together,* the chorus developed perfect harmony.

If the action of the participle happened before the action of the main verb, use the present perfect or past participle form.

➤ *Having breathed* the air of New York, I exulted in the possibilities for my life in the city.

➤ *Tinted* with a strange green light, the western sky looked threatening.

54j Use the subjunctive mood for wishes, requests, and conjecture.

The **mood** of a verb indicates the writer's attitude. Use the **indicative mood** to state or question facts, acts, and opinions (*Our collection is on display. Did you see it?*). Use the **imperative mood** for commands, directions, and entreaties. The subject of an imperative sentence is always *you,* but the *you* is usually understood, not written out (*Shut the door!*). Use the **subjunctive mood** to express a wish or a demand or to make a statement contrary to fact (*I wish I were a* *millionaire*). The mood that writers have the most trouble with is the subjunctive.

    Verbs in the subjunctive mood may be in the present tense, past tense, or perfect tense. Present tense subjunctive verbs do not change form to signal person or number. The only form used is the verb's base form: *accompany* or *be,* not *accompanies* or *am, are, is.* Also, the verb *be* has only one past tense form in the subjunctive mood: *were.*

1. Using the subjunctive mood to express a wish

WISH

If only I *were* more prepared for this test.

Note: In everyday conversation, most speakers use the indicative rather than the subjunctive when expressing wishes (*If only I was more prepared for this test*).

---

2. Using the subjunctive mood for requests, recommendations, and demands

Because requests, recommendations, and demands have not yet happened, they—like wishes—are expressed in the subjunctive mood. Words such as *ask, insist, recommend, request,* and *suggest* indicate the subjunctive mood; the verb in the *that* clause that follows should be in the subjunctive.

DEMAND

I insist that all applicants *find* their seats by 8:00 a.m.

3. Using the subjunctive in statements that are contrary to fact   Often such statements contain a subordinate clause that begins with *if:* the verb in the *if* clause should be in the subjunctive mood.

CONTRARY-TO-FACT STATEMENT

He would not be so irresponsible if his father *were* [not *was*] still alive.

Note: Some common expressions of conjecture are in the subjunctive mood, including *as it were, come rain or shine, far be it from me,* and *be that as it may.*

55 Problems with Pronouns

A **pronoun** (*he / him, it / its, they / their*) takes the place of a noun. The noun that the pronoun replaces is called its **antecedent.** In the following sentence, *snow* is the antecedent of the pronoun *it.*

www.mhhe.com/ awr
For information and exercises on pronouns, go to

Editing > Pronouns

➤ The *snow* fell all day long, and by nightfall *it* was three

feet deep.

Like nouns, pronouns are singular or plural.

SINGULAR   The *house* was dark and gloomy, and *it* sat in a

grove of tall cedars.

PLURAL   The *cars* swept by on the highway, all of *them*

doing more than sixty-five miles per hour.

A pronoun needs an antecedent to refer to and agree with, and a pronoun must match its antecedent in number (*plural / singular*) and gender (*he / his, she / her, it / its*). A pronoun must also be in a form, or case, that matches its function in the sentence.

For MULTILINGUAL STUDENTS

Nouns and Gender

In English, most nouns are neuter in gender. The exceptions are nouns that specifically name females or males, such as *woman, girl, sister, mother, man, boy, brother,* and *father,* and names like *Louis* and *Anna.*

The gender of a pronoun should match its antecedent, not the word it modifies.

➤ Penelope waited twenty years for *her* [not *his*] husband

Odysseus to return from Troy.

499

Pronoun Problems and Grammar Checkers

Do not rely on grammar checkers to alert you to problems in pronoun-antecedent agreement or pronoun reference. Some computer grammar checkers do reliably flag many errors in pronoun case, but by no means all. One grammar checker, for example, missed the case error in the following sentence: *Ford's son Edsel, who [should be whom] the auto magnate treated very cruelly, was a brilliant automotive designer. (See p. 510 for a discussion of the proper use of who and whom.)*

www.mhhe.com/
awr
For information
and exercises on
pronoun-antecedent
agreement, go to
Editing >
Pronoun-Antecedent
Agreement

55a   Make pronouns agree with their antecedents.

Problems with pronoun-antecedent agreement tend to occur when a pronoun's antecedent is an indefinite pronoun, a collective noun, or a compound noun. Problems may also occur when writers are trying to avoid the generic use of *he*.

1. Indefinite pronouns   **Indefinite pronouns** such as *someone, anybody,* and *nothing* refer to nonspecific people or things. They sometimes function as antecedents for other pronouns. Most indefinite pronouns are singular (*anybody, anyone, anything, each, either, everybody, everyone, everything, much, neither, nobody, none, no one, nothing, one, somebody, something*).

ALWAYS
SINGULAR   Did *either* of the boys lose *his* bicycle?

A few indefinite pronouns—*both, few, many,* and *several*—are plural.

ALWAYS
PLURAL   *Both* of the boys lost *their* bicycles.

The indefinite pronouns *all, any, more, most,* and *some* can be either singular or plural, depending on the noun to which the pronoun refers.

PLURAL   The students debated, *some* arguing that *their* positions on the issue were in the mainstream.

SINGULAR   The bread is on the counter, but *some* of *it* has already been eaten.

Problems arise when writers attempt to make indefinite pronouns agree with their antecedents without introducing gender bias. In the following sentence, for example, the writer chose to change the indefinite pronoun *none* to *all* instead of changing the plural pronoun *their* to a singular form. Why?

> *All*
> ~~None~~ of the great Romantic writers believed that their
> ^
>   *fell short of*
>   achievements ~~equaled~~ their aspirations.
>   ^

Replacing *their* in the original sentence with *his* would have made the sentence both untrue and biased: many women were writing and publishing during the Romantic Age. Changing *their* to *his or her* would avoid bias but sound awkward. Choosing an indefinite pronoun that can have a plural meaning (*all*) and revising the sentence is the best choice. An alternative would be to eliminate the indefinite pronoun altogether.

> The great Romantic writers believed that their
> achievements fell short of their aspirations.

2. Generic nouns

A **generic noun** represents anyone and everyone in a group—a typical doctor, the average voter. Because most groups consist of both males and females, using male pronouns to refer to generic nouns is usually sexist. To fix agreement problems with generic nouns, use one of the three options suggested in the box on page 502.

INCORRECT

A college *student* should have a mind of *their* own.

CHANGE TO PLURAL

College *students* should have minds of *their* own.

REWORD TO AVOID PRONOUN

A college student should have an independent point of view.

USE *HIS OR HER*

A college *student* should have a mind of *his or her* own.

IDENTIFY AND EDIT
Problems with Gender Bias and
Pronoun-Antecedent Agreement

agr

Try these three strategies for avoiding gender bias when an indefinite pronoun or generic noun is the antecedent in a sentence:

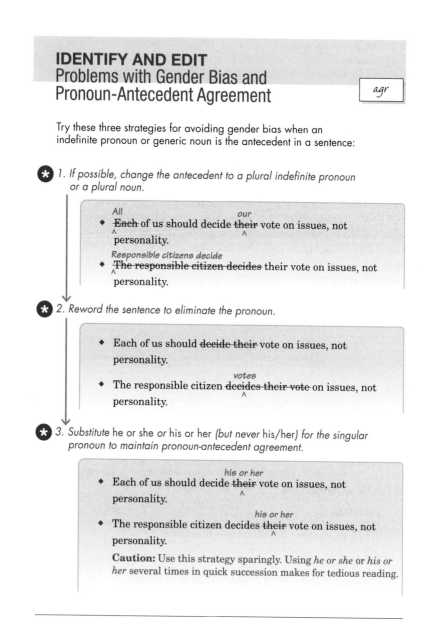

⭐ 1. If possible, change the antecedent to a plural indefinite pronoun or a plural noun.

> ◆ *All*
> ~~Each~~ of us should decide ~~their~~ *our* vote on issues, not personality.
>
> ◆ *Responsible citizens decide*
> ~~The responsible citizen decides~~ their vote on issues, not personality.

⭐ 2. Reword the sentence to eliminate the pronoun.

> ◆ Each of us should ~~decide their~~ vote on issues, not personality.
>
> ◆ The responsible citizen ~~decides their vote~~ *votes* on issues, not personality.

⭐ 3. Substitute he or she or his or her (but never his/her) for the singular pronoun to maintain pronoun-antecedent agreement.

> ◆ Each of us should decide ~~their~~ *his or her* vote on issues, not personality.
>
> ◆ The responsible citizen decides ~~their~~ *his or her* vote on issues, not personality.
>
> **Caution:** Use this strategy sparingly. Using *he or she* or *his or her* several times in quick succession makes for tedious reading.

3. Collective nouns

Collective nouns such as *team, family, jury, committee,* and *crowd* are treated as singular unless the people in the group are acting as individuals.

➤ **All together, the crowd surged through the palace gates,**

its
trampling over everything in ~~their~~ path.

The phrase *all together* indicates that this crowd is acting as a collection of individuals.

➤ **The committee left the conference room and returned to**

their
~~its~~ offices.

In this case, the members of the committee are acting as individuals: each is returning to an office.

If you are using a collective noun that has a plural meaning, consider adding a plural noun to clarify the meaning.

➤ **The *committee members* left the conference room and**

returned to *their* offices.

4. Compound antecedents
Compound antecedents joined by *and* are almost always plural.

➤ **To remove all traces of the crime, James put the book and**

their
the magnifying glass back in ~~its~~ place.

When a compound antecedent is joined by *or* or *nor,* the pronoun should agree with the closest part of the compound antecedent. If one part is singular and the other is plural, the sentence will be smoother and more effective if the plural antecedent is closest to the pronoun.

PLURAL   **Neither *the child nor the parents* shared *their* food.**

If the compound antecedent consists of a male and a female, however, the rule does not apply. Revise the sentence to avoid this situation.

and   *were late for their*   *s.*
➤ **~~Neither~~ José ~~nor~~ Laura ~~could make it to her~~ appointment**

~~on time.~~

> *Note:* When the two parts of the compound antecedent refer to the same person, or when the word *each* or *every* precedes the compound antecedent, use a singular pronoun.
>
> SINGULAR Being *a teacher and a mother* keeps *her* busy.
>
> SINGULAR *Every* poem and letter by Keats has *its* own special power.

www.mhhe.com/awr

For information and exercises on pronoun reference, go to

Editing >
Pronoun Reference

55b Make pronoun references clear.

If a pronoun does not clearly refer to a specific antecedent, readers can become confused. Two common problems are ambiguous references and implied references.

1. Ambiguous pronoun references
If a pronoun can refer to more than one noun in a sentence, the reference is ambiguous.

VAGUE The friendly banter between Hamlet and Horatio eventually provokes him to declare that his worldview has changed.

To clear up the ambiguity, eliminate the pronoun and use the appropriate noun.

CLEAR The friendly banter between Hamlet and Horatio eventually provokes Hamlet to declare that his worldview has changed.

Sometimes the ambiguous reference can be cleared up by rewriting the sentence.

VAGUE Jane Austen and Cassandra corresponded regularly when she was in London.

CLEAR When Jane Austen was in London, she corresponded regularly with Cassandra.

2. Implied pronoun references
The antecedent that a pronoun refers to must be present in the sentence, and it must be a noun or another pronoun, not a word that modifies a noun. Possessives and verbs cannot be antecedents.

> *his*   *Wilson*
> **In ~~Wilson's~~ essay "When Work Disappears," ~~he~~ proposes a**
>   ^   ^
>
> **four-point plan for the revitalization of blighted inner-city**
>
> **communities.**

Replacing *he* with *Wilson* gives the pronoun *his* an antecedent that is stated explicitly, not just implied. Note that in the revised sentence, the antecedent follows the pronoun.

> **Every weekday afternoon, my brothers skateboard home**
>   *their skateboards*
> **from school, and then they leave ~~them~~ in the driveway.**
>   ^

In the original sentence, *skateboard* is a verb, not a noun, and cannot act as a pronoun antecedent.

3. References for *this, that,* and *which*

The pronouns *this, that,* and *which* are often used to refer to ideas expressed in preceding sentences. To make the sentence containing the pronoun clearer, either change the pronoun to a specific noun or add a specific antecedent or clarifying noun.

> **As government funding for higher education decreases,**
>   *these higher costs*
> **tuition increases. Are we students supposed to accept ~~this~~**
>   ^
>
> **without protest?**

> **As government funding for higher education decreases,**
>
> **tuition increases. Are we students supposed to accept this**
> *situation*
> **without protest?**
> ^

4. References for *you, they,* and *it*

The pronouns *you, they,* and *it* should refer to definite, explicitly stated antecedents. If the antecedent is unclear, replace the pronoun with an appropriately specific noun, or rewrite the sentence to eliminate the pronoun.

>   *the government pays*
> **In some countries, such as Canada, ~~they pay~~ for such**
>   ^
>
> **medical procedures.**

> *students*
> According to college policy, ~~you~~ must have a permit to
>   ^
> park a car on campus.

> *The*
> ~~In the~~ textbook/ ~~it~~ states that borrowing to fund the
>   ^
> purchase of financial assets results in a double-counting
> of debt.

Note: You is not ambiguous when it is used to address the
reader: *Turn left when you reach the corner.*

Note: Writers sometimes use *one* as a generic pronoun. If you
use *one* in this way, follow one of the three strategies suggested
in the box on page 502 to avoid repeating the pronoun or introducing gender bias:

> *his or her*
> One should have a mind of ~~one's~~ own.
>   ^

The use of *one* as a pronoun usually seems pompous, however,
and is best avoided: *People should have minds of their own.*

55c Make your pronouns consistent within a sentence
or passage.

Keep the same point of view (first, second, or third person) and number (singular or plural) within a sentence or series of related sentences.

> Once you discover how easy it can be to download music,
>   *You*
> you will be hooked. ~~One~~ can easily find any type of music,
>   ^
>   *as well as*
> ~~and I have found~~ a number of sites that offer a good
>   ^
> selection.

(For more on confusing shifts, see Tab 9: Editing for Clarity, p. 413.)

55d Make pronoun cases match their function
(for example, *I* vs. *me*).

When a pronoun's form, or **case,** does not match its function in a sentence, readers will feel that something is wrong.

- Pronouns in the subjective case are used as subjects or subject complements: *I, you, he, she, it, we, they, who, whoever.*
- Pronouns in the objective case are used as objects of verbs or prepositions: *me, you, him, her, it, us, them, whom, whomever.*
- Pronouns in the possessive case show ownership: *my, mine, your, yours, his, hers, its, our, ours, their, theirs, whose*

1. Compound structures
Compound structures (words or phrases joined by *and, or,* or *nor*) can appear as subjects or objects. If you are not sure which form of a pronoun to use in a compound structure, treat the pronoun as the only subject or object, and note how the sentence sounds.

SUBJECT   Angela and ~~me~~ were cleaning up the kitchen.
                            I

If you treat the pronoun as the only subject, the original sentence is clearly wrong: *Me [was] cleaning up the kitchen.*

OBJECT   My parents waited for an answer from John
                  me
             and ~~I~~.

If you treat the pronoun as the only object, the original sentence is clearly wrong: *My parents waited for an explanation from I.*

Note: Do not substitute a reflexive pronoun for the pronoun you are unsure of: *Angela and I* [not *myself*] *were cleaning up the kitchen.*

---

2. Subject complements
A **subject complement** renames and specifies the sentence's subject. It follows a **linking verb**—a verb, often a form of *be,* that links the subject to its description or definition: *Children <u>are</u> innocent.*

IDENTIFY AND EDIT
Problems with Pronoun Case

case

Follow these steps to decide on the proper form of pronouns in compound structures:

 1. *Identify the compound structure (a pronoun and a noun or other pronoun joined by and, but, or, or nor) in the problem sentence.*

> compound structure
> PROBLEM SENTENCE [Her or her roommate] should call the campus technical support office and sign up for broadband Internet service.
>
> compound structure
> PROBLEM SENTENCE The director gave the leading roles to [my brother and I].

2. *Isolate the pronoun that you are unsure about, then read the sentence to yourself without the rest of the compound structure. If the result sounds wrong, change the case of the pronoun (subjective to objective, or vice versa), and read the sentence again.*

> PROBLEM SENTENCE [Her ~~or her roommate~~] should call the campus technical support office and sign up for broadband Internet service.
>
> *Her should call the campus technical support office* sounds wrong. The pronoun should be in the subjective case: *she.*
>
> PROBLEM SENTENCE The director gave the leading roles to [~~my brother and~~ I]
>
> *The director gave the leading roles to I* sounds wrong. The pronoun should be in the objective case: *me.*

3. *If necessary, correct the original sentence.*

> She
> ♦ ~~Her~~ or her roommate should call the campus technical
>   ^
>   support office and sign up for broadband Internet service.
>
>   me
> ♦ The director gave the leading roles to my brother and ~~I~~.
>   ^

SUBJECT   Mark's best friends are Jane and ~~me~~.

(I)

If you think the edited sentence sounds too awkward or formal, try switching the order to make the pronoun into the subject: *Jane and I are Mark's best friends.*

3. Appositives

Appositives are nouns or noun phrases that rename nouns or pronouns. They appear right after the word they rename and have the same function in the sentence that the word has.

SUBJECTIVE   The two weary travelers, Ramon and ~~me~~, finally

(I)

found shelter.

OBJECTIVE   The police arrested two protesters, Jane and ~~I~~.

(me)

4. *We* or *us*

When *we* or *us* comes before a noun, it has the same function in the sentence as the noun it precedes and renames.

SUBJECTIVE   ~~Us~~ students never get to decide such things.

(We)

OBJECTIVE   Things were looking desperate for ~~we~~ campers.

(us)

5. Comparisons with *than* or *as*

In comparisons, words are often left out of the sentence because the reader can guess what they would be. When a pronoun follows *than* or *as*, make sure you are using the correct form by mentally adding the missing word or words.

➤ Meg is quicker than she [is].

➤ We find ourselves remembering Maria as often as [we remember] her.

If a sentence with a comparison sounds too awkward or formal, add the missing words: *Meg is quicker than she is.*

6. Pronoun as the subject or the object of an infinitive

An infinitive has the word *to* plus the base verb (*to breathe, to sing, to dance*). Whether a pronoun functions as the subject or the object of an infinitive, it should be in the objective case.

subject   object

➤ We wanted our lawyer and *her* to defend *us* against this charge.

Note that in the example the subject of the infinitive is a compound noun. If a compound functioning as the subject or object of an infinitive has two pronouns, both should be in the objective case: *The nurse told her and me to go into the examining room.*

7. Noun or pronoun with an *-ing* noun (a gerund)

When a noun or pronoun appears before a **gerund** (an *-ing* verb form functioning as a noun), it should usually be treated as a possessive. Possessive nouns are formed by adding *'s* to singular nouns (*the teacher's desk*) or an apostrophe only (*'*) to plural nouns (*three teachers' rooms*). (*See Tab 11: Editing for Correctness, pp. 547–49.*)

> ➤ The ~~animals~~ fighting disturbed the entire neighborhood.
>   *animals'*

> ➤ Because of ~~them~~ screeching, no one could get any sleep.
>   *their*

Note: Possessive pronouns never contain an apostrophe and an *s*. Pronouns that appear with an apostrophe and an *s* are always part of a contraction. Be especially careful to use *its,* not *it's,* when the possessive form is called for: *The cat finally stopped its* [not *it's*] *screeching.*

55e Distinguish between *who* and *whom.*

The relative pronouns *who, whom, whoever,* and *whomever* are used to introduce dependent clauses and in questions. Their case depends on their function in the dependent clause or question.

- ▪ **Subjective:** *who, whoever*
- ▪ **Objective:** *whom, whomever*

1. Determining the pronoun's function in a clause   If the pronoun is functioning as a subject and is performing an action, use *who* or *whoever.* If the pronoun is the object of a verb or preposition, use *whom* or *whomever.*

> ➤ Henry Ford, *who* started the Ford Motor Company, was autocratic and stubborn.
>
> *Who,* which refers to *Henry Ford,* is performing an action in the dependent clause: starting a company.

> ➤ Ford's son Edsel, *whom* the auto magnate treated cruelly, was a brilliant automobile designer.
>
> *Whom,* which refers to *Edsel,* is the object of the verb *treated.* You can check the pronoun by changing the order within the clause: *The auto magnate treated whom* [*him*] *cruelly.*

2. Determining the pronoun's function in a question To choose the correct form for the pronoun, answer the question with a personal pronoun.

➤ ***Who* founded the General Motors Corporation?**

The answer could be *He founded it. He* is in the subjective case, so *who* is correct.

➤ ***Whom* did Chrysler turn to for leadership in the 1980s?**

The answer could be *It turned to him. Him* is in the objective case, so *whom* is correct.

56 Problems with Adjectives and Adverbs

Adjectives and **adverbs** are words that describe. Because they qualify the meanings of other words, we say that they *modify* them. Adjectives modify nouns and pronouns. Adverbs modify verbs, adjectives, and other adverbs.

www.mhhe.com/
awr
For information and
exercises on adjectives
and adverbs, go to

Editing >
Adjectives
and Adverbs

56a Use adverbs to modify verbs, adjectives, other adverbs, and whole clauses.

Adverbs tell where, when, why, how, how often, how much, or to what degree.

➤ The authenticity of the document is *hotly* contested.

➤ The water was *brilliant* blue and *icy* cold.

➤ Dickens mixed humor and pathos *better* than any other English writer after Shakespeare.

➤ *Consequently,* Dickens is still read by millions.

Adjectives, Adverbs, and Grammar Checkers

Computer grammar checkers are sensitive to some problems with adjectives and adverbs but miss far more than they catch. A grammar checker failed to flag the error in the following sentences (and, indeed, in most of the problem sentences throughout this chapter): *The price took a suddenly plunge* [should be *sudden*] and *The price plunged sudden* [should be *suddenly*].

56b Use adjectives to modify nouns or as subject complements.

Adjectives modify nouns and pronouns; they do not modify any other kind of word. Adjectives tell what kind or how many and may come before or after the noun or pronoun they modify.

➤ *Ominous gray* clouds loomed over the lake.

➤ The *looming* clouds, *ominous* and *gray,* frightened the children.

Some proper nouns have adjective forms. Proper adjectives, like the proper nouns they are derived from, are capitalized: *Victoria / Victorian, Britain / British, America / American, Shakespeare / Shakespearean.*

In some cases, a noun is used as an adjective without a change in form:

➤ *Cigarette* smoking harms the lungs and is banned in offices.

Occasionally, descriptive adjectives function as if they were nouns:

➤ The *unemployed* should not be equated with the *lazy.*

For MULTILINGUAL STUDENTS

Using Adjectives

In English, adjectives do not change form to agree with plural nouns or pronouns.

> The recipe calls for one green pepper and two ~~reds~~ ^{red}
>
> peppers.

(For more about adjectives in English, including rules about ordering adjectives when several act together to modify the same word, see Tab 12: Basic Grammar Review, pp. 612–14.)

1. Avoiding incorrect use of adjectives   In common speech, we sometimes treat adjectives as adverbs. In writing, this informal usage should be avoided.

> He hit that ball ~~real good.~~ ^{really well.}

   Both *real* and *good* are adjectives, but they are used as adverbs in the original sentence, with *real* modifying *good* and *good* modifying the verb *hit*.

Note that *well* can function as an adjective and subject complement with a linking verb to describe a person's health.

> After the treatment, the patient felt *well* again.

> She ~~sure~~ ^{certainly} made me work hard for my grade.

   In the original sentence, the adjective *sure* tries to do the work of an adverb modifying the verb *made*.

2. Using adjectives after linking verbs

Linking verbs connect the subject of a sentence to its description. The most common linking verb is *be*. Descriptive adjectives that modify a sentence's subject but appear after a linking verb are called **subject complements**.

➤ During the winter, both Emily and Anne *were sick.*

➤ The road *is long, winding,* and *dangerous.*

Linking verbs are related to states of being and the five senses: *appear, become, feel, grow, look, smell, sound,* and *taste.* Verbs related to the senses can be either linking or action verbs, depending on the meaning of the sentence.

> **ADJECTIVE** The dog smelled *bad.*

Bad modifies the noun *dog.* The sentence indicates that the dog needed a bath.

> **ADVERB** The dog smelled *badly.*

Badly modifies the verb *smelled,* an action verb in this sentence. The sentence indicates that the dog had lost its sense of smell.

3. Recognizing that some adjectives and adverbs are spelled alike

In most instances, *-ly* endings indicate adverbs; however, words with *-ly* endings can sometimes be adjectives (*the lovely girl*). In standard English, many adverbs do not require the *-ly* ending, and some words are both adjectives and adverbs: *fast, only, hard, right,* and *straight.* Note that *right* also has an *-ly* form as an adverb: *rightly.* When in doubt, consult a dictionary.

56c Use positive, comparative, and superlative adjectives and adverbs correctly.

Most adjectives and adverbs have three forms: positive (*dumb*), comparative (*dumber*), and superlative (*dumbest*). The simplest form of the adjective is the positive form.

1. Distinguishing between comparatives and superlatives

Use the comparative form to compare two things and the superlative form to compare three or more things.

➤ In total area, New York is a *larger* state than Pennsylvania.

➤ Texas is the *largest* state in the Southwest.

2. Learning when to use -er/-est endings and when to use more/most, or less/least

To form comparatives and superlatives of short adjectives, add the suffixes *-er* and *-est* (*brighter/brightest*). With longer adjectives (three or more syllables), use *more* or *less* and *most* or *least* (*more danger-ous*/*most dangerous*).

➤ Mercury is the ~~most near~~ planet to the sun.
               nearest

A few short adverbs have *-er* and *-est* endings in their comparative and superlative forms (*harder*/*hardest*). Most adverbs, however, including all adverbs that end in *-ly*, use *more* and *most* in their comparative and superlative forms. Negative comparatives and superlatives are formed with *less* and *least: less funny*/*least funny*.

➤ She sings *more loudly* than we expected.

Two common adjectives—*good* and *bad*—form the comparative and superlative in an irregular way: *good, better, best* and *bad, worse, worst.*

➤ He felt ~~badder~~ as his illness progressed.
         worse

These and other irregular adjectives and adverbs are listed in the box on page 516. When in doubt, consult a dictionary.

3. Watching out for double comparatives and superlatives
Use either an *-er* or an *-est* ending or *more*/*most* to form the comparative or superlative, as appropriate; do not use both.

➤ Since World War II, Britain has been the ~~most~~ closest ally

of the United States.

4. Recognizing concepts that cannot be compared
Do not use comparative or superlative forms with adjectives such as *unique, infinite, impossible, perfect, round, square,* and *destroyed.* These concepts are *absolutes.* If something is unique, for example, it is the only one of its kind, making comparison impossible.

➤ You will never find ~~a more unique~~ restaurant ~~than~~ this
              another   *like*

one.

5. Making sure your comparison is complete
Unless the context of your sentence makes the comparison clear, be sure to include both items you are comparing.

➤ Charles Dickens had more popular successes.
                   than any other British writer of his time

COMPARISON in ADJECTIVES and ADVERBS

Examples of Regular and Irregular Forms

Regular adjectives	Positive	Comparative	Superlative
One-syllable adjectives	red	redder, less red	reddest, least red
Two-syllable adjectives ending in –y	lonely	lonelier, less lonely	loneliest, least lonely
Other adjectives of two or more syllables	famous	more/less famous	most/least famous
Regular adverbs			
One-syllable	hard	harder, less hard	hardest, least hard
Most other adverbs	truthfully	more/less truthfully	most/least truthfully
Irregular adjectives			
	good	better	best
	bad	worse	worst
	little	less, littler	least, littlest
	many	more	most
	much	more	most
	some	more	most
Irregular adverbs			
	badly	worse	worst
	well	better	best

(*For more on making comparisons complete, see Tab 9, Editing for Clarity, pp. 408–9.*)

56d Avoid double negatives.

The words *no, not,* and *never* can modify the meaning of nouns and pronouns as well as other sentence elements.

NOUN	You are *no* friend of mine.
ADJECTIVE	The red house was *not* large.
VERB	He *never* ran in a marathon.

However, it takes only one negative word to change the meaning of a sentence from positive to negative. When two negatives are used together, they cancel each other out, resulting in a positive meaning. Unless you want your sentence to have a positive meaning (*I am not unaware of your feelings in this matter*), edit by changing or eliminating one of the negative words.

➤ They don't have <del>no</del> *any* reason to go there.

➤ He <del>can't</del> *can* hardly do that assignment.

Note that *hardly* has a negative meaning and cannot be used with *no, not,* or *never.*

The great twelfth century inventor al-Jazari designed many innovative mechanical devices. This plan for a water-operated automaton documents the engineering behind one invention's design; each working part relies on the precise placement of others.

It wasn't a matter of rewriting but simply of tightening up all the bolts.

—MARGUERITE YOURCENAR

Editing
for Correctness

Punctuation, Mechanics, and Spelling

Styles within Disciplines

The rules for capitalizing, abbreviating, and italicizing terms, as well as conventions for using numbers and hyphens, can vary from one course or discipline to another. If you are not sure about the conventions for a discipline, see what rules your course textbook follows. In particular, look for answers to these questions:

- Does the text use numerals or words for numbers under one hundred? Under ten?
- What abbreviations appear throughout the text?
- Does the book include a list of abbreviations for technical terms, as many books in the natural and applied sciences do?

If you cannot figure out the accepted practice from your texts, ask your instructor for help, or use the general rules presented in this book. You might also consult a style manual such as the *MLA Handbook for Writers of Research Papers,* sixth edition, used for literature, composition, and other humanities disciplines, or the *Publication Manual of the American Psychological Association,* fifth edition, used for the social sciences, such as psychology and sociology.

57 Commas

COMMON USES OF THE COMMA

You may have been told that commas are used to mark pauses, but that is not an accurate general principle. To clarify meaning, commas are used to set off sentence elements and in other conventional ways.

For MULTILINGUAL STUDENTS

Dealing with Punctuation, Mechanics, and Spelling

It is a challenge to write a thoughtful, well-organized paper and at the same time follow every rule of punctuation, mechanics, and spelling. To improve the accuracy of your paper, try going through an extra draft or two.

When you write your first draft, pay close attention to the content and organization of your paper, but do not focus on problems with punctuation, mechanics, and spelling. When you are satisfied that the content is sound, the writing is clear (*see Tab 9*), and your sentences are grammatically correct (*see Tab 10*), edit for correct punctuation, mechanics, and spelling.

Next, show your edited draft to a native speaker of English, and ask that person to read it and circle anything that does not seem right. When you get the paper back, try making the corrections yourself. If you do not understand why something has been circled, ask the reader to explain what is wrong and suggest possible solutions, or ask for help from a tutor in your campus writing center. Then prepare the final copy and review it one more time before handing it in.

57a Use a comma after an introductory word group that is *not* the subject of the sentence.

www.mhhe.com/awr
For information and exercises on commas, go to
Editing > Commas

Like an overture, an introductory word group must be distinct from, yet clearly attached to, what follows. A comma both attaches an introductory word, phrase, or clause to and distinguishes it from the rest of the sentence.

➤ **Finally, the car careened to the right, endangering passers-by.**

➤ **Reflecting on her life experiences, Washburn attributed her successes to her own efforts.**

➤ **Until he noticed the handprint on the wall, the detective was frustrated by the lack of clues.**

> *Note:* When the introductory phrase is less than five words long and there is no danger of confusion without a comma, the comma can be omitted.
>
> ➤ **For several hours we rode on in silence.**

Do not add a comma after a word group that functions as the subject of the sentence. Be especially careful with word groups that begin with *-ing* words.

➤ **Persuading constituents/ is one of a politician's most**

    important tasks.

Commas and Grammar Checkers

Because many decisions about comma use involve context and judgment calls, computer grammar checkers are of very limited value in helping you spot errors in your use of commas. They usually will not highlight missing commas following introductory elements or between independent clauses joined by a coordinating conjunction such as *and,* and they cannot decide whether a sentence element is essential or nonessential. Rely on your own judgment, not a grammar checker, to apply these rules and make these decisions.

57b Use commas between items in a series.

A comma should appear after each item in a series.

➤ **Three industries that have been important to New**

    England are shipbuilding, tourism, and commercial

    fishing.

Commas clarify which items are part of the series. In the following example, the third comma clarifies that the hikers are packing lunch *and* snacks, not chocolate and trail mix for lunch.

CHARTING the TERRITORY

Commas in Journalism

If you are writing for a journalism course, you may be required to leave out the final comma that precedes *and* in a series, just as magazines and newspapers sometimes do.

CONFUSING	For the hiking trip, we needed to pack lunch, chocolate and trail mix.
CLEAR	For the hiking trip, we needed to pack lunch, chocolate, and trail mix.

57c Use a comma in front of a coordinating conjunction (such as *and* or *but*) that joins two independent clauses.

When a coordinating conjunction (*and, but, for, nor, or, so, yet*) is used to join clauses that could each stand alone as a sentence, put a comma before the coordinating conjunction.

➤ **Injuries were so frequent that he began to worry, and his**
  ^

   style of play became more cautious.

If the word groups you are joining are not independent clauses, do not add a comma. (See *57m on p. 537.*)

> *Note:* If you are joining two short clauses, you may leave out the comma unless it is needed for clarity.
>
> ➤ **The running back caught the ball and the fans cheered.**

57d Add a comma between coordinate adjectives, unless they are joined by *and,* but do not separate cumulative adjectives with a comma.

Use a comma between **coordinate** adjectives that precede a noun and modify it independently (*a brave, intelligent, persistent woman*). Adjectives are coordinate if they can be joined by *and* (brave *and* intelligent *and* persistent) or if their order can be changed (*a persistent, brave, intelligent woman*).

➤ **This brave, intelligent, persistent woman was the first**

  female to earn a Ph.D. in psychology.

If you cannot add *and* between the adjectives or change their order, they are **cumulative,** with each one modifying the ones that follow it, and should not be separated with a comma or commas.

➤ **Andrea Boccelli, the world-famous Italian tenor, has performed in concerts and operas.**

   World-famous modifies *Italian tenor,* not just the noun *tenor.* You could not add *and* between the adjectives (world-famous *and* Italian tenor) or change their order (*Italian world-famous tenor*).

57e Use commas to set off nonessential additions to a sentence, but do not set off essential words or word groups with commas.

Nonessential, or **nonrestrictive,** words, phrases, and clauses add information to a sentence but are not required for its basic meaning to be understood. Nonrestrictive additions are set off with commas.

NONRESTRICTIVE

Mary Shelley's best-known novel, *Frankenstein or the*

Modern Prometheus, was first published in 1818.

   The sentence would have the same basic meaning without the title (*Mary Shelley's best-known novel was first published in 1818*).

Restrictive words, phrases, and clauses are essential to a sentence because they identify exactly who or what the writer is talking about. Restrictive additions are not set off with commas.

IDENTIFY AND EDIT
Commas with Coordinate Adjectives

Follow these steps if you have trouble determining whether commas should separate two or more adjectives that precede a noun:

1. *Identify the adjectives.*

> PROBLEM
> SENTENCE
> Ann is an [excellent art] teacher and a [caring generous] mentor.
>
> Note that nouns such as *art* can also be used as adjectives.

2. *Try changing the order of the adjectives or putting the word* and *between them. Then read the adjectives and noun to yourself. How do they sound?*

> PROBLEM
> SENTENCE
> Ann is an [art excellent] teacher and a [generous caring] mentor.
>
> We could say that Ann is a generous caring mentor, but it would be awkward to say that she is an art excellent teacher.

> PROBLEM
> SENTENCE
> Ann is an [excellent and art] teacher and a [caring and generous] mentor.
>
> We could say that Ann is a caring and generous mentor, but it would be awkward to say that she is an excellent and art teacher.

3. *If the phrase sounds wrong, the adjectives are cumulative and don't need a comma between them. If the phrase sounds right, the adjectives are coordinate and require a comma. If need be, correct the original sentence.*

> Ann is an excellent art teacher and a caring, generous mentor.
>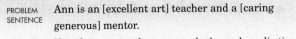
> ᴧ

RESTRICTIVE

Mary Shelley's novel *Frankenstein or the Modern Prometheus* was first published in 1818.

Without the title, the reader would not know which novel the sentence is referring to, so *Frankenstein or the Modern Prometheus* is restrictive.

Often, the context determines whether to enclose a word, phrase, or clause with commas. In the following examples, notice how a preceding sentence can affect the meaning and determine whether commas are needed:

> ➤ **Two customers with angry looks on their faces approached the check-out counter. The customers, demanding a refund, lined up by the register.**

> ➤ **The store opened at the usual time. The customers demanding a refund lined up by the register.**

Three types of additions to sentences often cause problems: adjective clauses, adjective phrases, and appositives.

1. Adjective clauses

Adjective clauses include a subject and verb, but they do not function independently. They begin with a relative pronoun or an adverb—*who, whom, whose, which, that, where,* or *when*—and modify a noun or pronoun within the sentence by telling *how many, what kind,* or *which one.* Adjective clauses can be either nonrestrictive or restrictive.

NONRESTRICTIVE

With his tale of Odysseus, *whose journey can be traced on modern maps,* Homer brought accounts of alien and strange creatures to the ancient Greeks.

RESTRICTIVE

The contestant *whom he most wanted to beat* was his father.

Note: Use *that* only with restrictive clauses. *Which* can introduce either restrictive or nonrestrictive clauses. Some writers prefer to use *which* only with nonrestrictive clauses.

---

2. Adjective phrases

Like an adjective clause, an adjective phrase also modifies a noun or pronoun in a sentence. Adjective phrases begin with a preposition (for example, *with, by, at,* or *for*) or a verbal (a word formed from a verb that can have various functions within a sentence). Adjective phrases can be either nonrestrictive or restrictive.

IDENTIFY AND EDIT
Commas with Nonrestrictive Words
or Word Groups

Follow these steps if you have trouble deciding whether a
word or word group should be set off with a comma or commas:

✱ 1. *Identify the word or word group that may need to be set off with commas.
Pay special attention to words that appear between the subject and verb.*

> PROBLEM
> SENTENCE
>
> subj
> Dorothy Parker [a member of the famous Algonquin
> verb
> Round Table] wrote humorous verse as well as short
> stories.
>
> PROBLEM
> SENTENCE
>
> subj   verb
> Her poem ["One Perfect Rose"] is a lament about a
> well-intentioned gift that falls short.

✱ 2. *Read the sentence to yourself without the word or word group. Does the
basic meaning stay the same, or does it change? Can you tell what
person, place, or thing the sentence is about?*

> SENTENCE
> WITHOUT
> THE WORD
> GROUP
>
> Dorothy Parker wrote humorous verse as well as
> short stories.
>
> The subject of the sentence is identified by name, and the
> basic meaning of the sentence does not change.
>
> SENTENCE
> WITHOUT
> THE WORD
> GROUP
>
> Her poem is a lament about a well-intentioned gift
> that falls short.
>
> Without the words "One Perfect Rose," we cannot tell what
> poem the sentence is describing.

✱ 3. *If the meaning of the sentence stays the same without the word or word
group, set it off with commas. If the meaning changes, the word or word
group should not be set off with commas.*

> ◆ Dorothy Parker, a member of the famous Algonquin Round
> Table, wrote humorous verse as well as short stories.
>
> ◆ Her poem "One Perfect Rose" is a lament about a well-
> intentioned gift that falls short.
>
> The sentence is correct. Commas are not needed to enclose "One
> Perfect Rose."

NONRESTRICTIVE

Some people, *by their faith in human nature or their general good will,* bring out the best in others.

The phrase does not specify which people are being discussed. The sentence would have the same meaning without it (*Some people bring out the best in others*).

RESTRICTIVE

People *fighting passionately for their rights* can inspire others to join a cause.

The phrase indicates which people the writer is talking about and therefore is restrictive. It is not set off with commas.

3. Appositives

Appositives are nouns or noun phrases that rename nouns or pronouns and appear right after the word they rename.

NONRESTRICTIVE

One researcher, *the widely respected R. S. Smith,* has shown that a child's performance on IQ tests can be very inconsistent.

Because the word *one* already restricts the word *researcher,* the researcher's name is not essential to the meaning of the sentence.

RESTRICTIVE

The researcher *R. S. Smith* has shown that a child's performance on IQ tests is not reliable.

The name *R. S. Smith* tells readers which researcher is meant.

57f Use a comma or commas with transitional expressions, parenthetical expressions, contrasting comments, and absolute phrases.

1. Transitional expressions

Transitional expressions show the relationship between ideas in a sentence. Conjunctive adverbs (*however, therefore, moreover*) and other transitional phrases (*for example, on the other hand*) are usually set off by commas when used at the beginning, in the middle, or at the end of a sentence. (*For a list of transitional expressions, see Tab 10: Editing for Grammar Conventions, p. 474.*)

➤ Brian Wilson, for example, was unable to cope with the
   pressures of touring with the Beach Boys.

➤ As a matter of fact, he had a nervous breakdown shortly
   after a tour.

➤ He is still considered one of the most important figures in
   rock and roll, however.

When a transitional expression connects two independent clauses, use a semicolon before and a comma after it.

➤ The Beatles were a phenomenon when they toured the
   United States in 1964; subsequently, they became the most
   successful rock band of all time.

Note: Short expressions such as *also, at least, certainly, instead, of course, then, perhaps,* and *therefore* do not always need to be set off with commas.

➤ I found my notes and *also* got my story in on time.

---

2. Parenthetical expressions

Parenthetical expressions are like whispered asides or a shrug in a conversation. The information they provide is relatively insignificant and could easily be left out. Therefore, they are set off with a comma or commas.

➤ Human cloning, so they say, will be possible within a decade.

➤ The experiments would take a couple of weeks, more or less.

3. Contrasting comments

Contrasting comments beginning with words such as *not, unlike,* or *in contrast to* should be set off with commas.

➤ As an actor, Adam Sandler is a talented comedian, not a

tragedian.

➤ Comedy, unlike tragedy, often has trouble gaining respect

from critics.

4. Absolute phrases

Absolute phrases usually include a noun (*sunlight*) followed by a participle (*shining*) and are used to modify whole sentences.

➤ The snake slithered through the tall grass, the sunlight

shining now and then on its green skin.

57g Use a comma or commas to set off words of direct address, *yes* and *no*, mild interjections, and tag questions.

Words that interrupt a sentence are set off by commas because they are not essential to the sentence's meaning.

➤ We have finished this project, Mr. Smith, without any

help from your foundation.

➤ Yes, I will meet you at noon.

➤ Of course, if you think that's what we should do, then

we'll do it.

➤ We can do better, don't you think?

57h Use a comma or commas to separate a direct quotation from the rest of the sentence.

Commas are used with quotation marks to set off what the source of the quotation says from the words identifying the source. (*See Chapter 61, pp. 553–61, for more on quotation marks.*)

➤ Irving Howe declares, "Whitman is quite realistic about

the place of the self in an urban world" (261).

➤ "Whitman is quite realistic about the place of the self

in an urban world," declares Irving Howe (261).

Note that the comma appears inside the closing quotation mark.

If the quoted sentence is interrupted, use commas to set off the interrupting words.

➤ "When we interpret a poem," DiYanni says, "we explain

it to ourselves in order to understand it."

If you are quoting more than one sentence and interrupting the quotation between sentences, the interrupting words should end with a period.

➤ "But it is not possible to give to each department an

equal power of self defense," James Madison writes in

The Federalist No. 51. "In republican government the

legislative authority, necessarily, predominates."

Note: A comma is not needed to separate an indirect quotation or a paraphrase from the words that identify its source. It is also not needed when a direct quotation is integrated into your sentence.

➤ Irving Howe notes/ that Whitman realistically depicts the

urban self as free to wander (261).

➤ Stanley Fish maintains that teaching content/ "is a lure

and a delusion."

57i Use commas with parts of dates, letters, and addresses, with people's titles, and in numbers.

1. Dates
Use paired commas in dates when the month, day, and year are included. Do not use commas when the day of the month is omitted or when the day appears before the month.

➤ **On March 4, 1931, she traveled to New York.**

➤ **She traveled to New York in March 1931.**

➤ **She traveled to New York on 4 March 1931.**

2. Parts of letters
Use a comma before the greeting in an informal letter and following the closing in any type of letter.

➤ **Dear Martha,   Sincerely yours,**

Note: In a business letter, use a colon following the greeting.

---

3. Addresses
Use commas to set off the parts of an address or the name of a state, but do not use a comma preceding a zip code.

➤ **He lived at 1400 Crabgrass Lane, Garrison, New York.**

➤ **At Cleveland, Ohio, the river changes direction.**

➤ **Here is my address for the summer: 63 Oceanside Drive, Apt. 2A, Surf City, New Jersey 06106.**

4. People's titles or degrees
Put a comma between the person's name and the title or degree when it comes after the name, followed by another comma.

➤ **Luis Mendez, MD, gave her the green light to resume her exercise regimen.**

5. Numbers
When a number has more than four digits, use commas to mark off the numerals by groups of three, beginning at the right.

➤ **Andrew Jackson received 647,276 votes in the 1828 election.**

If the number is four digits long, the comma is not required.

➤ **The survey had 1856 [or 1,856] respondents.**

Exceptions: Street numbers, zip codes, telephone numbers, page numbers (p. 2304), and years (1828) do not include commas.

For MULTILINGUAL STUDENTS

Long Numbers

In some other languages, periods, not commas, are used to mark off numerals by hundreds. However, in American English, periods are used for decimals only; commas are used in long numbers.

57j Use a comma to take the place of an omitted word or phrase or to prevent misreading.

When a writer omits one or more words from a sentence to create a special effect, a comma is often needed to make the meaning of the sentence clear for readers.

➤ **Under the tree he found his puppy, and under the car,**

his cat.

The second comma substitutes for the phrase *he found.*

Commas are also used to keep readers from misunderstanding a writer's meaning when words are repeated or might be misread.

➤ **Many birds that sing, sing early in the morning, before the**

sun rises.

➤ **Any offbeat items that can be, are sold at auction sites**

on the Web.

COMMON MISUSES OF THE COMMA

A comma used incorrectly can confuse readers. Commas should *not* be used in the following situations.

57k   Do not use commas to separate major elements in an independent clause.

Do not use a comma to separate a subject from a verb, a verb from its object, or a preposition from its object.

➤   **Reflecting on one's life,/ is necessary for emotional growth.**

The subject, *reflecting,* should not be separated from the verb, *is.*

➤   **Washburn decided,/ that her own efforts were key to**

   her success.

The verb *decided* should not be separated from its direct object, the subordinate clause *that her own efforts were key to her success.*

➤   **Although he is a famous actor he is in,/ emotional limbo.**

> *Note:* If a nonessential phrase appears between the subject and verb, it should be set off with a pair of commas (*see 57e on p. 526*).

57l   Do not add a comma before the first or after the final item in a series.

Use commas to separate items in a series but never before or after the series.

➤   **Americans work longer hours than,/ German, French, or**

   British workers,/ are expected to work.

> *Note:* Commas should never be used after *such as* or *like* (*see p. 539*).

57m Do not use commas to separate compound word groups unless they are independent clauses.

A comma should not be used between word groups joined with a coordinating conjunction such as *and* unless they are both full sentences.

➤ **Injuries were so frequent that he became worried,/ and**

started to play more cautiously.

Here, *and* joins two verbs (*became* and *started*), not two independent clauses.

➤ **He is worried that injuries are more frequent,/ and that**

he will have to play more cautiously to avoid them.

Here, *and* joins two subordinate clauses—both beginning with the word *that*—not two independent clauses.

57n Do not use commas to set off restrictive modifiers, appositives, or slightly parenthetical words or phrases.

If a word, phrase, or clause in a sentence is necessary to identify the noun or pronoun that precedes it, it is **restrictive** and should not be set off with commas. (*For more on restrictive and nonrestrictive elements, see pp. 526–30.*)

➤ **The applicants *who had studied for the admissions test* were restless and eager for the exam to begin.**

Because only those applicants who had studied were eager for the test to begin, the clause *who had studied for the admissions test* is restrictive and should not be set off with commas.

1. Appositives identifying nouns and pronouns
An **appositive** is a noun or noun phrase that renames a noun or pronoun and appears right after the word it renames.

➤ **The director,/ Michael Curtiz,/ was responsible for many**

great films in the 1930s and 1940s, including *Casablanca*.

The name *Michael Curtiz* identifies the director for readers.

2. Concluding adverb clauses

Adverb clauses beginning with *after, as soon as, before, because, if, since, unless, until,* and *when* are usually essential to a sentence's meaning.

RESTRICTIVE

I am eager to test the children's IQ again *because significant variations in a child's test score indicate that the test itself may be flawed.*

Clauses beginning with *although, even though, though,* and *whereas* present a contrasting thought and are usually nonrestrictive.

NONRESTRICTIVE

IQ tests can be useful indicators of a child's abilities, *although they should not be taken as the definitive measurement of a child's intelligence.*

> *Note:* An adverb clause that appears at the beginning of a sentence is an introductory element and is usually followed by a comma: *Until we meet, I'm continuing my work on the budget* (see pp. 523–24).

3. Words and phrases that are slightly parenthetical

Commas should be used for most parenthetical expressions (*see p. 531*). However, if setting off a brief parenthetical remark with commas would draw too much attention to the remark and interrupt the flow of the sentence, the commas can be left out.

➤ Science is *basically* the last frontier.

57o Watch out for and correct other common errors in using the comma.

- **Between cumulative adjectives:** Do not use a comma with **cumulative adjectives,** adjectives that cannot be reversed or joined with *and. (For more on cumulative adjectives, see p. 526.)*

  ➤ Three/ well-known/ American writers visited the

  artist's studio.

  You would not write *three American well-known writers.*

- **Between adjectives and nouns:**
  - ➤ An art review by a celebrated, powerful, writer would be guaranteed publication.

- **Between adverbs and adjectives:**
  - ➤ The artist's studio was a delightfully, chaotic environment, with canvases on every surface and spilled paints in a fiesta of color.

- **Between a noun and participle in an absolute phrase:**
  - ➤ My favorite singer, having lost the contest, I stopped paying attention.

- **After coordinating conjunctions** (*and, but, or, nor, for, so, yet*):
  - ➤ The *duomo* in Siena was begun in the thirteenth century, and, it was used as a model for other Italian cathedrals.

- **After *although, such as,* or *like:***
  - ➤ Stage designers can achieve many unusual effects, such as, the helicopter that landed in *Miss Saigon*.

- **Before *than:***
  - ➤ An appointment to the Supreme Court has more long-range consequences, than any other decision a President makes.

- **Before a parenthesis:**
  - ➤ When they occupy an office cubicle, (a recent invention), workers need to be especially considerate of their neighbors.

- **With a question mark or an exclamation point that ends a quotation** (*also see Chapter 61, p. 558*):
  - ➤ "Where are my glasses?," she asked in a panic.

58 Semicolons

Semicolons are used to join ideas that are closely related and grammatically equivalent. Usually, there must be a full sentence (independent clause) on each side of the semicolon.

www.mhhe.com/
awr
For information
and exercises on
semicolons, go to

Editing >
Semicolons

Semicolons and Grammar Checkers

Grammar checker programs will catch some comma splices that can be corrected by adding a semicolon between the two clauses. They will also catch some incorrect uses of the semicolon. They will not tell you when a semicolon *could* be used for clarity, however, nor will they tell you if the semicolon is the best choice. Rely on your own judgment, not the grammar checker, when deciding whether to add a semicolon to a sentence.

58a Use a semicolon to join independent clauses.

A semicolon should be used to join two related independent clauses when they are not joined by a comma and a coordinating conjunction (*and, but, or, nor, for, so, yet*). If readers are able to see the relationship between the two without the help of a coordinating conjunction, a semicolon is effective.

➤ **Before 8000 BC wheat was not the luxuriant plant it is**

today; it was merely a wild grass that spread throughout

the Middle East.

Sometimes, the close relationship is a contrast.

➤ **Philip had completed the assignment; Lucy had not.**

> *Note:* When a semicolon appears next to a quotation mark, it is always placed outside of the quotation mark: *My doctor advised me to "get plenty of rest"; my supervisor had other ideas.*

An occasional semicolon adds variety to your writing. Too many semicolons can make your writing seem monotonous, however. If you have used three or more semicolons in a paragraph, you should edit your sentences to eliminate most of them.

Note: If a comma is used between two clauses without a coordinating conjunction, the sentence is a comma splice, a serious error. One way to correct a comma splice is by changing the comma to a semicolon.

➤ **Tracy Kidder wanted to write about architecture,/; *House***

    is the result.

If no punctuation appears between the two clauses, the sentence is a run-on. One way to correct a run-on sentence is to add a semicolon between the two clauses.

➤ **Magnolias bloom in the early spring; daffodils blossom at**

    the same time.

(*For more on comma splices and run-on sentences, see Tab 10: Editing for Grammar Conventions, pp. 470–76.*)

58b Use semicolons with transitional expressions that connect independent clauses.

Transitional expressions, including transitional phrases (*after all, even so, for example, in addition, on the contrary*) and conjunctive adverbs (*consequently, however, moreover, nevertheless, then, therefore*), indicate the way two clauses are related to each other. When a transitional expression appears between two clauses, it is preceded by a semicolon and usually followed by a comma. (*For a list of transitional expressions, see Tab 10: Editing for Grammar Conventions, p. 474.*)

➤ **Sheila had to wait until the plumber arrived; consequently,**

    she was late for the exam.

Coordinating conjunctions (*and, but, or, nor, for, so, yet*) also indicate the way clauses are related. Unlike transitional expressions, however, they are preceded by a comma, not a semicolon, when they join two independent clauses. (*For more on comma splices and run-on sentences, see Tab 10: Editing for Grammar Conventions, pp. 470–76.*)

Note: The semicolon always appears between the two clauses, even when the transitional expression is in another position within the second clause. Wherever it appears, the transitional expression is usually set off with a comma or commas.

➤ **My friends are all taking golf lessons; my roommate and I,
  ^**

  however, are more interested in tennis.

58c Use a semicolon to separate items in a series or clauses when the items or clauses contain commas.

Because the following sentence contains so many elements, the semicolons are needed for clarity.

➤ **The committee included Dr. Curtis Youngblood, the county**

  **medical examiner; Roberta Collingwood, the director of
  ^**

  **the bureau's criminal division; and Darcy Coolidge, the
  ^**

  chief of police.

Note: This rule is an exception to the general principle that there should be a full sentence (independent clause) on each side of a semicolon.

A comma is the correct punctuation before a coordinating conjunction (*and, but, for, nor, or, so, yet*) that joins independent clauses: *Forsythia blooms in the early spring, but azaleas bloom later.* However, if the independent clauses already contain internal commas, a semicolon can help readers locate the point where the clauses are separated.

➤ **The closing scenes return to the English countryside, recalling the opening; but these scenes are bathed in a different, cooler light, suggesting that memories of her marriage still haunt her.**

58d Watch out for and correct common errors in using the semicolon.

▪ **Joining a dependent clause or a phrase to an independent clause:**

➤ **Professional writers need to devote time every day to their writing;, although doing so takes discipline.**

➤ **Seeming tame and lovable;, housecats can actually be fierce hunters.**

➤ **Foremost among the German competition horses is the Hanoverian;, a great show-jumping breed.**

The appositive phrase *a great show-jumping breed* should be set off with a comma, not a semicolon.

▪ **Joining independent clauses linked by a coordinating conjunction (*and, but, or, nor, for, so, yet*):** If the clauses contain commas, a semicolon is acceptable (*see p. 542*).

➤ **Nineteenth-century women wore colorful clothes;, but their clothes often look drab in the black-and-white photographs of the era.**

▪ **Introducing a series, an explanation, or a quotation:** A colon should usually be used for this purpose.

➤ **My day was planned;: a morning walk, an afternoon in the library, dinner with friends, and a great horror movie.**

➤ **The doctor finally diagnosed the problem;: a severe sinus infection.**

➤ **Boyd warns of the difficulty in describing Bach;: "Even his physical appearance largely eludes us."**

59 Colons

Colons function within sentences to introduce elements, and they also have other conventional uses. A colon always follows an independent clause in a sentence, but unlike the semicolon (*see pp. 540–43*), the element that follows it is not necessarily another independent clause.

www.mhhe.com/
awr
For information and exercises on colons, go to

Editing >
Colons

Colons and Grammar Checkers

A grammar checker may point out when you have used a colon incorrectly, but since colons are usually optional, most of the time you will need to decide whether a colon is your best choice in a sentence.

59a Use a colon after a complete sentence to introduce a list, an appositive, or a quotation.

Like an announcer on a television show, a colon draws readers' attention to what it is introducing. It is used after a complete sentence (independent clause) to introduce lists, **appositives** (nouns or noun phrases that appear right after the word they rename), and quotations.

> *independent clause*   *list*
> **Several majors interest me: biology, chemistry, and art.**

> *independent clause*   *appositive*
> **She shared with me her favorite toys: a spatula and a pot lid.**

If you use *that is* or *namely* with an appositive, it should follow the colon.

> *independent clause*   *quotation*
> **He said the dreaded words: "Let's just be friends."**

Note: If you introduce a quotation with a signal phrase such as *he said* or *Morrison comments* instead of a complete sentence, you should use a comma, not a colon. (*For more on introducing quotations, including block quotations, see pp. 553–56.*)

When you use a colon to introduce a sentence element, make sure that it is preceded by an independent clause.

>   *are*
> ➤ **Three kinds of futility ∧ dealt with in the novel: pervasive**
>
>   **poverty, lost love, and inescapable aging.**

The words *the following* or *as follows* often appear at the end of the introductory clause.

59b Use a colon when a second closely related independent clause elaborates on the first one.

Use a colon when you want to emphasize the second clause.

> ➤ **I can predict tonight's sequence of events: my brother will**
>
>   **arrive late, talk loudly, and eat too much.**

Note: When a complete sentence follows a colon, the first word may begin with either a capital or a lowercase letter. Whatever you decide to do, though, you should use the same style throughout your document.

59c Use colons in salutations in business documents, to indicate ratios, to indicate times of day, for city and publisher citations in bibliographies, and to separate titles and subtitles.

> ➤ **Dear Mr. Worth: To:**

> ➤ **The ratio of armed to unarmed members of the gang was 3:1.**

> ➤ **He woke up at 6:30 in the morning.**

> ➤ **New York: McGraw-Hill, 2007**

> ➤ *Possible Lives: The Promise of Public Education in America*

> *Note:* Colons are often used to separate biblical chapters and verses (John 3:16), but the Modern Language Association (MLA) recommends using a period instead (John 3.16).

59d Watch out for and correct common errors in using the colon.

- **Between a verb and its object or complement:**
  - ➤ **The elements of a smoothie are:/ yogurt, fresh fruit, and honey.**
- **Between a preposition and its object or objects:**
  - ➤ **Many feel that cancer can be prevented by a diet of:/ fruit, nuts, and vegetables.**
- **After *such as, for example,* or *including:***
  - ➤ **I am ready for a change, such as:/ a trip to the Bahamas or a move to another town.**
- **More than one colon in a sentence:**
  - ➤ **He was taken in by ~~a new con:~~ the Spanish lottery scam: victims are told they have won a big prize and asked to send financial information to a fake Spanish company.**

60 Apostrophes

Apostrophes show possession (*the dog's bone*) and indicate omitted letters in contractions (*don't*). They are also used in such a wide variety of other ways that they are frequently misused. The most common confusion is between plurals and possessives.

www.mhhe.com/
awr
For information
and exercises on
apostrophes, go to

Editing >
Apostrophes

Note: If you are wondering whether a particular noun should be in the possessive form, reword the sentence using the word *of* (*the bone of the dog*) to make sure that the noun is not plural.

Apostrophes and Grammar Checkers

A spelling checker will sometimes highlight *its* used incorrectly (instead of *it's*) or an error in a possessive (for example, *Englands' glory*), but this identification is not trustworthy or consistent. Spelling and grammar checkers will miss many apostrophe errors, so you should double-check all words that end in -*s* in your work.

60a Use apostrophes with nouns and indefinite pronouns to indicate possession.

For a noun to be possessive, two elements are usually required: someone or something is the possessor; and someone, something, or some attribute or quality is possessed.

POSSESSOR	PERSON, THING, ATTRIBUTE, QUALITY, VALUE, OR FEATURE POSSESSED	POSSESSION
woman	son	the woman's son
Juanita	shovel	Juanita's shovel
child	bright smile	a child's bright smile

547

Sometimes the thing possessed precedes the possessor.

> ➤ **The motorcycle is the student's.**

Sometimes the sentence may not name the thing possessed, but its identity (in this case, *house*) is clearly understood by the reader.

> ➤ **I saw your cousin at Nick's.**

Note: Possession can also be indicated using the preposition *of: the bright smile of a child.*

---

1. Deciding whether to use an apostrophe and an *s* or only an apostrophe

To form the possessive of all singular nouns, add an apostrophe plus *s* to the ending: *baby's.* Even singular nouns that end in -*s* form the possessive by adding *'s: bus's.*

Note: If a singular noun with more than two syllables ends in -*s* and adding *'s* would make the word sound awkward, it is acceptable to use only an apostrophe to form the possessive: *Socrates', Dickens', Moses', Jesus'.* Whatever your choice, be consistent.

- To form the possessive of a plural noun that ends in -*s*, add only an apostrophe to form the possessive: *subjects', babies'.*

- To form the possessive of a plural noun that does not end in -*s*, add an apostrophe plus *s* to form the possessive: *men's, cattle's.*

- To form the possessive of most indefinite pronouns, such as *no one, everyone, everything,* or *something,* add an apostrophe plus *s: no one's, anybody's.*

Note: Adding *'s* makes some indefinite pronouns sound awkward. In those cases, use *of* to form the possessive: *the wishes of a few, the parents of both.*

Forming Possessives

IF THE WORD IS A(N):	ADD:	EXAMPLE
singular noun	's	horse's Moore's
plural noun ending in -s	'	horses' Moores'
plural noun not ending in -s	's	children's
indefinite pronoun	's	everybody's

2. Using the apostrophe in tricky situations

- To express joint ownership, use the possessive form for the last name only; to express individual ownership, use the possessive form for each name.

  ➤ **Felicia and Elias' report**

  ➤ **The city's and the state's finances**

- To form the possessive of compound words, add an apostrophe plus *s* to the last word in the compound.

  ➤ **My father-in-law's job**

  ➤ **The editor-in-chief's decision**

- To form the possessive of proper names, follow the rules given above, with some exceptions. Some place or organizational names that include a possessive noun lack an apostrophe. In these cases, follow the established style rather than adding an apostrophe.

  ➤ **Kings Point**

  ➤ **Department of Veterans Affairs**

  ➤ **Pikes Peak**

Note: To form the possessive of buildings, machines, and other inanimate objects, use *of* if adding *'s* sounds awkward: *the window of the house* (not *the house's window*).

60b Use apostrophes to form contractions.

In a contraction, the apostrophe serves as a substitute for omitted letters.

we've = we have
weren't = were not
here's = here is

In informal writing, apostrophes can also substitute for omitted numbers in a decade: *the '50s*. It is usually better to spell out the name of the decade in formal writing, however: *the fifties*.

CHARTING the TERRITORY

Contractions in Academic Writing

Although the MLA and APA style manuals allow contractions in academic writing, some instructors think that they are too informal. Check with your instructor before using contractions.

60c Distinguish between contractions and possessive pronouns.

The following pairs of **homonyms** (words that sound alike but have different meanings) often cause problems for writers. Note that the apostrophe is used only in the contraction.

CONTRACTION	POSSESSIVE PRONOUN
it's (it is or it has)	its
It's too hot.	The dog scratched *its* fleas.
you're (you are)	your
You're a lucky guy.	Is that *your* new car?
who's (who is)	whose
Who's there?	The man *whose* dog was lost called us.
they're (they are)	their*
They're reading poetry.	They gave *their* lives.

*The adverb *their* is also confused with *there: She was standing there.*

60d Using an apostrophe with *s* to form plural numbers, letters, abbreviations, and words used as words is optional.

An apostrophe plus *s* ('s) can be used to show the plural of a number, a letter, or an abbreviation. Underline or italicize single letters but not the apostrophe or the *s*.

➤ **He makes his 2's look like 5's.**

➤ *Committee* **has two *m*'s, two *t*'s, and two *e*'s.**

➤ **Professor Morris has two Ph.D.'s.**

Exceptions: If an abbreviation does not have periods, the apostrophe is not necessary (*RPMs*). The apostrophe is also not necessary to form the plural of dates (*1990s*).

If a word is used as a word rather than as a symbol of the meaning it conveys, it can be made plural by adding an apostrophe plus *s*. The word should be italicized or underlined but the *s* should not be. If the word is in quotation marks, you should always use 's when you are forming the plural.

➤ **There are twenty-five** *no*'s **[or "no's"] in the first paragraph.**

Note: Style guides vary. The *MLA Handbook for Writers of Research Papers,* for example, no longer recommends using apostrophes to form plurals in most cases, except for plurals of letters treated as letters.

MLA STYLE   He makes his 2s look like 5s.

MLA STYLE   Committee has two m̲'s, two t̲'s, and two e̲'s.

Note the use of underlining instead of italics in MLA style. Whatever style you choose to follow, be consistent.

60e Watch out for common misuses of the apostrophe.

Never use an apostrophe with *s* to form a plural noun.

> *teachers*
> ➤ The ~~teacher's~~ asked the girls and boys for their attention.

(*See pp. 591–93 for more on forming plural nouns.*)

Never use an apostrophe with *s* to form the present tense of a verb used with a third-person singular subject (*he, she, it,* or a singular noun).

> *needs*
> ➤ A professional singer ~~need's~~ to practice different vocal
>
> techniques.

Never use an apostrophe with the possessive form of a pronoun such as *hers, ours,* or *theirs.*

> *ours*
> ➤ That cat of ~~our's~~ is always sleeping!

(*See 60c for advice on distinguishing contractions [*it's*] from possessive pronouns [*its*].*)

Never use an apostrophe with *s* to form the plural of a surname.

> *Clintons*
> ➤ The ~~Clinton's~~ again made history when Hillary was elected
>
> to the Senate during the same year Bill left the White
>
> House.

61 Quotation Marks

Quotation marks are used to enclose words, phrases, and sentences that are quoted directly; titles of short works such as poems, articles, songs, and short stories; and words and phrases used in a special sense.

www.mhhe.com/
awr
For information and exercises on quotation marks, go to

Editing > Quotation Marks

Quotation Marks and Grammar Checkers

A grammar checker cannot determine where a quotation should begin and end, but it can alert you to the lack of an opening or closing mark. Grammar checkers may not point out errors in the use of quotation marks with other marks of punctuation, however. For example, a grammar checker did not highlight the error in the placement of the period at the end of the following sentence.

➤ **Barbara Ehrenreich observes, "There are no Palm Pilots, cable channels, or Web sites to advise the low-wage job seeker".**

61a Use quotation marks to indicate the exact words of a speaker or writer.

Direct quotations from written material may include whole sentences or only a few words or phrases.

➤ **In *Angela's Ashes*, Frank McCourt writes, "Worse than the ordinary miserable childhood is the miserable Irish childhood" (11).**

➤ **Frank McCourt believes that being Irish worsens what is all too "ordinary"—a "miserable childhood" (11).**

Use quotation marks to enclose everything a speaker says in written dialogue. If the quoted sentence is interrupted by a phrase like *he said*, enclose the rest of the quotation in quotation marks. When another person begins to speak, start a new paragraph to indicate a change in speaker.

553

"I don't know what you're talking about," he said. "I did listen to everything you told me."

"If you had been listening, you would know what I was talking about."

If a speaker continues for more than a paragraph, begin each subsequent paragraph with an opening quotation mark, but do not insert a closing quotation mark until the end of the quotation.

Note: Do not use quotation marks to set off an indirect quotation, which reports what a speaker said but does not use the exact words.

> He said that ⸢he didn't know what I was talking about.⸤

Two or three lines of poetry may be run in to your text, much like any other *short* quotation. Line breaks are shown with a slash. Leave a space before and after the slash. (*See also Chapter 62, p. 569.*)

> **Wordsworth writes of the weary acquisitiveness of our modern age: "The world is too much with us; late and soon, / Getting and spending, we lay waste our powers" (lines 1–2).**

Note: In the style of the Modern Language Association (MLA), line numbers should appear in parentheses following the quotation. The word *lines* should precede the numbers the first time the poem is quoted.

61b Set off long quotations in indented blocks.

If you are using a quotation that is longer than four typed lines, set it off from the text as a block quotation. Start a new line for the quotation, type it double-spaced, and indent every line of the quotation one inch (ten spaces) from the left margin. Double-space above and below the quotation. Be sure that you indent every line in a block quotation.

A block quotation is *not* surrounded by quotation marks. If the text you are quoting includes a direct quotation, however, use quotation marks to set that off. If your quotation is more than one paragraph long, indent the first line of each new paragraph an extra quarter inch (three spaces). A block quotation is usually introduced by a sentence that ends with a colon.

As Carl Schorske points out, the young Freud was passionately interested in classical archeology:

> He cultivated a new friendship in the Viennese professional elite—especially rare in those days of withdrawal--with Emanuel Loewy, a professor of archeology. "He keeps me up till three o'clock in the morning," Freud wrote appreciatively to Fliess. "He tells me about Rome." (273)

CHARTING the TERRITORY

Documentation Styles

Providing the page number in parentheses after the quotation is a convention of the Modern Language Association (MLA), explained in the *MLA Handbook for Writers of Research Papers*. The American Psychological Association (APA) style, widely used in the social sciences, employs a different documentation convention: ". . . Rome" (p. 273). The APA and Chicago styles also have different rules for setting off long quotations. (*For more on the differences among documentation styles, see Tabs 6–8.*)

Longer verse quotations (four lines or more) are indented block style, like long prose quotations. (*For short quotations of poetry, see pp. 554 and 569.*) If you cannot fit an entire line of poetry on a single line of your typescript, you may indent the turned line an extra quarter inch (three spaces).

In the following lines from "Crossing Brooklyn Ferry," Walt Whitman celebrates the beauty of the Manhattan skyline and his love for that city:

> Ah, what can ever be more stately and
> admirable to me than mast-hemm'd
> Manhattan?
> River and sunset and scallop-edg'd waves of
> flood-tide?

> The sea-gulls oscillating their bodies, the
>> hay-boat in the twilight, and the belated lighter?
> What gods can exceed these that clasp me by
>> the hand, and with voices I love call me
>> promptly and loudly by my nighest name as
>> I approach? (lines 92-95)

(For more on when to use quotations, see Tab 5: Researching, pp. 262–63.)

61c Enclose a quotation within a quotation with single quotation marks.

Use single quotation marks to set off a quotation within a quotation.

➤ **In response to the press, the president of the university said, "I know you're saying to me, 'We want a winning football team.' But I'm telling you this: 'I want an honest football team.' "**

61d Use quotation marks to enclose titles of short works such as articles, poems, and stories.

The titles of long works, such as books, are usually underlined or put in italics. (*See Chapter 66, pp. 583–85.*) The titles of book chapters, essays, most poems, and other short works are usually put in quotation marks. Quotation marks are also used for titles of unpublished works, including student papers, theses, and dissertations.

Works That Should Be Enclosed in Quotation Marks

- **Essays:** "Once More to the Lake"
- **Songs:** "Seven Nation Army"
- **Short poems:** "Daffodils"
- **Short stories:** "The Tell Tale Heart"
- **Articles in periodicals:** "Scotland Yard of the Wild" (from *American Way*)

- **Book chapters or sections:** "The Girl in Conflict" (Chapter 11 of *Coming of Age in Samoa*)

- **Episodes of radio and television programs:** "I Can't Remember" (on *48 Hours*)

- **Titles of unpublished works, including student papers, theses, and dissertations:** "Louis Armstrong and Joe Glaser: More Than Meets the Eye" (Do not use quotation marks to enclose the title of your own paper on your title page.)

Note: If quotation marks are needed within the title of a short work, use single quotation marks: "The 'Animal Rights' War on Medicine."

61e Use quotation marks to indicate that a word or phrase is being used in a special way.

Put quotation marks around a word or phrase that someone else has used in a way that you or your readers may not agree with. Quotation marks used in this way function like raised eyebrows do in conversation and should be used sparingly.

➤ The **"worker's paradise"** of Stalinist Russia included slave-labor camps.

Words cited as words can also be put in quotation marks, although the more common practice is to italicize them.

➤ The words **"compliment"** and **"complement"** sound alike but have different meanings.

61f Place punctuation marks within or outside quotation marks, as convention and your meaning require.

As you edit, check all closing single and double quotation marks and the marks of punctuation that appear next to them to make sure that you have placed them in the right order.

1. Periods and commas

Always place the period or comma before the final quotation mark, even when the quotation is brief.

➤ **"Instead of sharing an experience the spectator must come to grips with things," Brecht writes in "The Epic Theatre and Its Difficulties."**

However, place the period or comma after a parenthetical reference.

➤ **Brecht wants the spectator to "come to grips with things" (23).**

2. Question marks and exclamation points

Place a question mark or an exclamation point after the final quotation mark if the quoted material is not itself a question or an exclamation.

➤ **How does epic theatre make us "come to grips with things"?**

Place a question mark or an exclamation point inside the final quotation mark when it is part of the quotation. No additional punctuation is needed after the closing quotation, unless you are adding a parenthetical citation in MLA style (see the third example below).

➤ **"Are we to see science in the theatre?" he was asked.**

➤ **Brecht was asked, "Are we to see science in the theatre?"**

➤ **Brecht was asked, "Are we to see science in the theatre?" (27).**

3. Colons and semicolons

Place colons and semicolons after the final quotation mark.

➤ **Dean Wilcox cited the items he called his "daily delights": a free parking space for his scooter at the faculty club, a special table in the club itself, and friends to laugh with after a day's work.**

4. Dashes

Place a dash outside either an opening or a closing quotation mark, or both, if it precedes or follows the quotation or if two dashes are used to set off the quotation.

➤ **One phrase—"time is running out"—haunted me throughout my dream.**

Place a dash inside either an opening or a closing quotation mark if it is part of the quotation.

➤ **"Where is the—" she called. "Oh, here it is. Never mind."**

61g Integrate quotations smoothly into your sentences, using the correct punctuation.

1. Formal introductions

When you introduce a quotation with a complete sentence, use a colon.

➤ **Hamilton credits the Greeks with a shift in the portrayal of gods: "Until then, gods had no semblance of reality."**

2. *She said* and similar expressions

If you introduce a quotation with a signal phrase such as *he said* or *she noted,* add a comma after the phrase and use a capital letter to begin the quotation.

➤ **Hamilton says, "That is the miracle of Greek mythology— a humanized world."**

If the phrase follows the quotation, add a comma at the end of the quotation, before the closing quotation mark. (If the quotation ends in a question mark or an exclamation point, however, do not add a comma.) Capitalize the first letter of the quotation even if the first word does not begin a sentence in the original source. If you change a lowercase letter to a capital letter, enclose the letter in brackets. (*See p. 568.*)

➤ **"The only white people who came to our house were welfare workers and bill collectors," James Baldwin wrote.**

Note: Do not use a comma after expressions such as *he said* or *the researchers note* if an indirect quotation or a paraphrase follows.

➤ **He said/ that he believed he could do it.**

3. Interrupted quotations

If you interrupt a quoted sentence with a signal phrase such as *she said,* place quotation marks around both parts of the quoted sentence and set the signal phrase off with commas. Note that the first word of the second part of the quoted sentence is not capitalized.

> ➤ **"The first thing that strikes one about Plath's journals,"
> writes Katha Pollitt in *The Atlantic*, "is what they leave
> out."**

To interrupt a quotation of two or more sentences with a signal phrase, attach the signal phrase to the first sentence with a comma, and put a period after it. The next sentence begins with an opening quotation mark and a capital letter.

> ➤ **"There are at least four kinds of doublespeak," William
> Lutz observes. "The first is the euphemism, an inoffensive
> or positive word or phrase used to avoid a harsh,
> unpleasant, or distasteful reality."**

4. Quotations that are integrated into a sentence

When a quotation is integrated into a sentence's structure, treat the quotation as you would any other sentence element, adding a comma or not as appropriate.

> ➤ **Telling me that she wanted to "play hooky from her life,"
> she set off on a three-week vacation.**

> ➤ **He said he had his "special reasons."**

61h   Edit to correct common errors
in using quotation marks.

> ■ **To distance yourself from slang, clichés, or trite expressions:** Avoid overused or slang expressions in college writing. If your writing situation permits slang, however, do not enclose it in quotation marks.

> > ➤ **Californians are so ⫽laid back.⫽**

> Revising the sentence is usually a better solution.

> > ➤ **Many Californians have a carefree attitude.**

■ **For indirect quotations:** Do not use quotation marks for indirect quotations. Watch out for errors in pronoun reference as well. (*See Tab 10: Editing for Grammar Conventions, pp. 504–6.*)

> ➤ He told his boss that ⸝the company lost its largest
>
> account.⸝

Another way to correct this sentence is to change to a direct quotation.

> ➤ He said to his boss, "We just lost our largest account."

■ **In quotations that end with a question mark or exclamation point:** Do not add another question mark or exclamation point to the end of a quotation that already ends in one of these marks.

> ➤ What did Juliet mean when she cried, "O Romeo,
>
> Romeo! Wherefore art thou, Romeo?"⸝

If you quote a question within a sentence that makes a statement, place a question mark before the quotation mark and a period at the end of the sentence.

> ➤ "What was Henry Ford's greatest contribution to the Industrial Revolution?" he asked.

■ **To enclose the title of your own paper on the title page or above the first line of the text:**

> ➤ ⸝Edgar Allan Poe and the Paradox of the Gothic⸝

If you use a quotation or a title of a short work in your title, though, put quotation marks around it.

> ➤ Edgar Allan Poe's "The Raven" and the Paradox of the Gothic

62 Other Punctuation Marks: Periods, Question Marks, Exclamation Points, Dashes, Parentheses, Brackets, Ellipses, and Slashes

Punctuation and Grammar Checkers

Your grammar checker will highlight a few errors in the use of the punctuation marks covered in this chapter. It might highlight a period used instead of a question mark at the end of a question, for example. The punctuation marks covered in 62d–62h involve judgment calls on the part of a writer, however. Grammar checkers will not tell you when you might use a pair of dashes or parentheses to set material off in a sentence, or when you need a second dash or parenthesis to enclose parenthetical material. You will need to check your writing carefully for problems with these marks of punctuation.

www.mhhe.com/
awr
For information and
exercises on other
punctuation marks,
go to

Editing >
End Punctuation

62a Use a period after most statements, polite requests, and indirect questions, and in abbreviations according to convention.

1. To end most statements, indirect questions, and polite requests

STATEMENT

There are more than one thousand periods in this book.

STATEMENT CONTAINING A QUOTATION

"What is the word count?" she asked.

STATEMENT CONTAINING AN INDIRECT QUESTION

She asked me where I had gone to college.

POLITE REQUEST

Please go with me to the lecture.

2. In abbreviations when convention requires them

A period or periods are used with the following common abbreviations, which end in lowercase letters.

Mr.	Dr.	Mass.
Ms.	i.e.	Jan.
Mrs.	e.g.	

If the abbreviation is made up of capital letters, however, the periods are optional.

RN (or R.N.)	BA (or B.A.)
MD (or M.D.)	PhD (or Ph.D.)

Periods are omitted in abbreviations for organizations, famous people, states in mailing addresses, and acronyms (words made up of initials).

FBI	JFK	MA	NATO
CIA	LBJ	TX	NAFTA

When in doubt, consult a dictionary.

When an abbreviation ends a sentence, the period at the end of the abbreviation serves as the period for the sentence. If a question mark or an exclamation point ends the sentence, place it *after* the period in the abbreviation.

➤ **When he was in the seventh grade, we called him "Stinky," but now he is William Percival Abernathy, Ph.D.!**

62b Use a question mark after a direct question.

➤ **Who wrote *The Old Man and the Sea*?**

Occasionally, a question mark changes a statement into a question.

➤ **You expect me to believe a story like that?**

When questions follow one another in a series, each one can be followed by a question mark even if the questions are not complete sentences, as long as the meaning is understood.

➤ **What will you contribute? Your time? Your talent? Your money?**

Use a question mark in parentheses to indicate a questionable date, number, or word, but do not use it to convey an ironic meaning.

➤ **Chaucer was born in 1340 (?) and lived until 1400.**

➤ **His yapping dog had graduated from obedience (?)**

   training.

> *Note:* Do not use a question mark after an indirect quotation, even if the words being indirectly quoted were originally a question.
>
> ➤ **He asked her if she would be at home later?.**

62c Use exclamation points sparingly to convey shock, surprise, or some other strong emotion.

➤ **Stolen! The money was stolen! Right before our eyes, somebody snatched my purse and ran off with it.**

> *Note:* Using numerous exclamation points throughout a document actually weakens their force. Try to convey emotion with your choice of words and your sentence structure instead of with an exclamation point.
>
> ➤ **Jefferson and Adams both died on the same day in 1826,**
>
> **exactly fifty years after the signing of the Declaration**
>
> **of Independence!.**
>
> The fact that the sentence reports is surprising enough without the addition of an exclamation point.

www.mhhe.com/
awr
For information and
exercises on dashes,
go to

Editing >
Dashes

62d Use a dash or dashes to set off words, phrases, or sentences that deserve special attention.

Think of the dash as a strong pause that emphasizes what follows—or sometimes what comes immediately before. A typeset dash, sometimes called an *em dash,* is a single, unbroken line about as wide as a capital M. Most word-processing programs provide the em dash as a special character or will convert two hyphens to an em dash automatically. Otherwise, you can make a dash with two hyphens in a row. Do not put a space before or after the dash.

1. Using a dash to highlight an explanation or a list
A dash indicates a very strong pause and emphasizes what comes immediately before or after it.

➤ Coca-Cola, potato chips, and brevity—these are the marks of a good study session in the dorm.

➤ I think the Comets will win the tournament for one reason—their goalie.

A colon could also be used in the second example. (*See Chapter 59, p. 544.*)

If an appositive consists of a list of items, use dashes to set it off more clearly for readers.

➤ The symptoms of hay fever / sneezing, coughing, itchy

eyes / can be controlled with over-the-counter medications.

Do not separate a subject and verb with a dash, however.

➤ Haydn, Mozart, and Beethoven—are the most famous

composers of the classical period.

2. Using a dash or dashes to insert—and highlight—a non-essential phrase or independent clause within a sentence

➤ All finite creations—including humans—are incomplete and contradictory.

➤ The first rotary gasoline engine—it was made by Mazda—burned 15 percent more fuel than conventional engines.

3. Using a dash or dashes to indicate a sudden change in tone or idea

➤ Breathing heavily, the archaeologist opened the old chest in wild anticipation and found—an old pair of socks and an empty soda can.

4. Using dashes sparingly

Used sparingly, the dash can be an effective mark of punctuation, but if it is overused, it can make your writing disjointed.

➤ After we found the puppy—shivering under the porch—we

brought her into the house—into the entryway, actually—

and wrapped her in an old towel—to warm her up.

www.mhhe.com/
awr
For information and
exercises on
parentheses, go to

Editing >
Parentheses

62e Use parentheses to set off relatively unimportant information.

Parentheses should be used infrequently and only to set off supplementary information, a digression, or a comment that interrupts the flow of thought within a sentence or paragraph.

➤ **The tickets (ranging in price from $10 to $50) go on sale Monday.**

When parentheses enclose a whole sentence by itself, the sentence begins with a capital letter and ends with a period before the final parenthesis. A sentence that appears inside parentheses *within a sentence* should neither begin with a capital letter nor end with a period.

➤ **Folktales and urban legends often reflect the concerns of a particular era. (The familiar tale of a cat accidentally caught in a microwave oven is an example of this phenomenon.)**

➤ **John Henry (he was the man with the forty-pound hammer) was a hero to miners fearing the loss of their jobs to machines.**

If the material in parentheses is at the end of an introductory or nonessential word group that is followed by a comma, the comma should be placed after the closing parenthesis. A comma should never appear before the opening parenthesis.

➤ **As he walked past/ (dressed, as always, in his Sunday**

   best), I got ready to throw the spitball.

Parentheses are used to enclose numbers or letters that label items in a list.

➤ **He says the argument is nonsense because (1) university presidents don't work as well as machines, (2) university presidents don't do any real work at all, and (3) universities would be better off if they were run by faculty committees.**

> *Note:* Parentheses are distracting to readers. If you find that you have used a number of parentheses in a draft, go over it carefully to see if any of the material within parentheses actually deserves more emphasis.

Parentheses also enclose in-text citations in many systems of documenting sources. (*For more on documenting sources, see Tabs 6–8.*)

62f When quoting, use brackets to set off material that is not part of the original quotation.

Use brackets to set off information you add to a quotation that is not part of the quotation itself.

➤ **Samuel Eliot Morison has written, "This passage has attracted a good deal of scorn to the Florentine mariner [Verrazzano], but without justice."**

In this sentence, the writer places the name of the "Florentine mariner"—Verrazzano—in brackets so that readers will know his identity.

Information that explains or corrects something in a quotation is also bracketed.

➤ **Vasco da Gama's man wrote in 1487, "The body of the church [it was not a church but a Hindu shrine] is as large as a monastery."**

Brackets are also used around words that you insert within a quotation to make it fit the grammar or style of your own sentence. If you replace a word with your own word in brackets, ellipses are not needed.

➤ **At the end of *Pygmalion*, Henry Higgins confesses to Eliza Doolittle that he has "grown accustomed to [her] voice and appearance."**

To make the quotation fit properly into the sentence, the bracketed word *her* is inserted in place of *your*.

Note: Brackets may be used to enclose the word *sic* (Latin for "thus") after a word in a quotation that was incorrect in the original. If you are following MLA style, the word *sic* should not be underlined or italicized when it appears in brackets. The three other styles covered in this book (APA, Chicago, and CSE) put *sic* in italics.

➤ **The critic noted that "the battle scenes in *The Patriot* are realistic, but the rest of the film is historically inacurate [sic]."**

Sic should be used sparingly because it can appear pretentious and condescending, and it should not be used to make fun of what someone has said or written.

If you change the first letter or a word in a quotation to a capital or lowercase letter, enclose the letter in brackets: *Ackroyd writes, "[F]or half a million years there has been in London a pattern of habitation and hunting, if not settlement."*

If you need to set off words within material that is already in parentheses, use brackets: *(I found the information on a Web site published by the National Institutes of Health [NIH].)*

62g   Use ellipses to indicate that words have been omitted.

Use three spaced periods, called ellipses or an ellipsis mark, to show readers that you have omitted words from a passage you are quoting. Some instructors suggest that you use brackets to enclose any ellipses that you add.

FULL QUOTATION FROM A WORK BY WILKINS

In the nineteenth century, railroads, lacing their way across continents, reaching into the heart of every major city in Europe and America, and bringing a new romance to travel, added to the unity of nations and fueled the nationalist fires already set burning by the French Revolution and the wars of Napoleon.

EDITED QUOTATION

In his account of nineteenth-century society, Wilkins argued that "railroads . . . added to the unity of nations and fueled the nationalist fires already set burning by the French Revolution and the wars of Napoleon."

If you are leaving out the end of a quoted sentence, the three ellipsis points are followed by a period to end the sentence.

EDITED QUOTATION

In describing the growth of railroads, Wilkins pictures them "lacing their way across continents, reaching into the heart of every major city in Europe and America. . . ."

When you need to add a parenthetical reference after the ellipses at the end of a sentence, place it after the quotation mark but before the final period: . . ." (253).

Ellipses are usually not needed to indicate an omission when only a word or phrase is being quoted.

➤   **Railroads brought "a new romance to travel," according to Wilkins.**

To indicate the omission of an entire line or more from the middle of a poem, insert a line of spaced periods.

> Shelley seems to be describing nature, but what's really at issue
>
> is the seductive nature of desire:
>
>> See the mountains kiss high Heaven,
>>
>> And the waves clasp one another;
>>
>> . . . .
>>
>> And the sunlight clasps the earth,
>>
>> And the moonbeams kiss the sea:
>>
>> What is all this sweet work worth
>>
>> If thou kiss not me? (1-2, 5-8)

Ellipses should be used only as a means of shortening a quotation, never as a device for changing its fundamental meaning or for creating emphasis where none exists in the original.

Ellipses may be used at the end of a sentence if you mean to leave a thought hanging. In the following passage, Dick Gregory uses an ellipsis to suggest that there was no end to his worries.

> ➤ **Oh God, I'm scared. I wish I could die right now with the feeling I have because I know Momma's gonna make me mad and I'm going to make her mad, and me and Presley's gonna fight … "Richard, you get in here and put your coat on. Get in here or I'll whip you."**

62h Use slashes to mark line divisions for poetry quotations that are less than four lines long, to separate options or combinations, and in electronic addresses.

Use the slash to show divisions between lines of poetry when you quote more than one line of a poem as part of a sentence. Add a space on either side of the slash. When you are quoting four or more lines of poetry, use a block quotation instead (*see pp. 555–56 and above*).

> ➤ **In "The Tower," Yeats makes his peace with "All those things whereof / Man makes a superhuman / Mirror-resembling dream" (163-165).**

The slash is sometimes used between two words that represent choices or combinations. Do not add a space on either side of the slash when it is used in this way.

➤ **The college offers three credit/noncredit courses.**

Slashes are also used to mark divisions in online addresses (URLs): *http://www.georgetown.edu/crossroads/navigate.html.*
Some writers use the slash as a marker between the words *and* and *or* or between *he* and *she* or *his* and *her* to avoid sexism. Most writers, however, consider such usage awkward. It is usually better to rephrase the sentence. (*See also Tab 10: Editing for Grammar Conventions, pp. 500–2.*)

➤ **A bill can originate in the House of Representatives,** ~~and/or~~ *in*

, or both
the Senate.

63 Capitalization

Many rules for the use of capital letters have been fixed by custom, such as the convention of beginning each sentence with a capital letter, but the rules change all the time. A recent dictionary is a good guide to capitalization.

www.mhhe.com/ awr
For information and exercises on capitalization, go to

Editing > Capitalization

63a Capitalize proper nouns (names), words derived from them, brand names, certain abbreviations, and call letters.

Proper nouns are the names of specific people, places, or things, names that set off the individual from the group, such as the name *Jane* instead of the common noun *person.* Capitalize proper nouns, words derived from proper nouns, brand names, abbreviations of capitalized words, and call letters of radio and television stations.

Capitalization and Grammar Checkers

Grammar checkers will flag words that should be capitalized or lowercase by convention, but they won't flag proper nouns unless the noun is stored in the program's dictionary, and they won't necessarily point out a noun that can be either proper or common, depending on the context. For example, a grammar checker flagged the capitalization error in the first sentence but not the second:

➤ **Maria is going to study the mammals of north America.**

➤ **The Darwin Martin House, designed by Frank Lloyd Wright, is located in buffalo, New York.**

- **Proper nouns:** Ronald Reagan, the Sears Tower
- **Words derived from proper nouns:** Reaganomics, Siamese cat
- **Brand names:** Apple Computer, Kleenex
- **Abbreviations:** FBI (government agency), A&E (cable television station)
- **Call letters:** WNBC (television), WMNR (radio)

TYPES and EXAMPLES of PROPER and COMMON NOUNS

- **People:** John F. Kennedy, Ruth Bader Ginsburg, Albert Einstein
- **Nationalities, ethnic groups, and languages:** English, Swiss, African Americans, Arabs, Chinese, Turkish
- **Places:** the United States of America, Tennessee, the Irunia Restaurant, the Great Lakes, *but* my state, the lake
- **Organizations and institutions:** Phi Beta Kappa, Republican Party (Republicans), Department of Defense, Cumberland College, the North Carolina Tarheels, *but* the department, this college, my hockey team
- **Religious bodies, books, and figures:** Jews, Christians, Baptists, Hindus, Roman Catholic Church, the Bible, the Koran *or* Qur'an, the Torah, God, Holy Spirit, Allah, *but* a Greek goddess, a biblical reference

(continued)

TYPES and EXAMPLES of PROPER and COMMON NOUNS (continued)

- **Scientific names and terms:** *Homo sapiens, H. sapiens, Acer rubrum, A. rubrum,* Addison's disease, Cenozoic era, Newton's first law, *but* the law of gravity
- **Names of planets, stars, and other astronomical bodies:** Earth (as a planet) *but* the earth, Mercury, Polaris *or* the North Star, Whirlpool Galaxy, *but* a star, that galaxy, the solar system
- **Computer terms:** the Internet, the World Wide Web, *or* the Web, *but* search engine, a network, my browser
- **Days, months, and holidays:** Monday, Veterans Day, August, the Fourth of July, *but* yesterday, spring and summer, the winter term
- **Historical events, movements, periods, and documents:** World War II, Impressionism, the Renaissance, the Jazz Age, the Declaration of Independence, the Constitution of the United States, *but* the last war, a golden age, the twentieth century, the amendment
- **Academic subjects, and courses:** English 101, Psychology 221, a course in Italian, *but* a physics course, my art history class

---

Note: Although holidays and the names of months and days of the week are capitalized, seasons, such as *summer,* are not. Neither are the days of the month when they are spelled out.

➤ **Why would *Valentine's Day,* the day representing love and romance, fall in *winter*—and in the coldest month of the year?**

➤ **She can meet with you on Sunday, the *seventh* of March.**

63b Capitalize titles when they appear before a proper name but not when they are used alone or after the name.

TITLE USED BEFORE A NAME

Every Sunday, *Aunt Lou* tells fantastic stories.

TITLE USED BEFORE A NAME

Everyone knew that *Governor Grover Cleveland* of New York was the most likely candidate for the Democratic nomination.

TITLE USED ALONE

My *aunt* is arriving this afternoon.

TITLE USED AFTER A NAME

The most likely candidate for the Democratic nomination was Grover Cleveland, *governor* of New York.

Exceptions: If the name for a family relationship is used alone (without a possessive such as *my* before it), it should be capitalized.

➤ **I saw *Father* infrequently during the summer months.**

Most writers do not capitalize the title *president* unless they are referring to the President of the United States: "The *president* of this university has seventeen honorary degrees." Although usage varies, you should be consistent. If you write "the President of the University," you should also write "the Chair of the History Department."

For MULTILINGUAL STUDENTS

Capitalizing the Pronoun I

Unlike other languages, English requires you to capitalize the first-person singular pronoun (*I*). All other pronouns are lower-case, unless they start a sentence or are part of the title of a work.

➤ **When *I* get home, *I* will call my doctor for the test results and let you know what she says.**

63c Capitalize titles of works of literature, works of art, and musical compositions.

Capitalize the important words in titles and subtitles. Do not capitalize articles (*a*, *an*, and *the*), the *to* in infinitives, or prepositions and conjunctions unless they begin or end the title or subtitle. Capitalize both words in a hyphenated word. Capitalize the first word after a colon or semicolon in a title.

- **Book:** *Two Years before the Mast*
- **Play:** *The Taming of the Shrew*
- **Building:** the Eiffel Tower
- **Ship or aircraft:** the *Titanic* or the *Concorde*
- **Painting:** the *Mona Lisa*
- **Article or essay:** "On Old Age"
- **Poem:** "Ode on a Grecian Urn"
- **Music:** "The Star-Spangled Banner"

63d Capitalize names of areas and regions.

Names of geographical regions are generally capitalized if they are well established, like *the Midwest* and *Central Europe*. Names of directions, as in the sentence *Turn south,* are not capitalized.

CORRECT   *East* meets *West* at the summit.

CORRECT   You will need to go *west* on Sunset.

Note: The word *western,* when used as a general direction or the name of a genre, is not capitalized. It is capitalized when it is part of the name of a specific region.

       western
➤ The ~~Western~~ *High Noon* is one of my favorite movies.

         Western
➤ I visited ~~western~~ Europe last year.

63e Follow standard practice for capitalizing names of races, ethnic groups, and sacred things.

The words *black* and *white* are usually not capitalized when they are used to refer to members of racial groups because they are adjectives that substitute for the implied common nouns *black person* and *white person.* However, names of ethnic groups and races are capitalized: *African Americans, Italians, Asians, Caucasians.*

Note: In accordance with current APA guidelines, most social scientists capitalize the terms *Black* and *White,* treating them as proper nouns.

TEXTCONNEX

Emphasis in E-Mail

When you are writing an e-mail message, you may be tempted to use all capital letters for emphasis when italics are not available. Although capital letters are sometimes used this way in print documents, they are not always welcome in online chat rooms and electronic mailing list postings, where participants may feel that they are equivalent to shouting. Also, strings of words or sentences in capital letters can be difficult to read. If you want to emphasize a word or phrase in an online communication, put an asterisk before and after it instead:

> ➤ I *totally* disagree with what you just wrote.

Many religious terms, such as *sacrament, altar,* and *rabbi,* are not capitalized. The word *Bible* is capitalized (though *biblical* is not), but it is never capitalized when it is used as a metaphor for an essential book.

> ➤ His book *Winning at Stud Poker* used to be the *bible* of gamblers.

63f Capitalize the first word of a quoted sentence but not the first word of an indirect quotation.

> ➤ She cried, "Help!"
> ➤ He said that jazz was one of America's major art forms.

The first word of a quotation from a printed source is capitalized if the quotation is introduced with a phrase such as *she notes* or *he concludes.*

> ➤ Jim, the narrator of *My Ántonia,* concludes, "Whatever we had missed, we possessed together the precious, the incommunicable past" (324).

When a quotation from a printed source is treated as an element in your sentence and not as a sentence on its own, the first word is not capitalized.

➤ **Jim took comfort in sharing with Ántonia "the precious, the incommunicable past" (324).**

If you need to change the first letter of a quotation to fit your sentence, enclose the letter in brackets.

➤ **The lawyer noted that "[t]he man seen leaving the area after the blast was not the same height as the defendant."**

If you interrupt the sentence you are quoting with an expression such as *he said,* the first word of the rest of the quotation should not be capitalized.

➤ **"When I come home an hour later," she explained, "the trains are usually less crowded."**

When quoting a text directly, reproduce the capitalization used in the original source, whether or not it is correct by today's standards.

➤ **Blake's marginalia include the following comment: "Paine is either a Devil or an Inspired Man" (603).**

63g Capitalize the first word of a sentence.

A capital letter is used to signal the beginning of a new sentence.

➤ **Robots reduce human error, so they produce uniform products.**

Sentences in parentheses also begin with a capital letter unless they are embedded within another sentence:

➤ **Although the week began with the news that he was hit by a car, by Thursday we knew he was going to be all right. (It was a terrible way to begin the week, though.)**

➤ **Although the week began with the news that he was hit by a car (it was a terrible way to begin the week), by Thursday we knew he was going to be all right.**

63h Capitalizing the first word of an independent clause after a colon is optional.

If the word group that follows a colon is not a complete sentence, do not capitalize it. If it is a complete sentence, you can capitalize it or not, but be consistent throughout your document.

➤ **The question is serious: do you think peace is possible?**

or

➤ **The question is serious: Do you think peace is possible?**

64 Abbreviations and Symbols

Unless you are writing a scientific or technical report, spell out most terms and titles, except in the cases discussed in this chapter.

www.mhhe.com/
awr
For information
and exercises on
abbreviations, go to

**Editing >
Abbreviations**

Abbreviations and Grammar Checkers

Computer grammar or spelling checkers may flag an abbreviation, but they generally will not tell you if your use of it is acceptable or consistent within a piece of writing.

64a Abbreviate familiar titles that always precede or follow a person's name.

Some abbreviations appear before a person's name (*Mr., Mrs., Dr.*) and some follow a proper name (*Jr., Sr., MD, Esq., PhD*). When an abbreviation follows a person's name, a comma is placed between the name and the abbreviation.

- ▪ **Before names:** Mrs. Jean Bascom; Dr. Epstein

- ▪ **After names:** Robert Robinson, Jr.; Elaine Less, CPA, LL.D.

Do not use two abbreviations that represent the same thing: *Dr. Peter Joyce, MD.* Use either *Dr. Peter Joyce* or *Peter Joyce, MD.* Spell out titles used without proper names.

>   *doctor.*
> **Mr. Carew asked if she had seen the ~~dr.~~**

64b Use abbreviations only when you know your readers will understand them.

If you use a technical term or the name of an organization in a report, you may abbreviate it as long as your readers are likely to be familiar with the abbreviation. Abbreviations of three or more capital letters generally do not use periods: *CBS, EPA, IRS, NAACP, USA.*

FAMILIAR ABBREVIATION   The EPA has had a lasting impact on the air quality of this country.

UNFAMILIAR ABBREVIATION   After you have completed them, take these
                           the Human Resources and Education Center.
                        forms to ~~HREC.~~

Write out an unfamiliar term or name the first time you use it, and give the abbreviation in parentheses.

> **The Student Nonviolent Coordinating Committee (SNCC) was far to the left of other civil rights organizations, and its leaders often mocked the "conservatism" of Dr. Martin Luther King, Jr. The SNCC quickly burned itself out and disappeared.**

Note: In the body of a paper, you can use *U.S.* as an adjective (*U.S. Constitution*) but not as a noun (*I grew up outside of the United States.*)

CHARTING the TERRITORY

Abbreviations and Symbols

Some abbreviations and symbols may be acceptable in certain contexts, as long as readers will know what they stand for. For example, a medical writer might use *PT* (*physical therapy*) in a medical report or professional newsletter.

CHARTING the TERRITORY

Scientific and Latin Abbreviations

Most abbreviations used in scientific or technical writing, such as those related to measurement, should be given without periods: *mph, lb, dc, rpm.* If an abbreviation looks like an actual word, however, you can use a period to prevent confusion: *in., Fig.*

In some types of scholarly writing, the use of Latin abbreviations is acceptable. When Latin abbreviations are used in scholarly work, they generally appear in parenthetical statements.

64c Abbreviate words typically used with times, dates, and numerals, as well as units of measurement in charts and graphs.

Abbreviations or symbols associated with numbers should be used only when accompanying a number: *3 p.m.*, not *in the p.m.; $500,* not *How many $ do you have?* The abbreviation *B.C.* ("Before Christ") follows a date; *A.D.* ("in the year of our Lord") precedes the date. The alternative abbreviations *B.C.E.* ("Before the Common Era") and *C.E.* ("Common Era") can be used instead of *B.C.* or *A.D.*, respectively.

> 6:00 p.m. or 6:00 P.M. or 6 PM
> 9:45 a.m. or 9:45 A.M. or 9:45 AM
> 498 B.C. or 498 B.C.E. or 498 BCE
> A.D. 275 or 275 C.E. or 275 CE
> 6,000 rpm
> 271 cm

> *Note:* Be consistent. If you use *a.m.* in one sentence, do not switch to *A.M.* in the next sentence.

In charts and graphs, abbreviations and symbols such as = for *equals, in.* for *inches,* % for *percent,* and *$* with numbers are acceptable because they save space.

64d Avoid Latin abbreviations in formal writing.

In formal writing, it is usually a good idea to avoid even common Latin abbreviations (*e.g., et al., etc.,* and *i.e.*). Instead of *e.g.,* use *such as* or *for example.*

cf.	compare (*confer*)
e.g.	for example, such as (*exempli gratia*)
et al.	and others (*et alia*)
etc.	and so forth, and so on (*et cetera*)
i.e.	that is (*id est*)
N.B.	note well (*nota bene*)
viz.	namely (*videlicet*)

64e Avoid inappropriate abbreviations and symbols.

Days of the week (*Sat.*), places (*TX* or *Tex.*), the word *company* (*Co.*), people's names (*Wm.*), disciplines and professions (*econ.*), parts of speech (*v.*), parts of written works (*ch., p.*), symbols (*@*), and units of measurement (*lb.*) are all spelled out in formal writing.

➤ The *environmental* (not *env.*) engineers from the Paramus Water *Company* (not *Co.*) are arriving in *New York City* (not *NYC*) this *Thursday* (not *Thurs.*) to correct the problems in the *physical education* (not *phys. ed.*) building in time for *Christmas* (not *Xmas*).

Exceptions: If an abbreviation such as *Inc., Co.,* or *Corp.* is part of a company's official name, then it can be included in formal writing: *Time Inc. announced these changes in late December.* The ampersand symbol (&) can also be used but only if it is part of an official name: *Church & Dwight.*

TextConnex

Digital Age Abbreviations and Acronyms

CD	compact disc
CD-ROM	compact disc read-only memory
DVD	digital videodisc
FTP	file transfer protocol
HTML	hypertext markup language
HTTP	hypertext transfer protocol
KB	kilobyte
MB	megabyte
MOO	multiuser domain, object-oriented
URL	uniform resource locator
WWW	World Wide Web

65 Numbers

www.mhhe.com/
awr
For information
and exercises
numbers, go to

Editing > Numbers

65a In nontechnical writing, spell out numbers up to one hundred and round numbers greater than one hundred.

➤ Approximately *twenty-five* students failed the exam, but more than *two hundred and fifty* passed.

When you are using a great many numbers or when a spelled-out number would require more than three or four words, use numerals.

➤ This regulation affects nearly *10,500* taxpayers, substantially more than the *200* originally projected. Of those affected, *2,325* filled out the papers incorrectly and another *743* called the office for help.

Round numbers larger than one million are expressed in numerals and words: 8 million, 2.4 trillion.

Use all numerals rather than mixing numerals and spelled-out words for the same type of item in a passage.

➤ We wrote to 132 people but only ~~sixteen~~ responded.
                                        16

65b Spell out a number that begins a sentence.

If a numeral begins a sentence, reword the sentence or spell out the numeral.

➤ *Twenty-five* children are in each elementary class.

65c In technical and business writing, use numerals for exact measurements and all numbers greater than ten.

➤ The endosperm halves were placed in each of 14 small glass test tubes.

581

➤ A solution with a GA_3 concentration ranging from 0 g/ml to 10^5 g/ml was added to each test tube.

➤ With its $1.9 trillion economy, Germany has an important trade role to play.

65d Use numerals for dates, times of day, addresses, and similar kinds of conventional quantitative information.

- **Dates:** October 9, 2002; 1558–1603; A.D. 1066 (*or* AD 1066); *but* October ninth, May first

- **Time of day:** 6 A.M. (*or* AM *or* a.m.), a quarter past eight in the evening, three o'clock in the morning

- **Addresses:** 21 Meadow Road, Apt. 6J; Grand Island, NY 14072

- **Percentages:** 73 percent, 73%

- **Fractions and decimals:** 21.84, 6½, two-thirds (*not* 2-thirds), a fourth

- **Measurements:** 100 miles per hour (*or* 100 mph), 9 kilograms (*or* 9 kg), 38°F, 15°Celsius, 3 tablespoons, 4 liters (*or* 4 l), 18 inches (*or* 18 in.)

- **Volume, chapter, page:** volume 4, chapter 8, page 44

- **Scenes in a play:** *Hamlet,* act 2, scene 1, lines 77–84

- **Scores and statistics:** 0 to 3, 98–92, an average age of 35

- **Amounts of money:** 10¢, (*or* 10 cents), $125, $2.25, $2.8 million (*or* $2,000,000)

- **Serial or identification numbers:** batch number 4875, 15.20 on the AM dial

- **Telephone numbers:** (716) 555-2174

Note: In nontechnical writing, spell out the names of units of measurement (*inches, liters*) in text. You can use abbreviations (*in., l*) and symbols (%) in charts and graphs to save space.

Dates and Decimals

In American English, the day usually follows the month in dates: *May 9, 2005; 5/9/05.* Decimals are preceded by a period (one-tenth = 0.1), and commas are used within whole numbers longer than four numerals (twenty-two thousand three = 22,003). In four-digit numbers, the comma is optional: *4,010* or *4010.*

66 Italics (Underlining)

Italics, a typeface in which the characters slant to the right, is used to set off certain words and phrases. If italics is not available, however, you can <u>underline</u> words that would be typeset in italics. Your instructor may <u>prefer</u> that you use underlining rather than italics, especially if you are following the MLA style of documentation. (*See Tab 6: MLA Documentation Style.*)

www.mhhe.com/
awr
For information
and exercises on
italics, go to
Editing > Italics

➤ **Tom Hanks gives one of his best performances in *Saving Private Ryan.***

➤ **Tom Hanks gives one of his best performances in <u>Saving Private Ryan.</u>**

66a Italicize (underline) titles of lengthy works or separate publications.

Italicize (or underline) titles of long works or works that are not part of a larger publication.

TEXTCONNEX

Italics and Underlining

Depending on the software you are using, italics or underlining may not be available for your e-mail messages. To indicate underlining, put an underscore mark or an asterisk before and after what you would italicize or underline in a manuscript: Tom Hanks gives one of his best performances in _Saving Private Ryan_.

To create Web sites, many people use HyperText Markup Language (HTML). In HTML, underlining indicates a hypertext link. If your work is going to be posted on the World Wide Web, use italics instead of underlining for titles to avoid confusion.

Works That Should Be Italicized (or Underlined)

- **Books (including textbooks):** *The Color of Water, The Art of Public Speaking*
- **Magazines and journals:** *Texas Monthly, College English*
- **Newspapers:** *Chicago Tribune*
- **Comic strips:** *Dilbert*
- **Plays, films, television series, radio programs:** *Death of a Salesman, On the Waterfront, The American Experience, Car Talk*
- **Long musical compositions:** Beethoven's *Pastoral Symphony* (*But* Beethoven's Symphony No. 6—the title consists of the musical form, a number, and/or a key.)
- **Choreographic works:** Balanchine's *Jewels*
- **Artworks:** Edward Hopper's *Nighthawks*
- **Web sites:** *The Motley Fool*
- **Software:** *Microsoft PowerPoint*
- **Long poems:** *Odyssey*
- **Pamphlets:** *Gorges: A Guide to the Geology of the Ithaca Area*

In titles of lengthy works, *a, an,* or *the* is capitalized and italicized (underlined) if it is the first word, but *the* is not generally treated as part of the title in names of newspapers and periodicals in MLA or Chicago style: the *New York Times.* If you are following APA or CSE style, however, you should treat *the* as part of the title.

> *Exceptions:* Do not use italics or underlining when referring to the Bible and other sacred books.

Court cases may also be italicized or underlined, but legal documents are not.

➤ **In *Brown v. Board of Education of Topeka* (1954), the U.S. Supreme Court ruled that segregation in public schools is unconstitutional.**

➤ **He obtained a writ of habeas corpus.**

Do not italicize or underline punctuation marks that follow a title unless they are part of the title: I finally finished reading *Moby Dick*!

Quotation marks are used for the titles of short works—essays, newspaper and magazine articles and columns, short stories, and short poems. Quotation marks are also used for titles of unpublished works when they are referred to within text, including student papers, theses, and dissertations. (*See Chapter 61, pp. 556–57, for more on quotation marks with titles.*)

66b Italicize (underline) the names of ships, trains, aircraft, and spaceships.

Queen Mary 2   *Montrealer*   *Spirit of St. Louis*   *Apollo 11*

Do not italicize any abbreviations used with the name, such as HMS or SS. Model names and numbers (such as Boeing 747) are not italicized.

66c Italicize (underline) foreign terms.

➤ **In the Paris airport, we recognized the familiar no smoking sign: *Défense de fumer.***

Many foreign words have become so common in English that everyone accepts them as part of the language and they require no italics or underlining: rigor mortis, pasta, and sombrero, for example.

66d Italicize (underline) scientific names.

The scientific (Latin) names of organisms, consisting of the genus and species, are always italicized.

> ➤ **Most chicks are infected with *Cryptosporidium baileyi*, a parasite typical of young animals.**

> *Note:* Although the whole name is italicized, only the genus part of the name is capitalized.

66e Italicize (underline) words, letters, and numbers referred to as themselves.

For clarity, italicize words or phrases used as words rather than for the meaning they convey. (You may also use quotation marks for this purpose.)

> ➤ **The term *romantic* does not mean the same thing to the Shelley scholar that it does to the fan of Danielle Steele's novels.**

Letters and numbers used alone should also be italicized.

> ➤ **The word *bookkeeper* has three sets of double letters: double *o*, double *k*, and double *e*.**

> ➤ **Add a *3* to that column.**

66f Use italics (underlining) sparingly for emphasis.

An occasional word in italics helps you make a point. Too much emphasis, however, may mean no emphasis at all.

WEAK	You don't *mean* that your *teacher* told the whole *class* that *he* did not know the answer *himself*?
REVISED	Your teacher admitted that he did not know the answer? That is amazing.

> *Note:* If you add italics or underlining to a quotation, indicate the change in parentheses following the quotation.
>
> ➤ **Instead of promising that no harm will come to us, Blake only assures us that we "need not *fear* harm" (emphasis added).**

67 Hyphens

67a Use hyphens to form compound words and to avoid confusion.

www.mhhe.com/
awr
For information
and exercises on
hyphens, go to
Editing > Hyphens

A hyphen joins two nouns to make one compound word. Scientists speak of a *kilogram-meter* as a measure of force, and professors of literature talk about the *scholar-poet*. Unlike a dash (-- or —), which is used *between* words, a hyphen is used *within* words. The hyphen lets us know that the two nouns work together as one. As compound nouns come into general use, the hyphens between them disappear: *firefighter, thundershower.*

A dictionary is the best resource when you are unsure about whether to use a hyphen. If you cannot find a compound word in the dictionary, spell it as two separate words. Whatever spelling you choose, be consistent throughout your document.

67b Use hyphens to join two or more words to create compound adjective or noun forms.

A noun can also be linked with an adjective, an adverb, or another part of speech to form a compound adjective.

accident-prone   quick-witted

Hyphens are also used in nouns designating family relationships and compounds of more than two words:

brother-in-law   stay-at-home

Note: Compound nouns with hyphens generally form plurals by adding *s* or *es* to the most important word.

attorney general/attorney<u>s</u> general
mother-in-law/mother<u>s</u>-in-law

Some proper nouns that are joined to make an adjective are hyphenated.

the Franco-Prussian war   of Mexican-American heritage   **587**

Hyphens often help clarify adjectives that come before the word they modify. Modifiers that are hyphenated when they are placed *before* the word they modify are usually not hyphenated when they are placed *after* the word they modify.

➤ **It was a *bad-mannered* reply.**

➤ **The reply was *bad mannered*.**

Do not use a hyphen to connect *-ly* adverbs to the words they modify.

➤ **They explored the newly⁄discovered territories.**

In a pair or series of compound nouns or adjectives, add suspended hyphens after the first word of each item.

➤ **The child care center accepted three-, four-, and five-year-olds.**

67c Use hyphens to spell out fractions and compound numbers.

Use a hyphen when writing out fractions or compound numbers from twenty-one to ninety-nine.

three-fourths of a gallon   thirty-two

Note: Use a hyphen to show inclusive numbers: *pages 100-140.*

67d Use a hyphen to attach some prefixes and suffixes.

Use a hyphen to join a prefix and a capitalized word.

un-American   pre-Columbian
mid-August   neo-Nazi

A hyphen is sometimes used to join a capital letter and a word.

T-shirt   V-six engine

The prefixes *all-, ex-, quasi-* and *self-,* and the suffixes *-elect, -odd,* and *-something)* generally take hyphens.

all-purpose   president-elect
ex-convict   fifty-odd
quasi-scientific   thirty-something
self-sufficient

Most prefixes, however, are not attached by hyphens, unless a hyphen is needed to show pronunciation, avoid double letters (*anti-immigration*), or reveal a special meaning that distinguishes the word from the same word without a hyphen: *recreate* (play) versus *re-create* (make again). Check a dictionary to be sure you are using the standard spelling.

67e Use hyphens to divide words at the ends of lines.

When you must divide words, do so between syllables. Pronunciation alone cannot always tell you where to divide a word, however. If you are unsure about how to break a word into syllables, consult your dictionary.

> ➤ **My writing group had a very fruitful *collab-***
> ***oration.* [not *colla-boration*]**

Never leave just one or two letters on a line.

> ➤ **He seemed so sad and vulnerable and so *discon-***
> ***nected* from his family. [not *disconnect-ed*]**

Compound words such as *hardworking, rattlesnake,* and *book-case* should be broken only between the words that form them: *hard-working, rattle-snake, book-case.* Compound words that already have hyphens, like *brother-in-law,* are broken after the hyphens only.

Note: Never hyphenate an acronym (CIA) or a one-syllable word.

TextConnex

Dividing Internet Addresses

If you need to divide an Internet address between lines, divide it after a slash. Do not divide a word within the address with a hyphen; readers may assume the hyphen is part of the address.

68 Spelling

Proofread your writing carefully. Misspellings creep into the prose of even the best writers. Use the following strategies to help you improve your spelling.

www.mhhe.com/
awr
For information
and exercises on
spelling, go to

Editing > Spelling

- Become familiar with major spelling rules (68a).
- Learn to distinguish **homonyms**—words that are pronounced alike but that have different meanings and spellings (68b).
- Keep a list of words that give you trouble. Include tricks to help you remember how to spell particular words—for example, there is "a rat" in *separate.*
- Keep a good college dictionary at hand. If you are not sure how a word is spelled, try looking up different combinations of letters, based on how you pronounce the word, until you hit the right one. You can also type a synonym for the word and use your word-processing program's thesaurus. The word you are looking for may be listed as an alternative.

Spelling Checkers

Computer spell checkers are helpful tools. The most recent versions of some commonly used word-processing programs will automatically correct obvious misspellings as you type them. Spell checkers will also give you a list of possible substitutes for a highlighted word if you right-click on the word. All spell checkers have limitations, however. They cannot tell *how* you are using a particular word. If you write *their* but mean *there,* spell checkers cannot point out your mistake. They also cannot point out many misspelled proper nouns. To catch these kinds of errors, you need to proofread your work yourself.

68a Learn the rules that generally hold for spelling, as well as their exceptions.

1. *i* before *e*
Use *i* before *e* except after *c* or when sounded like *a,* as in *neighbor* and *weigh.*

- *i* **before** *e:* believe, relieve, chief, grief, wield, yield
- **Except after** *c:* receive, deceive, ceiling, conceit
- **Exceptions:** seize, caffeine, codeine, weird, height

2. Adding suffixes

- **Final silent** *e:* When adding a suffix that begins with a vowel, drop the final silent *e* from the root word. Keep the final *e* if the suffix begins with a consonant.

  force/forcing   remove/removable
  surprise/surprising   care/careful

  Exceptions: argue/argument, true/truly, change/changeable, judge/judgment, acknowledge/acknowledgment

---

Exception: Keep the silent *e* if it is needed to clarify the pronunciation or if the word would be confused with another word without the *e*.

dye/dyeing (to avoid confusion with *dying*)
hoe/hoeing (to avoid mispronunciation)

- **Final** *y:* When adding the suffix *-ing* to a word ending in *y,* retain the *y.*

  enjoy/enjoying   cry/crying

  Change the *y* to *i* or *ie* when the final *y* follows a consonant, but not when it follows a vowel.

  happy/happier   defray/defrayed

- **Final consonants:** When adding a suffix to a word that ends in a consonant preceded by a vowel, double the final consonant if the root word has only one syllable or an accent on the last syllable.

  grip/gripping   refer/referred

  Exceptions: bus/busing, focus/focused

3. Forming plurals
Most plurals are formed by adding *s.* Some are formed by adding *es.*

When to Form the Plural with *es*

SINGULAR ENDING	PLURAL ENDING
s, sh, x, z, "soft" ch bus, bush, fox, buzz, peach	**es** buses, bushes, foxes, buzzes, peaches
consonant + o hero, tomato	**es** heroes, tomatoes
Exception: solo/solos	
consonant + y beauty, city	**change y to i and add es** beauties, cities
Exception: a person's name—Kirby, the Kirbys	
f, fe leaf, knife, wife	**change f to v and add s or es** leaves, knives, wives

Exception: Words that end in *ff* and some other words that end in *f* (*staff, roof*) form the plural by adding only an *s* (*staffs, roofs*).

Most plurals follow standard rules, but some have irregular forms (*child/children, tooth/teeth*), and some words with foreign roots create plurals in the pattern of the language they come from, as do these words.

addendum/addenda	datum/data
alumna/alumnae	medium/media
alumnus/alumni	phenomenon/phenomena
analysis/analyses	stimulus/stimuli
crisis/crises	thesis/theses
criterion/criteria	

Some nouns with foreign roots have regular and irregular plural forms (*appendix / appendices / appendixes*). Be consistent in using the spelling you choose.

> *Note:* Some writers now treat *data* as though it were singular, but the preferred practice is still to recognize that *data* is plural and takes a plural verb: *The data are clear on this point: the pass/fail course has become outdated by events.*

Compound nouns with hyphens generally form plurals by adding *s* or *es* to the most important word.

attorney general/attorneys general
mother-in-law/mothers-in-law

For some compound words that appear as one word, the same rule applies (*passersby*); for others, it does not (*cupfuls*). Consult a dictionary if you are not sure.

If both words in the compound are equally important, add *s* to the second word: *singer-songwriters*.

A few words such as *fish* and *sheep* have the same forms for singular and plural. To indicate that the word is plural, you need to add a word or words that indicate quantity: *five fish, a few sheep*.

For MULTILINGUAL STUDENTS

American and British Spelling

Standard British spelling differs from American spelling for some words—among them *color / colour, canceled / cancelled, theater / theatre, realize / realise,* and *judgment / judgement*.

68b Learn to distinguish words pronounced alike but spelled differently.

Homonyms sound alike but have different meanings and different spellings. Many are commonly confused, so you should check them when you proofread your work. The following is a list of common homonyms as well as words that are almost homonyms. For more complete definitions, consult the Glossary of Usage (*Chapter 50, pp. 449–58*) and a dictionary.

COMMON HOMONYMS and NEAR HOMONYMS

accept: "to take willingly"
except: "to leave out" (verb); "but for" (preposition)

affect: "to influence" (verb); "a feeling or an emotion" (noun)
effect: "to make or accomplish" (verb); "result" (noun)

all ready: "prepared"
already: "by this time"

discreet: "tactful" or "prudent"
discrete: "separate" or "distinct"

cite: "to quote or refer to"
sight: "spectacle, sense"
site: "place"

(*continued*)

COMMON HOMONYMS and
NEAR HOMONYMS (continued)

desert: "dry, sandy place" (noun); "to leave" (verb)
dessert: "after-dinner course"

hear: "perceive by listening"
here: "at this place"

it's: contraction for *it is* or *it has*
its: possessive pronoun

loose: "not tight"
lose: "to misplace"

passed: past tense of *pass*
past: "former time"

peace: "quiet, harmony"
piece: "part of"

plain: "simple"
plane: "aircraft" or "tool for leveling wood"

precede: "to come before"
proceed: "to go forward"

principal: "most important" (adjective); "the head of an organization" or "a sum of money" (noun)
principle: "a basic standard or law" (noun)

their: possessive pronoun
there: adverb of place
they're: contraction for *they are*

to: indicating movement
too: "also"
two: number

weather: "atmospheric condition"
whether: "if it is or was true"

who's: contraction for *who is*
whose: possessive of *who*

your: possessive pronoun
you're: contraction for *you are*

Shinjuku's Skyscraper District in Tokyo—featured in Lost in Translation—caters to an international, multilingual populace with signs in Japanese and English.

12

Grammar and rhetoric are complementary.... Grammar maps out the possible; rhetoric narrows the possible down to the desirable or effective.
—FRANCIS CHRISTENSEN

Basic Grammar Review

WITH TIPS FOR MULTILINGUAL WRITERS

12 Basic Grammar Review

What Was the Language of Your Ancestors?

Your native language or even the language of your ancestors may influence the way you use English. Even if English is your first language, you may be part of a group that immigrated generations ago but has retained traces of other grammatical structures. For example, the slang contraction *ain't,* brought here by Scottish settlers, may have meant *am not* at one time. Take note of the Tips for Multilingual Writers in this section. Some might help native speakers as well.

Written language, although based on the grammar of spoken language, has a logic and rules of its own. The chapters that follow explain the basic rules of standard written English.

Tip for Multilingual Writers:
Recognizing language differences

www.mhhe.com/
awr
For information
and exercises on
problem areas for
multilingual writers,
go to
Editing >
Multilingual/ESL
Writers

The standard structures of sentences in languages other than English can be very different from those in English. In other languages, the form of a verb can indicate its grammatical function more powerfully than can its placement in the sentence. Also, in languages other than English, adjectives may take on the function that articles (*a, an, the*) perform, or articles can be absent entirely.

If your first language is not English, try to pinpoint the areas of difficulty you have in English. See whether you are attempting to *translate* the structures of your native language into English. If so, you will need to learn more about English sentence structure.

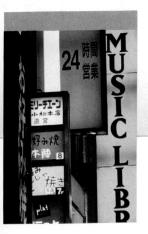

69 Parts of Speech

Grammar gives us a way of talking about how sentences are put together to make sense. Although *The toves gimbled in the*

597

www.mhhe.com/
awr
For information and
exercises on parts
of speech, go to

Editing >
Parts of Speech

wabe—from Lewis Carroll's poem "Jabberwocky"—is a group of words that in and of themselves do not make sense, the sentence does make grammatical sense. Because what makes a sentence meaningful is not just the individual words but also the pattern or ordering of its parts, you can answer questions like *What gimbled in the wabe? (the toves), What did the toves do in the wabe? (they gimbled),* and *Where did the toves gimble? (in the wabe).*

English has eight primary **parts of speech:** verbs, nouns, pronouns, adjectives, adverbs, prepositions, conjunctions, and interjections. All English words belong to one or more of these categories. Particular words can belong to different categories, depending on the role they play in a sentence. For example, the word *button* can be a noun *(the button on a coat)* or a verb *(he will button his jacket now).*

69a Verbs

Verbs carry a lot of information. They report action *(run, write)*, condition *(bloom, sit)*, or state of being *(be, seem)*. Verbs also change form to indicate person, number, tense, voice, and mood. To do all this, a **main verb** is often preceded by one or more **helping verbs,** thereby becoming a **verb phrase.**

> mv
➤ The play *begins* at eight.

> hv   mv   hv   mv
➤ I *may change* seats after the play *has begun.*

1. Main verbs

Main verbs change form (**tense**) to indicate when something has happened. If a word does not indicate tense, it is not a main verb. All main verbs have five forms, except for *be,* which has eight.

BASE FORM	*(talk, sing)*
PAST TENSE	Yesterday I *(talked, sang).*
PAST PARTICIPLE	In the past, I have *(talked, sung).*
PRESENT PARTICIPLE	Right now I am *(talking, singing).*
-S FORM	Usually he/she/it *(talks, sings).*

(For more on subject-verb agreement and verb tense, see Tab 10: Editing for Grammar Conventions, pp. 476–78 and 485–86, and the list of common irregular verbs on pp. 487–88.)

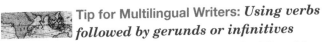 Tip for Multilingual Writers: *Using verbs followed by gerunds or infinitives*

Verbs in English differ as to whether they can be followed by a gerund, an infinitive, or either. Some verbs, like *avoid,* can be followed by a gerund but not an infinitive.

> We avoided ~~to climb~~ climbing the mountain during the storm.

Other verbs, like *attempt,* can be followed by an infinitive but not a gerund.

> We attempted ~~reaching~~ to reach the summit when the weather
>
> cleared.

Others can be followed by either a gerund or an infinitive with no change in meaning.

> We began climbing.

> We began to climb.

Still others have a different meaning when followed by a gerund than they do when followed by an infinitive. Compare these examples:

> She stopped eating.

She was eating but she stopped.

> She stopped to eat.

She stopped what she was doing before in order to eat.

The following lists provide common examples of each type of verb.

Some Verbs That Take Only an Infinitive

afford	hurry	promise
appear	intend	refuse
attempt	learn	request
choose	manage	seem
claim	mean	tend
decide	need	threaten
expect	offer	want
fail	plan	wish
hope	prepare	would like

Some Verbs That Take Only a Gerund

admit	finish	recommend
advise	forgive	regret
avoid	imagine	resist
consider	look forward to	risk
defend	mention	suggest
deny	mind	support
discuss	practice	tolerate
enjoy	propose	understand
feel like	quit	urge

Some Verbs That Can Take Either a Gerund or an Infinitive

An asterisk (*) indicates those verbs for which the choice of gerund or infinitive affects meaning.

begin	love	start
continue	prefer	*stop
hate	*remember	*try
like		

> *Note:* For some verbs, such as *allow, cause, encourage, have, persuade, remind,* and *tell,* a noun or pronoun must precede the infinitive: *I reminded my sister to return my sweater.* For a few verbs, such as *ask, expect, need,* and *want,* the noun may either precede or follow the infinitive, depending on the meaning you want to express: *I want to return my sweater to my sister. I want my sister to return my sweater.*
>
> *Make, let,* and *have* are followed by a noun or pronoun plus the base form without *to: Make that boy come home on time.*

2. Helping verbs that show time

Some helping verbs—mostly forms of *be, have,* and *do*—function to signify time (*will have been playing, has played*) or emphasis (*does play*). Forms of *do* are also used to ask questions (*Do you play?*). Here is a fuller list of such helping (**auxiliary**) verbs.

be, am, is	being, been	do, does, did
are, was, were	have, has, had	

Tip for Multilingual Writers: *Matching helping verbs* (do, have, be) *with the appropriate form of the main verb*

Do, Does, Did

The helping verb *do* and its forms *does* and *did* combine with the base form of a verb to ask a question or to emphasize something. It can also combine with the word *not* to create an emphatic negative statement.

QUESTION	*Do* you hear those dogs barking?
EMPHATIC STATEMENT	I *do* hear them barking.
EMPHATIC NEGATIVE	I *do not* want to have to call the police about those dogs.

Have, Has, Had

The helping verb *have* and its forms *has* and *had* combine with a past participle (usually ending in *-d, -t,* or *-n*) to form the *perfect tenses.* Do not confuse the simple past tense with the present perfect tense (formed with *have* or *has*), which is distinct from the simple past because the action can continue in the present. (*For a review of perfect tense forms, see Tab 10: Editing for Grammar Conventions, p. 493.*)

SIMPLE PAST	Those dogs *barked* all day.
PRESENT PERFECT	Those dogs *have barked* all day.
PAST PERFECT	Those dogs *had barked* all day.

Be

Forms of *be* combine with a present participle (ending in *-ing*) to form the *progressive tenses,* which express continuing action. Do not confuse the simple present tense or the present perfect with these progressive forms. Unlike the simple present, which indicates an action that occurs frequently and might include the present moment, the present progressive form indicates an action that is going on right now. In its past form, the progressive tense indicates actions that are going on simultaneously. (*For a review of progressive tense forms, see Tab 10: Editing for Grammar Conventions, pp. 493–94.*)

SIMPLE PRESENT	Those dogs *bark* all the time.
PRESENT PROGRESSIVE	Those dogs *are barking* all the time.
PAST PROGRESSIVE	Those dogs *were barking* all day while I *was trying* to study.

When *be* is used as a helping verb, it is preceded by a modal verb such as *can* or *may: I may be leaving tomorrow.* When *been* is the helping verb, it is preceded by a form of *have: I have been painting my room all day.*

Forms of *be* combine with the past participle (which usually ends in *-d, -t,* or *-n*) to form the passive voice, which is often used to express a state of being instead of an action.

BE + PAST PARTICIPLE

PASSIVE	The dogs *were scolded* by their owner.
PASSIVE	I *was satisfied* by her answer.

When *be, being,* or *been* is the helping verb, it needs another helping verb to be complete.

MODAL VERB	The dogs *will be scolded* by their owner.
ANOTHER FORM OF ***BE***	The dogs *were being scolded* by their owner.
FORM OF ***HAVE***	The dogs *have been scolded* by their owner.

3. Modals

Other helping verbs, called **modals,** express an attitude toward the action or circumstance of a sentence:

can	ought to	will
could	shall	would
may	should	must
might		

Modal verbs share several characteristics:

- They do not change form to indicate person or number.
- They do not change form to indicate tense.
- They are followed directly by the base form of the verb without *to*.

➤   **We must ~~to~~ study now.**

Some verbal expressions ending in *to* also function as modals, including *have to, be able to,* and *be supposed to.* These **phrasal modals** behave more like ordinary verbs than true modals, changing form to indicate tense and agree with the subject.

Tip for Multilingual Writers: *Understanding the form and meaning of modal verbs*

Modals are used to do the following:

- **Ask permission:** *may, might, can, could*
  May (Might / Can / Could) I come at five o'clock?

- **Pose a polite request:** *would*
  Would you please open the door?

- **Express ability:** *can, am/is/are able to; was/were able to*
  I *can (am able to)* take one piece of luggage.

- **Express possibility:** *may (might)*
  She *may (might)* return this afternoon.

- **Express expectation:** *should*
  I *should* finish my project today.

- **Express necessity:** *must (have to)*
  I *must (have to)* pass this test.

- **Express prohibition:** *must + not*
  You *must not* go there.

- **Express logical deduction:** *must (has to)*
  He *must (has to)* be there by now.

- **Express intention:** *will (shall)*
  I *will (shall)* go today.

69b Nouns

Nouns name people (*Shakespeare, actors, Englishman*), places (*Manhattan, city, island*), things (*Kleenex, handkerchief, sneeze, cats*), and ideas (*Marxism, justice, democracy, clarity*).

➤ ***Shakespeare*** lived in ***England*** and wrote ***plays*** about the human ***condition.***

1. Proper and common nouns

Proper nouns name specific people, places, and things and are always capitalized: *Aretha Franklin, Hinduism, Albany, Microsoft.* All other nouns are **common nouns:** *singer, religion, capital, corporation.*

2. Count and noncount nouns

A common noun that refers to something specific that can be counted is a **count noun.** Count nouns can be singular or plural, like *cup* or *suggestion* (*four cups, several suggestions*). **Noncount nouns** are nonspecific; these common nouns refer to categories of people, places, or things and cannot be counted. They do not have a plural form. (*The pottery is beautiful. His advice was useful.*)

Count Nouns

cars	facts	suggestions
clouds	machines	tables
computers	smiles	tools
earrings	stars	

Noncount Nouns

advice	information	rain
equipment	Internet	sunshine
furniture	jewelry	transportation
happiness	machinery	

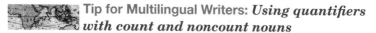 **Tip for Multilingual Writers:** *Using quantifiers with count and noncount nouns*

Consult an ESL dictionary if you have trouble determining whether a word is a count or noncount noun. If a word is a noncount noun, it will not have a plural form.

Note: Many nouns can be either count or noncount depending on the context in which they appear.

➤ **Baseball** [the game: noncount] **is never played with two**

 baseballs [the object: count] **at the same time.**

Count and noncount nouns are often preceded by **quantifiers,** words that tell how much or how many. Because noncount nouns are singular only and refer to things that cannot be counted, they require different quantifiers than count nouns, which refer to countable entities and can be plural. Following is a list of some quantifiers for count nouns and for noncount nouns, as well as a few quantifiers that can be used with both.

 ■ **With count nouns only:** *several, many, a couple of, a number of, a few, few*

■ **With noncount nouns only:** *a great deal of, much, not much, little, a little, less,* a word that indicates a unit (*a bag of sugar*)

■ **With either count or noncount nouns:** *all, any, some, a lot of*

Note: The quantifiers *a few* and *few* for count nouns and *a little* and *little* for noncount nouns all indicate a small quantity. In contrast to *a few* and *a little,* however, *few* and *little* have the negative connotation of *hardly any.*

➤ **The problems are difficult, and we have few options for solving them.**

The outlook for solving the problems is gloomy.

➤ **The problems are difficult, but we have a few options for solving them.**

The outlook for solving the problems is hopeful.

➤ **We have little time to find a campsite before sunset.**

The campers might spend the night in the open by the side of the trail.

➤ **We have a little time to find a campsite before sunset.**

The campers will probably find a place to pitch a tent before dark.

(*For help using articles with count and noncount nouns, see the section on pp. 606–8.*)

3. Concrete and abstract nouns

Nouns that name things that can be perceived by the senses are called **concrete nouns:** *boy, wind, book, song.* **Abstract nouns** name qualities and concepts that do not have physical properties: *charity, patience, beauty, hope.* (*For more on using concrete and abstract nouns, see Tab 9: Editing for Clarity, pp. 441–42.*)

4. Singular and plural nouns

Most nouns name things that can be counted and are singular or plural. Singular nouns typically become plural by adding *s* or *es*: *boy/boys, ocean/oceans, church/churches, agency/agencies.* Some have irregular plurals, such as *man/men, child/children,* and *tooth/teeth.* Noncount nouns like *intelligence* and *electricity* do not form plurals.

5. Collective nouns

Collective nouns such as *team, family, herd,* and *orchestra* are treated as singular. They are not noncount nouns, however, because collective nouns can be counted and can be made plural: *teams, families*. (*Also see Tab 10: Editing for Grammar Conventions, pp. 481 and 501–3.*)

6. Possessive nouns

When nouns are used in the **possessive case** to indicate ownership, they change their form. To form the possessive case, singular nouns add an apostrophe plus *s* (*'s*), whereas plural nouns ending in *-s* just add an apostrophe ('). (*Also see Tab 11: Editing for Correctness, pp. 547–52.*)

SINGULAR	insect	insect's sting
PLURAL	neighbors	neighbors' car

Tip for Multilingual Writers:
Using articles (a, an, the) *appropriately*

Some languages do not use articles at all, and most languages do not use articles in the same way as English. Therefore, articles often cause problems for multilingual writers. Articles in English express three basic meanings: indefinite (indicating nonspecific reference), definite (indicating specific reference), and generic (indicating reference to a general category).

Indefinite and definite meaning

A noun has an indefinite meaning, or a nonspecific reference, when it is first mentioned. To express an indefinite meaning with count nouns, use the **indefinite article** (*a, an*) for singular forms and no article for plural forms.

➤ I bought *a* new computer.

➤ I bought new computers.

Note: Noncount nouns *never* take the indefinite article.

    Knowledge
➤ A~~knowledge~~ is a valuable commodity.

To express a definite meaning or a specific reference, use the **definite article** (*the*) with both noncount nouns and singular and plural count nouns. A noun has a definite meaning or a specific reference in a variety of situations:

■ **When the noun identifies something previously mentioned:**

I was driving along Main Street when *a* car [nonspecific reference] pulled up behind me. *The* car [specific reference to the previously mentioned car] swerved into the left lane and sped out of sight.

■ **When the noun identifies something familiar or known from the context:**

We could not play today because *the* soccer field was wet.

■ **When the noun identifies a unique subject:**

The moon will be full tonight.

■ **When the noun is modified by a superlative adjective:**

We adopted *the* most economical strategy.

■ **When information in modifying phrases and clauses makes the noun definite:**

The goal *of this discussion* is to explain article use.

Generic meaning

A noun is used generically when it is meant to represent all the individuals in the category it names. Singular count nouns used generically can take either an indefinite article or a definite article depending on the context.

➤ *A student* **can use the Internet to research** *a topic* **efficiently.**

➤ *The university* **is an institution with roots in ancient times.**

Plural nouns used generically take no article.

➤ *Psychologists* **believe that** *children* **should reduce the amount of time they spend watching television.**

Articles and proper nouns

Most proper nouns are not used with articles.

➤ ~~The~~ **Arizona is a dry state.**

Some proper nouns, however, do take the definite article.

➤ ***The* Civil War was a watershed event in American history.**

Some other exceptions are the names of structures (*the White House*), names that include the word *of* (*the Fourth of July*), and many countries with names that are two or more words long (*the Dominican Republic*).

Whenever you encounter an unfamiliar proper noun, determine whether it is used with a definite article.

69c Pronouns

A **pronoun** takes the place of a noun. The noun that the pronoun replaces is called its **antecedent.** (*For more on pronoun-antecedent agreement, see Tab 10: Editing for Grammar Conventions, pp. 500–4.*)

➤ **The *snow* fell all day long, and by nightfall *it* was three feet deep.**

The box on pages 610–11 summarizes the different kinds of pronouns.

1. Personal pronouns
The **personal pronouns** *I, me, you, he, his, she, her, it, we, us, they,* and *them* refer to specific people or things and vary in form to indicate person, number, gender, and case. (*For more on pronoun reference and case, see Tab 10: Editing for Grammar Conventions, pp. 504–11.*)

➤ ***You* told *us* that *he* gave Jane a lock of *his* hair.**

2. Possessive pronouns
Like possessive nouns, **possessive pronouns** indicate ownership. However, unlike possessive nouns, possessive pronouns do not add apostrophes: *my/mine, your/yours, her/hers, his, its, our/ours, their/theirs.*

➤ **Brunch is at *her* place this Saturday.**

3. Reflexive and intensive pronouns
Pronouns ending in -*self* or -*selves* are either reflexive or intensive. **Reflexive pronouns** refer back to the subject and are necessary for sentence sense.

➤ **Many of the women blamed *themselves* for the problem.**

Intensive pronouns add emphasis to the nouns or pronouns they follow and are grammatically optional.

➤ President Harding *himself* drank whiskey during Prohibition.

4. Relative pronouns

The **relative pronouns** *who, whom, whose, that,* and *which* relate a dependent clause—a word group containing a subject and verb and a subordinating word—to an antecedent noun or pronoun in the sentence.

dependent clause

➤ In Kipling's story, Dravot is the man *who* would be king.

The form of a relative pronoun varies according to its **case**—the grammatical role it plays in the sentence. (*For more on pronoun case, see Tab 10: Editing for Grammar Conventions, pp. 507–11.*)

5. Demonstrative pronouns

The **demonstrative pronouns** *this, that, these,* and *those* point out nouns and pronouns that come later.

➤ *This* is the book literary critics have been waiting for.

Sometimes these pronouns function as adjectives: *This book won the Pulitzer.* Sometimes they are noun equivalents: *This is my book.*

6. Interrogative pronouns

Interrogative pronouns such as *who, whatever,* and *whom* are used to ask questions.

➤ *Whatever* happened to you?

The form of the interrogative pronouns *who, whom, whoever* and *whomever* indicates the grammatical role they play in a sentence. (*See Tab 10: Editing for Grammar Conventions, pp. 507–11.*)

7. Indefinite pronouns

Indefinite pronouns such as *someone, anybody, nothing,* and *few* refer to a nonspecific person or thing and do not change form to indicate person, number, or gender.

➤ *Anybody* who cares enough to come and help may take *some* home.

PRONOUNS

PERSONAL (INCLUDING POSSESSIVE)

SINGULAR	PLURAL
I, me, my, mine	we, us, our, ours
you, your, yours	you, your, yours
he, him, his	they, them, their, theirs
she, her, hers	
it, its	

REFLEXIVE AND INTENSIVE

SINGULAR	PLURAL
myself	ourselves
yourself	yourselves
himself, herself, itself	themselves
oneself	

RELATIVE

who	whoever	what	whatever	that
whom	whomever	whose	whichever	which

DEMONSTRATIVE

this, that, these, those

Most indefinite pronouns are always singular (*anybody, everyone*). Some are always plural (*many, few*), and a handful can be singular or plural (*any, most*). (*See Tab 10, pp. 482–83 and 500–1.*)

8. Reciprocal pronouns

Reciprocal pronouns such as *each other* and *one another* refer to the separate parts of their plural antecedent.

➤ **My sister and I are close because we live near *each other*.**

INTERROGATIVE

who	what	which
whoever	whatever	whichever
whom	whomever	whose

INDEFINITE

SINGULAR		PLURAL	SINGULAR/PLURAL
anybody	nobody	both	all
anyone	no one	few	any
anything	none	many	either
each	nothing	several	more
everybody	one		most
everyone	somebody		some
everything	someone		
much	something		
neither			

RECIPROCAL

each other, any other

69d Adjectives

Adjectives modify nouns and pronouns by answering questions like *Which one? What kind? How many? What size? What color? What condition?* and *Whose?* They can describe, enumerate, identify, define, and limit (*one person, that person*). When articles (*a, an, the*) identify nouns, they function as adjectives.

Sometimes proper nouns are treated as adjectives; the proper adjectives that result are capitalized: *Britain/British.* Pronouns can also function as adjectives (*his green car*), and adjectives often have forms that allow you to make comparisons (*great, greater, greatest*).

➤ The *decisive* and *diligent* king regularly attended meetings of the council. [What kind of king?]

➤ *These four artistic* qualities affect how an advertisement is received. [Which, how many, what kind of qualities?]

➤ *My little blue* Volkswagen died *one icy winter* morning. [Whose, what size, what color car? Which, what kind of morning?]

Like all modifiers, adjectives should be close to the words they modify. Most often, adjectives appear before the noun they modify, but **descriptive adjectives**—adjectives that designate qualities or attributes—may come before or after the noun or pronoun they modify for stylistic reasons. Adjectives that describe the subject and follow linking verbs (*be, am, is, are, was, being, been, appear, become, feel, grow, look, make, prove, taste*) are called **subject complements.**

BEFORE SUBJECT

The *sick* and *destitute* poet no longer believed that love would save him.

AFTER SUBJECT

The poet, *sick* and *destitute,* no longer believed that love would save him.

AFTER LINKING VERB

No longer believing that love would save him, the poet was *sick* and *destitute.*

Tip for Multilingual Writers: *Using adjectives correctly*

English adjectives do not change form to agree with the form of the nouns they modify. They stay the same whatever the number or gender of the noun.

➤ Juan is an *attentive* father. Alyssa is an *attentive* mother. They are *attentive* parents.

Adjectives usually come before a noun, but they can also occur after a linking verb.

➤ We had a *delicious* meal.

➤ The food at the restaurant was *delicious.*

The position of an adjective can affect its meaning, however. The phrase *my old friend,* for example, can refer to a long friendship (*a friend I have known for a long time*) or an elderly friend (*my friend who is eighty years old*). In the sentence, *My friend is old,* by contrast, *old* has only one meaning—elderly.

Adjective order
When two or more adjectives modify a noun cumulatively, they follow a sequence—determined by their meaning—that is particular to English logic:

1. Adjectives of size and shape: *big, small, huge, tiny, tall, short, narrow, thick, round, square*
2. Adjectives that suggest subjective evaluation: *cozy, intelligent, outrageous, elegant, original*
3. Adjectives of color: *yellow, green, pale*
4. Adjectives of origin and type: *African, Czech, gothic*
5. Nouns used as adjectives: *brick, plastic, glass, stone*
6. NOUN

Here are some examples:

➤ **the small, cozy red brick cottage**

➤ **the tall African statues**

Present and past participles used as adjectives
Both the present and past participle forms of verbs can function as adjectives. To use them properly, keep the following in mind:

▪ Present participle adjectives usually modify nouns that are the agent of an action.

▪ Past participle adjectives usually modify nouns that are the recipient of an action.

➤ **This problem is *confusing.***

The present participle *confusing* modifies *problem,* which is the agent, or cause of the confusion.

➤ **The students are *confused* by the problem.**

The past participle *confused* modifies *students,* who are the recipients of the confusion the problem is causing.

The following are some other present and past participle pairs that often cause problems.

amazing/amazed	frightening/frightened
annoying/annoyed	interesting/interested
boring/bored	satisfying/satisfied
depressing/depressed	shocking/shocked
embarrassing/embarrassed	surprising/surprised
exciting/excited	tiring/tired
fascinating/fascinated	

69e Adverbs

Adverbs often end in -ly (*beautifully, gracefully, quietly*) and usually answer such questions as *When? Where? How? How often? How much? To what degree?* and *Why?*

➤ **The authenticity of the document is *hotly* contested. [How is it contested?]**

Adverbs modify verbs, other adverbs, and adjectives. Like adjectives, adverbs can be used to compare (*less, lesser, least*). In addition to modifying individual words, they can be used to modify whole clauses. Adverbs can be placed at the beginning or end of a sentence or before the verb they modify, but they should not be placed between the verb and its direct object.

➤ **The water was *brilliant* blue and *icy* cold. [The adverbs intensify the adjectives *blue* and *cold*.]**

➤ **Dickens mixed humor and pathos *better* than any other English writer after Shakespeare. [The adverb compares Dickens with other writers.]**

➤ ***Consequently,* he is still read by millions.**

Consequently is a conjunctive adverb that modifies the independent clause that follows it and shows how the sentence is related to the preceding sentence. (*For more on conjunctive adverbs, see the material on conjunctions, pp. 617–22.*)

No, not, and *never* are among the most common adverbs.

SAY *NO* ONLY ONCE

It only takes one negator (*no/not/never*) to change the meaning of a sentence from positive to negative. In fact, when two negatives are used together, they may seem to cancel each other out.

➤ **They don't have ~~no~~ reason to go there.**
                           any

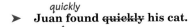

Tip for Multilingual Writers:
Putting adverbs in the correct place

Although adverbs can appear in almost any position within a sentence, they should not separate a verb from its direct object.

> *quickly*
> **Juan found ~~quickly~~ his cat.**
> ^

The negative word *not* usually precedes the main verb and follows the first helping verb in a verb phrase.

> *not*
> **I have been ~~not~~ sick lately.** ━━━━━━━━━━━
> ^

69f Prepositions

Prepositions (*on, in, at, by*) usually appear as part of a **prepositional phrase.** Their main function is to allow the noun or pronoun in the phrase to modify another word in the sentence. Prepositional phrases always begin with a preposition and end with a noun, pronoun, or other word group that functions as the **object of the preposition** (in *time,* on the *table*).

A preposition can be one word (*about, despite, on*) or a word group (*according to, as well as, in spite of*). Place prepositional phrases as close as possible to the words they modify. Adjectival prepositional phrases usually appear right after the noun or pronoun they modify and answer questions like *Which one?* and *What kind of?* Adverbial phrases can appear anywhere in a sentence and answer questions like *When? Where? How?* and *Why?*

AS ADJECTIVE   Many species *of birds* nest there.

AS ADVERB   The younger children stared *out the window.*

COMMON PREPOSITIONS

about	among	behind
above	apart from	below
according to	as	beside
across	as to	between
after	as well as	beyond
against	at	by
along	because of	by means of
along with	before	by way of

(continued)

COMMON PREPOSITIONS *(continued)*

down	in regard to	toward
during	inside	under
except	instead of	underneath
except for	into	until
excluding	like	up
following	near	upon
from	of	up to
in	on	via
in addition to	on account of	with
in case of	over	within
including	since	without
in front of	through	with reference to
in place of	to	with respect to

Tip for Multilingual Writers:
Using prepositions

Every language uses prepositions idiomatically in ways that do not match their literal meaning, which is why prepositional phrases can be difficult for multilingual writers. In English, prepositions combine with other words in such a variety of ways that the combinations can only be learned with repetition and over time (*see pp. 618–19*).

Idiomatic uses of prepositions indicating time and location

The prepositions that indicate time and location are often the most idiosyncratic in a language. The following are some common ways in which the prepositions *at, by, in,* and *on* are used.

TIME

AT The wedding ceremony starts *at two o'clock*. [a specific clock time]

BY Our honeymoon plans should be ready *by next week*. [a particular time]

IN The reception will start *in the evening*. [a portion of the day]

ON The wedding will take place *on May 1*. The rehearsal is *on Tuesday*. [a particular date or day of the week]

LOCATION

AT I will meet you *at the zoo*. [a particular place]

You need to turn right *at the light.* [a corner or an intersection]

We took a seat *at the table.* [near a piece of furniture]

BY Meet me *by the fountain.* [a familiar place]

IN Park your car *in the parking lot* and give the money to the attendant *in the booth.* [on a space of some kind or inside a structure]

I enjoyed the bratwurst *in Chicago.* [a city, state, or other geographic location]

I found that article *in this book.* [a print medium]

ON An excellent restaurant is located *on Mulberry Street.* [a street, avenue, or other thoroughfare]

I spilled milk *on the floor.* [a surface]

I watched the report *on television.* [an electronic medium]

Prepositions plus gerunds (*-ing*)

A gerund is the *-ing* form of a verb acting as a noun. A gerund can occur after a preposition (*thanks for coming*), but when the preposition is *to,* be careful not to confuse it with the infinitive form of a verb.

➤ I look forward to ~~win~~ at Jeopardy. *[winning]*

69g Conjunctions

Conjunctions join words, phrases, or clauses and indicate their relation to each other.

1. Coordinating conjunctions

The common **coordinating conjunctions** (or **coordinators**) are *and, but, or, for, nor, yet,* and *so.* Coordinating conjunctions join elements of equal weight or function.

➤ She was strong *and* healthy.

➤ The war was short *but* devastating.

➤ They must have been tired, *for* they had been climbing all day long.

(The section on conjunctions continues on page 620.)

COMMON IDIOMATIC EXPRESSIONS in ENGLISH

COMMON ADJECTIVE + PREPOSITION COMBINATIONS

afraid of: fearing someone or something

anxious about: worried

ashamed of: embarrassed by someone or something

aware of: know about

content with: having no complaints about; happy about

fond of: having positive feelings for

full of: filled with

grateful to (someone) (for something): thankful; appreciative

interested in: curious; wanting to know more about

jealous of: feeling envy toward

proud/suspicious of: pleased about/distrustful of

tired of: had enough of; bored with

responsible to (someone) (for something): accountable; in charge

satisfied with: having no complaints about

COMMON VERB + PREPOSITION COMBINATIONS

apologize to: express regret for actions

arrive in (a place): come to a city/country (*I arrived in Paris.*)

arrive at (an event at a specific location): come to a building or a house
  (*I arrived at the Louvre at ten.*)

blame for: hold responsible; accuse

complain about: find fault; criticize

concentrate on: focus; pay attention

consist of: contain; be made of

congratulate on: offer good wishes for success

depend on: trust

explain to: make something clear to someone

insist on: be firm

laugh at: express amusement

rely on: trust

smile at: act friendly toward

take care of: look after; tend

thank for: express appreciation

throw to: toss something to someone to catch

throw at: toss an object toward someone or something

throw (something) away: discard

throw (something) out: discard; present an idea for consideration

worry about: feel concern; fear for someone's safety or well-being

COMMON PARTICIPLES

Verb + preposition combinations that create *verb phrasals,* expressions with meanings that are different from the meaning of the verb itself. An askerisk (*) indicates a separable participle.

break down: stop functioning

*call off: cancel

*fill out: complete

*find out: discover

get over: recover

*give up: surrender; stop work on

*leave out: omit

look forward to: anticipate

look into: research

*look up: check a fact

look up to: admire

put up with: endure

run across: meet unexpectedly

run out: use up

stand up for: defend

turn down: reject

Tip for Multilingual Writers:
Using direct objects with two-word verbs

If a two-word verb has a direct object, the preposition (particle) may be either separable (*I filled the form out*) or inseparable (*I got over the shock*). If the verb is separable, the direct object can also follow the preposition if it is a noun (*I filled out the form*). If the direct object is a pronoun, however, it must appear between the verb and preposition.

                     it
➤   I filled out ~~it~~.
                   ^

2. Correlative conjunctions

The **correlative conjunctions** also link sentence elements of equal value, but they always come in pairs: *both . . . and, either . . . or, neither . . . nor,* and *not only . . . but also.*

➤ *Neither* the doctor *nor* the police believe his story.

3. Subordinating conjunctions

Common **subordinating conjunctions** (or **subordinators**) link sentence elements that are not of equal importance. They include the following words and phrases:

Subordinating Words

after	once	until
although	since	when
as	that	whenever
because	though	where
before	till	wherever
if	unless	while

Subordinating Phrases

as if	even though	in that
as soon as	even when	rather than
as though	for as much as	sooner than
even after	in order that	so that
even if	in order to	

Because subordinating conjunctions join unequal sentence parts, they are used to introduce dependent, or subordinate, clauses in a sentence.

➤ The software will not run properly *if* the computer lacks sufficient memory.

Tip for Multilingual Writers:
Using coordination and subordination appropriately

Do not use both subordination and coordination together to combine the same two clauses, even if the subordinating and coordinating words are similar in meaning. Some examples include *although* or *even though* with *but* and *because* with *therefore.*

➤ Although I came early, ~~but~~ the tickets were already

    sold out.

or

➤ ~~Although~~ I came early, but the tickets were already

    sold out.

➤ Because Socrates is human, and humans are mortal,

    ~~therefore~~ Socrates is mortal.

or

➤ ~~Because~~ Socrates is human, and humans are mortal,;

    therefore, Socrates is mortal.

When you use a coordinating conjunction (*and, but, or, for, nor, yet, so*), make sure that you use the conjunction that expresses the relationship between the two clauses that you want to show.

➤ My daughter's school is close to my house, ~~and~~ *but* my office

    is far away.

    In the revised version, *but* shows the contrast the writer is describing.

When you use a subordinating conjunction, make sure you attach it to the clause that you want to subordinate and not to the main idea. For example, if the main point is that commuting to work takes too much time, then the following sentence is unclear.

MAIN POINT OBSCURED	Although commuting to work takes two hours out of every day, I use the time to catch up on my reading.
MAIN POINT CLEAR	Commuting to work takes two hours out of every workday, although I use the time to catch up on my reading.

(*For help in punctuating sentences with conjunctions, see Tab 11: Editing for Correctness, pp. 525 and 537.*)

4. Conjunctive adverbs

Conjunctive adverbs indicate the relation between two clauses, but unlike conjunctions (*and, but*), they are not grammatically strong enough on their own to hold the clauses together. A period or semi-colon is also needed.

➤ **Swimming is an excellent exercise for the heart and for the muscles;** *however,* **swimming does not help a person control weight as well as jogging does.**

Common Conjunctive Adverbs

accordingly	however	now
also	incidentally	otherwise
anyway	indeed	similarly
as a result	instead	specifically
besides	likewise	still
certainly	meanwhile	subsequently
consequently	moreover	suddenly
finally	nevertheless	then
furthermore	next	therefore
hence	nonetheless	thus

69h Interjections

Interjections are forceful expressions. They are not often used in academic writing except in quotations of dialogue.

➤ *"Wow!"* **Davis said. "Are you telling me that there's a former presidential adviser who hasn't written a book?"**

➤ **Tell-all books are,** *alas,* **the biggest sellers.**

70 Parts of Sentences

Every complete sentence contains at least one **subject** (a noun and its modifiers) and one **predicate** (a verb and its objects, complements, and modifiers) that fit together to make a statement, ask a question, or give a command.

subject   predicate

➤ The *children* *solved* the puzzle.

Tip for Multilingual Writers: *Putting sentence parts in the correct order for English*

In some languages (such as Spanish), it is acceptable to omit subjects. In others (such as Arabic), it is acceptable to omit certain kinds of verbs. Other languages (such as Japanese) place verbs last, and still others (such as Hebrew) allow verbs to precede the subject. English, however, has its own distinct order for sentence parts that most sentences follow.

MODIFIERS + SUBJECT → VERB + OBJECTS, COMPLEMENTS, MODIFIERS

    mod   subj   verb   mod   obj   obj comp

➤ The playful kitten batted the crystal glasses on the shelf.

Changing a **direct quotation** (someone else's exact words) to an **indirect quotation** (a report on what the person said or wrote) often requires changing many sentence elements. When the quotation is a declarative sentence, however, the subject-before-verb word order does not change.

DIRECT QUOTATION	The instructor said, "You have only one more week to finish your papers."
INDIRECT QUOTATION	The instructor told the students that they had only one more week to finish their papers.

Note: In the direct quotation, the verb tense changes from present to past.

Changing a direct question to an indirect question, however, does require a word order change—from the verb-subject pattern of a question to the subject-verb pattern of a declarative sentence.

DIRECT QUESTION	The instructor always asks, "Are you ready to begin?"
INDIRECT QUESTION	The instructor always asks [us] if we are ready to begin.

In an indirect quotation of a command, a pronoun or noun takes the place of the command's omitted subject, *you,* and is followed by the infinitive (*to*) form of the verb.

DIRECT QUOTATION: COMMAND	The instructor always says "[*you*] Write down the assignment before you leave."

INDIRECT QUOTATION: The instructor always tells *us* to write
COMMAND down the assignment before we leave.

In indirectly quoted negative imperatives, the word *not* comes before
the infinitive.

DIRECT The instructor said, "Do not forget your homework."

INDIRECT The instructor reminded us *not* to forget our
homework.

70a Subjects

The **simple subject** is the word or words that name the topic of the
sentence; it is always a noun or pronoun. To find the subject, ask who
or what the sentence is about. The **complete subject** is the simple
subject plus its modifiers.

simple subject
➤ Did *Sir Walter Raleigh* give Queen Elizabeth I the
requisite obedience? [Who gave the queen obedience?]

complete subject

simple subject
➤ *Three six-year-old children* solved the puzzle in less than
five minutes. [Who solved the puzzle?]

A **compound subject** contains two or more simple subjects connected with a conjunction such as *and, but, or,* or *neither . . . nor.*

compound

simple simple
➤ *Original thinking* and *bold design* characterize her work.

In **imperative sentences,** which give directions or commands,
the subject *you* is usually implied, not stated. A helping verb is needed
to transform an imperative sentence into a question.

➤ *[You]* Keep this advice in mind.

➤ *Would* you keep this advice in mind?

In sentences beginning with *there* or *here* followed by some form
of *be,* the subject comes after the verb.

simple subject
➤ Here are the *remnants* of an infamous empire.

Tip for Multilingual Writers:
Including only one subject or there *or* it *in the subject position*

All English sentences and clauses except commands require an explicitly stated subject.

>   *She said*
> **The teacher told us to review sentence structure. ~~Said~~ we would have a quiz on it next class.**

Note: In commands, or imperative sentences, the subject, which is always *you,* is omitted.

> **[*You*] Read the instructions before using this machine.**

Unlike in some other languages, however, a pronoun cannot duplicate the subject.

> **The teacher ~~she~~ told us to review sentence structure.**

If the subject follows the verb, then the expletive *there* or *it* is needed in the subject position.

> *There is*
> **~~Is~~ a new independent radio station in our city.**
>
> *There* indicates existence or locality. The verb *is* agrees with the subject (*radio station*), which follows the verb.

> *It is*
> **~~Is~~ hard to find doctors who are willing to move to rural areas.**

Note: The pronoun *it* can also be the subject of a sentence about weather or environmental conditions (*It is cold in this house*), time (*It is three o'clock*), or distance (*It is five miles to the next filling station*).

70b Verbs and their objects or complements

In a sentence, the **predicate** says something about the subject. The verb constitutes the **simple predicate.** The verb plus its object or complement make up the **complete predicate.**

> **Tip for Multilingual Writers:**
> *Including a complete verb*

Verb structure, as well as where the verb is placed within a sentence, varies dramatically across languages, but in English each sentence needs to include at least one complete verb. (*See Chapter 69, pp. 598–603.*) The verb cannot be an infinitive—the *to* form of the verb—or an *-ing* form without a helping verb.

>   *is bringing*
> ➤ The caterer ~~to bring~~ dinner.

>   *are*
> ➤ Children running in the park.

In some languages, linking verbs (verbs like *be, seem, look, sound, feel, appear,* and *remain*) may sometimes be omitted, but not in English.

>   *look*
> ➤ They happy.

Verb functions in sentences

Based on how they function in sentences, verbs are linking, transitive, or intransitive. The kind of verb determines what elements the complete predicate must include and therefore determines the correct order of sentence parts. Most meaningful English sentences use one of five basic sentence patterns:

- **SUBJECT + LINKING VERB + SUBJECT COMPLEMENT**
  New Yorkers are busy people.

- **SUBJECT + TRANSITIVE VERB + DIRECT OBJECT**
  The police officer caught the jaywalker.

- **SUBJECT + TRANSITIVE VERB + INDIRECT OBJECT + DIRECT OBJECT**
  The officer gave the jaywalker a ticket.

- **SUBJECT + TRANSITIVE VERB + DIRECT OBJECT + OBJECT COMPLEMENT**
  The ticket made the jaywalker unhappy.

- **SUBJECT + INTRANSITIVE VERB**
  She sighed.

Linking verbs and subject complements A **linking verb** joins a subject to information about the subject that follows the verb. That information is called the **subject complement.** The subject complement may be a noun, a pronoun, or an adjective.

>   subj   lv   comp
> ➤ Ann Yearsley was *a milkmaid.*

The most frequently used linking verb is the *be* verb (*is, are, was, were*), but verbs such as *seem, look, appear, feel, become, smell, sound,* and *taste* can also function as links between a sentence's subject and its complement.

>   subj   lv   comp
> **That new hairstyle *looks* beautiful.**

Transitive verbs and direct objects A **transitive verb** identifies an action that the subject performs or does to somebody or something else—the receiver of the action, or **direct object.** To complete its meaning, a transitive verb needs a direct object, usually a noun, pronoun, or word group that acts like a noun or pronoun.

NOUN	I threw *the ball.*
PRONOUN	I threw *it* over a fence.
WORD GROUP	I put *what I needed* into my backpack.

Most often, the subject is doing the action, the direct object is being acted upon, and the transitive verb is in the **active voice.**

ACTIVE	*Parents* sometimes *consider* their *children* unreasonable.

If the verb in a sentence is transitive, it can be in the **passive voice.** In the following revised sentence, the direct object (*children*) has become the subject; the original subject (*parents*) is introduced with the preposition *by* and is now part of a prepositional phrase.

PASSIVE	Children are considered unreasonable by their parents.

Tip for Multilingual Writers:
Including only one direct object

In English, a transitive verb must take an explicit direct object. For example, *Take it!* is a complete sentence but *Take!* is not, even if *it* is clearly implied. Be careful not to repeat the object, especially if the object includes a relative adverb (*where, when, how*) or a relative pronoun (*which, who, what*), even if the relative pronoun does not appear in the sentence but is only implied.

> **Our dog guards the house *where* we live ~~there~~.**

Transitive verbs, indirect objects, and direct objects **Indirect objects** name to whom an action was done or for whom it was completed and are most commonly used with verbs such as *give, ask, tell, sing,* and *write.*

> subj   v   ind obj   dir obj
> **Coleridge wrote *Sara* a heartrending letter.**

Note that indirect objects appear after the verb but before the direct object.

Transitive verbs, direct objects, and object complements   In addition to a direct object and an indirect object, a transitive verb can take another element in its predicate: an **object complement.** An object complement describes or renames the direct object it follows.

>   dir obj   obj comp
> **His investment in a plantation made Johnson *a rich man*.**

Intransitive verbs   An **intransitive verb** describes an action by a subject that is not done directly to anything or anyone else. Therefore, an intransitive verb cannot take an object or a complement. However, adverbs and adverb phrases often appear in predicates built around intransitive verbs. In the sentence that follows, the complete predicate is in italics and the intransitive verb is underlined.

> **As a recruit, I *complied* *with the order mandating short hair.***

Some verbs, such as *cooperate, assent, disappear,* and *insist,* are always intransitive. Others, such as *increase, grow, roll,* and *work,* can be either transitive or intransitive.

TRANSITIVE   I *grow* carrots and celery in my victory garden.

INTRANSITIVE   My son *grows* taller every week.

Tips

LEARNING in COLLEGE

Using the Dictionary to Determine Prepositions and Transitive and Intransitive Verbs

Your dictionary will note if a verb is *v.i.* (intransitive), *v.t.* (transitive), or both. It will also tell you—or show by example—the appropriate preposition to use when you are modifying an intransitive verb with an adverbial phrase. For example, we may *accede to* a rule, but if and when we *comply,* it has to be *with* something or someone.

A **phrase** is a group of related words that
lacks either a subject or a predicate or both.
Phrases function within sentences but not
on their own. A **dependent clause** has a
subject and a predicate but cannot function as a complete sentence
because it begins with a subordinating word.

www.mhhe.com/
awr
For information
and exercises on
phrases and clauses,
go to
Editing > Phrases
and Clauses

71a Noun phrases

A **noun phrase** consists of a noun or noun substitute plus all of its
modifiers. Noun phrases can function as a sentence's subject, object,
or subject complement.

SUBJECT	*The old, dark, ramshackle house* collapsed.
OBJECT	Greg cooked *an authentic, delicious haggis* for the Robert Burns dinner.
SUBJECT COMPLEMENT	Tom became *an accomplished and well-known cook.*

71b Verb phrases and verbals

A **verb phrase** is a verb plus its helping verbs. It functions as the
predicate in a sentence: *Mary should have photographed me.* **Verbals**
are words derived from verbs. They function as nouns, adjectives, or
adverbs, not as verbs.

VERBAL AS NOUN	*Crawling* comes before walking.
VERBAL AS ADJECTIVE	Chris tripped over the *crawling* child.
VERBAL AS ADVERB	The child began *to crawl.*

Verbals may take modifiers, objects, and complements to form **verbal phrases.** There are three kinds of verbal phrases: participial,
gerund, and infinitive.

629

1. Participial phrases

A **participial phrase** begins with either a present participle (the
-*ing* form of a verb) or a past participle (the -*ed* or -*en* form of a verb).
Participial phrases always function as adjectives.

➤ *Working in groups,* **the children solved the problem.**

➤ *Insulted by his remark,* **Elizabeth refused to dance.**

➤ **His pitching arm,** *broken in two places by the fall,* **would
never be the same again.**

2. Gerund phrases

A **gerund phrase** uses the -*ing* form of the verb, just as some participial phrases do. But gerund phrases always function as nouns, not
adjectives.

➤ *Walking one hour a day* **will keep you fit.**
<small>subj</small>

➤ **The instructor praised** *my acting in both scenes.*
<small>dir obj</small>

3. Infinitive phrases

An **infinitive phrase** is formed using the infinitive, or *to* form, of a
verb: *to be, to do, to live.* It can function as an adverb, an adjective, or
a noun and can be the subject, subject or object complement, or direct
object in a sentence.

➤ *To finish his novel* **was his greatest ambition.**
<small>noun/subj</small>

➤ **He made many efforts** *to finish his novel* **for his publisher.**
<small>adj/obj comp</small>

➤ **He needed** *to finish his novel.*
<small>adv/dir obj</small>

71c Appositive phrases

Appositives rename nouns or pronouns and appear right after the
word they rename.

<small>noun   appositive</small>

➤ **One researcher,** *the widely respected R. S. Smith,* **has
shown that a child's performance on such tests can be
very consistent.**

71d Absolute phrases

Absolute phrases modify an entire sentence. They include a noun or pronoun, a participle, and their related modifiers, objects, or complements.

> ➤ **The sheriff strode into the bar,** *his hands hovering over his pistols.*

71e Dependent clauses

Although **dependent clauses** (also known as **subordinate clauses**) have a subject and predicate, they cannot stand alone as complete sentences. They are introduced by subordinators—either by a subordinating conjunction such as *after, in order to,* or *since (for a more complete listing, see p. 620)* or by a relative pronoun such as *who, which,* or *that (for more, see the box on p. 610).* They function in sentences as adjectives, adverbs, or nouns.

1. Adjective clauses

An **adjective clause** modifies a noun or pronoun. Relative pronouns (*who, whom, whose, which,* or *that*) or relative adverbs (*where, when*) are used to connect adjective clauses to the nouns or pronouns they modify. The relative pronoun usually follows the word that is being modified and also points back to the noun or pronoun. (*For help with punctuating restrictive and nonrestrictive clauses, see Tab 11, pp. 526–30 and 537–38.*)

> ➤ **Odysseus's journey,** *which can be traced on modern maps,* **has inspired many works of literature.**

In adjective clauses, the direct object sometimes comes before rather than after the verb.

dir obj   subj   v

> ➤ **The contestant** *whom he most wanted to beat* **was his father.**

2. Adverb clauses

An **adverb clause** modifies a verb, an adjective, or an adverb and answers the same questions adverbs answer: *When? Where? What? Why?* and *How?* Adverb clauses are often introduced by subordinators (*after, when, before, because, although, if, though, whenever, where, wherever*).

➤ *After we had talked for an hour,* he began to get nervous.

➤ He reacted *as if he already knew.*

3. Noun clauses

A **noun clause** is a dependent clause that functions as a noun. In a sentence, a noun clause may serve as the subject, object, or complement and is usually introduced by a relative pronoun (*who, which, that*) or a relative adverb (*how, what, where, when, why*).

SUBJECT	*What he saw* shocked him.
OBJECT	The instructor found out *who had skipped class.*
COMPLEMENT	The book was *where I had left it.*

As in an adjective clause, in a noun clause the direct object or subject complement can come first, violating the typical sentence order.

dir obj   subj

➤ The doctor wondered *to whom he* should send the bill.

![map graphic] Tip for Multilingual Writers: *Understanding the purposes and constructions of* if *clauses*

If clauses (also called **conditional clauses**) state facts, make predictions, and speculate about unlikely or impossible events. These conditional constructions most often employ *if,* but *when, unless,* or other words can introduce conditional constructions as well.

- Use the present tense for facts. When the relationship you are describing is usually true, the verbs in both clauses should be in the same tense.

  STATES FACTS

  If people *practice* doing good consistently, they *have* a sense of satisfaction.

  When Meg *found* a new cause, she always *talked* about it incessantly.

- In a sentence that predicts, use the present tense in the *if* clause. The verb in the independent clause is a modal plus the base form of the verb.

  PREDICTS POSSIBILITIES

  If you *practice* doing good through politics, you *will have* a greater effect on your community.

- If you are speculating about something that is unlikely to happen, use the past tense in the *if* clause and *could, should,* or *would* plus the base verb in the independent clause.

SPECULATES ON THE UNLIKELY

If you *were* a better person, you *would practice* doing good every day.

- Use the past perfect tense in the *if* clause if you are speculating about an event that did not happen. In the independent clause, use *could have, might have,* or *would have* plus the past participle.

SPECULATES ON SOMETHING THAT DID NOT HAPPEN

If you *had practiced* doing good when you were young, you *would have been* a different person today.

- Use *were* in the *if* clause and *could, might,* or *would* plus the base form in the main clause if you are speculating about something that could never happen.

SPECULATES ABOUT THE IMPOSSIBLE

If Lincoln *were* alive today, he *would fight* for equal protection under the law.

72 Types of Sentences

Classifying by the number of clauses they contain and how those clauses are joined, we can categorize sentences into four types: simple, compound, complex, and compound-complex. We can also classify them by purpose: declarative, interrogative, imperative, and exclamatory.

www.mhhe.com/
awr
For information and
exercises on types of
sentences, go to

Editing > Sentence
Types

72a   Sentence structures

A clause is a group of related words that includes a subject and a predicate. Some clauses are independent; others are dependent, or subordinate. **Independent clauses** can stand on their own as complete sentences. **Dependent, or subordinate, clauses** cannot stand alone. They function in sentences as adjectives, adverbs, or nouns. The presence of one or both of these two types of clauses, and their relation to each other, determines whether the sentence is simple, compound, complex, or compound-complex.

1. Simple sentences

A simple sentence has only one independent clause. Simple does not necessarily mean short, however. Although a simple sentence does not include any dependent clauses, it may have several embedded phrases, a compound subject, and a compound predicate.

INDEPENDENT CLAUSE

The bloodhound is the oldest known breed of dog.

INDEPENDENT CLAUSE: COMPOUND SUBJ + COMPOUND PRED

Historians, novelists, short-story writers, and playwrights write about characters, design plots, and usually seek the dramatic resolution of a problem.

2. Compound sentences

A compound sentence contains two or more independent clauses but no dependent clause. The independent clauses may be joined by a comma and a coordinating conjunction or by a semicolon with or without a conjunctive adverb.

➤   **The police arrested him for drunk driving, *so* he lost his car.**

➤   **The sun blasted the earth; *therefore*, the plants withered and died.**

3. Complex sentences

A complex sentence contains one independent clause and one or more dependent clauses.

independent clause   dependent clause

➤   **He consulted the dictionary *because he did not know how***

to pronounce the word.

4. Compound-complex sentences

A compound-complex sentence contains two or more coordinated independent clauses and at least one dependent clause (italicized in the example).

➤ **She discovered a new world of international finance, but she worked so hard investing other people's money *that she had no time to invest any of her own.***

72b Sentence purposes

When you write a sentence, your purpose helps you decide which sentence type to use. If you want to provide information, you usually use a declarative sentence. If you want to ask a question, you usually use an interrogative sentence. To make a request or give an order (a command), you use the imperative. An exclamatory sentence emphasizes a point or expresses strong emotion.

DECLARATIVE	He watches *Seinfeld* reruns.
INTERROGATIVE	Does he watch *Seinfeld* reruns?
IMPERATIVE	Do not watch reruns of *Seinfeld.*
EXCLAMATORY	I'm really looking forward to watching *Seinfeld* reruns with you!

This fourteenth-century map features Mansa Musa, the greatest ruler of the Empire of Mali in West Africa. During his reign, Mali prospered as a hub of trade and learning.

13

To be able to be caught up into the world
of thought—that is educated.

—EDITH HAMILTON

Further
Resources
for Learning

13 Further Resources for Learning

Timeline of World History

3000

ca. 3000 BCE City of Babylon is founded; cuneiform script, the earliest known fully developed system of writing, emerges in ancient Mesopotamia.

2500–2001 BCE Bow and arrow is first used in warfare; cotton is cultivated in Peru.

ca. 2660–1640 BCE Old and Middle Kingdoms of Egypt. Pyramids and grand monuments such as the Great Sphinx of Giza are built as royal tributes and burial structures.

2000 BCE *Gilgamesh,* ancient Mesopotamian epic, is composed (fullest extant *written* text of this epic dates from **seventh century** BCE): theme is futile human quest for immortality.

2000

ca. 1950 BCE Irrigation systems are in use in Chinese agriculture.

ca. 1850 BCE Oldest surviving Egyptian mathematics text shows that decimal system was in use.

1792–1750 BCE Rule of Babylonian king Hammurabi produces an orderly arrangement of written laws—the Hammurabi Code—among the first in the ancient world.

1200 BCE Olmec culture flourishes in Mexico (until **ca. 400 BCE**).

ca. 1000–80 BCE Varna system—precursor of caste system—evolves in India.

1000

776 BCE First recorded Olympic games are held at Olympia in Greece.

ca. 750 BCE *Iliad*—the earliest surviving example of Greek literature—and *Odyssey* are composed (ascribed to Homer).

700

Literary and cultural developments and events

Historical events

Advances in science and technology

Changes in everyday life

Break in timeline

600

551–479 BCE Life of Confucius, China's greatest philosopher.

ca. 560–480 BCE Life of Buddha (Siddhartha), founder of Buddhism.

508 BCE Athens becomes the world's first democracy.

500

ca. 500 BCE Many Old Testament books are transcribed.

ca. 500 BCE Greeks adopt Ptolemaic model of cosmos, in which the sun revolves around the earth.

461–429 BCE Reign of Pericles ushers in flowering of Athenian culture: Aeschylus, *Oresteia* (**458 BCE**); Sophocles, *Antigone* (**ca. 442–441 BCE**) and *Oedipus the King* (**ca. 429 BCE**); Euripides, *Medea* (**431 BCE**); Aristophanes, *Lysistrata* (**411 BCE**); Plato, *Republic* (**ca. 406 BCE**).

399 BCE Greek philosopher Socrates is tried and executed for corruption of youth.

400

404 BCE Golden age of Periclean Athens ends with fall of Athens to Sparta.

387 BCE Greek philosopher Plato founds the Academy.

350 BCE Aristotle, student of Plato, writes *Poetics*, founds rival school, Lyceum; earliest portion of *Mahabharata* (Sanskrit heroic epic) is composed mid-century.

356–323 BCE Life of Alexander the Great, king of Macedonia, who conquers the Persian Empire.

300

ca. 300 BCE Euclid writes *Elements*, seminal work of elementary geometry.

ca. 250 BCE Archimedes, founder of mathematical physics, writes *Measurement of the Circle* (includes concept of π).

ca. 250 BCE *Ramayana* (Sanskrit heroic epic) is composed mid-century.

215 BCE Construction of Great Wall of China begins.

200

ca. 200 BCE–500 CE Roman Empire encompasses the entire Mediterranean region.

100

23–13 BCE Roman poet Horace composes *Odes*.

27–19 BCE Roman poet Virgil composes the epic poem *Aeneid*.

0

8 Ovid composes *Metamorphoses*, a 15-volume poem based on Greek and Roman myths.

30 Jesus is crucified by the Romans in Jerusalem.

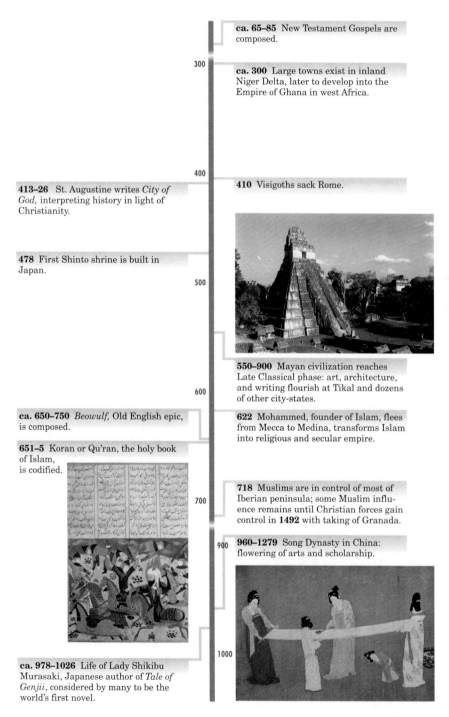

ca. 65–85 New Testament Gospels are composed.

ca. 300 Large towns exist in inland Niger Delta, later to develop into the Empire of Ghana in west Africa.

300

413–26 St. Augustine writes *City of God,* interpreting history in light of Christianity.

400

410 Visigoths sack Rome.

478 First Shinto shrine is built in Japan.

500

550–900 Mayan civilization reaches Late Classical phase: art, architecture, and writing flourish at Tikal and dozens of other city-states.

600

ca. 650–750 *Beowulf,* Old English epic, is composed.

622 Mohammed, founder of Islam, flees from Mecca to Medina, transforms Islam into religious and secular empire.

651–5 Koran or Qu'ran, the holy book of Islam, is codified.

718 Muslims are in control of most of Iberian peninsula; some Muslim influence remains until Christian forces gain control in **1492** with taking of Granada.

700

900

960–1279 Song Dynasty in China: flowering of arts and scholarship.

1000

ca. 978–1026 Life of Lady Shikibu Murasaki, Japanese author of *Tale of Genjii,* considered by many to be the world's first novel.

ca. 1100 *Song of Roland*, French epic poem, is composed.

1100

1096–1291 The Crusades, nine military expeditions in which European Christians attempted to reconquer the Holy Land (Palestine) from the Muslims, take place.

1200

ca. 1200 Zen Buddhism travels from China to Japan, becomes influential in Japanese politics, painting, landscape, and culture, especially in the tea ceremony.

ca. 1290–1918 Ottoman Empire, Muslim Turkish state comprising Anatolia, modern southeastern Europe, and the Arab Middle East and North Africa, is established.

ca. 1300–1650 Renaissance in Europe: "rebirth" of arts and culture.

1300

1307–21 Dante Alighieri composes *La Divina Commedia,* an epic poem describing his imaginary journey through heaven and hell.

1312–27 Empire of Mali in West Africa reaches its height under Mansa Musa, builder of the Great Mosque at Timbuktu.

1350

1347–51 "Black Death," an epidemic of the bubonic plague, rages in Europe, eventually claiming 25–50% of the population.

ca. 1370–1400 English poet Chaucer composes *The Canterbury Tales,* a collection of 24 tales with dramatic links.

ca. 1350–1400 Great Zimbabwe, a fabled stone city that controlled a large part of southeast Africa in medieval times, reaches its height.

1400

1431 Joan of Arc, leader of French army against the British in the Hundred Years' War, is burned at the stake for heresy by the British.

ca. 1438–1532 Inca Empire, largest native empire of the Americas, reaches its height in Central and South America; expansion ends with the Spanish invasion led by Pizarro.

1450

1453 Constantinople falls to Ottoman Turks, marking the end of the Byzantine Empire.

ca. 1455 Gutenberg Bible set and printed; Gutenberg's invention of movable type leads to book printing boom in Europe.

1484 Botticelli paints *Birth of Venus* for the Medici family of Florence.

ca. 1492 Christopher Columbus lands in the Bahamas.

1500

1499 Amerigo Vespucci lands in South America.

1503 Leonardo da Vinci, painter, inventor, and scientist, paints *Mona Lisa*.

1508–12 Michelangelo paints the ceiling of the Sistine Chapel in Rome.

1513 Niccolo Machiavelli writes *The Prince*, arguing for pragmatism over virtue in a ruler.

1517 Martin Luther's *95 Theses* introduces the Protestant Reformation in Europe.

1520 Gold, silver, and chocolate are brought from the Americas to Spain.

1532 Sugar cane is cultivated in Brazil.

1593–99 Shakespeare's sonnets are published, followed by *Hamlet* (**1600–1**) and *Othello* (**1604**).

1599 Globe Theater is built in London.

1600

1603 Kabuki is first performed in Japan by female entertainer Okuni.

1605 Miguel de Cervantes Saavedra writes his masterpiece *Don Quixote.*

1609 Tea is first shipped to Europe from China.

1611 King James Bible is published, becomes most popular version for more than three centuries.

1619 African captives are brought to Jamestown, Virginia, to be servants; slave system develops over the next 80 years.

1631–48 Taj Mahal, premier example of Mogul architecture, is built in Agra, India.

1637 René Descartes, called by some the founder of modern philosophy, writes *Discourse on Method* (from which comes "*Cogito, ergo sum*": "I think; therefore, I am").

1651 Thomas Hobbes writes *Leviathan,* portraying human life in a state of nature as "nasty, brutish, and short" and offering as a remedy a social contract in which the ruler's power—for the sake of expediency—is absolute.

1608 Galileo Galilei invents astronomical telescope, provides evidence to support Nicolaus Copernicus's theory that the earth and planets revolve around the sun.

1614 Pocahontas, Native American princess, marries tobacco planter John Rolfe.

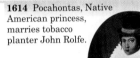

1625

1620 Pilgrims sail for America and found Plymouth Colony.

1632 Rembrandt van Rijn, prolific Dutch painter, paints his first major portrait, *The Anatomy Lesson of Dr. Tulp.*

1642–1648 English Civil War pits Parliamentary forces under Oliver Cromwell against Charles I: Charles I is defeated and beheaded in **1649.**

1650

1667 John Milton writes *Paradise Lost,* an epic poem describing man's "first disobedience" and the promise of his redemption.

1675

1687 Isaac Newton publishes *Principia,* in which he codifies laws of motion and gravity not modified until the twentieth century.

ca. 1688–1790 The Enlightenment, an intellectual movement committed to secular views based on reason, takes hold in Europe.

1690 John Locke publishes *Essay Concerning Human Understanding,* in which he espouses an empiricist view of philosophy (limiting true knowledge to what can be perceived through the senses or through introspection).

1700

ca. 1701 Peter the Great begins westernization of Russia.

ca. 1740s Culmination of the Baroque era in music: Vivaldi, *The Four Seasons;* Bach, *Brandenberg Concertos;* Handel, *Messiah.*

1740

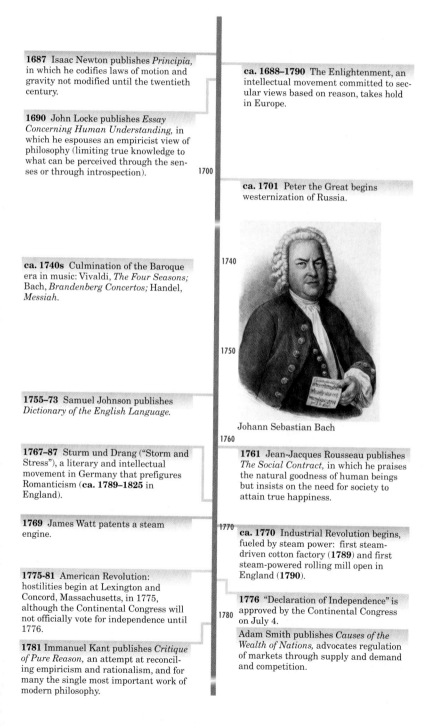

1750

1755–73 Samuel Johnson publishes *Dictionary of the English Language.*

Johann Sebastian Bach

1760

1767–87 Sturm und Drang ("Storm and Stress"), a literary and intellectual movement in Germany that prefigures Romanticism (**ca. 1789–1825** in England).

1761 Jean-Jacques Rousseau publishes *The Social Contract,* in which he praises the natural goodness of human beings but insists on the need for society to attain true happiness.

1769 James Watt patents a steam engine.

1770

ca. 1770 Industrial Revolution begins, fueled by steam power: first steam-driven cotton factory (**1789**) and first steam-powered rolling mill open in England (**1790**).

1775-81 American Revolution: hostilities begin at Lexington and Concord, Massachusetts, in 1775, although the Continental Congress will not officially vote for independence until 1776.

1780

1776 "Declaration of Independence" is approved by the Continental Congress on July 4.

Adam Smith publishes *Causes of the Wealth of Nations,* advocates regulation of markets through supply and demand and competition.

1781 Immanuel Kant publishes *Critique of Pure Reason,* an attempt at reconciling empiricism and rationalism, and for many the single most important work of modern philosophy.

1780s–90s Height of the Classical era in music: Mozart writes the opera *Don Giovanni* (**1787**); Haydn establishes the form of the symphony with *The Clock Symphony* (**1794**).

1788 Bread riots occur in France

1789 William Blake's *Songs of Innocence*, followed by *Marriage of Heaven and Hell* (**1790**) and *Songs of Experience* (**1794**), ushers in early Romanticism in England; Olaudah Equiano's *The Interesting Narrative of the Life of Olaudah Equiano, or Gustaus Vassa, the African,* one of the first slave narratives, is published.

1790

1789–99 French Revolution transforms France from a monarchy to a modern state.

1792 Mary Wollstonecraft publishes *A Vindication of the Rights of Woman,* an early work of feminism.

1793 Queen Marie Antoinette and King Louis XVI of France are guillotined.

ca. 1795–1825 English Romantic poetry flourishes with the work of William Wordsworth (**1770–1850**), Lord Byron (**1788–1824**), Percy Bysshe Shelley (**1792–1822**), and John Keats (**1795–1821**).

1798 Thomas Malthus's *An Essay on the Principle of Population* stirs interest in birth control and concerns about overpopulation.

1799 Rosetta Stone is found in Egypt, making it possible to decipher hieroglyphics; perfectly preserved mammoth is found in Siberia.

1800

1800 Alessandro Volta produces first battery of zinc and copper plates.

1803 Beethoven composes *Third Symphony (Eroica)*, marking the start of his dramatic middle period.

1804–6 Lewis and Clark expedition from St. Louis to the Pacific fuels westward expansion in the USA.

1804 Napoleon becomes emperor of France.

1807 Hegel publishes *Phenomenology of Spirit,* which introduces the concept of "master-slave" dialectic.

1808 Goethe publishes *Part 1* of *Faust,* a drama about a man who sells his soul for knowledge and power.

1810

1812 Noah Webster's *American Dictionary of the English Language* helps standardize spelling of American English.

1813 Mexico declares independence from Spain, becomes a republic in **1824**.

1813 Jane Austen publishes her novel *Pride and Prejudice.*

1815 Napoleon is defeated by British and Prussian forces at Waterloo.

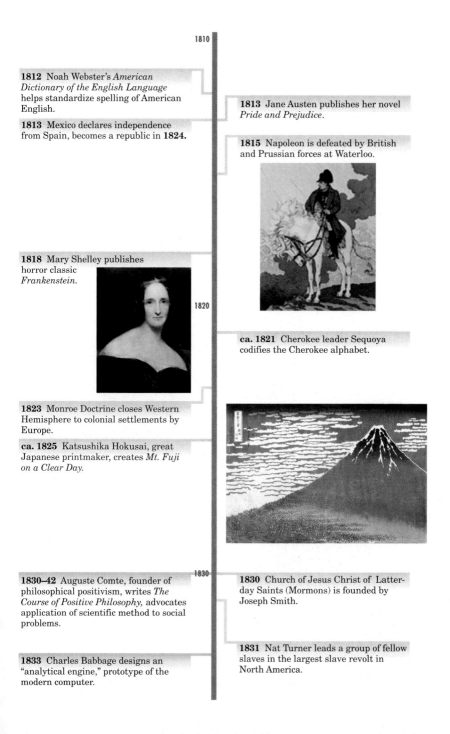

1818 Mary Shelley publishes horror classic *Frankenstein.*

1820

ca. 1821 Cherokee leader Sequoya codifies the Cherokee alphabet.

1823 Monroe Doctrine closes Western Hemisphere to colonial settlements by Europe.

ca. 1825 Katsushika Hokusai, great Japanese printmaker, creates *Mt. Fuji on a Clear Day.*

1830

1830–42 Auguste Comte, founder of philosophical positivism, writes *The Course of Positive Philosophy,* advocates application of scientific method to social problems.

1830 Church of Jesus Christ of Latter-day Saints (Mormons) is founded by Joseph Smith.

1831 Nat Turner leads a group of fellow slaves in the largest slave revolt in North America.

1833 Charles Babbage designs an "analytical engine," prototype of the modern computer.

1836 Samuel Colt puts his revolver into mass production, revolutionizes manufacture of small arms.

1837 Ralph Waldo Emerson, American transcendentalist, delivers "The American Scholar," an address expressing American literary independence.

1837–1901 Queen Victoria reigns in England, Ireland, and India.

1838 Charles Dickens publishes *Oliver Twist,* the first of many novels that sharply criticize abuses brought on by the Industrial Revolution in England.

1839 Daguerreotypes, forerunners of modern photographs, are developed by L. M. Daguerre and J. N. Niepce in France.

1840

1840s Rise of Romantic movement in France, Germany, and Italy.

1841 First university degrees granted to women in USA.

1843 Søren Kierkegaard, Christian existentialist philosopher, publishes *Either / Or.*

1843 Richard Wagner composes *The Flying Dutchman,* an opera expressing his ideal of the *Gesamtkunstwerk* ("total work of art").

1844 Samuel Morse invents the telegraph.

1847 Charlotte Brontë publishes *Jane Eyre*; Emily Brontë publishes *Wuthering Heights;* Anna Brontë publishes *Agnes Grey.*

1850

1848 Seneca Falls Convention for Women's Suffrage is held in USA; Karl Marx and Friedrich Engels write *Communist Manifesto,* a pamphlet exhorting workers to unite against capitalist oppressors.

1855 Walt Whitman publishes first edition of *Leaves of Grass,* creates a new American style for poetry.

1857 French poet Charles Baudelaire publishes *Flowers of Evil,* one of the seminal works of modern poetry.

1859 Charles Darwin publishes *On the Origin of Species,* establishes theories of evolution and natural selection ("survival of the fittest").

ca. 1860 Louis Pasteur invents pasteurization process, advances germ theory of infection, discovers rabies and anthrax vaccines (**1880s**).

1860

1860–65 Emily Dickinson writes most of her poetry; creates a new rhythm and vernacular for American verse.

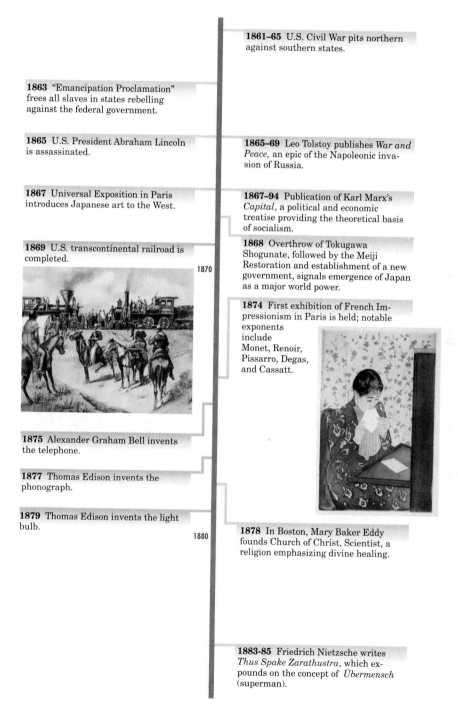

1861–65 U.S. Civil War pits northern against southern states.

1863 "Emancipation Proclamation" frees all slaves in states rebelling against the federal government.

1865 U.S. President Abraham Lincoln is assassinated.

1865–69 Leo Tolstoy publishes *War and Peace,* an epic of the Napoleonic invasion of Russia.

1867 Universal Exposition in Paris introduces Japanese art to the West.

1867–94 Publication of Karl Marx's *Capital,* a political and economic treatise providing the theoretical basis of socialism.

1869 U.S. transcontinental railroad is completed.

1868 Overthrow of Tokugawa Shogunate, followed by the Meiji Restoration and establishment of a new government, signals emergence of Japan as a major world power.

1870

1874 First exhibition of French Impressionism in Paris is held; notable exponents include Monet, Renoir, Pissarro, Degas, and Cassatt.

1875 Alexander Graham Bell invents the telephone.

1877 Thomas Edison invents the phonograph.

1879 Thomas Edison invents the light bulb.

1880

1878 In Boston, Mary Baker Eddy founds Church of Christ, Scientist, a religion emphasizing divine healing.

1883-85 Friedrich Nietzsche writes *Thus Spake Zarathustra,* which expounds on the concept of *Übermensch* (superman).

1890

1889 Eiffel Tower is built for Paris Exposition.

1893 Fabian Society, a socialist group that includes Irish playwright George Bernard Shaw, is established.

1893 X rays are discovered.

1895 Louis and Auguste Lumière project brief motion pictures on a screen to a paying audience in Paris; based on Thomas Edison's technology, their Cinématographe became the prototype of the movie camera.

ca. 1895 Charles "Buddy" Bolden, New Orleans cornet player and band leader, begins playing improvised music later known as jazz.

1898 Marie and Pierre Curie isolate radium and polonium.

1900

1903 Orville and Wilbur Wright make their debut power-driven flight near Kitty Hawk, North Carolina.

1907 Albert Einstein first publishes equation $E = mc^2$, deduced from his theory of special relativity, ushering in revolution in physics and astronomy.

1907 Pablo Picasso's *Les Demoiselles d'Avignon,* first Cubist painting, ushers in new artistic aesthetic.

1908 Henry Ford introduces the Model T; demand for cars induces the company to introduce assembly-line technique.

1910

1910 International Psychoanalytic Association is founded by Sigmund Freud and others; Freud's theories of the unconscious begin to gain popular recognition.

1913 *The Rite of Spring,* ballet with groundbreaking music by Igor Stravinsky and choreography by Vaslav Nijinsky, is first performed.

1914 Serbian nationalist assassinates heir to the Austro-Hungarian Empire in Sarajevo, sparking World War I.

1915 Margaret Sanger opens the first birth control clinic in USA.

1918 Romanian poet Tristan Tzara writes manifesto for Dada, avant-garde artistic movement established in part in reaction to the senseless slaughter of World War I.

1918–19 Influenza epidemic kills 22 million worldwide.

1922 First fascist government formed by Benito Mussolini in Italy.

1924 Joseph Stalin succeeds Lenin as head of Soviet Union.

1927 Martin Heidegger publishes *Being and Time,* a founding work of existentialist philosophy; Martha Graham, pioneer of modern dance, opens a dance studio in New York.

1929 Virginia Woolf, central to the Bloomsbury literary group, publishes feminist work *A Room of One's Own.*

1930s The Great Depression, precipitated by a stock market crash in **1929,** begins in USA and spreads abroad; in response, President Roosevelt introduces "New Deal" measures based on Keynesian economics.

1933 Adolf Hitler becomes chancellor of Germany, gradually assumes dictatorial power.

1936–39 Spanish Civil War.

1920

1914–21 James Joyce writes *Ulysses,* a masterpiece of modernist literature; publication in USA is delayed until **1933** because of obscenity charges.

1915 British passenger ship *Lusitania* sunk by German submarine, fueling American sympathy for war efforts of Britain, France, and Russia.

1917 USA enters World War I; Russian Revolution: Bolsheviks led by Vladimir Lenin seize power.

1918 Treaty of Versailles ends World War I; death toll approaches 15 million worldwide; race riots rock major U.S. cities.

1920 Nineteenth Amendment to the U.S. Constitution grants women suffrage.

ca. 1920 Arnold Schoenberg invents 12-tone system of musical composition.

1920s Harlem Renaissance: flowering of African American literature and the arts, particularly jazz, centered in New York City.

1927 Charles Lindbergh makes first solo, nonstop transatlantic flight; Werner Heisenberg develops Uncertainty Principle, which, together with Theory of Relativity, becomes basis of quantum physics; first successful transmission of an image via "television" occurs.

1931 Incompleteness Theorem is developed by the mathematician and philosopher Kurt Gödel.

1930

1935 African American Jesse Owens wins four gold medals in track at the Berlin Olympics.

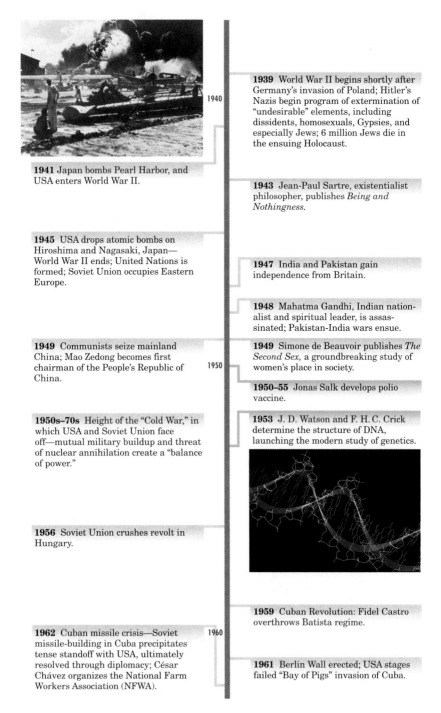

1940

1939 World War II begins shortly after Germany's invasion of Poland; Hitler's Nazis begin program of extermination of "undesirable" elements, including dissidents, homosexuals, Gypsies, and especially Jews; 6 million Jews die in the ensuing Holocaust.

1941 Japan bombs Pearl Harbor, and USA enters World War II.

1943 Jean-Paul Sartre, existentialist philosopher, publishes *Being and Nothingness.*

1945 USA drops atomic bombs on Hiroshima and Nagasaki, Japan—World War II ends; United Nations is formed; Soviet Union occupies Eastern Europe.

1947 India and Pakistan gain independence from Britain.

1948 Mahatma Gandhi, Indian nationalist and spiritual leader, is assassinated; Pakistan-India wars ensue.

1949 Communists seize mainland China; Mao Zedong becomes first chairman of the People's Republic of China.

1950

1949 Simone de Beauvoir publishes *The Second Sex,* a groundbreaking study of women's place in society.

1950–55 Jonas Salk develops polio vaccine.

1950s–70s Height of the "Cold War," in which USA and Soviet Union face off—mutual military buildup and threat of nuclear annihilation create a "balance of power."

1953 J. D. Watson and F. H. C. Crick determine the structure of DNA, launching the modern study of genetics.

1956 Soviet Union crushes revolt in Hungary.

1959 Cuban Revolution: Fidel Castro overthrows Batista regime.

1962 Cuban missile crisis—Soviet missile-building in Cuba precipitates tense standoff with USA, ultimately resolved through diplomacy; César Chávez organizes the National Farm Workers Association (NFWA).

1960

1961 Berlin Wall erected; USA stages failed "Bay of Pigs" invasion of Cuba.

1964 U.S. involvement in Vietnam War escalates with Tonkin Gulf Resolution; Malcolm X is assassinated in New York; Watts riots roil Los Angeles.

1966 Mao Zedong's Cultural Revolution begins, aiming to revitalize communist zeal; Black Panther Party is founded in Oakland, California.

1968 Martin Luther King, Jr. is assassinated in Memphis, Tennessee.

1969 American astronaut Neil Armstrong becomes first man to walk on the moon.

1970

1971 East Pakistan (now Bangladesh) declares independence from West Pakistan.

1974 President Richard Nixon resigns as a result of the Watergate scandal.

1975 Bill Gates and Paul Allen build and sell their first computer product, creating Microsoft.

1975–79 Vaccination programs against smallpox eradicate the disease worldwide.

1982 Benoit Mandelbrot publishes *The Fractal Geometry of Nature,* contributing to chaos theory.

1986 Chernobyl nuclear power plant disaster spreads fallout over Soviet Union and parts of Europe.

1963 Martin Luther King, Jr., delivers "I Have a Dream" speech to crowd of 250,000 at the Lincoln Memorial;

President John F. Kennedy is assassinated in Dallas.

1973 *Gulag Archipelego* by Alexander Solzhenitsyn is published in Paris; it is a massive study of Soviet penal system based on author's firsthand experience.

1975 Wave of former colonies—Mozambique, Surinam, Papua New Guinea—gain independence.

1979 Islamic revolution in Iran: Shah flees, Khomeini comes to power.

1980

1981 First cases of acquired immune deficiency syndrome (AIDS) in the USA are reported in New York and California.

1990

1989 Prodemocracy protests in Tiananmen Square, China, are quashed by government crackdown; Berlin Wall is demolished; Eastern Europe is democratized.

1991 Soviet Union is dissolved, making way for looser confederation of republics.

1995 Internet boom hits—number of people online grows exponentially.

2000

2000 Initial sequencing of human genome completed.

2001 Hijacked planes fly into 110-story World Trade Center Towers in New York City and the Pentagon in Washington, D.C.—thousands die; USA invades Afghanistan and later Iraq in "war on terrorism."

2004 Massive Indian Ocean tsunami devastates coastal communities from Indonesia to Somalia.

2005 Voters in France and Holland reject the proposed constitution for the European Union.

2005 Hurricane Katrina overwhelms U.S. Gulf coast and forces the evacuation of New Orleans.

Selected Terms from across the Curriculum

*Your professors will explain the vocabulary and concepts that are specific to the study of particular disciplines, but they might assume you understand certain terms that commonly appear in academic **discourse**. As you look at the sampling that follows, feel free to jump around among the words printed in bold, each of which has its own entry.*

alienation (from the Latin *alius,* "other") Being estranged from one's society or even from oneself. First used in psychology, the term was adapted by Karl **Marx** (1818–1883) in his writings on the relationship of workers to the products of their labor. In the twentieth century, **existentialist** philosophers used the word to mean an individual's loss of a sense of self, his or her *authenticity,* amid the pressures of modern society. *See also* **Marxism.**

Apollonian From *Apollo,* Greek god of prophecy, music, medicine, and poetry, often identified with the sun. Today Apollonian describes works of art or other cultural products characterized by clarity, harmony, and restraint. *See also* **Dionysian.**

archetype A model after which other things are patterned. The psychoanalyst Carl Jung (1875–1961) used the term to denote a number of universal symbols—such as the Mother or the universal Creator—that inhabit the **collective unconscious.**

Aristotelian Relating to the writings of Aristotle (384–322 BCE), Greek philosopher and author of works on logic, ethics, rhetoric, and the natural sciences. Aristotle established a tradition that values **empirical** observation, **deductive reasoning,** and science. This tradition can be contrasted with **Platonic idealism.**

arithmetic progression *See* **geometric progression.**

bell curve In statistics and science, a graph showing a normal distribution of results—in other words, a distribution in which the greatest number of results are grouped in the middle. If a math test is graded on a bell curve, for instance, most students will receive B's and C's, whereas only a few will receive A's or F's. Plotted on a graph, the curve will evoke the shape of a bell.

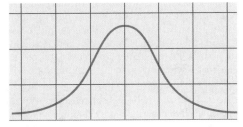

A bell curve.

Big Bang Theory A **hypothesis** about the origins of the universe: some 14 billion years ago, all the matter in the universe was concentrated in one almost infinitely dense point, which then exploded, dispersing matter in all directions at tremendous velocity. The Big Bang Theory implies a universe of finite size and age.

binary oppositions Paired terms conventionally treated as stable and logical opposites, such as *light/dark* and *man/woman.* Certain **postmodern** trends in philosophy and literary theory, notably **deconstruction,** seek to expose the "artificiality" of these and other **constructs** that shape the way we see the world. *See also* **structuralism.**

black hole From astronomy, a region in space-time where matter is infinitely dense and dimensionless and where the gravitational field is so strong that nothing can escape from it. The term is often used metaphorically to indicate something that is limitless or unresolvable.

Boolean logic (after the English mathematician George Boole, 1815–1864) A specialized algebra developed for the analysis of logical statements, used extensively in the development of the modern computer. A computer performs everything from simple math to Internet searches by means of Boolean logic, which uses **variables** and operators such as AND, OR, NOT, IF, THEN, and EXCEPT.

bourgeois Of or relating to the middle **class.** Although it originally referred to the artisans and craftsmen of medieval French towns, the term came into wide use with the Industrial Revolution, which created the modern middle class, and it is used in **Marxist** analysis to represent the capitalist class. *Bourgeois* commonly connotes an excessive concern with respectability and material goods.

canon Originally referring to a code of laws established by the church, the canon now typically refers to a collection of books deemed necessary for a complete education. What works are *canonical* is often debated and has changed over time. Current debate tends to focus on the exclusion from the canon of works by and about women and people of color. *See also* **multiculturalism.**

capitalism An economic system that emerged during the Industrial Revolution of the nineteenth century and offered private individuals the ownership of industry as well as unregulated market freedom. Today capitalism includes **Keynesian economic** models that allow government to regulate industry, particularly regarding such concerns as the minimum wage, tariffs, and taxes.

case study An intensive investigation and analysis of a person or group; often the object of study is proposed as the model of a certain phenomenon. Originally used in medicine, the term is now also common in psychology and business. Among the most famous and widely imitated case studies are those of Sigmund **Freud** (1856–1939), who used them to expound his theory of psychoanalysis. In business, a case study denotes a detailed examination of a corporation or enterprise with a view to determining the causes of its success or failure.

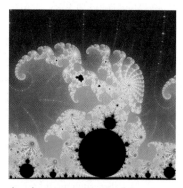

chaos theory A branch of mathematics used to describe highly complex phenomena such as weather or the flow of blood through the body. Chaos theory starts with the recognition that minute changes in a system can have large and unpredictable results. The *butterfly effect,* for instance, states that the flap of a butterfly's wings in China could theoretically cause a hurricane in New York. *See also* **iteration.**

class A term denoting social and/or economic standing in society (*upper class, lower class, middle class; working class, professional class, leisure class*).

An image generated from the Mandelbrot set, an aspect of chaos theory.

Karl **Marx** (1818–1883) argued that class conflict is economically based and so necessarily occurs between the working class and the capitalist class (those who control the means of production). Many have argued that economic standing alone does not determine class and that factors such as family, cultural background, and education play significant roles. *See also* **bourgeois, proletariat.**

classical Originally used to describe the artistic and literary conventions of ancient Greece and Rome. *Classical* (or *classicism / neoclassicism*) is also used for periods and products in the sciences, social sciences, philosophy, and music marked by straightforwardly rational models that describe the workings of the universe and human society as logical and ultimately harmonious. *See also* **modernism, postmodernism.**

coefficient In mathematics, a coefficient is a number or symbol multiplying a **variable** in an algebraic term, such as the 4 in $4x$. In the physical sciences, a coefficient is the numerical measure of a physical or chemical **constant.** In general usage, *coefficient* can denote factors working together to produce a result, as in "Jobs and longer prison terms are *coefficients* in the prevention of crime."

collective unconscious In the psychology of Carl Jung (1875–1961), the elements of the **unconscious** that are common to all humans. In the same way that each human body shares many features with others while at the same time being unique, the collective unconscious represents the general framework of the human unconscious, within which each individual's unconscious mind presents a unique pattern. *See also* **archetype.**

colonialism A policy by which a nation extends and maintains political and military control over a territory, often reducing it to a state of dependence. Begun as a way of acquiring resources such as spices, precious metals, and slaves, later instances of colonialism—such as the U.S. occupation of the Philippines from 1898 to 1946—have served mostly political or strategic purposes. *Postcolonial* refers to a state (or a cultural product or even a state of mind) that reflects former colonial occupation. *See also* **imperialism.**

constant In mathematics, science, and general usage, a factor that does not change. A mathematical or scientific constant is a quantity assumed to have a fixed value within a specific context. In physics, for example, the speed of light in a vacuum is 186,000 miles per second and is denoted by the constant c. Thus, in Einstein's famous equation $E = mc^2$, c is a constant and m, standing for any mass, is a **variable.**

construct (*noun*) Something that is shaped by culture ("constructed") but sometimes assumed to be "natural." For example, some might hold that the idea of gender ("maleness" and "femaleness") is a construct rather than the essential or inborn quality that past generations often assumed it to be.

contingent In logic, that which is true only under certain circumstances. In common usage, contingent often connotes that which has happened or can happen only as a result of a long, perhaps improbable sequence of events. Whenever you think, "It could easily have been different," you are feeling a sense of *contingency.*

correlation In statistics, a number that describes the relationship between two variables. In a *positive correlation,* the variables increase in tandem—for example, the higher a student's IQ, the better his or her scholastic performance. In a *negative correlation,* one variable increases while the other decreases—for example, the more green tea consumed, the lower the incidence of cancer.

counterculture *See* **culture.**

cross section A sample meant to be representative of a whole population. *See also* **longitudinal.**

culture Knowledge, beliefs, behavior, arts, institutions, and other products of work and thought that characterize a society. Within a dominant culture there may exist many *subcultures*: groups of particular ethnicity, age, education, employment, inclination, or other factors. A *counterculture* is a form of subculture whose values and lifestyle reject those of the dominant culture. *See also* **relativism.**

Darwinism British naturalist Charles Darwin's (1809–1882) theory of the historical evolution of species based on *natural selection,* or "the survival of the fittest." Where insects living within the bark of trees constitute a major food source, for instance, birds with longer, more pointed beaks tend to survive longer and produce more offspring, who then pass on longer, sharper beaks to ensuing generations.

deconstruction A method of literary criticism whose best-known theorist, Jacques Derrida (1930–2004), postulated that texts rest on **binary oppositions** such as *nature/culture, subject/object,* and *spirit/matter* that have been incorrectly assumed to be "true"; in exposing this fallacy, Derrida revealed the illogic of texts thought to be logical and coherent. Although often associated with **postmodernism** and the debate about the **canon,** deconstruction is in a philosophical sense a radical form of skepticism. In more common usage, to *deconstruct* something is to analyze it intensively, exposing it as (perhaps) something unexpected.

deductive reasoning Reasoning to a conclusion based on a previously held principle. *Inductive reasoning,* on the other hand, is the process of deriving a conclusion based on data. **Empiricism** holds that all knowledge is derived from sense experience by induction, whereas *rationalism* claims that knowledge can be deduced from certain a priori (presumptive) claims.

demographics (from the Greek *demos,* "people," and *graphia,* "writing") The quantitative study of human populations. A demographic study of a city might include the rate at which its population is growing, the size and distribution of its middle **class,** or the number of its families who have access to the Internet.

determinism In philosophy and science, the doctrine that every event is *determined,* or entirely shaped by earlier events, and that given complete knowledge of prior events and the laws that govern them, all future events can be predicted. Something described as *overdetermined* is thought to be shaped by more than one equally significant cause. Usually contrasted with *free will,* determinism is a feature of eighteenth- and nineteenth-century **classical** thought. In science, determinism has come to be opposed by the *indeterminism* of **quantum physics.**

dialectic In philosophy, history, and the humanities, the use of logical oppositions as a means of arriving at conclusions about ideas or events. *Dialectical reasoning* is most often associated with the philosophies of Georg Hegel (1770–1831)

FURTHER RESOURCES **FR-21**

and Karl **Marx** (1818–1883). According to Hegel, any human idea or *thesis* (for example, the sun circles the earth) naturally gives rise to an opposing idea or *antithesis* (the earth circles the sun), and these ideas resolve into a new idea or *synthesis* (the earth revolves around the sun but in an ellipse). Hegel's famous *master/slave dialectic* describes a seeming paradox: a slave holds power over his master because the master could not hold power without the slave. Marx extended dialectical reasoning in his theory of dialectical **materialism,** which analyzes not opposing ideas but contradictory **class** interests.

Dionysian That which embodies creativity, intuition, and, by extension, ecstasy, orgiastic release, and the irrational. The term is most often associated with the philosophy of Friedrich **Nietzsche** (1844–1900), where it opposes the **Apollonian.**

discourse (from the French *discours,* "speech" or "talk") *Discourse* is most often used in English to denote verbal expression in general, without distinguishing between writing and speech. *Discourse* can also refer to habits of expression characteristic of a particular community or to the content of that expression ("The *discourse* of experimental science does not often allow the use of the personal pronoun *I*").

disfranchise (also **disenfranchise**) Literally, to deprive of the right to vote; more loosely, to *disfranchise* means to deny rights or exclude from privileges, most often those associated with citizenship: "The rioters in Oklahoma felt themselves to have been effectively *disfranchised* by post–World War I economic and political change."

ecosystem A principal unit of study in ecology, the science of the relationships between organisms and their environments. All parts of an ecosystem are interdependent, and even small perturbations of one part (such as might be caused by pollution) can have profound effects on all of the other parts—a phenomenon often studied in **chaos theory.**

ego **Freudian** term for the "I" of mental functioning—that is, the capacity for realistic assessment of the needs of the self and the means of fulfilling these needs. *See also* **id, superego, repression, projection, unconscious.**

empiricism (from the Greek *empierikos,* "experienced") A philosophical trend, developed in large part by the philosophers John Locke (1632–1704) and David Hume (1711–1776), that data derived from experience or the senses are the ultimate source of knowledge, as opposed to reason, tradition, or authority. *Empirical* data are data gained through observation or experiment. Especially in medicine and psychology, *empirical* is often contrasted with *theoretical.* In its emphasis on observation and experience, empiricism is a conceptual cousin of **inductive reasoning** and **Aristotelianism.**

Enlightenment An intellectual movement committed to secular views based on reason that established itself in Europe in the eighteenth century (ca. 1688–1790).

epistemology The study of the nature of knowledge, its foundations and limits.

ethos (Greek for "character, a person's nature or disposition") The spirit or code of behavior peculiar to a specific person or group of people—for example, "part of the college student ethos is to stay up late drinking cola and eating

Captain Crunch." Ethos is one of the parts of Aristotle's **rhetorical triangle** (**ethos-logos-pathos**): in order to argue effectively, a speaker or writer must communicate a persuasive ethos, that is, a credible **persona** and a coherent perspective.

existentialism A strain in philosophy that emphasizes the isolation of the individual in an indifferent universe and stresses the individual's freedom (and responsibility) to determine his or her own existence. Having roots in the philosophies of Friedrich **Nietzsche** (1844–1900) and Martin Heidegger (1889–1976), existentialism was extremely influential in France after World War II, where French intellectuals like Jean-Paul Sartre (1905–1980) and Albert Camus (1913–1960) argued that by making conscious choices and taking responsibility for one's acts, one could overcome the otherwise absurd nature of the universe.

extrapolation In mathematics and computer science, the estimation of an unknown value using projections based on known information. For example, one might *extrapolate* the total number of votes cast for a political candidate nationwide based on a representative **sample.** *Interpolation,* on the other hand, is the estimation of an unknown value made by comparing known values that are closely related or nearby. The size of a colony of ants in June, for example, might be *interpolated* based on the numbers for May and July.

fascism (from the Italian *fascio,* "group") A name for the form of government established by Benito Mussolini (1883–1945) in Italy and Adolf Hitler (1889–1945) in Germany. Arising in response to economic and political upheaval in Europe after World War I, both governments centralized authority under a dictator, exerted strong economic controls, suppressed opposition through censorship and terror, and implemented belligerent nationalist and racist policies.

Mussolini and Hitler.

feminism The principle that women should enjoy the same political, economic, social, and cultural rights and opportunities as men. Mary Wollstonecraft's *A Vindication of the Rights of Woman* (1792) was a pioneering feminist work. The *suffrage movement,* which demanded that women be granted the right to vote, emerged following the first women's rights convention in Seneca Falls, New York, in 1848, and had achieved its goal in the United States and Europe by the early twentieth century. The *women's movement* that began in the 1960s initiated a new wave of feminism that focused on rectifying political, economic, social, and cultural inequalities between women and men. The many feminist thinkers who emerged from the women's movement have had a lasting impact in many academic fields, from the social sciences and humanities to the natural sciences.

formalism An approach to literary and art criticism that emphasizes rigorous attention to the structural elements and techniques of a work and de-emphasizes the historical or social contexts in which the work was created and its relationship to other works.

Freudian Relating to the theories of Sigmund Freud (1856–1939), the Viennese neurologist who invented psychoanalysis. A Freudian interpretation focuses on the unconscious emotional dynamics that are played out in a particular situation; in the study of literature, a Freudian interpretation focuses on such dynamics as they are represented in the **text.** *See also* **ego, id, superego, repression, projection, unconscious.**

game theory (also sometimes called *decision theory*) A mathematical method for analyzing situations of conflict or competition so as to determine a winning strategy. Game theory is useful not only in *true games* such as poker but also in business management, economics, and military strategy. *See also* **zero sum game.**

geometric progression A sequence of numbers determined by multiplying or dividing each number in succession by a **constant.** For example, *1, 4, 16, 64, 256* is a geometric progression with a constant multiplier, or **coefficient,** of 4. *Arithmetic progressions* proceed more slowly by adding or subtracting a constant: for example, *1, 4, 7, 10, 13* is an arithmetic progression with a constant *addend* of 3.

gestalt (German for "form" or "structure") The recognition of the whole of something that precedes the notice of any of its parts. In psychology, *Gestalt theory* asserts that psychological phenomena are irreducible and cannot be derived from the simple total of sensations a person experiences.

globalization The process by which communication and transportation technologies have made the world seem smaller and more interconnected. In economics, *globalization* refers to the way these advances have made national borders far less relevant in determining markets. The *anti-globalization* movement aims to protect workers from exploitation by multinational corporations, to prevent job loss among domestic workers, and to counter cultural homogenization. The presence of a McDonald's in Beijing is a good example of the effects of globalization.

hegemony Generally, the dominance of one nation or state over its neighbors. The Italian Marxist Antonio Gramsci (1891–1937) and his followers often used the term to refer to the dominance of the capitalists over the working **class.** *Hegemony* is now also used to describe a theory that has dominance in a particular field of study: "Dualism has long exercised hegemony in Western thought."

humanism (also *secular humanism*) A movement traditionally associated with Renaissance philosophers who deemphasized the role of religion or God in society while celebrating the achievements of human beings. There are *humanistic* branches of psychology, theology, and other disciplines that move the role of the human individual to the forefront of their studies.

hypothesis A statement that can be shown to be true or false either experimentally (in science) or through the use of logic (in other disciplines). For example, a simple hypothesis is that light is necessary for the survival of a certain plant. This hypothesis could be proved or disproved by the simple experiment of trying to grow the plant in a dark closet.

icon In **semiotics,** a **sign** that looks like what it refers to. A picture of the globe used to signify the earth or a line drawing of a suitcase indicating where to go to get your luggage at an airport are icons. Historically, an icon was a small picture of a religious figure, usually Jesus or the Virgin Mary.

id In **Freud**'s model of mental functioning, the raw desires and instincts of the individual, whose impulses are mediated by both the reality-testing capacities of the **ego** and the socializing function of the **superego.** *See also* **unconscious, projection, repression.**

idealism In philosophy and psychology, the notion that the mind determines ultimate reality, an idea that can be traced to **Plato** (428–347 BCE).

ideology A set of beliefs about the world (and often how it can be changed) espoused by an individual, group, or organization; a systematized worldview. **Capitalism,** for example, is an ideology. In the work of the Marxist critic Louis Althusser (1918–1990), an *ideology* is that which allows the individual to find his or her place and sense of self-worth within a given society.

imperialism One country's imposition of political and economic rule upon other countries. The British annexation of several countries in Africa in the nineteenth century is an example of this brand of imperialism. Today the term has been broadened to include the exportation of dominant cultural products and values. For example, some people in Europe and other parts of the world see the influx of American films into their markets as a form of *cultural imperialism. See also* **colonialism.**

inductive reasoning *See* **deductive reasoning.**

interpolation *See* **extrapolation.**

iteration Generally, the process of repeating steps over and over. In computer science, *iteration* refers to a computer's repeated looping through a set of programming instructions until it reaches the program's goal. In **chaos theory,** *iteration* involves getting data from an equation and repeatedly plugging the results back into the equation.

Keynesian economics The theory of economics developed by John Maynard Keynes (1883–1946), distinguished by the belief that government must intervene in the marketplace in order to promote stability and growth, specifically by increasing the money supply during economic downturns. *See also* **laissez-faire.**

laissez-faire (French for "allow to act") Generally, noninterference in the affairs or conduct of others. In economic and political theory, the idea that governments should not intervene in markets. The concept is based on the **classical** economic theory developed by Adam Smith (1723–1790) and others, which argues that an "invisible hand"—supply and demand, and competition—is sufficient to guide economic markets. *See also* **Keynesian economics.**

logos (Greek for "word") In Aristotle's **rhetorical triangle,** the topic of the argument or argument itself.

longitudinal A study in which the same group of subjects is examined over a long period of time. A *longitudinal study* could, for example, be conducted to test the rate of obesity over time among a certain group of schoolchildren.

Marxism The economic and political doctrine put forth by Karl Marx (1818–1883) and Friedrich Engels (1820–1895). Its basic teachings center around the **class** struggle between the **proletariat** (the working class) and the **bourgeoisie** (capitalists, those who own the *means of production*). Marxism predicts that in time the working class will inevitably revolt, wresting the means of production from the bourgeoisie and ceding them to the state, which will distribute goods equitably. A classless society will result.

materialism In philosophy, the belief that physical matter is all that exists and that so-called higher phenomena—for example, thought, feeling, mind, will—are wholly dependent on and **determined** by physical processes. Since the **Enlightenment,** almost all scientists have been materialists. In history and economics, the dialectical materialism of Karl **Marx** (1818–1883) held that **cultural** phenomena are determined wholly by economic conditions.

mean (also *average*) The sum of a set of numbers divided by the number of terms in the set. For example, the mean of the set (1, 2, 3) is 2 because its sum (6) divided by the number of terms (3) equals 2.

median The middle term in an ordered set of numbers. For example, the median of the ordered set (2, 6, 10, 12, 15) is 10 because there are two numbers (2 and 6) below 10 and two (12 and 15) above 10.

meta- A prefix often used to suggest "moving beyond," "going up a level," or "transcending." Thus, *metaphysics* is the branch of philosophy that deals with questions that cannot be resolved by physical observation, such as whether God exists. Similarly, *metapsychology* deals not with perception, emotion, or cognition per se, but rather with how such things are discussed and defined. **Freud**'s division of the psyche into **id, ego,** and **superego** is an example of metapsychology.

modernism Often used in opposition to classicism or neoclassicism when denoting periods in the sciences, social sciences, philosophy, and music, *modernism* as a trend in thought represents a break with the certainties of the past, among them a confidence that everything can be known. *Modern* science has been characterized by highly counterintuitive theories such as **relativity**—according to which there is no absolute way to measure time—and **quantum physics**—according to which you can know the speed or the position of a subatomic particle but never both. In literature, the **stream of consciousness** and/or *free association* style of *modernist* writers like Virginia Woolf (1882–1941) and James Joyce (1882–1941) broke decisively with the storytelling conventions of the late-nineteenth-century, or

Virginia Woolf.

Victorian, novel. Thus, some critics believe that **postmodernism** is really only the development of a trend begun in the modernist era.

multiculturalism The view that many cultures, not just the dominant one, should be given attention in the classroom and in broader society. The debate on multiculturalism is related to the debate on the **canon.**

nature-nurture controversy A debate about whether genetic (*nature*) or environmental (*nurture*) factors have the upper hand in determining human behavior. Experimental studies involving fraternal and identical twins raised together and apart have been undertaken to investigate the issue, but fundamental questions about method and the small **samples** involved have left the question unresolved. This debate pervades countless topics studied in the social sciences, among them questions of gender difference, intelligence, poverty, crime, and childhood development.

Nietzschean Following the ideas of Friedrich Nietzsche (1844–1900), a pioneering **existentialist** philosopher. Nietzsche believed that overemphasis on the Christian belief in the afterlife had led people away from what is real in the world. Nietzsche used the term *superman* (*Übermensch* in German) to apply to those who found the strength to cast aside these traditional social and moral values, using their **will to power.** *See also* **Apollonian, Dionysian.**

object/subject In philosophy and psychology, the *subject* does the observing or experiencing, while the *object* is that which is observed or experienced. Throughout history, this philosophical dualism has been studied, refined, and debated extensively. In **Freudian** and post-Freudian psychology, an *object* is an external person or thing that gratifies an infant and is therefore loved.

objective Pertaining to that which is independent of perception or observation, as opposed to *subjective,* which pertains to that which is determined by perception or observation. The old philosophical puzzle—If a tree falls in the woods, and no one is there to hear it, does it make a sound?—plays upon the notions of philosophical *objectivity* and *subjectivity.*

Oedipus complex The psychological notion expounded by Sigmund **Freud** (1856–1939) that describes the unconscious sexual longing of a son for his mother and his unconscious wish to kill his father, his rival for possession of the mother. The name is a reference to Sophocles' play *Oedipus Rex.* Freud also wrote of the *Electra* complex, which describes the similar sexual longing of a daughter for her father.

ontology Generally, the study of being and human consciousness.

paradigm A theoretical framework that serves as a foundation for a field of study or branch of knowledge. Darwinian evolution, Newtonian physics, and Aristotle's chemistry are all examples of scientific paradigms. *Paradigm shifts* designate the transition from one paradigm to another, usually with a profoundly transformative effect. For example, the shift from Newtonian physics to quantum physics might be termed a *paradigm shift.*

pathos (Greek for "suffering, experience, emotion") In Aristotle's **rhetorical triangle,** the feelings evoked in the audience by an argument.

persona (Latin for "mask") An assumed or public identity (as distinct from the *inner self*); a character adopted for a particular purpose; in literature, the voice or character of the speaker.

placebo effect A psychological process wherein subjects in medical research respond to an inactive compound, often a sugar pill, as if it contained active ingredients intended to treat a disease or condition.

Platonic Following the teachings of the Greek philosopher Plato (428–347 BCE), Platonic **idealism** is a system that attempts to show a rational relationship between the individual, the state, and the universe, governed by what is good, true, and beautiful. Basic tenets of this seminal branch of philosophy are that only a reflection of the truth can be perceived and that the gap between the ideal and its reflection motivates human consciousness. It can be contrasted with the **Aristotelian** tradition, which values empirical observation and scientific reasoning. In common usage, a *platonic relationship* is a close friendship that does not have a sexual component.

pluralism In everyday language, a condition of society in which multiple religions, ethnicities, and subcultures coexist peacefully. *Pluralism* can also refer to any philosophical system that proposes that reality is made up of a number of distinct entities. The pragmatist William James (1842–1910) and the analytic philosopher Bertrand Russell (1872–1970) were prominent *pluralist* thinkers.

postcolonial *See* **colonialism.**

postmodernism A cultural trend that seeks to expose the artificiality of the **constructs** that defined earlier periods of cultural production while confessing—indeed, in some cases even boasting of—an inability to replace them with an authentic substitute. One of the hallmarks of *postmodern* cultural products is *pastiche,* or *collage,* a form that borrows from other trends and emphasizes the disjuncture between disparate elements. *See also* **modernism.**

praxis Often used as a substitute for *practice* in ordinary usage, and opposed to **theory.** In the work of Antonio Gramsci (1891–1937), the "philosophy of praxis" outlined the refinements to Marxism that were necessary to make it relevant in the twentieth century.

projection In **Freudian** psychology, a mechanism by which the individual, unable to come to terms with his or her own fears and desires, imagines that these unwelcome impulses exist outside of him- or herself. *See also* **id, ego, superego, repression, unconscious.**

proletariat In **Marxism,** the *proletariat* is the downtrodden working **class,** who will revolt against the **bourgeois,** or capitalist, class, seizing from its members the means of production (factories and other industrial concerns).

quantum physics A theoretical branch of physics that deals with the behavior of atoms and subatomic particles. The work of such pioneers as Max Planck (1858–1947), Niels Bohr (1885–1962), and later Werner Heisenberg (1901–1976) has had a profound impact on the way we understand such things as the relationships between matter and energy. *See also* **relativity.**

relativism The belief that the meaning and value of all things are determined by their *context*—their relationship to other things in that time and place—rather than that things have inherent or absolute meaning or worth. *Moral relativism* is the idea that different people, groups, nations, or cultures have differing ideas about what constitutes good and evil and that those differences must be respected. *Cultural relativism* is the position that there is no absolute point of view from which one set of cultural values or beliefs can be deemed intrinsically superior to any other. *See also* **culture, humanism.**

relativity In physics, the theory expounded by Albert Einstein (1879–1955), which states that all motion is relative and that energy and matter are convertible. The famous formulation $E = mc^2$ equates energy (E) with matter (m) multiplied by the speed of light (c) squared. Einstein's work directly challenged two cornerstones of **classical** physics—that motion is an absolute and that energy and matter are two completely different entities.

repression In **Freudian** psychology, the process that keeps unacceptable desires, fears, and other troubling material (such as memories of traumatic experiences) from reaching (or returning to) consciousness. *See also* **unconscious, projection.**

Albert Einstein.

rhetoric In classical times, the art of public speaking. Currently, the term more broadly encompasses *language* or *speech,* often in a derogatory context (as in "The mayor's speech was so much empty *rhetoric*"), as well as the study of writing and the effective use of language.

rhetorical triangle Aristotle's description of the context of argument, consisting of **ethos** (roughly, the character of the speaker), **logos** (the topic of the argument or argument itself), and **pathos** (the feelings evoked in the audience).

sample A subset or selection of a group from a population. In a *random sample,* each subject is chosen in ways that replicate pure chance, and all members of the population have an equal chance of being selected for the sample.

scientific method A process involving observations of phenomena and the conducting of experiments to test ideas suggested by those observations. The development of the scientific method, a specialized form of trial and error, ushered in the scientific revolution of the seventeenth century. Francis Bacon (1561–1626), René Descartes (1596–1650), and especially Galileo Galilei (1564–1642) are most often credited with developing its constituent procedures: (1) choosing a question or problem (for example, what causes yellow fever); (2) developing a **hypothesis** (the disease is caused by a bacteria or virus transmitted by mosquitoes); (3) conducting observations and experiments (noting **correlations** between mosquito populations and incidence of yellow fever); (4) examining and interpreting the data (high correlations exist between incidence of yellow fever and that of the *A. aegypti* mosquito); (5) affirming, revising, or rejecting the hypothesis; and (6) deriving further experiments and hypotheses from it (microscopically examining the bodies of *A. aegypti* and yellow fever victims to try to find a virus or bacteria present in both).

secular Not having to do with religion or the church; deriving its authority from nonreligious sources. *See also* **humanism.**

semiotics The theory and study of **signs** and symbols. According to semiotics, meaning is never inherent but is always a product of social conventions, and **culture** can be analyzed as a series of **sign** systems. *See also* **structuralism.**

sign In **semiotics,** a constituent of a text—that is, any cultural product, including but not limited to language and human behavior—that derives its meaning only by means of its differentiation from surrounding signs. A recurring word in a poem can function as a sign, as can a wink or a nod; the meaning of each of these signs can be derived only from the study of their context.

skepticism The belief that nothing can be held true until grounds are established for believing it to be true. René Descartes (1596–1650), one of the founders of modern philosophy, expressed this attitude in his famous statement *"Cogito, ergo sum"* ("I think, therefore I am").

sociobiology The study of human behavior within an evolutionary/biological context. E. O. Wilson's *Sociobiology: The New Synthesis* (1975) provoked a controversial debate over the extent to which social behavior has a biological basis. *See also* **Darwinism.**

Socratic method Repeated questioning to arrive at implicit truths, a teaching method used by the Greek philosopher Socrates (470?–399? BCE), who influenced **Plato.**

solipsism Philosophical theory that the self is the only thing that can be known and verified and therefore is the only reality.

somatic (from the Greek for "body") Relating to the body. A *psychosomatic* illness is a physical condition that has a psychological origin.

standard deviation A measure of the degree to which data diverge from the **mean.** A high standard deviation means a greater range of results. Thus, in a **bell curve,** a tall, skinny curve represents a smaller standard deviation than does a wide, flat one.

statistical significance A value assigned to a research result as a measure of how likely it is that the result reflects mere chance. The higher the statistical significance, the less likely it is that chance determined the outcome. The results of studies employing large numbers of subjects typically have a higher statistical significance than do those from studies of a small number of subjects.

stream of consciousness A **modernist** literary technique in which the writer renders the moment-by-moment progress of a character's or narrator's thoughts. Among those writers who have used the technique are James Joyce (1882–1941) in *Ulysses,* Virginia Woolf (1882–1941) in *Mrs Dalloway,* and Marcel Proust (1871–1922) in *Remembrance of Things Past.*

structuralism An analytical method, today often subsumed under **semiotics,** that is used in the social sciences, the humanities, and the arts to examine underlying deep structures in a **text** by close investigation of its constituent parts (often termed **signs**). For example, in *narratology* (the study of narratives), myths, folktales, novels, paintings, and even comic books are reduced to their essential structures, from which are derived the rules that govern the different ways in which these narratives tell their stories. In *structural* approaches, the individual works under study are commonly considered less important than the universal structures that underlie them. This tendency has opened the approach to charges of anti-**humanism**. Michel Foucault (1926–1984) and other *poststructuralists* have challenged structuralists' belief in the possibility of revealing essential structures of knowledge and reality through this type of study. *See also* **semiotics, deconstruction, formalism, sign.**

subculture *See* **culture.**

subjective *See* **objective.**

sublimation A psychological concept describing the redirection of unacceptable feelings or impulses into socially acceptable behavior. For example, one might say that working long hours *sublimates* the desire to engage in adulterous exploits.

sublime Inspiring awe; impressive; moving; of high spiritual or intellectual worth. Michelangelo's painting on the ceiling of the Sistine Chapel is often cited as an example of the *sublime* in art; in nature, mountains such as Kilimanjaro have been described as *sublime*.

superego In the **Freudian** model of mental functioning, the mental agent responsible for keeping the desires of the **id** and the antisocial impulses **The ceiling of the Sistine Chapel.** of the **ego** in check. Religion and the law are two institutions that Freud identified as manifestations of the superego in society. *See also* **repression, projection.**

symbiosis In biology, a prolonged association and interdependence of two or more organisms, usually to their mutual benefit. *Parasitism* occurs when one organism benefits at the expense of another. In general usage, *symbiotic* is used metaphorically to denote a mutual dependency and benefit between people, organisms, or ideas.

taxonomy Any set of laws and principles of classification. Originating in biology, taxonomy includes the theory and principles governing the classification of organisms into categories such as species and phyla. Today a literary critic might compose a "taxonomy of literary styles."

teleology In philosophy, religion, history, and the social sciences, an explanation or theory that assumes movement or development toward a specific end. For instance, Christianity is profoundly *teleological* because it looks toward the second coming of Christ.

text In common academic usage, anything undergoing rigorous intellectual examination and analysis. Although commonly associated with printed or written works, texts may also be oral works such as speeches, visual works such as paintings, everyday objects like toys, and even human behavior. Analysis of such cultural products is often called "reading the text," even if the text is not a written work. *See also* **semiotics, sign.**

theory A statement devised to explain a collection of facts or observations; also, the systematic organization of such statements. Theory is commonly contrasted with *practice* or **praxis.**

topography The physical features of a region. In cartography and surveying, maps and charts are the graphic representations of topography.

totem/totemic (from the Ojibwa, a Native American tribal language) A bird, animal, or plant or a natural phenomenon that has a special meaning for an individual or social group and with which the individual or group claims a special relationship.

trope A figure of speech. In literary criticism, the term is often used to refer to any technique that recurs in a **text.** Comparing women's faces to flowers is a common trope in Renaissance poetry.

typology The systematic study and classification of individuals in a group according to selected characteristics. In psychology, Carl Jung (1875–1961) developed a personality typology that uses characteristics such as extraversion and introversion. The Myers-Briggs assessment tools, based on Jung's typologies, are used in psychotherapy and employment settings. *See also* **archetypes.**

uncertainty principle An important theory in **quantum physics** formulated by German physicist Werner Heisenberg (1901–1976) that places an absolute, theoretical limit on the accuracy of certain pairs of simultaneously recorded measurements. The significance of this principle is that it prevents scientists from making absolute predictions of the future state of certain systems. Heisenberg's principle has been applied to philosophy, where it is called the *indeterminacy principle.*

unconscious In the **Freudian** theory of the mind, the repository for repressed desires, fears, and memories. Ordinarily inaccessible to the conscious mind, the repressed material in the unconscious nevertheless has a powerful impact on conscious behavior and thoughts. *See also* **id, ego, superego, projection, repression.**

variable In mathematics, a variable is a term capable of assuming any set of values. In algebra, it is represented by a symbol such as x, y, p, or q. In experimental research, the *dependent variable* is measured for change precipitated by an *independent variable* determined by the experimenter. A *random variable* is a numerical value determined by chance-driven experiment or phenomenon. The value can be predicted according to the laws of probability but is usually not known until after the experiment has been completed.

will to power (from Friedrich **Nietzsche**'s *Thus Spake Zarathustra,*) The capacity to overcome the dictates of conventional morality in order to achieve a level of experience beyond the reach of the "common herd." The key quality of Nietzsche's *superman* (*Übermensch*), the will to power manifests itself in creativity, independence, and originality. The association of this concept with Nazism has long made Nietzsche's ideas the focus of heated debate. *See also* **Apollonian, Dionysian, Nietzschean.**

zero sum game   Any competitive situation where a gain for one side results in a loss for the other side. This term originated in **game theory** but is now in common use. In a *zero sum economy,* any economic gain is offset by an economic loss.

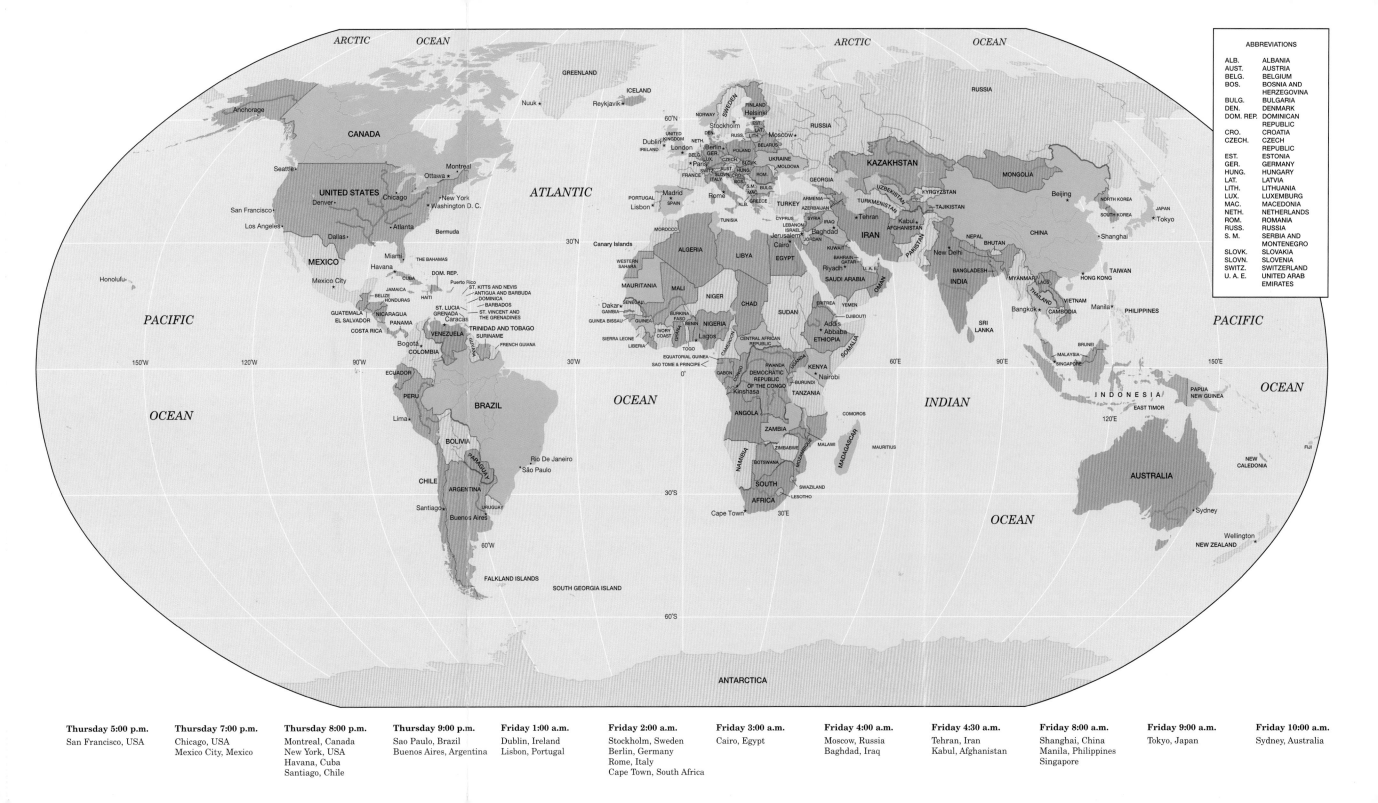

Thursday 5:00 p.m.	**Thursday 7:00 p.m.**	**Thursday 8:00 p.m.**	**Thursday 9:00 p.m.**	**Friday 1:00 a.m.**	**Friday 2:00 a.m.**	**Friday 3:00 a.m.**	**Friday 4:00 a.m.**	**Friday 4:30 a.m.**	**Friday 8:00 a.m.**	**Friday 9:00 a.m.**	**Friday 10:00 a.m.**
San Francisco, USA	Chicago, USA	Montreal, Canada	Sao Paulo, Brazil	Dublin, Ireland	Stockholm, Sweden	Cairo, Egypt	Moscow, Russia	Tehran, Iran	Shanghai, China	Tokyo, Japan	Sydney, Australia
	Mexico City, Mexico	New York, USA	Buenos Aires, Argentina	Lisbon, Portugal	Berlin, Germany		Baghdad, Iraq	Kabul, Afghanistan	Manila, Philippines		
		Havana, Cuba			Rome, Italy				Singapore		
		Santiago, Chile			Cape Town, South Africa						

Quick Reference for Multilingual Writers

Many multilingual students encounter problems when they try to transfer their thoughts from one language into another. For example, some languages, like Russian and Chinese, do not include articles such as *a, an,* and *the* (English: *The flowers are beautiful*); other languages, such as Arabic and French, do not use definite articles to introduce a profession (English: *Here is the doctor*); still others, such as Spanish, include articles to indicate a generalization, whereas English does not (English: *time flies*). More tips for multilingual writers are included in the review of basic grammar in Tab 12 and in *For Multilingual Students* boxes found throughout this handbook, but here is a quick reference for dealing with some of the common issues that come up when you are transferring your first language into English.

Nouns and Pronouns

Count and Noncount Nouns

Count nouns name persons, places, or things that can be counted. Count nouns can be singular or plural.

Noncount nouns name a class of things. Usually, noncount nouns have only a singular form.

COUNT	NONCOUNT
cars	information
table	furniture
child	humanity
book	advice

Pronouns

Common Problem: Personal pronoun restates subject.

INCORRECT My sister, *she* works in the city.

CORRECT My sister works in the city.

Pronouns replace nouns. They stand for persons, places, or things and can be singular or plural.

Personal pronouns act as subjects, objects, or words that show possession.

- *Subject pronouns:* I, we, you, he, she, it, one, they, who
- *Object pronouns:* me, us, you, him, her, it, one, them, whom
- *Possessive pronouns:* my, mine, our, ours, your, yours, his, her, hers, its, their, theirs, whose

Relative pronouns introduce dependent clauses.

Relative pronouns: that, whatever, which, whichever, who, whoever, whom, whomever, whose

EXAMPLE His sister, *who* lives in Canada, came to visit.

Articles

Common Problem: Article is omitted.

INCORRECT Water is cold. I bought watch.

CORRECT *The* water is cold. I bought *a* watch.

Using Articles with Count and Noncount Nouns

Definite article (*the*): used for specific reference with all types of nouns.

The car I bought is red. [*singular count noun*]

The dogs howled at the moon. [*plural count noun*]

The furniture makes the room appear cluttered. [*noncount noun*]

Do not use *the* before most singular proper nouns, such as names of people, cities, languages, and so on.

~~The~~ Dallas is a beautiful city.

Indefinite articles (*a, an*): used with singular count nouns only.

Use *a* before a word that begins with a consonant sound.

a pencil

a sports car

a tropical rain forest

Use *an* before a word that begins with a vowel sound.

an orange

an hour

an instrument

Do not use an indefinite article with a noncount noun.

  Water
~~A water~~ is leaking from the faucet.

No article: Plural count nouns and noncount nouns do not require *indefinite* articles. Plural count nouns and noncount nouns do not need *definite* articles when they refer to all of the items in a group.

Plural count nouns and noncount nouns

Every night I hear ~~a~~ dogs barking.

I needed to find ~~an~~ information in the library.

Plural count nouns

SPECIFIC ITEM *The* dogs next door never stop barking.

ALL ITEMS IN A GROUP Dogs make good pets.

Noncount nouns

SPECIFIC ITEM *The* jewelry she wore to the party was beautiful.

ALL ITEMS IN A GROUP Jewelry is expensive.

Verbs

Common Problem: *be* verb is left out.

INCORRECT He sleeping now. She happy.

CORRECT He *is* sleeping now. She *is* happy

Verb Tenses

Tense refers to the time of action expressed by a verb.

Present tense (base form or form with -s ending): action taking place now.

I *sleep* here. She *sleeps*. We *sleep* late every weekend.

Past tense (-d or -ed ending): past action.

I *laughed*. He *laughed*. They *laughed* together.

Future tense (*will* + base form): action that is going to take place.

I *will go* to the movie. He *will run* in the marathon. You *will write* the paper.

Present perfect tense (have or has + past participle): past action that was or will be completed.

I *have spoken*. He *has washed* the floor. We *have made* lunch.

Past perfect tense (had + past participle): past action completed before another past action.

I *had spoken*. She *has been* busy. They *had noticed* a slight error.

Future perfect tense (will + have + past participle): action that will begin and end in the future before another action happens.

I *will have eaten*. She *will have danced* in the recital by then. You *will have taken* the train.

Present progressive tense (am, are, or is + present participle): continuing action.

I *am writing* a novel. He *is working* on a new project. They *are studying* for the test.

Past progressive tense (was or were + present participle): past continuing action.

I *was cleaning* the house. She *was working* in the yard. You *were making* dinner.

Future progressive tense (will + be + present participle): future continuing action

I *will be traveling* to Europe. She *will be sightseeing* in New York. They *will be eating* together tonight.

Present perfect progressive tense (have or has + been + present participle): past action that continues in the present.

I *have been practicing*. He *has been sleeping* all morning. They *have been coming* every weekend.

Past perfect progressive tense (had + been + present participle): continuous action completed before another past action.

I *had been driving* for six hours. She *had been reading* when I arrived. They *had been singing*.

Future perfect progressive tense (will + have + been + present participle): action that will begin, continue, and end in the future.

I *will have been driving* for ten hours. He *will have been living* there for three years. You *will have been studying* for the test all afternoon.

Sentence Structure

Subjects and Verbs

English requires both a subject and a verb in every sentence or clause.

S V   S V
She slept.   He ate.

Direct and Indirect Objects

Verbs may be followed by *direct* or *indirect objects*. A *direct object* receives the action of the verb.

S V   DO
He drove the car.

An *indirect object* is the person or thing to which something is done.

S V   IO   DO
She gave her sister a birthday gift.

A Guide to Weights and Measurements

The United States is one of only a few countries in the world that have not converted to the International System of Units (SI), otherwise known as the modern metric system. You will encounter this system of measurement in all science courses. Following is a helpful conversion chart for many common units of metric measurement. (*Source:* Merriam-Webster online dictionary and the U.S. Metric Association Web site)

Length

1 kilometer (km) = 0.62 mile

1 hectometer (hm) = 328.08 feet

1 decameter (dam) = 32.81 feet

1 meter (m) = 39.37 inches

1 decimeter (dm) = 3.94 inches

1 centimeter (cm) = 0.39 inch

1 millimeter (mm) = 0.039 inch

1 micrometer (μm) = 0.000039 inch

Area

1 square kilometer (sq km *or* km^2) = 0.3861 square mile

1 hectare (ha) = 2.47 acres

1 are (a) = 119.60 square yards

1 square centimeter (sq cm *or* cm^2) = 0.155 square inch

Volume

1 cubic meter (m^3) = 1.307 cubic yards

1 cubic decimeter (dm^3) = 61.023 cubic inches

1 cubic centimeter (cu cm *or* cm^3, *also* cc) = 0.061 cubic inch

Capacity (liquid)

1 decaliter (dal) = 2.64 gallons

1 liter (l) = 1.057 quarts

1 cubic decimeter (dm^3) = 1.057 quarts

1 deciliter (dl) = .21 pint

1 centiliter (cl) = 0.338 fluid ounce

1 milliliter (ml) = 0.27 fluid dram

1 microliter (μl) = 0.00027 fluid dram

Mass and Weight

1 metric ton (t) = 1.102 short tons

1 kilogram (kg) = 2.2046 pounds

1 hectogram (hg) = 3.527 ounces

1 decagram (dag) = 0.353 ounce

1 gram (g) = 0.035 ounce

1 decigram (dg) = 1.543 grains

1 centigram (cg) = 0.154 grain

1 milligram (mg) = 0.015 grain

1 microgram (μg) = 0.000015 grain

Index

Index for Multilingual Writers

For MULTILINGUAL STUDENTS

Credits

Text Credits

Tab 1: p. 5: Adapted from Robert S. Feldman, *P.O.W.E.R. Learning: Strategies for Success in College and Life,* 2nd ed. Copyright © McGraw-Hill Companies, Inc. Used with permission of The McGraw-Hill Companies. **p. 8:** Currency graph from *Wall Street Journal: Eastern Edition* [Only Staff-Produced Materials May Be Used] by Frederick C. Klein. Copyright © 1979 by Dow Jones & Co. Inc. Reproduced with permission of Dow Jones & Co. Inc. in the format textbook via Copyright Clearance Center; Revised graph adjusted for deflation. Copyright © 1987 From *Misused Statistics* by Herbert F. Spirere, Louise Spirer, and Abram J. Jaffe. Reproduced by permission of Taylor & Francis Books, Inc. **p. 12:** Screenshot of course home page created in PageOut by Dr. Susan P. Sullivan, Professor of Accounting, University of Massachusetts Dartmouth. Copyright © McGraw-Hill Companies, Inc. Used with permission. Screen shot of Microsoft® Internet Explorer used by permission of Microsoft Corporation. **p. 14:** Screenshot from Catalyst. Copyright © McGraw-Hill Companies, Inc. Reprinted by permission of the McGraw-Hill Companies, Inc. **p. 17:** Definition of "haze." Copyright © 2000 by Houghton Mifflin. Reprinted by permission from *The American Heritage Dictionary of the English Language,* Fourth Edition; Definition of "pig out." *ESL Learner's Edition, Random House Webster's Dictionary of American English* 1997; Definition of "academic." *ESL Learner's Edition, Random House Webster's Dictionary of American English* 1997.

Tab 2: pp. 24–25: Hentoff, Nat. "Misguided Multiculturalism," *The Village Voice,* July 19–25, 2000, pgs 29–30. Copyright © 2000 by Nat Hentoff. Reprinted by permission of the author. **p. 55:** Used with permission from Gary Klass. **p. 57:** From Clarke & Cornish, "Modeling Offenders' Decisions," in *Crime and Justice,* volume 6, Tonry & Morris, eds., 1985, p. 169. Copyright © 1985 University of Chicago Press. Used by permission of the publisher, University of Chicago Press. **p. 62:** Excerpt from Robert Reich, "The Future of Work," as found in *Harper's Magazine,* 1989. Reprinted with permission. **p. 65:** From Bentley and Zieger, *Traditions and Encounters: A Global Perspective on the Past,* 2nd ed. Copyright © McGraw-Hill Companies, Inc. Used with permission of The McGraw-Hill Companies. **p. 67:** Graph as found in the State of the News Media report by the Project for Excellence in Journalism, www.stateofthemedia.com. Based on Nielsen Media Research data. Reprinted with permission. **p. 68:** NASA. **p. 69:** Cintara Corporation, a full service branding agency. **p. 71:** U.S. Global Change Research Program http://www.usgrcrp.gov/usgrcrp/Library/nationalassessment/overviewhealth.html. **p. 72:** From Jonathan Fast's "After Columbine: How People Mourn Sudden Death" in *Social Work,* October 2003. Copyright 2003, National Association of Social Workers, Inc., Social Work; From Damian Robinson's "Riding into the Afterlife" in *Archaeology,* Volume 57, Number 2, March/April 2004. Courtesy of Archaeology Magazine. **pp. 72–73:** From J. Jill Suitor, Rebecca Powers, and Rachel Brown's "Avenues to Prestige among Adolescents" in *Adolescence,* Summer, 2004, v39 i154 p229(13). Reprinted with permission from Libra Publishers. **pp. 79–80:** Screen shot of Microsoft® Word used by permission of Microsoft Corporation. **p. 89:** © 1998 Glencoe/McGraw-Hill. Adapted from *Mathematics: Applications and Connections, Course 2.* Used with permission. **p. 99:** Screen shot of Microsoft® Word used by permission of Microsoft Corporation.

Tab 3: p. 120: From "Love and Achievement Motives in Women's and Men's Suicide Notes," by Canetto, Silvia Sara, Lester David, in *Journal of Psychology,* Vol. 136, Issue 5, September 2002. Reprinted with permission of the Helen Dwight Reid Educational Foundation. Published by Heldref Publications, 1319 Eighteenth St., NW, Washington, DC 20036-1802. Copyright (c) 2002. **p. 145:** From Gloria Ladson Billings, *The Dreamkeepers: Successful Teachers of African American Children,* San Franscico: Jossey-Bass, 1994, 35–36. Copyright © 1994 by Jossey-Bass Inc. Reprinted with permission of John Wiley & Sons, Inc. **p. 175:** Screenshot of the home page for the National Museum of the American Indian. Courtesy, National Museum of the American Indian, Smithsonian Institution.

Screen shot of Microsoft® Internet Explorer used by permission of Microsoft Corporation. **p. 176:** Vietnam Women's Memorial, Copyright 1993, Vietnam Women's Memorial Foundation, Glenna Goodacre, Sculptor, courtesy, Vietnam Women's Memorial Foundation, Inc. 1735 Connecticut Av NW, 3rd Floor, Washington, DC 2009. Screen shot of Microsoft® Internet Explorer used by permission of Microsoft Corporation. **p. 178:** Screen shot from University of Alaska Anchorage web site used with permission. Screen shot of Microsoft® Internet Explorer used by permission of Microsoft Corporation. **p. 179:** Screen shot of Library of Congress homepage. Http://www.loc.gov. Screen shot of Microsoft® Internet Explorer used by permission of Microsoft Corporation. **p. 180:** As found on http://cedarmesa.blogspot.com. Used by permission of Cedar Mesa Music. Screen shot of Microsoft® Internet Explorer used by permission of Microsoft Corporation.
Tab 5: p. 214: Screenshot of ASU West Library's Reference Source page. Reprinted with permission. **p. 220:** Image published with permission of ProQuest Information and Learning Company. Further reproduction is prohibited without permission. **pp. 224 and 225:** Reproduced with permission of Google. Screen shot of Microsoft® Internet Explorer used by permission of Microsoft Corporation. **pp. 228 and 229:** Copyright 2002 The City University of New York. Used with permission. Screen shot of Microsoft® Internet Explorer used by permission of Microsoft Corporation. **p. 232:** Gridded Population of the World, CIESIN, Columbia University. Used with permission. **p. 234:** Image Courtesy SkeetobiteWeather.com **p. 243:** Reprinted with permission from the Virginia Center for Digital History, University of Virginia. Screen shot of Microsoft® Internet Explorer used by permission of Microsoft Corporation. **p. 256:** Copyright 2002 The City University of New York. Used with permission. Screen shot of Microsoft® Internet Explorer used by permission of Microsoft Corporation. **p. 257:** Screen shot of New Orleans Online. Photos from Louis Armstrong Archives, Queens College, City University of New York, Flushing. Courtesy of the Louis Armstrong House & Archives, Queens College. **pp. 260–261:** Ephland, John. From "Down Beat Jazz 101: The Very Beginning," *Down Beat Magazine,* http://www.downbeat.com/default.asp?sect=education&subsect=jazz. **Tab 6: p. 328:** Anonymous watercolor caricature of Armstrong with his manager, Joe Glaser, c. 1950. Louis Armstrong Archives, Queens College, City University of New York, Flushing. Courtesy of the Louis Armstrong House & Archives, Queens College. **MLA foldout:** Image produced by ProQuest Information and Learning Company. Inquiries may be made to: ProQuest Information and Learning Company, 300 North Zeeb Road, Ann Arbor, MI 48106-1346 USA. Telephone (734) 761-7400; Email: info@il.proquest.com; Webpage: www.il.proquest.com. Screen shot of Microsoft® Internet Explorer used by permission of Microsoft Corporation. From *Louis Armstrong: An Extravagant Life* by Lawrence Bergreen. Copyright © 1997 by Lawrence Bergreen. Used by permission of Broadway Books, a division of Random House, Inc.; "Heebie Jeebies" By Boyd Atkins. © 1926, 1953 by MCA Music Publishing, All rights administered by Universal Music Corp. / ASCAP. Used By Permission. All Rights Reserved. Table of content and introductory page from Hayes, Brent Edwards. "Louis Armstrong and the Syntax of Scat." *Critical Inquiry* 28 (2002): 618–49. Copyright © 2002 by The University of Chicago Press. Reprinted with permission from the publisher, The University of Chicago Press. Table of contents and article excerpt from Epstein, J. (2002). A voice in the wilderness. *Latin Trade,* 10(12), 26. Reprinted with permission of Latin Trade.
Tab 7: p. 360: From National Institute of Space Research (2002). In D. Kalmowitz, B. Mertens, S. Wunder, and P. Pacheco, *Hamburger Connection Fuels Amazon Destruction: Cattle Ranching and Deforestation in Brazil's Rain Forest.* Reprinted with permission from the Center for International Forestry Research (CIFOR). **APA foldout:** From *Exploring Agrodiversity* by H. Brookfield. Copyright © 2001 Columbia University Press. Reprinted with permission of the publisher. Reprinted with permission from EBSCO. Screen shot of Microsoft® Internet Explorer used by permission of Microsoft Corporation.
Tab 9: pg. 446: Definition of "compare" from *Random House Webster's College Dictionary.*
Tab 11: p. 569: Reprinted with the permission of Scribner, an imprint of Simon & Schuster Adult Publishing Group, from *The Collected Works of W. B. Yeats, Volume I: The Poems, Revised,* edited by Richard J. Finneran. Copyright © 1928 by The Macmillan Company; copyright renewed (c) 1956 by Georgie Yeats.

Photo Credits

Abbreviations and Symbols for Editing and Proofreading

abbr	Faulty abbreviation **64**	*p*	Punctuation error
ad	Misused adjective or adverb **56**		⌃ Comma **57a–k**
agr	Problem with subject-verb or pronoun agreement **53, 55a**	*no ,*	Unnecessary comma **57 l–o**
appr	Inappropriate word or phrase **47**		; Semicolon **58**
			: Colon **59**
art	Incorrect or missing article **69b**		⌄ Apostrophe **60**
awk	Awkward		" " Quotation marks **61**
cap	Faulty capitalization **63**		. ? ! Period, question mark, exclamation point **62a–c**
case	Error in pronoun case **55d**		
cliché	Overused expression **48d**		— ( ) [ ] Dash, parentheses, brackets, ellipses, slash **62d–h**
coh	Problem with coherence **7f**		. . . /
com	Incomplete comparison **39c**		
coord	Problem with coordination **44**	*para*	Problem with a paraphrase **23b, d, e**
cs	Comma splice **52**		
d	Diction problem **47, 48**	*pass*	Ineffective use of passive voice **46b**
dev	More development needed **6b, c**		
dm	Dangling modifier **43e**	*pn agr*	Problem with pronoun agreement **55a**
doc	Documentation problem	*quote*	Problem with a quotation **23d, 61b, g**
	APA **31, 32**		
	Chicago **35**	*ref*	Problem with pronoun reference **55b**
	CSE **36, 37**		
	MLA **26, 27**	*rep*	Repetitious words or phrases **38b**
emph	Problem with emphasis **44**		
exact	Inexact word **48**	*run-on*	Run-on (or fused) sentence **52**
exam	Example needed **6b**	*sexist*	Sexist language **47e, 55a**
frag	Sentence fragment **51**	*shift*	Shift in point of view, tense, mood, or voice **41**
fs	Fused (or run-on) sentence **52**		
hyph	Problem with hyphen **67**	*sl*	Slang **47a**
inc	Incomplete construction **39**	*sp*	Misspelled word **68**
intro	Stronger introduction needed **6c**	*sub*	Problem with subordination **44**
		sv agr	Problem with subject-verb agreement **53**
ital	Italics or underlining needed **66**		
jarg	Jargon **47c**	*t*	Verb tense error **54f**
lc	Lowercase letter needed **63**	*trans*	Transition needed **7f**
mix	Mixed construction **40**	*usage*	See Glossary of Usage **50**
mm	Misplaced modifier **43a–d**	*var*	Vary your sentence structure **45**
mng	Meaning not clear	*vb*	Verb problem **54**
mood	Error in mood **54j**	*w*	Wordy **38**
ms	Error in manuscript form **8**	*ww*	Wrong word **48**
	APA **33**	//	Parallelism needed **42**
	Chicago **35d**	#	Add a space
	MLA **29**	^	Insert
num	Error in number style **65**	⌒	Close up space
		x	Obvious error
¶	Paragraph **6c**	??	Unclear

Contents